Communication Between
CULTURES

EIGHTH EDITION

Larry A. Samovar

San Diego State University, Emeritus

Richard E. Porter

California State University, Long Beach, Emeritus

Edwin R. McDaniel

California State University, San Marcos

Assisted By:

Carolyn S. Roy

San Diego State University

WADSWORTH
CENGAGE Learning·

Australia • Brazil • Japan • Korea • Mexico • Singapore • Spain • United Kingdom • United States

WADSWORTH
CENGAGE Learning·

Communication Between Cultures,
Eighth Edition, International Edition
Larry A. Samovar, Richard E. Porter, Edwin
R. McDaniel & Carolyn S. Roy

Publisher: Monica Eckman

Senior Assistant Editor: Rebekah Matthews

Editorial Assistant: Colin Solan

Media Editor: Jessica Badiner

Marketing Program Manager: Gurpreet Saran

Manufacturing Planner: Doug Bertke

Art Director: Linda May

Rights Acquisition Specialist: Jessica Elias

Design Direction, Production Management,
and Composition: PreMediaGlobal

Cover Image: © Shutterstock

Chapter Opener Image & Title Page
Image: © Shutterstock

International Edition:

ISBN-13: 978-1-133-49216-0

ISBN-10: 1-133-49216-9

Cengage Learning International Offices

Asia
www.cengageasia.com
tel: (65) 6410 1200

Australia/New Zealand
www.cengage.com.au
tel: (61) 3 9685 4111

Brazil
www.cengage.com.br
tel: (55) 11 3665 9900

India
www.cengage.co.in
tel: (91) 11 4364 1111

Latin America
www.cengage.com.mx
tel: (52) 55 1500 6000

UK/Europe/Middle East/Africa
www.cengage.co.uk
tel: (44) 0 1264 332 424

Represented in Canada by Nelson Education, Ltd.
www.nelson.com
tel: (416) 752 9100/(800) 668 0671

Cengage Learning is a leading provider of customized learning solutions with
office locations around the globe, including Singapore, the United Kingdom,
Australia, Mexico, Brazil, and Japan. Locate your local office at:
www.cengage.com/global

For product information and free companion resources:
www.cengage.com/international
Visit your local office: **www.cengage.com/global**

Printed in China
1 2 3 4 5 6 7 16 15 14 13 12

CHAPTER 4   Cultural History: Our Antecedents   85

CHAPTER 5   Culture, Life and Death   114

CHAPTER 7	Identity and Culture: Situating the Individual 204

CHAPTER 8	Verbal Messages: Language 234

CHAPTER 9   Nonverbal Communication: The Messages of Action, Space, Time, and Silence 254

Every tale can be told in a different way.

GREEK PROVERB

If we are to achieve a richer culture, rich in contrasting values, we must recognize the whole gamut of human potentialities, and so weave a less arbitrary social fabric, one in which each diverse gift will find a fitting place.

MARGARET MEAD

The opportunity to write an eighth edition of *Communication Between Cultures* filled us with feelings of gratitude and caution. The realization that earlier texts had been so well received by our peers and students that another edition was warranted left us with a sense of appreciation. We interpreted this measure of success to mean that during the past forty years our message regarding the importance of intercultural communication appears to have resonated with an approving audience. We welcomed the prospect of being able to refine and improve upon what we had done in seven previous editions. We did, however, realize the requirement to exercise prudence when advancing new perspectives and material while concomitantly retaining the focus that had contributed to the popularity of earlier editions. For this edition, we have sought to fuse the past, present, and future prospects of intercultural communication. We have retained the core concepts of the discipline, added contemporary perceptions and research, and ventured into some new territory.

This book is still about the synergy between communication and culture and how that interface influences human interactions. More specifically, it is about what happens when people of different cultures engage in communication with the objective of sharing ideas, information, and perspectives, while working to understand and appreciate their differences. Knowing that the concepts of communication and culture inextricably intertwine, we have endeavored to incorporate the basic principles of both topics throughout the text. Informed by the understanding that intercultural interactions are a daily occurrence for an ever growing number of people, we designed this book for those individuals whose professional or private lives bring them into contact with members of cultures or co-cultures different from their own.

RATIONALE

Global interest in, and the study of, intercultural communication arises from two fundamental but interrelated premises. First, you live in a dynamic, rapidly evolving era characterized by dramatic changes in technology, travel, economic and political institutions, immigration patterns, growing demographic diversity, and population density. These changes have created a world that requires regular interaction with people of different cultural origins—be they next door, across town, or thousands of miles away. Whether or not you embrace these "conversations," they will continue to increase in both frequency and intensity and grow in importance. Huston Smith succinctly summarized these circumstances when, in *The World's Religions*, he wrote, "When historians look back on [the twentieth] century they may remember it most, not for space travel or the release of nuclear energy, but as the time when the peoples of the world first came to take one another seriously." His reflections on the past century remain equally valid for our current globalized society.

The second premise is that people now have a greater appreciation of the truism that culture and communication work in tandem. In equally subtle and profound ways, your cultural background and life experiences largely determine your worldview, your perception of others, and how you choose to engage with others in that world.

APPROACH

Our approach is underpinned by the belief that all forms of human communication require some type of action. Stated in different terms, your communicative actions affect you as well as the people with whom you interact. Whether you are generating or receiving words or body movements, you are creating and producing messages that influence someone else. Any study of communication must include information about the choices that are made in selecting your messages, as well as a discussion of the consequences of those choices. Hence, this book advances the view that engaging in intercultural communication is pragmatic (you do something), philosophical (you make choices), and ethical (your selected actions have consequences).

PHILOSOPHY

A dual philosophy has guided the preparation of this edition. First, we hold that it is advantageous, if not a requirement, for the seven billion of us sharing this planet's limited resources to improve our intercultural communication skills. Globalization has created a world so small and interdependent that we must rely on each other— whether we want to or not. As simplistic as it may seem, what occurs in one place can now have a major impact on people in countless other parts of the world. Second, many of the obstacles to understanding others can be mitigated through motivation, knowledge, and an appreciation of cultural differences. Our objective is to provide you with all three.

We believe that writing about culture and communication involves personal decisions and a specialized point of view. As scholars and authors we have developed that point of view and a mutual philosophy about intercultural interaction. We contend that the first commandment of any civilized society should be: *Allow people to be different as long as those dissimilarities do not create hardships for others.* At times you will find that we have openly stated our personal positions, and for those convictions we make no apologies. Concurrently, we have made a concerted effort to check our own ethnocentrism. For those instances where it unintentionally surfaces, we apologize.

NEW FEATURES

As with our earlier efforts, this new edition contains numerous changes, including new content, updated materials, and revisions. Throughout preparation of this eighth edition, we have kept in mind the constructive comments made by users and reviewers of the previous editions of *Communication Between Cultures*. In response to several reviewers' suggestion, we have increased the number of photographs and replaced many of the older ones. In another significant change, new content on how to acquire and improve intercultural communication skills has been incorporated throughout the book. Additional new features include the following:

- While continuing to address globalization, introductory sections also focus on U.S. domestic intercultural issues. Data from the 2010 census is used to illustrate the dramatic changes in U.S. demographics, and projections of population changes are employed to demonstrate the increasing criticality of intercultural communication.
- The technology section has been expanded to address the role of contemporary information technology in the increasing interconnectivity of people worldwide, enabling the reconstitution of cultures, abetting the polarization of some segments of society, and fostering social and cultural changes.
- Communication and culture are now treated in a single chapter, which also includes new material on interpersonal communication.
- The dynamic nature of the contemporary world order and evolving cultural patterns within the United States demanded that we increase the scope of our analysis to demonstrate how globalization and social changes are having impacts on traditional family structures.
- We feel strongly that history provides a map of where a culture has been and a blueprint for its future. Accordingly, history is now a standalone chapter. A "Country Statistics" table has been added for each national history. Also, every topic contains a new section, called "Contemporary Social Issues," which discusses current social conditions and how they may affect the future. All of the history topics were updated, and Islamic history was extensively revised.
- Worldview and religion remain salient issues in contemporary society. Continuing media focus and growing misconceptions mandated we offer a more in-depth examination of Islamism. Our expanded discussion of secularism was prompted by the increasing numbers of people moving away from organized religion.
- Four new taxonomies were added to the cultural values chapter. An older value cataloguing explains thirteen values central to the U.S. dominant culture. Two new value dimensions complementing Hofstede's work have been included. Also included is a comprehensive overview of the GLOBE Study—research on personal values, institutionalized values, and managerial leadership across 61 societies.
- The role of identity in intercultural communication has been updated with new examples and references. The discussion of stereotyping, prejudice, racism, and ethnocentrism has also been revised.
- New content has been added to the language chapter. How culture is reflected through language usage is illustrated by examples from six different languages. There is a new section discussing how various conversational topics are taboo in different cultures. The treatment of translation and interpretation was also revised and expanded.

- In addition to revising and updating the content of the nonverbal chapter, we included a new section on improving nonverbal communication skills.
- Aware of the time instructors now need to utilize material from the plethora of current multimedia offerings, we have condensed the chapters on business, education, and health care into a single unit treating intercultural communication in contexts. In this new chapter, Brazil, China, and India, all growing world economic powers, are used as models to explain culture's impact on negotiations and conflict resolution in the business context.
- As with each previous edition, all retained material has been updated, new examples integrated throughout, and a host of new references were used.

ACKNOWLEDGEMENTS

No book is the sole domain of the authors. Many people contributed to this new edition, and we would like to acknowledge them. We are especially pleased with our publisher for the past forty years. While we have experienced and survived numerous changes in ownership, editors, and management, and even corporate name changes, the professional focus and dedication of the company have remained intact.

We begin our specific expressions of appreciation with a sincere "thank you" to Rebekah Matthews, our Senior Assistant Editor. From inception to completion, she offered us direction and support. Whether our problems, questions, or grumblings were major or minor, Rebekah always responded with great wisdom, good humor, and infinite patience. Also, we wish to recognize the hard work and contributions of Colin Solan, editorial assistant; Jessica Badiner, media editor; Margaret Bridges, senior content project manager; Kalpana Venkataramani, content project manager, PreMediaGlobal; and Gurpreet Saran, program marketing manager. Also, many thanks to Alan Heisel for writing the Instructor's Resource Manual. We also extend our sincere thanks to the reviewers of the previous text. Their suggestions contributed significantly to any improvements found in this edition.

We need to convey our gratitude to Carolyn Sexton Roy, friend and personal copy editor. As a historian Carolyn has had a keen interest in people and culture for many years, and she brought that passion to this edition. We are especially grateful for the time she spent on the final preparations of the manuscript. On countless occasions she fine-tuned entire chapters so that our message would be clearer and more succinct.

Finally, we express our appreciation to the tens of thousands of students and the many instructors who have used past editions. For forty years they have enabled us to "talk to them" about intercultural communication, and, by finding something useful in our exchange, they have allowed us to produce yet another edition of *Communication Between Cultures*.

Larry A. Samovar
Richard E. Porter
Edwin R. McDaniel
Carolyn S. Roy

CHAPTER 1

Intercultural Communication: Interaction in a Multicultural World

Globalization makes multicultural increasingly normative.

MARCELO SUÁREZ-OROZCO

What we have to do … is to find a way to celebrate our diversity and debate our differences without fracturing our communities.

HILLARY CLINTON

What appear to us as reasonable conclusions from within the perspective of our own culture may in fact look different from another cultural perspective.

NINIAN SMART

The process commonly referred to as "globalization" has entered its third decade and continues to accelerate. It is obvious that fewer and fewer people live in only a local, regional, or even national societal order. More than ever before, the world is now characterized by an interrelated, interdependent global community. The seamless movement of capital, labor, people, and data across national borders has become commonplace. Increased domestic diversity resulting from immigration and shifting birth patterns has made intercultural activities a daily event for a large percentage of the world's population, which now surpasses seven billion. The rapidly changing complexion of the U.S. domestic population reflected in the 2010 census vividly demonstrates the need to develop and competently employ intercultural communication skills.

An objective of this text is to provide you with an understanding of the evolving social environment you live in, the role that culture plays in your life, and how that role can produce different results for people belonging to other cultures. This book is about your adapting, adjusting, and participating in a globalized society. Because people's most significant values, beliefs, attitudes, behaviors, and especially communication practices are products of culture, it is beneficial to understand how cultural knowledge can provide an understanding of why people perceive the world and conduct their daily lives differently than you. A more specific aim of this book is to provide you with the cultural knowledge and communicative skills needed to interact successfully in a multicultural environment.

THE GLOBAL COMMUNITY

Communication between people from different cultures is not new. It has been occurring for thousands of years as cultural groups waged war, conducted commercial activities, and engaged in social exchanges with each other. Now, we have reached a point in history where the latter two interactions have become not only ordinary but are necessities, creating an interdependent global community. In the commercial arena, this interdependence was seen in the aftermath of the 2011 Great Eastern Japan Earthquake and tsunami, which disrupted the supply of Japanese manufactured products to businesses around the globe, resulting in worldwide production slowdowns. Another example of economic interconnectedness is the negative impact on world financial markets stemming from the European Union nations' sovereign debt crisis in 2011. Even Hollywood has yielded to the forces of economic globalization. Today, the foreign market represents 68 percent of the income from films. To maintain this revenue, U.S. studios are using foreign actors in large budget films and "cutting back on standard Hollywood fare like romantic comedies because foreign movie-goers often don't find American jokes all that funny."[1] The growth of international tourism is also bringing people from varying cultures into contact with each other. In 2010 there were some 940 million international tourist arrivals worldwide, with over 59 million in the United States, the second most popular destination.[2]

Modern transportation systems make it easy for tourists to travel long distances to experience new and exciting cultures.

Edwin McDaniel

Globalization has internationalized the workforce. Competition for jobs, especially those requiring technological skills or advanced degrees, is now worldwide. Even low-skilled labor is being outsourced. For instance, approximately 10 percent of the Filipino labor force work outside their homeland, with over a million employed in Saudi Arabia.[3] The field of education is also experiencing the influences of globalization. Between 1980 and 2010 the number of students studying at higher education institutions outside their home country tripled to approximately three million. In 2008, nearly 30 percent of students attending the Massachusetts Institute of Technology (MIT) were from abroad.[4] And this trend is likely to increase. According to one university administrator, "Higher education is going to become more global."[5] That assertion was borne out by a recent International Institute of Education study that reported joint- and dual-degree programs between universities from different nations were becoming common as a way "to further the internationalization of their campuses and raise their global profile."[6]

Naturally, there are many other examples of the increasing interaction between peoples around the world. Moreover, world population growth, projected to surpass

People throughout the world are becoming aware of the social and economic problems created by overpopulation.

Steve Harrington

nine billion by 2050,[7] will increase international competition for the resources necessary to support the basic needs of that number of people. According to one estimate, this will require a 70 percent rise in worldwide food production.[8] There are numerous other issues as well. Climate change, natural disasters, health epidemics, cyberspace security, immigration, and financial regulations will require cooperative international governances. In each instance, the success or failure may well rest on the ability to communicate effectively across cultural differences.

GROWING DOMESTIC DIVERSITY

Although all of the globalization issues just discussed have impacts on the United States, the growing diversity of U.S. demographics makes multicultural awareness and intercultural communication skills more immediate concerns in your life. Data from the 2010 census have disclosed major population shifts among minority groups and age cohorts, making it clear that the complexion of the U.S. population is undergoing rapid, dramatic change. These changes will bring into contact population segments holding different worldviews and often contrasting values. The ability to prevent potential conflicts and foster productive, cooperative relations will depend largely on effective intercultural communications.

Minorities now represent 35 percent of the U.S. population.[10] Between 2000 and 2010, the non-Hispanic White portion of the total population decreased from 69 percent to 64 percent. This decline was offset by significant increases among Asians and Hispanics. While Asians grew to almost 5 percent, Hispanics accounted for the majority of the U.S. population growth—increasing from 13 to 16 percent of the overall population. This represents a 43 percent growth over the 10-year period between censuses. In Texas, Hispanics are the majority population in 51 counties.[11] California, Hawaii, New Mexico, and Texas are considered "minority majority" states. Due to declining birthrates among non-Hispanic Whites, minority children comprise the majority of youths in 10 states and 35 major metropolitan areas, with Hispanic children accounting for most of the growth.[12] By the year 2023, minorities are projected to constitute the majority of all U.S. children under the age of 18.[13]

Accompanying this shift in the U.S. ethnic population is the growth of what has been termed the "cultural generation gap."[15] As shown in Table 1.1, the 45~64 age

TABLE 1.1	U.S. Population by Age Group—2000 & 2010[14]	
AGE GROUP	**PERCENT OF TOTAL POPULATION—2000**	**PERCENT OF TOTAL POPULATION—2010**
Under 18	25.7	24.0
18~44	39.9	36.5
45~64	22.0	26.4
65 and over	12.4	13.0

Source: © Cengage Learning 2013

cohort increased noticeably between 2000 and 2010, while the under 45 age group experienced a decline. This increase in older Americans is due largely to the Baby Boom Generation moving into retirement, and according to Brownstein, fully four-fifths of this rapidly expanding senior population is white.[16] This is in contrast to the younger generation of Americans, whose growth is largely a

product of Hispanic and Asian births. This disparity in age groups and ethnicity raises the potential for conflict in an era of limited public resources. Older Americans are more prone to give priority to entitlement programs such as Social Security and Medicare. Conversely, the younger generations will no doubt see greater value in funding education, health care, and social programs.[17] Without competent intercultural communication initiatives, these demographics could well polarize major segments of the population.

U.S. IMMIGRATION

Immigration is another major influence on U.S. demographics, and one that continues to bring people from different cultures into contact. Large scale immigration to the United States began with the arrival of the first Europeans just over 400 years ago. Since those early arrivals, immigrants have continued to arrive in varying numbers, and recently those numbers have been rising. Census data from 2009 revealed foreign-born immigrants represented 12 percent of the U.S. population and an additional 11 percent "were native-born with at least one foreign-born parent."[19] Unlike in the past when new arrivals tended to gather together in large urban areas, today's immigrants are locating into suburbs and small towns. In many cases, they are moving into areas where immigrants have not previously concentrated.[20] This change carries a distinct possibility of intercultural friction. How will long-time residents unfamiliar with outsiders react to people from diverse ethnic groups, dressing differently, practicing a religion other than Christianity, speaking little or no English, often poorly educated, and holding varied values and worldviews?

The near constant stream of U.S. media reports associating immigrants with crime, the political drumbeat to secure the borders, and the claim that illegal arrivals are taking U.S. jobs only serve to create a negative perception. In actuality, immigrants have made and continue to make significant contributions to the economy and welfare of the United States, as illustrated by the following statistics.

- In recent years, immigrants have been responsible for 25 percent of all U.S. patents.
- Chinese and Indian immigrants accounted for 40 percent of the patents coming from work at Intel Corporation.
- In 2006, 40 percent of the Ph.D.s awarded by U.S. universities in science and engineering, and 65 percent in computer science, went to foreign-born students.

• During the period 1995–2005, 25 percent of all engineering and technology companies started in the United States had at least one immigrant as a founder, and an additional 27 percent had a foreign-born Chief Executive Officer or Chief Technology Officer.[21]

TECHNOLOGY

Advances in information technology (IT) are bringing about changes in contemporary society that pose new situations requiring intercultural communication expertise. The scope of the extensive interconnectivity now available around the world is highlighted by Friedman.

> It starts with the fact that globalization and the information technology revolution
> have gone to a whole new level. Thanks to cloud computing, robotics, 3G wireless
> connectivity, Skype, Facebook, Google, LinkedIn, Twitter, the iPad, and
> cheap Internet-enabled smartphones, the world has gone from connected to
> hyper-connected.[23]

Facebook, for instance, has over 800 million active subscribers, of which 70 percent are outside the United States, and the site offers in excess of 70 language translations.[24] This broad IT reach is being used to facilitate cohesion among previously disparate groups and individuals, creating societal changes, and in some instances bringing about the polarization of different groups.

Technology has enabled ordinary individuals to cheaply and quickly organize themselves around a common interest, ideology, or social cause. An obvious example is the 2011 Arab Spring, when people in the Middle East used Facebook, Twitter, and other media to organize and rise up against repressive, authoritarian governmental rule. In India, followers of the social activist Anna Hazare used Facebook and Twitter to mobilize large sections of the population in a nationwide anti-corruption protest.[25] IT is also helping people around the world maintain or reestablish contact for political activism, social interaction, and cultural preservation. An example of this is found in the reemergence of the Circassian diaspora, descendants of a Caucasus nation destroyed in the mid-1800s by the Russian tsar. In 2010, "Facebook groups and Twitter feeds enabled Circassians to coordinate the protests held [concurrently] in Berlin, Istanbul, New York, The Hague, and Washington, D.C." to mark the anniversary of their country's destruction. In addition, they are using the Internet to reassemble their culture by posting Circassian music, dance, and language dictionaries online.[26] Rather than moving the global community toward the single, homogenized culture decried by many globalization opponents, technology is actually providing a means to reaffirm and extend cultural awareness, identity, and practices.

In some instances, media technology is also bringing about a more polarized society, particularly in the United States. The availability of varied information sources on the Internet is enormous, making it quite easy to find material that confirms and solidifies almost any conviction. As described by one journalist,

The Internet and cellular phones allow people everywhere to exchange ideas and information.

Bill Bachmann/PhotoEdit

Out in cyberspace, facts are movable objects, pushed aside when they don't fit beliefs, political leanings or preconceived notions. Everybody's an expert. The like-minded find each other and form communities online, reinforcing their biases and their certitude.[27]

Individuals no longer find it necessary to seek compromises with people who hold perceptions and attitudes that differ from their own. As a result, "Americans increasingly are segregating themselves into communities, clubs and churches where they are surrounded by people who think the way they do.... The result is polarization and intolerance."[28] Evidence of this is seen in a wide range of forums, such as conservative vs. liberal, pro-life vs. freedom of choice, anti-immigration vs. immigration rights, reduced government spending vs. social welfare programs, and the schism surrounding gay marriage rights. It is also evident in the vitriolic exchanges often posted on entertainment blogs, even on such mundane issues as what is a good or bad YouTube music video. The Internet offers a degree of anonymity that can be used to strip away social civility. Amelioration of these divergent perspectives will be achieved only by understanding that people have varying values and worldviews and by acquiring the ability to communicate across those differences.

The continuing growth of digital technology is also bringing about profound social and cultural changes. For instance, readers are turning away from hardcopy publications like newspapers and books in favor of portable electronic devices. All the courses at the Massachusetts Institute of Technology are now also available online. According to one survey, in 2009 the Internet was the third most common means of meeting someone among U.S. heterosexuals. In India, where parents continue to view dating with disfavor and arranged marriages are still quite common, mobile devices allow young couples to interact beyond the watchful eyes of family members. Concomitantly, Indian dating websites have adapted to the culture by allowing parents and relatives to create a profile for a marriage eligible family member.[29]

The foregoing offers only a small sampling of the countless examples of how society is evolving as the world becomes metaphorically smaller. Our intent was to illustrate some of the numerous and varied challenges you will encounter during your lifetime. A constant theme associated with these demands is the interconnectedness and interdependence of contemporary society. This means that people of varied nationalities and ethnic origins, sometimes speaking other languages and holding different, possibly divergent convictions, must learn to live together despite the likelihood of conflict. We hope that by now you are convinced of the need to expand your cultural awareness and improve your intercultural communication skills. If so, you are ready to begin studying intercultural communication.

DEFINING THE CONCEPTS

Before you begin that study, however, we need to define some concepts that you will encounter throughout this text. While Chapter 2 provides an in-depth discussion of culture and communication, an appreciation of the following four terms will help in understanding the remainder of this chapter.

INTERCULTURAL COMMUNICATION

Since you are probably enrolled in a course dealing with *intercultural communication* and we use the term throughout the text, it seems appropriate that we take a moment to give meaning to the two words. Additionally, the terms *dominant culture* and *co-culture* are used extensively, and it is important to have an early understanding of those concepts. For us, intercultural communication occurs when a member of one culture produces a message for consumption by a member of another culture. More precisely, *intercultural communication involves interaction between people whose cultural perceptions and symbol systems differ enough to influence the communication event*.

THE DOMINANT CULTURE

When referring to a group of people as a *culture*, we are applying the term to the dominant culture found in most societies. In the United States, a variety of terms have been coined to represent this group, such as *umbrella culture, mainstream culture, U.S. Americans*, and *Euro-Americans*. We prefer to use *dominant culture* because it clearly indicates that the group we are referring to generally exercises the greatest influence on the beliefs, values, perceptions, communication patterns, and customs of the culture. A dominant group is characteristic of all cultures, and this collective of people possesses those instruments of power that allow it to set the broad societal agenda the majority of others will commonly follow. The power we are referring to does not necessarily reside in numerical dominance but in the ability to control the major institutions within the culture—governmental, educational, mass media, economic, military, religious, and the like. What a dominant cultural group uses as the basis of power (money, fear, the military, and such) may differ from culture to culture, but in every case, the group determines the political, economic, and social agenda. Regardless of the source of power, certain people within every culture possess and exercise disproportionate influence, and that influence is translated into how other members of the culture shape their lives.

Adult white males have exercised dominance in the United States since the country was established. While they constitute less than 40 percent of the total U.S. population, white males continue to monopolize the positions of national power, which enables them to determine and manipulate the content and flow of messages produced by the various societal institutions. However, the shifting U.S. ethnic demographics discussed earlier portend a diffusion of the power historically held by white males.

CO-CULTURES

As just pointed out, a dominant culture exists in every society, but that collective is not monolithic. That is, within the dominant culture are numerous co-cultures and specialized cultures. We believe the best way to identify these groups is with the term *co-culture*, because it calls attention to the idea of dual membership. Therefore, we use co-culture when discussing groups or social communities exhibiting perceptions, values, beliefs, communicative behaviors, and social practices that are sufficiently different as to distinguish them from other groups and communities and from the dominant culture.

Co-cultures may share many of the characteristics of the dominant culture, but their members also exhibit distinct and unique patterns of communication. Co-cultural affiliation can be based on ethnic heritage, gender, age cohort, sexual preference, or other criteria. What is important about all co-cultures is that being gay, disabled, Latino, African American, Chinese American, American Indian, female, young, or old, to name a few examples, exposes a person to a specialized set of messages that helps determine how some aspects of the external world are perceived. It also significantly influences how members of that co-culture communicate those perceptions.

SOCIETY

Providing an uncomplicated definition of the term *society*, and one that readily distinguishes society from culture, is a demanding task. However, because we use the term throughout this book, a definition is in order. Like culture, which we discuss fully in the next chapter, society is an abstract concept that scholars have constructed to help explain various aspects of human activity. *Society* can be defined from a general and a specific perspective. In the general sense, we are referring comprehensively to organized human interactions, such as social structure, organizations, and institutions. When used from a specific perspective, we are denoting a group or groups of interdependent, self-perpetuating, relatively autonomous people within a specified geographical area. In this sense, a society may consist of multiple cultures. Depending on the size, a society may extend across national borders and share some degree of culture and language. Thus, global society, European society, or U.S. society would refer to the organized human social interactions within those geographic boundaries and encompass many cultures. The geographical region could also be much smaller.[30]

In the remainder of this chapter we bring out some of the difficulties you might encounter when entering a new cultural environment and offer a discussion on ethics in the intercultural communication context. It is important to recognize the indications of culture shock, and an ability to manage those symptoms is a necessity for effective intercultural interactions. Your study of intercultural communication will bring you both new communicative skills and new ethical responsibilities.

VENTURING INTO A NEW CULTURE

The English Renaissance composer William Byrd once said, "That song is best esteemed with which our ears are most acquainted." This adage underscores the notion that people tend to enjoy and feel comfortable with the familiar. When communicating with close friends you usually know how to act and what to expect. It is the same with being a member of a particular culture. Put in slightly different terms, culture contributes to a feeling of familiarity. In fact, one of the "obligations" of all cultures is to assure that their members share many of the same experiences. From learning a common language to establishing a collective set of values, a culture creates common bonds among its members. When you leave the known dimensions of your culture, harking back to our opening quotation, "the song" is unfamiliar, and the strangeness can produce problems. These foreign predicaments might be only minimal if you were spending merely a week in Paris or a weekend at Cancun. However, if you are entering a new culture for a prolonged period of time, you will usually have to adapt to that culture, a process that can be difficult and stressful. As Nolan points out, "Your new environment makes demands for which you have no ready-made responses; and your responses, in turn, do not seem to produce the desired results."[31] *Culture shock* is a part of the process of trying to adjust and adapt to a new culture. Specifically, culture shock is a mental state caused by the transition that occurs when you go from a familiar cultural environment to an unfamiliar one and discover that your normative, established patterns of behavior are ineffective. Because some degree of culture shock is a common response to sustained contact with a new cultural environment, we will examine the phenomenon in more detail.

REACTIONS TO CULTURE SHOCK

The reactions associated with culture shock may vary widely among individuals and can appear at different times. According to Ferraro and Andreatta, "When culture shock sets in, everything seems to go wrong. You often become irritated over minor inconveniences. The food is strange, people don't keep their appointments, no one seems to like you, everything seems so unhygienic, people don't look you in the eye, and on and on."[32]

When confronting some of the effects associated with culture shock, it is not uncommon for people to experience a sense of disorientation, feelings of rejection, homesickness, withdrawal, irritation, and physical and mental fatigue. This cataloging of tensions connected to culture shock is not intended to overwhelm you or make you apprehensive about venturing into another culture, but rather to help you be prepared should you experience some of these reactions.

THE PHASES OF CULTURE SHOCK

Although there are variations in both how people respond and the amount of time they need to adjust, most of the early literature addressing culture shock suggested that people normally experience four phases and a U-model was used to illustrate the progression of those phases. A few introductory remarks will be helpful before we explain the overall concept of the U-curve. First, the lines separating the phases a person goes through are not at all distinct—that is to say, the transition from one stage to another is not as clear-cut as our description might imply. From a broad perspective, the U-curve seeks to demonstrate an initial decline in the level of cultural adaptation, followed by a steady period of recovery and adjustment to the host culture. This can be visualized as beginning at the top left side and moving downward before climbing back up the right side toward the top of the "U." A bit more detail will give you a better understanding of the culture shock process.

The first phase, which we call the *exhilaration stage,* is usually filled with excitement, hopefulness, and even a feeling of euphoria as the individual anticipates being exposed to a different culture. People see their cultural experience as a time to explore everything from new foods to a different pace of life. The second phase (*disenchantment stage*) begins when they recognize the reality of the new setting, start to encounter some difficulties, and adaptation and communication problems begin to emerge. As Triandis notes, "The second phase is a period when difficulties of language, inadequate schools for the children, poor housing, crowded transportation, chaotic shopping, and the like begin taking their toll."[33] This is the crisis period of culture shock. Confused and baffled by their new surroundings, people can easily become irritated, hostile, impatient, angry, and even lonely. The *adjustment stage,* the third phase, is when the sojourner gains some cultural insight and gradually begins to make some adjustments and modifications in coping with the

Language difficulties often produce culture shock as the "guest" attempts to become functional in a new culture.

Edwin McDaniel

new surroundings. Events and people now seem much more predictable and less stressful, and adaptation begins to occur. In the final phase, the *effective functioning stage*, people understand the key elements of the new culture (special customs, behaviors, communication patterns, and such) and feel comfortable in the surroundings. Early research also postulated that sojourners returning to their home country after extended periods abroad experienced reentry shock and went through another U-shaped experience, and a W-model was used to illustrate the process.[34]

Although they continue to enjoy popularity, perhaps because of their ease of understanding and illustration, subsequent research has failed to confirm the U- and W-models of culture shock and adaptation. The early models lacked methodological rigor and tended to oversimplify the complex processes of cultural integration. More recent studies have disclosed that culture shock can affect sojourners very differently based on personal and situational factors. For instance, one later investigation found that difficulties commenced immediately upon arrival in a new culture. Similar findings have shown that reentry shock can take a variety of forms.[35] Newer models, such as those offered by Adler and by Kim suggest that the adaptation process is cyclic with intermittent periods of adaptation and stress, with the latter attenuating the longer the sojourner remains in the new culture.[36]

BEYOND CULTURE SHOCK

As we noted earlier, people are moving from place to place throughout the world in larger numbers and with greater regularity. These people, and you might well be one of them, are faced with the monumental task of adapting to a new culture. Their new "homes" are often for an extended period of time, perhaps permanent. The impact and the importance of having to adapt to a new culture are clearly articulated by Kosic and Phalet:

> International migration creates culturally and ethnically diverse societies. As people from different cultures interact with each other, they face not only different belief systems, values, customs, and behaviors, but unfortunately also prejudice towards each other. It seems that social relationships between immigrants and local populations often lack cohesion and sometimes show strong antagonism or even racism underneath an outward appearance of tolerance. In political and public debates, immigrants are often depicted as trouble-makers.[37]

Many of these newcomers experience difficulty while adapting to the host culture. Some of these difficulties are in fact much like the ones associated with culture shock. As Mak, Westwood, Ishiyama, and Barker point out, "Newcomers may not be ready to learn and practice social behaviors appropriate to the new culture in the initial period of settlement. It is not unusual for recent arrivals to be overwhelmed by the immediate demands and challenges in orienting to living in a new place."[38] The name given to the process of learning to live in a new culture is *acculturation*. Berry defines acculturation as "the dual process of cultural and psychological change that takes place as a result of contact between two or more cultural groups and their individual members.... At the individual level it involves changes in a person's behavioral repertoire."[39] This process of adjustment is a lengthy ordeal that requires gaining a large body of useful knowledge about the new culture. As Ward, Bouchner, and Furnham note, "A necessary condition of functioning effectively in a second-culture environment is to acquire relevant social skills through behavioural culture training, mentoring, and learning about the historical, philosophical and sociopolitical foundations of the host culture."[40] The recommendations generated by Ward and his associates will now be elaborated and made more specific.

Learn about the Language of the Host Culture

It is obvious that someone living in a new culture will face numerous challenges as they attempt to deal with language differences. Noting this difficulty, Ralph Waldo Emerson once wrote, "No man should travel until he has learned

the language of the country he visits. Otherwise he makes himself a great baby—so helpless and so ridiculous." When we talk of problems associated with being exposed to a new language, we are talking about two ideas: language acquisition and the ways of speaking unique to the new culture. Both of these can contribute to culture shock and can delay the adaptation process. Harper summarizes this view when she notes, "Lack of language skills is a strong barrier to effective cultural adjustment and communication, whereas lack of knowledge concerning the ways of speaking of a particular group will reduce the level of understanding that we can achieve with our counterparts."[41] People trying to adjust to and interact with a new culture must face challenges associated not only with learning an additional language, but also with the unique cultural patterns within each language. As we will point out in Chapter 8, cultural variations in the use of language can mean many things, from the use of idioms and "conversational taboos" to linguistic ways of showing respect.

Guard against Ethnocentrism

Throughout this book we will talk about *ethnocentrism* (a conviction that one's own culture is superior to all other cultures). Problems adapting to a new culture are often hindered by ethnocentrism, and excessive ethnocentrism can lead to prejudice, which in turn results in mistrust, hostility, and even hate.[42] One aspect of ethnocentrism is that it can affect everyone—"guests," immigrants, and even members of the host culture. This can result in members of the host culture passing judgment on outsiders while the person trying to adapt cannot, or will not, sublimate his or her native culture. The key to effective adaptation is for all parties to recognize the strong pull of ethnocentrism and attempt to keep it in check.

Learn about the Host Culture

One of the major themes throughout this book is the notion that developing a fund of knowledge about other cultures is a useful first step toward improving intercultural communication. Culture shock and adaptation may be less troublesome if you become aware of the fundamental characteristics of the culture in which you will be living. Cultural awareness refers to understanding the culture's religious orientation, historical background, political system, key values and beliefs, verbal and nonverbal behaviors, family organization, social etiquette, and other similar aspects.

Work to Maintain Your Culture

People are less overwhelmed by another culture, and tend to be more comfortable moving into a new culture, if they maintain their own culture. Often this simply means finding other people who share your culture and spending time with them. It is very common for people from a particular culture to move to a specific neighborhood so they can continue to share everything from familiar foods to religious affiliations. Today, unlike in the past, modern technology has made staying in touch with family members and friends in one's home country both affordable and easy. "A 19th-century Russian immigrant might never see or speak to his family again. A 21st-century migrant can Skype them in the taxi from the airport."[43]

To this point we have spent a great deal of time discussing some of the issues involved when people from different cultures attempt to communicate with one another. Much of this analysis centered on what you should do and how you should act. Because those actions have consequences, we suggest your decisions include an ethical dimension. Put in slightly different terms, the messages you send to other people have the potential to change them in both subtle and easily discernible ways. This assertion leads us to a point in the chapter where we feel compelled to examine the ethical questions involved with your producing a response from your communication partners. More specifically, these changes have ethical overtones.

ETHICAL CONSIDERATIONS

As an introduction to the study of intercultural ethics we advance a series of contentions:

- Only God should decide when it is time to die.
- Assisted suicide should be made legal.
- America needs to stop allowing immigrants into this country.
- America should have an open border policy with Mexico.
- Racial profiling is necessary and justified.
- Racial profiling violates the personal freedom of some Americans.
- War is appropriate in some circumstances.
- War is always wrong.
- Women always have the right to control their reproductive behaviors.
- Abortion is always wrong.
- Sending production overseas is good for the economy.
- Sending production overseas takes jobs away from hardworking Americans.

Deciding how you feel about these positions involves having to make judgments that contain some ethical implications and focus on questions of what is right and wrong, and proper and improper. These questions may also require that you think about them in a global sense, considering what is appropriate for your society or for the global society as a whole, rather than what might apply to one or a few individuals. Ethics can be seen as a reflection of your convictions, which are rooted in your culture. As a set of principles, it also provides guidelines that influence the manner in which you communicate with other people. Ethics, therefore, helps you determine what you ought to do, how you ought to act, and how you should interact with people.

Ethics refers to judgments that focus "on degrees of rightness and wrongness, virtue and vice, and obligations in human behavior."[44] Because these judgments are a precursor to action, ethical decisions often have impacts on the thoughts and behaviors of other people. The ramifications of these "impacts" are so profound that ethics has been a topic of concern for thousands of years. Religious thinkers, philosophers, and ordinary people have been struggling to answer the difficult and complex questions we face when deciding how to treat other people. From the Ten Commandments to the Buddha's Eightfold Path, to the writings of the Koran, to Epicurus' justification of egotistical behavior, to Martin Buber's "ethics with heart," to Confucius' *Analects*, people have endeavored to decide on a code of ethics. Answers range from simplistic and selfish observations ("It is a dog-eat-dog world"), to religious mandates that speak of the "oneness" of all human beings.

You can tell from the last paragraph that ethics is an elusive, multifaceted topic. And while the motivations for your ethical decisions come from a host of sources (parents, church, school, mass media, and the like), in the final analysis the resolution to act in one way or another rests with you. What complicates the decision-making process is that many ethical decisions are so automatic that you are not even aware of them. In addition, a person's set of ethics seeks to offer them "instructions" on how to make difficult moral decisions in both their professional and private lives. These choices are made even more challenging when ethical practices collide—as they often do in intercultural interactions. What we are suggesting is that cultural diversity also exists among ethical systems. This observation of seemingly diverse moral systems raises the question of whether there is an absolute morality and set of universal ethical principles. We aver that the answer is, "No." While people hold many of the same ethical precepts, they advance diverse arguments about what is the "true" morality, whether morality is absolute, or whether it is relative to specific cultures. It is not our purpose here to settle the dispute. Rather, we will give you a brief overview of two of the most common perspectives (*fundamentalism* and *relativism*) employed by people and cultures to deal with ethical issues.

FUNDAMENTALISM

The first approach, often associated with various religions, is known as fundamentalism or moral absolutism. In this view, expressed by Harper, "ethical principles are universally applicable ... [and] timeless moral truths are rooted in human nature and independent of the conventions of particular societies."[45] Brannigan expands this notion by saying that adherents to this position "believe that there are definitive, true moral rules and codes that apply to all people at all times. These rules constitute objective moral standards and they are exceptionless."[46] These writers are implying that there is a universal morality that applies to all people at all times, everywhere.

RELATIVISM

Unlike the absolutist worldview described above, the second approach follows from a relativistic worldview. This orientation is often referred to as *moral relativism* and has as its core the view that deciding what is right or wrong and good and bad behavior is not absolute, but instead changeable and relative. More specifically, this orientation holds that ethical principles are culturally bound, context dependent, and only applicable to their respective cultures.[47] Relativism underscores the fact that cultures not only often fail to agree on specific practices and beliefs, but also with respect to moral codes as they apply to topics focusing on what is right and

REMEMBER THIS

A fundamentalist perspective holds that there is a timeless absolute morality that applies to everyone everywhere and is independent of the conventions of individual cultures.

wrong, good and bad, and virtue and vice. The philosophical premise behind this perspective may be summarized succinctly as: "There is no single true morality. There are many different moral frameworks, none of which is more correct than the others."[48]

A more specific view of relativism, and one that applies directly to this book, is what is known as cultural relativism. Haviland and his associates maintain that cultural relativism is: "The idea that one must suspend judgment of other people's practices in order to understand them in their own cultural terms."[49] This philosophy affirms that ethical standards vary from culture to culture. If, for example, bribery, or *bustarella*, were to be an acceptable and expected behavior in Italy, then under the ethical relativistic view, the intolerance of bribery in the United States would be no more or less ethical than the toleration of bribery in Italy. A secondary dynamic that follows from cultural relativism is that ethical standards are subject to change. Robertson and Crittenden suggest that the dynamic of convergence will cause standards and norms everywhere to shift as globalization leads to common values regarding economic and work-related behavior.[50]

It is not our purpose to argue for either the correctness, or your acceptance, of the fundamentalist or relativistic worldview. We will defer to the Taoist philosophic tradition, which holds that humans exist simultaneously in both a real world and an ideal world. In a simplified explanation, the world of reality is the world that is, and the idealized world is the world that ought to be. In the world that is, ethics and morality are culturally relative. Perhaps, in the world that ought to be, ethics and morality would be absolute. But, as we primarily exist in the real world, we will proceed on the assumption that rightly or wrongly, ethics and morality are culturally relative. We will further advance the notion that regardless of one's basic religious or philosophical view of the world, ethical decisions—and how they are determined— are part of everyone's daily life. Hence, the remainder of this section will focus on some guidelines and behaviors you may adopt as you attempt to practice ethical behavior when interacting with people of diverse cultures.

ETHICS IN INTERCULTURAL COMMUNICATION

BE MINDFUL THAT COMMUNICATION PRODUCES A RESPONSE

One of the basic premises of this book is that the messages you produce create a response from other people. Even when communicating within your own cultural sphere, it is sometimes difficult to predict what response you may elicit. And in the intercultural environment, where cultural diversity is a factor, it is much more difficult to foretell the type of response your messages will produce. For example, you have learned, as part of your cultural endowment, the appropriate way to respond to, and thank someone for, a compliment or a gift. You can gauge with a high degree of accuracy what others expect from you as well as how they will respond to your signs of appreciation. Predicting the responses of people from other cultures is far more difficult. Let us for a moment stay with our simple example of thanking someone for a gift. In Arab cultures gift recipients are expected to be profuse in offering thanks, whereas, in English culture recipients are expected to offer restrained thanks because too much exuberance is considered offensive.

The point is that it is difficult to always know how people will react to messages. Therefore, we recommend that you try to concentrate on both the other person and your surroundings. This focus on actions and the results of those actions is called, in the Buddhist tradition, *being mindful*. "Mindfulness is the aware, balanced, acceptance of the present experience."[51] Obviously, concentrating on personal actions is far more complicated than can be expressed in a single sentence. Yet the central message is clear: Being mindful during a communication encounter means giving full attention to the moment. By being mindful you can adjust your messages to both the context and the person. But most importantly, you can be aware of what you are doing to another person—and that is a matter of ethics.

SHOW RESPECT FOR OTHERS

How would you respond if someone embarrassed you in front of others, put you down, or treated you as if you were insignificant? The answer is obvious: Your feelings would range from anger to emotional hurt. No one likes being denigrated. Each and every person seeks respect, dignity, and a feeling of worth, regardless of their culture. From an ethical perspective this means that during your interactions you display respect for the dignity and feelings of all people. Burbulies refers to this behavior as employing "the rule of reciprocity," in which you develop a "reversible and reflexive attitude and reciprocal regard for others."[52] Burbulies is not alone in his conviction of the importance of respect for other people. Johannesen uses words such as "devalues," "ridicule," and "excluding" when he speaks of ethical guidelines regarding respecting one another.[53] Confucius has much the same message concerning the ethical treatment of others when he tells us that "Without feelings of respect, what is there to distinguish men from beasts?" In intercultural interactions this means that you must reach beyond your own cultural norms and respect the norms of other cultures.

SEARCH FOR COMMONALITIES AMONG PEOPLE AND CULTURES

Throughout this book we will spend considerable time talking about cultural differences that influence intercultural communication. Yet we must not overlook the similarities among people and cultures, because those similarities can act as an ethical guide. DeGenova offers some words that illustrate this suggestion:

> No matter how many differences there may be, beneath the surface there are even more similarities. It is important to try to identify the similarities among various cultures. Stripping away surface differences will uncover a multiplicity of similarities: people's hopes, aspirations, desire to survive, search for love, and need for family—to name just a few.[54]

This search for similarity is an important ethical component because it enables you to seek out common ground that helps you decide how to treat other people,

At the core of a meaningful ethic is the belief that all cultures share many basic beliefs about children and family.

Robert Fonseca

regardless of their culture. The similarities that unite people, and in a real sense make everyone part of "the global village," may range from the obvious to the subtle. For example, it is apparent that all seven billion people inhabit the same planet for a rather short period, and all people share the same desire to be free from external restraint—the craving for freedom is basic.

The world's great religious traditions have also recognized the values that bind people and make for a more just society. They all offer tutoring to their followers as it applies to correct moral precepts. For example, they all denounce murder, stealing, bearing false witness, adultery, and the like. In addition, these traditions also agree on the significance of the "Golden Rule." Although the words are different, the wisdom contained within the words is universal.[55]

- Buddhism: "Hurt not others in ways you yourself would find harmful."
- Christianity: "All things whatsoever ye would that men should do to you, do ye even so to them."
- Confucianism: "Do not do unto others what you would not have them do unto you."

- Hinduism: "This is the sum of duty: Do naught unto others which would cause you pain if done to you."
- Islam: "No one of you is a believer until he desires for his brother that which he desires for himself."
- Judaism: "What is hateful to you; do not to your fellow man. This is the law; all the rest is commentary."

From this brief sample you can recognize that in many significant ways people are very much alike. It is important that in a multicultural world you begin to observe these commonalities. Huntington expressed the same ideas when he wrote, "People in all civilizations should search for and attempt to expand the values, institutions, and practices they have in common with people of other civilizations."[56]

RESPECT CULTURAL DIFFERENCES

Although we just discussed the need to seek out similarities among people and cultures, we now ask that you not ignore cultural differences. Think about the words of former President Shimon Peres of the State of Israel, who said. "All people have the right to be equal and the equal right to be different." In short, while seeking commonalities you need to be aware and respectful of cultural differences. By developing this awareness, you will begin to develop an intercultural ethical perspective. Keep in mind a recurring theme in this book: People are both alike and different. Barnlund wrote of this double-sided nature of cultures:

> If outwardly there is little to distinguish what one sees on the streets of Osaka [Japan] and Chicago—hurrying people, trolleys and buses, huge department stores, blatant billboards, skyscraper hotels, public monuments—beneath the surface there remains great distinctiveness. There is a different organization of industry, a different approach to education, a different role for labor unions, and a contrasting pattern of family life, unique law enforcement and penal practices, contrasting forms of political activity, different sex and age roles. Indeed, most of what is thought of as culture shows as many differences as similarities.[57]

We conclude this section on cultural differences and ethics by again stressing that a complete and honest intercultural ethical perspective grants similarities and recognizes differences. By accepting and appreciating both, you are better able to assess the potential consequences of your communicative acts and to be more tolerant of those of others. Thomas Jefferson said much the same thing about accepting differences when he wrote, "It does me no injury for my neighbor to say there are twenty gods, or no God."

ACCEPT RESPONSIBILITY FOR YOUR BEHAVIOR

Earlier we mentioned that you should be aware that communication elicits responses and that your choice of communicative behaviors can cause both intended and unintended consequences for other people. This notion is predicated on the belief that we are all given the gift of "free will." From a communication perspective this also "recognizes that while we are each situated in a particular culture and socialized into certain norms, we are nevertheless able to reflect on those norms and change them if necessary."[58] This means that your decisions, actions, and even failures, have consequences—consequences over which you have some control. The obvious intercultural import of this fact leads us to what the Dalai Lama has called "our universal responsibility." That responsibility means that if we are going to live in this crowded, interconnected world, we should recognize our individual roles within that world. Remember, as we will demonstrate throughout this book, people and cultures are inextricably linked. As the English anthropologist Gregory Bateson queried, "What pattern connects the crab to the lobster and the orchid to the primrose and all four of them to me? And me to you?"

STUDYING INTERCULTURAL COMMUNICATION

If we have been successful in our endeavors, you should now be convinced of three important points. First, learning how to become successful in your future intercultural interactions is a necessary and worthwhile pursuit. Second, venturing in and out of cultures different from your own can involve culture shock and other issues related to acculturation. And third, the study of intercultural communication requires that you develop a set of ethical standards because your interactions with other people will influence them in both minor and major ways. In our zeal to convince you of these three premises, we might have unintentionally been guilty of overstating the magnitude of culture in human behavior. That is to say, while we strongly hold to the notion that culture is an instrumental variable in human interaction, there are a number of potential problems that can be encountered as you make culture the centerpiece in your study of intercultural communication. Specifically, we need to offer four caveats that will clarify the crucial link between culture and communication. These qualifications deal with (1) the uniqueness of each individual, (2) the perils of generalizing and (3) the need for objectivity.

INDIVIDUAL UNIQUENESS

The American philosopher and psychologist William James wrote, "In every concrete individual, there is a uniqueness that defies formulation." In a very real sense that "formulation" is another way of saying that there have never been two people exactly alike. The reason is simple: Our behavior is shaped by a multitude of sources, and culture is just one of those sources. Put in slightly different terms, we remind you, we are more than our cultures. Although all cultures offer people a common frame of reference, people are not captives of their culture, nor are they subject to all the lessons of that culture. In fact, it is folly to think of people in terms of being blank slates. As Pinker points out, "The mind cannot be a blank slate, because blank slates don't do anything."[59] Instead, people are thinking, feeling individuals whose biology and history interact and play crucial roles in their social collective behavior. Consequently, the values and behaviors of a particular culture may not be the values and behaviors of all the individuals within that culture.

To further clarify the notion of individual uniqueness, we ask you to reflect for a moment on all the potential responses that could be generated by the simple phrase, "I am going to the racetrack and will make some bets." Depending on the listener's background, one person might believe that horse racing is an evil form of gambling; another might maintain that horse racing is animal abuse; and yet another, hearing the same words, could respond by saying, "I love horse races." The reason, of course, is that the world does not look the same to all people. Think for a moment about how the following can influence your behavior. Your genetic makeup, social group experiences, language, gender, age, individual and family history, political affiliation, educational

level, perceptions of others, current circumstances, the region and neighborhood where you grew up, your religious experiences, and many other aspects are at play every moment of your life. All of these factors (along with culture) form your individual personality. Hooker does an excellent job of drawing attention to the interplay of personality and culture, and the hazards of relying solely on culture when studying intercultural communication, when he writes:

> Personality consists of the traits that are unique to an individual human being. It is partly genetic and partly learned. Because much of personality is acquired, it is strongly influenced by culture. Yet a very wide range of personalities can develop within a given culture, whence the danger of placing too much emphasis on "national character." [60]

We have been stressing that although all learned behavior takes place within a cultural setting, every person has a unique personality. Therefore, you must be cautious and prudent when making cultural generalizations. What we said earlier is worth repeating: Always keep in mind that culture is a powerful force in the shaping of human behavior, but people are more than their cultures.

GENERALIZING

When people from other cultures conclude that all Americans wear baseball caps everywhere they go and eat mostly fast food, they are generalizing. When Americans conclude that Germans and Irish spend most of their time drinking beer and singing old folk songs in beer halls and pubs, they are generalizing. And when people say that Muslims do not have time to do anything but pray because they pray five times a day, they are also generalizing. These examples are representative of an endless number of cultural generalizations people use when talking about other groups. Just what is the practice of overusing and misusing generalizations? When we generalize, we are allowing a few instances to represent an entire class of events, people, or experiences. It is easy to fall into the trap of employing generalizations since they are easy to arrive at. For example, think how quickly you can make a decision about another culture if, after meeting someone from India who is studying computer science, you conclude that all students from India only want jobs working with computers. As we noted, these sorts of cultural generalizations are popular because they are easy to create—easy, because they rely on limited samples. In addition, when repeated with enough regularity, they become a shorthand representing an entire collection of people. As you might expect, the study of intercultural communication, which, of course, implies learning about other people and their cultures, is the perfect arena to misuse generalizations, since it is tempting to generalize about an entire collectivity of people when discussing their qualities and "typical" behaviors.

Generalizations are based on a limited amount of data and then applied to a larger population. In intercultural communication, this means ascribing characteristics to a larger group of people based on attributes displayed by a smaller group. Stereotypes differ from generalizations in that they may not be based solely on conjecture and usually appeal to the audience's positive or negative emotions. For example, "all Asian students make good grades" is a stereotype. A generalization would be "Records indicate that Asian students are likely to make good grades."

While we grant that generalizing can be a problem when studying intercultural communication, you can take certain precautions (as we have endeavored to do in this book) to minimize the misleading effects of generalizing. First, cultural generalizations must be viewed as approximations, not as absolute representations. Your personal experiences have taught you that people often do not follow the prescribed and accepted modes of cultural behavior. You may read about conformity as a trait of the Japanese people, but while in Tokyo see a group of motorcycle riders dressed like Hell's Angels. In instances such as these, remember the admonition of the English writer Robert Burton: "No rule is so general, which admits not some exception."

Second, when you do make generalizations, they should deal with primary values and behaviors of a particular culture. It is these core values and learned behaviors that occur with enough regularity and over a long enough period of time that tend to correctly identify the members of a particular culture. If you examine the dominant culture of the United States, you would have little trouble noticing the importance placed on individualism in everything from dress to outward behavior. In the same manner, you could begin to get insight into the role of women in Saudi Arabia by

CONSIDER THIS

Think about the problems associated with generalizing as you read the following brief narrative:

Mr. Thomas was senior vice president of a major oil company that had recently purchased a competing company and was now about to merge the two businesses into a single large international firm. His company sent Mr. Thomas to Kenya for an indefinite time so that he could institute all of the major changes needed to make the operation work smoothly and be profitable. He wanted to make a good impression and establish friendly relationships with all his staff—a staff composed of people from many parts of the world. Mr. Thomas called his new employees into his office individually so that he could build rapport with them on a one-to-one basis. Below is a summary of some of his encounters, none of which produced the results Mr. Thomas wanted.

a. *As an employee from China was leaving the office after a very productive visit, Mr. Thomas said, "It was nice working with you. You remind me of all the people I worked with when I was in Japan."*

b. *Mr. Thomas noticed a strange look on the face of the assistant manager from Germany when he said, "Remember, this is an informal company. No suits and ties, and we will call everyone by their first name."*

c. *When the worker from Saudi Arabia arrived for the one-on-one meeting, the first thing Mr. Thomas said was "How are your wife and family?"*

d. *The administrator from Bolivia was reminded that this new company "runs a tight ship" and that "all work has to be completed on time."*

e. *Mr. Thomas told his new American administrative assistant that one of her duties would involve preparing coffee for all the executives.*

f. *When meeting the new foreman from Kuwait, Mr. Thomas greeted him by extending his left hand.*

g. *Mr. Thomas's advice to the Japanese manager was to make sure his opinions were expressed in forceful terms at all their staff meetings.*

What went wrong?

noticing how few women drive cars, hold public office, or dress in Western attire. What you will notice about our two examples, while there might be exceptions, is that the behaviors in both are easily recognizable. You even see a somewhat consistent pattern in something as simple as greeting behavior. For example, in Mexico people usually embrace, in India people bow, and in the United States people typically shake hands. These kinds of behaviors are recognizable because of their consistency over an extended period, usually involving generation after generation.

Third, when employing generalizations try to use those that can be supported by a variety of sources. Insufficient and/or limited samples often produce unwarranted conclusions. As you read this book you will notice that we have attempted to use hundreds of reliable references to validate many of our conclusions. This sort of "research" is especially useful when seeking to substantiate a generalization concerning a culture where one's fund of knowledge might be limited.

Finally, conclusions and statements about cultures should be qualified so that they do not appear to be absolutes, but only cautious generalizations. For example, although this is only the first chapter of the book you might have noticed how frequently we have used words such as "often," or "usually" so as to avoid speaking in unconditional terms. Coles adds to our list of qualifying terms suggesting phrases such as "on average," "more likely," and "tend to" as a way of moderating the generalization being advanced.[61] These sorts of qualifiers allow thinking and talking about other cultures without implying that every member of the group is exactly alike. We also add that the validity of the generalization often shifts from culture to culture. That is to say, if the culture is somewhat homogeneous, such as that of Japanese or Koreans, references to group characteristics tend be more accurate. However, heterogeneous cultures, like the United States, are far more difficult to generalize about because of the variety of backgrounds, religions, ethnic groups, and the importance placed on each person's individuality.

OBJECTIVITY

Our next consideration when studying intercultural communication involves the issue of objectivity, one of those concepts that is easier to talk about than to attain. The very definition of objectivity ("The state of being objective, just, unbiased and not influenced by emotions or personal prejudices")[62] should alert you to the difficulty of trying to communicate with other people while suspending personal judgment. The problem, of course, is complicated when you engage in intercultural communication, since you approach and respond to other cultures from the perspective of your own culture—and often, consciously or unconsciously, it is difficult to be objective when you perceive the actions of other cultures. As mentioned earlier, this method of using your own culture as an anchor for assessing other cultures is called ethnocentrism. Specifically, as Ferraro and Andreatta note, ethnocentrism is "the belief that one's culture is superior to all other's."[63] Notice in the following brief example, advanced by Tischler, how ethnocentrism and a lack of objectivity operate: "An American might call a Guatemalan peasant's home filthy because the floor is made of packed dirt or believe that the family organization of the Watusi (of East Africa) is immoral because a husband may have several wives."[64]

As evidenced by what we have said thus far, being objective is no simple assignment. For example, it is difficult, if not impossible, to see and to give meaning to words and behaviors unfamiliar to you. How, for instance, do you make sense of someone's silence if you come from a culture that does not value silence? You might make the mistake of

THE USES OF COMMUNICATION

COMMUNICATION AND IDENTITY

One is born into this world without a sense of self. "Self is not innate, but is acquired in the process of communication with others."[2] With this declaration Wood is saying that through contacts with others, information is accumulated that helps define who you are, where you belong, and where your loyalties rest. Identity is multi-dimensional, since an individual has numerous identities ranging from concepts of self, emotional ties to family, attitudes toward gender, to beliefs about one's culture. Regardless of the identity in question, notions regarding all your identities have evolved during the course of interactions with others. So important is identity to the study of intercultural communication that Chapter 6 will examine the link between identity and intercultural communication.

COMMUNICATION AND PERSON PERCEPTION

Not only does communication allow gathering information about personal and cultural identity, it also assists in collecting data about other people. Personal experience reveals that when you meet someone for the first time, gathering information about that individual begins immediately. That information serves two purposes. First, it enables you to learn about the other person. Second, it assists in deciding how to present yourself to that person. These judgments affect everything from the discussion topics selected to whether you decide to continue the conversation or terminate it. This information, collected from both verbal and nonverbal messages, is essential in intercultural communication because in many instances you are dealing with "strangers."

COMMUNICATION AND INTERPERSONAL NEEDS

While there might be many occasions when frustration with other people causes one to find comfort in solitude, in most instances people are social creatures; therefore, communicating with others satisfies a basic social need. Conversation with others creates an enjoyable experience as it produces a feeling of warmth and friendship. In short, communication is one of the major ways to fulfill a social component within you. This linking up with others provides a sense of inclusion and affection. Although cultures might express these feelings and emotions differently, all people, both by nature and nurture, have a need to communicate and interact with others.[3]

COMMUNICATION AND PERSUASION

This final function suggests that communication allows you to send verbal and non-verbal messages that can shape the behavior of other people. Adler and Proctor describe this function thusly: "Besides satisfying social needs and shaping identity, communication is the most widely used approach to satisfying what communication scholars call instrumental goals: getting others to behave in ways we want."[4] If you

Communicating with others satisfies some basic social needs by producing feelings of warmth, friendship, and a sense of inclusion and affection.

Don Smetzer/PhotoEdit

take a moment to reflect on the activities of a normal day, you will discover that you engage in innumerable face-to-face situations intended to influence others. They range from selling products at work, to asking someone for directions when lost, to soliciting a higher grade from a professor, to rallying a group of friends to work for a charitable cause. In all of these instances you are using communication as a tool that allows you to exercise some degree of control over your environment.

Having reviewed the purposes of communication, we are ready to define communication and to discuss some of the basic principles of communication.

CONSIDER THIS

What is meant by the phrase, "People engage in communication for a variety of purposes"?

DEFINING COMMUNICATION

There was good reason for the English statesman Benjamin Disraeli to write, "I hate definitions." While definitions are necessary (they help establish boundaries), finding a single definition for the word "communication" can be troublesome. For example, nearly forty years ago Dance and Larson perused the literature on communication and found 126 definitions of the word.[5] Since then, because the word communication is abstract, countless other definitions have been added to their list. If you type the words "definition of communication" into a search engine on the Internet you will find hundreds of attempts at trying to define this word. In our effort to develop a single definition we have endeavored to isolate the commonalities of many of these definitions. We propose that *human communication is a dynamic process in which people attempt to share their thoughts with other people through the use of symbols in particular settings.*

THE COMPONENTS OF COMMUNICATION

The brevity of our definition has forced us to omit important specifics regarding how communication operates in real-life. Some of those specifics contribute a more complete understanding of how communication operates when people attempt to share what they know, what they want to know, and how they feel. In addition, because of limitations inherent in all definitions, it might seem from our definition that communication is a linear process with each phase of the interaction progressing as one thing happens at a time. This false notion fails to portray human interaction accurately. In most instances the eight stages of communication that make up the components occur almost simultaneously. An awareness of the interacting components promotes understanding the way communication functions when people exchange ideas and feelings.

SOURCE

We begin with the *source*—a person who has an idea, feeling, experience, etc., that they wish to share with another person. The source, as well as the other person, sends and receives messages, since communication is an interactive process. Put in slightly different terms, while you are sending messages you are also observing the messages being generated by your communication partner.

ENCODING

Because what you are feeling and thinking cannot be shared directly (no direct mind-to-mind contact), you must rely on symbolic representations of your internal states. This brings us to our second component—*encoding*. Encoding is an internal activity. It occurs when the source creates a message through the selection of verbal or nonverbal symbols. By employing vocabulary, rules of grammar, and syntax that are relevant to the sender's language, he or she attempts to symbolize what is going on inside them. What this means is that while the process of converting feelings into words and actions is universal, the words and actions selected and how they are strung together have their origins in the culture of the language being used. A member of one culture observes a close friend and makes a decision to smile, whereas, a member of another culture places their hands in front of their chest and slightly bows in the direction of their friend.

MESSAGES

Encoding leads to the production of the *message*, which is a set of written, pictorial, verbal, and/or nonverbal symbols that represent a source's particular state of being at a specific moment. While encoding is an internal act (finding a code that represents a personalized reality), the sending of messages is an external undertaking—it is the subject matter to be communicated.

CHANNEL

Messages must have a means of moving from person to person. It is the *channel* that provides that necessary connection. The channel can take a variety of forms. For instance, as you read this book, the words on the printed page constitute our message, while the printing on these pages is the channel. Channels, in face-to-face interaction, are sights and sounds. However, channels can include a host of types of media. From television to the Internet, messages get moved from place to place.

RECEIVER

After a message has been generated and moved along through a channel, it must encounter a *receiver*. The receiver is the person who takes the message into account, and thereby is directly linked to the source. Receivers may be those whom the source intended to interact with or they may be other people who, for whatever reason, came in contact with the source's message.

DECODING

In the next stage of the communication process the receiver *decodes* the message. This operation (the converting of external stimuli to meaningful interpretations) is akin to the source's act of encoding, since both are an internal activity. The decoding process within the receiver is often referred to as *information processing*. In this stage the receiver attributes meaning to the behaviors generated by the sender.

FEEDBACK

When you send a message to another person you usually perceive the response that person makes to your actions. That response may be words, a nonverbal reaction, or even silence. It matters little; what is important is that your message produced some response that you took into account. The perception of the response to your message is called *feedback*. Feedback typically has two stages. First, it applies to the reactions you obtain from your communication partner. Second, in most instances you use that reaction to decide what to do next. In this way feedback controls the ebb and flow of the conversation. You smile at someone. Your smile is greeted with a frown. You respond by asking, "Are you okay?"

NOISE

The source is not alone in sending messages to the receiver. In actuality, every communication event is characterized by a multitude of competing stimuli. We intentionally use the word "competing" as a way of calling attention to the fact that numerous stimuli are seeking to get noticed. Among communication scholars, this notion of competing stimuli is referred to as *noise*. It is defined and explained as: "any intended or unintended stimulus that affects the fidelity of a sender's message,

[and] disrupts the communication process. Noise is often thought of as interference to the communication process. Noise can be external or internal, and it can influence our ability to process information."[6] Noise can be produced by people sitting behind you talking on a cell phone or by an air conditioner in need of servicing.

Before leaving our discussion of the components of communication we offer a caveat. As you know from personal experience, trying to communicate is not a simple matter. Communication is a highly complex and multidimensional activity. Hence, our enumeration of the components of communication could be extended for the remainder of the book. Factors such as perception, gender, race, culture, motivation, illness, communication skills, funds of knowledge, social systems, and self-concepts may all play roles in the communication experience.

CHARACTERISTICS OF COMMUNICATION

REMEMBER THIS

Communication is a complex behavior that involves numerous interrelated processes.

Having defined communication, and briefly explained its major components, we now expand our analysis to include a discussion of the basic characteristics of communication. As was the case with our examination of definitions and components, a few introductory remarks are in order. First, communication has more characteristics than we can discuss in the next few pages. Just as a description of a forest that mentions only the trees and flowers—but omits the wildlife and lakes—does not do justice to the entire setting, our inventory is not exhaustive. We, too, are forced to leave out some of the landscape. Second, as noted in the introduction to this section on communication, while the linear nature of language forces us to discuss one principle at a time, keep in mind that in reality the elements of communication are in continuous interaction with one another.

COMMUNICATION IS A DYNAMIC PROCESS

You will notice that the words *dynamic process* were contained in our earlier definition of communication. The words *dynamic* and *process* were linked to remind you of a number of things about communication. First, the words indicate that communication is an ongoing activity that has no beginning or end. Put in slightly different terms, *communication is not static*. Communication is like a motion picture, not a single snapshot. A word or action does not stay frozen when you communicate. It is immediately replaced with yet another word or action. Second, communication is a dynamic process because once a word or action is produced, it cannot be retracted. Once an event takes place, that *exact* event cannot happen again. The judge who counsels the jury to "disregard the testimony just given" knows that such a mental activity is impossible. The poet T.S. Eliot said it far more eloquently when he wrote, "In the life of one person, never the same time returns." Third, the phrase *dynamic process* conveys the idea that sending and receiving messages involves a host of variables, *all in operation at the same time*. Each of the parties to the transaction is reacting to the other by seeing, listening, talking, thinking, perhaps smiling and touching the other, all at once. According to Trenholm and Jensen, "To understand communication, we have to look at how what we do and say is connected to what others do and say. We have to view communication as an ongoing process."[7]

COMMUNICATION IS SYMBOLIC

You will recall that our definition of communication mentioned the importance of symbols to human interaction. We noted that there is no direct mind-to-mind contact between people. You cannot directly access the internal thoughts and feelings of other human beings; you can only infer what they are experiencing by what you see and hear. Those inferences are drawn from the symbols people produce. *In human communication a symbol is an expression that stands for or represents something else.* Other animals may engage in some form of communication, and even make use of some symbols, but none has the unique communication capabilities found among humans. Through millions of years of physical evolution, and thousands of years of cultural development, humans are able to generate, receive, store, and manipulate symbols. This sophisticated system allows people to use symbols—be it sounds, marks on paper, letters on the screen of a cell phone, sculptures, Braille, movements, or paintings—to represent something else. Reflect for a moment on the wonderful gift you have that allows you to hear the words, "The kittens look like cotton balls," and like magic, you have an image in your head. Because the image you conjure up for "kittens" and "cotton balls" is inside of you, it is important to remember that each person "defines" those words and phrases from their own cultural perspective. Although all cultures use symbols,

> **CONSIDER THIS**
>
> *What is meant by the phrase "communication is a dynamic process"?*

> **REMEMBER THIS**
>
> *Because you cannot directly access the internal thoughts of another person, you must rely on and interpret their use of verbal and nonverbal symbols to represent those thoughts.*

they assign their own meanings to the symbols. Not only do Spanish speakers say *perro* for "dog," but the mental image they form when they hear the sound is probably quite different from the one Chinese speakers form when they hear *gŏu*, their word for "dog." So important is the notion of symbols to the study of intercultural communication that later in this chapter, and again in Chapters 8 and 9, we will return to the topic of symbols.

COMMUNICATION IS CONTEXTUAL

The heading declares communication is *contextual* as a way of informing you that communication does not occur in a vacuum. Communication is part of a larger system composed of many ingredients, all of which must be considered. As Littlejohn states, "Communication always occurs in a context, and the nature of communication depends in large measure on this context."[8] What this implies is that setting and environment help determine the words and actions you generate and the meanings you give to the symbols produced by other people. Context provides what Shimanoff calls a "prescription that indicates what behavior is obligated, preferred, or prohibited."[9] Attire, language, nonverbal behavior, topic selection, and vocabulary are all adapted to the context. Reflect for a moment on how differently you would behave in each of the following settings: a classroom, a church, a courtroom, a funeral, a wedding, a sporting event, a hospital, or a nightclub. For example, a male would not attend a university lecture, even in hot weather, without wearing a shirt. However, at a football stadium, you might find a whole row of males without shirts on (possibly with letters painted on their chests), and this would be socially acceptable. Even the words we exchange are contextual. The simple phrase, "How are you?" shifts meaning as you move from place to place and person to person. To a friend it can be a straightforward expression used as a greeting. Yet during a doctor's appointment, the same three words ("How are you?") uttered by the physician call for a detailed response regarding your physical condition.

This contextualization of communication involves a number of variables we need to examine.

Location

Brief introspection should tell you that your behavior is not the same in every environment. Whether it is an auditorium, an employment interview, an upscale restaurant, a group meeting, or an office, the location of your interaction provides guidelines for your behavior. Either consciously or unconsciously, you know the prevailing rules, many of which are fixed by your culture. Most cultures, for example, have classrooms, but the rules for behavior in those classrooms are rooted in culture. In Mexico, children are encouraged to move around the room and to interact verbally and physically with their classmates. In China, students remain in their seats nearly all of the day and seldom talk to one another.

Occasion

The occasion of a communication encounter also controls the behavior of the participants. The same auditorium or sports arena can be the occasion for a graduation ceremony, concert, pep rally, convocation, dance, or memorial service. Each of these occasions calls for distinctly different forms of behavior. For example, somberness and silence are usually the rule at a solemn American Protestant funeral, while an Irish wake calls for music, dancing, and a great deal of merriment. A pep rally or dance would be an occasion in the same sports arena venue for raucous activity and much movement.

Time

Time is another crucial element that can influence the communication event. Yet the influence of time on communication is so subtle that its impact is often overlooked. To understand this concept, answer these questions: How do you feel when someone keeps you waiting for a long time? Do you respond to a phone call at 2:00 AM the same way you do to one at 2:00 PM? Do you find yourself rushing the conversation when you know you have very little time to spend with someone? Your answers to these questions reveal how often the clock controls your actions. Every communication event takes place along a time-space continuum, and the amount of time allotted, whether it is for social conversation or a formal presentation, affects that event. Cultures, as well as people, use time to communicate. In the United States, schedules and time constraints are ever present. "For Americans, the use of appointment-schedule time reveals how people feel about each other, how significant their business is, and where they rank in the status system."[10]

Number of Participants

The number of people with whom you communicate also affects the flow of communication. You feel and act differently if you are speaking with one person, in a group, or before a large audience. Cultures also respond to changes in number. For example, people in Japan find small-group interaction much to their liking, yet they often feel extremely uncomfortable when they have to give a formal public speech.

MOST COMMUNICATION BEHAVIOR IS LEARNED

Your ability to communicate is a complex interplay between biology and culture. Without describing the complexities of genetic science or the evolution of culture, what we are saying is that human beings are equipped with the necessary anatomy, physiology, and chemistry to learn new information throughout their lives. In addition, there is no upper limit to how much you can learn. This notion is often referred to as the brain being an "open-ended system." We can tell you one fact after another, and your brain can store these facts away. You may have trouble remembering it, but the information is there. For example, if we write that over fifty years ago Leon Festinger developed the theory of cognitive dissonance, "Star of the Class" is a celebrated race horse, and Ulan Bator is the capital of Mongolia, and you did not know these facts prior to reading them, you now have the three items stockpiled somewhere in your brain. This idea that the brain is an open system has direct implications for intercultural communication. Being able to learn nearly any kind of information and numerous behavior patterns has resulted in your knowing how to communicate. If you were reared in a home where your family spoke Spanish, you learned to communicate in that language. If your family spoke in hushed tones, you learned to speak softly. If your family engaged in a great deal of touching, you learned about touch as a form of communication. Even what you learned to talk about was part of your learning experiences. If your family discussed politics and believed people should never gossip, you too, at least early in your life, held these beliefs about appropriate and inappropriate topics for discussion. What we are suggesting is that all people have learned, and carry around, an assorted fund of knowledge about communication. However, it is obvious that not all people and cultures have gathered the same information. In one culture people might have received information on how to use camels or horses for transportation, while in another people have received instructions on how to drive automobiles. Some people have learned to talk to God, while others sit quietly and wait for God to talk to them. We conclude this section by reminding you that people of cultures different from your own might have distinctive views about transportation and God, but also unique ways of communicating.

COMMUNICATION HAS A CONSEQUENCE

As part of our last discussion on the workings of communication we inserted the idea that people can learn something from every experience to which they are exposed. An extension of this concept is stated by Berko and his associates when they write, "All of our messages, to one degree or another, do something to someone else (as well as to us)."[11] Obviously, your response to messages will fluctuate in both degree and kind. If someone sends you a message by asking directions to the library, your response is to say, "It's on your right." You might even point to the library. The message from the other person has thus produced an observable response. If someone says to you, "The United States is spending too much money fighting wars thousands of miles away," and you only think about this statement, you are still responding, but your response is not an observable action. There are also thousands of responses that are harder to detect. These are responses to messages that you receive by observing, imitating, or interacting with others. Generally, you are not even aware that you are receiving these messages. Your parents act out their gender roles, and you receive messages about your gender role. People greet you by shaking hands instead of hugging, and without being aware of it, you are receiving messages about forms of address.

The response you make to someone's message does not have to be immediate. You can respond minutes, days, or even years later. For example, your second-grade teacher may have asked you to stop throwing rocks at a group of birds. Perhaps the teacher added that the birds were part of a family and were gathering food for their babies. She might also have indicated that birds feel pain just like people. Perhaps twenty years later you are invited to go quail hunting. You are about to say "yes" when you remember those words from your teacher and decide not to go on the "expedition." This decision reflects the principle that all communication has a consequence.

One of the most important implications of this principle is that you are changing other people each time you exchange messages with them. Wood buttresses this view when she writes, "What we say and do affects others: how they perceive themselves, how they think about themselves, and how they think about others. Thus, responsible people think carefully about ethical guidelines for communication."[12]

REMEMBER THIS

a. Perception is a highly personal matter.
b. People as well as cultures differ in the manner in which they communicate.

We conclude this section on communication by again reminding you that *communication is complex*. It is even more complex when the cultural dimensions are included. Although all cultures use symbols to share their realities, the specific realities and the symbols employed are often quite different. In one culture you smile in a casual manner as a form of greeting, while in another you bow formally in silence, and in yet another you acknowledge your friend with a full embrace. From our discussion you should now have an understanding of the concept of communication and the role it plays in everyday interaction. With this background, we now turn to the topic of culture.

CULTURE

Moving from communication to culture provides us with a rather seamless transition, for as Hall points out, "Culture is communication and communication is culture."[13] In fact, when examining communication and culture it is hard to decide which is the voice and which is the echo. The reason for the duality is that you "learn" your culture via communication, while at the same time communication is a reflection of your culture. This book manifests the authors' strong belief that you cannot improve your intercultural communication skills without having a clear understanding of this phenomenon called culture. The following examples demonstrate the powerful link between communication and culture:

- Some people scratch their ears and cheeks as a sign of happiness, but people in other places of the world smile when they are happy. Why?
- Some people in many parts of the world put dogs in their ovens, but people in the United States put them on their couches and beds. Why?
- Some people in Kabul and Kandahar pray five times each day while kneeling on the floor, but some people in Jerusalem pray while standing erect and slightly rocking back and forth. Why?
- Some people speak Tagalog and others speak English. Why?
- Some people paint and decorate their entire bodies, but others spend hundreds of dollars painting and decorating only their faces. Why?
- Some people shake hands when introduced to a stranger, but other people bow at such an encounter. Why?

The general answer to all these questions is the same—*culture*. As Peoples and Bailey point out, "cultures vary in their ways of thinking and ways of behaving."[14] That sentence is not only the answer to our initial question, but it also serves as one of the basic premises of this entire book. Rodriguez punctuates the influence of culture on human perception and actions when she writes, "Culture consists of how we relate to other people, how we think, how we behave, and how we view the world."[15] Although culture is not the only stimulus behind your behavior, its omnipresent quality makes it one of the most powerful. Hall underscores this point when he concludes, "There is not one aspect of human life that is not touched and altered by culture."[16] Wood further speaks to this notion when she writes, "We are not born knowing how, when, and to whom to speak, just as we are not born with attitudes about cooperating or competing. We acquire attitudes as we interact with others, and we then reflect cultural teachings in the way we communicate."[17] Wood is reminding you that although you enter this world with all the anatomy and physiology needed to live in the world, you do not arrive knowing how to dress, what toys to play with, what to eat, which gods to worship, what to strive for, how to spend your money or your time, or how to define the questions surrounding death.

CULTURE IS SHARED

Your culture is shared with other people who have been exposed to similar experiences. While your personal experiences and genetic heritage form the unique *you*, culture unites people with a collective frame of reference. "Culture is to a human collective what personality is to an individual."[18] Nolan reaffirms this idea when he suggests that "culture is a group worldview, the way of organizing the world that a particular society has created over time. This framework or web of meaning allows the members of that society to make sense of themselves, their world, and their experiences in that world."[19] It is this sharing of a common reality that gives people within a particular culture a common fund of knowledge, a sense of identity, shared traditions, and specific behaviors that are often distinct from other collections of people. Haviland and his associates explain this "sharing" process: "As a shared set of ideas, values, perceptions, and standards of behavior, culture is the common denominator that makes the actions of individuals intelligible to other members of their society. It enables them to predict how other members are most likely to behave in a given circumstance, and it tells them how to react accordingly."[20]

What this sharing of experiences means is that culture allows for the behaviors of one individual to be comprehensible to the other members of that culture. Chiu and Hong offer an excellent summary of some of the activities and perceptions that grow out of a shared way of experiencing the world:

> Shared knowledge gives rise to shared meanings, which are carried in the shared physical environment (such as the spatial layout of a rural village, the subsistence economy) social institutions (e.g., schools, family, the workplace), social practices (e.g., division of labor), the language, conversation scripts, and other media (e.g., religious scriptures, cultural icons, folklores, idioms).[21]

We have tried to convince you that culture is a powerful force on how people view the world and interact in that world. To further that idea let us now (1) define culture, (2) explain the basic functions of culture, (3) highlight the essential elements of culture, and (4) discuss the major characteristics of culture.

CULTURE DEFINED

The preceding discussion on the topic of culture should enable you to see that culture is ubiquitous and complex. It is also difficult to define. As Harrison and Huntington note, "The term 'culture,' of course, has had multiple meanings in different disciplines and different contexts."[22] These meanings "range from complex and fancy definitions to simple ones such as 'culture is the programming of the mind' or 'culture is the human-made part of the environment.'"[23] The media also use the word to portray aspects of individual sophistication such as classical music, fine art, or exceptional food and wine. You also hear the words "popular culture" when people are discussing current trends within the culture. This, of course, is not the way we use the word. For our purposes, we are concerned with a definition that contains the recurring theme of how culture and communication are linked. One definition that meets our needs is advanced by Triandis:

> **CONSIDER THIS**
>
> Using the examples offered by Chiu and Hong, how would you explain the following "shared meanings" to someone from another culture: (a) typical arrangement of American cities, (2) some general characteristics of American schools and families, (3) perceptions of various jobs and professions, and (4) the place of religion in American culture?

> Culture is a set of human-made objective and subjective elements that in the past have increased the probability of survival and resulted in satisfaction for the participants in an ecological niche, and thus became shared among those who could communicate with each other because they had a common language and they lived in the same time and place.[24]

We are partial to this definition because it highlights the essential features of culture. First, specifying that it is "human-made" clarifies that culture is concerned with non-biological parts of human life. This distinction allows for explanations of behavior that must be learned while at the same time eliminating (at least from our study) innate acts that are not learned (such as eating, sleeping, crying, speech mechanisms, and fear). "Second, the definition includes what can be termed "subjective" elements of culture—these include such concepts as values, beliefs, attitudes, behaviors and those foundational conventions most prevalent in a social order." Think for a moment of all the subjective cultural beliefs and values you hold that influence your interpretation of the world. Your views about the American flag, work, immigration, freedom, aging, ethics, dress, property rights, etiquette, healing and health, death and mourning, play, law, individualism, magic and superstition, modesty, sexual taboos, status differentiation, courtship, formality and informality, and bodily adornment are all part of your cultural membership. Finally, the definition also calls attention to the importance of language as a symbol system that allows culture to be transmitted and shared. This means that a collection of people has established not only a set of symbols, but rules for using those symbols.

THE FUNCTIONS OF CULTURE

Perhaps at this stage in our discussion about culture it is wise to ask the following question: *What are the basic functions of culture?* In its most uncomplicated sense, culture, for over forty thousand years until today, is intended to make life unproblematic for people by "teaching" them how to adapt to their surroundings. The English writer Fuller echoed the same idea in rather simple terms when he wrote, "Culture makes all things easy." A more detailed explanation as to the functions of culture is offered by Sowell:

> Cultures exist to serve the vital, practical requirements of human life—to structure a society so as to perpetuate the species, to pass on the hard-learned knowledge and experience of generations past and centuries past to the young and inexperienced in order to spare the next generation the costly and dangerous process of learning everything all over again from scratch through trial and error—including fatal errors.[25]

Culture serves a basic need by laying out a somewhat predictable world in which each individual is firmly grounded. It thus enables you to make sense of your surroundings by offering a blueprint of not only how to behave but also what results you can anticipate for that behavior. While people in every culture might deviate from this blueprint, they at least know what their culture expects from them. Try to imagine a single day in your life without the guidelines of your culture. From how to earn a living, to how an economic system works, to how to greet strangers, to explanations of illness and death, to how to find a mate, culture provides you with structure and direction.

THE ELEMENTS OF CULTURE

While culture is composed of countless elements (food, shelter, work, defense, social control, psychological security, forms of governing, social harmony, purpose in life, and so on), there are five that relate directly to this book. Understanding these will enable you to appreciate the notion that while all cultures share a common set of perceptions and behaviors, these five particular aspects often distinguish one culture from another. We introduce these early in our analysis of intercultural communication because these aspects will become major topics and even individual chapters later in the book.

Early in life children learn about appropriate and inappropriate ways of acting so that they will know how to adapt to their surroundings.

Edwin McDaniel

Religion

We begin with one of the most important of all components of culture—religion. For thousands of years religion has been used by people to assist them in understanding the universe, natural phenomena, what to die for, and how to dwell among other people. The influence of religion can be seen in the entire fabric of a culture since it serves so many basic functions. These functions include "social control, conflict resolution, reinforcement of group solidarity, explanations of the unexplainable, and emotional support."[26] In many ways religion is like culture itself, since it provides the followers of the faith with a set of values, beliefs, and even guidelines for specific behaviors. These guidelines consciously and unconsciously impact everything from business practices (the Puritan work ethic), to politics (the link between Islam and government), to individual behavior (codes of personal ethics). This multidimensional aspect of religion, and its relationship to culture, means that to understand any culture you must also understand how the members of that culture provide explanations for how the world operates and how they believe they fit into that process.

History

Over two thousand years ago the Roman orator Cicero remarked, "History ... provides guidance in daily life, and brings us tidings of antiquity." Cicero was correct; all cultures believe in the idea that history provides stories about the past that serve as lessons on how to live in the present. These stories also help cement people into what is called "a common culture." This "common culture" creates a strong sense of identity. As these descriptions of significant historical events get transmitted from generation to generation, people begin to perceive "where they belong" and where their loyalties lie.

Robert Fonseca

Religion is an essential part of every culture and has been used by people to assist them in understanding the universe, natural phenomena, what to die for, and how to dwell among other people.

These stories of the past also provide members of a culture with large portions of their values and rules for behavior. History highlights the culture's origins, "tells" its members what is deemed important, and identifies the accomplishments of the culture of which they can be proud. While all cultures use history to transmit important messages about that culture, each set of messages is unique to a particular culture. The "lessons" of the Holocaust, the Spanish conquest of Mexico, the motivation behind the building of the Great Wall of China, the Indian and Pakistani Conflict of 1947, and the events of September 11, 2001, are stories that carry a unique meaning and varied level of importance for their respective cultures. These events also help explain contemporary perceptions held by members of those cultures. In short, the study of history links the old with the new while serving as a pointer for the future.

Values

Values are another key feature of every culture. Bailey and Peoples emphasize the role values play in culture when they write, "Values are critical to the maintenance of culture as a whole because they represent the qualities that people believe are essential to continuing their way of life. It is useful to think of values as providing the ultimate standards that people believe must be upheld under practically all circumstances."[27] The connection between values and culture is so strong that it is hard to talk about one without discussing the other. As Macionis notes, values are "culturally defined standards of desirability, goodness, and beauty that serve as broad guidelines for social living."[28] The key word in any discussion of cultural values is "guidelines." In other words, values help determine how people within a particular culture ought to behave. To the extent that cultural values differ, you can expect that participants in intercultural communication will tend to exhibit and to anticipate different behaviors under similar circumstances. For example, while all cultures value the elderly, the strength of this value is often very different as you move from culture to culture. In the Korean, Chinese, Japanese, Mexican, and American Indian cultures, the elderly are highly respected and revered. They are even sought out for advice and counsel. This is in stark contrast to the United States, where the emphasis is on youth.

Social Organizations

Another feature found in all cultures is what we call "social organizations." These organizations (sometimes referred to as social systems or social structures) represent the various social units within the culture. These are institutions such as family, government, schools, tribes, and clans. The basic premise that underlies all these organizations is the need for and reality of interdependence. As Lavenda and Schultz point out, "Human interdependence means that we cannot survive as lone individuals but need to live with others."[29] This "living with others" means that there are patterned interactions that are "rule governed," which all members of these organizations have learned and display. These social systems establish communication networks and regulate norms of personal, familial, and social conduct.[30] "They also establish group cohesion and enable people to consistently satisfy their basic needs."[31] The ways these organizations function and the norms they advance are unique to each culture. Nolan underscores the nature of these organizations in the following illustration: "Social structures reflect our culture, for example, whether we have kings and queens, or presidents and prime ministers. Within our social structure, furthermore, culture assigns roles to the various players—expectations about how individuals will behave, what they will stand for, and even how they will dress."[32]

Language

Language is yet another feature that is common to all cultures. In fact, as Haviland and his associates note, "Language is fundamental to the functioning of human culture."[33] Language and culture are connected in a number of ways. Whether they are English, Swahili, Chinese, or French, most words, how they are used, the meanings assigned, the grammar employed, and the syntax bear the identification marks of a specific culture. Bailey and Peoples further develop the important role language plays in the existence of a culture when they write: "Language underlies every other aspect of a people's way of life—their relationship with the natural environment, family life, political organizations, worldview, and so forth. Most socialization of children depends on language, which means language is the main vehicle of cultural transmission from one generation to the next."[34]

CHARACTERISTICS OF CULTURE

We begin this next section with this obvious, yet often overlooked, truism: The seven billion people in the world are both alike and different from each other. You can find that same amalgamation among cultures. While this book basically focuses on the differences that influence communication, it is useful to examine a series of characteristics that all cultures have in common. We believe an examination of these traits is useful for a number of reasons. First, "A careful study of these characteristics helps us to see the importance and the functions of culture itself."[35] Second, as we review these commonalities the strong connection between culture and communication will become apparent. Most experts agree: "The heart of culture involves language, religion, values, traditions, and customs."[36] These are the very topics treated throughout this book. Finally, this may be the first time you have been asked to seriously look at your own culture. As Brislin points out, "People do not frequently talk about their own culture or the influence that culture has on their behavior."[37] Remember, most of culture is in the taken-for-granted realm and below the conscious level. Learning about culture can be an energizing awakening as you develop understanding of your actions and the actions of others. Shapiro offered much the same pep talk when he wrote: "The discovery of culture, the awareness that it shapes and molds our behavior, our values and even our ideas, the recognition that it contains some element of the arbitrary, can be a startling or an illuminating experience."[38]

Culture Is Learned

Perhaps the most important characteristic of culture is that *it is not innate; it is learned*. Imagine what a confusing place this world must be to a newborn. After living in a peaceful environment for nine months, the infant is thrust into this novel place called "the world." It is a world filled with sights, sounds, tastes, and other sensations that, at this stage of life, have no meaning. As the psychologist William James noted, what greets the newborn is a bubbling, babbling mass of confusion. From the moment of birth to the end of life you seek to overcome that confusion and make sense of the world. It is culture that assists you in that sense-making process. "When an infant is born, he or she enters a cultural environment in which many solutions already exist to the universal problems facing the human population. The child merely needs to learn or internalize those solutions in order to make a reasonable adjustment to his or her surroundings."[39]

In some ways this entire book is about how and what members of particular cultures have learned, and how that "learning" might influence intercultural communication. When we speak of "learning," we are using the word in a rather broad sense. We are talking about both informal and formal learning.[40] *Informal learning* is often very subtle and normally takes place through interaction (your parents kiss you and you learn about kissing—whom, when, and where to kiss), observation (you observe your parents kneeling at church and learn about correct behavior in a religious setting), and imitation (you laugh at the same jokes your parents laugh at and you learn about humor).

The *formal* teaching of a culture is far more structured and is often left to the various social institutions of the culture, such as schools and churches. When a school system teaches computer skills, American history, or mathematics, it is giving the members of a culture the tools and information the culture deems important. When a child has a

Sunday school lesson focusing on the Ten Commandments, he or she is learning about ethical behavior. As you might expect, it is often difficult to distinguish between informal and formal learning, since culture influences you from the instant you are born. In addition, much of cultural learning is subconscious, and in most instances you are rarely aware of many of the messages that it sends. This unconscious or hidden dimension of culture leads many researchers to claim that culture is invisible. There is even a well-respected book about culture by Edward T. Hall, titled *The Hidden Dimension*.[41] The title is intended to call attention to the important premise that the "messages" and "lessons" of culture are so subtle that you seldom see them "coming in" or getting acted out. Most of you would have a difficult time pointing to a specific event or experience that taught you to stand when an important person enters the room or how to employ direct eye contact during a job interview. The roles of silence and space, the importance of attractiveness, your view of aging, your ability to speak one language instead of another, your preference for activity over meditation, or your preference for using one mode of behavior over another when dealing with conflict are all rooted in culture. Try to isolate where you learned what is considered "cool" in your culture. You might be able to point to what you think is "cool," but telling someone how you learned to be "cool" would be a near-impossible task.

While you could readily recognize how you learned to solve a specific chemistry problem, you would have a much harder time with your culture's more subtle "teachings." Reflect for a moment on the learning that is taking place in the following examples:

- A young boy in the United States whose grandfather reminds him to shake hands when he is introduced to a friend of the family is learning good manners.
- An Arab father who reads the Koran to his daughter and son is teaching the children about God.
- An Indian child who lives in a home where the women eat after the men is learning gender roles.
- A Jewish child who helps conduct the Passover ceremony is learning about traditions.
- A Japanese girl who attends tea ceremony classes is learning about patience, self-discipline, and ritual.
- A fourth-grade student watching a film on George Washington crossing the Delaware River is learning about patriotism and fortitude.

In these examples, people are learning their culture through various forms of communication. That is why, earlier in this chapter, we said that culture is communication and communication is culture. Wood establishes this important link between culture and communication when she writes, "We learn a culture's views and patterns in the process of communicating. As we interact with others, we come to understand the beliefs, values, norms, and language of our culture."[42]

A number of points should be clear by now. First, learning cultural perceptions, rules, and behaviors usually

CONSIDER THIS

Using the list of "learning" examples we just offered, stop now and reflect on your own background and try to recall any specific events where you were "learning" about your culture and did not realize it at the time. For instance, what experiences taught you about good manners, the treatment of the elderly, the importance of an education, sportsmanship, that it is wrong to steal, and the importance of being charitable.

takes place without your being aware of it. Second, the essential messages of a culture get reinforced and repeated. Third, you learn your culture from a large variety of sources, with family, schools, church, and community being the four most powerful institutions of culture. Let us look at a few of the specific ways those institutions "teach" their most essential messages.

Learning Culture through Proverbs. Even before a very young child can read, he or she is hearing "lessons about life" transmitted through proverbs. "Whether called maxims, truisms, clichés, idioms, expressions, or sayings, proverbs are small packages of truth about a people's values and beliefs."[43] Proverbs are so important to a culture that there are even proverbs about proverbs. A German proverb states: "A country can be judged by the quality of its proverbs." And the Yoruba of Africa teach that "A wise man who knows proverbs, reconciles difficulties." Both of these proverbs emphasize the idea that you can learn about a people through their proverbs. These proverbs—communicated in colorful, vivid language, and with very few words—reflect the wisdom, biases, and even superstitions of a culture.

Proverbs are learned easily and repeated with great regularity. Because they are brief (a line or two), their influence as "teachers" is often overlooked. Yet, many religious traditions use proverbs to express important messages about life. The Proverbs in the Old Testament represent a collection of moral sayings and "wisdom" intended to assist the reader to behave in a particular and honorable way. Chinese philosophers such as Confucius, Mencius, Chung Tzu, and Lao-tzu also used proverbs and maxims to express their thoughts to their disciples. These proverbs survive so that each generation can learn what a culture deems significant. "Proverbs reunite the listener with his or her ancestors."[44] Seidensticker notes that "[proverbs] say things that people think important in ways that people remember. They express common concerns."[45]

The value of proverbs as a reflection of a culture is further underscored by the fact that "interpreters at the United Nations prepare themselves for their extremely sensitive job by learning proverbs of the foreign language"[46] that they will be interpreting. As Mieder notes, "Studying proverbs can offer insights into a culture's worldview regarding such matters as education, law, business, and marriage."[47] Roy offers a summary as to why understanding cultural proverbs is a valuable tool for students of intercultural communication. "Examination of these orally transmitted traditional values offers an excellent means of learning about another culture because these oft-repeated sayings fuse past, present, and future. These sayings focus our attention on basic principles accepted within the culture."[48]

Because all people, regardless of their culture, share common experiences, many of the same proverbs appear throughout the world. For example, in nearly every culture some degree of thrift and hard work is stressed. Hence, in Germany the proverb states, "One who does not honor the penny is not worthy of the dollar." In the United States people are told, "A penny saved is a penny earned." Because they value silence, the Chinese have a proverb that says: "Loud thunder brings little rain." Taking responsibility for one's actions is also a universal value. Hence, in English, it is "God helps those who help themselves." For Indians, the proverb is "Call on God, but row away from the rocks." However, our concern is not with the commonality of cultural proverbs, but rather the use of these proverbs to teach lessons that are unique to that particular culture. By examining some of these proverbs you will be able to accomplish two purposes at once. First, you will discover the power of proverbs as a teaching device. Second, an examination of proverbs will help you learn about other cultures' worldviews, beliefs, values, and communication patterns.

The following are but a few of the hundreds of proverbs and sayings from the United States, each of which attempts to instruct about an important value held by the dominant culture.

- *Time is money, Strike while the iron is hot, Actions speak louder than words,* and *He who hesitates is lost.* These proverbs underscore the idea that, in the United States, people who do not waste time and make quick decisions are highly valued.
- *God helps those who help themselves, Pull yourself up by your bootstraps,* and *No pain, no gain.* These three sayings highlight the strong belief held in America that people should show individual initiative and never give up.
- *A man's home is his castle.* This expression not only tells us about the value of privacy, but also demonstrates the male orientation in the United States by implying that the home belongs to the man.
- *The squeaky wheel gets the grease.* In the United States people are encouraged to be direct, speak up, and make sure their views are heard.

The following are a few proverbs from some non-U.S. cultures.[49] While we could have selected thousands of proverbs to illustrate our point about the link between these sayings and the teaching of key elements of a culture, we have selected but a few that stress important values associated with intercultural communication.

- Many cultures prefer **silence** over an abundance of talk. They believe silence is associated with wisdom. Tanzanian: *The wisest animal is the giraffe; it never speaks.* Thai: *A wise man talks a little, an ignorant one talks much.* Peruvian: *From the tree of silence hangs the fruit of tranquility.* Hopi Indian: *Eating little and speaking little can hurt no man.*
- Respect for the wisdom of the **elderly** is found in many collective cultures. Chinese: *To know the road ahead, ask those coming back.* Spanish: *The devil knows more because he's old than because he's the devil.* Portuguese: *The old man is the one who makes good food.* Greek: *The old age of an eagle is better than the youth of a sparrow.* Nigerian: *What an old man will see while seated, a small child cannot see even standing.*
- Many cultures teach the value of **collectivism** and **group solidarity** over individualism. Chinese: *A single bamboo pole does not make a raft.* Ethiopian: *When spider webs unite, they can tie up a lion.* Japanese: *A single arrow is easily broken, but not ten in a bundle.* Russian: *You can't tie a knot with one hand.* Brazilian: *One bird alone does not make a flock.*
- For many cultures there is the belief that **fate**, rather than one's own devices, controls much of life. Japanese: *One does not make the wind, but is blown by it.* Spanish: *Since we cannot get what we like, let us like what we can get.* Mexican: *Man proposes and God disposes.* Or, *I dance to the tune that is played.*
- Cultures that place a premium on **education** use proverbs to assist in the teaching of this important value. Jewish: *A table is not blessed if it has fed no scholars.* Chinese: *If you are planning for a year, sow rice: if you are planning for a decade, plant a tree; if you are planning for a lifetime, educate people.*
- Some cultures stress **social harmony** over direct confrontation. Chinese: *A harsh word dropped from the tongue cannot be brought back by a coach and six horses.*

Japanese: *The spit aimed at the sky comes back to one.* Korean: *Kick a stone in anger and harm your own foot.*

- **Privacy** is a key value is some cultures. Here again you can observe the use of proverbs to teach that value. German: *Sweep only in front of your own door.* Swedish: *He who stirs another's porridge often burns his own.*

Learning Culture through Folktales, Legends, and Myths. While the words *folktales*, *legends*, and *myths* have slightly different meanings, we use the three words interchangeably because they all deal with narratives that are intended to transmit the important messages each culture seeks to teach its members. "Often such tales are described as 'cultural history.'"[50] These "tales" are frequently simple morality lessons focusing on good and evil and right and wrong. However, in many instances "Myths, legends, and folktales also provide a way of addressing the existential questions people have asked throughout time."[51] Hence, these stories "are designed to explain some of the really big issues of human existence such as where we came from, why we are here, and how we can account for the things in our world."[52] These three narrative forms are used in a variety of settings (such as at home, in school, and at church), at all stages of language development (oral, written, etc.), and at each stage of life (infancy, childhood, and adulthood).

The customs, traditions, and beliefs expressed in folktales link people to their history and root them to their past. Thus, "these cultural components are passed on through generations in the retelling of the tales."[53] Rodriguez mentions some of the specific purposes of these stories that help contribute to their longevity: "Folktales are not only regarded as some of the best keepers of our language and cultural memories, they are also great helpers in the process of socialization, they teach our children the sometimes difficult lessons about how to interact with other people and what happens when virtues are tested or pitted against one another."[54]

Whether it tells of Pinocchio's nose growing longer because of his lies, Columbus's daring voyage, Captain Ahab's heroics as he seeks to overcome the power of nature, Abraham Lincoln learning to read by drawing letters on a shovel by the fireside, Robin Hood helping the poor, or Davy Crockett as the courageous frontiersman fighting to save the Alamo, folklore constantly reinforces important cultural lessons. In passing, observe that some of these lessons are very subtle. Notice, for example, the built-in gender bias in these few examples. In each story, males are the main characters and heroes. When females appear in cultural stories ("Cinderella," "Snow White," "Little Red Riding Hood," and many others), they are often portrayed as submissive and docile.

The stories that are passed from generation to generation are entertaining and captivating, but in nearly all cases they are also used to stress moral messages. Americans revere the tough, independent, fast-shooting cowboy of the Old West; the Japanese learn about the importance of duty, obligation, and loyalty from "The Tale of the Forty-Seven Ronin"; and the Sioux Indians use the legend of "Pushing up the Sky" to teach that people can accomplish much if they work together. For the Australian

In Western cultures that stress the importance of the individual, people are often the main focus of the message being created by the artist.

Kathleen K. Parker

As already indicated, art is a relevant symbol, a forceful teacher, and an avenue for transmitting cultural values. We need only look at the art on totem poles to see what matters to American Indians of the northwestern United States. The carvings on these poles chronicle how deeply these people are concerned about their ancestors, family, history, identity, wildlife, and nature.[71] "Erected in front of the homes of chiefs, these poles are inscribed with symbols that are visual reminders of the social hierarchy."[72] This Indian art, whose purpose is to tell stories, is very different from the art of Islam. Since the Koran forbids the depiction of human figures; calligraphy, geometric designs, pottery, and carpets are esteemed fine art. Even inscriptions from the Koran are a form of art. [73]

It should be clear from our brief discussion of art that "through the cross-cultural study of art—myths, songs, dances, paintings, carvings, and so on—we may discover much about different worldviews and religious beliefs, as well as political ideas, social values, kinship structures, economic relations, and historical memory."[74]

Learning Culture through Mass Media. Obviously, this is not a book about mass media or folktales or art. We examine mass media simply as a way of calling your attention to the many "teachers" and "messages" used to pass on culture. When we speak of mass media, we are talking about those media that are created, designed, and used to reach very large audiences. The impact of these devices on a population, particularly young people who are learning about culture, is now common knowledge. While mass media are used for a host of reasons, we are concerned with this mode of communication as a purveyor of culture. Wood amplifies this view when she writes, "Mass media is a major source of information and entertainment. Yet that's not all we get from mass communication. We also get ideas about who we are and should be, and we form impressions of people, events, issues and cultural life."[75] As a means of presenting this "cultural life," mass media transmit images and stories that contribute to a sense of cultural identity while at the same time shaping beliefs and values. Mass media are, as Williams notes, "mass social learning."[76]

The over-abundance of media in daily life is perhaps most evident when applied to young people. A report by the Kaiser Family Foundation highlights the overwhelming number of cultural messages young people receive in the following summary:

> Two-thirds of infants and toddlers watch a screen an average of 2 hours a day. Kids under age 6 watch an average of 2 hours a day of screen media, primarily TV and videos or DVDs. Kids and teens 8-18 years spend nearly 4 hours a day in front of a TV screen and almost two additional hours on a computer (outside of schoolwork) playing video games.[77]

An average American spends about 1,600 hours a year watching television, and it is estimated that by the time a student graduates from the twelfth grade he or she will have spent more time watching television than in the classroom. It is easy to understand how these images affect attitudes and perceptions toward leisure time, gender, sexuality, race, the elderly, and drugs and alcohol. In blatant and in subtle terms children are told what is and is not important. Delgado offers a summary of the power of mass media outlets by noting that they "help constitute our daily lives by shaping our experiences and providing the content for much of what we talk about (and how we talk) at the interpersonal level."[78] Perhaps the clearest explanation of the role mass media plays in learning about culture is found in Cultivation Theory, which was developed by Gerbner and Gross.[79] This theory is directly linked to the learning of culture, since at its heart is the idea that television helps shape future perceptions.[80] Specifically, the theory asserts that over time television fosters the viewers' notion of reality. The words "over time" are important to Cultivation Theory since "the greater the amount of television you watch, the more your worldview comes to accord with the beliefs, values, and attitudes you see on the screen."[81]

Because the messages you receive are so diverse, and come from a host of sources, it is difficult to make a direct cause-and-effect link to television's role in the socialization process. Yet there are thousands of studies that attempt to document the part television plays in the life of young children. The Kaiser Family Foundation and the American Academy of Child and Adolescent Psychiatry offer the following summary of how television viewing among young children gets reflected in their perceptions of the world.

- Extensive viewing of television violence by children causes greater aggressiveness. In addition, children who watch more than four hours of TV a day have lower grades in school and are often overweight.
- Television viewing takes the place of activities such as playing with friends, being physically active, reading, and doing homework.[82]

Gender roles are also learned and reinforced by mass media. Although there are many exceptions, most studies reveal that in the United States men are valued over women. Women are seen as caring, emotional, socially skilled, and family oriented, while men are taken to possess the opposite set of traits.[83] These same characteristics are stressed by most of the mass media.[84]

We conclude our description of the initial, and perhaps most important characteristic of culture, by reminding you of a few key points. First, children are born without any cultural knowledge. However, because they have the biological "tools" necessary to learn, they quickly discover that the sounds and actions around them have meaning. The same learning process applies to the cultural attributes and characteristics that confront them. In short, the location of your birth sets the tone for what you learn and what you will not learn. Second, most of the behaviors we label as "cultural" are automatic, invisible, and usually performed without our being aware of them. For example, in North American culture, women "are more likely than men to initiate hugs and touches that express support, affection, and comfort, whereas men more often use touch to direct others, assert power, and express sexual interest."[85] What we are suggesting is that these—and thousands of other behaviors—are learned consciously and unconsciously and are performed almost habitually. Third, it is important to repeat that the methods of learning culture we have mentioned are only a few of the many ways culture "is taught." Space constraints have forced us to leave out many subtle yet powerful "teachers." For example, sports are much more than simple games. Football in America is popular because it illustrates important themes of the culture. Notice the inconspicuous messages contained in some of the language surrounding the broadcasting of a professional football game. You will hear statements such as "he has the killer instinct," "they are all warriors," "he is a real head hunter," "they are out for blood," and "they all play smash-mouth football." You can observe in every culture a variety of activities that have significant meanings that go beyond the actual endeavor. There are "lessons being taught" by Spanish bullfighting, Japanese gardens, French wine, German symphonies, and Italian operas.[86] These cultural metaphors represent and teach, according to Gannon, "the underlying values expressive of the culture itself."[87]

Culture Is Transmitted from Generation to Generation

The American philosopher Thoreau once wrote, "All the past is here." As it applies to culture, Thoreau is correct. For a culture to endure it must make certain that its crucial messages and elements are not only shared, but are passed to future

Sports are much more than simple games to a culture in that there is often a hidden message in the behavior of the participants.

Clayton Sharrard/PhotoEdit

generations. In this way the past becomes
the present and helps create the future. As
Brislin notes, "If there are values considered
central to a society that have existed
for many years, these must be transmitted

from one generation to another."[88] This process of transmitting culture can be seen
as a kind of "social inheritance."[89] Charon elaborates on this idea when he writes:
"Culture is a social inheritance; it consists of ideas that may have developed long
before we were born. Our society, for example, has a history reaching beyond any
individual's life, the ideas developed over time are taught to each generation and
'truth' is anchored in interaction by people long before dead."[90]

It is communication that makes culture a continuous process, for once cultural
habits, principles, values, and attitudes are formulated, they are communicated
to each member of the culture. While the immediate family begins the "education"
process, you need to remember that most of the crucial "lessons" of a culture continue
to be emphasized throughout the person's life. Infants, held and touched by parents,
do not consciously know they are learning about family and touch, but they are. The
essential cultural values continue to be reinforced as children share holidays, both
religious and secular, with grandparents, aunts, uncles, and other relatives. So strong
is the need for a culture to bind each generation to past and future generations, it is
often asserted that a fracture in the transmission process would contribute to a culture's extinction.

Culture Is Based on Symbols

Our discussion of how culture is transmitted from generation to generation allows for
an easy transition to our next characteristic—*culture is based on symbols*. The relationship between culture and symbols is made apparent by Ferraro when he writes, "symbols tie together people who otherwise might not be part of a unified group."[91] Bailey
and Peoples expand on the link between symbols and culture in the following:

> Just as we learn norms and values as we grow up, we learn the meanings that people in our
> culture attach to symbols. The understandings people share about symbols and their meaning affect the patterns of behavior found in a culture. In fact, if individuals did not agree
> that certain kinds of behaviors communicate certain meanings; social interaction would be
> far more difficult than it usually is.[92]

The portability of symbols allows people to package, store, and transmit them. The
mind, books, pictures, films, computer memory chips, and videos enable a culture to
preserve what it deems important and worthy of transmission. This makes each individual, regardless of his or her generation, heir to a massive repository of information
that has been gathered and maintained in anticipation of his or her entry into the
culture.

Cultural symbols, as we have noted, can take a host of forms, encompassing gestures, dress, objects, flags, and religious icons. However, it is words, both written and
spoken, that are most often used to symbolize objects and thoughts. Notice the link
between symbols and culture in the definition of the word *symbol* advanced by Macionis: "A symbol is anything that carries a particular meaning recognized by people who
share culture."[93] It is language that enables you to share the speculations, observations, facts, experiments, and wisdom accumulated over thousands of years—what

the linguist Weinberg called "the grand insights of geniuses which, transmitted through symbols, enable us to span the learning of centuries."[94] Bates and Plog offer an excellent summary of the importance of language to culture:

> Language thus enables people to communicate what they would do if such-and-such happened, to organize their experiences into abstract categories ("a happy occasion," for instance, or an "evil omen"), and to express thoughts never spoken before. Morality, religion, philosophy, literature, science, economics, technology, and numerous other areas of human knowledge and belief—along with the ability to learn about and manipulate them—all depend on this type of higher-level communication.[95]

So important are symbols to the study of intercultural communication that we have set aside Chapters 8 (verbal messages) and 9 (nonverbal messages) to further develop this connection between symbols and human behavior.

Culture Is Dynamic

The Greek philosopher Heraclitus might well have been talking about culture when, more than two thousand years ago, he observed: "You cannot step twice into the same river, for other waters are continually flowing in." What he was telling us then is true even today—cultures do not exist in a vacuum; because of "other waters continually flowing in," they are subject to change. Simply reflect for a moment on the countless cultural changes you have observed in your life. We are not only speaking of surface changes in fashion and music, but also those alterations in culture brought about by new technology and globalization. You have lived not only through the ongoing impact of these two forces in the world, but have witnessed cultural changes that have altered perceptions of gays, immigrants, and various religions. While some cultures change more than others, because of isolation or design, all cultures have been subject to change since the earliest hunter-gatherers moved from place to place. However, never in recorded history have these changes been so widespread and profound. Angrosino notes, "The intensity of change seems to have increased; no longer restricted to isolated historical moments of conflict and crisis, change seems to be pushing us relentlessly."[96] As we noted, these changes have been promoted by the rise of American capitalism, worldwide population growth, large movements of immigrants, and the constant improvement and proliferation of information technology systems. Whether it comes in small increments or dramatic bursts, cultural change is inevitable. Our premise is simple: Cultures, more than ever before, are subject to fluctuations and seldom remain constant. Haviland and his associates summarize this important assertion in the following manner. "Cultures have always changed over time, although rarely as rapidly or as massively as many are doing today. Change takes place in response to such events as population growth, technological innovations, environmental crisis, the intrusion of outsiders, or modifications of behavior and values within the culture."[97]

We conclude this section on the dynamic nature of culture by mentioning a few ideas about cultural change that are directly related to intercultural communication. First, because much of culture is habitual and deeply rooted in tradition, you can find countless examples where *change is not welcomed* and is *even confronted with hostility*. In France you find a type of "language police" whose duty it is to monitor outside "infiltration" of their language. The French it seems are ever vigilant to keep their language (and their culture) "pure" and free from outside corruption. In the United States there are still large numbers of people who rail against women having equal rights with men. In much of the Arab world, some of the aggression aimed at the West can be traced to a fear of having Western values imposed on traditional Islamic beliefs. Many Arabs believe that is what happened as part of the "contact" with the West during the Christian Crusades, the Ottoman Empire, and the occupation of much of the Middle East by the West in the early twentieth century.

Second, since cultures seek to endure, they often adopt those outside elements that are compatible with their existing values and beliefs, or that can be modified or incorporated into their culture without causing much disruption. For example, because of contact via increased commerce, American businesses embraced some Japanese quality control practices. At the same time, the Japanese started using new American marketing techniques. Our point is that eating a Papa John's pizza, drinking a Coke, or wearing Levi's jeans does not alter the inherent value system of a culture. In fact, in most instances cultures find a way to use these types of activities to "preserve and enhance" what is already part of their culture.[98]

Finally, and perhaps most importantly, although many aspects of culture are subject to change, *the deep structure of a culture resists major alterations*. Most of the changes you observe are likely part of what is called "popular culture." This level of culture changes regularly, but that is not the content of culture we are talking about. Beamer and Varner explain this idea of levels of culture and change in the following manner: "Popular culture, which includes consumer products—for example, music, food, hairstyles, clothing, recreational activities, and their equipment, styles of cars, and furnishings—constantly change[s]. But backstage culture—the values, attitudes, and cultural dimensions that have been learned from birth—change[s] very little and very, very slowly."[99]

What Varner and Beamer are saying is that changes in dress, music, food, transportation, mass entertainment, and housing are exterior changes and do not go to the root of the culture. In most instances they are simply blended into the existing culture. However, values and behaviors associated with such things as ethics and morals, definitions of the role of government, the importance of family and the past, religious practices, the pace of life, folklore, and attitudes toward gender and age are so deeply embedded in a culture that they persist generation after generation. This continual embracing of one's culture is called "cultural boundary maintenance." It is the manner in which a culture maintains "its distinctiveness by imposing certain cultural boundaries that strengthen and glorify its own cultural traditions and discourage cultural borrowing from other groups."[100] Barnlund offers a religious example of cultural maintenance when he writes, "The spread of Buddhism, Islam, Christianity, and Confucianism did not homogenize the societies they enveloped. It was usually the other way around: societies insisted on adapting the religions to their own cultural traditions."[101]

In the United States, studies conducted on American values show that most contemporary core values are similar to the values of the last 250 years. In short, when assessing the degree of change within a culture, you must always consider what is changing. Do not be fooled into believing that major cultural shifts are taking place in Japan because people in Tokyo dress much like the people in Paris. Or that Germans are abandoning their love of soccer because people now play basketball in Germany. These are "front-stage behaviors." Most of what we call

CONSIDER THIS

How would you explain Hall's phrase, "You touch a culture in one place and everything else is affected"? Can you think of some examples from your culture that illustrate Hall's assertion?

culture is below the surface, like an iceberg. You can observe the tip, but there are other dimensions and depths that you cannot see. That is the subterranean level of culture.

Culture Is an Integrated System

Throughout this chapter we have isolated various aspects of culture and talked about them as if they were discrete units. The nature of language makes it impossible to do otherwise; yet in reality, it is more accurate to perceive culture from a holistic perspective. Hall says it this way: "You touch a culture in one place and everything else is affected."[102] Ferraro and Andreatta expand on Hall's premise when they point out that "cultures should be thought of as integrated wholes, the parts of which, to some degree, are interconnected with one another. When we view cultures as integrated systems, we can begin to see how particular cultural traits fit into the whole system and consequently, how they tend to make sense *within that context*."[103]

Values regarding materialism stem from a variety of sources (history, family, and religion) and can influence family size, work ethic, use of time, and spiritual pursuits. A complex example of the interconnectedness of cultural elements is the civil rights movement of the United States in the 1960s. This movement brought about changes in housing patterns, discrimination practices, educational opportunities, the legal system, and career opportunities. In more recent times, in the last decade of the twentieth century you can observe how the convergence of "new technologies" mingled with a host of other cultural values, attitudes, and behaviors. Modes of communication brought about by digital technology and the Internet have produced and influenced issues concerning privacy, language, and the use of face-to-face communication.

We conclude this section on the characteristics of culture by reminding you that the pull of culture begins at birth and continues throughout life—and some cultures say even after life. Using the standard language of her time (sexist by today's standards), the famous anthropologist Ruth Benedict offered an excellent explanation of why culture is such a powerful influence on all aspects of human behavior. What is intriguing about Professor Benedict's quote is that although she wrote it over sixty years ago, it is as true today as it was then. Actually, it would be accurate if she were describing events forty thousand years ago.

> The life history of the individual is first and foremost an accommodation to the patterns and standards traditionally handed down in his community. From the moment of his birth the customs into which he is born shape his experience and behavior. By the time he can talk, he is the little creature of his culture, and by the time he is grown and able to take part in its activities, its habits are his habits, its beliefs his beliefs, its impossibilities his impossibilities. Every child that is born into his group will share them with him, and no child born into the opposite side of the globe can ever achieve the thousandth part. [104]

The important point to take away from our entire discussion of culture is eloquently expressed in the following sentences: "God gave to every people a cup, a cup of clay, and from this cup they drank life.... They all dipped in the water, but their cups were different." [105] This book is about how those "different cups" influence how people perceive the world and behave in that world.

Structure of Culture: Family Lessons

Children have never been very good at listening to their elders, but they have never failed to imitate them.

JAMES BALDWIN

In every conceivable manner, the family is a link to our past and a bridge to our future.

ALEX HALEY

Call it a clan, call it a network, call it a tribe, call it a family. Whatever you call it, whoever you are, you need one.

JANE HOWARD

W hy do members of some cultures seek solitude, whereas those of other cultures become dejected if they are not continuously in the company of others? Why do people of some cultures frantically cling to youth, whereas others welcome old age and even death? Why do some cultures worship the earth, whereas others mistreat it? Why is it that in some cultures individuals seek material possessions, while in other cultures people believe wealth is a hindrance to a "settled" life? Why do some believe that great insight can be found in silence, while others feel that words contain the world's great wisdom? Why do families in some cultures have children living at home even after marriage, while in others children can scarcely wait to flee their homes? These and countless other such questions need to be answered in order to understand how people of different cultures see the world, live in that world, and communicate with other people about that world. In the study of intercultural communication it is not enough simply to know that some people bow, while others shake hands, or that some exchange gifts as an important part of a business transaction, while others perceive such an act as bribery. Although these specific behaviors are significant, it is more important to know what motivates people to engage in one action rather than another. The key to how members of a culture view the world can be found in that culture's *deep structure*. It is this deep structure, the conscious and unconscious assumptions about how the world works, that unifies a culture, makes each culture unique, and explains the "how" and "why" of a culture's collective action—an action that is often difficult for "outsiders" to understand. The aspects of deep structure are sources of insight because they not only deal with significant universal questions, but examining ethics, notions about God, nature, aesthetics, and even death leads to helping people understand "the meaning of life."

At the core of any culture's deep structure are the *social organizations* we introduced in Chapter 2. These organizations, sometimes referred to as *social institutions*, are the groups that members of a culture turn to for lessons about how to live their lives. Thousands of years ago, as cultures became more and more advanced and their populations grew, they began to realize that there was a need to organize in a collective manner. These collective institutions, which offer their members "rule-governed relationships," serve the purpose of holding "members of a society together."[1] Bates and Plog repeat this important notion about social organizations when they note, "Our ability to work in cooperation with others in large social groupings and coordinate the activities of many people to achieve particular purposes is a vital part of human adaptation."[2] There are a number of groups within every culture that help with that adaptation process while also giving members of that particular culture guidance on how to behave. The three most enduring and influential social organizations that deal with deep structure issues are (1) *family* (clans), (2) *state* (community), and (3) *religion* (worldview). These three social organizations—working in concert—define, create, transmit, maintain, and reinforce the basic and most crucial elements of every culture.

Before examining these institutions, note that they go by a variety of names. For example, a larger analysis of religion would embrace spirituality and a culture's worldview. And when speaking of community in the cultural sense, concepts related to country, state, and the history of the culture are included. Regardless of what we call the three deep structure institutions, they form the roots of every culture and provide the fundamental values and attitudes that are most critical to that culture. This chapter looks at how families shape the social perceptions and communication behaviors of members in a particular culture. In the next chapter the topic of a culture's collective history gets linked to the deep structure of a culture. And finally, in Chapter 5, it will be worldview and religion that connect to the topic of intercultural communication.

THE DEEP STRUCTURE OF CULTURE

Although many communication problems occur on the interpersonal level, most serious confrontations and misunderstandings can be traced to cultural differences that go to the core of a culture. When Al Qaeda attacked the United States on the morning of September 11, 2001, this act of violence was linked more to cultural and religious differences than to political ones. And when Americans were exuberant over the killing of Osama bin Laden on May 1, 2011, they reflected American values of retribution and justice, both part of the historical worldview of the United States. These sorts of deep structure examples that pit one set of cultural values against another can be found throughout the world. News reports abound with stories of the ongoing persecution of the Kurds in Turkey, Iran, and Iraq. In Kosovo, ethnic Albanians declared independence from Serbia—not for economic reasons, but for cultural reasons. A kind of "ethnic cleansing" has been occurring in the Sudan for decades as the north and south struggle over divergent cultural norms. In China "ethnic clashes between Han Chinese and Muslim Uighurs,"[3] as well as with Tibetans, continue to occur on a somewhat regular basis. Israel and much of the Arab world continue a deep structure dispute that goes back thousands of years.

Hostility and brutality over two contradictory worldviews are as commonplace today as they were thousands of years ago. Christians on a number of fronts are facing oppression and physical abuse around the world. In Malaysia, Iraq, and Nigeria, Christians and their churches have been under attack. In Sudan the "conflict nurtured by racial and religious hostility"[4] goes back to the early twentieth century. What we are suggesting is that wherever or whenever there are ethnic and cultural confrontations, be it in Boston, Beirut, Burundi, or Mumbai, it is a culture's deep structure that is being acted out.

Although many of our examples demonstrate clashes that have long historical traditions, Huntington speaks to the future of intercultural contact and the potential problems that can arise when deep structure beliefs clash: "The great divisions among humankind and the dominating sources of conflict will be cultural."[5] While Huntington advanced his proposition nearly twenty years ago, his words are as timely today as when he wrote them. As he explains his thesis in the following statement, we add that even today it can serve as the central theme of this chapter: "The people of different civilizations have different views on the relations between God and man, the individual and the group, the citizen and the state, parents and children, husband and wife, as well as differing views of the relative importance of rights and responsibilities, liberty and authority, equality and hierarchy."[6]

The issues Huntington cites, as well as the examples we provided earlier, all penetrate to the very heart of culture. They are what we call in this chapter the deep structure of a culture. Such issues (God, loyalty, duty, family and kinship, community, state, allegiance, etc.) have been part of every culture for thousands of years. In fact, when the world's first cultures started forming—over forty thousand years ago—these same elements were at the core. That is to say, the earliest expressions of culture reveal that our "ancestors" had interests in spiritual practices, kinship relations, and even formed communities. Delgado points out, "Culture produces and is reproduced by institutions of society, and we can turn to such sites to help re-create and represent the elements of culture."[7] The aim of this chapter is to look at those "sites" so that you may better understand how and why cultures have different visions of the world. We suggest four important reasons family, community, and religion hold such prominent sway over the actions of all cultures. By looking at these four you can begin to appreciate the importance of a culture's deep structure to any study of intercultural communication.

DEEP STRUCTURE INSTITUTIONS CARRY CULTURE'S MOST IMPORTANT MESSAGES

The social institutions of family, state, and religion carry the messages that matter most to people. Whether you seek material possessions to attain happiness or choose instead to seek spiritual fulfillment, the three deep structure institutions help you make major decisions regarding how to live your life. These cultural institutions, and the messages they generate, tell you whether you should believe

CONSIDER THIS

What about the institutions of family, state, and religion makes them endure?

in fate or the power of free choice, notions about right and wrong, why there is suffering, what to expect from life, where your loyalties should reside, and even how to prepare for death.

DEEP STRUCTURE INSTITUTIONS AND THEIR MESSAGES ENDURE

The three institutions that compose a culture's deep structure endure. They work in harmony to preserve the wisdom, traditions, and customs that make a culture unique. From the time early Cro-Magnon cave drawings appeared in southern France until the present, we can trace the strong pull of family, community, and religion. Generations of children are told about the messages of Abraham, Confucius, Moses, the Buddha, Christ, Muhammad, and other spiritual leaders. Whether it is the Eightfold Path, the Ten Commandments, the Analects, the Five Pillars of Islam, or the Vedas, the meanings of these writings survive. Just as every American knows about the values conveyed by the story of the Revolutionary War, every Mexican is aware of the consequences of the Treaty of Guadalupe Hidalgo. Likewise, in China students are being taught about the "one hundred years of humiliation" suffered under Western and Japanese imperialists in the nineteenth and twentieth centuries.

DEEP STRUCTURE INSTITUTIONS AND THEIR MESSAGES ARE DEEPLY FELT

The content generated by these institutions, and the institutions themselves, arouse profound and emotional feelings. Looking around the world, deeply rooted loyalty and nationalism can be observed on every continent. The emotional response associated with deep structure issues surfaced when a Danish newspaper printed caricatures of the prophet Muhammad, which millions of Muslims found offensive, since most Muslims consider any depiction of the prophet to be sacrilegious. Days of rioting followed in Pakistan, India, Bangladesh, the Philippines, Indonesia, and many other countries. Hundreds of thousands of Muslims took to the streets "demonstrating against the cartoons by burning, trampling and spitting on Danish flags while chanting 'God is Great' and 'Down with Denmark.'"[8] Moreover, think for a moment about the fierce reactions that can be produced in the United States when someone takes God's name in vain, calls someone's mother an obscene name, or burns the American flag. Countries and religious causes have sent young men and women to war and politicians have attempted to win elections by inciting people to recognize the importance of God, country, and family. Regardless of the culture, in any hierarchy of cultural values, love of family, God, and country top the list.

DEEP STRUCTURE INSTITUTIONS SUPPLY MUCH OF A PERSON'S IDENTITY

One of the most important responsibilities of any culture is to assist its members in forming their identities. You are not born with an identity, but through countless interactions you discover who you are, how you fit in, and where to find security. Charon makes much the same point when he notes, "We learn our identities—who we are—through socialization."[9]

As mentioned elsewhere, the family is most instrumental in the early stages of the socialization process that establishes a child's personal identity. However, once you encounter other people, you begin to develop a variety of identities. As Huntington points out, "Everyone has multiple identities which may compete with or reinforce each other: kinship, occupational, cultural, institutional, territorial, educational, partisan, ideological, and others."[10] These and countless other memberships help define you. However, the most significant identities, the ones that mean the most, are filtered through deep structure institutions. In this sense, culture—through family, church, and state—becomes the defining feature in your identity. At some point in your life you move from identities based only on the "I" ("How attractive am I?" "Am I a good student?") to identities linked to the "we." That is to say, you begin to realize that while you still have a personal identity, you also have shared identities. You belong to a "community" and relate to its norms, values, communication behaviors, and the like. We are stressing that you begin to see yourself as part of a larger unit, and thus have loyalties to it. Kakar explains this transition in the following: "At some point of time in early life, the child's 'I am!' announces the birth of a sense of community. 'I am' differentiates me from other individuals. 'We are' makes me aware of the other dominant group (or groups) sharing the physical and cognitive space of my community."[11] This "we" identity connects the individual to cultural groups and the main institutions of the culture.

"People define themselves in terms of ancestry, religion, language, history, values, customs, and institutions."[12] This means that when you think about yourself, you most likely conclude that you are a member of a family ("my name is Jane Smith"), that you have a religious orientation ("I am a Christian"), and that you live in the United States ("I am from Idaho"). String these three institutions together and you can observe how people throughout the world employ these cultural organizations for their identity. Those different identities are important to the study of intercultural communication because, according to Guirdham, they "can be used to identify similarities and differences in behaviors, interpretations, and norms."[13] Lynch and Hanson agree when they point out, "A person's cultural identity exerts a profound influence on his or her lifeways."[14] For the purposes of this book, those "lifeways" offer insights into how people communicate with one another. The notion of identity is so crucial to the study of intercultural communication that all of Chapter 7 examines this topic in detail.

FAMILY

The Chinese say that if you know the family, you do not need to know the individual. A Hebrew proverb states, "My father planted for me, and I planted for my children." In Africa the saying is, "A person who has children does not die." And in the United States children are told, "The apple does not fall far from the tree." Although these ideas differ slightly, they all call attention to the importance and enduring quality of family life in every culture. The family is the oldest and most fundamental of human institutions. More importantly, "As a social institution, the family is intertwined with other social institutions."[15] It is also a universal experience found in every culture.[16] Kim endorses these same notions when she notes, "The family is the basic unit of society and it is at the heart of its survival."[17] You constantly see specific forms of government evolving, and even disappearing, in places like Iran, Cuba, Iraq, China, the old Soviet Union, and numerous countries in Africa; yet in each of these nations "families survive."[18] Because it has survived for thousands of years, the family unit "is a very effective means of providing social regulation and continuity."[19] And while family arrangements and patterns take a variety of forms, Nye and Berardo rightly propose that "without the family, human society as we know it could not exist."[20]

THE IMPORTANCE OF FAMILY

The seventeenth-century English cleric Charles Colton offered an excellent introduction to the importance of family when he noted, "The family is the most basic unit of government. As the first community to which a person is attached and the first authority under which a person learns to live, the family establishes society's most basic values."[21] He is saying that the individual, the family, and the culture work together to teach the "essentials" of the culture. Smith and Mosby underscore this point when they write, "The family is the most prominent social group that exists. It prepares its members for the various roles they will perform in society."[22] Perhaps the most import and powerful influence of the family is in its transformation of a biological organism into a human being who must spend the rest of his or her life around other human beings. It is the family that greets you once you leave the comfort of the womb. In this sense the family is the first and chief socializing agent. As DeGenova and Rice point out: "The family is the principal transmitter of knowledge, values, attitudes, roles, and habits from one generation to the next. Through word and example, the family shapes a child's personality and instills modes of thought and ways of acting that become habitual."[23]

The significance of family is eloquently highlighted by Swerdlow, Bridenthal, Kelly, and Vine: "Here is where one has the first experience of love, and of hate, of giving, and of denying; and of deep sadness.... Here the first hopes are raised and met—or disappointed. Here is where one learns whom to trust and whom to fear. Above all, family is where people get their start in life."[24]

DEFINITION OF FAMILY

Because we have been discussing families during the last few pages, we will pause and define just what a family is; however, familial patterns have evolved over time and vary across cultures, making a single definition difficult, even within the United States. As Strong and his associates note, "As contemporary Americans, we live in a society composed of many kinds of families—married couples, stepfamilies, single-parent families, multigenerational families, cohabiting adults, child-free families, families headed by gay men or by lesbians, and so on. With such variety, how can we define family?"[25] While there is no simple answer to the question just posed, a definition advanced by Lamanna and Riedman is helpful: "A family is any sexually expressive or parent-child or other kin relationship in which people— usually related by ancestry, marriage, or adoption—(1) form an economic unit and care for any young, (2) consider their identity to be significantly attached to the group, and (3) commit to maintaining that group over

CONSIDER THIS

Why do you think families, in one form or another, are found in every culture?

time."[26] We like the Lamanna and Riedman definition because it is broad enough to include most types of family configurations found all over the world. That is to say, their definition is descriptive and non-ethnocentric because it "Combines some practical and objective criteria with a more social-psychological sense of family."[27]

FORMS OF FAMILY

Although all cultures deem family one of their most important social institutions, the form and type of the family manifest the collective and historical beliefs of each culture. Yet even with some cultural variations, most people encounter two families during the course of their life: (1) the family they are born into (the family of orientation) and (2) the family that is formed when and if they take a mate.

In the last few decades families throughout the world have undergone numerous changes that have altered the two prevailing forms of family. Before turning to those alterations, let us briefly mention the two common forms of families found in most cultures. The two types are *nuclear* ("typically identified as a parent or parents and a child or children") and *extended* ("typically includes grandparents and relatives").[28]

Nuclear Families

Nuclear families, often referred to as "two-generation families," are the most typical pattern found in most Western cultures. Ferraro and Andreatta offer an excellent summary of nuclear families when they write, "The everyday needs of economic support, child care, and social interaction are with the nuclear family itself rather than by a wider set of relatives."[29] The nuclear family, like all of the deep structure institutions, manifests many of the values of the culture that stresses this family pattern. For example, the nuclear family is usually characterized by a great deal of geographic mobility[30]—a trait found in American culture ever since the founding of the country. Cultural values of the nuclear family are also reflected in child-rearing practices. According to Triandis, "there is less regimentation and less emphasis on obedience, while exploration and creativity are encouraged."[31] Part of that exploration and creativity can be seen in how soon children reared in nuclear families move away from home to "experience life" on their own. As Haviland and his co-authors state, "Once children reach the age of majority (18), parents have no further legal obligation to them, nor do the children to their parents."[32] American cultural values toward, and treatment of, the elderly are likewise replicated in nuclear families. In these families older members of the family do not normally spend their "senior" years living with their children.

Extended Families

As mentioned earlier, extended families differ from nuclear families, and Tischler offers an excellent description of the former: "Extended families include other relations and generations in addition to the nuclear family, so that along with married parents and their offspring, there might be the parents' parents, siblings of the spouses and children, and in-laws. All members of the extended family live in one house or in homes close to one another, forming one cooperative unit."[33]

Historically, the cooperative units mentioned by Tischler usually have gathered for economic reasons and share the workload and rearing of children. In an extended family a set of behaviors and values may be acted out that differ from those found in nuclear families. For instance, "extended families insist on obedience and are more organized around

Extended families connect a great many generations into a single unit.

Patrick Olear/PhotoEdit

In what major ways do extended families differ from nuclear families?

rules than are nuclear families."[34] Regardless of the culture or the configuration, the family teaches you your culture and "provides you with the foundation of your self-concept and communication competencies."[35]

TRANSFORMING FAMILIES IN THE UNITED STATES

To this point we have only mentioned the two most common types of families—nuclear and extended. It would be misleading if we concluded our discussion without mentioning the wide range of families currently found in the United States. American culture, for a host of reasons, has seen many families transform in structure and form during the last four decades. Tischler notes, "By the 1970's radical changes were becoming evident. The marriage rate began to fall; the divorce rate, which had been fairly level, began accelerating upward, and fertility began to decline."[36] It might be useful to review a few of those changes before we move to a more detailed analysis of how child-rearing practices affect communication.

We begin by repeating this declaration: There are now fewer "typical" American families in the United States than ever before. Almost since the founding of the United States, religious traditions, laws, and cultural values and attitudes defined what form the "accepted" American family would take until social changes in the United States forced people to rethink the definition and configuration of what a family is. Most of these modifications, according to Strong, DeVault, and Cohen, were brought about by the following four factors: "(1) economic changes, (2) technological innovations, (3) demographics, and (4) gender roles and opportunities for women."[37] You can observe a major change in

the American family by comparing the
census of 2000 with the census of 2010
as it applies to children living with
both parents—a so-called "traditional"
family. The Census Bureau reported
that "The percentage of households
headed by a married couple who had
children under the age of 18 living

CONSIDER THIS

*Why do you think there are so many different forms of families
throughout the world? And why does the institution of family continue to endure in spite of all these changes?*

with them declined to 21 percent in 2010, down from 24 percent in 2000."[38] There are,
of course, other variations on the American family. For example, in the United States we
now see some of the following types of families: (1) "traditional" married couples, (2) children living with one parent, (3) a heterosexual woman and man who have cohabited and
have children, but have never married, (4) two gay men or two lesbians who have
adopted a child, (5) and a single woman or man who has adopted a child.[39]

Many of the transformations facing families in the United States involve race and ethnicity, which relate directly to this book. Lamanna and Riedman speak to this same point
when they note, "There is more racial and ethnic diversity among American families than
ever before, and much of this diversity results from immigration. The foreign-born now
constitute 12 percent of the U.S. population."[40] Just in the area of interracial marriages,
a 2007 Stanford University study calculated that "more than 7 percent of America's 59
million married couples were interracial, compared to less than two percent in 1970."[41]

We conclude this section as we began it, with a reminder that the structure and
workings of American families have experienced major transformations that affect
intercultural communication. However, we want to add that in spite of these changes,
"Family—in all its emerging varieties—remains resilient."[42] In fact, a major study
conducted by the Pew Research Center revealed that most adults "say their family is
the most important element in their life."[43]

GLOBALIZATION AND FAMILIES

To this point we have discussed how families in the United States have changed in the last
four decades. For a variety of reasons, families throughout the entire world are also encountering forces that are changing how they appear and function. While there are many reasons
families have been altered in recent years, the major catalysts for many of the worldwide
shifts in family structure can be found in *globalization*. Although we discussed globalization
in Chapters 1 and 2, and will revisit the concept in other chapters, we now briefly touch on
some of the effects of this phenomenon on families. The rationale is simple—globalization
is much more than "the process through which diverse peoples and nations are integrated
into a single system involving flows of technology, transportation, communications, travel,
and market exchanges."[44] Globalization has a series of consequences and effects that go well
beyond the exchange of goods and services. Instead, as McGregor writes, "The phenomenon of globalization covers a wide variety of changes in various aspects of social, cultural,
political, religious, and economic life."[45] To be more specific, some of the effects of globalization have altered the idea of traditional families for millions of people. As Trask points
out: "Globalization is the critical driving force that is fundamentally restructuring the social
order around the world, and families are at the center of this change. In every society, traditional notions about family life, work, identity and the relationships of individuals and
groups to one another are being transformed due to globalizing forces."[46]

To further explain Trask's assessment, note that two aspects of globalization have been partially responsible for some of the changes in the structure of families throughout the world: (1) *mass media* and (2) *migration patterns*.

Mass Media

One of the many expressions of globalization has been the explosion of mass media across cultures. Lavenda and Schultz declare: "People need not even leave their homes to be buffeted by the forces of globalization."[47] Computers, cell phones, and television now can "link people who have never seen one another, creating global networks, or *virtual communities*, that reach beyond the boundaries of nation-states."[48] But what about the sway of the messages being sent via this new technology? Many scholars believe that some of those messages, dominated by Western cultures, can have a profound influence on many non-Western cultures. Bailey and Peoples note, "Western cultural norms, values, and behaviors, beliefs, technology, and material culture are replacing existing cultural practices of non-Western peoples and non-Western peoples are being acculturated and assimilated into a global community that shares a basically Western culture."[49] While millions of messages are sent via mass media, we are interested in those that affect the family. As noted in Chapter 2, drawing a straight line from this technology to family behavior is often difficult to document. Yet the following question is worth posing: What happens when a culture with a well-established set of family values is exposed to a different set of values that are introduced by media from another culture? Think for a moment about what you see on American television, YouTube, Facebook, and in American films that directly and indirectly applies to modesty, the judgment of beauty, materialism, violence, competition, and the treatment of the elderly. As Chapter 6 will show, cultures differ greatly in how they respond to the values previously mentioned. Families in all parts of the globe are seeing images that stress nudity instead of modesty, anorexic thinness instead of health, materialism instead of spirituality, competitiveness instead of cooperation, assertiveness instead of social harmony, and mocking of the elderly instead of respecting them. One set of values is not better than another, but globalized media sources have created an alternative set of values that are now offered to families throughout the world. Many of these families are struggling to blend traditional patterns with the new ones being thrust upon them by globalization. As Ingoldby and Smith point out, "Families around the world are richly varied, responding to rapid social and demographic changes, and both maintaining and adapting traditional ways of life to present-day circumstances and demands."[50]

Migration

Globalization has created a world where millions of workers leave their families and move from one country to another to seek jobs and higher wages. The United Nations noted in the 2010 Human Development Report that "the number of people living outside their country of birth is larger than at any other time in history."[51] In fact, "migrants now account for approximately 3.1 percent of the world population."[52] For many "migration is one way that men and women try to escape poverty."[53] However, when they "escape," they often transform the

CONSIDER THIS

Can you think of any specific examples in recent American films or television programs where the following Western values were shown in a positive manner?

- Nudity
- Materialism
- Anorexic thinness
- Competitiveness
- Assertiveness
- Mocking the elderly

makeup and character of their family. As Hefti clearly states, "Migration has an impact on the social lives of both the migrants and the families they left behind."[54] These are often extended families where for centuries both parents have taken an active role in child rearing. However, when the father or mother migrates to another country seeking work, the entire dynamic of an extended family changes. Haviland and his co-authors speak of this change when they note that there are millions who now live in "new, single-generation households that stand in stark contrast to the multi-generation extended family households in which they were raised."[55]

The Philippines present a vivid example of how migration, stimulated by globalization, has changed many extended families. In the Philippines, mothers now leave home to take low-paying jobs in Hong Kong, Singapore, Middle East nations, and many other parts of the world in order to support their families. As Basker reports: "Many of the Filipino *amahs* [maids] here [Hong Kong] are mothers who have left their husbands and children to come and work as maids—six days a week—for less than the equivalent in United States currency of $400 a month."[56] Unfortunately, according to Hefti, the personal closeness of the family "deteriorates due to the long separation."[57] This corrosion of traditional families caused by economic migration is not confined to one culture. Countless people from Africa, Asia, and Latin America leave their homes because they believe they can have "a better life if only they could migrate to Western Europe or the United States."[58]

Perhaps one of the most vivid examples of the lure of jobs away from one's family can be found in the porous U.S.-Mexican border. Here you see a situation where millions of Mexicans and Central and South Americans have come, both legally and illegally, to the United States in search of employment. When this happens, as Bunim points out, "it is the families that suffer the greatest consequences."[59] The central question behind all these instances is: *What happens to the core family values as people leave their traditional families in search of employment?* It may take decades to answer this question, but we tend to agree with Giddens when he writes about the worldwide influence of globalization on our lives: "The traditional family is under threat, is changing, and will change much further."[60]

FUNCTIONS OF THE FAMILY

All families, regardless of type, form, or culture, perform similar functions. Nearly all of these functions are intended to teach new members of the culture, from the moment of birth, what they need to know to survive and live in societal harmony. In this sense, cultures use the family as one of their social institutions to tutor people in proper ways of thinking and behaving so its members become the kind of human beings valued by the particular culture. Some of the functions that seem to be common to all cultures merit examination.

Reproductive Function

The most important function of the family in any culture is reproduction. While modern technology has added some new dimensions to reproductive methods (artificial insemination,

CONSIDER THIS

Families are changing because of globalization, modernization, and a shift in traditional values. How do you think these changes might influence the following?

- *Gender roles*
- *Treatment of the elderly*
- *Socialization of young children*
- *Family size*

in vitro fertilization), a new infusion of infants is necessary for all cultures. Strong and his colleagues point out, "The family makes society possible by producing (or adopting) and rearing children to replace the older members of society as they die off."[61] As simple and obvious as it sounds, this essential function allows a culture to perpetuate itself. Without the infusion of new life, the culture would soon disappear.

Economic Function

An important task given to all families is teaching economic sharing and responsibility. While the methods for generating goods and services, and even the means of distribution, vary from culture to culture, "In almost all societies, the family consumes food and other necessities as a social unit. Therefore, a society's economic system and family structures often are closely correlated."[62] This means that one of the functions of nearly every family is to supply the basic needs of food, clothing, and shelter.[63] Later in the chapter you will notice how variations in family economic functions often teach important cultural values such as materialism, thrift, sharing, and hard work.

Socialization Function

As mentioned in Chapter 2, the family is one of the "teachers" that pass on the important elements of culture from generation to generation. Part of that instruction is identified by Strong and his associates when they write: "Children are helpless and dependent for years following birth. They must learn to walk and talk, how to care for themselves, how to act, how to love, and to touch and be touched. Teaching children how to fit into their particular culture is one of the family's most important tasks."[64]

Part of a family's socialization process is teaching the culture's core values and worldview. Obviously the "lessons" on how to be an effective member of a culture come from a variety of sources, yet it is the family that initially exposes the child to the ideas "that matter most." That is to say, not only are norms and values passed along by families to children, but families also "give them their initial exposure to questions of faith."[65] Children are not born into a world that automatically disposes them to believe in one God, many gods, or no gods. Devotion to a "higher power," be it Allah or Christ, the words of Buddha or Confucius, or the forces of nature, must be learned—and that teaching process begins in the home. Barry and associates offer yet another catalogue of the values usually assigned to the family. These include training in obedience, responsibility, nurturing achievement, self-reliance, and general independence.[66] In short, we agree with Al-Kaysi when he writes, "The family provides the environment within which human values and morals develop and grow in the new generation; these values and morals cannot exist apart from the family unit."[67]

Identity Function

As you learned earlier in this chapter, people have multiple identities—individual, national, cultural, sexual, ethnic, social class, and familial. We maintain that family is perhaps the most important of all identities since it is a precursor to other identities. Simply put, the family is the first institution that sends messages about identity. Burguiere makes this point in the following way: "Before we become ourselves, we are a son or daughter of X or of Y; we are born into a family, and

> ### REMEMBER THIS
>
> *In many ways it is the socialization function of the family that teaches young people how to live among other people besides their immediate family.*

are identified by a family name before becoming a separate social being."[68] In this sense family is not only the basic unit of a society, but it also provides each individual with their most essential social identity.[69] The family does this by giving children knowledge about their historical backgrounds, information regarding the permanent nature of their culture, and specific behaviors, customs, traditions, and language associated with their ethnic or cultural group.[70] Because of the importance of identity to intercultural communication, we will have much more to say on the topic when we move to Chapter 7.

COMMUNICATION, CULTURE, AND FAMILY

To this point we have not discussed specific cultural differences in child-rearing practices, particularly those that get reflected in communicative behavior. However, we are now ready to establish a link between the family and intercultural communication. But before discussing these differences, we need to make it clear that in many ways families, at least with regard to child-rearing practices, have many similarities. For example, "All cultures rely on the social unit of the family for the generation and perpetuation of the economic, political, artistic, educational vitality, and well-being [of the culture]."[71] There are, of course, some other basic parallels shared by all cultures. As Smith and his associates

By observation, imitation, and practice, each family introduces young children to many of the values and behaviors that are important to the culture.

Robert Fonseca

point out, "There is much commonality across cultures in the construal of infancy and early childhood, based on biological needs for care, nutrition, protection, etc."[72]

Having established that there are similarities among most families, regardless of the culture, we now turn to *cultural variations* regarding how family communication patterns get acted out. The connection between families and communication is made clear by Trenholm and Jensen when they write, "The family is a social construction, both a product of communication and a context in which communication takes place. In fact, it is one of the richest sources of communication patterns we have."[73] The family teaches a host of communication skills. Chapter 2 mentioned that the family introduces people to language and tells them how to employ that language. By observation, imitation, and practice, you are introduced to the entire spectrum of communication behaviors. As Gamble and Gamble note, "It is in the family that we first learn how to create, maintain, and end relationships; how to express ourselves; how to argue; how to display affection, how to choose acceptable topics for mixed company...."[74]

CULTURAL VARIANTS IN FAMILY INTERACTION

Before beginning this section on the role of family in cultural interaction patterns, three disclaimers are in order. First, all of the major institutions of a culture are linked. While the concept of family as a single social organization is used, you should be aware that it works in conjunction with other aspects of a culture. As Houseknecht and Pankhurst note, "Family and religion must be viewed in terms of their interactions with other institutions."[75] For example, when a Christian family sits down to dinner and says grace before eating, the children are learning about the importance of God and family rituals at the same time. And when those same children assist their mother in displaying the American flag for a Fourth of July picnic, and later sing "God Bless America," they are also learning about three deep structure institutions at once—church, community, and family.

Second, families within a culture may also display a range of differences. It would be naïve to assume that every family in the United States stresses the value of hard work, since there are families where servants pamper even the youngest children. In short, there are variations among and within cultures. As Rodriguez and Olswang observe, "Societies differ, between and within cultures, in their conceptions of the desired traits in children, and therefore, parental beliefs and values might reasonably differ as parents seek to develop culturally defined traits in their children."[76]

Finally, because of space considerations, no attempt to offer an in-depth exploration of the family has been made. You should be conscious of the cause-and-effect relationship between interacting with one's family and the manner in which one interacts with other people. The basic assumption of this section is simple: Interaction patterns within the family offer clues to communication patterns found outside the family, or, as the Swedish proverb says, "Children act in the village as they have learned at home."

GENDER ROLES

One of the most important family patterns is the teaching of accepted gender roles. As Wood notes, "Families, particularly parents and stepparents, are a primary influence of gender identity."[77] The learning of acceptable gender roles begins as soon as the announcement is made proclaiming that a newborn is a boy or a girl. Robbins observes,

"The infant is given a gender-appropriate name, dressed in properly designed or colored clothing, and spoken to in gender-appropriate language."[78] The task of teaching what is "appropriate" language and behavior falls on the family regardless of the culture. As this next section will reveal, in different cultures boys and girls grow up with very distinct gender identities. These differences are more influenced by culture than biology. Tischler underscores this important idea when he writes: "Most sociologists believe that the way people are socialized has a greater effect on their gender identities than do biological factors. Cross-cultural and historical research offer support for this view, revealing that different societies allocate different tasks and duties to men and women and that males and females have culturally defined views of themselves and of one another."[79]

United States

To this point we have talked in broad terms about gender differences across cultures. Let us now turn to some specific differences. We begin with the socialization process that yields gender differences among children in the dominant culture in the United States. Children begin to learn how to differentiate between masculine activities and feminine activities when they are just infants. Studies reveal, "At 24 months children were aware that labels, such as boy, girl, mommy and daddy, are applied to certain classes of people."[80] These learned perceptions influence how members of a culture interact with both genders. In the last twenty years, interest in gender roles has increased. The reason for the attention to gender behavior should be obvious. As Coles points out, "These socially constructed gender expectations for girls and boys frequently translate into different experiences and roles throughout the life course."[81] Knowing these expectations offers clues as to how interaction is carried out. In the United States, at least among the dominant culture, "appropriateness" is rather specific. Summarizing the research on gender socializing, Galvin and Cooper offer the following synopsis: "In our society males are socialized to be successful, aggressive, sexual, and self-reliant, whereas females are socialized to be nurturing, sensitive, interdependent, and concerned with appearance."[82]

Later in this section we will talk about how gender roles, like culture, are dynamic and subject to change. However, it is appropriate at this point to observe that nowhere is that change more obvious than in the United States. Events in the United States have brought about conditions that have influenced the notion of gender among many families. From the start of the twentieth century to the early 1960s, with the exception of World War II when many women replaced men in factories to support the war effort, most females were reared to be wives and assume the roles associated with that position. This, of course, is no longer the case. From being a member of the Supreme Court, to being part of a police SWAT team, or a military combat pilot, females are now socialized to assume a host of different roles. Men have also been affected by a shift in gender roles. As Wade and Tavris point out, "It is no longer news that many men, whose own fathers would no more have diapered a baby than jumped into a vat of boiling oil, now want to be involved fathers."[83]

Having examined some of the research involving gender development and family in the United States, we are now ready to examine gender roles in other cultures.

Asian

The fusing of many social organizations into a single concept can be seen in the gender interpretations found in cultures such as Japan, Vietnam, China, and Korea. In many instances, the history of these roles can be traced to the influence of

Confucianism. The basic Confucian assumption was "that men's and women's social places and expected behaviors were quite distinct."[84] So prescriptive and dissimilar were the behaviors that they were reinforced in guidance manuals such as *Lesson for Girls*, written between ca. 45-120 CE.[85] Writing about Korea's Confucian legacy, Kim notes that "Confucianism made men alone the structurally relevant members of the society and relegated women to social dependence."[86] In early Confucian families, Korean or Chinese boys studied the classics and played indoors and out, while "girls were confined to the inner quarters of the house where they received instruction in womanly behavior and tasks, such as domestic duties, embroidery, and cooking."[87] Even today, while many young girls work in China, gender roles are still rather rigid. According to Davis and Proctor, "Males are primarily responsible for task functions, while females attend to social and cultural tasks."[88] Jankowiak maintains that at the core of these gender attitudes, at least for the Chinese, is the belief that both biological and cultural forces contribute to these differences.[89]

Many of the gender attitudes we have just described for Korea and China can be found in other Asian and East Asian cultures. Among Vietnamese, "Women are raised more strictly and given less freedom than men."[90] While the practice has changed among Vietnamese-Americans, it was the practice in traditional Vietnamese families that only males were educated.[91]

In Japan, a highly industrialized nation where a great many women are in the work force, there are still major gender differences within the family that go back thousands of years. As Schneider and Silverman point out, "Despite change, sex remains a master status [determiner] in Japanese society, defining gender roles that men and women play in school, work, and other areas."[92] Within the home children often see the father served first at meals, getting the first bath, and receiving nods and deep bows from the rest of the family. All of these activities call attention to the importance of males in Japan. Young boys are indulged, pampered, and even allowed to be a little unregulated. All of this is intended to teach them what it means to become a Japanese man. Young girls receive very different treatment as the family attempts to instruct them in the values associated with being modest and respectable Japanese women. Hall, referring to work by Takie Sugiyama Lebra, offers a clear depiction of that treatment:

> The training young girls receive at home instills cultural values and conditions them to proper comportment. These values include modesty, reticence, elegance in handling such things as chopsticks and dishes, tidiness, courtesy, compliance, discipline for self-reliance, diligence, endurance, and a willingness to work around the house. Japanese girls are groomed to be skilled wives and mothers.[93]

What is interesting about gender roles in most Asian cultures, Hendry says, is that although the family system perceives men as being superior to women, "the duty of care within the family falls almost automatically to women, whether it is in times of sickness, injury, or senility."[94] This is exemplified in the Chinese saying, "Strict father, kind mother."

Latino

The sacredness and importance of the family is at the core of Latino cultures. It is within the context of the family that the individual finds security, emotional support, and a sharp distinction as to how gender roles are defined. In Mexican culture the father is placed in the dominant role. And as Hildebrand and his associates note, "The authority of the husband and father is seldom questioned or disputed. The father's role is expected to be one of breadwinner and protector of the family. He provides for the family's physical needs and monitors and controls all members' participation in the world outside the home."[95] Very early in life Mexican children learn that "the father makes all of the major decisions, and he sets the disciplinary standards. His word is final and the rest of the family looks to him for guidance and strength."[96] So strong is the male role in the Mexican household that in the absence of the father the "power position reverts to the oldest son."[97]

The notion of *machismo* in Mexican culture is often misconstrued and subject to numerous stereotypes. Becerra notes that some exaggerated myths paint a picture of "excessive aggression, little regard for women, and sexual prowess."[98] In stark contrast, most of the research regarding *machismo* maintains that "genuine *machismo* is characterized by true bravery or valor, courage, generosity, and a respect for others. The *machismo* role encourages protection of and provision for family members, use of fair and just authority, and respect for the role of the wife and children."[99]

Just as Confucian philosophy influenced the shaping of Asian gender roles, the conception of female roles within Christianity derives in part from the masculine representation of God as Father.[100] That is to say, the male and female roles within Latino families are defined by tradition and religion. Strong and his co-authors develop this idea when they note, "In traditional Latina gender roles, the notion of *marianismo* has been the cultural counterpart to *machismo*. Drawn from the Catholic ideal of the Virgin Mary, *mariansimo* stresses women's roles as self-sacrificing mothers suffering for their children and subordinating themselves to males."[101] It is the mother who nurtures and educates the children while allowing the father to be "the provider and disciplinarian."[102] You can observe the same view of women in Spain, where "the Spanish husband accords his wife due respect as stronghold of the family; he thinks of her as if she were a saint."[103] Children observe a mother who is willing to sacrifice, is strong, and has great perseverance. These "behaviors ensure survival and power through the children."[104]

We should point out as we conclude this section that changes in migration patterns have altered the role of women in many Latin American cultures. Perhaps the link between gender roles and migration is most vivid as it applies to the United States and Mexico. Writing about this connection Schneider and Silverman observe, "When men migrate alone, the women left behind assume new responsibilities and freedoms. They must make decisions for their families, and usually they must work."[105] Summarizing the overall impact of migration on Latino families and gender roles, it appears that "Given class and cultural diversity among Latinos, continued immigration, family change in the home countries, and increasing intermarriage, the future direction of the Latino family is difficult to predict."[106]

Indian

You have already seen how history, family, and religion are powerful forces in every culture and work in tandem. In each of the cultural families we have talked about, you saw the link between these social institutions and gender roles. When we look at the

---

CONSIDER THIS

Felicita, from Mexico, and her roommate Maria, from Costa Rica, were both entering their freshman year at a major university. This was the first time either of them had been away from home. They were delighted when they were asked by some other students to go out on a Friday night. When the other students, a mix of males and females, arrived at Felicita and Maria's dorm room, they asked if the two of them were ready to go. Both girls looked at each other and were somewhat confused. When the other students asked what was wrong, Felicita and Maria responded that they could not go. When the students inquired why they had changed their minds, Felicita and Maria said it was because there was not a chaperone to join them for the evening. What happened?

role of gender in India, the connection between a culture's history, religion, and its worldview is also apparent. Henderson writes, "Women's status stems from the convergence of historical and cultural factors."[107] Tischler develops this important point in more detail in the following manner: "In traditional India, the Hindu religion conceived of women as strongly erotic and thus a threat to male asceticism and spirituality. Women were cut off physically from the outside world. They wore veils and voluminous garments and were never seen by men who were not members of the family. Only men were allowed access to and involvement with the outside world."[108] Such an orientation and "ideology separates women and men from one another. Masculinity and femininity become defined as distinct, if not opposing, entities."[109] While strict adherence to this kind of dogma no longer exists, the residual influence has tended to create a culture where males are considered the superior sex. Male children are thought to be entrusted to parents by the gods. Gannon offers the following summary of this particular view of gender in India: "The preference for a son when a child is born is as old as Indian society. A son guarantees the continuation of the generations, and he will perform the last rites after his parent's death. This ensures a peaceful departure of the soul to its next existence in the ongoing cycle of life. The word *putra*, or son, literally means 'he who protects from going to hell.'"[110]

The type of family described above has for thousands of years produced a culture where "Men act as head of the household, primary wage earners, decision makers, and disciplinarians. Women are subordinate and serve as caretakers; as children they are groomed to move into and contribute to the well-being of the husband's family."[111] The roles just mentioned are learned very early in life. Boys are given much more freedom of expression than are girls; boys are encouraged to take part in the religious festivals and activities as a means of introducing them to the spiritual world, and girls are asked to help with the chores that keep the family functioning. It is also hoped that a girl will grow up to be a good wife who devotes herself to her husband's welfare through her performance of religious ritual, household duties, and chastity.[112]

To assist their sons in securing "good wives," arranged marriages are still commonplace in India—as well as complicated. As Ferraro and Andreatta explain, "In addition to making certain that a mate is selected from one's own caste, parents must be careful to arrange marriages for their children that take into consideration such factors as level of education, physical attractiveness, compatibility with future in-laws, and level of maturity."[113]

As is the case in so many cultures, globalization has had an impact on the Indian workforce which in turn has brought about some minor changes in gender stratification throughout India. Today, the number of young women in India becoming scholars, scientists, and medical doctors is greater than their American counterparts.[114] However, as is the case in many countries, while the proportion of working women in India has increased, it is still only around 25 percent.[115] And much of the increase has been in agricultural areas as the men moved to the cities for better jobs.

The Muslim Community

One of the clearest delineations of gender roles can be found in Arab society. This attitude can be traced to religious issues associated with being Muslim. "Clear Islamic teachings spell out the roles of women and their rights and duties in the patrilineage. When women marry, they retain their father's name and seldom adopt their husband's name. Father and brothers are expected to assume protection over girls and women."[116] Sedgwick explains some of these religious underpinnings in more detail when he reports, "Islam takes it as axiomatic that men are stronger than women, not only physically but also mentally and morally, and that women are, therefore, in need of male protection and guidance."[117] So strong is this decree to protect women that "Young unmarried women need permission from their parents or even their brothers when they seek to venture from their home."[118] Women are expected to live in a way that upholds and furthers the honor of their families. Daniel and Mahdi offer the following insight: "The most important cultural norm affecting a woman's life is the cultural association of a married woman with family honor."[119] The Koran is filled with specific messages for women telling them how they can preserve that honor. These messages range from admonitions against using cosmetics or perfume outside the home, to rules about avoiding bathing in public places.[120]

So conspicuous is the preference for male heirs that on the wedding day, friends and relatives of the newlyweds wish them many sons. An Arab proverb states, "Your wealth brings you respect, your sons bring you delight." This preference for males even extends to the weaning of the child. As Patai says, "Weaning comes much earlier in the life of a girl than of a boy."[121] Sait points out just how strong the partiality for males is when he writes, "traditional Palestinian society views women largely through the prism of family, honor, and chastity, and those violating those traditional social norms face reprisals."[122] Men are expected to marry, support their families, and defend the honor of the family.[123]

In Pakistan, which also has deep Islamic roots, you can see a specific example of how gender differences are acted out in the perception and treatment of boys and girls. Irfan and Cowburn explain the Pakistani family and gender: "In Pakistani culture males are more highly valued. They act as the head of the household, the primary wage earner, decision-maker, and disciplinarian. Elder brothers, or on some occasions even younger brothers, take over the role of father and never get challenged by the parents."[124]

Changing Gender Roles

As we move toward the conclusion of this section on gender roles across cultures we need to remind you of two important points. First, gender is a significant component to any study of intercultural communication. As Lamanna and Riedmann note, "Gender is important to discussions of family power, communication, and parental roles, as well as to work and family roles."[125] Our second point is that, for a host of reasons, gender roles in families are being forced to change. Trask reinforces this important idea when she writes: "Westernization and globalization have differentially affected all families with respect to gender roles, child rearing, and maintenance of aging parents."[126] Shifts in gender roles throughout the world, including in the United States, can be easily observed. Discussing these changes in the United States, Tischler writes:

> Female gender roles are changing rapidly, although traditional attitudes toward careers and marriage undoubtedly remain part of the thinking of many people in our society. Girls are being encouraged not to limit themselves to these stereotyped roles and attitudes. More and more young women expect to pursue careers before and during marriage and child rearing. Work fields that in the past have been traditionally male, such as medicine, law, or pharmacy, are now seeing either equal enrollments of men and women or majority women in their training schools.[127]

The United States is not the only nation witnessing transformations regarding gender roles. From Brazil electing its first female President, to a movement among African young women to question the notion of female circumcision, the entire

Female gender roles are changing rapidly as girls are encouraged not to limit themselves to stereotyped roles and attitudes.

Michael Newman/PhotoEdit

world is experiencing a shift in the perception of established female roles. In Egypt, as "the economy modernizes, women are drawn more and more into public roles, and they find new opportunities for self-expression."[128] In other Middle East countries women are asking for the right to vote. Recently a controversy surfaced in Saudi Arabia when newspapers "broke with tradition and … [began] printing photographs of Saudi women" and also carried stories about debates focusing on gender issues. One debate centered on "whether bans on women driving and working in some retail shops should be reversed."[129] The issue of women driving, according to a report on National Public Radio, is gaining some momentum: Saudi women are employing various social networking sites to air their arguments for easing the driving bans.

As observed earlier in the chapter, the rise of a global economy has also contributed to a re-evaluation of females' roles within the family. As Nanda and Warms note, "Women are being increasingly incorporated into the world economy, especially working in multinational corporations in developing countries."[130] These new economic roles influence what happens in the family. For example, studies have shown that when Mexican-American women secure employment outside the home, there arise within the family "joint decision making and greater equality of male and female roles."[131] In short, you

must be careful when thinking about gender roles in a dynamic world, and must guard against applying Western standards to the rest of the world.

INDIVIDUALISM AND COLLECTIVISM

Of great importance to the study of intercultural communication are the notions of individualism and collectivism. These two orientations will occupy a large portion of Chapter 6. We want to introduce the terms now, however, for they play a significant role in child-rearing practices and in the interaction that takes place within a family. Before we begin, it is important to realize that although the terms *individualism* and *collectivism* seem to be polar opposites, they are actually the end values of a continuum along which cultures can be situated. As Triandis points out, "Most cultures include a mixture of individualistic and collective elements."[132] What are these elements? In general, according to Schmidt and his associates, "The *individual-collective* dimension assesses a culture's tendency to encourage people to be unique and independent or conforming and interdependent."[133] More specifically, cultures classified as *individualistic* value the individual over the group. The individual is perceived as a sovereign stand-alone entity. Each person's uniqueness is of paramount value in individualistic cultures. Summarizing some of the characteristics associated with this value, West and Turner note, "When a culture values individualism, it prefers competition over cooperation, the individual over the group, and the private over the public. Individualistic cultures have an 'I' communication orientation, emphasizing self-concept and personal achievement."[134]

Collective cultures have a view of the world that is rather different from that of cultures that value individualism. For collective cultures the emphasis is on the needs and goals of the group rather than the self. Thomas and Inkson summarize this orientation with the following: "In collective cultures, people primarily view themselves as members of groups and collectives rather than as autonomous individuals. They are concerned about [the effect of] their actions on their groups. Their activities are more likely to be taken in groups on a more public basis."[135]

Individualism and the Family

It is not surprising that the two orientations we have just described get manifested in the family environment. That is to say, within each family, children begin to learn (unconsciously at first) values associated with individualism or collectivism. The enactment of these lessons takes a variety of forms. Let us look at some of those forms.

As we have stressed throughout this chapter, most cultural characteristics have their roots in the deep structure of a culture. For Americans, individualism, as it applies to families, is partially linked to the history of the United States. From earliest colonial times through the Industrial Revolution period, the nuclear family has been prominent in American culture. In these first nuclear families, early travelers to the

United States would report that parents were proud of their "wildly undisciplined, self-assertive offspring."[136] While families in the United States take a host of different designs, individualism is still the hallmark of most families. This kind of family tends to "emphasize independence and individual autonomy."[137] A subtle example of this nurturing of independence is the sleeping arrangement of children in America. "Even when dealing with children, North Americans try to provide them with a bedroom of their own, respect their individual right to privacy, and attempt to instill in them a sense of self-reliance and independence by encouraging them to solve their own problems."[138] Triandis underscores this North American attitude toward individualism within the family when he writes, "In individualistic cultures independence is expected and valued, and self-actualization is encouraged. Mother and child are distinct and the child is encouraged to leave the nest."[139] This independence and autonomy encourage self-reliance. Nomura and his colleagues expand this idea when they write, "children in America appear to be encouraged to 'decide for themselves,' 'do their own things,' 'develop their own opinion,' or 'solve their own problems.'"[140]

Of course, North Americans are not the only people whose families reflect an individualistic orientation. In Germany, where personal achievement and individual rights are emphasized, "it is not unusual or deviant behavior to belong to no group beyond the family, friendship circles, and rather formal work group membership."[141] The reason behind this view toward individualism is that the people perceive themselves as autonomous individuals with the liberty to select one group over another or to remain separate.

Collectivism and the Family

An Asian-Indian proverb states, "An individual could no more be separated from the family than a finger from the hand." The proverb serves as an excellent introduction to our discussion of collectivism and the family, since it demonstrates that "family interdependence is stronger in collective societies than in those families that stress individualism."[142] As we noted at the outset of this section, in collective cultures people experience a profound allegiance and attachment to their families. You can see that interdependence when Wolpert tells us that, in India, family members "share property, all material possessions, food, work, and love, perform religious rituals together, and often live under the same roof."[143]

The contrast between individualistic and collective extended families is vivid when we turn to Latino cultures. "Extended family members rely on one another to take care of children, [and]...provide friendship and support."[144] Ingoldsby offers a synopsis of the Latino experience within the family as a "type of social organization that places the family ahead of the individual's interests and development. It is part of a traditional view of the society that highlights loyalty and cooperation within the family."[145]

As is the case with a great deal of culture, the collective view of family has deep historical roots. Regarding Mexico, for example, Rodriguez ties together the three ideas of history, collectivism, and family: "From the time of our ancestors, the community has taken care of its children. The Aztecs accepted the children from the village into the clan and gave them *cara y corazón*. They socialized them, teaching them the traditions, to be self-disciplined and obedient.... It was the group that gave the child life and sustained him." [146]

What we have been discussing in regard to families in Mexico also applies to Mexican-American families. Sanchez writes, "While it often consists of a household of husband, wife, and children, people of Mexican origin are more likely to live in an extended family context, which includes parents, grandparents, brothers and sisters, cousins, and other blood relatives—commonly referred to as *la familia*, the greater family."[147] The idea of collectivism among Mexican families is further strengthened by a system of godparenting called *compadrazgo*. Godparents, in most instances, are not blood relations, but are part of the extended family. Zinn and Pok explain this broadening of the Mexican family in the following manner: "The *compadrazgo* system of godparents established connections between families and in this way enlarged family ties."[148] Godparenting is also an important social institution in Brazilian culture.[149] This same strong family linkage and bond is seen in Cuban-American families even when these families attempt to adapt to new American lifestyles.[150]

Puerto Rican culture is another example of the socialization process involving a collective orientation. According to Carrasquillo, "For the Puerto Rican, the family is an extended social unit that encompasses a wide variety of relationships. The extended family functions as a primary agent of socialization, as a safety net for its members in times of need, and as a means for obtaining protection, companionship, and social and business contact."[151]

This same idea of an extended collective family is also found in sub-Saharan African culture. In fact, Wilson and Ngige write, "The nuclear family of husband, wife, and their children (i.e., family of procreation) was considered incomplete without the extended family."[152] The collective nature of this family structure encourages everyone "to contribute meaningfully toward the common good of the family institution, strengthening the cohesion and sense of belonging of all members in the community."[153] In these types of families children are reared and nurtured by a series of adults. For example, according to Peltzer, child-rearing practices include "mothering by several adults during infancy and early childhood."[154] Richmond and Gestrin underscore this notion when they note, "The African extended family is extended indeed. Among its members are parents and children, grandparents, uncles and aunts, in-laws, cousins of varying degrees, as well as persons not related by blood."[155] You can observe the collective nature of these families in the Maasai proverb, "The child has no owner." The meaning, of course, is that all members of the tribe are responsible for socializing the children.

Three more cultures (Arab, Japanese, and Chinese) and one co-culture (American Indian) should be examined before we conclude our section on collectivism and the family. An excellent preview of the Arab view toward collectivism is stated by Esherick:

> Unlike the rugged individualism we see in North America (every person for him or herself, individual rights, families living on their own away from relatives, and so on), Arab society emphasizes the importance of the group. Arab culture teaches that the needs of the group are more important than the needs of one person.[156]

In collective and extended Arab families people "share work, income, and expenses as a single economic unit."[157] In Egypt, for example, "Extended family members carry out household tasks, work in fields, and take care of the very young and the very old."[158] Arab families, as part of their collective orientation, have through the centuries developed a keen sense of family loyalty. In the Bedouin tribes of Saudi Arabia, "Intense feelings of loyalty and dependence are fostered and preserved" by the family.[159] Not only has the Arab view of collective families been a tradition for thousands of years, but this value seems to travel with families as they move from place to place in the twenty-first century. For example, Arab-Americans maintain a very traditional view of the collective family, even in the United States. They continue to have "large families in which all aunts, uncles, cousins and grandparents are considered part of the immediate family, even if there is only one breadwinner in the household."[160]

Japan is another culture where collectivism is manifested in the family. As Ferraro and Andreatta point out, "In group-oriented cultures such as Japanese, people strive for the good of the larger group—such as the family or the community."[161] More specifically, as it applies to the Japanese family, "individuals are encouraged to find fulfillment for their needs within the family and to put the collective interests of the group before their own personal interests."[162] This means that children are brought up "to seek fulfillment with others rather than individually."[163] This emphasis on collectivism within the family fashions children into adults who are part of a culture that holds loyalty to family and groups in high esteem.[164] Japanese parents also expect their children to be compliant "and avoid confrontations" that might disturb the harmony within the family.[165] So important are these traditional family values of loyalty, collectivism, and harmony that the Japanese expect them to be part of a person's entire life. The Japanese have a saying that reaffirms these values: "Even if an extended family does not live together, parents and grandparents should live near enough to offer a bowl of hot soup."[166]

The Chinese perception of collectivism is deeply rooted in Confucianism, and "family interests are placed above those of society and other groups within it."[167] The importance of the family has historically not only been linked to Confucianism, but also to the geographic nature of China. Because vast areas of the country are widely separated, most Chinese have always felt detached from the central government. Hence, family loyalty supersedes all other institutions. As this Chinese proverb makes clear, "Heaven is high and the Emperor is far away." So strong is the value of loyalty that ethnographic studies suggest that Chinese children are raised in a manner that teaches them that they should not bring shame to their family, which would be perceived as a lack of devotion. Hence, in China, "Children are socialized to be conscious of what others think of them and are expected to act so as to get the most out of approval of others while trying to avoid disapproval."[168] Chu and Ju make much the same point: "An important Chinese cultural value is filial piety. Traditionally, Chinese children feel a lifelong obligation to their parents, ideally exemplified by an unreserved devotion to please them in every possible way."[169]

For American Indians, "extended family members are important teachers for transmitting ways and values."[170] However, what is interesting about collectivism among American Indians is that "despite nearly five hundred years of destructive contact with Anglo-European cultures, important differences in family practices persist among Native Americans."[171] Speaking of this difference, Cheshire writes, "Individuals identify themselves not only as members of specific families, but as members of a tribe, which creates a larger kinship structure to draw upon, with many families interrelated."[172] Because of this expanded definition of an extended family, "it is not unusual to have youngsters stay in a variety of different households."[173]

REMEMBER THIS

Some cultures engage in child-rearing practices that are characterized as dependence training, while other cultures emphasize independence-training routines.

THE ELDERLY

The family is the first institution to introduce the child to the notion of age grouping. Classifying people by age is common in all cultures, and "age grouping is so familiar and so important that it and sex have been called the only universal factors that determine a person's position in society."[174] As you might expect, there are vast cultural differences in how age is valued. "In most cultures, the elderly are responsible for passing down oral traditions and teaching and instructing younger members."[175] For "these societies old age often has profound significance, bringing with it the period of great respect."[176] In the United States, for a number of reasons, most members of the dominant culture have a somewhat negative perception of the elderly. For many, death is not seen as a natural stage in the life process, so many people in the dominant culture do all they can to avoid growing old. As Andersen and Taylor explain, "We are taught to fear aging in this society, and many people spend a lot of time and money trying to keep looking young. Unlike many other societies, ours does not revere the elderly, but instead devalues them, making the aging process even more difficult."[177] Even the English language has created "derogatory terms" for the elderly.[178] Reflect on the images created by the following terms: "codger," "fuddy-duddy," "geezer," "fossil," "blue-hair," "cotton-top," "old coot." The age bias in the United States is so blatant that during retirement years the elderly are often isolated from the rest of the culture and enter retirement communities and convalescent homes instead of moving in with their children. In general, we "who reside in the western world do not see the value of having our elderly family members in our lives."[179]

Perceptions of the elderly that are common in the dominant culture in the United States are not the rule in many other cultures. In fact, "It is interesting to note how North American stereotypes of the elderly have influenced societal views of the aging process, especially when we consider how the elderly are perceived and treated in other countries."[180] Let us pause for a moment and look at some of these other countries and cultures.

We begin with a group of cultures that have a long tradition of positive perceptions of the elderly—Latino cultures. These perceptions are translated into actions that see the elderly being respected, playing a dominant role in the family, and being cared for. In most Latin families, "special authority is given to the elderly."[181] Part of the authority comes from the perception of the elderly as being wise and possessing a great deal of the culture's history. That wisdom is reflected in a Spanish proverb: "The devil knows more because he's old than because he is the devil." Translated, the elderly have acquired a large fund of knowledge. This positive view of old age is seen in many Latin cultures. In Puerto Rican families, grandparents not only live with the extended family, they also help with child-rearing activities.[182] So strong is the bond between the elderly and the family in Latino cultures that "placing elderly parents in nursing homes or centers for the aged is virtually unknown. To do so may be looked on as abandonment or rejection of a loved one and as a serious shirking of family responsibility."[183]

An Arab proverb states: "A house without an elderly person is like an orchard without a well." This proverb serves as an

REMEMBER THIS

A culture's perception and treatment of its elderly is a reflection of what members of that culture have "learned" about the aging process.

excellent introduction to yet another society that greatly respects the elderly. For example, Hildebrand and his colleagues point out, "Prestige and power are attached to age, and especially to Arab grandparents. The grandfather is the undisputed head of the household or clan, and everyone submits to his authority. He passes on the oral traditions of the Arab peoples, using parables for the moral guidance and character development to younger generations."[184] This deference to the elderly is not only embedded in a culture's deep structure institution of the family but also is part of religious training. For example, Mir states, "Both the Qur'an and the Prophet emphasized the importance of caring for the elderly. In Islamic teaching, it is the responsibility of each individual to care for and honor his or her parents as they age."[185] So strong is that responsibility that "in the Muslim world, there seems to be no such thing as a nursing home."[186] You can observe the effects of this attitude toward the elderly when you look at Saudi Arabian culture. There, "the authority, wisdom, and counsel of elder family members are still to a great extent accepted, and younger family members must wait sometimes far into middle age before being accorded that status."[187] Lutfiyya speaks of this early socialization when he writes, "Children are often instructed to kiss the hands of older people when they are introduced to them, to be polite in the presence of elders, and to stand up and offer them their seats. Young people are encouraged to listen to and to learn from their elders. Only from the older people who have lived in the past can one learn anything of value, they are told."[188]

This same respect for the elderly is taught in most Asian cultures. Tischler offers an excellent introduction to the Asian view of the elderly in the following paragraph:

> In many societies, such as Japan and China, age brings respect and honor. Older people are turned to for advice and their opinions are valued because they reflect a full measure of experience. Often, older people are not required to stop their productive work simply because they have reached a certain age. Rather, they work as long as they are able to, and their tasks might be modified to allow them to continue to work virtually until they die. In this way, people maintain their social identity until they die.[189]

In places such as China, Korea, and Japan, one reason for the respect and reverent attitude toward the elderly is that ancestor worship and the past are highly valued. There is even a belief that if someone "lived so long they must possess some special life force."[190] In all three of these cultures (Chinese, Korean, Japanese), the family's belief in that "special force" is deeply entrenched in Confucian philosophy—particularly, the Confucian notion of filial piety that is concerned with the correct way to treat one's parents and grandparents. Confucius believed that filial piety served as the root of all other values. So powerful is this philosophical tradition that it is even extended after the death of a person's parents,[191] which is illustrated by the proverb, "When eating bamboo sprouts, remember who planted them."

Elderly people are not only venerated in Asian cultures, but they are also influential, both in and out of the family. In Korean culture, children are taught at a young age that grandparents and other older members of the family are the authority figures.[192] This same attitude is found in China. As Wenzhong and Grove note, "Perhaps the chief determinant of relative power in China is seniority."[193] The hierarchy associated with age in Chinese culture is clear. After the father, the eldest male has most of the authority. Even when Chinese families resettle in the United States they still follow the customs associated with respecting the elderly. Chinese-American families reportedly experience a sense of guilt and shame if their elderly parents are placed in nursing homes.[194]

Steve Harrington

In many cultures the elderly are not only respected and venerated, they are also active members of the family and help "teach" young children about the culture.

During this chapter we have alluded to some obvious and subtle changes to families throughout the world. Japan represents a clear example of change as it applies to how the elderly are perceived and treated. While the Japanese still embrace the view that there should be "obedience and deference to senior persons,"[195] certain events have altered the notion of family in Japan and treatment of the elderly. Izuhara summarizes the causes for those alterations, "There are a number of common pressures and processes confronting family structures and resources. Social change, demographic shifts, and changes in economies and the labor market are some of the key drivers of family change."[196] We need to mention once again that these changes have not produced a decline in filial devotion, but rather a need to adapt to an ever-changing world. For instance, a continually declining birthrate means "Japan will have to become a pioneer in figuring out how to run a society top heavy with older people."[197]

Before concluding this section we need to mention two co-cultures within the United States. We begin with Native American Indian families. As is the case with all of the families we have examined, any cultural generalizations need to arrive with a series of disclaimers. For example, Native American Indians are a very heterogeneous co-culture. Not only are there approximately 530 different tribes, but you also find dissimilarity between those Indians who live on reservations and those who have relocated to urban areas.[198] However, in spite of these differences, attitudes involving the elderly have remained in place for hundreds of years. At the heart of those views is the same positive perception of the elderly that we have seen in other cultures typified by extended families. That is, there is a deep and clear deference regarding the elderly within Native American Indian culture—a respect and admiration that can be traced to that culture's deep structure. The elderly, both men and women, have a number of roles within the family. They are part of the decision-making process,[199] and are also responsible for transmitting the collective knowledge and wisdom that each tribe has accumulated over thousands of years. As "carriers" of the culture "Native American elders are the safe-keepers of tribal stories and songs and are held in the highest respect in tribal groups. Forming an indispensable part of the community, the elders share and pass on to each new generation the tribal oral traditions. The tradition of passing information orally from one generation to the next is typical of all tribes."[200]

African-Americans represent another co-culture in the United States that has a view toward the elderly that differs slightly from the one held by the dominant culture, a view that has been influenced by the history of this co-culture. As McAdoo notes, "The historical past of many African-American families is uniquely different from all the other immigrant groups that have come to the United States. The American experience has resulted in many of the strengths that have helped families to cope with adversities."[201] Part of this past has fashioned a situation where "The elders in an African-American community are valued and treated with respect. The role of grandmother is one of the most central roles in the African-American family."[202] Speaking of this essential role, Ruiz notes:

Historically, the African-American grandmother has played important roles within the extended family network. She has been guardian and caregiver for her children, grandchildren, great-grandchildren, nieces, and nephews, as well as fictive kin. She represents wisdom and strength while serving as keeper of the family values, and conveyer of African-American culture.[203]

CONSIDER THIS

Recall as much as you can about your personal family history. Record your answers to the following questions as they apply to the conscious and unconscious learning that took place. It might be interesting to compare your answers with someone from a different culture.

a. *In general, could my family be classified as formal or informal?*
b. *What or who were the subjects of jokes?*
c. *What was the attitude toward the elderly?*
d. *Was conflict dealt with in a direct or indirect manner?*
e. *Who made the major decisions in your family? Mother? Father? Both? Other family members?*
f. *If you had siblings of the opposite sex, did you notice different child-rearing practices being acted out? What were those differences?*
g. *Was competition or cooperation stressed?*
h. *How did you learn about religious matters?*
i. *How were you rewarded?*
j. *How were you punished?*

SOCIAL SKILLS

Earlier in this chapter we discussed how families are important to all cultures for a host of reasons. The reason most germane to this chapter is succinctly stated by Andersen and Taylor: "For most people, the family is the first source of socialization. Through families, children are introduced to the expectations of society."[204] The key word in Andersen and Taylor's sentence is "expectations." The "expectation" that we are concerned with is the socialization regarding communication activity. That is, how and what do families teach the child about verbal and nonverbal skills. The connection between family and communication is further clarified in the following paragraph:

> The family is the most basic of all human groups. It is the context within which the first steps toward communication take place. The family is a great teacher of the symbols and rules of meaning that are the foundation of social life. Thus, the family has always been the principal source for learning vocabulary and linking symbols, meanings, and referents so the new members of society could take the first steps in communicating.[205]

A family's communication responsibilities are numerous. Taylor offers a rather comprehensive listing of many "cultural rules" a person has to learn to function effectively within society. They include:

- How to start and end conversation
- Taking turns when interacting
- When not to interrupt
- The use of silence
- Knowing appropriate and inappropriate topics of conversation
- How to use humor
- Correct use of nonverbal communication
- Appropriate use of laughter[206]

The family introduces children to notions of power, assertiveness, control, negotiation styles, role relationships, and feedback rules, among other variables.[207]

We will look now at two of the general social skills the family "teaches."

Aggression

Because all cultures prepare their members to live among other people, it should not be surprising that many of the same social skills are taught in every family. For example, instruction in good manners is stressed in every culture, for without some degree of civility you would have chaos and confusion. Yet the emphasis placed on many common child-rearing "messages" differs in degree and intensity as you move from culture to culture. A good example of cultural differences can be seen in a culture's acceptance or rejection of aggressive behavior. For instance, some studies of American family life have shown that parents encourage, approve, and reward aggressive behavior.[208] This tendency is even more pronounced with young males who learn to dominate others as a way to increase their status.[209] In short, among members of the dominant culture, children are often instructed to "stand up for their rights" and not let anyone "push them around." You can even see the mixing of values when the young boy is told "to fight back and not act like a sissy."

Many cultures take the opposite view toward aggressive behavior from the one found in the dominant culture of the United States. In many Asian cultures even the word "no" is seen as a sign of being forceful, belligerent, rude, impolite and, of course, aggressive.[210] In these cultures, children are taught the social skills necessary for group harmony, family interdependence, respect for the elderly, and the importance of saving face. Avoidance of the word "no" is just one of many ways this value is made manifest. Another vivid example of how each family teaches various social skills can be seen among the Thai, where the family teaches patterns of interaction that avoid aggressive behavior: "The child quickly learns that by behaving in a way that openly demonstrates consideration for the feelings of others, obedience, humility, politeness and respect, he can make people like him and be nice to him. This behavior may be summed up in one Thai word, *krengjai*, which is usually translated as 'consideration.'"[211]

Let us briefly mention two other cultures (Mexican and Native American Indian) where aggressive behavior within the family is discouraged. One study found that "Mexican parents were the most punitive for aggression against other children, while the American parents stand out as particularly tolerant of aggression against other children."[212] Native American families also try to avoid aggression and conflict within the family and seek to maintain harmony among all relationships.[213]

Decision Making

The methods and techniques people employ to make decisions is yet another action that is learned very early in life—and most likely within the family environment. As Sparks points out, "Decision-making describes the process by which families make choices, judgments, and ultimately come to conclusions that guide behavior."[214] The process most often employed by families of the dominant culture in the United States is referred to as "person-oriented" decision making. Some of the "persons" who are verbal are often children, for in "person-oriented" families, "children are allowed greater opportunities to influence one another and their parents. In any given person-orientated family, a more verbal and expressive child or spouse may play a larger role in decision making than less verbal members."[215] This emphasis on allowing children to make personal choices on their own is not the case in other cultures and co-cultures. It seems that while "Anglo-American children perform best when they choose their own tasks, Asian-American children perform best in mom-chosen tasks."[216] You can find this same lack of child-centered decision making in Mexican-American and Japanese families where authority is highly concentrated in the head of the family and children have far less influence.

The goal of this chapter has been to demonstrate the prominence of the family in the enculturation process, particularly as it applies to social interaction. The importance and enduring nature of the family is clearly captured by the Chinese proverb: "To forget one's ancestors is to be a brook without a source, a tree without a root."

CHAPTER 4

Cultural History: Our Antecedents

We learn history not in order to know how to behave or how to succeed, but to know who we are.

LESZEK KOLAKOWSKI

History should not be written to make the present generation feel good but to remind us that human affairs are complicated.

MARGARET MACMILLAN

THE IMPORTANCE OF HISTORY

As you begin this chapter, you are probably wondering what history has to do with intercultural communication. It is a fair question and one the next few paragraphs will try to answer. Over two thousand years ago the Roman philosopher Cicero wrote: *History is the witness that testifies to the passing of time; it illumines reality, vitalizes memory, provides guidance in daily life, and brings us tidings of antiquity.* The importance of history to the study of culture and communication is clearly illustrated by that proclamation, and it takes on added meaning when you realize that the word *culture* can be easily substituted for the word *history*.

Among more recent statements attesting to the role history plays in understanding human society, Stearns writes, "The past causes the present, and so the future."[1] For the study of culture, knowledge of your historical heritage helps you understand current values and institutions. As you will learn in the section on U.S. history, the majority of the early immigrants to the United States were from Europe, and they brought with them historically influenced traditions and worldviews. Huber has pointed out that Europe's philosophical and scientific foundation came from Greece and was strongly influenced by Medieval Islam. The Western legal system is a product of ancient Rome, and Christianity came from Jerusalem.[2] An understanding of these connections can provide insight into the values, traditions, and social institutions that govern your life today.

A study of a people's history can provide insight into the values, traditions, and social institutions that a culture deems important.

Robert Fonseca

GUEST

History also provides identity, which can help unify people from differing backgrounds and cultures. Bender reports that in the nineteenth and twentieth centuries the national history of the United States became an important force in unifying the nation's varied social strata.

> It [U.S. national history] became the core of civic education in schools and other institutions devoted to making peasants, immigrants, and provincial peoples into national citizens. A common history, which involved both common memory and a tacit agreement to forget differences, was intended to provide a basis for a shared national identity.[3]

The discussion of history presented here involves much more than a chronology of events and dates. Granted, these are important, but taken in isolation they paint a rather limited picture. Characterizing history as one of the deep structures of a culture incorporates a culture's formal and informal governmental procedures, its sense of community, its political and economic processes, its key historical heroes, and even its geography. All of these factors work in combination to provide the members of every culture with their identity, values, goals, and expectations. For example, a consistent theme in U.S. history is that anything is possible—one can even become president. History books are full of accounts of Abraham Lincoln's backwoods upbringing in Illinois, Harry Truman working in a clothing store, and Bill Clinton's path from rural Arkansas to the White House. Future texts will describe how Barack Obama overcame the divisive issue of racism to become president. Any study of U.S. business history will highlight how Steve Jobs began in a garage and went on to build Apple, or how Larry Page and Sergey Brin's initial work on Google began in their dormitory room. Such stories are examples of how history can influence perception, behavior, and national character.

The progression of history is important when reflecting on Middle East current events as well. The long-standing conflict between Israel and Palestine becomes more understandable—if mistrust, animosity, and violence can be understood—when you know that the area has long been considered sacred by Christians, Muslims, and Jews alike.[4] The public demonstrations in Bahrain in early 2011 were not a result of recent contentious relations between the Shiite Muslim majority and the Sunni monarch. Differences between these two sects can be traced to the seventh century.[5] On a larger scale, Stearns believes that understanding the contemporary tensions between Christians and Muslims, "requires some knowledge of patterns that took shape over 12 centuries ago."[6]

Interest in the study of history is predicated on two assumptions. The first is that historical events help explain the character and actions of a culture. As Kerblay notes, "For all people, history is the source of the collective consciousness."[7] From the earliest westward movement away from the initial east coast settlements, to the explorations of outer space, Americans have agreed on a history of embracing new challenges. The second assumption is that what a culture seeks to remember and pass on to following generations is significant in accounting for the character of that culture. For instance, U.S. history books abound with examples of how a single determined individual can make a difference in the world. Everyone has heard how Rosa Parks, Martin Luther King, Jr., and César Chávez brought about social changes that significantly improved the lives of many Americans. The prevalence of these stories demonstrates the significance of "the individual" in U.S. culture.

In addition to learning about the historical foundations of U.S. culture, the following sections will provide you greater insight to historical events that shaped the national character of the countries discussed and give you an understanding of Islamic civilization. The following are examples of what this chapter discusses.

- How centuries of authoritarian rule molded the Russian national character
- How China's pride in their historical achievements can produce ethnocentric feelings
- How early Japanese agricultural practices contributed to a preference for group activity
- The historical event that initiated Hindu-Muslim animosity long before the 1947 Partition of India
- How the Spanish conquest contributed to the Mexican sense of fatalism
- How a simple question of leadership resulted in the Sunni-Shiite schism

UNITED STATES HISTORY

This examination of U.S. history will focus less on discussing actual historical events, and instead, will emphasize the cultural traits that emerged from those events to form the contemporary U.S. national character. Those cultural traits are primarily a product of the people who created the United States, especially the first immigrants who set the pattern for what was to follow from 1607 to the present. McElroy maintains that the "primary American cultural beliefs derive from" the initial settlers and that they "began the process of distinguishing American behavior from European behavior, which during the next eight generations led to the formation of a new American culture."[8] McElroy is suggesting that much of what is considered the U.S. national character can be traced to the European people who arrived in the early years of the nation's formation—a population that came holding many of the values that continue to characterize the United States, such as hard work, self-improvement, practicality, freedom, responsibility, equality, and individuality.[9]

The initial settlers were predominantly Anglo-Saxons who brought with them selected English values, the English system of law, and the basic organization for commerce used during the sixteenth century. As they were beginning to establish their culture, these first immigrants were confronted with a wave of non-Anglo-Saxon newcomers, a development that grew and continues even today with the arrival of new immigrants. This ongoing influx of immigrants, both legal and illegal, has produced what is sometimes referred to as the first multicultural nation in the world. Remarkably, the later arriving immigrants have adapted to the larger U.S. culture. In his examination of U.S. history, Fischer is struck by "the extent to which the American mainstream has overflowed and washed away that [ethnic] diversity, leaving behind little but food variety and self-conscious celebrations of multiculturalism."[10] Fischer is referring to the many immigrant ethnic cultures being subsumed by, and incorporated into, the dominant U.S. culture.

While cultural integration does not come easily, then or now, the shared desire of the first immigrants to be free from the oppressive dictates of such English institutions as "the Crown," "divine right," and the Church of England, motivated them to seek unity. This impetus led, in part, to the binding of the early English settlers with Germans, Irish, and other ethnicities that were fleeing the repressive governance of monarchs and religious authorities. The result was a social fabric flexible enough to enfold Catholics, Congregationalists, Methodists, Lutherans, Presbyterians,[11] and a host of others, and to unite North, South, East, and West within a national framework.

Country Statistics: United States of America[12]	
Location	North America
Size	9,826,675 sq. km
Population	>313.23 million (July 2011 est.)
Ethnic Groups	White 79.96%, Black 12.85%, Asian 4.43%, Amerindian and Alaska native 0.97%, native Hawaiian and other Pacific islander 0.18%, two or more races 1.61% (July 2007 estimate). **Note:** About 15.1% of total population is Hispanic who may be of any race or ethnic group.
Government	Constitution-based federal republic
Language	English 82.1%, Spanish 10.7%, other Indo-European 3.8%, Asian and Pacific island 2.7%, other 0.7%

These early Americans wanted to separate alienable rights (those that could be voluntarily surrendered to the government) from inalienable rights (those that could not be surrendered or taken away, even by a government of the people).[13] The fundamental American proposition became "life, liberty, and the pursuit of happiness" for each individual, and those liberties had to be secured against the potentially abusive power of government. The common desire to escape religious authoritarianism and monarchy rule also gave rise to what is referred to as the doctrine of separation of church and state, which prohibits the government from supporting any single form of religion or from preventing anyone from practicing his or her chosen religion.[14] This doctrine is currently at the forefront of U.S. political activity, as questions of abortion rights, school prayer, and religious displays on government property are publicly and passionately debated.

As noted, the people who established the initial settlements, and later colonies, integrated selected English values with a new set of beliefs. Chief among these were individuality, a lack of formality, and efficient use of time. Centuries later these values endure. Individualism was perhaps among the initial values to emerge in the new country. As McElroy notes, "The self-selecting emigrants who left Europe for America manifested individualism by their emigration. When they got on the ships, they were already individualists."[15] This sense of individualism also strongly influenced the nation's early political formation. The founders of the United States sought to establish a nation based on "political freedom, personal liberty, rule of law, social mobility, and egalitarianism."[16] A rich, spacious land with abundant natural resources encouraged implementation of these ideals, and personal liberty continues to be a hallmark of contemporary American society.

The value placed on individuality in the United States has been heightened through folklore and the popular media. For example, novels often portray the American settler as moving westward into new lands, carving out a homestead in the wilderness remote from others. Rugged individualism is exemplified in the image of the American cowboy—someone unencumbered by restrictive obligations or personal ties, free to roam the spacious American West at will, and able to surmount all challenges single-handedly. Stewart and Bennett, however, have pointed out that the early frontier individualism, so commonly portrayed in the media, was more myth than reality.[17] Early settlers actually came together in loosely formed, informal groups to help each other accomplish various tasks, such as harvesting crops, building a church or barn, to barter for goods, or simply to socialize. Indeed, the role of groups in early and present-day American life has led Fischer to consider U.S. culture as characterized by *voluntarism* rather than individualism, where the self-reliant, independent individual recognizes the benefits of communal activity but engages in those activities on a self-selective, voluntary basis.[18]

Distaste for formality and wasting time was also part of the colonial experience. Settling a new, undeveloped land required a great deal of effort be devoted to the daily activities of surviving, a situation that did not lend itself to formality. There was no time to be squandered on the nonsense of the rigid European and British rules of formality. Only resourceful, determined people survived. The difficult geographical factors of the Western frontier also had a far reaching influence on the settlers. The behaviors of survival based on individualism, a lack of formality, and efficiency soon gave rise to corresponding beliefs, values, and attitudes. In this way, independence and individualism became even more pronounced in the American culture. Anything that might violate free expression and the right to think for yourself was considered morally wrong.

United States history is also replete with instances of violence and war, experiences that shaped both the culture and the geographical borders. The early history of the United States witnessed the taking of American Indian lands by force; the capture, importation, and enslavement of Africans; and numerous wars, such as the

Revolutionary War, the War of 1812, the Civil War, the Mexican-American War, and the Spanish-American War. The latter two profoundly changed U.S. national borders and its overseas domain. The Mexican-American War and its consequences are discussed further in the section on Mexican history. The Spanish-American War placed several of Spain's colonial holdings under U.S. control, where Puerto Rico and Guam remain today. There are, of course, many other examples that reflect the American belief in possessing and using military force. As McElroy points out, "The most remarkable cultural feature of American behavior in the twentieth century is repeatedly deploying huge armies and other military forces on far-distant continents and seas and in transferring colossal quantities of war supplies to distant allies."[19] That pattern has continued into the twenty-first century as witnessed by the conflicts in Iraq and Afghanistan. The United States also continues to maintain an extensive global military presence, with forces in 144 countries.[20]

Expansion has also been an important part of U.S. history and began when the early English settlers "took possession of lands they alleged to be empty and unused."[21] Bender tells you, "Americans came to associate the meaning of America with an entitlement to unrestricted access to land and markets. Land, freedom, opportunity, abundance, seemed a natural sequence, which nourished something of an American compulsion to use new lands and opportunities to achieve wealth."[22]

This perspective was clearly evident in the U.S. adoption of the concept of Manifest Destiny, a philosophy applied in the early 1800s to justify an aggressive campaign of westward expansion and territorial acquisition. Although originally used to dispossess American Indians and Mexicans, this philosophy stressed that Americans were the people "who would inevitably spread the benefits of democracy and freedom to the lesser peoples inhabiting the region."[23] The frequent U.S. calls for free markets and democratic reforms in other nations, especially the Middle East, can be construed as a continuing application of Manifest Destiny.

Notions of freedom and independence were continually reinforced during the United States' formative period, as settlers restlessly moved westward into new territories. The challenge of developing a sparsely populated land also produced a culture with a strong love of change and progress. Today, change is commonly associated with progress, especially when economically driven.[24] The ability to conceive new ideas and innovative ways of accomplishing tasks is regarded as a highly desirable attribute. The expectation of frequent changes designed to improve products, processes, and individual conditions represents normality among U.S. Americans. The desire for change and innovation pushed early settlers across the vast wilderness of the North American continent and produced a national restlessness that now sends men and women on explorations of space. This can be seen as a continuing manifestation of a cultural heritage that emphasizes egalitarianism, independence, frequent change, and a willingness to engage the unknown.

Contemporary Social Issues

The U.S. is currently confronted with a host of social issues that could ultimately have an impact on established societal norms, and the two that carry the greatest potential for intercultural conflict are mentioned here. The first is immigration, which is significantly changing the ethnic composition of the population. Data from the 2010 census shows that, collectively, minorities now constitute the majority in many parts of the United States. Members of different ethnicities, particularly those newly arrived, often bring with them worldviews and practices dissimilar from those of the established majority. This population shift clearly carries the possibility of intercultural discord. A second prominent source of disharmony is the pronounced ideological differences behind a number of social issues that are proving exceptionally divisive. Three of the most

contentious issues are the right to life versus freedom of choice debate, the argument over same-sex marriage, and the question of school prayer. The ideological divide behind these differences is primarily along secular and religious beliefs, and those on either side of the arguments show little inclination to seek a middle ground.

RUSSIAN HISTORY

Perhaps the most prominent aspect of Russia's history is its geography. The largest country in the world, almost twice the size of the United States, Russia encompasses eleven time zones stretching across the northern tier of the European and Asian continents. This geo-location has played a major role in shaping the history and culture of the Russian peoples,[25] and understanding that link is essential to appreciating Russian culture. The vast harshness of Russia's steppes and forests and the sheer enormity of their country created a people who "would rather settle down by a warm stove, break out a bottle of vodka, and muse about life."[26]

Lacking any significant barriers to passage, geography has left the country vulnerable to historical invasions by armies from both Europe and Asia. The Russian "Motherland" (*Rodina*) has been invaded and occupied by the Mongols, Germans, Turks, Poles, Swedes, French, Japanese, and English—subjecting the Russian peoples to war, persecution, and intense suffering. Cities have been brutally occupied and cruelly governed, with the population of entire towns and villages slaughtered. Consequently, Russians have developed a perception of the world that frequently incorporates a sense of distrust toward outsiders.[27] While it is difficult for most Americans to understand this national paranoia, Daniels summarizes these differences in perception and history:

> It is of greatest importance for Americans to appreciate how different was Russia's international environment from the circumstances of the young United States. Russia found itself in a world of hostile neighbors, the United States in secure continental isolation. Living under great threats and equally great temptations, Russia had developed a tradition of militarized absolutism that put the highest priority on committing its meager resources to meet those threats and exploit those temptations.[28]

Russia's historical political heritage has helped mold the contemporary Russian worldview. Esler depicts that heritage in the following manner: "Russia's political tradition has historically been autocratic, from the legacy of the Byzantine emperors and Tartar khans, through the heavy-handed authoritarianism of Peter the Great, to the totalitarian regime of Joseph Stalin."[29] To give you a fuller appreciation of the tradition of Russia being governed by an autocratic, centralized government, a brief overview of the establishment and development of the Russian state is provided.

Country Statistics: Russian Federation	
Location	Europe and Northern Asia
Size	17,098,242 sq. km
Population	>138.74 million (July 2011 est.)
Ethnic Groups	Russian 79.8%, Tatar 3.8%, Ukrainian 2%, Bashkir 1.2%, Chuvash 1.1%, other or unspecified 12.1% (2002 census)
Government	Federation
Language	Russian (official); more than 140 other languages and dialects

Early historical records indicate that during the ninth century a series of city states were established along the waterways of the western Russian plain, with Novgorod and Kiev being the most prominent. These city states were ruled by princes, and Kiev developed into a major center of government until the late twelfth century, when political decay set in. The arrival of the Mongols in 1240 brought about the final collapse of the Kievan state. Although the Mongols maintained a military presence in Russia for well over 200 years, they were generally satisfied to rule from a distance as long as tribute was paid. Mongol rule was replaced in the fifteenth century by the rise and ultimate establishment of a consolidated Russia governed from Moscow. From the early sixteenth century until the Bolshevik Revolution in 1917, the Russian peoples were subjected to the heavy-handed rule of an authoritarian, centralized government headed by an often despotic "tsar."[30] The Russian Revolution replaced the tsarist rulers with a Soviet regime but brought little improvement to ordinary Russians' lives. It was not until 1991 when the Communist Party lost power that the Russian peoples achieved a democratic government.

These experiences instilled within Russians traits that enabled them to accept the dictates of their leaders and endure incredible hardship. One of the most vivid examples of the Russians being dominated by harsh, authoritarian rule had its beginning in the 1917 Bolshevik Revolution, which was supposed to overturn the oppressive tsarist regime, eliminate economic inequities, and give the working class a political voice. Instead, much of the country was destroyed and the entire socio-cultural structure was changed in the name of Communism. Stalin's program of state agricultural and industrial collectivization disrupted the lives of "tens of millions.... Millions more died in the political purges, the vast penal and labor system, or in state-created famines."[31] World War II brought added suffering when some 27 million Soviet citizens perished in the struggle against fascist Germany.[32] In 1991, due to economic stagnation and popular demand for greater freedom, the repressive Communist system collapsed and was replaced by the Russian Federation, an independent nation. From this sketch of Russian political history, it is easy to understand why Bergelson says that even today many Russians feel they have "no control over the world."[33] The long legacy of centralized, repressive rule and unwarranted suffering has imparted a sense of fatalism that has become a part of Russian culture.

The Russian historical tradition is also marked by a deep appreciation of, and devotion to, the arts. During the tenth century, Greek Orthodox Christianity was imported from the Byzantine Empire and made the state religion. "Consequently, Byzantine culture predominated, as is evident in much of Russia's architectural, musical,

and artistic heritage."[34] The performing and cultural arts remain an
important part of Russian life today.
Since its inception in the early
1700s, the world-famous Bolshoi
Ballet has been a source of great
pride and object of esteem among all

> **REMEMBER THIS**
>
> *Much of the history of Russia has been shaped by wars, invasions, and persecutions it has endured during its long history.*

Russians. Classical music by Tchaikovsky, Rachmaninoff, Rimsky-Korsakov, and
Stravinsky is admired and enjoyed throughout the world. In the field of literature,
Russia has produced such literary giants as Chekhov, Dostoevsky, Gogol, Pushkin,
and Tolstoy, and five Russian authors have been awarded the Nobel Prize for
Literature—Ivan Bunin (1933), Boris Pasternak (1958), Mikhail Sholohov (1965),
Alexander Solzhenitsyn (1970), and most recently, Joseph Brodsky (1987).

Although two decades have passed since the collapse of communist rule, Russia
remains in transition. With very little historical experience of democracy or capitalism to draw on, Russia has encountered many problems in adapting to the "new
world." Following the establishment of the federation in 1991, Russia was in turmoil
until Putin became president in 1999. He quickly moved to consolidate and centralize
political and economic power over the entire country. In an early speech, Putin
acknowledged people's universal values, but also asserted three distinctly Russian
values—(1) patriotism, (2) the state should play a role in world affairs, and
(3) "state-centeredness." The latter refers to the belief that the state should be a central
influence in Russian society. According to Putin, "It is a fact in Russia the tendency
toward collective forms of activity have always dominated over individualism. It is
also a fact that in Russian society paternalistic sentiments are deeply embedded."[35]

This perception helps explain the continuing movement away from a liberal
democratic form of governance in favor of returning to a more authoritarian central government, a structure that has long characterized Russia's history. This has moved Russia
toward "state capitalism" and brought about a diminution of political freedom.[36]

Contemporary Social Issues

The Russian Federation is presently grappling with numerous social issues, some of
which are common throughout globalized society and others that are uniquely Russian.
Most prominent of these concerns is the prevalence of widespread official corruption.[37]
The personal benefits gained by corrupt officials has made government employment
highly desirable and increased the number of bureaucrats by 66 percent over a ten-
year period ending in 2010.[38] The country is beset with a declining population. The
combination of a falling birthrate and a rising mortality level, exacerbated by poor
health practices, has significantly contracted the national workforce, placing "constraints on economic productivity and growth."[39] The nation is also seeing growing
resentment and violence directed toward ethnic groups by Russian nationalists.[40] Professor Daniel Treisman summarized the difficulties facing Russia:

> a country struggling with a combination of challenges, governed under a system that is part
> democratic, part authoritarian; informed by a press that is only partly free; powered by an
> economy cued to world commodity cycles; inhabited by citizens who judge their leaders on
> the basis of economic performance; where alcoholism, encouraged by the extremely low cost
> of vodka, is taking an extraordinary toll on life expectancy and aggravating crime.[41]

CHINESE HISTORY

An appreciation of China's history is central to any understanding of Chinese culture. Even in today's rapid pace, interconnected, digital world, China's long record of achievements and experiences form an important part of how the more than 1.33 billion contemporary Chinese perceive and experience the world. One reason for this importance is: "The past obsesses the Chinese in part because there is so much of it."[42] Archeological data suggest that the prehistoric origins of Chinese society extend back to 7000 BCE.[43] The documented historical record began approximately 3,500 years ago, during the Shang Dynasty (1523–1027 BCE), and continues unbroken to current times, which makes China the world's oldest continuous civilization.[44]

Geography has played a significant role in China's uninterrupted record of cultural development, because, as Hucker indicates, it served to both confine and unify on a national scale but led to differentiation on a regional level.[45] The world's third largest country, slightly bigger than the United States, China has extensive and formidable borders—vast, desolate plateaus and desert to the north, high mountain ranges to the west and southwest, mountains and deep valleys to the south, and the sea to the southeast and east. Geographically remote until the development of modern communication and transportation systems, ancient China developed politically, economically, and culturally in relative isolation, with little awareness of early civilizations in other parts of the world. This seclusion contributed to China's sense of cultural superiority and helped form Imperial China's worldview. Secure in the perception of their

An appreciation of China's history is central to understanding Chinese culture.

Noriko McDaniel

cultural greatness, ancient rulers referred to the country as the "Middle Kingdom" located at the center of the world, or *tianxia* ("under Heaven"), and considered anything beyond their borders of little importance.[46]

Internally, China's irregular topography gave rise to regional separation and differentiation in customs and dialects. In overcoming these impediments to unification, dynastic rulers instituted a bureaucratic system of government that enabled control of the predominantly agrarian population. The adoption of Confucianism as a state ideology and development of a written language common to all facilitated the consolidation of control under a centralized ruler.[47] Thus, while China presented an outward model of uniformity, internally it was marked by social and linguistic diversity.

Country Statistics: People's Republic of China

Location	Eastern Asia
Size	9,596,961 sq. km
Population	>1.33 billion (July 2011 est.)
Ethnic Groups	Han Chinese 91.5%; Zhuang, Manchu, Hui, Miao, Uighur, Tujia, Yi, Mongol, Tibetan, Buyi, Dong, Yao, Korean, and other nationalities 8.5% (2000 census)
Government	Communist state
Language	Mandarin (70%), 6 other major Chinese dialects. Ethnic minority languages include Mongolian, Tibetan, Uyghur and other Turkic languages (in Xinjiang), and Korean.

China's contemporary worldview is strongly influenced by historical events of the past two hundred years. By the early 1800s, colonial Western powers (e.g., English, Dutch, Portuguese, French, U.S., and others) had established themselves in the East Asian region and had begun to demand that China open its borders to unrestricted trade. These demands, coupled with the ineffectiveness of the weak and corrupt Chinese imperial court, ultimately led to the Western nations creating individual "spheres of influence" within China. In effect, these areas closely resembled colonies, where foreign residents enjoyed special privileges and extraterritoriality. It took World War II and a subsequent civil war for China to rid itself of the foreign powers, and today China refers to this period in its history as an era of "national humiliation."[48]

Since 1949 China has been governed by the Chinese Communist Party (CCP). The early years of CCP rule, particularly those under Mao Zedong, were characterized by internal strife and political turmoil. Left with a backward and underdeveloped nation, postwar Communist leaders initiated a series of reform programs—the Great Leap Forward and the Cultural Revolution—which had disastrous effects on the nation and the populace. While figures vary, a recent study by Professor Dikötter estimates that the Great Leap experiment (1958~62) may have resulted in the premature deaths of as many as 45 million people.[49]

In the early 1970s China began to move away from the debilitating "revolutionary" programs and responded to political overtures from the United States, which led to President Richard Nixon's historic visit to Beijing in 1972. Following Mao's death in 1976 more pragmatic leaders recognized the need for economic and political reforms, and China began to modernize. In the 1990s Chinese leaders opted for a market-driven economy which has proven enormously successful and improved the lives of millions of China's citizens. In less than twenty years the nation has become a major player in the global economy. In 2010 China became the world's second largest economy, following only the United States, and the leading exporting country.[50]

Communicating History

The importance placed on the family offers an example of the bond that exists between a culture's history and how the world is perceived. Historically, Chinese society has been predominantly agricultural, with people maintaining strong ties to their home village and the land. Extending over thousands of years, coupled with the influence of Confucianism, the labor-intensive agrarian lifestyle explains the Chinese traditional cultural orientation toward collectivism and hierarchy. These two values are exemplified through the Chinese patriarchal family, or clan, as the basic social unit and the acceptance of centralized patrimonial governance.

China also offers us an example of how governments can use history as a form of communication to promote nationalism and foreign policy goals. China's growing economic strength, trade imbalances, and plans for military expansion have become a source of concern for its neighbors as well as the United States. The desire for increased military strength and international recognition can be seen, in part, as arising from China's humiliating experience at the hands of Western powers in the 1800s and 1900s. The Chinese take great pride in their long history, and they well remember the lessons of the past, and their "humiliation" by outside powers has instilled "a sense of entitlement growing out of historical victimization."[51] These nineteenth-century injustices are often used to defend current Chinese policy, promote nationalism, and are the subject of displays in numerous Chinese museums.[52]

The Chinese feeling of historical humiliation is so great that in November 2010, during a state visit, the Prime Minister of the United Kingdom and his party were asked to remove the poppies they were wearing to honor veterans killed in war. Perhaps unaware of this annual tradition, the Chinese conveyed the message that wearing the flowers "would cause grave offence because it would remind Chinese ministers and officials of the Opium Wars,"[53] in which Chinese forces were defeated by the British during the mid-1800s.

Contemporary Social Issues

China's rapid rise to a prominent position in the global economic and diplomatic community has brought unprecedented changes to Chinese society. Many of these changes are positive, but some present the country's leadership with a variety of problems. These include the perception of widespread official corruption, growing social inequality between the rich and poor, and rising unemployment in urban areas.[54] Of the many social shifts, the one with the greatest potential for transforming traditional cultural norms is the changing structure and location of the Chinese population. Due to the cultural imperative for sons and availability of selective abortion, China's official one-child policy, instituted over 30 years ago, has resulted in a disproportionate number of males among the younger generations. This has "forcefully altered the family and kin structure of hundreds of millions of Chinese families."[55] The many potential problems resulting from this imbalance are further aggravated by the current rural-to-urban population shift, as China continues to move from agrarianism to industrialization. One report discloses that, "China is preparing, by 2025, for 350 million people to live in

cities that don't exist now."[56]
As greater numbers of young men
and women leave their farming villages for the cities, the traditional
concept of the extended family, and
attendant values, will begin to erode,
just as it has in Japan.

CONSIDER THIS

What events in China's history have moved it toward the status of being one of the world's superpowers?

JAPANESE HISTORY

The history of Japan is a product of geography. Proximity to its two closest Northeast Asian neighbors—China and Korea—produced a lengthy historical record of interaction. Approximately 100 miles of ocean separate Japan from the Korean peninsula, and China is just 500 miles to the east across the Yellow Sea. This nearness facilitated the importation of ideas and artifacts from the two nations, particularly China. For example, Confucianism and Buddhism, both brought from China through Korea, exerted a significant and enduring influence on the development of Japanese society. The use of Chinese ideograms is a daily reminder to contemporary Japanese of their nation's historical connection to China. Despite this legacy, however, the Japanese are defined by cultural characteristics quite different from those of its two nearby neighbors.

Country Statistics: JAPAN	
Location	Northeast Asia
Size	377,916 sq. km
Population	>126.47 million (2011 est.)
Ethnic Groups	Japanese 98.5%; Koreans 0.5%; Chinese 0.4%; other 0.6%
Government	Parliamentary
Language	Japanese

A relatively small nation composed of four major islands and several thousand smaller ones, Japan was accessible only by sea until the early part of the twentieth century. This insularity also made Japan relatively immune to large-scale immigration from the Asian mainland, and invading foreign armies were often stymied by the sea. This natural isolation, further encouraged by over 250 years of governmental imposed national seclusion during the *Tokugawa* or *Edo* era (1603–1867), was instrumental in the development of Japan's cultural distinctiveness and self-image.

Historical isolation, low numbers of immigrants, and a feudal-based system of governance produced a society characterized by its relative cultural homogeneity. This sense of ethnic similarity has become a defining characteristic among the Japanese, as Dower writes: "Although all peoples and cultures set themselves apart (and are set apart by others) by stressing differences, this tends to be carried to an extreme where Japan is concerned."[57]

One expression of cultural homogeneity is the Japanese attitude toward foreigners. As a result of the country being closed to outsiders until the mid-nineteenth century, when it was forcibly opened by Western powers, the Japanese developed ambivalence

For centuries the Japanese have had a strong sense of self-identity.

Edwin McDaniel

toward foreigners. Demographic separation and geographic isolation "produced in the Japanese a strong sense of self-identity and also an almost painful self-consciousness in the presence of others."[58] This self-consciousness persists today and can sometimes be encountered by foreigners traveling outside Japan's major urban areas, where they may find themselves treated as curiosities or even ignored. Such behavior is frequently a result of uncertainty on the part of the Japanese about how to interact with a non-Japanese individual. While their culture specifies the appropriate behavior for working and socializing with other Japanese, no established "correct" way of dealing with foreigners has evolved. The Japanese uncertainty toward foreigners continues today, as evident in contemporary attitudes toward immigration. In a 2010 survey of over 2,000 voters, "65 percent of the respondents opposed a more open immigration policy."[59]

Another important link between Japan's long history and its contemporary cultural values is the *Tokugawa* historical legacy. In the early 1600s, following a period of debilitating civil wars, Japan was politically unified under the leadership of a military-style governor (*shogun*). The Japanese population, much of which resided in or around castle towns, was divided into four specific, hierarchical groups—*samurai*, farmer, artisan, and merchant (*shi-nō-kō-shō*)—each with its own set of subgroups and hierarchy (the Imperial Court was above these and several lower status groups were below).[60] The central government specified strict codes of behavior to regulate the conduct of every aspect of personal and public life. In other words, the Japanese formed a culture where in many contexts there was a single correct way to perform a task, be it sitting, eating, dressing, living, or even thinking, and any other type of behavior was considered deviant.[61] The objective of these protocols was to ensure external peace and internal group stability by subordinating the individual to the central authority and the greater social order. Societal stability was the paramount objective, and this continues to be a central focus of Japanese social activity, demonstrated by an adherence to established norms, a resistance to rapid change, and an aversion to risk.[62]

The *Tokugawa* era castle town residents relied on benevolent feudal lords for protection and civil administration. In return for these benefits, the people professed a strong loyalty to the warlords (*daimyo*). This cultural characteristic is evident in modern Japanese social relationships, where workers continue to demonstrate dedication and loyalty to their school, company, and other in-groups. Modern corporations and government institutions became substitutes for the castle town and have traditionally offered lifetime employment, although three decades of economic stagnation have forced changes to this practice. Feudalism also inculcated in the Japanese an acceptance of discipline, sacrifice, and conformity. People were required to conduct every aspect of their lives in a highly proscribed manner, depending on their social class membership. These conditions have been translated into contemporary Japanese dedication to societal and organizational formality and an acceptance of higher authority, status differentials, and conformity to group expectations.[63]

As noted previously, a culture's history is just one of many sources contributing to the character of the people of that culture. This concept is demonstrated with regard to the Japanese attitude toward *collectivism*, or group orientation. Here again, the link between culture and geography is evident. In total land area Japan is slightly smaller than Montana, but over 70 percent of the country is mountainous. Since people began inhabiting the islands, the rugged topography has forced the majority of the population to live communally in the narrow valleys and along the few coastal plains, where today almost 127 million people[64] are crowded together.

Japanese "premodern village life was a community enterprise"[65] where the people depended on cooperative efforts to carry out labor intensive wetland (rice) cultivation. As Reischauer and Jansen point out, "Probably such cooperative efforts over the centuries contributed to the notable Japanese penchant for group identification and group action."[66] Group affiliation was also inculcated by the feudal government organization and class system, discussed above, which lasted until the *Meiji* Restoration in 1868.

Due to the necessity of group cooperation in early Japanese village life, exclusion, or the threat thereof, became a form of punishment. Unlike early U.S. settlers, whose life was characterized by frontier semi-isolation, self-reliance, and independence, premodern Japanese farmers were reliant on other villagers. The demands of wetland cultivation made an isolated existence essentially impossible. As a result, group exclusion became "a powerful sanction throughout rural [Japanese] society"[67] to maintain order and punish social deviance. To some degree, various forms of social exclusion remain a means of social punishment in modern Japan.[68] Group orientation continues to guide contemporary Japanese society, where one's status is based more on the schools attended, profession, or employer than on individual achievement.

World War II (1941–45) was a historical event that greatly impacted Japanese society. Motivated by an inability to resist incursions by Western powers in the mid-1800s, Japan immediately instituted comprehensive national programs to modernize itself in the image of the United States and European nations. Along with economic industrialization, educational restructurings, and social transformation, Japanese leaders also sought to build a powerful military, capable of not only defending the island nation, but also of providing Tokyo a voice in international affairs. This led to imperialistic expansion into Asia in the 1930s and ultimately entry into World War II. At the end of the war Japan's industrial and military capacity was virtually nonexistent. Almost one hundred years of modernization and industrialization efforts had been comprehensively and completely destroyed. However, drawing on their cultural traits of discipline, the ability to endure hardship (*gaman*), and strong sense of national identity, the Japanese began a wide-reaching program of reconstruction, aided by Allied Occupation Forces, and by the mid-1980s, Japan had become one of the world's leading economies. The aftermath of World War II, especially the impact of the atomic bombs dropped on Hiroshima and Nagasaki, also instilled in the Japanese a strong feeling of pacifism[69] and a reluctance to engage in military operations not directly related to national self-defense.[70]

The point being made should be transparent. The cultural characteristics discussed in this section have endured in Japan for centuries. They have guided the social organization and conduct of the Japanese people through periods of prosperity and of devastation, and they remain a constant influence even today.

Contemporary Social Issues

The era of globalization has given rise to societal problems that are straining the fabric of contemporary Japanese social order and, in some instances, bringing change to traditional values. These problems include (1) demographic changes, (2) immigration issues, and (3) risk management.

Japan's once rural society, characterized by interdependent extended families, now consists largely of urban nuclear families. The nation has the world's highest percentage of elderly population (over 65), whose numbers are growing rapidly. The situation is exacerbated by increased longevity, a rising marriage age, and a severely falling birthrate.[71] These developments will ultimately exert a significant burden on social programs as the native workforce declines. The obvious solution is increased immigration, but this course faces considerable difficulty, as Kingston points out, "The growing presence of foreigners in Japan is generally unwelcome and seen as a risk not only in terms of crime rates, but also to a national identity rooted in a sense of homogeneity."[72] For Japan's consensus-based, conformist, and highly risk-avoidance culture, change comes gradually,[73] even in the face of crisis. However, in the dynamics of the globalized world, change is constant and often rapid, requiring governments and corporations to either adapt or be left behind. Sugimoto indicates that "contemporary Japanese society is caught between the contradictory forces of narrow ethnocentrism and open internationalization."[74]

INDIAN HISTORY

Many aspects of your everyday life are a result of events that took place in India thousands of years ago. Each time you pull on your cotton jeans, eat chicken, or use the decimal system, you are enjoying the benefits of developments that arose in ancient India.[75] Modern India is no less influential in your life. No doubt you have already had experience talking with a company's representative in India while getting help with an IT problem or making an airline or hotel reservation for your Spring Break trip. And while you sleep, someone in Mumbai, Kolkata, or Noikda may be processing your credit card account, developing a new website for use next semester when you register for classes, or reviewing the legal details of the contract for your new job.[76] These scenarios illustrate why an appreciation of India's history and culture is important today. In addition to these examples, there are many other reasons for learning about India.

Some 2.2 million Indian Americans currently live in the United States, and over 60 percent have college degrees. While these educated professionals love their adopted nation, they also maintain a strong attachment to India and their heritage.[77] Indian Americans are also becoming active in U.S. politics. In 2011 the governors of both Louisiana and South Carolina were first-generation Indian Americans; and in 2010, six Indian Americans ran for seats in the U.S. Congress.[78] As more Indian Americans become part of the United States' diversity, it behooves us to have an awareness of the origins of their culture.

Anyone beginning a study of the Republic of India will be immediately struck by the rich diversity that characterizes the geography, peoples, cultures, languages, and history of the world's largest democracy. Starting in the towering Himalayan Mountains to the north, the Indian subcontinent extends southward for almost two thousand miles into the Indian Ocean, passing through a variety of terrain and climatic zones including deserts, tropical forests, alluvial plains, plateaus, and mountain ranges. The more than 1.18 billion people inhabiting this land constitute 15 percent of the world's population and consist of over two thousand ethnic groups and tribes, speak eighteen official languages, and practice a multiplicity of religions, which include Hinduism, Islam, Christianity, Sikhism, Buddhism, Jainism, Parsi, and a number of other belief traditions.[79]

Country Statistics: Republic of India

Location	Southern Asia
Size	3,287,263 sq. km
Population	>1.18 billion (July 2011 est.)
Major Ethnic Groupings	Indo-Aryan 72%, Dravidian 25%, Mongoloid and other 3% (2000 census)
Languages	Hindi, Bengali, Telugu, Marathi, Tamil, Urdu, Gujarati, Malayalam, Kannada, Oriya, Punjabi, Assamese, Kashmiri, Sindhi, and Sanskrit; Hindustani, English as *lingua franca*

India's contemporary multicultural society is an outgrowth of its long and varied historical legacy, a product of influences from South and Northeast Asia, Central Asia, the Middle East, and Europe. The archeological record indicates hunter-gatherers were active on the subcontinent as early as two million years ago. By approximately 2600 BCE these early groups had evolved into urban dwellers, living in houses along grid-patterned streets with drainage systems. Archeological data also suggest they engaged in long-distance trade with Middle Eastern societies. These early inhabitants, who left no written record, are commonly referred to as the Indus River Valley Civilization because they lived along the Indus River in what is now Pakistan. Although the exact cause of its demise remains unclear, the civilization appears to have succumbed to a cataclysmic natural disaster and subsequent climate change.[80]

The subcontinent next witnessed the arrival of nomadic Aryans coming from the west, bringing with them cattle and horses. These pastoral tribes conquered and settled northern India, establishing various warring principalities. When Alexander the Great crossed into India in 327 BCE, he found a politically and territorially divided land, highly vulnerable to conquest. Following Alexander's departure, most of the subcontinent was consolidated into the Maurya Empire (321–185 BCE), India's first unified state. The decline of Mauryan culture left the land politically fragmented until the second unification of northern India, the Gupta Dynasty (320–550 BCE). During these two eras Buddhism and Hinduism arose and flourished in India. The various rulers practiced religious tolerance, which became one of India's principal values. However, it was Hinduism that "provided a unifying framework through which diverse merchant, noble, and artisan groups were integrated into large-scale polities."[81]

Islam first arrived in the southern part of present-day Pakistan as early as 711 CE, but its influence was initially contained within that region. It was later Muslim invaders, arriving from the west via the Khyber Pass, who established an enduring presence on the subcontinent. These early Muslim raiders set about conquering the Hindus and destroying their temples, thus planting the seeds of "communal hatred in the hearts and minds of India's populace,"[82] a historical legacy that today continues to divide Muslim and Hindu. The presence and influence of Muslims grew to such proportions that the Delhi Sultanate, established in north-central India in the early thirteenth century, lasted for over three hundred years. Concurrently, the south remained an agrarian Hindu state.[83]

The Delhi Sultanate was deposed in 1526 by a new wave of Muslim invaders. Mongols from Central Asia established the Mughal Empire, which ultimately ruled most of the subcontinent. The Mughals established "the strongest dynasty in all of Indian history" and nominally held power until the mid-1800s.[84] Indian culture flourished under Mughal rule. A civil service was established to administer the country, religious and ethnic differences were tolerated, meritocracy was practiced, and Persian became the language of the court. The arts were encouraged and thrived.[85] The famous Taj Mahal, a monument to the wife of one of the Mughal rulers, was built during this era.

The decline of Mughal rule opened the door for Western powers to establish a foothold on the subcontinent and ultimately enabled England to make India a colony. Western nations had long sought access to the spices of Southeast Asia, historically monopolized by Arab traders using the Silk Road to transport goods to Europe. With the development of sea power, the Western Europeans were able to circumvent the overland route by sailing around Africa to reach Indian Ocean littoral lands. Portuguese ships arrived on the west coast of India in 1510, and Dutch, French, and English vessels soon followed. Capitalizing on the political disorder in the failing Mughal Empire, England's East India Company gained power through a military takeover and established itself as the dominant trader on India's southeast coast.[86]

The East India Company maintained a trade monopoly until 1813, focusing on commercial enterprise with little regard for the native peoples' welfare, economic infrastructure, or culture. Grihault writes "At the time of the British arrival, India had a strong mercantile capitalist economy. Britain, however, restructured the economy to serve her own imperial interests, disrupting much of the indigenous infrastructure and impeding the development of India's own culture."[87] This transformation is illustrated by British merchants exporting Indian cotton to England, where it was made into cloth and sent back to India, thus displacing millions of "Indian spinners, weavers and other handicraftsmen."[88] Ultimately, British commercial activities proved economically disastrous for the Indian populace, and at the end of the nineteenth century the nation was "less urbanized than it had been at the beginning [of the century], with over ninety percent of its much larger population dependent upon the land alone for support."[89]

The Indian National Congress was established in 1885 by young, educated Indians with the objective of redressing the excesses of British colonial rule. As a political organization, it was largely ineffective until Mohandas Gandhi was able to build an effective coalition. Gandhi's campaign of passive resistance, which influenced the U.S. civil rights movement of the 1960s, led to India's independence from British rule in 1947. However, due to the long-standing discord between Hindus and Muslims, India was "partitioned" into two separate, sovereign states—India and Pakistan. The partition displaced some ten million people and unleashed widespread political violence between Hindus and Muslims, resulting in the loss of as many as one million lives. The enduring conflict between India and Pakistan over the Kashmir region is a legacy of the partition.[90]

Following partition, India instituted a government-controlled, socialist-oriented economy, which was characterized by marginal growth, budget deficits, a bloated bureaucracy, and high levels of unemployment. Finally, in the 1990s, effective economic reforms were undertaken that led to India's current rise in the global economy. Based on Gross Domestic Product (GDP) measurements, India is now the world's fifth largest economy.[91] Unfortunately, benefits derived from this economic growth have been felt disproportionately among the population, which remains predominantly rural, poor, and often illiterate.[92]

For some, however, the digital age is bringing significant cultural change to traditional Indian society. The many large Indian and multinational IT companies have provided employment to many educated, English-speaking young women and men. For the women, traditionally accustomed to assuming a submissive role in marriage, economic security has brought empowerment, independence, and ideas of equality with their spouse.[93] The digital revolution is also changing Indian courtship practices. Dating is not a traditional Indian custom and arranged marriages are common. However, the digital age has enabled young couples to communicate via email, social networking sites, and mobile phones—all beyond the watchful eye of their parents.[94]

Contemporary Social Issues

Despite its recent economic successes, India remains a nation of remarkable contrasts. The highly educated Indian workers supporting the information technology and service industries account for only a small portion of the nation's inhabitants. Over half of the population continues to live in rural villages and almost 40 percent remain illiterate, a condition afflicting over half the women.[95] India is also beset with extensive, persistent poverty, with as much as 25 percent of the population living below the official poverty line, a condition exacerbated by high unemployment.[96] Widespread official corruption, which trickles all the way down to the village level, further adds to the burden borne by the poor.[97] The lack of adequate primary school education in many of the Indian states[98] is an additional impediment to lowering the levels of poverty and unemployment. The long-standing schism between Muslim and Hindu remains a serious problem, occasionally erupting into violent conflict. The two sides are divided by such issues as religion, social class, language, educational levels, and rising Hindu nationalism. While Muslims represent approximately 13 percent of the population, they remain underrepresented in government agencies.[99]

MEXICAN HISTORY

Reasons for learning about the history of Mexico are numerous and obvious. You are probably well aware of the close relationship between the United States and Mexico which exists due to their common border almost 2,000 miles in length. On a daily basis, nearly one million people and one billion dollars in business goods cross the border legally. U.S.-Mexican interaction along the border occurs at federal, state, and local levels; it requires effective intercultural communication to coordinate and manage mutual economic interests, legal matters, environmental problems, health issues, law enforcement, and many other interests. Some facts below demonstrate the importance of this relationship and the mutual, effective communication that must occur:

• There are 39 bilateral agreements that govern telecommunication operations.
• Mexico is the United States' third largest trading partner.
• More than 18,000 corporations with U.S. ties operate in Mexico.
• Upwards of one million U.S. citizens have their primary residence in Mexico.[100]

Within the United States, Mexican-Americans account for 63 percent of the U.S. Hispanic population, and according to Census Bureau reports, Hispanics comprised over 16 percent of the total U.S. population in 2010.[101] There are, of course, many more issues that tie the two nations, and knowledge of Mexico's history can provide insight into the Mexican worldview, enhance mutual understanding, and improve communicative interactions. For instance, "Mexicans themselves believe that their history holds the key to their character."[102] With this in mind, let us examine the history of Mexico and how that history continues to influence the Mexican people. The discussion is divided into six major periods: (1) the pre-Columbian, (2) the invasion by Spain, (3) independence from Spain, (4) the Mexican-American War, (5) the revolution, and (6) modern Mexico.

Country Statistics: United Mexican States	
Location	North America
Size	1,964,375 sq. km
Population	>113.72 million (July 2011 est.)
Ethnic Groups	Mestizo (Amerindian-Spanish) 60%, Amerindian or predominantly Amerindian 30%, white 9%, other 1%
Government	Federal republic
Language	Spanish only 92.7%, Spanish and indigenous languages 5.7%, indigenous only 0.8%

Archeological evidence dates human existence in Mexico and Central America back at least fifty thousand years, but most historians begin the story of the Mexican peoples with what is called the pre-Columbian era (300 BCE–1951 CE), during which the agriculturally based Olmec, Maya, Toltec, and Aztec civilizations flourished in different parts of what is now Mexico. With achievements that equaled or exceeded their counterparts in Europe, each of these great societies made unique contributions to modern Mexican culture. Collectively they constitute an important part of contemporary Mexican worldview and identity. Even today their legends, artistic heritages, architecture, and foods remain "an integral part of the [Mexican] national identity."[103]

Gloria Thomas

All cultures are proud of their historical traditions.

It is important to remember that Mexicans are extremely proud of this period of their history, not only for its achievements in agriculture, creative arts, and the establishment of large urban settlements, but also for scientific advancements. For example, the Mayas, who were advanced in astronomy and mathematics, developed the concept of zero before it was discovered in Europe and created one of the world's most accurate calendars.[104] Mexicans are also aware of the many accomplishments of the Aztecs, whose social and religious structure, as well as art, has survived for thousands of years. Even today, a common trait among Mexicans is their great pride in the legacy of Mexico's early history.

The pre-Columbian period was brought to an end by the Spanish Conquest, which began in 1519 when Hernando Cortés invaded the Yucatan Peninsula on the southeast coast of Mexico. The arrival of the Spanish conquerors resulted in death, destruction, and subjugation of the native inhabitants. Using the advantages of naval power, horses, guns, interpreters, and alliances with local enemies of the Aztecs, Cortés eventually defeated the indigenous people. Especially devastating were the diseases brought by the Europeans, such as smallpox, to which the natives had no immunity.[105] It is estimated that slayings, starvation, disease, and overwork destroyed about 90 percent of the native population by 1650.[106] The Spanish occupation of Mexico and subsequent colonization profoundly changed the country and the people forever.

REMEMBER THIS

As is the case with all cultures, Mexicans take great pride in their history.

To illustrate this transformation, three major changes arising from Spain's military conquest of the land and the peoples are examined. The first was the introduction of Catholicism. In the beginning it was left to the Spanish army to destroy Indian idols and replace them with Christian crosses. It was the Spanish friars, following in the wake of the soldiers, who spread throughout the countryside to convert the conquered natives. The conversions proved rather easy because the Indians adapted the new religion to meet their needs, and both cultures "believed in an afterlife and a world created by god(s)."[107] The second consequence of the Spanish colonization of Mexico was the development of a rigid social class system that some historians see as imposing great hardship on the indigenous population. As Foster observed, "The Spanish caste system spread illiteracy, racism, and official corruption through the land, setting one group against the others."[108] A third effect of Spain's occupation was the granting of vast tracts of land to the Spanish conquerors. This created a large status and socioeconomic gap between the upper and lower classes in much of Mexico and engendered a highly stratified social order—characteristics that remain a part of Mexican society.[109]

For almost three hundred years Mexico suffered under Spanish rule as a feudal and deeply Catholic country where landed aristocrats dominated a population of primarily agrarian peasants under what was called the *hacienda* system.[110] This social organization endured until the summer of 1810, when Miguel Hidalgo y Costilla, a Criollo parish priest, rallied a group of followers and started the fight for Mexican independence. Although Hidalgo was executed in 1811, he is known as the "Father of Mexican Independence." Actual independence, however, was not achieved until 1821 when Spain and Mexico negotiated a treaty, called the Plan of Iguala,[111] sometimes referred to as the Plan of Three Guarantees. Final freedom came in 1824, when Mexico became a federal republic under its own constitution. During this period Mexico abolished titles of nobility and attempted to introduce measures that would produce a more democratic society. However, as Johns points out, "Neither independence from Spain nor the Mexican Revolution changed the basic structure of social relations in which a small, largely Hispanic elite presided over the exploitation of the impoverished populace."[112] The historical legacy of class separation remains evident in contemporary Mexico's hierarchical social structure.

The next twenty years witnessed great upheaval in Mexico as the people attempted to adapt to a new form of government. It was during this period that the territory of Texas declared its independence from Mexico. Coupled with the U.S. doctrine of Manifest Destiny, this event proved to be a major cause of the Mexican-American War, which began on May 13, 1846. In addition to Texas, President Polk, with the backing of the American people, sought to acquire what amounted to half of Mexico's territory. The two countries fought over the land for two years (1846–48) in a war that is seldom remembered in the United States, but which Mexico considers "its greatest disaster."[113]

On February 2, 1848, the war ended with the signing of the Treaty of Guadalupe Hidalgo. Its provisions called for Mexico to cede 55 percent of its territory (present-day Arizona, California, New Mexico, and Texas, and parts of Colorado, Nevada, and Utah) in exchange for 15 million dollars in compensation for war-related damage to Mexican property.[114] For Mexicans the war was a bitter defeat. But for the United States it was an example of Manifest Destiny—"to spread the benefits of democracy to the lesser peoples of the continent."[115] The war had an impact that is still felt today. Samora and Simon write that, "The Mexican-American War created unparalleled bitterness and hostility toward the United States, not only in Mexico but throughout Latin America…. Even today, Latin American relationships with the United States are often marred by suspicion and distrust."[116]

Our next period of Mexico's history centers on the Revolution of 1910. After over 30 years of a near continuous, repressive dictatorship under President Porfirio Diaz, the Mexican people revolted. During Diaz's rule, Mexico's elite saw their wealth grow, but the living standards of the poor continually declined. At the time of the Revolution "90 percent of Mexico's mestizos and Indians were still desperately poor on the ranches and haciendas of a handful of wealthy land owners."[117] The Revolution ushered in widespread social change because it "rejected Europe as a model, asserted an Indian identity for Mexico, and committed the government to providing security for peasants and workers by redistributing land and income."[118] One of the revolt's leading figures, Emiliano Zapata, remains a national hero among the Mexican general populace.

The last phase of Mexican history—that of contemporary Mexico—remains a work in progress. Huge oil and natural gas reserves, manufacturing, agriculture, tourism, and the hundreds of maquiladora factories along the U.S.-Mexico border have made Mexico a major economic force. In addition, with the 1994 passage of the North American Free Trade Agreement (NAFTA), Mexico, the United States, and Canada became free-trade partners. Although the passage of time and the implementation of economic agreements have improved relations between the governments of Mexico and the United States, there are still critical issues that require effective intercultural interaction. These include border security, drug trafficking, the movement of guns from the United States to Mexico, and, perhaps the most salient, illegal immigrants.

Contemporary Social Issues

Today Mexico is struggling with a number of social issues, but two primary causes underlie many of the problems. First, poverty and unemployment, especially in the rural areas, continue to suppress the standard of living for large numbers of Mexicans. Lacking jobs, many elect to leave their homes and join the flow of illegal immigrants seeking work in the United States. Initially, the immigrants were men, but some estimate that now 35–45 percent are women.[119] Regardless of gender, they all make the arduous and dangerous trip north for similar reasons—to find employment in order to provide their families a better life. These families are dependent on the remittances the immigrants send back, which collectively total approximately 21 billion dollars a year.[120] The long separations between the immigrants in the United States and their loved ones in Mexico place considerable strain on the traditional Mexican family social structure. A second issue adversely impacting Mexico is directly tied to the smuggling of illegal drugs carried out by the various organized crime cartels. In recent years the level of narco-violence has risen dramatically, and reportedly has led to the deaths of nearly 35,000 people over a four-year period beginning in 2006.[121] The escalating violence, coupled with growing evidence of widespread corruption of government officials by the cartels, has seriously eroded public confidence. The effectiveness of law enforcement agencies and the legal system to provide law enforcement and public protection has become questionable. This has resulted in a general sense of insecurity and disillusionment at all levels of society, leaving the people to rely on their extended families for support.[122]

CONSIDER THIS

What is the primary source of your information about Mexican history and culture?

ISLAMIC CIVILIZATION

Previous history sections focused on how past events influence the cultural characteristics of individual countries. For the last section, however, we will take a broader perspective and examine the sweeping history of Islamic civilization and how it continues to be a major factor in the lives of more than one and a half billion people. Events such as the tragedy of September 11, 2001, U.S. military conflicts in Iraq and Afghanistan, the ongoing global fight against terrorism, and the early 2011 uprisings in North Africa and the Middle East should serve as motivation for you to learn about Islam. But there are numerous additional reasons for acquiring an appreciation of Islamic history and culture. Muslims are part of the U.S. social fabric. They are your coworkers, your neighbors, your sports stars, and most importantly, they form an integral part of society.

Muslim Demographics

As we will discuss in Chapter 5, Islam is the world's second largest religion, exceeded only by Christianity, with Muslims representing the majority of the population in 49 nations. Islam is the predominant religion of most North African and Middle Eastern countries, and several nations in South and Southeast Asia. Additionally, there are large, growing populations of Muslims in Europe and North America. Worldwide, Muslims now number approximately 1.6 billion, constituting over one-fifth of the entire population. These numbers are expected to grow between now and 2030 before leveling off at more than 2.1 billion, exceeding one quarter of humankind. Over the next 20 years "The Muslim share of the U.S. population (adults and children) is projected to grow from 0.8% in 2010 to 1.7% in 2030, making Muslims roughly as numerous as Jews or Episcopalians are in the United States today."[123]

Muslim Population as Percent of Total Population 2010 and 2030[124]		
SELECTED NATIONS	**2010**	**2030**
U.S.	0.8	1.7
Canada	2.8	6.6
United Kingdom	6.4	8.2
Austria	5.7	9.3
Belgium	6.0	10.2
France	7.5	10.3
Germany	5.0	7.1
Sweden	4.9	9.9

The Age of Ignorance

In order to better understand the history of Islam and its influence in the contemporary world, it is helpful to have an overview of the early Middle East, particularly the Arabian Peninsula where Islam originated. The geography and climate of the region can be described as generally semi-arid and arid, with insufficient rainfall to support agriculture except along river valleys or near oases. This is especially true of the Arabian Peninsula, historically the domain of the nomad. Domestication of the camel around 3000 BCE allowed nomadic groups to move across the peninsula's arid vastness in search of water and fodder for their herds. Constantly on the move, these pastoralists were unable to develop the architectural and cultural artifacts that characterized the great early civilizations of the Middle East, such as the Sumerian and Babylonian to the east and the Egyptian to the west. Instead, they developed cultural expressions more suitable to their mobile lives and what was necessary for survival in the harsh desert environment.[125] During this pre-Islamic era, which Muslims refer to as the "age of Ignorance" (*jahiliya*),[126] "early Arabs composed poems that embodied their code of values: bravery in battle, patience in misfortune, persistence in revenge, protection of the weak, defiance of the strong, loyalty to the tribe, hospitality to the guest, generosity to the needy, and fidelity in carrying out promises."[127] Loyalty to one's tribe was paramount, and intertribal wars and raids against trade route caravans were common. These early groups practiced a variety of religions, including Judaism, Christianity, animism, and ancestor worship, but a tradition developed among the tribes to annually suspend hostilities and conduct a pilgrimage to an ancient shrine in the city of Mecca.[128] This became an important part of Islamic history and remains the destination of today's Muslim pilgrimages (*hajj*).

The Rise and Spread of Islam

Islamic civilization began in the early seventh century and stretches across more than 1,400 years, encompassing far more events than space and time allow for examination here. Thus, the focus here will be on the rise of Islam in the Middle East, with only brief mention of its spread to other parts of the world. However, you should keep in mind this is but one part of the story of Islam. Chapter 5 discusses the establishment of Islam as a religion by the Prophet Muhammad. Therefore, all you need remember here is that Muhammad, from a merchant family in Mecca, received his heavenly revelations about 610 CE and began recruiting followers. Our historical examination of the rise and spread of Islam will begin with his death, in 632 CE.

There was no clear line of succession for the Islamic leadership when Muhammad died. He left no male heir and did not designate anyone to take his place. This void was filled by a series of Caliphs (Arabic for "successor" or "representative"),[129] a role assumed by successive leaders of Islam until the demise of the Ottoman Empire in 1923, in the aftermath of the First World War. The first caliphs were drawn from those who had directly served Muhammad and were known as the Patriarchal Caliphate or "Rightly Guided Caliphs" (CE 632–661).[130] Soon after Muhammad's death, many of the Arab groups that had previously submitted to his teachings and leadership sought to disassociate themselves from the new caliphs. Armed groups of "believers" were quickly dispatched to suppress these dissenters, and within a few years the many nomadic tribes and the urban areas of the Arabian Peninsula had been completely subdued. By the middle of the seventh century the "believers" held control of most of what is now called the Middle East.[131] As Donner points out, these conquests "established a large new empire in the Near East, with a leadership 'committed to a new religious ideology.'"[132] The new empire provided the political order and organizational structure necessary for the spread of the Islamic religion.

Eras of Islamic Civilization	
Prophet Mohammad	610~632
Patriarchal Caliphate (Rightly Guided Caliphs)	632~601
Umayyad Caliphate	661~750
Abbasid Caliphate	750~1258
Medieval Islam	1259~1300?
Ottoman Empire	1301~1923
Nation States	1923~Present

The death of the last of the caliphates who had known Muhammad ended the era of the Patriarchal Caliphate and ushered in the Umayyad Caliphate (CE 661–750). This period brought many changes to Islam, one of which was the relocation of the capital from Medina in Arabia to Damascus in Syria. Of greater consequence, consolidation of the Middle East enabled Muslims to embark on the conquest of more distant lands. To the west, Muslims spread across all of North Africa, crossing into southern Europe in 710, where they remained a significant presence until 1492 when Christian armies forced them to abandon the city of Granada (in present day Spain), the last Muslim bastion on the Iberian Peninsula.[133] To the east, Islam moved across what is now Iran, Afghanistan, Pakistan, and into India and Central Asia, ultimately reaching western China. Southward, Islam extended to present day Indonesia and the Southern Philippines, where it continues to command a dominant position.

Despite the geographical advances of Islam during this period, the Umayyad Caliphate was not without internal problems. Questions of leadership succession persisted and ultimately led to civil wars and the division of Islam into its two major branches—Sunni and Shiite. Today, Sunnis represent 87–90 percent of all Muslims and Shiites compose 10–13 percent,[134] with the latter concentrated in Iran, Iraq, Pakistan, and India. The fundamental difference separating these two divisions has its roots in the question of leadership of the Muslim community, and the historical basis of those differences justifies a brief review.

Sunnis believe that the leader of Islam should be whoever is best qualified. The Shiites, however, contend that leadership is a function of heredity, through lineage traced to Muhammad. Originally, the two groups saw themselves divided not by ideology but by a question of politics, but over time, varied theological and religious practices have evolved.[135] Moreover, because the Shiites have always been a minority, they have developed an interpretation of history quite different from the Sunnis. Esposito provides an insightful summation of the two groups' varied worldviews:

> While Sunni history looked to the glorious and victorious history of the Four Rightly Guided Caliphs and then the development of imperial Islam ... [Shiite] history was the theater for the struggle of the oppressed and disinherited. Thus, while Sunnis can claim a golden age when they were a great world power and civilization, which they believe is evidence of God's favor upon them and a historic validation of Muslim beliefs, [Shiites] see in these same developments the illegitimate usurpation of power by Sunni rulers at the expense of a just society. [Shiites] view history more as a paradigm of the suffering, disinheritance, and oppression of a righteous minority community who must constantly struggle to restore God's rule on earth under His divinely appointed Imam.[136]

These contrasting perspectives should provide you with greater insight to the historical enmity influencing relations between Sunnis and Shiites worldwide. Their religious differences played a major role during the Iraqi conflict, and the early 2011 protests in Bahrain were partly the result of a Shiite majority living under the autocratic rule of a Sunni monarch.

In the mid-eighth century the Umayyad Caliphate was succeeded by the Abbasid Caliphate (749–1258), the seat of government was moved to Baghdad, and the ruling Arab hierarchy was supplanted by a cadre of multiethnic Muslims of non-Arab origin. With Islam as the uniting force, all believers, regardless of ethnicity or place of origin, were considered equal. Under the Abbasids, Baghdad became one of the world's most important cities, and its wealth enabled Muslim emissaries to continue to expand Islamic influence. But this preeminence could not be sustained. As a result of political decline, agricultural failure, and the rise of numerous independent Islamic dynasties in other regions, Baghdad's control of the Islamic empire had become decentralized by the tenth century. These new outlying dynasties continued to expand Islamic culture as they sought to emulate Baghdad, becoming new centers for learning, art, and craftsmanship.[137]

The early years of the eleventh century saw the onset of history's most storied clash between Christianity and Islam—the Crusades, which lasted almost 200 years. Although Muslims had occupied Jerusalem, the seat of both Christianity and Judaism, in 638, they ruled without religious persecution, and the city remained open to Christian and Jewish pilgrims.[138] Arrival of the Seljuk Turks, however, brought change to the Islamic world. Pushing outward from Central Asia, the Seljuks assumed a position of power in the Abbasid Caliphate in Baghdad in 1055 and drove the Byzantines from their lands in Asia Minor (now part of Turkey). This gave them control over the Christian pilgrimage routes connecting Europe with Jerusalem. The Byzantine rulers appealed to Rome for assistance, hoping for trained armies. In response, Pope Urban II in 1095 called for the masses to help in "saving fellow Christians" and liberating the Holy Land.[139] Thus were the Crusades launched. Christian forces comprised of nobles, mercenaries, and adventurers were able to gain control of isolated pockets in the Holy Land before ultimately being defeated by the Arab ruler Saladin in the late twelfth century. Smith notes, "Saladin's treatment of the Christian population [in Jerusalem] was humane and reasonable, in notable contrast to the way in which Christians had earlier dealt with Muslims and Jews upon their arrival in Jerusalem."[140]

The final era of unified Islamic governance was brought about by Mongol invaders moving out of Central Asia through Afghanistan and Persia into the Middle East. Reaching Baghdad during the mid-thirteenth century, Mongol warriors destroyed the city and all its inhabitants, bringing an end to the Abbasid Caliphate. The devastation brought by the Mongol armies pushed the Turkish nomads into the eastern regions of modern day Turkey, where they met and defeated the last of the Byzantine forces. These nomads became known as the Ottomans, and they ruled Islam for more than six hundred years. During their reign, Ottoman armies advanced into Europe as far as Vienna, Austria, and took control of the Balkans, where large communities of Muslims remain today. In the seventeenth and eighteenth centuries the European powers began to challenge the Ottoman Empire, then beset by internal decay and unable to hold back the Christian nation forces. As the Ottomans retreated, European powers rushed in to fill the void. The extent of this change is pointed out by Bernard Lewis:

> By the early twentieth century—although a precarious independence was retained by
> Turkey and Iran and by some remoter countries like Afghanistan, which at that time

did not seem worth the trouble of invading—almost the entire Muslim world had been incorporated into the four European [colonial] empires of Britain, France, Russia, and The Netherlands.[141]

The defeat of the Ottomans at the end of the World War I concluded more than thirteen centuries of a unified Islam and replaced it with nation-states, many of which remained under the domination of Western colonial masters until after World War II.[142] Since then, relations between the West and the Muslim world have traveled a bumpy road, with the focal point often being oil and the Israeli-Palestine problem.

Legacy of History

This brief chronology illustrates the richness of Islamic history, which helps shape the identity and worldview of modern Muslims. History is particularly significant to Muslims, as noted by Lewis, "Islamic history, for Muslims, has an important religious and also legal significance, since it reflects the working out of God's purpose for His Community—those that accept the teachings of Islam and obey its law."[143] From the Muslim perspective, the early era of the caliphates represents a period of one ruler exercising dominion over a single state. The perception of unity persisted even after the caliphate had splintered into a variety of dynastic states, and the people of the Islamic domain identified themselves not by nationality or ethnicity but as Muslims.

For contemporary Muslims, the history of Islam is continually reinforced through (1) language, (2) geography, and (3) tribal affiliation, all of which are derived from the religion's Arabic origins.[144] Classical Arabic was the original language of the Koran, and Arabic became the language of the Middle East and North Africa as a result of the early Islamic conquests. Located in southeast Saudi Arabia, Mecca remains the holiest of all Arab sites and the annual destination of well over a million Muslims who make the pilgrimage (*hajj*) each year. Tribal affiliation, the basis of ancient Arabia's societal organization, continues to exert a strong influence among contemporary Muslims. The importance and role of tribal organization has been vividly demonstrated in both Iraq and Afghanistan, where U.S. forces belatedly realized the need to work through tribal leaders.

The history of Islamic civilization can easily be oversimplified into a tale of conquest and colonization. One can also use that same lens to view the history of Western civilization, as Lewis indicates: "From the end of the fifteenth century, the peoples of Europe embarked on a vast movement of expansion—commercial, political, cultural, and demographic—which by the twentieth century had brought almost the whole world into the orbit of European civilization."[145]

Space limitations preclude a discussion of the lasting achievements in the sciences, arts, literature, philosophy, and architecture that are a product of Islam. These accomplishments came from the early Islamic centers of civilization, where art, scholarship, craftsmanship, and intercultural borrowing were encouraged. Unification facilitated the spread of advancements in any field throughout the Islamic realm. Whatever your personal history and culture, it likely bears an Islamic influence. Muslims have been

REMEMBER THIS

Islamic history and religion are directly linked.

coming to the United States since well before the nineteenth century. They were among the early explorers, traders, and settlers. It is also estimated that Muslims constituted 14 to 20 percent of the slaves brought from Africa.[146] Words we use every day, such as *algebra, average, lemon,* and *magazine,* have Arabic origins. And the next time you are sipping your favorite coffee drink, recall that coffee, along with coffeehouses, was introduced to the West through Islam.

Contemporary Social Issues

Today, Muslims look on Islamic history with both pride and humiliation. Pride is taken in the fact that while Europe was mired in the Dark Ages, Islam represented "the most advanced civilization in the world."[147] However, as witnessed by the uprisings across North Africa and the Middle East, many Muslims are largely dissatisfied with current social conditions in their countries. With few exceptions, Muslim nations in North Africa and the Middle East are plagued by a host of similar conditions inhibiting the ability to improve living standards and participate in democratic institutions. Common problems include authoritative, repressive regimes, official corruption, absence of viable democratic processes, stagnant economic development, lack of women's equality, and an expanding population, a majority of which are under 25 years of age and see little opportunity for economic advancement.[148]

For a variety of reasons, many Muslims associate Arabic countries' failures with the West and Western values.[149] This has given rise to groups, referred to as Islamist, calling for a return to the golden age of Islamic civilization; the reinstitution of strict Islamic law, values, and principles; and the exclusion of Western ways.[150] So strong is the influence of history that these groups romanticize the past as the way to a better future; however, the Islamists have a limited following. In recent polls only about 20 percent of the Arab world electorate supported Islamist parties, such as the Muslim Brotherhood.[151] Technology has robbed both autocratic leaders and extremist groups of the ability to control, manipulate, or restrict communication directed to the populace. "Access to the airwaves and the internet has democratized Islam, forcing rival interpreters of the faith to compete on their own merits for an audience that crosses sects and borders."[152]

to the following admonition from Genesis that they believe promotes a worldview placing "man" above nature and the environment. "Then God blessed them, and God said to them, be fruitful and multiply, fill the earth and subdue it; have dominion over the fish of the sea, over the birds of the air, and over every living thing that moves on the earth."[11]

- Shintoism is another worldview that produces a unique attitude toward nature. The Shinto religion encourages an aesthetic appreciation of nature in which the focus is on reality and not heaven—a reality that makes nature supreme. Shintoism prescribes an aesthetic love of the land. Every hill, lake, mountain, and river is treasured. Cherry trees, shrines, and scenic resorts are indispensable to a full life. People perceive them as lasting icons among which their ancestors lived and died. People thus preserve nature so that nature can preserve the family.[12]

- A very different worldview emerges on examination of American Indians' perceptions. In most Western logic and science, people move from the specific to the general. American Indians begin with an apprehension of the whole (general) and move to specifics. This worldview reasons that to the extent the Universe is a whole, dimensions such as location and time (both specific) become irrelevant.[13] It is the "big picture" that gives meaning to life, not the bits and pieces.

Another link between worldview and behavior can be seen in how a culture perceives the business arena. In two classic texts, Weber's *The Protestant Ethic and the Spirit of Capitalism* and Tawney's *Religion and the Rise of Capitalism*, the bonds among religion, commerce, and production are examined. In both of these historical works the authors conclude that there are connections among a culture's history, religion, and worldview. Bartels reaffirms these bonds when he writes, "The foundation of a nation's culture and the most important determinant of social and business conduct are the religious and philosophical beliefs of a people. From these beliefs spring role perceptions, behavior patterns, codes of ethics and the institutionalized manner in which economic activities are performed."[14] Even the way a culture conducts its business can reflect its worldview. If a culture values "out-of-awareness" processes and intuitive problem solving, it might reach conclusions through processes much different from a culture that values the scientific method. Nisbett provides a summary of these differences:

> Thus, to the Asian, the world is a complex place, composed of continuous substances, understandable in terms of the whole rather than in terms of the parts, and subject more to collective than to personal control. To the Westerner, the world is a relatively simple place, composed of discrete objects that can be understood without undue attention to context, and highly subject to personal control. Very different worlds indeed.[15]

This introduction has attempted to demonstrate that worldview, perception, and communication are associated. This association can be manifested as worldview determines how people see their place in the world. The following example helps explain the way some cultures employ their worldview to understand the universe.

> Ask any Tibetan or Navajo about one's place in the scheme of things and the answer will inevitably be that we must act, speak, and think respectfully and reasonably toward others.

REMEMBER THIS

A culture's worldview is directly linked to how members of that culture perceive the world and live in that world.

Navajos say that we are all people: earth-surface walkers, swimmers, crawlers, flyers, and sky and water people. Tibetans know that we are humans, animals, worldly gods and demigods, ghosts and hell beings, and a host of aboriginal earth powers. Regardless of category or description, we're all inextricably connected through a system of actions and their effects, which can go according to cosmic order or fall out of synchrony with it.[16]

CONSTRUCTS OF WORLDVIEWS

We have already mentioned that your worldview originates in your culture, is transmitted via a multitude of channels, is composed of numerous elements, and can take a variety of forms.[17] Most of these forms can be classified into three categories: traditional religions, secular humanism, and spirituality. These orientations obviously intersect on a number of important questions. And in many instances, individuals select a portion of all three orientations to construct their view of reality. However, these three constructs have dissimilar answers for inquiries concerning life, death, human nature, and ways of knowing. Let us briefly introduce these three worldviews in general terms before we explain religious traditions in more detail.

Religion as a Worldview

Some Africans say, "There is no distinction between religion and the rest of life. All of life is religious." Although that might be an overstatement, it is true that as a worldview, religion is an important part of life for billions of people. The connections among worldview, religion, and culture are made clear by Roberts: "A distinguishing characteristic of religion is that it provides a worldview."[18] At the core of this worldview is a "belief in the existence of a reality greater than humans."[19] There are other distinguishing characteristics of a religious worldview.

A major characteristic of a religious worldview is that it provides a belief in the existence of a reality greater than humans.

Robert Fonseca

In most religions there is a universal spirit, God, or deity that is sacred and looked to for guidance and salvation. This divinity, while it may go by different names, has established a moral classification and set of "instructions" that people can discover. Part of that discovery process asks people to follow certain eternal moral decrees. The motivation for following the wisdom of these religious worldviews is that "human conduct has long-term (beyond individual death) significance."[20] We will return to the specifics of that "significance" when we examine six of the major religious traditions.

Secularism as a Worldview

The idea of secularism as a worldview has been a part of the human experience for as long as people have been concerned with questions about the meaning of life and explanations about death. As early as circa 400 BCE, Plato talked about the portion of humankind that did not believe in the existence of any of the gods. Hence, this worldview "traces its roots from ancient China, classical Greece and Rome, through the Renaissance and the Enlightenment, to the scientific revolution of the modern world."[21] Like traditional religions, secularism has experienced periods of great interest as well as phases of decline. The past two decades have witnessed renewed and intense interest in secularism, and Tischler tells us that "many scholars have noted that modern society is becoming increasingly secularized, that is, less influenced by religion."[22] There are numerous surveys that buttress Tischler's generalization. The Pew Forum on Religion and Public Life estimated that in 2007 over 16 percent of the population of the United States would fall into the general category of "unaffiliated" with any religion.[23] In 1990 that number was just 8 percent.[24] Worldwide there are over a billion people who fall into this category.[25] What all these people have in common is a worldview that claims a denial of the existence of God. More specifically, "Secular humanism is philosophically *naturalistic*. It holds that nature (the world of everyday physical experience) is all there is, and that reliable knowledge is best obtained when we query nature using the scientific method."[26]

There are many definitions for the term *secularism*, as well as many words that are used to describe this worldview (*atheism, agnosticism, rationalism, deism*). However, regardless of the name it goes by, there are some core beliefs that explain this worldview. The most fundamental of these beliefs is that there is a social order and explanation of life that can exist *without* God or organized religion. Not only do secularists deny the existence of God, but they believe in other fundamental truths. Let us look at three of these truths.

Rejection of "Miracles" and Supernatural Beings.   Secularists begin with the premise that religion, and the various deities and Gods associated with it, are a projection of humankind's own aspirations and yearnings. Therefore, the "stories" of visions and unnatural occurrences associated with those Gods cannot be believed.[27] Hitchens asserts, "Religion is man-made. Even the men who made it cannot agree on what their prophets, or redeemers, or gurus actually said or did."[28] Because of this attitude, secularists hold that "**Science** provides the only reliable source of knowledge about this universe."[29] An extension of this position would, of course, lead to a firm belief in evolution.

A Set of Ethical Standards.   Like all worldviews, secularism espouses a set of ethical standards. Many of those standards are universal and can also be found in religious traditions. If there are differences, it is because "their values are simply grounded in earthly concerns rather than in anticipation of heavenly rewards or fear of infernal punishment."[30] Or as orator Robert Ingersoll, noted, "Secularism teaches us to be good here and now."[31] In one of its Manifestos, The American Humanist Association (a major secularist organization) was specific on the subject of ethics when it stated,

> "We assert that humanism will: (a) affirm life rather than deny it, (b) seek to elicit the possibilities of life, not flee from them, (c) endeavor to establish the conditions of a satisfactory life for all, not merely for the few. By this positive morale and intention we will be guided, and from this perspective and alignment the techniques and efforts of humanism will flow."[32]

The Finality of Death. As a secular humanist, the physicist Stephen Hawking's description of death in many ways summarizes the secularist's concept of death when he writes of heaven as a "fairy tale for people who are afraid of the dark." For those who hold this view, death is the end of this life and there is no other life after this one: "At death, the individual ceases to exist in any cohesive or conscious form."[33] Because of this interpretation of dying, secularists believe that death is not a spiritual matter, but rather an undeniable truth about our existence. Markham and Lohr repeat this basic aspect of secularism when they write, "At death, everything that comprised our being and consciousness is totally dissolved."[34] When there are funerals they are kept very simple. They are intended to offer support to the family by recalling the accomplishments of the deceased.

Spirituality as a Worldview

While the notion of spirituality has been discussed for thousands of years, recently the concept has gained a large following, especially in the United States. This recognition has produced two very different approaches to spirituality. First, because of its popular culture exposure, the concept and the use of the word have become fashionable and trendy. Many people now use the word to describe their belief system. It is generally regarded as a system that stresses the idea that a person does not need formal religion to live a life of faith. A different and more formalized view of spirituality also exists. It is a "concern with the scared, as distinguished from material matters. In contrast to religion, spirituality is often individual rather than collective and does not require a distinctive format or traditional organization."[35] It is this idea of having a personalized worldview that appeals to the American value of individualism. The notion of a "religion," wherein each person can turn to themselves to discover "inner peace," combines this value of individualism with the value of free choice. Carl Jung, the famous Swiss psychiatrist and popular figure among contemporary spiritualists, expressed this same view when he remarked somewhat poetically, "Your vision will become clear only when you look into your heart. Who looks outside, dreams. Who looks inside, awakens." Underscoring the distinction between religion and personal spirituality is the idea of emphasis on the individual versus the institution.

> Religion is typically experienced within a social institution with commonly shared traditions, sacred texts, beliefs, and worship practices. Religious institutions usually have a governing structure with designated leaders. Spirituality, on the other hand, is part of each person that searches for purpose, meaning, worth, and wonder, often in quest of an ultimate value or the holy.[36]

From the few lines above that describe modern spirituality, you can observe that it is a personal search for finding the answers to life's essential questions. Followers of this approach suggest that to experience the world personally one should adhere to some of the following guidelines:[37]

- Self-discovery is important. Think not only about what you are but what you choose to be.
- Learn to value silence, solitude, and quiet meditation.
- Practice mindfulness. Learn to observe your environment and how you behave when you are in that environment.
- Engage is creative self-expression. Connect yourself to activities such as yoga, dance, music, and other such activities.
- Seek simplicity in your lifestyle.

This brief analysis of spirituality should demonstrate that it contains a number of notions that are general and difficult to pin down, which for some people is part of its appeal. Note that spirituality has many of the same goals found in organized religions (inner peace, a link with nature, a search for meaning in life, among others). The major difference is that spirituality uses some atypical methods of achieving those goals and places emphasis on the individual being part of the "discovery process."

RELIGION

By now it is likely that you have asked yourself: "Why am I studying worldviews and religions in a course dealing with intercultural communication?" Such a query merits an answer, and our reply comes in two parts. First, religion, perception, and behavior are inextricably intertwined. Second, never in the history of civilization has the behavioral dimension of religion been so widespread, relevant, and volatile. Let us explain those two ideas in more detail before we examine the world's six major religious traditions.

You will recall that Chapter 3 discussed the importance of a culture's social institutions. Religion, as we pointed out, is one of those institutions. Kimball assists us in making this important point: "For the vast majority of people worldwide, their religious tradition—like family, tribe, or nation—anchors them in the world. Religious traditions provide structure, discipline, and social participation in a community."[38] Friedman used the image of an olive tree and its deep and stable roots in the title of his book, *The Lexus and the Olive Tree*, to underscore the powerful and enduring quality of religion to a collection of people.[39] Witness the importance of religion's collective force in the word "religion" itself. "The word *religion* comes from the Latin word *religare*, which means 'to tie.'"[40] The obvious implication is that religion ties people to what is sacred.

RELIGION AND THE SACRED

An intriguing aspect of religion is that it has attempted to explain the workings of the world—and in some cases the next world—for thousands of years. Whether through institutions such as the Catholic Church, spiritual and social leaders like Buddha and Confucius, or the teachings of the *Bible, Vedas, Koran, Torah*, and *I Ching*, people have always felt a need to look outside themselves and seek help when addressing questions about mortality and immortality, suffering, and the origins of the universe.

Malefijt notes, "Religion provides explanations and assigns values to otherwise inexplicable phenomena."[41] Nanda and Warms are more specific regarding how these phenomena "help" religion with what it offers its followers: "Religion provides a cosmology, or set of principles or beliefs about the nature of life and death, the creation of the universe, the origin of society and groups within the society, the relationship of individuals and groups to one another, and the relation of humankind to nature."[42] Notice that the items highlighted by Nanda and Warms give credence to the basic theme of this chapter: *The deep structure of culture deals with issues that matter most to people*. Whether they are wondering about the first cause of all things, or the reason for natural occurrences such as comets, floods, lightning, thunder, drought, famine, or disease, many people rely on religious explanations. Smith eloquently expresses the steadfast importance of religion to the psychological welfare of most people: "When religion jumps to life it displays a startling quality. It takes over. All else, while not silenced, becomes subdued and thrown into a supporting role.... It calls the soul to the highest adventure it can undertake, a proposed journey across the jungles, peaks, and deserts of the human spirit."[43]

RELIGION AND PERSONAL CONDUCT

Religion not only deals with the sacred, but it also helps its adherents deal with issues related to human conduct by serving "as a mechanism of social control." This role is fulfilled by establishing notions of right and wrong, transferring part of the burden of decision making from individuals to supernatural powers, and reducing "stress and frustration that often lead to social conflict."[44] The idea of the social dimension of religion is explained by Tischler: "Religion responds to the basic human need to understand the purpose of life. This means creating a worldview that can have social, political, and economic consequences."[45] What history tells us is that religion has

A shared religion reinforces group norms and links followers to a common purpose as they search for guidance and counsel.

M. Freeman/PhotoLink/Getty Images

been a major source of cultural values, beliefs, and attitudes for as long as humans have used religion as a way of understanding how to function among other people. "A shared religion reinforces group norms, provides moral sanctions for individual conduct, and furnishes the ideology of common purpose and values that support the well-being of the community."[46] From this paragraph it should be clear that for the religious individual, theology and everyday experiences cannot be separated.

THE STUDY OF RELIGION IN THE TWENTY-FIRST CENTURY

We ended the last section by noting the tandem relationship between religious activity and many of the dimensions of culture. Or as Roberts notes, "Religion, in turn, is part of a larger system, the nation, and it interacts with economic, health care, political, and educational institutions."[47] As these systems, and the entire world, become more complex, religion is undergoing a kind of modern-day reassessment. From globalization, to the rise of religious extremism, to domestic changes in demographics, to debates between secularists and Evangelical Christians, the world is confronted with an excess of events that are affecting religion in this century. It seems that "peoples of religion are no longer long distances from each other. Hindus, Buddhists, Muslims, and Christians are highly mobile populations that have crossed geographical and cultural boundaries to meet and live among each other."[48]

Globalization and Religion

As you learned in previous chapters, globalization has both economic and social consequences. As Ferraro and Andreatta point out, "In much the same way that markets have been globalizing over the past decade, the revolution in information and communication has had far-reaching effects on the various ecclesiastical religions of the world."[49] The idea that globalization should have effects on religion should not be surprising, since globalization, combined with the forces of modern technology, has made human contact inevitable. In the past, religions have usually consisted of the beliefs, values, and practices of a particular religious community. However, now those religious communities are confronted with messages being sent via new technologies, as well as the challenges created by major shifts in international migration patterns. Because of these two forces, religious institutions have had to adapt to a series of novel and often troubling sets of images and ideas. According to Roberts, one of the most troubling new concepts faced by religion today is secularism. He notes, "Globalization impacts religion in a number of ways. The emerging global culture is a highly secularized one stressing a rational-utilitarian outlook on the world and calling for institutional differentiation of religion from other spheres."[50] What is troublesome to many religious leaders is that these "other spheres" pull their adherents away from well-established doctrines and values.

Conflict and Religion

The long span of religion has always had to explain the dichotomy between preaching about peace while engaging in bloody and brutal wars. It seems that not much has changed, since in this century we have seen an unprecedented wave of violence among people of various religious convictions. There are multitudinous examples where religious clashes can be observed. The Religious Tolerance Organization each year identifies large numbers of "wars and conflicts that have religious intolerance as an element."[51] Add to these their reports on the worldwide increase in anti-Semitism[52] and the numerous accounts documenting the negative treatment of American Muslims,[53] and you can understand why we see connections between globalization, religion, and violence. You should also be able to appreciate why, as we start our examination of religious traditions, we echo and support the words of Paden: "The study of religion…prepares us to encounter not only other centers and calendars, and numerous versions of the sacred and profane, but also to decipher and appreciate different modes of language and behavior. Toward that end, knowledge about others plays its indispensable role."[54]

SELECTING WORLDVIEWS FOR STUDY

It is obvious that we must omit numerous worldviews and religions from our analysis. From animism to Zoroastrianism, from Rastafarianism to Scientology, there is no shortage of religions. Even within the United States there are thousands of religious denominations. For example, there are millions of people who are Mormons, Jehovah's Witnesses, and Unitarians. Yet, for reasons we will explain later, we placed them under the general category of Christians. There are also people who follow New Age philosophies as a worldview, or who practice Wicca (a modern pagan tradition). Turning to Asia, we did not include Sikhism, Taoism, Baha'i, or Shintoism. We also omitted primal religions practiced in parts of Africa, Australia, and the Pacific Islands, as well as in the native Indian cultures of North and South America. In short, with thousands of religions, cults, movements, philosophies, and worldviews to choose from, how can we decide which orientations to examine? Drawing on the research of religious scholars, we have decided to examine Christianity, Judaism, Islam, Hinduism, Buddhism, and Confucianism. And while we grant the importance of other religious traditions and worldviews, our decision was based on three widely accepted criteria—*numbers*, *diffusion*, and *relevance*.

First, while statistics of the world's religions are only approximations, most studies reveal that worldwide, Christianity and Islam have over a billion adherents each, and Hinduism is rapidly approaching that number.[56] Second, by including diffusion as a criterion, we are referring to the notion of dispersion of a religion throughout the world. For example, while the Jewish population is numerically small (approximately 14 million—less than 0.22 percent worldwide), Jews can be found in nearly every country in the world. In fact, because of thousands of years of persecution and a long history of migrating from country to country, only one-third of all Jews live in Israel. Propelled by missionary zeal, Christianity and Islam are also diffused throughout the world. In fact, although many Africans, such as the Yoruba and the Nuer, still follow traditional religions, most Africans, because of colonization and missionaries, are either Christians or Muslims.[57]

Finally, the six traditional religions are worthy of serious study because they are as influential and relevant today as they were thousands of years ago. As Carmody and Carmody note: "When we speak of the great religions we mean the traditions that have lasted for centuries, shaped hundreds of millions of people, and gained respect for their depth and breadth."[58] Because of this respect and longevity these "are the faiths that every citizen should be acquainted with, simply because hundreds of millions of people live by them."[59] The remainder of this chapter seeks to introduce you to them so that you can understand how members of these religious traditions might perceive and participate in this world.

THE ELEMENTS OF RELIGION

It should not be surprising that similar elements characterize all of the world's religions since they all have the same major goal—to make living life more meaningful and death more comprehensible. Let us now look at some of these common elements.

Speculation

Most people, from the moment of their birth to the time of their death, face many of the same challenges concerning the uncertainties of life. "Religion is psychologically comforting because it helps us explain the unexplainable. Every society must deal with imponderable questions that have no definitive logical answers: When did life begin? Why do bad things happen to good people?"[60] In this capacity, religion provides a blueprint for those parts of the world that people do not understand, and thus lessens feelings of bewilderment. From creation stories to detailed descriptions of heaven and hell, all religions assist us in understanding where people came from, why they are here, what happens when they die, and why there is suffering. In the course of answering these questions, religions provide their members a sanctuary. Macionis summarizes this sense of security: "Religious beliefs offer the comforting sense that the vulnerable human condition serves a great purpose. Strengthened by such beliefs, people are less likely to collapse in despair when confronted by life's calamities."[61]

Sacred Writings

At the heart of each of the world's religious traditions lies a body of sacred wisdom— wisdom that must be transmitted from generation to generation. Van Voorst speaks to the importance of these sacred writings, noting:

> The major living religions of the world have all expressed their teachings and practices in writings. Over the course of time some of these writings gained unique standing in their traditions and scriptures. As scriptures, they continue to influence the course of their religions. To read the scriptures of the world, therefore, is to encounter world religions in a direct and meaningful way.[62]

These sacred writings become a repository for a religion's essential principles and teachings. It is important to notice that the word "sacred" is used when describing these writings. Matthews clearly identifies why that word is used: "Each religion believes its sacred writings have divine or spirit-inspired origin. They were either written or spoken by God, written by divinely guided humans, or spoken by teachers of deep spiritual insight."[63] You will notice that in the last sentence Matthews is alluding to the variety of forms these scriptures can take. Some of those forms are:

CONSIDER THIS

Locate a copy of scriptures from two religions different from your own. Read parts of those scriptures and try to locate a creation story. How do the stories differ from your tradition?

- Scriptures, such as those found in Judaism, Christianity, and Islam. These often employ historical narratives that are usually associated with individuals. These individuals are authority figures who provide guidance and instruction. For Jews, these figures are Abraham and Moses. For Christians, it is Jesus, the Son of God. In the Muslim faith, it is a supreme all-knowing God, called *Allah* in Arabic, who used Muhammad as a conduit to deliver his message.
- "Messages" of faith contained in the "books" of each religion. These "books" are the Old Testament for the Jews, originally written in Hebrew; the New Testament, first written in Greek, for Christians; and the Koran, written in classical Arabic, for Muslims.
- "Scriptural books [that] ... have philosophy about the nature of reality (for example, the Hindu *Upanishads*), [or] ... [that] have moral philosophy (for example, the Confucian *Analects*)."[64]
- In the case of Buddhism, not a universal scripture written down by Buddha, but The Pali Canon, which is based on oral tradition and contains the teachings of Buddha.
- Scriptures that can take the form of poetry, myth, legends, prophecy, and the like.

Religious Rituals

We begin our discussion of religious rituals by turning to one of the "authorities" we have just mentioned—Confucius. In Analects 8.2, Confucius notes the value of ritual when he says, "Without ritual, courtesy is tiresome; without ritual, prudence is timid; without ritual, bravery is quarrelsome; without ritual, frankness is hurtful."[65] Rituals are practiced by all religions. Smart offers an excellent restatement of this idea when she writes:

> Most place a heavy emphasis on ritual. The Catholic is enjoined to attend Mass weekly. The Muslim is told to pray five times daily, according to a set formula. The Hindu attends temple rituals frequently. The Theravada Buddhist will often make a trip to the temple to pay his or her respects to Buddha. The Protestant typically has a worship service with a sermon as a vital part of their ritual.[66]

In their strictest form, "Rituals are actions that are repetitive, prescribed, and ceremonial."[67] By engaging in rituals, members not only recall and reaffirm important beliefs; they also feel spiritually connected to their religion, develop a sense of identity by increasing social bonds with those who share their views, and sense that their life has meaning and structure. "Ritual serves to relieve social tensions and reinforce a group's collective bonds. More than this, it provides a means of marking many important events and lessening the social disruption and individual suffering of crises such as death."[68] Rituals, like so many aspects of culture, are not instinctive, so in order to endure they must be passed from one generation to the next.

Rituals are repetitive, prescribed, and ceremonial actions that allow members of a particular faith to reaffirm important beliefs and feel spiritually connected to their religion.

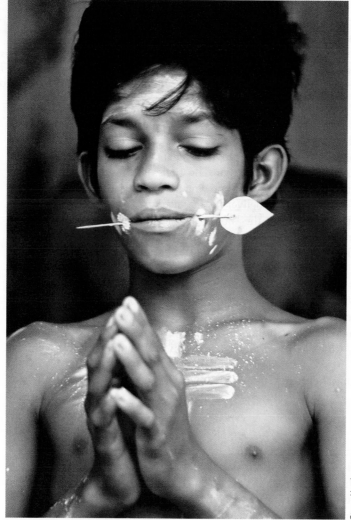

Steve Harrington

The most common of all rituals are rites of passage that mark key stages in the human cycle of life. "Rites of passage are social occasions marking the transition of members of the group from one important life stage to the next. Birth, puberty, marriage, and death are transition points that are important in many different cultures."[69] There are thousands of rituals dealing with the sacred that bring families and the religious community together at the same time they are teaching important lessons. There are rituals dealing with space (Muslims turning toward Mecca when they pray), and others that call attention to important events (Christian baptisms, Jews marking the importance of Passover, the Hindu young boy engaging in the *Unpanayanam* ceremonial rite of entering manhood).

Rituals can be indirect as well as direct. A good example of an indirect ritual is the Japanese tea ceremony. At first glance it would appear that the tea ceremony is simply the preparation and drinking of tea, but the importance of the ritual to Buddhism is far greater. "Every detailed act, every move and position, embodies humility, restraint, and awareness. This framing of ordinary action in order to reveal some deeper significance—in this example the values are related to the Zen Buddhist idea of immanence of the absolute in the ordinary—is a common element of ritual behavior."[70]

Ethics

Robinson and Rodrigues correctly write, "Religion has played a prominent role in the regulation of human behavior. Almost every religious tradition discriminates between acceptable and unacceptable conduct."[71] In Matthew 19:16, when Jesus is asked, "Teacher, what good deed must I do to have eternal life?" you can see the link between ethics and religion. The person raising the question uses religion in seeking guidance regarding what is moral and immoral conduct. The bond between religion and ethics can be seen in a variety of ways. It is often clear and simple advice, such as Confucius stressing moral honesty, but can also extend to more complex and specific religious laws. In Judaism, for example, there are "not merely the Ten Commandments but a complex of over six hundred rules imposed upon the community by a Divine Being."[72] In Islamic ethics, the association of religion, regulations, and actions is also apparent. "For Muslims, the teaching of the Quran (Islam's sacred book) and *hadith* (stories or traditions about the Prophet Muhammad) exemplify the moral way of life that God expects of human beings."[73] Smart underscores this powerful link between religion, law, and moral behavior when she writes: "Islamic life has traditionally been controlled by the Law, or *sharia*, which shapes society as both a religious and a political society, as well as shaping the moral life of the individual—prescribing that he should pray daily, give alms to the poor, and so on, and that society should have various institutions, such as marriage, modes of banking, etc."[74]

Hindus also have ethical precepts attached to their religion. As Matthews points out: "Hinduism has a rich moral code.... In the Vedas, Rita is the principle of right order in the universe; all things conform to its control. For the individual, the principle of right action is Dharma. Dharma is Rita incorporated in the life of individuals."[75] Because of the strong belief in reincarnation, each life must manifest empathy and reciprocity toward all living creatures—people and animals. If not in the next life, we experience the consequences of ill deeds in this life. This view toward ethics is clearly expressed in the Hindu admonition: "This is the sum of Dharma: do not do to others what would cause pain if done to you."

For the Buddhist, ethical values can be found in Buddha's listing of the four great virtues that people should strive for: "benevolence, compassion, joy in others' joy, and equanimity."[76] While the words might change, the central message about ethics from Confucius is much the same as the one found in other traditions. Matthews summarizes those principled words in the following sentences. "The word *reciprocity* is a good description for Confucian ethics. People should avoid doing to others what they would not want done to them. They should do those things that they would like done to themselves."[77]

You can observe by now that the message of ethics "pretty much tells a cross-cultural story."[78] From warnings to avoid murder, thieving, lying, and adultery, to stressing the virtues of "humility, charity, and veracity,"[79] a similar basic core of moral guidelines

CONSIDER THIS

All religious traditions treat the topic of ethics and offer specific advice on how to live an ethical life. Why do you think ethics and religion are linked?

is found in all cultures. According to Coogan, what they all seek to accomplish by the formation of ethical principles is to "enable their adherents to achieve the ultimate objective of the tradition—the attainment of salvation, redemption, enlightenment, and the 'liberation of the soul.'"[80]

Before we begin our discussion of the great religions of the world, we urge you to keep a few points in mind. First, remember that religion is but one kind of worldview, and even a secular person who says, "There is no God," has likely sought answers to the large questions about the nature of truth, how the world operates, life, death, suffering, and ethical relationships.

Second, remember that "religion pervades many spheres that others might call secular and it cannot easily be separated from them."[81] It is often difficult to draw a line between secularism and a subtle manifestation of religion. What one person might call "religion" or "worldview," another person might call "philosophy." For example, when a group of people prefers intuitive wisdom to "scientific facts" as a means of discovering reality, they may do so without invoking the teachings of Buddhism or Hinduism. For our purposes, labeling is not nearly as important as the notion that a culture's heritage includes ways of dealing with timeless and fundamental questions.

Finally, it is not our intent to offer a course on world religion. Therefore, we have omitted much of the theology and doctrine of the world's great religions and instead concentrated on ways in which religion "gets acted out." We, like Smith, believe that the locus of religion is in the person and in human interaction.[82]

CHRISTIANITY

We start with Christianity, a faith that took its name from Jesus Christ, who with a small band of disciples travelled throughout the Holy Land preaching, teaching, and healing the sick. Today, with over two billion adherents (one-third of the world's population) it is the largest of all the traditions[83] and has seen its ideology spread throughout the world. For example, there were 10 million Christians in Africa in 1990—now there are over 360 million. That same explosion in growth can be seen in South America, Asia, and even China.[84] The diversity of people who are Christians produces a multiplicity of denominations. By some estimates there are 33,800 different Christian denominations.[85] However, Christianity has historically been composed of three major branches: the Roman Catholic Church, under the guidance of the papacy in Rome; the Eastern Orthodox Churches, with members concentrated in Eastern Europe, Russia, Ukraine, the Balkans, and Central Asia; and Protestantism, which embodies a host of denominations such as Baptists, Presbyterians, Methodists, Lutherans, and Episcopalians.[86] While each of these branches and their numerous subsets boasts some unique features, they all share many of the same rituals, beliefs, traditions, basic characteristics, and tenets. In fact, one of the strengths of Christianity throughout the centuries has been its ability to maintain its basic core while being adaptive and varied. As Wilson points out, "Christianity can be seen for what it was historically and what it continues to be today: a living, ever-changing religion which, like any other religion, owes its vitality to its diversity."[87] Prothero highlights that diversity when he writes, "Christianity is now so elastic that it seems a stretch to use this term to cover the beliefs and behaviors of Pentecostals in Brazil, Mormons in Utah, Roman Catholics in Italy, and the Orthodox of Moscow."[88]

Core Assumptions

In spite of the assortment of Christian denominations we just mentioned, this tradition has a basic core of beliefs that offers its followers a guideline for understanding life and death. Three of the most common guidelines can be found in a few basic tenets and ideologies. Hale expands on these in the following:

> Essentially, Christianity is a monotheistic tradition centered on faith in God (the eternal creator who transcends creation and yet is active in the world) and in Jesus Christ as the savior and redeemer of humankind. Christianity holds that God became incarnate—fully human—as Jesus of Nazareth. Christians believe that Jesus died on a cross and was resurrected, physically rising from the dead. The belief in the Trinity, the sacred mystery of Father, Son, and Holy Spirit as one, triune ("three-in-one") God is central to the Christian tradition.[89]

A number of important precepts emerge from Hale's summary.

- There is a single God who created the universe and also "gave the world" his only son, Jesus Christ. Part of this "giving" involves Jesus giving his life on the Cross (the Crucifixion).
- "Christians believe that the gravest problem in human life is sin—the failure to live in harmony with the will of God."[90]
- Christianity is a total worldview that includes both the religious and the secular dimensions of life. Part of this unification of the ways of life is drawn from the belief that Jesus lived among the people and suffered, hence, he understands human pain, problems, and enticements.
- "Man and woman are created in God's image. People have been made as the crowning glory of God's creative activity, to act as God's representatives in this world."[91]
- "God is personal, that is to say, Trinitarian. This God who acts is not only a God of energies, but a personal God."[92]

Cultural Expressions of Christianity

An important question to examine is how are these basic tenets of Christianity reflected in daily life? While there are thousands of directives that Jesus and his apostles carried to the world, we have selected a few of those that have not only shaped the Christian tradition, but apply to the study of intercultural communication.

Christianity and Community. In the introduction to this section we pointed out that community was an essential component of Christianity. The link between the community and Christianity has roots that go back to the inception of the religion. For example, from the beginning of his practice, Jesus gathered others to share in his ministry. These relationships were "not a nebulous affiliation, but a concrete group of people that entered into a relationship with Jesus and with other people."[93] The gatherings of these people came to be known as "communion" and "fellowship." These important occasions within the community contributed to feelings of interdependence and group cohesion. This notion of community as part of Christianity goes back to the apostles who used these communities to take care of the poor (II Cor. 8:24), provide hospitality to travelers (Rom 16:2), and generally comfort one another.

For Christians, the church is a key element in how community is revealed. Not only is it a "house of worship" and a place of great reverence, but it is also a place where people gather in groups and share a common identity. For our purposes it is the social dimension of Christianity that offers insight into the communication aspects of this tradition. Even today you can observe the strong influence of cooperative spirit in how churches have special services for young children, sanctuaries for baptisms, meeting halls, and countless social gatherings.

Of course, the church has a theological function as well as a social purpose that ties the community to the sharing of God's message. "Jesus' view of the self was relational. The self was not a monad existing in isolation."[95] Jesus believed that "the closer people drew to God, the closer they could draw to one another."[96] Even at the Last Supper, Jesus shared his final meal with his twelve disciples rather than being alone. Our point is that a sense of community and organized worship has contributed to the social dimension found in Western cultures. Americans are social creatures and belong to numerous clubs, committees, and organizations. The French historian de Tocqueville pointed out over two hundred years ago that Americans had a large series of networks and associations that went well beyond their family unit.

Christianity and Individualism.   At the same time that Christianity encourages community, it also stresses the importance and uniqueness of each individual. Most scholars maintain that Christianity and Judaism were the first religions that placed "greater emphasis on the autonomy and responsibility of the self."[97] As McGuire points out, Christianity "is characterized by an image of the dynamic multidimensional self, able (within limits) to continually change both self and the world."[98] In short, Christianity and Judaism are the religious traditions that "discovered the individual."[99] Before the arrival of these two religions, people were seen as members of tribes, communities, or families, and behaved in ways that reflected the collective nature of their existence. While family and community remained important, Christianity highlighted the significance of each person. An example of the power of self can be seen in the view of salvation, particularly for Protestants. Salvation "is achieved by our own efforts alone and there is a tendency for deeds to count more than prayers."[100] Even the Bible carries examples of individualism. "The Gospels are replete with scenes in which Jesus works one-on-one healing this woman's sickness, forgiving that man's sins, and calling each to personal conversion."[101] Summarizing this important point, Woodward writes, "Christianity discovers individuality in the sense that it stresses personal conversion."[102] You also can see the importance of the individual in the part of Christian theology that begins with the assumption that the world is real and meaningful because God created it. An extension of that idea is that human beings are significant because God created them in his image. Hence, the Christian God is a personal God who desires a relationship with his creation.[103] In a culture that values individualism, Christianity is an especially appealing religion as each person can have a one-on-one bond with God.

Christianity and "Doing."   Western culture, as will be discussed in detail in Chapter 6, is one that encourages activity and action. Some of the roots of this philosophy can be traced to Christianity. We begin with how Jesus lived his life. In Christianity, "living in the world" rather than withdrawal from the world is emphasized.[104] From its beginning "the Jesus movement began to send out emissaries" to bring the news about Jesus to all who would listen.[105] Peter, one of Jesus' disciples, once said of Jesus, "He went about doing good."[106] Weaver and Brakke speak of this doing when they write, "From the earliest days of the Christian movement, evangelization was important."[107] Going out into the world was seen as "missionaries were sent to the furthest reaches of the Roman world to bring Christianity to various people; Patrick in Ireland, Boniface in German, and Augustine of Canterbury in England were effective missionaries, able to adapt their message to the needs of their audiences."[108]

There are, of course, many other examples demonstrating Christianity as having a long tradition of action. In the Roman era, sick people were cast into the streets because the Romans feared death might result if they remained near a sick person. Christians would take them in and nurse them. There are also numerous stories of how Jesus would speak with prostitutes, visit people in their homes, and travel from place to place talking to strangers along the way.

Christianity, as a statement of "doing," also stressed hard work. The argument was that "material success was taken to be one clue that a person was among the elect and thus favored by God, which drove early Protestants to relentless work as a means of confirming (and demonstrating) their salvation."[109] Even today, hard work is commonly valued in the West. When meeting a person for the first time you will often hear the following question being asked: "What do you do?" It is the "doing" that can be partially linked to Christianity.

Christianity and the Future. Throughout this book we discuss cultural attitudes toward time. From those discussions, and from your own observations, you can conclude that Americans are future oriented—they are concerned with what will happen next, rather than what is happening in the present. We suggest that one of the reasons for this behavior might have some of its roots in Christianity, as one of the lessons of Christianity is that the future is important. For Christians "no matter what happened in the past, it is the future that holds the greatest promise."[110] God forgives mistakes and offers repentance and incentives to move forward. "Christians hold that those who repent of their sins and turn to Jesus Christ will be forgiven and will join him in heaven after death."[111] In this sense, the individual is destined to move on. Even the notion of a heaven accents the future. You can see that emphasis on the future in Romans 6:23: "For the wages of sin is death, but the gift of God is eternal life in Christ Jesus our Lord." In short, built into Christian ideology is a positive and optimistic outlook toward the future—a belief that *things will be better in the future.*

Christianity and Courage. One of the most enduring legacies of the Jesus story is the message of courage in the face of adversity. In how he lived and how he died "Jesus was courageous."[112] A careful reading of the life of Jesus reveals a man who would not be intimidated by his opponents and who repeatedly demonstrated strength and daring in the face of overwhelming odds. Without fear, Jesus preached against what was established doctrine during his entire adult life. This not only made him a prophet, but also a hero. France, writing about Jesus, notes, "He aroused the opposition of leaders,"[113] and "He seemed to delight in reversing accepted standards, with his slogan: 'The first shall be last, and the last first.'"[114] You can conclude that his practice of mixing with ostracized groups (such as the unfortunate and prostitutes) was a brave and courageous act. These same two attributes represent powerful values in American culture.

Christian Notions about Death

While death is a universal experience, nearly every worldview and religious tradition has discovered a way to mark the event with its own interpretation. That is to say, regardless of the explanation advanced, religious and secular traditions attempt to enlighten their members about death. Explanations of death, regardless of the tradition, examine the following six questions: "What is the purpose of death? Does existence end at death? If not, what happens after death? Are we reembodied in a similar form or in a different form? Is there a final judgment? And how are we to prepare for our own dying?"[115]

The Christian answers to these six questions are not simple for two reasons. First, there is a great variety of Christian denominations. And second, interpretations of the Old and New Testaments often differ. However, regardless of the name of the Christian denomination, or the teachings it follows, there is a theme about death that links them all. All explanations begin with the clear admonition in Ecclesiastes 3:2: There is "a time to be born, and a time to die." From this scripture grows the core for the explanations about death and the afterlife. Matthews summarizes this core when he writes, "Most Christians believe that those who have lived a righteous life will live happily in the presence of God in heaven; those who are wicked will endure hell."[116] In short, there is eternal life, and salvation is possible through the caring and loving creator. Many turn to John 11:25–26 for the following words of guidance and inspiration: "I am the resurrection. If anyone believes in me, even though he dies, he will live, and whoever lives and believes in me will never die. Do you believe this?"[117] A similar passage is found in I Peter 1:3–4: "...God has something stored up for you in heaven, where it will never decay or be ruined or disappear."[118] These words tell Christians that death is not something to be feared. As Wilson points out, "The Christian churches teach that the human soul is immortal and was originally destined to spend eternity in the presence of God in heaven."[119] Some denominations are even more

While death is a universal experience, each religious tradition has discovered a way to mark the event with its own interpretation.

Edwin McDaniel

specific in their explanation of heaven. For example, some Baptists believe: "Heaven is a place where the redeemed go to receive the reward of eternal companionship with God. It is depicted as being filled with mansions and golden streets."[120] So important is the notion of heaven that religious scholars have found the words *heaven* and *eternal life* mentioned over six hundred times in the New Testament.[121]

While heaven awaits those who have lived virtuous and righteous lives, "those who are wicked will endure in hell."[122] Because the idea of hell was a late arrival to Christianity (not introduced until the writings of Luke and Matthew), there are a number of versions and descriptions of what hell is and how one becomes a candidate for this "nightmare." In some of the early descriptions, particularly those advanced by Luke, details are scarce and never graphic.[123] But other accounts of hell, especially those suggested by Matthew, are much more explicit and detailed. "Matthew argues, again and again, that Hell exists, is sheer torture, and is reserved for the damned who will be cast 'into the furnace of fire; where there will be wailing and gnashing of teeth.'"[124] Not only do portrayals of hell differ, but who goes to hell instead of heaven is also left to some mild speculation. In most accounts, hell is reserved for people who die without accepting Christ or who have "sinned" and not repented. Hell is most of all "the separation from the love of God."[125] There is yet another more modern argument that suggests that a loving God would not be party to anything as cruel and sordid as hell, and therefore, God needs to be trusted. Regardless of how heaven and hell are defined in various Christian traditions, one conclusion is obvious—Christian doctrine maintains that there is an afterlife, which, as we shall see later in the chapter, is not the case in all religious traditions.

JUDAISM

There are fewer than fourteen million Jews worldwide, representing less than 0.22 percent of the world's population.[126] However, their interest in politics, literature, education, medicine, finance, and law have, for thousands of years, made them an important and influential group no matter in which country they have lived. As Prothero notes, "This tiny religion has wielded influence far out of proportion to its numbers. It started a monotheistic revolution that remade the Western world."[127] Smith estimates "that one-third of our Western civilization bears the marks of its Jewish ancestry."[128] In addition, Judaism was the prototype and forerunner to both Christianity and Islam.

It is difficult to be specific concerning the roots of Judaism as a religion. Matthews mentions this problem when he writes, "When did Judaism begin? With the creation of the world more than five thousand years ago, or with the exodus from Egypt? Did Judaism proper begin in Jerusalem after leaders returned from exile in Babylon, or only after the destruction of the Temple in 70 CE?"[129] In spite of these questions, scholars can agree on the following set of facts. Judaism was founded in approximately 1300 BCE, when twelve Israelite tribes came to Canaan from Mesopotamia. Later, many of them settled in Egypt where they were held as slaves until they fled to Jerusalem in about 1200 BCE. One of the most significant events in the forming of this religion is the role played by the prophet Abraham. According to Jewish history, God chose Abraham to function as the "father" of the Jewish people, a people that God designated as his "chosen people." To be the recipients of this honor, Jews entered into a sacred *covenant* with God. "The covenant was repeatedly renewed. Unlike a contract, the covenant had no date of expiration."[130] Matlins and Magida offer an excellent summary of the covenant: "Central to this covenant is the concept of being 'chosen' as a people. For as Moses tells his people in the Bible: 'The Lord has chosen you to be a people for His own possession, out of all the peoples that are on the face of the earth' (Deuteronomy 12:2)."[131] In Jewish theology, this distinctive consideration was never meant to give special advantages to the Jews, but only to increase their responsibilities and therefore their hardships.[132] From circumcision to the keeping of the Sabbath, signs of the covenant abound in Jewish culture and religion.[133] It is this covenant that is at the heart of why Jews consider themselves God's "chosen people."

In the nearly four thousand years of historical development, the people who practice the Jewish religion have exhibited not only a penchant for continuity but also a remarkable adaptability. Torstrick speaks of this persistent ability to adapt in the following: "The Jewish faith developed over a 4,000-year period. Over that span of time, it has demonstrated a remarkable capacity to adapt and persevere, to absorb elements from the civilizations and cultures which it has come into contact with, but to also retain its own unique identity and heritage."[134]

Core Assumptions

The Jewish worldview is expressed through a number of basic principles.

- Jews "believe in one universal and eternal God, the creator and sovereign of all that exists."[135] This creed is clear and brief. It is expressed in Deuteronomy 6:4: "Hear, O Israel: The Lord our God, the Lord is one."
- There is no belief in original sin; however, a person can commit sin by breaking the commandments.[136] This means each person must be obedient to God-given commandments in the Torah (the first five books of the Bible).
- Humans are inherently pure and good and are given free will.[37] They "can live any way they choose; they have only to bear the consequences."[138]

These core assumptions compose a belief system stressing the secular notion that places great emphasis on this life rather than an afterlife.

Branches of Judaism

Judaism, like the other major traditions, has experienced a variety of configurations and divisions since its inception. While the core of the religion has remained the same since its beginning, Judaism has now branched into three large groups: *Orthodox*, *Reform*, and *Conservative* Judaism. What is unique about these three groups is that "while Christian denominations distinguish themselves largely on the basis of faith and belief, these branches differ more on ritual and ethics."[139] The *Orthodox* branch is the most traditional and the oldest of the three branches, "and was the only form of Jewish practice prior to the eighteenth century."[140] It is also the only branch of

Judaism that is officially acknowledged in Israel. Orthodox Judaism retains as much as possible from the traditional religious teachings found in classical and ancient writings. This means following dietary laws such as not eating shellfish or pork, not allowing men and women to sit together in the synagogue, not working or driving on the Sabbath, and having men wear skull caps (yarmulkes) and prayer shawls.[141]

Reform Judaism was an attempt in the late eighteenth century to modernize many of the long-established Jewish practices so that Jews worldwide could assimilate into non-Jewish communities without losing their Jewish identity.[142] Prothero notes, "Pioneers in the Reform movement wanted to be modern Germans or modern Americans without ceasing to be Jews."[143] Conducting prayer services in the local language, not requiring men to wear yarmulkes, the use of choirs and musical instruments, and allowing men and women to sit together are part of the Reform movement. Reformed congregations even allow ordained women rabbis.

Conservative Judaism, particularly in the United States, was intended to find a middle ground between holding onto the basic traditions of the Orthodox while still employing some modern changes associated with the Reform movement. This means that Conservatives believe many of the rules, rituals, and traditions of Orthodox practice are necessary if Jewish identity is to be maintained.[144]

Regardless of which branch of Judaism one follows, it is clear that the Jewish faith is unique in that it is both a culture and a religion. It is common, for example, to find nonreligious Jews who identify fully with the culture but not with the theology. Fisher and Luyster elaborate on this point: "Judaism has no single founder, no central leader or group making theological decisions; Judaism is a people, a very old family. This family can be defined either as a religious group or a national group."[145] In short, Judaism penetrates every aspect of human existence for the Jews and provides a means of living with both the secular and religious worlds.

Cultural Expressions of Judaism

As was the case with Christianity, the issue for students of intercultural communication is simply: How does Judaism become reflected in the manner in which Jews perceive the world and interact with other people within that world? We now offer a few answers to those questions.

Oppression and Persecution. One of the most enduring and horrific manifestations of Jewish history has been the countless examples of oppression, genocide, and persecution. As Van Doren points out: "The history of Judaism and the Jews is a long complicated story, full of blood and tears."[146] As far back as 1500 BCE the pharaoh of Egypt made an effort to kill all Jewish males. In 70 CE "The Roman Army destroyed Jerusalem, killed over 1 million Jews, took about 100,000 into slavery and captivity, and scattered many from Palestine to other locations in the Roman Empire."[147] More hatred and massive killings of Jews occurred during the Spanish Inquisition in 1478. During that same period in other parts of Europe "Laws were passed that prohibited descendants of Jews or Muslims from attending university, joining religious orders, holding public office, or entering any of a long list of professions."[148] In 1523, in an essay titled *Jews and Their Lies*, Martin Luther further intensified hostility against the Jews by insisting that they convert to Christianity.[149] Prager and Telushkin offer an excellent summary of this long-standing persecution of Jews we have just touched upon: "Only the Jews have had their homeland destroyed (twice), been dispersed wherever they have lived, survived the most systematic attempt in history (aside from that of the Gypsies) to destroy an entire people, and been expelled from nearly every nation among whom they have lived."[150]

While repression, genocide, and discrimination have punctuated Jewish history for thousands of years, it was the Holocaust, and the mass killing of six million Jews (1.5 million of them children) that told Jews that anti-Semitism follows them wherever they go. In just a single paragraph, Esposito and his co-authors capture the horrors:

> When the Nazi party came to power, the Jews were stripped of their citizenship and all their legal rights; their homes and businesses were appropriated; and they were herded into box-cars that delivered them to an elaborate system of death camps, where they were worked to death as slaves or murdered in specially designed gas chambers made to order for mass killings.[151]

Even today, when reflecting on the Holocaust, Jews are still troubled by two aspects of this hideous portion of their history. The first is the silence of the world leading up to the Holocaust and the lack of response once what was taking place was known by outsiders. Markham and Lohr point out, "When the Jews were seeking escape from Germany, other countries closed their borders. Although the Allies knew about the death camps, they took no special measures to destroy them."[152] Second, they see the Holocaust as a natural outgrowth of centuries of anti-Semitism. They still observe outbursts of this hostility in this century as they listen to words of Iran's President Ahmadinejad calling for Israel to be "wiped off the map," or read a report from the U.S. State Department referring to the fact that in 2006 nearly 600 major anti-Semitic incidents against Jewish individuals and facilities were reported.[153]

The result of the experiences we have just mentioned is that today many Jews have a difficult time trusting non-Jews. Yet, in spite of these suspicions and hardships, "Jews are still essentially the same stubborn, dedicated people, now and forever affirming the same three things. First, they are a people of the law as given in the only books of Moses. Second, they are the chosen people of God, having a covenant with him. Third, they are a witness that God is and will be forevermore."[154]

Learning. The Jewish essayist and Nobel laureate Elie Wiesel quotes a Jewish saying: "Adam chose knowledge instead of immortality." This saying highlights that a love of learning has been a hallmark of the Jewish religion and culture since its very beginning. As Braswell notes, "Judaism centers on the worship of God, the practice of good deeds, and the love of learning."[155] For thousands of years Jews have made the study of the Talmud (a holy book of over 5,000 pages) an important element of Jewish life.[156] The Jewish prayer book even speaks of "the love of learning" as one of three principles of faith.[157] This important ingredient of Jewish culture is underscored by the fact that "As early as the first century, Jews had a system of compulsory education."[158] Jews even have a proverb: "Wisdom is better than jewels."

Because of this cultural and religious characteristic regarding learning, Jews have stressed education throughout their history. When the first Jews arrived in the United States, they immediately realized that education was the path to a good life for them and their children. Today the Jewish population is one of the most well-educated groups in the United States. One-third of all Jews have advanced graduate degrees, and 55 percent have earned at least a bachelor's degree.[159] It is common for Jews to seek professions centering on education, law, medicine, and literature.

Justice. The idea of justice is deeply rooted in the Jews' traditions. An individual's responsibility and moral commitment to God and other people is even detailed in Jewish religious writings. Markham and Lohr point out that "The God of Israel taught through his prophets that worship of God without social justice is worthless."[160] In fact, one of the four categories of Jewish law is actually "to ensure moral treatment of others."[161] You can see this concern for justice in everything from ancient Jewish writings to the active role Jews played during the civil rights movement of the 1960s. So deep-seated is this basic precept that Smith believes much of Western civilization owes a debt to the early Jewish prophets for establishing the notion of justice as a major principle for the maintenance of "social order."[162]

Family and Community. As you saw in Chapter 3, all societies value the family, but for Jews the family is the locus of worship and devotion. When we speak of the Jewish family we are actually talking about two interrelated families—the larger community of Jews and a person's immediate family. One of the ways Jews have dealt with centuries of hardships was to turn to both of these families for strength and courage. As Prothero notes, "Judaism centers on the community rather than the individual."[163] Most Jews have always felt a sense of connectedness with other Jews regardless of where they lived. Being referred to as "The Children of Israel" speaks to the fact that as Jews they believe "they are all the physical or spiritual descendants of the same family,"[164] and as such "They share a sense of community with and responsibility for Jews throughout the world."[165]

Each Jewish family, in addition to the larger Jewish community, plays a key role in the life of all Jews. That is, "The center of Jewish religious life is the home. Great emphasis is placed on the family and its relationships."[166] On nearly every occasion, be it in the home or the synagogue, the family is an active participant in Jewish life. That life is linked to the larger community by a host of religious traditions and rituals. From circumcisions to Passover seders (ceremonial dinners), to bar or bat mitzvahs, to marriage and death, to the treatment of the elderly, the family and religion are strongly bound together. Rosten offers a summary of this link: "For 4,000 years, the Jewish family has been the very core, mortar, and citadel of Judaism's faith and the central reason for the survival of the Jews as a distinct ethnic group. The Jewish home is a temple, according to Judaic law, custom, and tradition."[167]

Jewish Notions about Death

An aspect of Judaism and death is that there are very few references to death or an afterlife in traditional Jewish writings. As Rabbi Ponn notes, "The first and primary responsibility of the Jew is this life and not the world to come."[168] This attitude is seen in the fact that "The *Torah*, the most important Jewish text, has no clear reference to afterlife at all."[169] Because of this lack of specific material in religious literature, Jews view death as a natural process. As Kramer points out, "The writer of 2 Samuel 14:14 says: 'We must all die; we are like water spilt on the ground, which cannot be gathered up again.'"[170]

An important aspect of Jewish notions regarding death is the role of family and community that we discussed earlier. "Judaism meets this important passage, as all others in a person's life, with distinctive ritual that reinforces identity with the community of believers. The identity is not only with the present community but also with past communities of Jews."[171] Even after the regular seven days of mourning, people continue to come together in "the context of a loving and supporting community."[172] Not only does the family gather at the cemetery, but shortly after the ceremony larger numbers of guests are invited to take part in a social gathering to have refreshments and share stories about the deceased.

ISLAM

We begin our analysis of Islam with this assertion: For a host of reasons, a large percentage of non-Muslims do not fully understand the Islamic faith. Prothero reaffirms our contention in the following:

> Most Europeans and North Americans have never met a Muslim, so for them, Islam begins in the imagination, more specifically in that corner of the imagination colonized by fear. They see Islam through a veil hung over their eyes centuries ago by Christian Crusaders intent on denouncing Islam as a religion prone to violence, its founder, Muhammad, as a man of the sword, and its holy book, the Quran, as a text of wrath.[173]

Perceptions of the Islamic faith are often colored by hysteria, generalizations, and oversimplifications. Not only are these misperceptions the fault of media frenzy, but there are no simple explanations to explain this religion since "the images and realities of Islam and of Muslims are multiple and diverse."[174] Despite the bombings on September 11, 2001, the harsh rhetoric coming from Iran, and stories concerning ayatollahs ordering the stoning of prostitutes, it is misleading to equate all these acts directly to the Islamic faith. Such a blanket condemnation of all Muslims is disingenuous on two counts. First, when taken as a whole, and compared to other faiths, "The Islamic religion is no more prone to violence than any other religion."[175] Second, terrorism and "suicide attacks are more directed toward secular ends than religious ones."[176] Whether or not you agree with our conclusions regarding violence and Islam, it is a critical worldview that must be understood if you are to become a successful intercultural communicator in the twenty-first century.

The statistical and demographic impact of Islam throughout the world only serves to underscore the need to learn more about what Belt calls the "most misunderstood religion on earth."[177] Islam is the fastest-growing of all the religions, with approximately 1.6 billion followers scattered throughout the world. This figure includes over 23 percent of the world's population. We used the word "scattered" as a way of pointing out that the largest share of Muslims, nearly 80 percent, live in places other than Arab lands.[178] Because of immigration, a substantial portion of that percentage lives in the United States. In fact, Islam will soon be the second most commonly practiced religion in the United States, with approximately seven million members. In 2010 there were more Muslims in the United States than there were Jews.[179] All these numbers imply that whether on the international level, in your neighborhood, or on college campuses, contact with Muslims has become a fact of life.

Origins

One of the major contentions of this book is that there is a connection between culture, history, family, and religion. You can see this point reflected in the Islamic faith. As Sedgwick notes: "Just as the events of Jesus' life matter to a Christian, and just as the history of Israel matters to a Jew, so the events of early Islam matter to a Muslim."[180]

So essential is history to the study of Islam that we dedicated an entire section to this topic in the previous chapter. However, now we need to return briefly to that history, this time from a religious perspective. Woodward provides a summary of the events that led to the creation of Islam:

> The Arabs were mostly polytheists, worshiping tribal deities. They had no sacred history linking them to one universal god, like other Middle Eastern peoples. They had no sacred text to live by, like the Bible; no sacred language, as Hebrew is to Jews and Sanskrit is to Hindus. Above all, they had no prophet sent to them by God, as Jews and Christians could boast.[181]

The need for a prophet to carry the message from God was resolved with the arrival of Muhammad, who in 610 CE received a revelation from God. According to the stories of Muhammad, he was a person with a curious mind who would retreat into a cave near his home and engage in prayer and meditation. It was during one of these meditative periods that "the angel Gabriel appeared to him and told him that God had chosen him to be His messenger to all mankind."[182] This epic event was to cast Muhammad forever as the messenger of God. Muslims believe Allah (Arabic for God) had spoken to human beings many times in the past through other prophets. However, it was Muhammad who delivered the religious messages until his death in 623. These messages were to become recorded in the Koran. Not only did these messages reveal "words from God," but they also established the social order that was to become Islam. Muhammad believed that community and religion were one and the same. Muhammad established the city-state that became known as Medina. This fusion of church and state was unique in Muhammad's time and remains one of the central characteristics of Islam today.

Muhammad's message was so powerful that when combined with the missionary zeal found in Islam, it was able to establish a presence in Europe, North Africa, Persia, Jerusalem, Damascus, the Caucasus, Central Asia, Egypt, and Turkey.[183] The growth of Islam continues; Muslims now form the majority in forty-nine countries and a substantial minority in many others.[184]

Core Assumptions

As is the case with all religious traditions, the major premises at the heart of the Islamic worldview are complex and numerous. We have selected six that deserve to be called "core assumptions," for they are the most basic articles of faith and those help explain some of the perceptions and actions of people who call themselves Muslims.

One God.   The central pronouncement of Islam is that there is only one God. "Islam always has taught that Allah is One, that there is only One God. The first half of the Muslim creed says: 'There is no god at all but Allah.'"[185] In the Koran the idea is stated as follows: "He is God, the One God to Whom the creatures turn for their needs. He begets not, nor was He begotten, and there is none like Him."[186] So powerful is this simple premise that Muslims believe the greatest of all sins occurs when a person gives even the smallest share of Allah's exclusive and unique sovereignty to something else or to another body.[187] Regardless of your personal reaction to the specific event, you can recall the protests and even violence that erupted in Pakistan, Afghanistan, Indonesia, and countless other Arab countries following publication by a Danish newspaper of cartoons satirizing the Prophet Muhammad. For the protestors, the cartoons diminished the spirituality and uniqueness of Muhammad.

Belief in Angels.   Angels play an important role in the theology of Islam. They were created by Allah to serve and worship him. Of all the angels, Gabriel occupies the most important position.[188] As noted, it was the angel Gabriel who informed Muhammad that God had chosen him to bring forth the message of Islam. Throughout the Koran angels "are presented as invisible, abstract symbols of God's power."[189] Angels are often presented as somewhat ethereal and unearthly. To demonstrate just how powerful God is, angels in the Koran worship and obey only one God.

The Koran.   We have already referred to the Koran and noted it is for Muslims the most sacred of all texts. Written in classical Arabic, "Muslims believe that the Koran (also written *Qur'an*) is the infallible Word of God, expressing God's will for all humankind: final, perfect, and complete."[190] The story of the inception of the Koran is a simple one, and one we alluded to earlier. "Muslims believe that the angel Gabriel revealed the *Qur'an* to Muhammad over an approximately twenty-year period, from his call to be a prophet until his death in 632 CE. The words of the *Qur'an* were *given to* Muhammad, not *written* by him. Its only author is God, and every word comes from God."[191]

Unlike the Hebrew Bible and the Christian New Testament, the Koran has very little narrative. Its 114 chapters (often called *surahs*) contain the "wisdom" that Muhammad proclaimed during his life. This makes the Koran a manual on how to live, since it treats topics ranging from how to lead a holy life to proper conduct of social matters. The Koran offers counsel in both spiritual and practical topics because Islam does not distinguish between religious, social, and political life. Prothero expands on this idea when he writes, "Islam is a way of life as well as a religion. The Quran tells Muslims not just how to worship Allah, but also how to lend money, divide estates, enter into contracts, and punish criminals."[192] The eclectic nature of the Koran has led some observers to suggest that the Koran is the most memorized book in the world. "To this day there is great prestige in memorizing the text, and one who knows it in its entirety is called *hafiz* (literally 'guardian')."[193] The Koran is so venerated by Muslims that they would never write in the book or damage it in any way. In 2011 this uncompromising devotion to the Koran caused violence to erupt in Afghanistan and other places after an evangelical Protestant pastor in Florida burned a copy of the Koran.

Submission.   In its most basic form, Islam is a religion based on the idea of *submission*. It is often said that people who are Muslims are those who have submitted themselves to God. This notion is tied to the overarching precept of one God. Daniel and Mahdia offer a synopsis of this important belief: "*Islam* itself means 'submission' to God and His will. The Koran emphasizes over and over the majesty of God, the beneficence that He has shown to human beings in particular, the acts of obedience and gratitude that creatures owe in return to their Creator, and the rewards that await the faithful at the end of time."[194]

Predestination.   So prevailing is their belief in the supremacy of God that Muslims believe that Allah is aware of everything that happens and that events in life are predestined by his will. This conception of a "Divine Creed" (called *Al-Qadar*) is predicated on four important Islamic principles:

- God is aware of everything.
- God is the creator of everything.
- God has documented all that has happened.
- "Whatever God wills to happen happens, and whatever He wills not to happen does not happen."[195]

Demonstrating their strong belief in fate, Muslims frequently employ the phrase "*in sha'a Allah*" (if God wills it) and the word *inshalle* ("God willing"). These utterances represent the Islamic theological concept that destiny unfolds according to God's will. Farah points out that "The sayings of the Prophet are replete with his insistence on God's role as preordainer and determiner of all that takes place."[196] For example, the Koran admonishes: "No soul can ever die except by Allah's leave and at a time appointed...."[197] "Thy God hath created and balanced all things, and hath fixed their destinies and guided them...."[198] The devout Muslim accepts that God's will directs everything.

Judgment

For Muslims, their present life is only preparation and trial for their next domain of existence. "Muslims believe in a Judgment Day on which each person will be sent by God to either paradise or to hell."[199] Hence, for Muslims life is a kind of "impending judgment." The Koran states this crucial core concept in many different places and in a variety of ways. Here is but a small sampling:

- "And those who believe and do good deeds, they are the dwellers of Paradise, they dwell therein forever." (Koran 2:82)
- "And whoever seeks a religion other than Islam, it will not be accepted from him and he will be one of the losers in the Hereafter." (Koran 3:85)
- "Those who have disbelieved and died in disbelief, the earth full of gold would not be accepted from any of them if it were offered as a ransom. They have a painful punishment, and they will have no helpers." (Koran 3:91)

The message in all the above is clear—have one's good deeds outweighed the bad deeds? As we will see later in the chapter, Paradise awaits those who have followed God's wishes, while hell is the place where all others must spend eternity. The Koran makes it very clear that merely professing Islam is not enough. In fact, some of the cruelest of all punishments in the afterlife fall on those who were hypocrites during their lives.

Five Pillars of Islam

An important core assumption for Muslims deals with the *Five Pillars of Islam*. These five pillars disclose important beliefs, values, and perceptions of how Muslims see both this world and the next. The pillars are thought of as an "outline of specific patterns for worship as well as detailed prescriptions for social conduct, to bring remembrance of God into every aspect of daily life and practical ethics into the fabric of society."[200] Because the pillars are the umbrella under which all Muslims stand, Muslims who are scattered throughout the world are able to see themselves as a "family of believers."

Because the pillars are translated into action, it is important for students of intercultural communication to be aware of the content of these precepts. "The Five Pillars of Islam" are (1) statement of belief, (2) prayer, (3) alms, (4) fasting, and (5) pilgrimage.

Statement of Beliefs (Shahadah).   Repetition of the creed (*Shahadah*), often called the *Profession of Faith*, means uttering the following statement: "There is no God but Allah, and Muhammad is the Prophet of Allah." This short sentence represents a condensed synopsis of basic Islamic beliefs. The first part of this pronouncement expresses the primary principle of monotheism, and the second element reinforces the Muslim trust in Muhammad, thus validating the Koran. These words, in Arabic, are heard everywhere Muslims practice their faith. They are also the first words a child hears at birth and are repeated throughout life.[201] These declarations affirm the notion that the person accepts the idea of one God and that Muhammad was that God's messenger to humanity. The next four pillars are often conceived of as the "action" dimension of *Shahadah* since they demand a series of specific behaviors.

Prayer (Salat).   Prayer is a central ritual, performed five times a day—at dawn, at noon, in the mid-afternoon, after sunset, and before retiring. The prayer ritual is very structured, as described by Nydell:

> Prayer is regulated by ritual washing beforehand and a predetermined number of prostrations and recitations, depending on the time of day. The prayer ritual includes standing [facing toward Mecca], bowing, touching the forehead to the floor (which is covered with a prayer mat, rug, or other clean surface), sitting back, and holding the hands in cupped position, all while reciting sacred verses. Muslims may pray in a mosque, in their home or office, or in public places.[202]

Even when there is no mosque available, Muslims will stop what they are doing and pray. As Prothero notes, "Muslims can…be seen putting down prayer rugs at taxi stands at London's Heathrow Airport and inside office buildings in Dubai."[203]

Almsgiving (Zakat).   The rationale for almsgiving is deeply rooted in the Islamic tradition, and is predicated on the notion that everything is part of God's domain. This means that even wealth and material possessions are only held by human beings because of God's will. "Alms are related to the nature of God, who is merciful and requires mercy in his worshipers toward one another. Compassion toward weak and defenseless persons of the community is a reflection of the compassion of God."[204] Like so much of ritual, there are some deeper meanings imbedded in the act of almsgiving. "Consideration for the needy is part of Islam's traditional emphasis on equality. In the mosque, all are equal; there are no preferred pews for the rich or influential—all kneel together."[205]

Fasting (Sawm).   Fasting is a tradition observed throughout the holy month of Ramadan. During this period, Muslims do not eat, drink, engage in sexual activity, or smoke between sunrise and sunset. People who are in ill health, women who are pregnant or nursing, and the elderly are excused from fasting. While Muslims believe that fasting has health benefits, "the primary emphasis is less on abstinence and self-mortification as such than on spiritual self-discipline, reflection, and the performance of good works."[206]

Ramadan is also used to encourage families to emphasize family and social relationships during this period. "In the evening after breaking the fast, Muslims socialize, discussing family, community, national and international affairs and reaffirming their values, customs and traditions."[207]

Pilgrimage (Hajj).   The fifth pillar of Islam involves a pilgrimage to Mecca (in Saudi Arabia) that every Muslim, if financially and physically able, is to make as evidence of his or her devotion to Allah. The trip involves a series of highly symbolic rituals designed to "both celebrate and reinforce the unity of Muslims."[208] This feeling of unity is reinforced by the fact that all the participants, who number in the millions, wear the same color garments. The pilgrims circle the *Kabha* (a square stone building believed to have been built by Abraham, who struggled against idol worship) seven times.[209] This act, much like the actions associated with all the other pillars of Islam, reaffirms the strong belief Muslims have in their religion. Caner and Caner speak of the power of these pillars noting, "The five pillars act as a tapestry that gives Muslims a portrait of their task in life, a journey that they hope ends as it begins—as a newborn baby free from all sins."[210]

Cultural Expressions of Islam

The question now is, how does theology get translated into the way Muslims live their lives? We admit that the line between religion and worldly events is often a thin one, yet there are clues that unite the two. We now search for some of those clues.

The Message and Response to *Jihad*.   What we are seeing this decade is that "Of all the terms used in the world's religions, none is as controversial as *jihad*."[211] A *National Geographic* article echoes the notion: "*Jihad* is a loaded term—and a concept that illustrates a deep gulf of miscommunication between Islam and the West. There are those in each community who see jihad as a clash of civilizations—and act on those beliefs."[212] This debate over what *jihad is* plagues U.S. foreign policy as well as the perceptions of most American citizens.[213] Part of the misinterpretation and fear is due in part to the Islamic extremists who employ the word *jihadists* as a rhetorical device to inflame the passions of their followers and to threaten their adversaries. The world has seen this confrontational use of the word on numerous occasions. Osama bin Laden used the word as a rallying cry to justify numerous attacks against the United States and other countries. Even today, Iran's leaders and the opposition forces fighting in Afghanistan are invoking the notion of a *jihad* against Israel and the United States. By linking *jihad* to martyrdom, they create a powerful weapon.

The variety of meanings for the word *jihad* goes back centuries. A reading of the Koran, and interpretations advanced by *imams* (Muslim prayer leaders), reveals two meanings for the word, both of which are used by followers of the faith. One, *inner jihad*, deals with the individual, and describes "the internal struggle each Muslim should engage in to improve himself or herself, to submit to God and restrain from sinful impulses."[214] It is "the battle all individuals wage against their own baser instincts."[215]

It is the second interpretation, the *outer jihad*, which causes problems both in and out of the Islamic faith. This meaning "covers all activities that either defend Islam or else further its cause."[216] Hence, early wars that Muslims engaged in to bring new lands or peoples under Islam were known as *jihad wars*. Muslims suggest that these wars were similar to the Christian crusades. One of the most famous of these wars is discussed by Armstrong who points out that Arabs, in the name of Islam, "waged a Jihad against their imperial masters the Ottomans, believing that Arabs, not Turks, should lead the Muslim peoples."[217] Even today many Arab Muslims believe that

> ## CONSIDER THIS
>
> The Islamic notion of jihad *includes more than one interpretation.*
> *What are some of those interpretations?*

their land and their faith are in danger if they do not wage war against the West. It is easy to see how this orientation contributes to a militant vision of the Islamic tradition. Regardless of the merits of this line of reasoning, it behooves you to understand the importance that *jihad* carries in the Islamic tradition and to try to discover which of the two meanings is being employed when a person speaks about a *jihad.*

A Complete Way of Life. Another significant cultural manifestation of Islam is that it is a complete way of life. It must be remembered that Muhammad was both a political figure and a religious prophet. In Islam, religion and social membership are therefore inseparable. Islam instructs people on the best way to carry out their lives in private, social, economic, ethical, political, and spiritual arenas. That is, "Islamic law makes no distinction between religion and society, but governs all affairs, public and private."[218] Nydell further develops this idea in the following: "An Arab's [Muslim's] religion affects his or her whole way of life on a daily basis. Religion is taught in schools, the language is full of religious expressions, and people practice their religion openly, almost obtrusively, expressing it in numerous ways."[219] Viewed from this perspective, Islam is a codification of all values and ways to behave in hundreds of circumstances, ranging from child rearing to eating practices, to preparing for bed, to the treatment of homosexuals, to views toward modesty.[220] This sort of all-inclusive theological orientation provides its members with "an immense body of requirements and prohibitions concerning religion, personal morality, social conduct, and political behavior. Business and marital relations, criminal law, ritual practices, and much more were covered in this vast system."[221]

We can turn to Sharia Law (often spelled Shariah) as yet another example of how Islam is a complete way of life that fuses religious theology directly with worldly affairs. That is, "Historically, Muslims have not separated the sacred and secular, so Shariah extends into all aspects of life—family, society, economics and politics."[222] Just what is Sharia law and why has it been a major topic of discussion in the media? Sharia law (often referred to as Muslim or Islamic law) is a legal code derived basically from three sources, the Koran, the *Hadith* (sayings from Muhammad), and *fatwas* (rulings of Islamic scholars).[223] These are very specific laws that deal with nearly all phases of human behavior. They fall into five categories: obligatory, meritorious, permissible, reprehensible, and forbidden. The controversy surrounding these laws centers on two related issues. The first is the degree of influence they have over contemporary Muslims and some of the "punishments" associated with violating any of the laws. Many people in the West, and some in the Muslim community, believe these laws violate basic human rights, particularly when applied to the treatment of women and those people being punished for what would be considered minor crimes by Western standards. The second half of the controversy is a relatively new one. Simply stated, there is a belief among some Americans that these laws will find their way into non-Muslim countries. Many states and communities in the United States believe that Sharia law requires that it be imposed on non-Muslims as well as Muslims.[224] Muslims, of course, see Sharia law differently. They turn to the actual meaning of the Arabic word *Sharia* ("a clear path") to help explain its importance in the life of all Muslims. For them, the "path" is a series of mandates that benefits humanity by offering people structure, specific guidelines, and a divine connection to the past.

CONSIDER THIS

What is meant by the phrase "Islam is a complete way of life"? What are some examples that would validate the truth of this assertion?

Gender

Although we discussed gender and Islam as it applied to families in Chapter 3, we now look at the religious aspects of this topic. The subject of gender is difficult to examine and is also charged with controversy. It seems that "of all the Western criticism of Islam, one of the most persistent has been that it is hostile to women."[225] The criticism and confusion surrounding this topic have made it hard to study the tie between gender and Islam objectively. It appears that "A priori assumptions, preconceptions, and stereotypes regarding Middle Eastern women abound, and generalizations about women in a region as internally diverse as the Middle East continue to predominate in current discourse."[226] Part of the confusion, both within and outside the Islamic world, stems from the fact that the Koran, as well as other religious teachings, offer a variety of interpretations on the subject of women. Those who support a traditional and strict reading of the Koran point to 4:34, which states: "Men are superior to women on account of qualities with which God has gifted the one above the other, and on account of the outlay they make from their substance for them." Sedgwick summarizes this restricted view of women, by Western standards, when he writes, "Islam takes it as axiomatic that men are stronger than women, not only physically but also mentally and morally, and that women are therefore in need of male protection and guidance."[227] There are, of course, other signs of this viewpoint within the Muslim faith. For example, according to Islamic tradition, women cannot teach men, "so Muslim women who have trained in the ways of the Koran teach only girls and other women."[228] In most countries, "Islam encourages women to pray at home" instead of at the mosques with men.[229]

As noted, there are millions of Muslims, both men and women, who have a different interpretation, not only of what the Koran says, but also of the role of women in daily life. With regard to the Koran, many Muslims turn to 33:35, which "teaches that men and women are equal before God in terms of their religious and moral obligations and rewards."[230] They also believe that the Koran's position on women is one that seeks to protect them. In addition, as Elias writes, "Despite the inegalitarian social structure that dominates the majority of Islamic societies, women from all backgrounds usually embrace rather than reject their religious tradition."[231]

In spite of these different perceptions and interpretations of the Koran, worldwide attitudes regarding gender roles in many Islamic countries are in a state of flux. In places such as Syria, Saudi Arabia, and Indonesia[232] women are actively protesting and demanding more rights. Recently in Egypt, hundreds of women marched in support of International Women's Day.[233] Many of these protests are producing results. Within Iraq, women are now taking a role in the new National Assembly, and women in Kuwait were granted voting rights.[234] Women have held high governmental positions and even been heads of state in places such as Pakistan, Bangladesh, Indonesia, and Turkey.[235] And "in Morocco, Tunisia, Egypt, Lebanon, Syria, Jordan and Iraq, educated women have been active at all levels of society."[236] In the United States, not only was Miss USA an Islamic woman, but modest swimsuits are now being sold so that Muslim women can enjoy the beach. While these changes seem minor, they do reflect, at least in the United States, a view that many "more Muslim women are joining the debate on gender issues."[237]

This section on Islam and gender ends reminding you of two points. First, when observing any cultural difference, it is important not to allow ethnocentrism to direct your evaluation. As an "outsider," you are applying Western models to the Islamic culture's attitude toward women. While you might find it strange for women to cover their hair with the *hijab*, Muslim women might have a difficult time understanding why so many women in the United States use dye to alter the natural color of their hair. Finally, broad generalizations regarding gender often overlook regional differences. For example, the life of a village woman residing in rural Afghanistan is very different from the life of a well-educated Palestinian who is socially and politically active within her community.

Islamic Notions about Death

The idea of death and an afterlife are crucial elements of the Islamic religion. We highlighted some of those elements when we discussed the Islamic view of "judgment." It is important that we return to that topic, particularly due its current relevance; this issue has been the subject of countless news reports due to the prominence of suicide bombers. Part of the curiosity stems from attempts to comprehend the motivation behind bombings that take the lives of women and children, as well as that of the bomber. Looking at the concepts of the "final judgment" and afterlife offers some clues to this complex question. The theology of Muslims, Jews, and Christians, with some variation, all include the Day of Judgment (the Day of Resurrection) when all people will be resurrected for God's judgment according to their beliefs and deeds. However, as Robinson and Rodrigues point out, "Of the western religious traditions, Islam offers the most detailed description of the afterlife, where a beautiful paradise awaits the righteous and a hideous hell imprisons and punishes the wicked."[238] As we noted elsewhere, this concept of a moral code, and its tie to an afterlife, is one of the most fundamental and crucial elements of Islamic doctrine. That is to say, "Judgment, reward, and punishment are central points in Islam and are the foundation upon which its entire system of ethics is based."[239] The result of Allah's judgment determines whether each person will be sent to heaven or hell. Islamic teaching makes it very clear that these two places are poles apart. "Heaven abounds in deep rivers of cool, crystal water, lush fruit and vegetation, boundless fertility, and beautiful mansions with gracious attendants. Hell's portrayal is at times equally graphic with its account of molten metal, boiling liquids, and the fire that splits everything to pieces."[240]

While many Muslim scholars point out that these two descriptions are only metaphors for an afterlife, the two depictions nevertheless underscore the importance of good and evil, and the consequences of each, in Islamic teaching. We should also note that there is debate among Muslim *imams* and scholars on the issues of suicide bombers, martyrdom, and heaven. Many *imams* in the leadership of Al Qaeda see the actions of these bombers as an extension of a *jihad* against the enemies of Islam. They tell suicide bombers that they are dying to save Islam from the West. Other Muslims maintain that the Koran does not approve of the killing of innocent people. Regardless of the authenticity of these positions, one thing seems certain: Those who become suicide bombers and engage in these horrific and gruesome acts do so because they believe their actions will be rewarded in heaven. For this group, death in the name of Allah assures a place in heaven.

HINDUISM

Hinduism, with almost a billion followers, is the world's oldest known religion—dating back almost 4000 years.[241] In spite of its many followers and long history, Hinduism, because it is so very different from Western worldviews, remains a mystery to most "outsiders." Part of that mystery is that Hinduism as a "religion has no single founder, creed, teacher, or prophet acknowledged by all Hindus as central to the religion, and no single holy book is universally acclaimed as being of primary importance."[242] Boorstin explains this view when he writes:

> Western religions begin with a notion that One—One God, One Book, One Son, One Church, One Nation under God—is better than many. The Hindu, dazzled by the wondrous variety of the creation, could not see it that way. For so multiplex a world, the more gods the better! How could any one god account for so varied a creation?[243]

Hinduism is difficult to pin down. As Smart points out, "Even to talk of a single something called Hinduism can be misleading, because of the great variety of customs, forms of worship, gods, myths, philosophies, types of rituals, movements, and styles of art and music contained loosely within the bounds of a single religion."[244] In short, Hinduism "lacks both a single canonical text accepted by all followers and an elite who exert control over the development of its fundamental beliefs and practices."[245]

A fascinating aspect of Hinduism is that despite the diversity we have been talking about, there are some precepts and concepts that partially explain the worldview.

Origins

Providing an accurate history of Hinduism is problematic. First, Hinduism had its creation long before people were maintaining written records. Second, the lack of a single founder and text makes it difficult to isolate a specific chronology. Even with these limitations, most historians trace the origins of Hinduism to a time four thousand years ago when a group of light-skinned Aryan Indo-European tribes invaded what is now northern India.[246] As these Aryans moved into the Indus Valley, a blending of cultures took place, since as "they mixed with native peoples, they shared customs, traditions, rites, symbols, and myths."[247] These beginnings were "marked not by remarkable personalities (although there must have been many) and great proselytizing movements, but rather by the composition of orally transmitted sacred texts expressing central concepts of what we now call Hinduism."[248] Because of the message contained in these texts, and their significance to Hinduism, we now examine some of those "central concepts."

Sacred Texts

We have already mentioned that Hinduism is not only the oldest of all religions, but also the most diverse. Van Voorst speaks of that diversity when he writes, "Vast in size, varied in usage, and profound in influence, many scriptures have been chanted, heard, taught, and repeated for three thousand years."[249] Looking at some of the scriptures will help to develop insight into this intriguing religion.

The Vedas. The oldest and most fundamental scriptures are called the *Vedas*. For thousands of years the wisdom concerning what is now Hinduism was transmitted orally. In fact, one definition of *Vedas* actually means "hearing." The Vedas are composed of four books that seek to "transmit the ancient revelations in a series of hymns, ritual texts, and speculations composed over a period of a millennium beginning ca. 1400 BC."[250] These four books, with their philosophical maxims and spiritual guidance, are important because they not only deal with the spiritual dimensions of Hinduism, but they also offer insights into the cultural life in India thousands of years ago.

The Upanishads. Sometime between 800 and 400 BCE another important group of Hindu texts appeared. They are called the *Upanishads*. These books, written in both prose and verse, are highly metaphysical. These texts were instrumental in shaping many of the philosophical beliefs of the Hindu religion. These are the texts that teachers use to pass on the messages of *Upanishads*. In fact, "The literal meaning of *Upanishad*, 'sitting near devotedly,' brings picturesquely to mind an earnest disciple learning from his teacher."[251] The text stresses issues of faith dealing with notions of reality, the "Oneness" of everything in the universe, the role of one's soul, and the importance of contemplation and mediation. Usha elaborates on the power of the *Upanishads* when he writes, "The *Upanishads* teach the knowledge of God and record the spiritual experiences of the sages of ancient India."[252]

The Bhagavad-Gita. Written around 540 to 300 BCE, the *Bhagavad-Gita* is a lengthy poem of dialogue between a warrior, Prince Arjuna, and the god Lord Krishna.[253] This eighteen-chapter book, revealing the wisdom of Krishna, teaches how to become aware of the "Supreme Reality," a reality that can be known through the pursuit of knowledge, devotion, altruistic behavior, and contemplation. Robinson and Rodrigues speak to the importance of the *Bhagavad-Gita* when they write, "In the two millennia since its composition, the *Gita*, as it is often called, has served as a source of inspiration for countless numbers, from Hindu philosophers and politicians such as Shankara and Mahatma Gandhi, to Western authors and poets such as Henry David Thoreau and T.S. Eliot."[254] A major characteristic of the text is that it reinforces the very core of Hinduism: that God is an exalted, stirring, and sublime force within us. Because God is within us, we can rise above our mortal limitations and be liberated. The *Bhagavad-Gita* also speaks of three courses you can follow to accomplish this liberation: (1) the discipline of knowledge, *jnana-yoga*, (2) the discipline of action, *karma-yoga*, and (3) the discipline of devotion, *bhakti-yoga*.[255]

Core Assumptions

As is the case with all religions, the messages and lessons advanced by the sacred texts, teachers, and prophets of Hinduism are diverse, numerous, and beyond the scope and purpose of this chapter. However, Hinduism does contain some central teachings that you will find useful when interacting with someone who is Hindu.

Divine in Everything. For Hindus "The universe is interconnected across time and space. Rocks, plants, animals and human are all interrelated."[256] The essence of this worldview is a belief that God is within each being and object in the universe, and that the spirit of each soul is divine. Further, Hindus hold that the goal of life is to become sensitive to the divine in its many forms. Narayanan further develops this concept of the divine when he writes, "The belief that the divine is not only beyond gender and name, but also beyond number, has resulted in its manifestation in many shapes and forms: as human or animal, as trees, or as combinations of these beings."[257] This view of a vast number of deities makes Hindus among the most religious people in the world because they find the divine in everything. As Boorstin notes, "The Hindu is dazzled by a vision of the holy, not merely holy people but places like the Himalayan peaks where the gods live, or the Ganges which flows from Heaven to Earth, or countless inconspicuous sites where gods or goddesses or unsung heroes showed their divine mettle."[258]

Ultimate Reality.   Hinduism is based on the fundamental assumption that the material world, the one we can touch and see, is not the only reality. Instead, they hold that there are other realities that lead to spiritual advancement, and reveal the true nature of life, the mind, and the spirit. The Hindu view is that a person's perception of the world is simply an illusion. Hence, Hindus are not satisfied with what they see or hear. This view is reflected in the Hindu saying, "Him the eye does not see, nor the tongue express, nor the mind grasp." Counsel for such an orientation even comes from the *Bhagavad-Gita* in the following advice: "A man of faith, intent on wisdom, His senses restrained, will wisdom win."[259] An extension of this point of reference leads Hindus to believe that finding satisfaction in the material and physical world (the Western notion of reality) might gratify you temporarily, but eventually the satisfaction of that world will "wear out." To experience true happiness, bliss, or liberation (what Hindus call *nirvana*), one needs to discover the spiritual existence found outside traditional concepts of reality. Kumar and Sethi summarize this orientation in the following: "The normative implication of this principle is that individuals should strive to unite their inner self with the ultimate reality. The attempt to realize this unity constitutes the heart of spiritualism in the Indian subcontinent."[260]

Brahman.   The notion of *Brahman* is actually an extension of the previous paragraph, since many Hindus believe "reality is Brahman."[261] Hence, Brahman becomes an all-inclusive, transcendental reality that sustains and supports everything. This definitive reality is seen as "the sacred Power which is both the sacrificial process and in the cosmos."[262] It is a special knowledge about "the truth of things" that allows someone to be enlightened. Jain and Kussman offer a summary of this important concept: "Brahman is the ultimate level of reality, a philosophical absolute, serenely blissful, beyond all ethical or metaphysical limitations. The basic Hindu view of God involves infinite being, infinite consciousness and infinite bliss."[263]

Multiple Paths.   In many respects, Hinduism is a conglomeration of religious thought, values, and beliefs. As we discussed earlier, Hinduism does not have a single founder or an organizational hierarchy. Among Hindus one may find magic, nature worship, animal veneration, and an unlimited number of deities. Because of this eclectic approach to "God," Hinduism has been able to present various paths to those asking

CONSIDER THIS

What do Hindus mean when they say, "Truth does not come to the individual; it already resides within each of us"?

the eternal questions about life and death. There is even a famous Hindu expression: "Truth is one, but sages call it by various names."[264] McGuire offers an explanation of the diverse nature of Hinduism in the following paragraph: "Indeed, Hinduism is a way of life that encourages acceptance of multiple representations of deity, multiple religious functionaries and multiple authorities, multiple understandings of duty and proper devotion, multiple allegiances to autonomous congregations, and multiple (and changeable) devotional practices and holy places."[265]

Because of this multiple-paths approach of Hinduism, it has been called a "religion which offers many beliefs and practices to all comers."[266] This all-inclusive orientation has been responsible for Hinduism's popularity even outside of India.

Cultural Expressions of Hinduism

As we have stressed throughout this chapter, a person's religion is never entirely confined to a church, mosque, synagogue, or temple. Our thesis has been that religion is something people do. This is particularly true of Hinduism. Let us now turn to some of the ways the religion is reflected in everyday life.

Complete Way of Life.   It has been said that Hinduism is a holistic way of life. This idea is also expressed in the Hindu saying by Swami Vivekananda: "The Hindu man drinks religiously, sleeps religiously, walks religiously, marries religiously, and robs religiously." The reason behind Vivekananda's observation is that Hinduism pervades every part of a person's life. In "Hinduism religion is not separate from living. It is living itself. God does not exist in temples and sacred places only."[267] One of the reasons Hinduism is so pervasive in a Hindu's life is because the early stages of Hinduism saw a mixing of cultures and of gods.[268] In this sense, as Venkateswaran points out, "Hinduism is not merely a religion. It encompasses an entire civilization and a way of life, whose roots date back prior to 3000 BCE."[269]

As we have been highlighting, Hinduism is not simply a theology; it is a complete way of life that shows itself in a multiplicity of ways. The sacred writings of this tradition, for example, speak of the arts, medicine, health, science, governance, and a host of other cultural issues. In addition, while temples are a popular place for worship, it is the daily activity in the home that best reflects Hindu practices as an important and integral part of life. Henderson indicates the significance of the home in the following explanation: "Hinduism wears the face of family and home. A home's most sacred spot is its hearth. Most rituals occur amid daily life. The acts of bathing, dressing, and eating are connected to ritual purity."[270]

Dharma.   *Dharma*, because of its influences on how people live and treat each other, represents an important concept of Hinduism. As DeGenova points out, "Dharma is perhaps the most influential concept in Indian

CONSIDER THIS

Below is a list of some of the issues that all worldviews and religious traditions deal with. Think about your own worldview and religious tradition as you examine the list. Compare your answers to those of two other traditions.

a.   Which are supreme, the laws of God or the laws of nature?
b.   Is unhappiness an accepted part of life?
c.   Is there an afterlife?
d.   What is the role of fate in life? What is the role of free will?
e.   Are women superior to men?
f.   Is one's station in life determined by birth?
g.   What is evil?

culture and society."[271] In fact, Dharma is actually "a Sanskrit term variously translated as duty, law, justice, truth, order, righteousness, virtue, ethics and even religion."[272] The applications of Dharma pertain to both religious and communal responsibilities. There are, in fact, three rather specific applications of Dharma contained within the various sacred writings: "The first relates to natural law or the laws governing the spiritual-physical universe, the second relates to the laws governing society; and the third relates to the laws governing the individual."[273] The laws of Dharma provide people guidance on how to behave, perform their vocational obligations, act during various life cycles, and even how old people should treat those younger than they.[274]

An extension of the belief and command of Dharma is the idea that if you go against Dharma, which is seen as a cosmic norm, you will produce bad Karma. Because Karma affects this life and subsequent lives (through reincarnation), most Hindus seek to live a virtuous life and follow their Dharma.

Karma. Having just alluded to Karma we now explain the concept in more detail, especially since the term is generally misunderstood by non-Hindus. The word is now part of popular culture and takes on a host of meanings that only serve to distort the concept. In its general sense, Karma, which comes from a Sanskrit word meaning "action," refers to the idea that every action has an equivalent reaction that can either be immediate or at some future time. The future time can even be in a different lifetime. At the heart of the belief in Karma is the view that reaction and action can have either good or bad consequences. Prothero expands on these ideas, writing: "Just as, according to the law of gravity, what is dropped from a tree will fall to the ground, according to the law of Karma, evil actions produce punishments and good actions produce rewards."[275] The final resolution to a person's Karma has long-range implications. That is to say, a person "with bad Karma could be reborn many times into lower castes of humans, or even lower animals, and then not released until he or she has been reborn in the Brahmin, or priestly caste."[276] The ethical implications of Karma are obvious. Each new birth is not a matter of chance, but rather results from good or bad actions in prior lives.

Four Stages of Life. Another cultural manifestation of Hinduism is referred to as the "Duties of the Four Stages of Life." While the writings concerning these stages go back thousands of years, many Hindus attempt to carry out the specific duties even today. These stages represent phases the individual passes through as a means of gathering enough wisdom to become "free" and "spiritual." People have "specific responsibilities associated with each of these phases, and it is their duty to fulfill them."[277] Before we mention the four stages, we should point out that very few people make it past stages one and two, since the last two stages make enormous demands on the individual. However, the specific guidelines for each stage continue to help shape a Hindu's life. In somewhat abbreviated form let us look at these four stages: (1) In the *student* stage a young boy, usually between the ages of eight and twelve, studies the Vedas while serving an apprenticeship with a teacher. (2) The *householder* is that phase in a male's life when he builds his family and attempts to live a highly spiritual and ethical life while meeting his obligations as husband and father. (3) The *forest dweller* is one who has met his obligations to his family and society and is now ready to leave all personal attachments and begin intensive study and meditation. (4) The *ascetic*, an optional state, is when the Hindu denounces the

For Hindus, "Four Stages of Life" represent phases the individual passes through as a means of gathering enough wisdom to become "free" and "spiritual."

Steve Harrington

world and is completely independent from all people and possessions and unites with Brahman. In short, he is liberated from ordinary life.[278]

There are many women who also seek to carry out the duties associated with the Four Stages of Life. In most instances, they only follow the first three stages. They become students and take instruction in the religious duties associated with this first stage. As a householder, a woman's duties are somewhat different from those of her husband, yet she still strives to live a spiritual life. Some women even attempt to become forest dwellers. However, as noted, they are not expected to enter the ascetic stage.[279]

Notions about Death

Although we have already mentioned some perceptions regarding death and Hinduism when we discussed Dharma and Karma, we now return to that topic since it is instrumental in how Hindus approach life. The core of a Hindu's conviction regarding death is summarized by Narayanan in one short statement: "Hindus believe in the immortality of the soul and in reincarnation."[280] With this basic belief as their anchor, Hindus learn not to fear death or even grieve over the death of loved ones. The rationale is clear: even though the physical body dies, a person's soul does not have a beginning or an end but simply passes into another reincarnation at the end of this life.[281] That is to say, the individual does not actually die, but rather takes on a new body—"the Eternal Self"—which cannot be destroyed. Hindus believe that the state of mind of the person just before death is imperative, demonstrating their conviction that the person continues living on after death. Were the person's thoughts at the moment of death about family and spiritual matters, or was the person thinking "evil thoughts"? The answer to this question is important to the Hindu.

Once the person dies, the body is wrapped in white cloth and cremated as quickly after death as possible. The funeral procession and ceremony are very ritualistic and involve everything from washing the deceased, to mourners bathing, to stories being told about the deceased.[282] In India, if at all possible, the ashes of the deceased person are taken by relatives and scattered into a holy river such as the Ganges.

BUDDHISM

A fifth major religious tradition that can influence intercultural communication is Buddhism. Although the followers of Buddhism are small in number (about 400 million) when compared to those of Christianity, Islam, or Hinduism, Buddhism's impact on civilization has been profound. Not only has Buddhism extended itself over cultural areas in South and East Asia, but because it is so adaptable, it has millions of followers all over the world, including over two million in the United States. What appeals to many Westerners is that, unlike most Western religions, Buddhism is "grounded in reason not faith and therefore is in harmony with the prevailing spirit of scientific empiricism."[283] Yet in spite of its popularity, many Westerners do not fully understand Buddhism. Thera, quoting the philosopher T.H. Huxley, mentions some of the reasons Westerners are bewildered by Buddhism: "Buddhism is a system which knows no God in the Western sense, which denies a soul to man, which counts the belief in immortality a blunder, which refuses any efficacy to prayer and sacrifice, which bids men look to nothing but their own efforts for salvation."[284]

Origins

While it is true that Western religions and Buddhism present very different ways of seeing the world, both share a profound core belief in the influence of a single individual who lived among the people. For Christians, Jesus offers personal guidance as a means of understanding each person's place in the world. In Buddhism, it is Buddha who is "the person who has epitomized the human situation."[285]

In spite of the fact that oral histories associated with most religious founders have often been altered and embellished, a clear picture of the history of Buddhism is accessible. Buddhism was founded by an Indian prince named Siddhartha Gautama. The story of how he became known as the Enlightened One has four essential features. The first involves his birth and his given name. "According to legendary accounts, Siddhartha's birth was accompanied by auspicious celestial signs and a wise man's prediction that the child would be successful as either a universal monarch or a great ascetic."[286] The second element in the Buddha story centers on the fact that at the time of his birth, his father was a king and the prince was born into great luxury and opulence, which he would later reject. As Siddhartha himself said, "I wore garments of silk and my attendants held a white umbrella over me."[287] The third part of the Buddha story explains that even with all his lavish surroundings, the prince felt a deep discontentment with his life. Garfinkel offers an account of what was to become a major event in the founding of Buddhism: "At age 29 the married prince, disillusioned with his opulence, ventured out of his palace and for the first time encountered old age, sickness, and death. So moved was he by this brush with the painful realities of life that he left his comfortable home to search for an end to human suffering."[288]

For the next six years, often called The Period of Enquiry, the prince engaged in deep meditation and lived an austere life as he searched for answers to explain the suffering he saw. After examining his thoughts during this period, he emerged from his self-imposed seclusion and became Buddha. As Clark notes, "Siddhartha became a Buddha (Enlightened One) in a flash of insight one day while meditating. He immediately gathered his disciples and began to teach them what he had learned."[289] This Great Renunciation produced an emotion within Siddhartha that some say formed one of the elements of Buddhism. The emotion was the feeling of complete calm and "sense of serene confidence (*prasada*) the prince experienced when he discovered there was a way to overcome the suffering of life."[290]

The fourth and final feature of the story of Buddha focuses on how he spent his life after his personal revelation. Until his death at 80 in 483 BCE, Buddha traveled throughout the Ganges Valley sharing his insights with anyone who would listen. After his death, his message was carried by his students. Buddhist missionaries were sent all through Asia, and during the next centuries Buddhism spread and took hold in Southeast Asia, China, Japan, and Korea.

Core Assumptions

As is the case with all religious traditions, there are multiple forms of Buddhism (such as Theravada, Mahayana, Zen, Pure Land, Vajrayana, and Tibetan Buddhism). Over the centuries, each culture and country adapted their existing belief system to what Buddhism had to offer. However, in spite of some minor differences, all the major schools of Buddhism share the same basic assumptions. Let us look at two of those assumptions before we examine some of the specific precepts associated with Buddhism.

First, Buddha made it clear that *he was not a God, but simply a man,* and never claimed "to be a god or savior. He [was] simply a pathfinder."[291] In fact, Buddha went so far as to suggest that "a belief in god is itself a form of human desire and clinging, a product of the ego and another cause of suffering in that it prevents a person from becoming an autonomous and free human being."[292] When Buddha was asked if he was God, the answer he offered his followers demonstrates the importance of this crucial concept to the practice of Buddhism:

"Are you a god?" they asked.

"No."

"An angel?"

"No."

"A saint?"

"No."

"Then what are you?"

Buddha answered, "I am awake."[293]

That simple response, "I am awake," tells all those who seek Buddha that the answer to life can be found in the simple act of "waking up" and becoming aware of the truths that accompany being enlightened.[294]

Second, Buddha taught that *all individuals have the potential to seek the truth on their own*. Buddha believed that people should never take any religious teaching on faith alone.[295] It is often difficult for Westerners to understand this orientation, since many Western religions stress religious direction from the clergy. Buddhism, on the contrary, challenges individuals to do their own religious seeking. Two famous Buddhist sayings reaffirm this key point: "Be lamps unto yourselves," and "Peace comes from within. Do not seek it without." This emphasis on self-reliance is explained by the Buddhist teacher Bhikkhu Bodhi when he writes, "For the Buddha, the key to liberation is mental purity and correct understanding, and for this reason he rejects the notion that we gain salvation by learning from an external source."[296] The words "external source" represent the essential message in Buddha's teaching, as you can observe in two more celebrated Buddhist maxims that stress the same point: "Betake yourself to no external refuge. Work out your own salvation with diligence," and "You are your own refuge; there is no other refuge." Bodhi explains this core assumption in the following:

> The Buddha rests his teaching upon the thesis that with the right method man can change and transform himself. He is not doomed to be forever burdened by the weight of his accumulated tendencies, but through his own effort he can cast off all these tendencies and attain a condition of complete purity and freedom.[297]

The Four Noble Truths. Once Buddha sensed he had become enlightened, he was determined to share his wisdom with others. Many of the essentials of that wisdom are found in the Four Noble Truths. As Powell notes, "The Four Noble Truths is nothing less than a distillation of the wisdom which the Buddha had gained through Enlightenment."[298] These Noble Truths, "stand as the axioms of his (Buddha's) system, the postulates from which the rest of his teachings logically derive."[299] It is important to keep in mind that while the Four Noble Truths, and the discussion of the Eightfold Path that follows, are treated as separate categories, they are interrelated in that each flows seamlessly into the other.

The First Noble Truth is that life is "suffering." Buddha speaks of the major cause of suffering, noting that "Birth is suffering, aging is suffering, illness is suffering, worry, misery, pain, distress, and despair are suffering; not attaining what one desires is suffering."[300] The basic rationale for Buddha's assertion that life is suffering is further explained by Bodhi: "The reason all worldly conditions are said to be *dukkha*, inadequate and unsatisfactory, is because they are all impermanent and unstable; because they lack any substantial or immutable self; and because they cannot give us lasting happiness; secure against change and loss."[301]

The teachers of Buddhism point out that if your life is not characterized by some degree of suffering at the moment, you only need look at the world to see the suffering of others. Contrary to Western interpretation, Buddha's philosophy is not a negative one, in spite of this first admonition using the word suffering. "The intention of this first truth is not to induce pessimism but to encourage clear, realistic observation."[302]

The Second Noble Truth concerns the roots of suffering. Buddha taught that much of our suffering is caused by craving, self-desire, attachment, anger, envy, greed, ignorance, and self-delusion regarding the nature of reality.[303] Throughout the writings of Buddha, students encounter advice regarding how to learn to see the world as it is. Buddha believed that accepting the world was a major step toward enlightenment. He would tell his students: See the false as false. The true as true. Look into your heart. Follow your nature.

The Third Noble Truth is an extension of the first two truths. It asserts that because suffering has a cause it can be eliminated. Put in slightly different terms, "If we wake up to the way the world really is, in all its flux and flow, and stop clinging to things that are by their nature running through our fingers, we can achieve nirvana."[304] Since nirvana means reaching enlightenment and moving beyond suffering, Buddhists believe it is a goal worth pursuing. By clearly seeing truth, you can put an end to suffering, ignorance, and craving. As is the case in nearly all of Buddha's counsel, the key component is the person. Notice how ideas become reinforced in the following famous instruction advanced by Buddha:

> *By your own efforts*
> *Waken yourself, watch yourself.*
> *And live joyfully.*
> *You are the master.*

The Fourth Noble Truth is often called "the remedy," since it is an explanation and prescription for the end of suffering and a path to nirvana. In many ways the central core of the teaching of Buddha deals with the Eightfold Path. Because of the importance to the Buddhist worldview, and the practical application to how one lives life, we turn to a brief discussion of the tenets of the Eightfold Path.

The Eightfold Path. As noted, the Four Noble Truths speak to the symptoms that create unhappiness and suffering, in this sense the Eightfold Path is the antidote. The Eightfold Path is a practical guide to correct behavior, and it contains the essential steps that allow each individual to be free from troublesome attachments and delusions about the nature of reality. The various elements that make up the Path are not seen as single steps, but rather they are fused—learned and practiced simultaneously. In addition, the steps are usually reduced to three categories: Wisdom, Ethical Conduct, and Mental Discipline.[305]

Wisdom

1. *Right view is achieving a correct understanding and accepting the reality and origins of suffering and the ways leading to the cessation of suffering.* This first Path sets the tone for all the others that follow, since it asks the individual to see the universe (reality) as it really is: impermanent, imperfect, and elusive.

2. *Right purpose is being free from ill will, cruelty, and untruthfulness toward the self and others*. To follow in "the path," Buddha encouraged his followers to discover any "unwholesome" ways of thinking they might have and discard them. Instead, they should develop an attitude toward the world filled with loving kindness and compassion.

Ethical Conduct

3. *Right speech.* Buddha stressed that people should use discourse that is truthful and considerate. Right speech should be free of falsehoods and slander, be honest, promote harmony, not be divisive, and be void of idle chatter.

4. *Right action* is Buddha's version of the Ten Commandments, for this principle seeks to promote moral, honorable, and peaceful behavior. Among other things, this path calls for abstaining from the taking of life, from stealing, from sexual misconduct, from lying, and from drinking intoxicants.

5. *Right livelihood* asks all disciples to avoid occupations that harm living beings and animals. That means refraining for stealing, exploiting people, and selling weapons or intoxicants. Buddha believed that these forms of livelihood were not conducive to spiritual progress.

Mental Discipline

6. *Right efforts* means cultivating and maintaining wholesome thoughts. It was Buddha's belief that allowing the mind to experience anger, agitation, and even dullness, would keep a person from cultivating mindfulness and concentration.

7. *Right mindfulness* refers to being able to manage your mind. Buddha strongly believed in mental control. He continuously urged his students to concentrate on the "here and the now." This, according to Buddha, allows one to see things as they are. There is a rather famous Buddha saying: "Do not dwell in the past, do not dream of the future, concentrate the mind on the present moment."

8. *Right concentration*, although it comes as the final entry in the Eightfold Path sequence, is one of the most important. It reminds students to aim for a calm, meditative mind. This means complete attentiveness to a single object and the achievement of purity of thought, free from all hindrances and distractions. When the mind is made still through mediation, according to Buddha, the true nature of everything is revealed.

Cultural Expressions of Buddhism

The Use of Silence. One of the teachings of Buddha that can influence intercultural communication centers on the Buddhist view toward language and silence. You got a clue regarding Buddha's view of silence in the final item of the Eightfold Path that stressed the importance of meditation. Specifically, meditation that is carried out in silence. One of the reasons for the emphasis on silence is that Buddhism requires abandonment of views generated by the use of ordinary words and scriptures. In Buddhism, language can be deceptive and misleading when a person is trying to understand the universe as it really is. Brabant-Smith explains this idea when he notes, "Ordinary language tends to deal with physical things and experiences, as understood by ordinary man; whereas Dharma language (Buddha's teaching) deals with the mental world, with the intangible non-physical world."[306] This notion finds expression in three well-known Buddhist admonitions: "Beware of the false illusions created by words," "Do not accept what you hear by report," and "Peace comes from within. Do not seek it from without." These sayings reflect Buddhists' belief that there is a supreme and wonderful truth that words cannot reach or teach. A Buddhist teacher expressed it this way: "A special transmission outside the scriptures; No dependence upon words or letters; Direct pointing at the mind of man; Seeing into one's nature and the attainment of Buddhahood."[307]

A view of language that maintains words can distort reality leads to a position that values silence as a tool for discovering truth. Echoing this notion, Chandrakanthan writes, "In the life and teachings of Buddha, true Silence leads to Truth by avoiding wordiness and wordlessness because such Silence is Truth."[308] The Dalai Lama enhances this point of view when he states, "Remember that silence is sometimes the best answer."

Impermanency. While we have already alluded to the notion of impermanency, we briefly return to it since it is a fundamental Buddhist idea. Buddha's premise is clear and simple—all events and people are subject to change, always in a state of flux, and fleeting. To present the premise more eloquently we find the words of Buddha: "Snow falls upon the river, white for an instant then gone forever."[309] He made the point that whether it be a fleeting moment in time or life's stages from birth, to childhood, to adulthood, to old age, nothing remains the same. Buddha believed that recognizing the truism that nothing is permanent would encourage his followers to appreciate the moment, and accept the tentative nature of life. By reminding his followers of the transitory nature of life Buddha was able to speak to the subject of a code of conduct that could influence human interaction. He told his followers that if you always consider that each life ends, then it will be simple to remember that even "quarrels come to an end."[310]

Karma. Buddha's teaching regarding Karma is important because it sets the tone for ethical behavior. Buddha repeatedly stressed that a person's actions had consequences. One of his most famous teachings stated: "Speak or act with a pure mind and happiness will follow you, as your shadow, unshakable." The words "follow you" offer insight into Buddha's notion of Karma, since the result of your action "can either manifest its effect in this very life or in the next life or only after several lives."[311] Buddhists have a strong belief in free-will and therefore your actions, over which you have control, determine your Karma. In fact, the actual word *Karma* "is used to denote volitional acts which find expression in thought, speech or physical deeds, which are good, evil or a mixture of both and are liable to give rise to consequences, which partly determine the goodness or badness of these acts."[312]

Buddha's way of thinking about Karma is referred to as the *law of action and reaction*. Because he did not believe in a higher being or divine intervention, he taught that people have within themselves the potential to control their own Karma. For Buddha, "All beings are the owners of their deeds (Karma), the heirs of their deeds; their deeds are the womb from which they sprang.... Whatever deeds they do—good or evil—of such they will be the heirs."[313] When Buddha speaks of "heirs," he is referring to the concept that the manifestations of one's Karma remain beyond the physical death of the person. Bogoda underscores this key point when he writes: "The only thing we own that remains with us beyond death is our Karma, our intentional deeds. Our deeds continue, bringing into being a new form of life until all craving is extinguished. We are born and evolve according to the quality of our Karma. Good deeds will produce a good rebirth, bad deeds a bad rebirth."[314]

Buddhist Notions about Death

A large portion of Buddha's teaching focuses on death. In fact, it was an awareness of the inevitability of death that prompted Buddha to engage in his quest for the "true meaning of life." Buddha believed one could not be happy in this life nor create good Karma without understanding the reality of impermanence. He once told his students, "Who, unless he be quite mad, would make plans which do not reckon with death, when he sees the world so unsubstantial and frail, like a water bubble."[315] One of the most often quoted sayings in Buddhism is the one that states, "Like a fish which is thrown on dry land, taken from his home in the waters, the mind strives and struggles to get away from the power of Death." Carse rephrases this view of Buddha's attitude about facing death as, "The classical Buddhist view of death is that it is an unavoidable feature of existence and it can cause anguish only when one attempts, in whatever way, to elude it, even if it is by way of mental speculation on the nature of death or of an eternal soul."[316]

As noted earlier, according to Buddhism, death is only an end to a temporary phenomenon. In some ways Buddhists perceive death as ending one chapter and starting another. When the organic life ends, the forces of Karma take over because they have not been destroyed—*this is rebirth*. As Ottama states it, "our past Karma is rebirth itself."[317] As pointed out during our examination of Karma, it is believed that the person's past deeds, both wholesome and unwholesome, play a role in how many times he or she is reborn. As long as the person is greedy, manifests hatred, does not control immoral behavior, and continues to engage in self-delusion, he or she will continue to produce bad Karma. Once there is enough good Karma, the person will experience nirvana. As we also noted earlier, nirvana in its unadorned state is complete bliss that releases a person from all unhappiness.

The state of a person's mind approaching death is also important in the Buddhist tradition. Most religions hold that even a seriously ill person should "keep fighting" to stay alive and avoid death as long as possible. The underlying premise for this philosophy is that death should be avoided at all costs.[318] Buddhism rejects trying to cling to life. But the idea of suicide is contrary to Buddhist teaching since the person contemplating suicide is experiencing feelings of fear, anxiety, and desperation. All of these reactions affect the person's state of mind as they approach death. For Buddha, the state of mind in which one dies is a powerful determinant of the next rebirth. At death the person should be at peace with themselves and the entire universe. While such a state is indeed difficult to accomplish, it is nevertheless what Buddha taught his students to strive for.[319]

Buddhism has no specific or dogmatic regulations regarding funerals. In fact, most funerals vary according to the type of Buddhism the deceased practiced, but in most instances the body is cremated. Buddhist families attempt to have a monk preside over the service. However, as Lamb points out, "The purpose of monks at funerals is not to pray for the deceased but to aid the bereaved and transfer 'merit' to the dead person."[320]

CONFUCIANISM

Confucianism, like all the major traditions, has played a principal role in shaping the culture of billions of people for thousands of years. Taylor reinforces the point when he writes, "The Confucian influence has stretched across the broad sweep of history from its founding to the contemporary age. Today, it is even discussed in Western circles because of its global impact on the diversity of cultures and their worldviews."[321] The breadth of those cultures is explained by Prothero when he observes: "It is impossible to understand contemporary life in mainland China, Taiwan, Hong Kong, Japan, South Korea, North Korea, Singapore, or Vietnam without reckoning with the long shadow of Confucianism."[322] Some experts have even concluded that the economic success of many of these countries over the past few decades is, in part, due to Confucianism and its emphasis on values such as concern for the future, hard work, achievement, education, merit, frugality, and cooperation.[323] The reason is that Confucianism brings its adherents "a personal and social morality that stresses the practice of key virtues such as filiality, humaneness, propriety, and faithfulness."[324]

At the outset we should point out that Confucianism, at least in the conventional sense, is not thought of as a formal religion since "Confucianism has no formal religious hierarchy such as the Vatican, no official priesthood, and almost no congregational life."[325] Confucianism began as a series of ethical precepts for the appropriate way of managing a society. If Confucianism is not a religion, what is it? Taylor gives a partial answer when he writes that it is a "system of social, political, ethical, and religious thought based on the teachings of Confucius and his successors."[326] Notice that he uses the words "religious thought" instead of the word "religion."

Confucius the Man

As was the case with Buddhism, Confucianism centers on the teachings of a single man: Confucius. The importance of this man is noted by Scarborough when he writes, "Confucius is perhaps the most influential individual in Asian history, not so much for his views on government as for his teachings on the proper relationships and conduct among people."[327] Confucius was born in China in 551 BCE. He attempted various careers early in his life, and held several government positions. However, at around the age of thirty he turned to teaching. Confucius believed that because education taught character and created a better society, it should be available to everyone. What Confucius taught grew out of his observations about the human condition in China during his lifetime. "Confucius was witness to the political disintegration of the feudal order, an era characterized by the hegemony of various states and almost constant internecine warfare."[328] In response to these observations, "Confucius asserted that government must be founded on virtue, and that all citizens must be attentive to the duties of their position."[329] McGreal points out, "People were impressed by his integrity, honesty, and particularly his pleasant personality and his enthusiasm as a teacher. Three thousand people came to study under him and over seventy became well-established scholars."[330] Those followers are important to Asian history because they carried on the work of Confucius after his death.

Core Assumptions

There are a number of principles that help explain Confucianism. First is the supposition that people are basically good and only have to learn, by example, what constitutes correct behavior.[331] Confucius suggested how to bring about this correct behavior. Specifically, he said that the best "way to actualize this goodness is through education, self-reflection, self-cultivation, and by behavior in accordance with the established norms of the culture."[332] Second, because Confucius had great faith in education, he "taught that by education even a common man could become superior."[333] Third, Confucius stressed a deep commitment to social harmony. That harmony meant fulfilling the familial and secular obligations needed to live and work together. In carrying out these relationships, Confucianism "emphasizes the individual's social relations and social responsibility over self-consciousness: people perceive themselves according to their social relationships and responsibilities as opposed to their individual being."[334] Yum notes, "Confucianism is a philosophy of human nature that considers proper human relationships as the basis of society."[335] These "proper" relationships involve such things as the protection of "face," dignity, self-respect, reputation, honor, and prestige. Finally, because Confucius strongly believed in a rigid hierarchy for all relations, he put forth five specific relationships where lower members had "the duty to honor and obey the upper members."[336] These relations were "son and father, minister and ruler, wife and husband, young and old, friend and friend."[337] This notion of "honoring upper members" often affects how Chinese interact with people of another culture. For example, Chinese students who attend universities in the United States might be reluctant to contradict, question, or even approach an American professor for fear that their action might be taken as displaying a lack of respect.

The Analects

While there are many writings attributed to Confucius, it is the wisdom contained in the *Analects* (sayings) that have been the most influential and far-reaching. Because Confucius did not write down his philosophy, it was his students and disciples who compiled his advice. These books were not written in a systematic and structured fashion, instead, the Analects were written over a fifty-year period that produced twenty books. Today, the Analects continue to exert considerable influence on East Asian values and behavior. The books teach basic Confucian values and virtues such as respect, honor, filial piety, duty, humanity, propriety, and ritual.[338] These ideals are presented in the form of aphorisms, sayings, stories, and proverbs. The importance of this work to Chinese culture was demonstrated when quotes from the *Analects* were read by hundreds of performers at the opening ceremonies of the 2008 Olympics in Beijing.

Cultural Expressions of Confucianism

As we have indicated, Confucianism teaches that the proper and suitable foundation for society is based on respect for human dignity. That dignity means respecting the proper hierarchy in social relationships among family members and within a community. Confucius set forth a series of ideals that describe his thoughts regarding these relationships. An understanding of these teachings will help you appreciate Asian perception and interaction patterns.

Jen (humanism). Most scholars agree that the idea of *jen* is the cornerstone of what Confucius taught. This core concept is directly related to the notion of reciprocity. In simple terms, *jen* "is the ideal relationship which should pertain between individuals."[339] In Confucian philosophy, *jen* is often referred to as the "humane principle." Essentially it is based on "Deep empathy or compassion for other humans."[340] This fundamental belief in the integrity of all people is a reflection of the premise that people are by nature good, and *jen* is meant to mirror that goodness. This means that regardless of one's status or personality, conflict can and should be avoided. In its place people should strive for harmony in their interactions with other people.

Li (rituals, rites, proprieties, conventions). *Li* is the outward expression of good manners. It is often thought of as the rules to be followed so that "things" are done correctly. The words associated with *li* are "*propriety, appropriateness, and conformity* (to prevailing customs)."[341] In contemporary times *li* could be as straightforward as not interrupting the person who is talking, or making sure your bow is performed properly.

Te (power). *Te* literally means power. For Confucius, it was power that was properly employed for the betterment of everyone. He strongly believed that to use power correctly, "leaders must be persons of character, sincerely devoted to the common good and possessed of the character that compels respect."[342]

Wen (the arts). Confucius had great reverence for the arts. He saw the "arts as a means of peace and as an instrument of moral education."[343] You can further observe that veneration in the following quotation attributed to Confucius: "By poetry the mind is aroused; from music the finish is received. The odes quicken the mind. They induce self-contemplation. They teach the art of sensibility. They help to restrain resentment. They bring home the duty of serving one's parents and one's prince."[344]

Confucianism and Communication

As is the case with all worldviews, Confucianism influences perception and communication in a variety of ways. Let us mention four of those ways that most directly relate to intercultural communication. First, Confucianism teaches *empathy* as it encourages people to understand the feelings of others. Perhaps you noticed that when we discussed *jen*, the word "empathy" appeared. Second, when communicating with someone who adheres to the Confucian philosophy, you should be aware of *status and role relationships*. Remember, it was the goal of Confucius "to make social relationships work without strife."[345] To accomplish that goal it was important that proper status and role relationships be maintained. Chiu and Hong explain this key element noting that Confucianism "prescribes different obligatory requirements for different role relationships; for example, loyalty of the ruled to their ruler, filial piety of sons and daughters to their parents, respect for brothers, and trust for friends."[346] Even today, these different role behaviors influence such things as using language that shows respect and status, how leaders are selected, and seating arrangements in business and educational settings.[347]

> **REMEMBER THIS**
>
> *Confucius was primarily concerned with maintaining social harmony in all interpersonal relationships.*

Third, Confucian principles manifest great concern for *ritual and protocol*. As noted earlier, social etiquette was an important part of Confucian teaching. Novak writes that "in Confucius's view, attentive performance of social ritual and everyday etiquette shapes human character in accordance with archetypal patterns."[348] In the business context, ritual and protocol are manifested in the fact that when negotiating, the Chinese feel uncomfortable if there is not structure, form, and correct manners. They believe these characteristics will preserve harmony among the participants.

Finally, Confucian philosophy tends to encourage the *use of indirect instead of direct language*. In the United States people often ask direct questions, are sometimes blunt, and frequently use the word "no." Confucian philosophy, on the other hand, encourages indirect communication. For example, "In Chinese culture, requests often are implied rather than stated explicitly for the sake of relational harmony and face maintenance."[349] Yum makes much the same point while demonstrating the link between Confucianism and talk:

> The Confucian legacy of consideration for others and concern for proper human relationships has led to the development of communication patterns that preserve one another's face. Indirect communication helps to prevent the embarrassment of rejection by the other person or disagreement among partners.[350]

Confucian Notions about Death

Our discussion of death as applied to Confucianism will be very brief when compared to other traditions. There is even a story that "when asked questions about death and an afterlife it was reported Confucius would respond with a yawn."[351] The reason for such a noncommittal response is simple. Confucius was not interested in death or an afterlife. For Confucius, a person should strive to live the best possible life while here on earth. When urged by his disciples to speak on the subject he would often offer two responses. One rather simple and one linguistically adorned. His uncomplicated explanation would say he had not finished studying about life so why delve into questions about death. The longer reply actually offered a hint into his view of the inevitability of death: "The great mountain must crumble; The strong beam must break; And the wise man withers away like a plant."[352]

While Confucius showed little interest in the topic of death, "Rites for the dead are by no means neglected by Confucians."[353] Because of his strong belief in such virtues as filial piety, honor, and formal ritual, Confucius urged his followers to engage in formal practices ranging from funerals to the building of small family shrines to honor the dead.

> **CONSIDER THIS**
>
> *Why do cultures conceive of death in so many different ways? Which orientation comes closest to your conception of death?*

RELIGION AND WORLDVIEW: A FINAL THOUGHT

It seems Homer was right when he noted that "all men need their Gods." In this chapter we demonstrated that there are a variety of those gods, some with names and some without names. As you saw, people turn to these gods to help them deal with the cosmic questions of how to live life and cope with death. We attempted to make it clear that our approach was similar to Friedman's when he wrote, "God speaks multiple languages."[354] One problem, of course, is that in the twenty-first century there are thousands of people who do not welcome a bilingual or multicultural God. This disagreement over who God is and what he or she is saying has created a number of problems. That is to say, we are now experiencing a major collision of religious and spiritual beliefs. We have seen discord and conflict between "fundamentalism and modernism," conflicts involving "the sacred and the secular," and debates full of vitriol between "religious exclusivism and religious pluralism."[355] Those who become swayed by these dichotomies do so for a host of reasons. As Prothero notes, some people seek vehemently to advance a theological point while "others stress religious differences in order to make the political point that religious civilizations are fated to clash."[356] Regardless of their motives, trying to advance rigid, extreme, and dichotomized positions in the name of a single ideology has made this a very dangerous world. It is a world where, fearing for all of us, the Dalai Lama appeals for everyone to meet their "universal responsibility" and find harmony among all the world's religions. The question we face is clear—can the world's great religions and multiple worldviews find the harmony the Dalai Lama seeks? Friedman poses the same question slightly differently: "Can Islam, Christianity, and Judaism know that God speaks Arabic on Fridays, Hebrew on Saturdays, and Latin on Sundays, and that he welcomes different human beings approaching him through their own history, out of their own history, out of their language and cultural heritage?"[357] That answer is yet to be determined.

Cultural Values: Guidelines for Behavior

There is an objective reality out there, but we view it through the spectacles of our beliefs, attitudes, and values.

DAVID G. MYERS

Values provide perspective in the best of times and the worst.

CHARLES GARFIELD

The preceding chapters provided an appreciation of the basic components of communication and culture, explained different ways culture is acquired, and outlined factors that contribute to how people from a culture see the world. This information should have provided you an understanding of culture's role in guiding your daily life. Factors such as family, history, religion, and cultural identity influence your decisions as to what to think about and how to act. It may be something mundane, such as what to wear to a summer concert, or whether to use "yes sir/ma'am" during a job interview. On the other hand, it can be quite complex, such as influencing your opinion on birth control, the Tea Party, or collective bargaining. What you think and how you react to events is based in part on how you perceive the world, which is strongly influenced by cultural values. What you consider important is often a product of values learned during childhood and these values motivate your behavior. Values are what "give a culture its distinctive quality."[1] A preference for individual freedom, such as in the United States, over collective social stability, such as in China, is normally based on cultural values.

Is there one God or many? Is it acceptable to burn the American flag? Would you eat whale meat? The attitude you hold about an opinion, a moral issue, some question of ethics, a proposed course of action, or how to behave in a particular context is strongly influenced by cultural values, and your values can conflict with those from another culture. The ability to recognize and manage this conflict plays a central role in successful intercultural communication exchanges. This chapter will make you aware of the impact of cultural values and provide understanding on how values can be different across cultures. To accomplish this we will (1) examine perception,

(2) link perception to culture (3), briefly discuss values, and (4) look at different patterns, or dimensions, of cultural values.

UNDERSTANDING PERCEPTION

The distinguished theoretical physicist Steven Hawking and his colleague contend that just as models are used in science, people construct "mental models ... in order to interpret and understand the everyday world" and the resulting perceptions are subjectively influenced because they are "shaped by a kind of lens, the interpretive structure of our human brains."[2] We agree with this and suggest that culture plays a very large role in the process. A simple illustration of culture's influence on perception is what you see when looking at the moon. Most native born Americans will visualize a human face, but many American Indians, as well as Japanese, perceive a rabbit; the Chinese claim to see a lady fleeing her husband; and Samoans report a woman weaving. What is the cause of these very different views? The reason is perception—how diverse cultures have taught their members to look at the world in different ways. Perception is how you make sense of your physical and social world, how you construct reality. As the German novelist Hermann Hesse wrote, "There is no reality except the one contained within us," and that reality has been placed in you, in part, by your culture. Perceptions give meaning to external forces by allowing you to interpret, categorize, and organize the stimuli you choose to monitor. In other words, perception is the process whereby people convert external events and experiences into meaningful internal understanding. Although the physical dimension is an important phase of perception, you must realize that the psychological aspects of perception are what help you understand intercultural communication.

As pointed out in Chapter 1, by exposing a large collection of people to *similar* experiences, culture generates *similar* meanings and *similar* behaviors. This does not mean, however, that everyone in a particular culture will see things in exactly the same way, as is discussed later in this chapter. Two examples will illustrate the interaction between culture and perception. The first contrasts culturally based communication styles.

> "As is well known, Americans and most Europeans prize frankness, detailed presentations, and lively debate based on facts as well as assumptions. In contrast, for more than a thousand years the Japanese were programmed to speak publicly only in *tatemae* [emphasizing social expectations] terms, and reveal their *honne* (real thoughts) only in private settings."[3]

From this, it is easy to imagine how a culturally uninformed American might perceive a typical Japanese speaker as being evasive, ambiguous, or even duplicitous.

The second example concerns how age is perceived across cultures. In the United States culture teaches the value of youth and rejects growing old. According to one communication researcher, "young people view elderly people as less desirable interaction partners than other young people or middle-aged people."[4] This negative view of the elderly is not found in all cultures. For example, in Middle Eastern, Asian, Latin American, and American Indian cultures, older people are perceived in a very positive light. Notice what Harris and

CONSIDER THIS

"Nigeria's ideals vary from place to place: the north is mostly Muslim, the south is mostly Christian or animist. Young and old, rural and urban, Ibo, Hausa, and Yoruba: each group sees the world differently."

The Economist, April 2011, p. 72

Moran say about the elderly in Africa. "It is believed that the older one gets, the wiser one becomes—life has seasoned the individual with varied experiences. Hence, in Africa age is an asset. The older the person, the more respect the person receives from the community, and especially from the young."[5]

It is clear from these examples that culture influences one's subjective reality and that there are direct links among culture, perception, and behavior. A more comprehensive appreciation of perception, its functions, and deficiencies can be acquired by understanding the following five characteristics offered by Alder and Gunderson.[6]

- *Perception is selective*—Because there are too many stimuli competing for the attention of your senses at the same time, you focus on selected information and filter out the rest.
- *Perception is learned*—Life's experiences teach you to see the world in certain ways.
- *Perception is culturally determined*—Culture teaches you the meaning of most of your experiences.
- *Perception is consistent*—Once you perceive something in a particular manner that interpretation does not usually change.
- *Perception is inaccurate*—You view the world through a subjective lens influenced by culture, values, and personal experiences, which tends to make you see what you want to see.

UNDERSTANDING VALUES

What you believe in becomes the foundation for your values. What you find desirable for yourself and for the society you live in is a result of your values. More precisely, "culturally shaped personal values determine how we live our lives," and people normally think these values should be adhered to not only by themselves but also by everyone else.[7] For instance, people in the United States place great value on personal freedom and individual rights, and they think people all over the world should enjoy those same opportunities. In China, however, the conservative leadership sees "social harmony and moral rectitude" taking precedence over the individual.[8] The Communist Party also rejects the Western view of human rights as an individualistic concept and considers the task of "lifting millions from poverty and ensuring [societal] stability" to be much more important than individual rights.[9]

Values are not only held by individuals, they are also the domain of the collective. Andersen and Taylor make this point clear by stating, "Values guide the behavior of people in society" and "shape the social norms in a given culture."[10] In short, values underlie the qualities and actions that people consider necessary and vital to sustain their culture. They establish the standards for maintaining a culture.[11]

The significance of values is that they inform members of a culture as to what is considered right and wrong, good and bad, correct and incorrect, appropriate and inappropriate, in almost every context of human endeavor. The following statement offers a clear explanation on the role of values: "In any society, tribal or modern, there will be values concerning how people should treat each other, how … people should work, the proper kinds of recreation, the correct relation to the supernatural, the best ways to relate to other societies, the best kinds of artifacts, how to socialize children, and so on."[12]

Institutionalized cultural values define what is worth dying for, what is worth protecting, what frightens people, what subjects are worthy of study, and which topics deserve ridicule. As discussed in Chapter 2, your values—like all important aspects of culture—are gained through a variety of sources (family, history, proverbs, media, school, church, state, etc.) and therefore tend to be broad-based, enduring, and relatively stable. When enacted, a culture's value system establishes the expected, normative modes of behavior for members of that culture and institutes the criteria used to judge people's conduct. Unfortunately, those criteria are often applied to members of other cultures who have different values, and this frequently results in misunderstandings and even conflict. Clashes arising from varying cultural values can be related to something as seemingly inconsequential as the appropriateness of eating certain foods (e.g., American and Hindu attitudes toward beef) or a more substantial matter such as capital punishment. A good rule of thumb for any intercultural encounter is, "If you consider the other person strange, they probably consider you strange."

CULTURAL PATTERNS

People and cultures are extremely complex. To help reduce this complexity, the expression *cultural patterns*, sometimes called value orientations, is used as an umbrella term to collectively talk about values, beliefs, and other orientations that characterize the dominant group within a culture. When used here, the term refers to culturally based beliefs, values, attitudes, and behaviors shared by members of a particular culture. These patterns encompass the conditions that contribute to a social group's perception of the world and how they live in that world. Cultural patterns are useful in the study of intercultural communication because they provide a systematic structure to help identify and examine reoccurring values.

Before discussing cultural patterns, a few cautionary remarks will help you to better use the patterns presented in this chapter. When using cultural patterns to help gain added insight to various ideas and activities exhibited by other cultures, you should keep in mind the following four caveats.

- *You are more than your culture*: As pointed out in Chapter 1, the dominant values of a culture may not be shared by all individuals within that culture. Factors as diverse as age, gender, education, income level, personal experiences, and others influence your view of the world. Because people are more than their culture, delineating national characteristics or typical cultural patterns is a risky endeavor due to the heterogeneity of almost all societies. Think of the many ethnic groups, religious orientations, and political perspectives that make up the U.S. population. Therefore, cultural patterns used to characterize an entire country should generally be limited to the members of the dominant culture in that nation.
- *Cultural patterns are integrated*: Because language is linear in nature, we are forced to talk about only one cultural pattern at a time. It is important, however, to realize that the patterns do not operate in isolation; they are interrelated and integrated. In other words, they act in concert. If a culture values the elderly that value gets attached to yet other values related to respect and decision making.
- *Cultural patterns are dynamic*: Any review of world history will tell you that values can evolve and produce

> ### REMEMBER THIS
>
> Cultural patterns can be seen as systems of integrated beliefs and values working in combination to provide a coherent, if not always consistent, model for perceiving the world. These patterns contribute to the way you see, think, and feel about the world and how you live in it.

cultural changes. The U.S. civil rights movement gave rise to actions that led to equal rights for women, which in turn became a model for gay rights. As globalization creates a more interconnected world, people become aware of different values. The unrest that swept many of the Arab speaking nations in early 2011 was in part a result of young people who embraced freedom, independence, and democracy—values significantly at odds with those held by the authoritarian elites. Even after recognizing the dynamic nature of culture and value systems, you need to remember that the deep cultural structures always resist change and evolve very slowly. Recall that many of the Egyptian young men demonstrating for freedom and democracy later declared that a woman's place was in the home.

• *Cultural patterns can be contradictory*: In many instances, you can find contradictory values in a particular culture. A frequent refrain in the United States is "all people are created equal," but racial prejudice toward minorities and violence directed against gays continues. Some of the most divisive issues now facing the U.S. society—abortion, gay marriage, gun rights, and school prayer—are a result of contrasting values. Indeed, the divide between conservatives and liberals is at its core a difference of ideologically based values. These types of contradictions are found in all cultures. The Bible advocates helping others and the Koran teaches brotherhood among all people. Yet, in both America and in many Muslim nations, some segments of the population are very rich and others are extremely poor.

Even with the reservations just offered, the study of cultural patterns is a worthwhile endeavor. However, when engaged in any intercultural endeavor, you should keep in mind that you are dealing with an individual and that individual may or may not evince the traits generally ascribed to that culture.

SELECTING CULTURAL PATTERNS

There are a number of cultural pattern typologies that have been compiled by scholars from various disciplines. In almost all cases, the goal was to discern patterns that would help identify and understand dissimilar cultural values. Clearly, there is some degree of overlap among the different classification systems, but each also has its own merits. For obvious reasons, we have selected cultural pattern typologies that are most often seen in the work of intercultural communication scholars. Thus, the remainder of this chapter presents a comprehensive examination of the following seven value taxonomies.

• Kohls' list of **Values Americans Live By**
• Hofstede's set of **Value Dimensions**
• Minkov's **Monumentalism versus Flexhumility**
• The Kluckhohn and Strodtbeck classification of **Value Orientations**
• The **GLOBE Study**
• Hall's categorization of **High-Context and Low-Context Orientations**
• Ting-Toomey's explanation and application of **Face and Facework**.

As you go through these different systems, two assumptions should be apparent. First, values presented in cultural patterns are points lying along a continuum rather than polar opposites. The rationale is simple—cultural differences are usually a matter of degree. Second, there is a great deal of duplication and commonality between the different cultural patterns. In fact, many of the patterns discussed here are also part of other taxonomies. This will become evident as you read through the different value classifications.

KOHLS' "THE VALUES AMERICANS LIVE BY"

Attempting to provide an overall classification for U.S. values is challenging due to the nation's diverse, multiethnic population. This problem is acknowledged by Charon's statement: "Listing American values is a difficult task because there are so many exceptions and contradictions." However, he adds, "On a general level, Americans do share a value system."[13] Kim points out that "There are similar characteristics that all Americans share, regardless of their age, race, gender, or ethnicity."[14]

Although this book leans more toward explaining other cultures, a section exploring American cultural values is also essential. For people who are not members of the dominant culture, this information will provide new insights and understanding. For members of the dominant culture, this analysis of U.S. cultural values is provided for three reasons. First, people carry their culture wherever they go, and that culture influences how they respond to the people they meet. Second, examining one's own values can reveal cultural information that is often overlooked or taken for granted. Finally, personal cultural values can serve as an important reference point for making comparisons with cultures.

Professor Kohls spent much of his life working to improve cross-cultural understanding. After living in Korea, he returned to the United States and began conducting cultural workshops for the Peace Corps. He also spent time at the U.S. Information Agency (USIA) as Director of Training. Kohls authored *The Values Americans Live By*, a 1980s monograph, intended to help expatriates adjust to living in the United States,[15] and it remains widely available on the Internet. Although written nearly 30 years ago, the thirteen values Kohl ascribed to Americans (see Figure 6.1) continue to provide an accurate characterization of the dominant U.S. culture. Each value is discussed individually.

FIGURE 6.1	Kohls' American Values Comparison[16]		
US VALUES		**FOREIGN COUNTERPART VALUES**	
Personal Control over the Environment	1	Fate	
Change	2	Tradition	
Time & Its Control	3	Human Interaction	
Equality	4	Hierarchy/Rank/Status	
Individualism/Privacy	5	Group's Welfare	
Self-Help	6	Birthright Inheritance	
Competition	7	Cooperation	
Future Orientation	8	Past Orientation	
Action/Work Orientation	9	"Being" Orientation	
Informality	10	Formality	
Directness/Openness/Honesty	11	Indirectness/Ritual/"Face"	
Practicality/Efficiency	12	Idealism	
Materialism/Acquisitiveness	13	Spiritualism/Detachment	

Source: © Cengage Learning 2013

PERSONAL CONTROL OVER THE ENVIRONMENT

The earliest European settlers arrived in America confident they could tame this wild new land and imbue it with political and religious institutions of their own choosing. No doubt many felt they were simply following God's directive in Genesis 1:28: "And God blessed them, and God said to them, Be fruitful, and multiply, and replenish the earth, and subdue it: and have dominion over the fish of the sea, and over the fowl of the air, and over every living thing that moves on the earth." The idea of exercising domain over nature and bending the environment to one's own will underwrote the physical and political resolve required to move the American frontier westward. In the United States today, the value of mastering nature can be seen in the construction of highways that crisscross the nation, dams that hold back the waters of large rivers, tunnels that go through mountains, bridges that cross wide bays, and spaceships that take men and women into outer space. The ability to control nature is considered normal and even right. This results in bold approaches to overcome all obstacles and the belief that an individual should have control over their personal environment and the ability to achieve any goal.

CHANGE

Closely aligned with control of the environment is the value of change and progress. Ever since the country's earliest days, people have subscribed to a body of forward looking beliefs and attitudes that promote progress. Various aspects of this orientation are optimism, receptivity to change, emphasis on the future rather than the past or present, faith in an ability to control all phases of life, and confidence in the perceptual ability of the common person. This passion for change and progress is evident in the way that Americans have traditionally approached the environment—as something to be conquered, tamed, or harnessed for social or personal benefit.

As discussed later in the chapter, many older, more traditional cultures, which have witnessed the rise and fall of civilizations and believe in fatalism, view change and progress as detrimental, and they often have difficulty understanding American's general disregard for history and tradition.

> This fundamental American belief in progress and a better future contrasts sharply with the fatalistic (Americans are likely to use that term with a negative or critical connotation) attitude that characterizes people from many other cultures, notably Latin, Asian, and Arab, where there is a pronounced reverence for the past. In those cultures the future is considered to be in the hands of "fate," "God," or at least the few powerful people or families that dominate the society. The idea that people in general can somehow shape their own futures seems naïve, arrogant, or even sacrilegious.[17]

TIME AND ITS CONTROL

For Americans, time is a valuable commodity, something to be measured and used wisely. Americans manage their lives according to schedules which are often divided into hourly, daily, weekly, monthly, and even yearly segments.[18] Deadlines and due dates are a constant reminder of when projects must be completed. U.S. business representatives tend to quickly move past introductory formalities and rapidly "get down to business." This is in contrast to other cultures, such as Mexico, where it is considered important to get to know the other person before initiating business discussions. In the United States, schedules are generally inflexible with meetings starting on time, moving through a defined agenda, and ending promptly. In other cultures, time is seen as more malleable, and spending time with someone can take precedence over a schedule. Even America's founding fathers considered time to be important, as this quotation from Benjamin Franklin demonstrates: "Lose no time; be always employed in something useful." The continuing value Americans place on time is illustrated by corporate practices. For instance, "Wal-Mart … pioneered the daily early-morning meeting at which all stand so as to get down to business quickly, shorten the meeting time, and then go out and execute agreements made."[19]

EQUALITY/EGALITARIANISM

Equality is perhaps the most prized American value and is enshrined in the preamble to the United States *Declaration of Independence*, which states that "all men are created equal."[20] The concept is further preserved in the *Constitution*, which states, "No Title of Nobility shall be granted by the United States."[21] The founders of our nation sought to ensure that the English social caste system (a landed, hereditary aristocracy) they had escaped could not develop in America.

Rather than focus on the literal meaning of "created equal," let us look at the ideals behind those words, which we believe were best explained by Abraham Lincoln in 1860, when he said, "We do wish to allow the humblest man an equal chance to get rich with everybody else." Thus, the value that pervades contemporary U.S. society can be termed "equal opportunity." All people should have the same opportunity to succeed in life, and the state, through laws and educational opportunities, is expected to guarantee that right.

The American value of equal opportunity translates into equality and informality in social relationships. For instance, most of the primary social relationships within a family tend to promote egalitarianism rather than hierarchy. Formality is generally not important. In secondary relationships, most friendships and coworkers are also treated as equals, usually interacting on a first name basis. People from cultures that adhere to formal social structures often find it disconcerting to work with Americans, whom they believe diminish the value of social status differences. We are not implying that Americans completely ignore hierarchy, but it is usually a secondary consideration or applied only in specific contexts, such as seating arrangements and formal introductions.

Please remember that contradictions often exist within U.S. values. The history of the United States is replete with examples of discrimination based on skin color, ethnicity, gender, level of education, social class, sexual preference, and even choice of religion. Unfortunately, today some people still continue to use these criteria to evaluate others. While she acknowledges that many Americans have experienced periods of inequality, Hanson points out "Not all citizens have had equal rights throughout the course of the country's history, but Americans nevertheless value the notion highly and strive toward this ideal."[22]

INDIVIDUALITY AND PRIVACY

Another important cultural value in the United States is individuality, often referred to as "freedom" by Americans.[23] Broadly speaking, individualism, as developed in the works of the seventeenth-century English philosopher John Locke, holds that each person is unique, special, completely different from all other individuals, and the basic unit of nature."[24] Locke's view is simple: The interests of the individual are or ought to be paramount, and all values, rights, and duties originate in individuals. Individualism commands so much influence among Americans that it gives rise to other U.S. values, such as personal initiative, self-reliance, and equal opportunity.

The emphasis on the individual is also found elsewhere in the world, but it has emerged as the cornerstone of American culture. The origin of this value has a long history. As mentioned in the discussion on U.S. history in Chapter 4, the emphasis on individualism arose from the early settlers' desire to escape the repressive conditions that then characterized European society.[25] Whether one is considering sexual, social, or ethical matters, among Americans the self holds the pivotal position. This notion is so strong that some Americans see a person who fails to demonstrate individuality as being out of step with society. Regardless if conveyed by literature, art, or American history, the message is the same—individual achievement, sovereignty, and freedom are the virtues most glorified and canonized.

Despite today's stress on personal freedom and individual rights, Americans also have a very distinct group orientation. Chapter 4 reported that one scholar had characterized the United States as a culture of voluntarism, where people participate in groups of their own choosing.[26] Gannon and Pillai bring this point out. "Americans

One indication of individualism among Americans is how they use space.

Edwin McDaniel

are also group-oriented and being part of a group or network and identifying with it is essential for success in almost all instances. Within the group structure specialization is exalted and everyone is expected to add value to the final product or service because of it."[27]

This concept is easily illustrated by using sports as a metaphor. Baseball has designated hitters, pinch hitters, and relief pitchers. Football has place kickers, specialty teams, punt returners, and others specialists. In each case, a person's specialty is used to benefit the entire team (group) while concurrently providing a degree of individual identity.

SELF-HELP CONTROL

The importance Americans place on self-help and personal achievement is an outgrowth of the values of independence, equality, and individuality, which are exemplified in commonly heard expressions such as "being self-reliant," "stand on your own two feet," or "don't depend on others." In the United States, your family name or the school attended will normally only help you to get an initial introduction or interview. Any subsequent gain must be earned through personal merit. Theoretically, the concept of equality underlying U.S. societal organization provides everyone the same opportunity for material and social improvement. One just has to work for it. The opportunity to go from rags to riches remains a fundamental American belief and can actually be seen in the political careers of Presidents Clinton and Obama. Both started from humble beginnings and went on to ultimately sit in the Oval Office. The nineteenth-century English poet William Henley succinctly captured this U.S. value of self-mastery when he wrote, "I am the master of my fate, I am the captain of my soul."

COMPETITION AND FREE ENTERPRISE

A positive attitude toward competition is an integral part of life in the United States and is taught from early childhood on. Whether it is through childhood games or being continually asked to answer questions in the classroom, a competitive nature is encouraged among American children. People are ranked, graded, classified, and evaluated so that everyone will know who the best is. The media continually provides "Top 10" lists of people, schools, hospitals, movies, vacation locations, and endless others. The U.S. economic system—free market enterprise—is based on competition, and the U.S. government is constantly touting free and open markets. The assumption is that individuals, left to their own means, can more ably and quickly achieve their desired goals. Moreover, the system is considered "fair" because everyone has the same opportunity.

This competitive spirit can create problems for Americans when they interact with people who do not share the value. For instance, in some cultures, a person's social and economic stature can be a product of family connections, schools attended, length of time with an organization, or even age. In these cultures, competition based on personal merit can be a secondary consideration. Additionally, cultures that promote interdependency and cooperation take a negative view of intra-group competition.

FUTURE ORIENTATION

An old adage holds that Americans are not especially interested in history because they have so little of it. While that is somewhat of an overstatement, it does point out that in the United States what lies ahead usually takes precedence over the past. What is going to happen holds the greatest attraction because, it seems, whatever we are doing is not quite as good as what we could otherwise be doing or will be doing in the future. Change, taking chances, a stress on youth, and optimism are all hallmarks of U.S. culture and reflect the value placed on the future. As a people, Americans are constantly thinking about what is coming. Very young children even play with the toys (dolls, cars, guns, and so on) that rush them toward, and prepare them for, adulthood. What you want, you want now, so you can dispose of this moment and move on to the next. In the classroom, U.S. students longingly watch the clock as it counts the minutes to the end of class—and cues them to move on to another class or activity. Adler and Gunderson aptly capture the U.S. forward-looking focus when they observe, "Future-oriented cultures justify innovation and change mostly in terms of future economic benefits."[28] We will return to this topic when we discuss the Kluckhohn and Strodtbeck's value orientations later in the chapter.

ACTION/WORK ORIENTATION

The value associated with work is so important in the United States that people meeting for the first time frequently ask each other, "What do you do?" or "Where do you work?" Embedded in this simple query is the belief that working (doing something) is important. For most Americans, work represents a cluster of moral and affective conditions of great attractiveness, and voluntary idleness is often seen as a severely threatening and damaging social condition. Unlike cultures where physical labor is considered the providence of the less privileged, Americans place considerable value on the "dignity of human labor." This value can be seen in the activities of U.S. presidents—Reagan chopped wood, G.W. Bush cleared brush, and President Obama has spent time helping Habitat for Humanity construct homes for the less fortunate.

A major reward for this hard work, and an important aspect of life in the United States, is time away from the job. For Americans, leisure time is something they have earned. It is relief from the demands and stress of work. This emphasis on recreation and relaxation takes a wide variety of forms. Each weekend people rush to get away in their RVs, play golf or tennis, go skiing, ride their mountain bikes, go to the beach, or "unwind" at a gambling casino, a racetrack, or a movie. Vacations are usually spent "doing" something. Americans commonly relax by engaging in some form of activity. However, leisure time is generally seen as an opportunity to "refresh," so one can return to work with rededicated enthusiasm.

INFORMALITY

When placing an order at nearly any Starbucks© in southern California you are almost always asked to provide your name, and the expectation is that it will be your first name. Shortly thereafter, you will likely hear your name shouted out as your order is completed. In U.S. restaurants the waitstaff will often introduce themselves using their first name. These practices are examples of the informality that characterizes U.S. culture and are in contrast with what you would experience in other, more formal cultures.

This informality is a reflection of the equality that Americans value. Everyone, regardless of position, rank, or wealth is considered as equal and there is no need for titles of distinction. The exception to this practice is for those in certain professions, such as military, medical, courts, clergy, high government official, and a few others. This informality does not connote a lack of respect toward others. Rather, it conveys the feeling of equality and individuality inherent in the dominant U.S. culture.

DIRECTNESS, OPENNESS, AND HONESTY

Americans often use phrases like, "Just tell it like it is," or "Don't beat around the bush." In these instances, the speaker is indicating a desire to quickly get to the heart of the matter. This illustrates the value placed on direct, open, and honest communication, which takes precedence over politeness and face saving measures. Here again, you can see the influence of equality, informality, the importance of time, and the feeling that each person can take care of themselves. Americans see no need to use elaborate courtesy protocols because everyone is equal and honesty is a positive mark of one's character.[29]

PRACTICALITY AND EFFICIENCY

Practicality and efficiency are also hallmarks of the dominant culture. Unlike some Asian cultures, gift giving in the United States is usually kept within the limits appropriate to the giver's budget. In America garage sales are common and people are not embarrassed to buy used items. At a restaurant with a large group, people usually "go Dutch," with everyone paying for their own meals. It is easy to see that individuality, independence, and self-reliance are central considerations in the pragmatic attitude evinced by Americans. Because strong group ties do not play a major role in U.S. societal activities, there is no need to build interpersonal relations based on a system of mutual obligations, as is done in many collectivistic cultures. The role of efficiency in America can also be seen in the highly structured use of time, discussed earlier. Americans also tend to be very rational or logical when working on problems. "Just give me the facts," an often heard phrase in the U.S., illustrates the importance of objectivity when making a decision or a judgment. Reason takes precedence over emotionality, subjectivity, or sentimentality.

MATERIALISM/ACQUISITIVENESS

Acquiring material possessions has always been an integral part of life for most Americans. "Americans consider it almost a right to be materially well off and physically comfortable."[30] In fact, Americans consider their materialistic nature "natural and proper."[31] From Bender's perspective, U.S. materialism is a natural outgrowth of the nation's philosophy of equal opportunity for all.[32] However, Americans have historically been willing to work hard to realize their dreams. Thus, the acquisition of material possessions, such as a large home, a variety of clothes for every occasion, convenient personal transportation, and a large selection of foods, is considered just reward for hard work. The American preference for a large selection of material items to choose from is clearly illustrated in your typical supermarket, which carries over 48,000 items,[33] and the number of sandwich and condiment choices available at Subway©.

OTHER CULTURAL PATTERNS

With this understanding of the dominant U.S. culture values, you are now ready to make some cross-cultural comparisons. As mentioned earlier in this chapter, scholars have devised a number of taxonomies that can be used to analyze key behavioral patterns found in almost every culture. Among those classification listings, several seem to be at the core of most intercultural communication studies and we will look at six of them.

HOFSTEDE'S VALUE DIMENSIONS

Developed by Hofstede,[34] the first classification identifies six value dimensions (individualism/collectivism, uncertainty avoidance, power distance, masculinity/femininity, long-term/short-term orientation, and indulgence/restraint) that are influenced and modified by culture. Hofstede's research was one of the earliest attempts to use statistical data to examine cultural values. He surveyed more than one hundred thousand IBM employees from 50 countries and three geographical regions. After careful analysis, each country and region was assigned a rank of 1 through 50 in four identified value dimensions (individualism/collectivism, uncertainty avoidance, power distance, masculinity/femininity). Subsequent research involving participants from 23 nations revealed a fifth dimension (long-term/short-term orientation) and these countries were ordered 1 through 23. Recent work with World Values Survey data from 93 nations has disclosed the indulgence/restraint dimension. The country rankings provided by this research not only offer a clear picture of what was valued in each culture, but also help you see comparisons across cultures. However, it is important to keep in mind that Hofstede's work measured cultural dimensions at a national rather than individual level,[35] which means that his value dimensions characterize the dominant culture in that society. Within every culture you will find individuals all along a particular value continuum. For example, in the United States, some members of the dominant culture possess strong collective tendencies. Conversely, in a group-oriented culture such as South Korea, you can find individuals that subscribe to, and assert, individuality. Therefore, in any intercultural encounter, you must be mindful that the other person or persons may not adhere to the norm for their culture.

INDIVIDUALISM/COLLECTIVISM

The cultural dimensions of individualism and collectivism were previously mentioned in Chapters 2 and 3 while examining the functions of family. Here the values receive a more comprehensive examination. Based on numerous scholarly studies, individualism versus collectivism (individual orientation versus group orientation) is thought of "as one of the basic pattern variables that determine human action."[36] The two values produce variations in family structures, how classroom activities are conducted, the way organizations manage workgroups, and even how the individual conducts social relations. The individualism/collectivism continuum can be defined in the following manner: "Collectivistic cultures emphasize community, collaboration, shared interest, harmony, tradition, the public good, and maintaining face. Individualistic cultures emphasize personal rights and responsibilities, privacy, voicing one's own opinion, freedom, innovation, and self-expression."[37] This synopsis should prepare you for a more in depth study of the two dimensions.

Individualism

Having already touched on individualism in the examination of American cultural values, here some of its components are identified. First, the individual is the single most important unit in any social setting. Second, independence rather than interdependence is stressed. Third, individual achievement is rewarded. Lastly, the uniqueness of each individual is of paramount value.[38] A person's rights and privacy prevail over group considerations in an individualistic culture.[39] Individualists are likely to belong to many groups but retain only weak ties, changing membership when desired. Hofstede's findings (see Table 6.1) indicate that Western democracies tend toward strong individualism.

Individualism in the United States is seen in the expectation that employees will change jobs in order to advance their careers. The individual is first, and the organization and co-workers are a secondary consideration. Conversely, in Japan individuals have traditionally expected to retain affiliation with the same company throughout

TABLE 6.1	Individualism/Collectivism Values for Fifty Countries and Three Regions				
RANK	**COUNTRY**	**RANK**	**COUNTRY**	**RANK**	**COUNTRY**
1	United States	19	Israel	37	Hong Kong
2	Australia	20	Spain	38	Chile
3	Great Britain	21	India	39~41	Singapore
4/5	Canada	22/23	Japan	39~41	Thailand
4/5	Netherlands	22/23	Argentina	39~41	West Africa
6	New Zealand	24	Iran	42	El Salvador
7	Italy	25	Jamaica	43	South Korea
8	Belgium	26/27	Brazil	44	Taiwan
9	Denmark	26/27	Arab countries	45	Peru
10/11	Sweden	28	Turkey	46	Costa Rica
10/11	France	29	Uruguay	47/48	Pakistan
12	Ireland	30	Greece	47/48	Indonesia
13	Norway	31	Philippines	49	Colombia
14	Switzerland	32	Mexico	50	Venezuela
15	Germany	33~35	Yugoslavia	51	Panama
16	South Africa	33~35	Portugal	52	Ecuador
17	Finland	33~35	East Africa	53	Guatemala
18	Austria	36	Malaysia		

The lower the number, the more the country promotes individualism; a higher number means the country is more collective. Source: Adapted from G. Hofstede, *Culture's Consequences: Comparing Values, Behaviors, Institutions and Organizations Across Nations*, 2nd ed. (Thousand Oaks, CA: Sage Publications, 2001).

their working career. To change jobs would be disloyal to the company and the other employees.

Collectivism

The majority of the world's population live in collectivistic societies where group interests take precedence over those of the individual.[40] In collective cultures, relationships form a rigid social framework that distinguishes between in-groups and out-groups. People rely on their in-groups (e.g., family, tribe, clan, organization) to look after them, and in exchange they believe they owe loyalty to that group. The following behaviors are often found in collective cultures:

> Collectivism means greater emphasis on (a) the views, needs, and goals of the in-group rather than oneself; (b) social norms and duty defined by the in-group rather than behavior to get pleasure; (c) beliefs shared with the in-group rather than beliefs that distinguish the self from in-group; and (d) great readiness to cooperate with in-group members.[41]

In collective societies, people are born into extended families, clans, or tribes that support and protect them in exchange for their allegiance. As events in Iraq, Afghanistan, and Libya have demonstrated, tribalism is an important social factor in many Arab nations and in African societies, "African thought rejects any view of the individual as an autonomous and responsible being."[42] In collective cultures, the individual is emotionally dependent on organizations and institutions, and group membership is emphasized. Organizations and the groups to which individuals belong also affect private life, and people generally acquiesce to group decisions, even if they are counter to personal desires. The importance of the group in collective societies is shown by a Chinese proverb: "No matter how stout, one beam cannot support a house." As is the case with all cultural

Collective cultures value the group as the most important social unit.

Edwin McDaniel

CONSIDER THIS

There are numerous U.S. co-cultures that can be classified as collective. African Americans, for instance, exhibit many of the traits attributed to collective societies,[44] and Hispanics and Asian Americans place great value on their extended families.

patterns, collectivism influences how communication is used. For example, "following traditional Korean values, communicating to become part of an in-group and to strengthen intragroup bonds is more important than communicating for information exchange and persuasion."[43]

Collectivism is also contextual. In a learning environment, a collective classroom will stress harmony and cooperation rather than competition. In the health care setting, a hospital patient is likely to receive a continual stream of visitors consisting of family members and friends. The sense of collectivism is so strong among the Japanese that following the March 2011 earthquake, tsunami, and nuclear accident disaster, a national consensus of self-restraint quickly developed. The population as a whole voluntarily became more conservative in their consumption and entertainment activities, wishing to evince a sense of selflessness and a feeling of solidarity with the disaster victims.[45]

UNCERTANITY AVOIDANCE

At the core of uncertainty avoidance is the inescapable truism that the future is unknown. Though you may try, you can never predict with 100 percent assurance what someone will do or what might happen in the future. As the term is used in Hofstede's research, uncertainty avoidance can be defined as "the extent to which the members of a culture feel threatened by ambiguous or unknown situations."[46] As you will learn below, cultures vary in their ability to tolerate ambiguity and unpredictability.

High Uncertainty Avoidance

High uncertainty avoidance cultures endeavor to reduce unpredictability and ambiguity through intolerance of deviant ideas and behaviors, emphasizing consensus, resisting change, and adhering to traditional social protocols. These cultures are often characterized by relatively high levels of anxiety and stress. People with this orientation believe that life carries the potential for continual hazards, and to avoid or mitigate these dangers, there is a strong need for laws, written rules, planning, regulations, rituals, ceremonies, and established societal, behavioral, and communication conventions, all of which add structure to life. Social expectations are clearly established and consistent. Nations with a strong uncertainty avoidance tendency are listed in Table 6.2.

Japan is a high uncertainty culture with many formal social protocols that help to predict how people will behave in almost every social interaction. Japan's high uncertainty avoidance was illustrated in a poll taken in 2007 which revealed that for Japanese in their 20s, over 42 percent of males and more than 38 percent of females had reservations about living overseas.[47]

Low Uncertainty Avoidance

At the other end of the continuum are low uncertainty avoidance cultures. They more easily accept the uncertainty inherent in life, tend to be tolerant of the unusual, and are not as threatened by different ideas and people. They prize initiative, dislike the structure

TABLE 6.2	Uncertainty Avoidance Values for Fifty Countries and Three Regions				
RANK	**COUNTRY**	**RANK**	**COUNTRY**	**RANK**	**COUNTRY**
1	Greece	19	Israel	37	Australia
2	Portugal	20	Colombia	38	Norway
3	Guatemala	21/22	Venezuela	39/40	South Africa
4	Uruguay	21/22	Brazil	39/40	New Zealand
5/6	Belgium	23	Italy	41/42	Indonesia
5/6	El Salvador	24/25	Pakistan	41/42	Canada
7	Japan	24/25	Austria	43	United States
8	Yugoslavia	26	Taiwan	44	Philippines
9	Peru	27	Arab Countries	45	India
10~15	Spain	28	Ecuador	46	Malaysia
10~15	Argentina	29	Germany	47/48	Great Britain
10~15	Panama	30	Thailand	47/48	Ireland
10~15	France	31/32	Iran	49/50	Hong Kong
10~15	Chile	31/32	Finland	49/50	Sweden
10~15	Costa Rica	33	Switzerland	51	Denmark
16/17	Turkey	34	West Africa	52	Jamaica
16/17	South Korea	35	Netherlands	53	Singapore
18	Mexico	36	East Africa		

The lower the number, the more the country can be classified as one that dislikes uncertainty; a higher number is associated with a country that feels comfortable with uncertainty. Source: Adapted from G. Hofstede, *Culture's Consequences: Comparing Values, Behaviors, Institutions and Organizations Across Nations*, 2nd ed. (Thousand Oaks, CA: Sage Publications, 2001).

associated with hierarchy, are willing to take risks, are flexible, think that there should be as few rules as possible, and depend not so much on experts as on themselves. As a whole, members of low uncertainty avoidance cultures are less constrained by social protocol.

As with other value dimensions, differences in uncertainty avoidance influence communication and activities in varied contexts. In a classroom composed of children from a low uncertainty avoidance culture, such as Britain, you would expect to see students feeling comfortable dealing with unstructured learning situations, being rewarded for innovative approaches to problem solving, and learning without strict timetables. A different behavior is the case in high uncertainty avoidance cultures like Germany, where you find that students expect structured learning situations, firm timetables, and well-defined objectives.[48]

POWER DISTANCE

Another cultural value dimension revealed by Hofstede's research is power distance, which classifies cultures on a continuum of high and low power distance (Some scholars use the terms "large" and "small" power distance). Power distance is concerned with how societies manage "the fact that people are unequal."[49] The concept is defined as, "the extent in which the less powerful members of institutions and organizations within a country expect and accept that power is distributed unequally."[50]

In this sense, institution refers to family, school, and community, while organizations represent places of employment. The premise of the dimension deals with the extent to which a society prefers that power in relationships, institutions, and organizations be distributed equally or unequally. Although all cultures have tendencies toward both high and low power distance relationships, one orientation seems to dominate.

High Power Distance

"Individuals from high power distance cultures accept power as part of society. As such, superiors consider their subordinates to be different from themselves and vice versa."[51] People in high power distance countries (see Table 6.3) believe that power and authority are facts of life. Both consciously and unconsciously, these cultures teach their members that people are not equal in this world and that everybody has a rightful place, which is clearly marked by countless societal hierarchies. In organizations in high power distance cultures, you find a greater centralization of power, more recognition and use of rank and status, and adherence to established lines of authority.

Low Power Distance

Low power distance countries hold that inequality in society should be minimized. "Cultures referred to as 'low power distance' are guided by laws, norms, and everyday behaviors that make power distinctions as minimal as possible."[52] Subordinates and superiors consider each other as equals. People in power, be they supervisors, managers, or government officials, often interact with their constituents and try to look less powerful than they really

TABLE 6.3	Power Distance Values for Fifty Countries and Three Regions				
RANK	**COUNTRY**	**RANK**	**COUNTRY**	**RANK**	**COUNTRY**
1	Malaysia	18/19	Turkey	37	Jamaica
2/3	Guatemala	20	Belgium	38	United States
2/3	Panama	21~23	East Africa	39	Canada
4	Philippines	21~23	Peru	40	Netherlands
5/6	Mexico	21~23	Thailand	41	Australia
5/6	Venezuela	24/25	Chile	42~44	Costa Rica
7	Arab countries	24/25	Portugal	42~44	Germany
8/9	Ecuador	26	Uruguay	42~44	Great Britain
8/9	Indonesia	27/28	Greece	45	Switzerland
10/11	India	27/28	South Korea	46	Finland
10/11	West Africa	29/30	Iran	47/48	Norway
12	Yugoslavia	29/30	Taiwan	47/48	Sweden
13	Singapore	31	Spain	49	Ireland
14	Brazil	32	Pakistan	50	New Zealand
15/16	France	33	Japan	51	Denmark
15/16	Hong Kong	34	Italy	52	Israel
17	Colombia	35/36	Argentina	53	Austria
18/19	El Salvador	35/36	South Africa		

The lower the number, the more the country can be classified as a high power distance culture; a higher number is associated with countries that have low power distance culture. Source: Adapted from G. Hofstede, *Culture's Consequences: Comparing Values, Behaviors, Institutions and Organizations Across Nations*, 2nd ed. (Thousand Oaks, CA: Sage Publications, 2001).

are. We can observe signs of this dimension in nearly every communication setting, and the following provides an example from the educational context.

> In large power distance societies, the educational process is teacher centered. The teacher initiates all communication, outlines the path of learning students should follow, and is never publicly criticized or contradicted. In large power distance societies, the emphasis is on the personal "wisdom" of the teacher, while in small power distance societies the emphasis is on impersonal "truth" that can be obtained by any competent person.[53]

In low power distance work centers, you might observe decisions being shared, subordinates being consulted, bosses relying on support teams, and status symbols being kept to a minimum.[54]

MASCULINITY/FEMININITY

Hofstede uses the words masculinity and femininity to refer to the degree to which masculine or feminine traits are valued and revealed. His rationale, one that is supported across several academic disciplines, is that many masculine and feminine behaviors are learned and mediated by cultural norms and traditions. Adler and Gunderson feel that the terms masculinity and femininity do not adequately convey the full meaning behind this dimension and choose to use the terms "career success" and "quality of life."[55]

Masculinity

Masculinity is the extent to which the dominant values in a society are male-oriented. A masculine oriented culture can be defined as, "A society is called *masculine* when emotional gender roles are clearly distinct: men are supposed to be assertive, tough, and focused on material success, whereas women are supposed to be more modest, tender, and concerned with the quality of life."[56]

Adler and Gunderson report that masculine, or career success, oriented cultures have highly defined gender roles and promote achievement in the workplace. "Assertiveness and the acquisition of money and things (materialism)"[57] are emphasized and often take precedence over interpersonal relationships. The United States offers an example of the influence of strong gender roles in a masculine-based culture (see Table 6.4 for rankings). Despite the high level of economic development and stress on gender equality, in 2011 women were elected to only 88 (16.4 percent) of the 535 combined seats available in the U.S. Senate and the House of Representatives, which demonstrates a disproportionately low level of female political empowerment.[58]

Femininity

Cultures that value femininity as a trait stress nurturing behaviors. "A society is called *feminine* when emotional gender roles overlap: Both men and women are supposed to be modest, tender, and concerned with the quality of life."[59] A feminine worldview

TABLE 6.4	Masculinity Values for Fifty Countries and Three Regions				
RANK	**COUNTRY**	**RANK**	**COUNTRY**	**RANK**	**COUNTRY**
1	Japan	18/19	Hong Kong	37/38	Spain
2/3	Austria	20/21	Argentina	37/38	Peru
2/3	Venezuela	20/21	India	39	East Africa
4/5	Italy	22	Belgium	40	El Salvador
4/5	Switzerland	23	Arab countries	41	South Korea
6	Mexico	24	Canada	42	Uruguay
7/8	Ireland	25/26	Malaysia	43	Guatemala
7/8	Jamaica	25/26	Pakistan	44	Thailand
9/10	Great Britain	27	Brazil	45	Portugal
9/10	Germany	28	Singapore	46	Chile
11/12	Philippines	29	Israel	47	Finland
11/12	Colombia	30/31	Indonesia	48/49	Yugoslavia
13/14	South Africa	30/31	West Africa	48/49	Costa Rica
13/14	Ecuador	32/33	Turkey	50	Denmark
15	United States	32/33	Taiwan	51	Netherlands
16	Australia	34	Panama	52	Norway
17	New Zealand	35/36	Iran	53	Sweden
18/19	Greece	35/36	France		

The lower the number, the more the country can be classified as one that favors masculine traits; a higher score denotes a country that prefers feminine traits. Source: Adapted from G. Hofstede, *Culture's Consequences: Comparing Values, Behaviors, Institutions and Organizations Across Nations,* 2nd ed. (Thousand Oaks, CA: Sage Publications, 2001).

maintains that men need not be assertive and that they can assume nurturing roles. It also promotes sexual equality and holds that people and the environment are important. Interdependence and androgynous behavior are the ideal, and people sympathize with the less fortunate. In contrast to the masculine culture reflected by the number of women in the U.S. Congress, in Norway, which had the second highest ranking in the femininity category (see Table 6.4), women occupied 67 (40 percent) of the 169 Parliament seats following the 2009 election, suggesting a high level of female political empowerment.[60]

The impact of masculinity/femininity on a culture can also be observed in the "gender gap" survey. To determine the gender gap in countries, The World Economic Forum conducts a yearly survey to measure these four categories: (1) economic participation and opportunity; (2) educational attainment; (3) health and survival; and (4) political empowerment. In the political empowerment category of the 2010 report (which assessed 134 nations), Iceland, Norway, Finland, and Sweden were ranked as the top four; the United States was 40, Italy 54, Mexico 61, and Japan 101.[61] These rankings generally parallel Hofstede's findings.

LONG- AND SHORT-TERM ORIENTATION

Over the years, Hofstede's work has been widely critiqued, and one major complaint concerned the Western bias which influenced data collection.[62] To resolve this problem,

Hofstede offered a new dimension called long- versus short-term orientation, also referred to as "Confucian work dynamism."[63] Identification of this dimension came from a study of 23 countries using an assessment called the Chinese Value Survey (CVS) developed from values suggested by Chinese scholars.[64] While admitting that Westerners might find this fifth orientation perplexing, Hofstede originally linked the dimension to Confucianism, because it appeared "to be based on items reminiscent of the teachings of Confucius, on both poles."[65]

Recognizing the inherent weakness of basing the dimension on data from only 23 nations, Minkov and Hofstede drew on World Values Survey (WVS)[66] data to replicate and extend the study to 38 nations.[67] Reporting the results of their analysis in late 2010, the two researchers disclosed, "China and other East Asian countries tended to score high on the dimension, suggesting a long-term orientation. Continental European countries had average scores, whereas Anglo, African, and South Asian countries had low scores, suggestive of a short-term orientation."[68] The research was subsequently extended to encompass 93 countries, and the dimension was recently defined as follows:

> Long-term orientation stands for the fostering of virtues oriented toward future rewards—in particular, perseverance and thrift. Its opposite pole, short-term orientation, stands for the fostering of virtues related to the past and present—in particular, respect for tradition, preservation of "face," and fulfilling social obligations.[69]

After identifying high scores among some East European nations, Hofstede and his colleagues no longer consider the dimension's association with Confucianism to be appropriate. Rather, they now see the long-term/short-term orientation to be "a universal dimension of national culture, underpinned by concepts that are meaningful across the whole world."[70]

You might easily envision how these patterns could influence communication in a business context. Corporate organizations in cultures that rank high on the long-term orientation scale, such as in China and South Korea, would be characterized by a focus on obtaining market share, rewarding employees based on organizational loyalty, strong interpersonal connections, situational ethics, adaptability, and self-discipline. Leisure time would not be a central concern. In contrast, organizations possessing a short-term orientation, like those in Mexico, the U.S., and Egypt, would emphasize short-term profits, use merit to reward employees, experience transient organizational loyalty, and consider ethics to be based on a set of universal principles. Personal freedom and leisure time would be a significant value.[71]

INDULGENCE/RESTRAINT

Using World Values Survey data from 93 nations/regions, Michael Minkov, a Bulgarian academic, recently disclosed a sixth dimension, termed indulgence versus restraint. This is defined as, "Indulgence stands for a tendency to allow relatively free gratification of basic and natural human desires related to enjoying life and

TABLE 6.5	Selected Characteristics of Indulgent and Restrained Cultures
INDULGENT CULTURE	**RESTRAINED CULTURE**
• Thrift unimportant	• Thrift important
• Moral discipline relaxed	• Moral discipline observed
• Positive attitude prevalent	• Cynicism prevalent
• Optimism prevalent	• Pessimism prevalent
• Relaxed gender roles	• Defined gender roles
• Smiling a norm	• Smiling considered suspect
• Freedom of speech primary value	• Freedom of speech secondary value
• Maintaining national order secondary concern	• Maintaining national order primary concern

Source: Adapted from G.Hofstede, G.J. Hofstede, and M. Minkov, *Cultures and Organizations: Software of the Mind,* 3rd ed. (New York: McGraw-Hill, 2010).

having fun. Its opposite pole, restraint, reflects a conviction that such gratification needs to be curbed and regulated by strict social norms."[72] As used in this sense, gratification refers to overall enjoyment of life.

In an indulgent society, people will place a priority on their sense of freedom and personal enjoyment through leisure time and interacting with friends. Consumption and spending would take precedence over fiscal restraint. In contrast, members of a restrained society would feel they had less freedom to enjoy themselves, consider frugality to be important, and that social order and discipline were more important than individual freedoms. In indulgent cultures, individuals are encouraged and expected to smile at everyone, but in a restrained culture, receiving a smile from a stranger would be viewed with suspicion (see Table 6.5). Looking at Table 6.6, think for a moment how someone from a culture with a strong sense of restraint, like Russia, may react to the typical greetings from waitstaff in a U.S. restaurant.

TABLE 6.6		Indulgent versus Restraint Ranking for 30 of 93 Countries			
RANK	**COUNTRY**	**RANK**	**COUNTRY**	**RANK**	**COUNTRY**
1	Venezuela	36	Greece	67/69	Czech Republic
2	Mexico	37/38	Taiwan	67/69	Poland
3	Puerto Rico	37/38	Turkey	75	China
8	Sweden	44	Thailand	77/80	Russia
9	New Zealand	49/51	Philippines	77/80	Montenegro
11	Australia	49/51	Japan	77/80	Romania
15/17	Canada	49/51	Germany	77/80	Bangladesh
15/17	Netherlands	54	Iran	83/84	Hong Kong
15/17	United States	66	Italy	83/84	Iran
26	Brazil	67/69	South Korea	92	Egypt

Lower numbered countries are seen as favoring indulgent traits; a higher score denotes a preference for restraint traits. Source: Adapted from G. Hofstede, G.J. Hofstede, and M. Minkov, *Cultures and Organizations: Software of the Mind,* 3rd ed. (New York: McGraw-Hill, 2010).

Minkov's Monumentalism/Flexhumility

Minkov's analysis of WVS data identified another cultural dimension which he labeled "monumentalism versus flexhumility," and established rankings for 57 nations and provinces. He likened "monumentalism" to monuments or statues, which are created to reflect pride in a person, event, or thing, and once erected, are relatively unchangeable. "Flexhumility" is a combination of the words self-flexible and humility. In monumentalism cultures, people usually possess and openly demonstrate pride in themselves, their achievements, families, and other social institutions. Conversely, people from flexhumility cultures typically exercise humility, situational flexibility, and readily adapt to changing conditions.[73] Table 6.7 contains lists of selected traits for this dimension.

TABLE 6.7	Selected Characteristics of Monumentalism and Flexhumility Cultures
MONUMENTALISM	**FLEXHUMILITY**
• Self-pride/self-promotion	• Humility
• Self-concept is consistent/fixed	• Self-concept is flexible/fluid
• Truth is absolute	• Truth is relative
• Absolutist cognition	• Holistic cognition
• Religion is important	• Religion less important
• Interpersonal competition valued	• Interpersonal competition problematic
• Lower value on education	• Higher value on education
• Difficulty in adapting to another culture	• Easily adapts to another culture
• Suicide taboo	• Suicide accepted
• Tipping expected/prevalent	• Tipping not expected/rarely done

Adapted from M. Minkov, "Monumentalism versus Flexumility," SIETAR Europa Congress (2007). Link: www.sietar-europa.org/congress2007/files/congress2007_paper_Michael_Minkov.doc.

Latin American and Middle East countries scored the highest on the monumentalism scale. At the lower end, indicating a flexhumility culture, were Slavic countries (e.g., Russia, Bulgaria, Ukraine, Belarus), the Baltic states (Estonia, Latvia, and Lithuania), and Northeast Asia nations (China, Japan, and South Korea). The U.S. ranked in the upper middle of the scale, which reflects how U.S. Americans balance self-promotion and humbleness. In the United States, individuals are often told "you have to toot your own horn," meaning some degree of self-promotion is required and expected. If that horn is tooted too loud, however, a person risks being labeled a braggart. Consider the potential for intercultural communication failure when a monumentalism interviewer asks a flexhumility interviewee to talk about personal achievements.

Kluckhohn and Strodtbeck's Value Orientations

The next taxonomy of orientations (human nature, person/nature orientation, time, activity, and relational orientation) comes from the anthropological work of Kluckhohn and Strodtbeck. They based their research on the notion that every individual, regardless of culture, must deal with five universal questions, referred to as "value orientations." These "orientations," or patterns, inform members of a culture

TABLE 6.8	Five Value Orientations from Kluckhohn and Strodtbeck		
ORIENTATION		**VALUE AND BEHAVIOR RANGE**	
Human nature	Basically evil	Mixture of good and evil	Basically good
Humans and nature	Subject to nature	Harmony with nature	Master of nature
Sense of time	Past	Present	Future
Activity	Being	Being-in-becoming	Doing
Social relationships	Authoritarian	Group	Individualism

Source: F.R. Kluckhohn and F.L. Strodtbeck, *Variations in Value Orientations* (New York: Row and Peterson), 1960.

what is important and provide them guidance for living their lives.[74] After extensive study, they concluded that all people turn to their culture to help them in answering the same five basic questions:

1. What is the character of human nature?

2. What is the relation of humankind to nature?

3. What is the orientation toward time?

4. What is the value placed on activity?

5. What is the relationship of people to each other?

As with Hofstede's dimensions, Kluckhohn and Strodtbeck's orientations (see Table 6.8) are best visualized as points along a continuum. Moving through the five orientations, you will notice that some of the characteristics, although they have different names, are similar to the ones discussed by Hofstede. This is understandable because both approaches are talking about the meaningful values founding all cultures. Hence, both sets of research track many of the same patterns.

HUMAN NATURE ORIENTATION

Nearly all judgments about human behavior, be they moral or legal, begin with this core question: What is the character of human nature? Was Anne Frank right when she wrote in *The Diary of a Young Girl*, "In spite of everything, I still believe that people are really good at heart"? Or was the philosopher Immanuel Kant correct when he observed, "Out of the crooked timber of humanity no straight thing can ever be made"? For centuries, religious leaders, philosophers, scholars, and others have pondered questions concerning human nature, answers to which represent a powerful force in how one lives life. Although all people individually answer questions about human nature, there are also cultural explanations for why people act as they do. Since discussions of human nature often deal with divisions of evil, good and evil, and good, each of those issues are examined below to see how they can differ across cultures.

Evil

Some cultures believe that people are intrinsically evil. Brought by the early Puritans, this view prevailed in the United States for many years. In the last century, however,

Americans have come to consider themselves as a mixture of good and evil. That is, most Americans now believe that by following certain rules they can change and improve themselves. According to this idea, with constant hard work, control, education, and self-discipline, people can achieve goodness. A more restrictive view of human nature as good or evil is found in parts of the world where Islam is strong. There, you can find cultures that are imbued with the notion that people have a penchant for evil and therefore cannot, when left to their own resources, be trusted to make a correct decision. Hence, to help control the actions of their members, numerous social institutions, ranging from the religious to the political, are designed to monitor and manage behavior.

Good and Evil

People holding a Taoist worldview believe the universe is best seen from the perspective of *yang* and *yin*, an infinite system of opposing elements and forces in balanced, dynamic interaction. Two of the forces are good and evil, and since humanity is part of the universe, these forces are naturally present in humankind. This idea is exemplified in the notion of the *yin* and *yang* cycle. Periodic increases in *yin* are accompanied by corresponding decreases in *yang*; this is followed by an opposite cycle in which *yang* increases while *yin* decreases. This view of the good and evil nature of humanity proposes that people cannot eliminate evil, because it is an integral part of the universe. For very different reasons, many Europeans also have a dualistic (good/evil) approach to human nature. Specifically, they believe that while we might be born with a propensity for evil, through learning and education people can become good.

Good

Perhaps the most extreme view of the innate goodness of human nature is found in the philosophies of Confucianism and Buddhism. According to the Lu Wang school of Confucianism, "Human nature is originally good." Contemporary Chinese scholar Pei-Jung Fu echoes this belief when he writes, "there is solid foundation for claiming that Confucius regarded human nature as tending toward goodness."[75] Buddhism also maintains that you are born pure and are closest to what is called "loving kindness" when you enter this world. Hence, people are good, but their culture often makes them evil.

Cutting across the arguments concerning the good and evil of human nature is the question of the essential rationality of human nature. Throughout history, there has been tension between those who believe in fate or mystic powers and those who feel that the intellect can solve any problem and discover any truth. Imagine, for a moment, your perceptions of reality if you are French and take the rational approach reflected in Descartes' philosophy, or if you are an American Indian and believe that external forces control much of your thinking and behavior. To cite another example, the Hindu relies on mysticism, intuition, and spiritual awareness to understand the nature of reality. A belief in fate, as opposed to one that stresses freewill, is bound to yield different conclusions.

PERSON/NATURE ORIENTATION

Humans Subject to Nature

Different conceptions of the relationship between humanity and nature produce distinct frames of reference for human desires, attitudes, and behaviors. At one end of the scale devised by Kluckhohn and Strodtbeck is the view that humans

Many groups teach their members to live in harmony with nature.

Robert Fonseca

are subject to nature. Cultures holding this orientation believe the most powerful forces of life are beyond control. Whether the force is a god, fate, or magic, it cannot be overcome and must therefore be accepted. This perspective is found in India and parts of South America. For the Hindu, because everything is part of a unified force, "the world of distinct and separate objects and processes is a manifestation of a more fundamental reality that is undivided and unconditional."[76] This "oneness" with the world helps create a vision of a world operating in harmony. In Mexico and among Mexican Americans, there is a strong tie to Catholicism and the role of fate in controlling life and nature, which leads to a general acceptance of things as they are.

Harmony with Nature

The middle or cooperative view is widespread and often associated with East Asians. In Japan and Thailand, there is a perception that nature is part of life and not a hostile force waiting to be subdued. This orientation affirms that people should, in every way possible, live in harmony with nature. To cite another example, the desire to be part of nature and not control it has always been strong among American Indians. Even today, many tribes practice conservation of natural resources and protest disruption of ancestral lands.

Master of Nature

At the other end of the scale is the view that compels us to conquer and direct the forces of nature to our advantage. This orientation is characteristic of the Western approach, which, as noted earlier in the chapter, has a long tradition of valuing technology, change, and science. Americans have historically believed that nature was something that could and had to be mastered. Even our language reflects this orientation. Early West European immigrants to North America encountered a vast, unforgiving wilderness that they set about to "tame," and modern astronauts are working to "conquer" space. People with this orientation see a clear separation between humans and nature.

TIME ORIENTATION

People's fixation with time and the power they afford it are obvious, and as you would expect by now, cultures vary widely in their perspective toward time. The greatest differences are in the respective values placed on the past, present, and future and on how each influences interaction. This section will highlight some of the major cultural differences in the perception of time as it applies to the Kluckhohn and Strodtbeck taxonomy.

Past Orientation

In past-oriented cultures, history, established religions, and tradition are extremely important. There is an intense belief that contemporary perceptions of people and events, decision making, and determinations of truth should be guided by what happened in the past. Respect for the past is especially evident in most Asian nations because of their long and eventful histories. Chu and Ju found that respect for their historical heritage was considered the most important traditional value among Chinese.[77] There is even a famous Chinese proverb that states, "The past is as clear as a mirror, the future as dark as lacquer." A similar adage from India advises, "Learn about the future by looking at the past." Great Britain remains devoted to tradition, including the maintenance of a monarchy, and continues to value its historical achievements. France is yet another culture that can be understood by exploring its view of the past. As Hall and Hall disclose, the French, on many levels, venerate the past.

> The importance of French history to the average French person can hardly be overstated. The French live surrounded by thousands of monuments to their glorious past. Every quarter in Paris has its historically important statues, buildings, or fountains, daily reminders of past achievements. French villages have statues to local heroes and important political leaders. As a result of this constant immersion in history, the French tend to see things in their historical context and relate contemporary events to their origins.[78]

Present Orientation

Present-oriented cultures hold that the immediate moment carries the most significance. The future is seen as ambiguous, capricious, and, in a sense, beyond the control of the individual. Because the past is over and the future is unpredictable, present cultures, such as Filipinos and Latin Americans, enjoy living in the moment. These cultures tend to be more impulsive and spontaneous than others and often have a casual, relaxed lifestyle. Mexicans and Mexican Americans believe in living in the present moment, and this view is also characteristic of the African-American co-culture.[79]

Future Orientation

In future-oriented cultures, what is yet to come is most valued and the future is expected to be grander than the present or past. Change, taking chances, a stress on youth, and optimism are all hallmarks of cultures that hold this orientation. This view toward the future is held by most Americans, who are constantly thinking about what is ahead. This does not mean that Americans have no regard for the past or no thought of the present, but it is certainly true that many Americans, in thought or action, tend to have a short-term, forward-looking orientation. The effect on communication can be seen in business negotiations between a long-term future-oriented country like China and a short-term future-oriented nation such as the United States. Whereas the Chinese side would be looking to establish a relationship that would carry into the future, the U.S. team would be more focused on the immediate project and have much less concern for the future.

ACTIVITY ORIENTATION

Activity orientation refers to how people of a culture view activity. Kluckhohn and Strodtbeck detailed three common approaches to activity—being, being-in-becoming, and doing.

Being

A being orientation refers to spontaneous expression of the human personality. "People in being-orientated cultures accept people, events, and ideas as flowing spontaneously. They stress release, indulgence of existing desires, and working for the moment."[80] Most Latino cultures consider the current activity as the one that matters the most. In Mexico, for example, interpersonal relations are valued more than accomplishments and people take great delight in the simple act of conversation

In many cultures people welcome solitude and spend portions of their lives in meditation and contemplation.

Edwin McDaniel

with family and friends. Mexicans will talk for hours with their companions, for they believe that the act of "being" is one of the main goals and joys of life.

Being-in-Becoming

Being-in-becoming stresses the idea of development and growth. It emphasizes the kind of activity that contributes to the development of all aspects of the self as an integral whole. This usually correlates with cultures that value a spiritual life over a material one. For example, in both Hinduism and Buddhism, people spend a portion of their lives in meditation and contemplation in an attempt to purify and fully advance themselves. The New Age movement in the United States also stresses the need to develop the being-in-becoming approach to daily life.

Doing

The doing orientation describes activity in which accomplishments are measurable by standards external to the individual. The key to this orientation is a value system that stresses activity and action. It is the doing orientation that most characterizes the dominant American culture. Americans' attitude toward doing and activity is best summed up by Kim:

> Americans are action oriented; they are go-getters. They get going, get things done, and get ahead. In America, people gather for action—to play basketball, to dance, to go to concert. When groups gather they play games or watch videos. Many Americans don't have the patience to sit down and talk…. Life is in constant motion.[81]

A doing perspective affects many other cultural beliefs and values. Your definition of activity affects your perception of work, efficiency, change, time, and progress. Even the pace at which you live your life—from how fast you walk to how quickly you make decisions—is related to where you fall on the being/doing

"Doing" cultures stress activity and action, usually in the company of others.

Jeff Greenberg/PhotoEdit

scale. Americans admire and reward people who can make quick decisions and "get things done."

HALL'S HIGH-CONTEXT AND LOW-CONTEXT ORIENTATIONS

Anthropologist E.T. Hall categorizes cultures as high- or low-context, depending on the degree to which meaning comes from the contextual environment rather than the words exchanged during communicative interaction.[82] The assumption underlying Hall's classifications is that "one of the functions of culture is to provide a highly selective screen between man and the outside world. In its many forms, culture therefore designates what we pay attention to and what we ignore."[83]

Hall saw context as "the information that surrounds an event; it is inextricably bound up with the meaning of the event."[84] His work revealed that cultures were often characterized by high- or low-context communication, which he described in the following manner:

> A high-context (HC) communication or message is one in which most of the information is already in the person, while very little is in the coded, explicitly transmitted part of the message. A low-context (LC) communication is just the opposite; i.e., the mass of the information is vested in the explicit code.[85]

Although all cultures possess some characteristics of both high- and low-context variables, most can be ranked along a scale for this particular dimension (see Table 6.9). To emphasize this fact, various cultures have been placed on a continuum rather than using only two opposing categories.

HIGH-CONTEXT

In high-context cultures, most of the meaning exchanged during an encounter is often not communicated through words. One reason that meanings frequently do not have to be stated verbally in high-context cultures is because there is normally a strong level of similitude among the people. This leads to similar perceptions, experiences, and societal expectations, which produces well defined social protocols. Because high-context cultures are usually quite traditional, they change little over time and produce consistent responses to the social environment. "As a result, for most normal transactions in daily life they do not require, nor do they expect, much in-depth background information."[86] Because meaning is not necessarily contained in words, in high-context cultures, information is provided through inference, gestures, and even silence.

People from high-context cultures tend to be attuned to their surroundings and can easily express and interpret emotions nonverbally. Meaning in high-context cultures is also conveyed "through status (age, sex, education, family background, title, and affiliations) and through an individual's informal friends and associates."[87] Because of the subtle "messages" used by high-context cultures, members of these groups often "communicate in an indirect fashion."[88] They rely more on how something is said, rather than what is said, and are acutely aware of nonverbal cues.

TABLE 6.9	Cultures Arranged Along the High-Context and Low-Context Dimension

HIGH-CONTEXT CULTURES

Japanese
|
Chinese
|
Korean
|
African American
|
Native American
|
Arab
|
Greek
|
Latin
|
Italian
|
English
|
French
|
North American
|
Scandinavian
|
German
|
German/Swiss
|

LOW-CONTEXT CULTURES

Source: Adapted from E.T. Hall, *Beyond Culture* (Garden City, NY: Doubleday, 1976), 91.

The high-context nature of Asian cultures shown in Table 6.9 is, according to Chang, a result of Confucian philosophy, which inclines "Asian culture toward high-context and collectivist communication that emphasizes role hierarchy and relations rather than the expression of self through direct communication."[89]

LOW-CONTEXT

Low-context cultures typically have considerable population diversity and tend to compartmentalize interpersonal contacts. Lack of a large pool of common experiences means that "each time they interact with others they need detailed background information."[90] In low-context cultures, the verbal message contains most of the information and very little is embedded in the context or the participant's nonverbal activity. This characteristic manifests itself in a host of ways. For example, the Asian mode of communication (high-context) is often vague, indirect, and implicit, whereas Western communication (low-context) tends to be direct and explicit. "Americans depend more on spoken words than on nonverbal behavior to convey messages. They think it is important to be able to 'speak up' and 'say what's on their mind.' They admire a person who has a large vocabulary and who can express him- or herself clearly and cleverly."[91] As suggested at the end of this quote, differences in perceptions of credibility are another aspect of communication associated with these two orientations. In high-context cultures, people who rely primarily on verbal messages for information are perceived as less credible. They believe that silence often sends a better message than words, and that anyone who needs words does not have the requisite information. As the Indonesian proverb states, "Empty cans clatter the loudest."

THE GLOBE STUDY

The most recent listing of values is a product of the Global Leadership and Organizational Effectiveness Research Program. GLOBE, as it is more commonly called, is an ongoing research project investigating the relationship between social culture, organizational culture, and leadership within organizations. Data collection and analysis has involved approximately 170 international researchers and over 17,000 managers from more than 900 organizations across 61 societies.[92] This is a massive project and reaches far beyond the scope and available space of this text. Accordingly, the discussion here is limited in coverage and designed to provide you only a succinct overview of the study and some selected results.

GLOBE STUDY CULTURAL DIMENSIONS

The investigation focused on nine cultural dimensions (see Table 6.10) derived from work by earlier researchers such as Hofstede and Kluckhohn and Strodtbeck, which you will recognize from previous discussions in this chapter. However, the GLOBE research extended the dimensions by asking the participants to indicate both their personal desires (values) and what was considered appropriate in their societies (actual practices). While expecting to find congruence between these two value sets, the results disclosed disagreement across seven of the dimensions.[93] This differentiation is similar to D'Andrade's distinction between *personal* and *institutionalized* values.[94]

Institutionalized values can be illustrated with an example from the Japanese culture. Japanese co-workers often go out together for drinks at the end of the workday, a practice intended to strengthen group ties. This normally delays their return home by several hours. The Japanese employees recognize the necessity of participating in this practice as it frequently involves important, informal work-related discussions and decisions. However, many have informally expressed a preference to return home directly from work and spend time with their families or engage in non-work related pursuits rather than go out with co-workers.[96] In this sense, we see personal values subordinated to institutionalized values, a situation like that found by the GLOBE study.

TABLE 6.10	GLOBE Study Cultural Dimensions
Uncertainty Avoidance	The extent that societal or organizational members work to reduce uncertainty about future events through the use of social norms, protocols, and established practices.
Power Distance	The degree that societal or organizational members acquiesce to the unequal distribution of power.
Collectivism – Societal	The degree that established social and organizational practices condone and reward collective actions and resource distribution.
Collectivism – In-group	The degree of pride, loyalty, and interconnectedness that people have in their family or organization.
Gender Egalitarianism	The degree that a society or organization minimizes differences in gender roles and gender inequality.
Assertiveness	How assertive, confrontational, and aggressive are members of a society or organization in their social interactions.
Future Orientation	The extent that people take part in future orientated actions, such as planning and investing for the future and delaying gratification.
Performance Orientation	The degree that a society or organization rewards members for improvement and excellence.
Humane Orientation	The degree that a society or organization promotes and rewards displays of fairness, altruism, generosity, caring, and kindness toward others.

Adapted from multiple sources.[95]

GLOBE SOCIETIES AND GEOGRAPHICAL GROUPS

The study's 61 societies came from 58 nations, with dual societies drawn from within three of the countries: Switzerland was separated into French speaking and the remainder. Germany was divided along the old Cold War political boundary of East (GDR) and West (FDR). South African participants were placed into black and white categories. In addition to classifying the societies across the different dimensions, the research also examined managerial leadership behaviors. Another feature of the study was an effort to examine cultural similarities and differences across the societies collectively. Thus, the 61 societies were placed into cultural geographical groups based on a variety of factors, such as similar ethnic and linguistic patterns, religion, ideology, customs, historical migration patterns, and shared historical experiences.[97] This resulted in the 10 societal geographical groups listed in Table 6.11.

The survey data was then statistically analyzed to determine the predominant cultural dimensions for each grouping. Results of that analysis are provided in Table 6.12 and the following paragraphs, with each grouping being rated as high, middle, or low for each of the nine cultural dimensions. It should be noted, however, that while the groupings do offer a general overview of the principal cultural traits for an entire collectivity the procedure can also obscure potential differences between the individual countries.[98]

As you can see in Table 6.12, there is considerable variation between the different groups. To provide additional understanding of these differences a narrative description of the institutionalized cultural characteristics of each cultural geographical group is provided below.

TABLE 6.11	GLOBE Societal Geographical Groups	
White Dominant Cultures	• Canada • England • Ireland	• New Zealand • South Africa[A] • United States
Scandinavia	• Finland • Sweden	• Denmark
Central Europe	• Germany (GDR) • Germany (FDR)	• Netherlands • Switzerland
Eastern Europe	• Albania • Georgia • Greece • Hungary	• Kazakhstan • Poland • Russia • Slovenia
Southern Europe	• France • Italy • Portugal	• Spain • Switzerland[B] • Israel
Africa	• Namibia • Nigeria • Zambia	• Zimbabwe • South Africa[C]
Middle East	• Turkey • Egypt • Morocco	• Kuwait • Qatar
Central and South America	• Mexico • Guatemala • El Salvador • Costa Rica • Colombia	• Venezuela • Ecuador • Bolivia • Brazil • Argentina
Northeast Asia	• China • Japan • South Korea	• Taiwan • Hong Kong • Singapore
South and Southeast Asia	• Iran • India • Indonesia	• Malaysia • Thailand • Philippines

[A]*White sample,* [B]*French speaking sample,* [C]*Black sample*
Source: Adapted from V. Gupta and P.H. Hanges, "Regional and Climate Clustering of Societal Cultures," in *Culture, Leadership, and Organizations: The GLOBE Study of 62 Societies,* R.J. House, P.J. Hanges, M. Javidan, P.W. Dorfman, and V. Gupta, eds. (Thousand Oaks, CA: Sage Publications, 2004), 191.

White Dominant Cultures: This group consists of developed nations with predominantly English speaking populations. A major characteristic is an individualistic, performance based orientation, with a forward looking perspective. Rewards are a result of merit and there is less dependence on formal rules and established procedures. While gender equality is valued, in practice the countries are male-dominated.[99]

Scandinavia: The Scandinavia group is marked by its high scores on gender equality, future orientation, and uncertainty avoidance. The group is characterized by an

TABLE 6.12 GLOBE Societal Geographical Groups on Institutionalized Values

	UNCERTAINTY AVOIDANCE	POWER DISTANCE	COLLECTIVE-SOCIETAL	COLLECTIVISM-IN-GROUP	GENDER EGALITARIANISM	ASSERTIVENESS	FUTURE ORIENTATION	PERFORMANCE ORIENTATION	HUMANE ORIENTATION
White Dominant Cultures	Middle	Middle	Middle	Low	Middle	Middle	Middle	High	Middle
Scandinavia	High	Low	High	Low	High	Low	High	Middle	Middle
Central Europe	High	Middle	Low	Low	Middle	High	High	High	Low
Eastern Europe	Low	Middle	Middle	High	High	High	Low	Low	Middle
Southern Europe	Middle	Middle	Low	Middle	Middle	Middle	Middle	Middle	Low
Africa	Middle	Middle	Middle	Middle	Middle	Middle	Middle	Middle	High
Middle East	Low	Middle	Middle	High	Low	Middle	Low	Middle	Middle
Central and South America	Low	Middle	Low	High	Middle	Middle	Low	Low	Middle
Northeast Asia	Middle	Middle	High	High	Middle	Middle	Middle	High	Middle
South and Southeast Asia	Middle	Middle	Middle	High	Middle	Middle	Middle	Middle	High

Source: Adapted from V. Gupta and P.H. Hanges, "Regional and Climate Clustering of Societal Cultures," in *Culture, Leadership, and Organizations: The GLOBE Study of 62 Societies*, R.J. House, P.J. Hanges, M. Javidan, P.W. Dorfman, and V. Gupta, eds. (Thousand Oaks, CA: Sage Publications, 2004), 3–193.

"underplaying of assertiveness, familial, and masculine authority and emphasis on certainty, social unity and cooperation"[100] The welfare state found in all Scandinavian nations may contribute to the group's weaker performance orientation scores.

Central Europe: High scores on assertiveness, uncertainty avoidance, and future orientation, along with low scores on gender equality distinguish the cultural practices of this group. This helps explain the reliance on well-defined rules and standards, masculinity, and the assertive approach taken by members of these nations, along with their technocratic orientation.[101]

Eastern Europe: Societies in the Eastern European group are marked by a preference for hierarchical organizational leadership practices, strong in-group collectivism, and gender equality.[102] It is useful to note that many of the nations in this group were once part of the former Soviet Union, a historical legacy that no doubt continues to play a role in shaping their institutionalized values.

Southern Europe: A distinctive feature of the Southern Europe group is the reliance on the state to provide a wide range of social support services, which tends more toward collectivism than individualism. Of the nine cultural dimensions, gender equality was the lowest statistical score of the group and power distance was the highest. This may be related to the strong role of Catholicism in all the countries of this group.[103]

Africa: This group is characterized by a strong humane orientation, which is perhaps an outgrowth of life's difficulties in these societies. People from the Sub-Saharan Africa societies tend to subordinate self-interest and value social interdependence and reciprocity.[104]

Middle East: The five nations of this group share a common historical, religious, and socio-cultural heritage. Arabic is the common language in all but Turkey, and Islam is the dominant religion. Societies of the Middle East grouping exercise strong in-group collectivism, which centers on the family and attachments to other groups such as tribe, sect, village, neighborhood, or classmates. These societies also follow well-defined power distance hierarchies in their relationships and have very distinct gender roles, with masculinity being predominant. Many of these institutionalized values can be attributed to the Koran, which teaches that leadership authority should be respected and provides clear definitions of the different roles for men and women.[105]

Central and South America: A paternalistic perspective is a central theme among these societies. This is reflected in the desire to sustain personal social status and a predilection for in-group collectivism. Latin Americans often tend to have a sense of fatalism and prefer to live life in the present, rather than projecting into the future.[106]

Northeast Asia: A defining feature of this group is the pervasive influence of the Chinese historical legacy and enduring influence of Confucianism shared by all the countries. Confucianism contributes to the contemporary practice of strong societal and in-group collectivism in these nations. Indeed, performance rewards are associated less with individual achievement and more with attainment of collective goals.[107]

South and Southeast Asia: Societies in this group are noted for their practices of strong in-group collectivism, humanism, preference for social hierarchy, and a tendency toward male domination. Within the workforce, women commonly have to rely on family connections or a lengthy work history in order to compete with their male counterparts. It appears that modern South Asian women can have outside accomplishments, but are expected to concurrently maintain strong family ties.[108]

Before ending this review of the GLOBE values research, you should recall that the study was very extensive and explored a large number of topics, many of which are not covered in this overview. Additionally, you should remember that the use of cultural geographical grouping provides a convenient means of identifying societal similarities and differences from a regional perspective, but also runs a very distinct danger of masking intergroup variances.

FACE AND FACEWORK

The final cultural pattern was developed by intercultural communication scholar Ting-Toomey, whose work highlights the role of "face" and "face-work" in intercultural communication. Here we use the term face as a metaphor for the self-image you want to project to other people; face is your public identity. Since face is how *others* see you, it is acquired, maintained, and lost through social interaction. This process is referred to as facework, which Domenici and Littlejohn define as "a set of coordinated practices in which communicators build, maintain, protect, or threaten personal dignity, honor, and respect."[109] In other words, facework consists of those actions you engage in to acquire or maintain face for yourself or give face to someone else.

For a job interview, you will probably wear your best suit and arrive a few minutes before the scheduled time. During the interview, you will remember to sit erect, maintain eye contact, respond to questions with thoughtful answers, use formal terms of address, and avoid slang. These efforts amount to self-directed facework because you want to make a positive impression. As the old saying goes, you will try to "put on your best face." Complimenting a friend's new clothes, on being accepted to graduate school, or for landing a new job are examples of other-directed facework.

Ting-Toomey and her colleagues have conducted extensive research into the role of face and facework in intercultural communication, especially in conflict situations. Her work assumes that people from all cultures strive to "maintain and negotiate face in all communication situations."[110] Face and facework, however, are influenced by cultural values and vary across cultures.[111] In individualistic cultures, for example, a person's face is usually derived from his or her own self-effort and is normally independent of others. Accordingly, people from individualistic groups are more concerned with maintaining their own face. Because U.S. Americans do not normally rely on group affiliation for their identity or social support, they are less concerned with how they influence someone else's face. This results in a direct, forthright communication style. Common expressions in the United States such as "tell me what you really think," and "don't hold anything back" demonstrate the value placed on open, candid communication. In some instances, harmonious interpersonal relations may become secondary to frankness.

In collectivistic cultures, group membership is normally the primary source of identity and status. Considerable value is placed on establishing and sustaining stable, harmonious relationships with in-group members. This is evident in what constitutes face in collectivistic societies. Among the Japanese, face involves "honor, appearance of propriety, presence, and the impact on others."[112] Among the Chinese, according to Gao and Ting-Toomey, "gaining and losing face is connected closely with issues of social pride, honor, dignity, insult, shame, disgrace, humility, trust, mistrust, respect, and prestige."[113] As you might expect, extreme politeness and positive interpersonal relations is an important part of face-saving in collective social groups. "The preference for harmony in collectivistic groups is focused around anticipating and forestalling any loss of face within one's dyad or group. The focus upon context and upon indirect styles of communication can therefore be seen as forms of preventive facework."[114]

Varying attitudes as to what represents face and how facework is conducted have a very noticeable impact on how a culture views and approaches conflict. Kim tells us that in collective cultures, in-group conflict "is viewed as damaging to social face and relational harmony, so it should be avoided as much as possible."[115] As a result, in collectivistic cultures maintenance of mutual and other-face receives greater emphasis than self-face.

The different values placed on face, what constitutes face, and how it is managed have a very noticeable influence on facework. Drawing on the individualism/collectivism cultural pattern, Ting-Toomey posits that when confronted with the potential for conflict, collectivists will be more inclined toward avoidance and obligating measures.[116] This is a result of concern for both mutual face and others' face, and how one's actions may affect others. Individualists, however, are concerned primarily with self-face and tend to favor confrontational and solution-oriented approaches to resolve conflicts.[117] This attitude toward problem solving by individualistic cultures is evident in the number of U.S. lawyers, frequency of law suits, and the requirement to sign a lengthy contract for such basic services as cable TV or a mobile phone account. Collectivistic nations, such as Japan, have far less lawyers and prefer to resolve disputes through intermediaries.

These contrasting attitudes toward conflict give rise to quite different culturally based communication styles. During intercultural communication events, these divergent styles can result in confusion, misinterpretation, or even animosity among the participants. Adherence to an indirect communication style to sustain amicable relations, as used in high-context cultures, can actually produce the opposite effect among individualistic participants. Conversely, the use of open, direct, forthright communication, common in low-context cultures, can be perceived as rude and inconsiderate by collectivistic participants, who will likely consider the interaction as face threatening.

The differences between face and facework across cultures are a function of different cultural values. Just as we have discussed throughout this chapter, the variation in cultural values has a direct and continuing influence on how you perceive the world, behave, and communicate. The hope is that you will be motivated to learn more about variations in cultural patterns so that you will be able to understand, predict, and even adapt to the behavior of people from different cultures.

Cultural Patterns and Communication

By now, you have probably realized that cultural patterns occupy a very prominent position in the field of intercultural communication. This chapter has provided only a preliminary overview of how those patterns can help you understand and anticipate varied communicative behaviors that may arise during an intercultural exchange. A succinct overview of the most common patterns and their influence on behavior and communication is provided in Table 6.13.

TABLE 6.13	The Influence of Cultural Patterns

CULTURAL PATTERNS

Individualism vs. Collectivism

Individualism (e.g., USA, Australia, Canada)	*Collectivism* (e.g., Korea, China, Mexico)
• Focus is on the individual & self-promotion • Independency • Task dominates relationship • Social obedience through sense of guilt	• Focus is on the group/affiliations & self-criticism • Interdependency • Relationship dominates task • Social obedience through sense of shame

Egalitarian vs. Hierarchical (Power Distance)

Egalitarian (e.g., Australia, Canada, USA)	*Hierarchical* (e.g., Mexico, India, Korea)
• Horizontal relationships • Subordinates consulted • Equality expected	• Vertical relationships • Subordinates informed • Inequality accepted

Low vs. High Uncertainty Avoidance

Low Uncertainty Avoidance (e.g., India, USA)	*High Uncertainty Avoidance* (e.g., Japan, Spain)
• Change is normal and good • Few behavioral protocols • Greater cultural diversity	• Change is disruptive and disliked • Many behavioral protocols • Less cultural diversity

Monochronic vs. Polychronic (Use of Time)

Monochronic (e.g., Germany, USA)	*Polychronic* (e.g., Arabs, Africans)
• Time is linear and segmented • Focus on a single task • Adherence to schedules	• Time is flexible • Focus on multiple tasks • Weak ties to schedules

Low vs. High Context Communication

Low Context (Direct) (e.g., Germany, USA)	*High Context (Indirect)* (e.g., Korea, Japan)
• Meaning reliant on verbal message • Nonverbal communication low importance • Silence is avoided	• Meaning can be derived from context • Nonverbal communication high importance • Silence is normal

Low vs. High Face Concerns

Low Face Concerns (e.g. Canada, USA)	*High Face Concerns* (e.g., Korea, China)
• Conflict/disagreement is constructive • Concern for self-face	• Conflict/disagreement is threatening • Concern for mutual/other-face

Source: E. McDaniel, "Crossing Cultural Borders: Intercultural Communication from the Interpretation and Translation Perspective," *Journal of Interpreting and Translation Studies*, 14:2 (2011), 359.

CHAPTER 7

Identity and Culture: Situating the Individual

A people must have dignity and identity.

ANDREW GOODMAN

An identity would seem to be arrived at by the way in which the person faces and uses his experience.

JAMES BALDWIN

Identity is a word that has gained increased media usage over the past decade, but it is seldom defined or fully explained. And you are probably asking how identity relates to intercultural communication. A very good question, and by the end of this chapter, you should have an answer to that query as well as a greater appreciation for the complexity of identity.

Identity is a multifaceted, abstract concept that plays an important role in daily communicative interactions and especially in intercultural communication. Globalization is adding even greater complexity to cultural identities by the increased mixing of cultures through cross-cultural marriage, international adoption, immigration, and an overall broadening of opportunities for people of different cultures to meet and interact across a variety of work and leisure contexts. With this in mind, this chapter will focus on some of the more salient aspects of identity.

Because the concept is so pervasive, it is necessary to have an appreciation of exactly what identity entails. To provide that understanding, we begin by pointing out the growing need to understand the role of identity in our culturally diverse global society. This is followed by a theoretical definition of identity, a discussion of some of your many identities, and an examination of a few of the different ways identity is acquired. We then address the many ways in which you establish and enact your cultural identities and the role of identity in communication. Next, we look at the growing phenomenon of bicultural and multicultural identities that are being produced by a globalized social order. The chapter concludes with an examination of stereotyping, prejudice, racism, and ethnocentrism.

THE ROLE OF IDENTITY

According to Pinney, the formation of an identity is a principal objective of the adolescent years, and "those who fail to achieve a secure identity are faced with identity confusion, a lack of clarity about who they are and what their role is in life."[1] This suggests that identity development plays a critical role in the individual's psychological well-being. Thus, the necessity of understanding your sense of identity is self-evident.

The 2010 census was only the second time that respondents could report belonging to more than a single race. Some 2.7 percent of the survey respondents, representing over nine million U.S. Americans, identified themselves as belonging to two or more races. This was a 32 percent increase from the 2000 census.[2] Although not included on the 2010 census form, a question on the 2000 census form allowed individuals to write in their "ancestry or ethnic origin." That query produced about 500 different categories,[3] and more than 90 of those categories had populations in excess of 100,000.[4] The results illustrated the ethnic diversity in the United States and the level of awareness that people have about their identities. The ever changing, technology-driven world is, in part, influenced by adherence to varying perceptions of identity. In other words, as people struggle to adapt to the dynamic changes of modern social life, characterized by the push of globalization and pull of traditional norms, identity is becoming an important factor in how they live their lives and with whom they associate.

For the study of intercultural communication, the concern is how identity influences and guides expectations about your own and others' social roles and provides guidelines for communication interaction with others.[5] For example, in the United States the cultural model for university classroom interaction is defined as student-centered. Students are free to interrupt lectures to ask questions and respectfully question the professor's assertions. Students are aware that the professor may call on them to answer questions about the lesson, and this anticipation instills a motivation to be prepared. Identity as a professor or a student provides the blueprint for classroom behavior. However, that blueprint is designed for a U.S. classroom. Collective cultures, such as Korea and Japan, adhere to an instructor-centered blueprint. The identity roles are the same, but the culturally formed expectations are quite different. Japanese university students do not normally expect to be called on to answer questions, and they seldom raise questions during class. Varied guidelines can also be seen in how occupational identity may influence intercultural interactions. In many cultures, teachers are afforded great social respect and deference by both students and the population as a whole. But in the U.S., where status is more a function of material gain, educators do not normally occupy an elevated position in the social hierarchy. These examples are somewhat oversimplified, but they demonstrate the importance of understanding the role of identity in an intercultural situation. There are many more reasons behind the need to gain an awareness of identity and its influence on intercultural interactions. We believe, however, that the above discussion should convince you of the benefits of becoming better acquainted with both your own identity and that of others. To help you with that task, we will begin with a definition of identity.

DEFINING IDENTITY

As mentioned earlier, identity is abstract, complex, dynamic, and socially constructed. Because of those characteristics, identity is not easily defined, and scholars have provided a variety of descriptions, such as the following offered by Marranci:

> Identity has fascinated intellectuals, such as philosophers (e.g., Locke … and Hume …), psychologists (e.g., James …) and sociologists (e.g., Goffman …) for centuries. Each discipline, and within it each school and scholar, has provided an interpretation, theory and model. With them, they also provide terminologies that have proliferated into a confusing list…. 'identity,' 'self-identity,' 'personal identity,' 'self,' 'selfhood,' 'personhood,' 'I,' 'me,' and a plethora of other terms….[6]

To illustrate this profusion of explanations, Gardiner and Kosmitzki see identity as "a person's self-definition as a separate and distinct individual, including behaviors, beliefs, and attitudes."[7] Ting-Toomey considers identity to be the "reflective self-conception or self-image that we each derive from our family, gender, cultural, ethnic, and individual socialization process. Identity basically refers to our reflective views of ourselves and other perceptions of our self-images."[8] In a more concise definition, Martin and Nakayama characterize identity as "the concept of who we are."[9] While all of these definitions treat identity in its broadest sense, some communication scholars address cultural identity more specifically. Fong contends that "culture and cultural identity in the study of intercultural relations have become umbrella terms that subsume racial and ethnic identity."[10] She defines cultural identity as:

> The identification of communications of a shared system of symbolic verbal and nonverbal behavior that are meaningful to group members who have a sense of belonging and who share traditions, heritage, language, and similar norms of appropriate behavior. Cultural identity is a social construction.[11]

Lustig and Koester view cultural identity as "one's sense of belonging to a particular cultural or ethnic group."[12] Ting-Toomey and Chung see cultural identity as "the emotional significance that we attach to our sense of belonging or affiliation with the larger culture."[13] For Klyukanov, "cultural identity can be viewed as membership in a group in which all people share the same symbolic meanings."[14]

This plethora of definitions is not intended to confuse you, but instead to demonstrate the abstractness of identity, which makes it difficult to construct a single, concise description agreeable to all. Part of the difficulty stems from the long history of identity study across many scholarly disciplines, as stated above. Only recently has it become a subject of investigation for intercultural communication scholars, who began to examine the cultural components of identity. As a result, some definitions address "identity" and others speak of "cultural identity." However, as we will demonstrate throughout the chapter, we believe that culture influences all facets of your many identities.

We have repeatedly pointed out that identity is dynamic. By this we mean that your identities are not static. You continually acquire new identities as a natural process of life experiences. Also, you have more than a single identity. To consider these two points—dynamic and multiple identities—recall how you identified yourself in grade school, in high school, and after entering college. During that time you acquired some new identities and set aside some old ones. For example, you left behind the identity of a high school student and assumed that of a university student.

However, you retained the regional identity of your hometown and state. Perhaps you gave up your identity as a member of a high school sports team, such as swimming or volleyball, and took on the identity of a sorority or fraternity member. As you can see, identity is a composite of multiple, integrated identities; they do not work in isolation, but operate in combination based on the context or situation. As an illustration, when you are in the classroom, your identity as a student is prominent, but you are still a male or a female, a friend of some of your classmates, an employee, a son or daughter, and perhaps even a wife or a husband, to list just a few of your other identities.

In an effort to better understand people's multiple identities, some researchers have constructed taxonomies for the different types. For instance, Turner offers three identity categories: human, social, and personal.[15] *Human identities* are those perceptions of self that link you to the rest of humanity and set you apart from other life forms. *Social identities* are represented by the various groups you belong to, such as racial,

People have a number of identities, and they are acquired as a natural process of life experiences.

Kathleen K. Parker

ethnic, occupational, age, hometown, and others. Social identity is a product of the contrast between membership in some social groups and non-membership in others (i.e., the in-group/out-group dichotomy). *Personal identity* is what sets you apart from other in-group members and marks you as special or unique. These markers may be innate talents, such as the ability to play a musical instrument without formal training; special achievements, like winning an Olympic gold medal; or something as intangible as a gregarious personality.

Hall offers a similar categorization when he writes, "Each of us has three levels of identity that, depending on the context, may or may not be salient in our interactions with others. These three levels are personal, relational, and communal."[16] *Personal identities* are those that make you unique and distinct from others. *Relational identities* are a product of your relationships with other people, such as husband/wife, teacher/ student, or executive/manager. *Communal identities* are "typically associated with large-scale communities, such as nationality, ethnicity, gender, or religious or political affiliation."[17]

Hall's communal identity is essentially the same as Taylor's social identity, and Gudykunst provides a further classification of communal or social identity. These identities are considered important during intercultural communication interactions.

> Our social identities can be based on our memberships in demographic categories (e.g., nationality, ethnicity, gender, age, social class), the roles we play (e.g., student, professor, parent), our membership in formal or informal organizations (e.g., political parties, social clubs), our associations or vocations (e.g., scientists, artists, gardeners), or our memberships in stigmatized groups (e.g., homeless, people with AIDS).[18]

This discussion has offered a theoretical understanding of identity and attempted to show that an individual's identity is "made up of numerous overlapping aspects or subidentities."[19] Because differences in identity are relevant to intercultural communication interaction and study, we now look at some social identities and examine how they are influenced by culture.

EXAMPLES OF SOCIAL IDENTITY

We use the terms identity and identities interchangeably, but point out that one's identity actually consists of multiple identities acting in concert. The importance and saliency of any single identity is a function of the context. As the situation varies, you may choose to emphasize one or more of your identities. At work, your occupational and organizational identity is paramount, but when visiting your parents, you are first a son or a daughter. In both environments, however, other identities, such as race and biological sex, are also present, although in a secondary role. Regardless of the identity or identities on display, all are influenced to various degrees, by culture. In this section we will examine a few of your many identities and illustrate how culture influences each.

RACIAL IDENTITY

The most important aspect to remember about race is that it is a social construct arising from historical attempts to classify people into different groups. The concept grew out of efforts by eighteenth-century European anthropologists to place peoples into different categories based largely on their outward appearance. During that era, race was also used "as a device for justifying European dominance over Africans and American Indians."[20] In retrospect, it is easy to see how those early endeavors were influenced by feelings of prejudice and ethnocentrism grounded in a strong sense of Western superiority.

Today, racial identity is usually associated with external physical traits such as skin color, hair texture, facial appearance, and eye shape.[21] Modern science, however, has found that there is very little genetic variation among human beings, which undermines the belief that race can be used to categorize peoples. The idea has been further eroded by centuries of genetic intermixing,[22] which is becoming an increasing occurrence in contemporary society through intercultural marriage. However, the socially constructed concept of racial identity persists in the United States, no doubt abetted by the historical legacy of conditions such as slavery, the early persecution of American Indians, issues of civil rights, and most recently, a growing influx of immigrants. The lingering effects are seen in question nine of the 2010 census form, which offered respondents a choice of 15 different racial categories. These categories clearly confused race (e.g., White, Black) with nationality and ethnicity (e.g., Chinese, Guamanian).[23]

Although race remains a commonly used term in the United States, it is ill defined and often interchanged with the term ethnic group. This lack of a clear definition and resulting confusion leads us to agree with Kottak and Kozaitis' suggestion that "it is better to use the term *ethnic group* instead of *race* to describe *any* such social group, for example, African Americans, Asian Americans, Irish Americans, Anglo Americans, or Hispanics."[24]

ETHNIC IDENTITY

As we have just stated above, from our perspective, racial identity is traditionally tied to one's biological ancestry that produces similar physical characteristics. Ethnicity or ethnic identity, on the other hand, is derived from a sense of shared heritage, history, traditions, values, similar behaviors, area of origin, and in some instances, language.[25]

Some people take their ethnic identity from a regional grouping that transcends national borders and is grounded in common cultural beliefs and practices. This is illustrated by the three groups below. In each case, a shared language constitutes an additional dimension of their ethnic identity.

- The Basques, located along the Spanish-French border, who speak Euskara
- The Kurds, a large ethnic group in northeast Iraq with communities in Turkey, Iran, and Syria, who speak Kurdish
- The Roma (commonly called Gypsies), scattered across Eastern and Western Europe, who speak Romani

The ethnicity of many U.S. Americans is tied to their ancestors' home of origin before immigrating to the United States, such as Germany, Italy, Mexico, China, or one of a host of other places. Generations subsequent to the original immigrants often refer to themselves using terms such as "German-American," "Italian-American," "Mexican-American," or "Chinese-American." As Chen explains, the hyphen both separates and connects the two cultural traditions.[26]

CONSIDER THIS

Maria was born in Mexico and immigrated to the United States with her parents when she was two years old and settled in rural Vermont. Her elementary through high school classmates were predominantly white, most of her friends were Anglos. Determined to assimilate, Maria's parents celebrated only U.S. holidays and always spoke English at home. As a result, she has only a limited ability in using Spanish and a passing knowledge of Mexican culture. Now a junior in college, Maria recently discovered she entered the United States illegally and is in danger of being deported to Mexico.

What is Maria's ethnic identity? What cultural problems might she encounter if she is sent to Mexico?

During the formative years of the United States, immigrants often grouped together in a particular region to form ethnic communities, and some of these continue today, such as Chinatown in San Francisco and Little Italy in New York. Newer ethnic enclaves, like Little Saigon in the Los Angeles area, have developed in the wake of more recent immigrants. In these areas, the people's sense of ethnic identity tends to remain strong, because traditional cultural practices, beliefs, and often language are followed and perpetuated. But as time passes, members of younger generations tend to move to areas of greater ethnic diversity and frequently marry into other ethnic groups. For some, this can dilute their feelings of ethnic identity, and today, it is not uncommon to hear U.S. Americans refer to their ethnicity by providing a lengthy historical account of their family's many ethnic mergings. Others, especially those with a Euro-American heritage, will often simply refer to themselves as "just an American" or even "a white American." Frequently, they are members of the U.S. dominant culture, which grew out of Judeo-Christian religious traditions imported from Western Europe, and whose lineage is characterized by an extensive history of interethnic Euro-American marriages. Martin and Nakayama write that many cultural practices associated with "whiteness" are beyond the awareness of the actual participants, but are more discernible by members of excluded minority culture groups.[27] Thus, "whiteness" can frequently be associated with positions of privilege.

GENDER IDENTITY

Gender identity is quite different from biological sex or sexual identity. Gender is a socially constructed concept that refers to how a particular culture differentiates masculine and feminine social roles. Ting-Toomey sees gender identity as "the meanings and interpretations we hold concerning our self-images and expected other-images of 'femaleness' and 'maleness.'"[28]

What constitutes displays of gender identity varies across cultures and is constantly changing, often in response to mass media content. For instance, the appearance of U.S. men in the 1960s and 70s was characterized by long hair, often with beards and mustaches. Today, however, fashion dictates little or no hair. Additionally, a Google search of "men's nail polish" will produce over 18 thousand hits. Language is another means of expressing gender differences. In Japanese, certain words are traditionally used exclusively by women, while men employ entirely different words to express the same meaning. In English, there is little or no distinction between words used by women and those used by men. A culture's gender norms can also influence career decisions. For instance, males represent less than 6 percent of nurses in the

Dennis MacDonald/PhotoEdit

Gender identity refers to the ways particular cultures differentiate between masculine and feminine roles.

United States. This disparity, according to Cohen, is because "most people consider nursing to be a woman's career."[29]

In contrast to the rather rigid classifications of either male or female used by the United States and most Western European nations, some cultures offer a socially acceptable middle ground for transgender individuals. Some of the Native American Indian tribes accepted transgenders and even considered them to have special powers.[30] Thailand's *kathoeys*, or "lady boys," do experience some discrimination but enjoy more social acceptance than their U.S. counterparts.[31] In South Asia, the *hijras*, generally men who assume feminine identities, are not viewed as male or female but as a third gender.[32]

NATIONAL IDENTITY

National identity refers to nationality, which the majority of people associate with the nation where they were born. But national identity can also be acquired by immigration and naturalization. People who have taken citizenship in a country different from their birthplace may eventually begin to adopt some or all aspects of a new national identity, depending on the strength of their attachment to their new homeland. Alternatively, people residing permanently in another nation may retain a strong connection to their homeland. National identity usually becomes more pronounced when people are away from their home country. When asked where they are from, international travelers normally respond with their national identity—e.g., "We are from Canada." There are, however, many instances where local affiliation outweighs nationality. Texans, for instance, are noted for identifying themselves as being from Texas rather than from "the States." Strong feelings of national identity are often on display at international sporting events, such as the World Cup or the Olympics.

As we have indicated, identity is dynamic and can change contextually over time. A particularly interesting example of this dynamism is ongoing in the European Union, where younger generations are moving away from the national identity of their parents and adopting what might be termed a "transnational" identity. Reid reports that young adults from European Union nations tend to "think of 'Europe' as their native land."[33] Concern about national identity is so great in France that the government has established a Ministry of Immigration and National Identity, which is tasked with "better integrating newcomers and protecting French identity."[34] In an effort to heal the wounds of the 1994 conflict between the Hutu and Tutsi tribes, the Rwandan government has outlawed ethnicity and is seeking to have new generations see themselves only as Rwandans.[35] A similar effort is underway in Afghanistan where U.S. military trainers are attempting to create a sense of nationality among Afghan soldiers that will transcend culturally instilled tribal loyalities.[36]

Most nations are home to a number of different cultural groups, but one group usually exercises the most power and is often referred to as the dominant culture because its members maintain control of economic, governmental, and institutional organizations. This control leads to the establishment of a "national character," defined by Allport as:

> "National character" implies that members of a nation, despite ethnic, racial, religious, or individual differences among them, do resemble one another in certain fundamental matters of belief and conduct, more than they resemble members of other nations.[37]

In the United States the dominant culture is considered to be people with Western European ethnicity, and the cultural traits arising from that heritage are ascribed to the nation as a whole and referred to as the "national character." The advent of globalization, however, has brought challenges to the primacy of U.S. dominant cultural values as people of different nationalities, ethnicities, and varied beliefs and values increasingly come into contact with each other.

REGIONAL IDENTITY

With the exception of very small nations like Andorra, Lichtenstein, or Monaco, every country can be divided into a number of different geographical regions, and often those regions reflect varying cultural traits. The cultural contrasts among these regions may be manifested through ethnicity, language, accent, dialect, customs, food, dress, or different historical and political legacies. Residents of these regions use one or more of those characteristics to demonstrate their regional identity. For example, although the total population of Belgium is just over 10 million, the country has three official languages—Dutch, French, and German.

In the United States many regional identities are delimited by state boundary lines, and almost everyone is proud of his or her home state. Residents of Alaska, California, and Texas offer prime examples of pride in regional identity. Louisiana is marked by a distinct cultural tradition derived from its French historical heritage. Regional identity can also be based on a larger or smaller geographical area, such as New England, "down South," "back East," "West Texas," or "Southern California."

In Japan regional identity is marked by a variety of different dialects (e.g., Tokyo, Kansai, Tohoku, etc.), and some of those dialects (e.g., Kagoshima and Okinawa) are difficult for Japanese from other regions to understand. Japanese living overseas often form clubs based on their home prefecture and hold periodic gatherings to celebrate their common traditions. Despite reunification, separate East and West German identities remain a reality. Mexicans demonstrate their regional identity when they tell people they are from Sinaloa, Michoacán, Oaxaca, or Mexico City. In China people from different regions often speak mutually unintelligible languages (e.g., Mongolian, Tibetan, Uyghur) or dialects (e.g., Mandarin, Cantonese, Hakka). Political division resulting from war has imposed different national identities on residents of North and South Korea and divided regional identities.

ORGANIZATIONAL IDENTITY

In some cultures a person's organizational affiliation can be an important source of identity. This is especially true in collectivistic cultures, but far less so in individualistic cultures. To illustrate this dichotomy, we will contrast organizational identity practices in Japan, a collectivistic culture, and the United States, an individualistic culture.

Although becoming less prevalent among younger workers, Japanese businessmen employed by large corporations have traditionally worn a small lapel pin to signal their company affiliation. There is no similar practice among managers and executives in the United States. Although some in the United States occasionally may wear a polo shirt or a tie with a company logo, this is not a common or habitual practice. In Japan a person's organizational identity is so important that during introductions the company's name is given before the individual's name. For example, Mrs. Suzuki, an employee at the Tokyo Bank, would be introduced as *Tōkyō Ginkō no Suzuki san* ("Ms. Suzuki of Tokyo Bank").[38] In the United States an individual is introduced first by his or her name, followed by the organization. On business cards the Japanese company and the individual's position are placed above his or her name. On American business cards the company name is normally at the top, followed by the individual's name in large, bold letters, with organizational position under the name in smaller type. These examples offer insight into how collective cultures stress identity through group membership, and individualistic cultures emphasize individual identity.

PERSONAL IDENTITY

Earlier in this chapter we noted that personal identity consists of those characteristics that set one apart from others in his or her in-group, those things that make one unique, and how one sees oneself. Cultural influences also come into play when determining personal identity. Markus and Kitayama report that "people in different cultures have strikingly different construals of the self, of others, and of the interdependence between the two."[39] People from individualistic cultures like the United States and Western Europe work to exemplify their differences from others, but members of collectivistic cultures tend to emphasize their group membership or connection to others. While still slaves to fashion, most U.S. Americans try to demonstrate their personal identity in their dress and appearance. In collective cultures, like China, Korea, and Japan, people tend to dress in a similar conservative fashion because it is important to blend in.

Personal identity arises from those objects and ideas that help set you and others apart from the dominant culture while also marking you as a member of a specific group.

Rudi Von Briel/PhotoEdit

CYBER AND FANTASY IDENTITY

The Internet allows you to quickly and easily access and exchange information on a worldwide basis. As Suler, a psychologist, informs us, the Internet also provides an opportunity to escape the constraints of everyday identities:

> One of the interesting things about the Internet is the opportunity it offers people to present themselves in a variety of different ways. You can alter your style of being just slightly or indulge in wild experiments with your identity by changing your age, history, personality, physical appearance, even your gender. The username you choose, the details you do or don't indicate about yourself, the information presented on your personal web page, the persona or avatar you assume in an online community—all [are] important aspects of how people manage their identity in cyberspace.[40]

The Internet allows individuals to select and promote what they consider the positive features of their identity and omit any perceived negative elements, or even construct entirely new identities. Some online groups require participants to assume an "imaginary persona," and infatuation with these invented identities can become so strong they can "take a life of their own."[41] The Internet is replete with "virtual world" websites, such as Second Life, that allow users to construct a cyber identity, which may or may not correspond to their actual identity. According to one report, in Indonesia, with the world's largest Muslim population and the second largest Facebook market, people are constructing cyber, or virtual, identities that are very different from their actual identities. Some may elect to create a cyber persona with physical characteristics entirely different from their own features.[42]

Fantasy identity, which also extends across cultures, centers on characters from science fiction movies, comic books (*manga*), and *anime*. Every year people attend domestic and international conventions devoted to these subjects. For example, the 2011 Hong Kong Ani-Com & Games convention drew almost 700,000 attendees over a five-day period, and the 1,100 people with the best costumes were admitted free.[43] Comic-Con International has been held annually in San Diego, California, since 1970; in 2011 ticket sales were capped at 130,000.[44] At these gatherings some attendees come dressed, individually or in groups, as their favorite fantasy character(s). For a few hours or days they assume, enact, and communicate the identity of their favorite media character. But conventions are not the only opportunity for people to indulge their fantasy identities. "Cosplay" (short for costume play) is another venue that lets people attend events or parties dressed as media characters.

There are many other forms of identity that play a significant role in the daily lives of people. For example, we have not examined the functions of age, religion, political affiliation, socio-economic class, physical ability, or minority status, all of which are part of most individuals' identity and are influenced by culture. Nor have we addressed the very influential role that tribal identity plays in many places, such as Afghanistan, Iraq, Libya, and Pakistan. However, the various identities discussed here should give you an awareness of the complexity of the topic and of how culture influences identity. Now, let us look at how we acquire our identities.

ACQUIRING AND DEVELOPING IDENTITIES

As discussed earlier, identities are largely a product of group membership. Ting-Toomey sees identities as being acquired and developed "through interaction with others in their cultural group."[45] Identity development, then, becomes a process of familial influences, cultural socialization, and personal experiences. We have already looked at the family in Chapter 3, but familial influence on identity is so great that we need to touch on a few points here. The initial exposure to your identity came from your family, where you began to learn culturally appropriate beliefs, values, and social roles.[46] Development of gender identity begins at a very early age when family members begin to teach children behaviors specific to boys and girls. Interacting with extended family members instills age-appropriate behaviors. It is also the family that first begins to inculcate the concept of an individual- or group-based identity.

Upon entering school, you were required to learn and demonstrate the culturally ascribed behaviors of a student. The media also played a considerable role in your identity development. The near-constant exposure to media stereotypes creates a sense of how you should look, dress, and act in order to display age and gender appropriate identities. Media is also used to recruit people to join different groups, such as those for or against a specific activity, like gay marriage, abortion, or the war in Afghanistan; and inclusion in such a group imparts another identity.

From a theoretical perspective, Phinney offers a three-stage model to help explain identity development.[47] Although the model focuses on ethnic identity among adolescents, it is equally applicable to the acquisition and growth of cultural identity. *Unexamined ethnic identity*, the initial stage, is "characterized by the lack of exploration of ethnicity."[48] During this phase individuals are not particularly interested in exploring or demonstrating their personal ethnicity. For members of minority cultures the lack of interest may result from a desire to suppress their own ethnicity in an effort to identify with the majority culture. Majority members in the United States, on the other hand, seem to take for granted that their identity is the societal norm and give little thought to their own ethnicity.[49]

The second stage, *ethnic identity search*, begins when individuals become interested in learning about and understanding their own ethnicity. Movement from stage one to stage two can result from a variety of stimulations. An incident of discrimination might move members of a minority to reflect on their own ethnicity. This could lead to a realization that some beliefs and values of the majority culture can be detrimental to minority members[50] and motivate movement toward one's own ethnicity. Dolores Tanno grew up in northern New Mexico and had always considered herself Spanish. After leaving New Mexico, she discovered that some people saw her as Mexican rather than Spanish, and this motivated her ethnic identity search.[51] Increased interest in ethnic identity could come from attending a cultural event, taking a culture class, or some other event that produces a greater awareness of one's cultural heritage. *Ethnic achievement*, Phinney's final stage of identity development, is reached when individuals have a clear and confident understanding of their own cultural identity. For minority members, this usually comes with an ability to effectively deal with discrimination and negative stereotypes.[52] Identity achievement can also provide one with greater self-confidence and feelings of personal worth.

Adding to the work of other scholars, Martin and Nakayama present separate, multi-stage identity development models for minority, majority, and biracial individuals. In the **minority development** model, the initial stage, *unexamined identity*, is similar to Phinney's model, in which individuals are unconcerned with identity issues. During stage two, *conformity*, minority members endeavor to fit in with the dominant culture and may even possess negative self-images. *Resistance and separatism*, stage three, is usually the result of some cultural awakening that stimulates a greater interest in and adherence to one's own culture. Concurrently, rejection of all or selected aspects of the dominant culture may occur. In the final stage, *integration*, individuals have a sense of pride in, and identify with, their own cultural group and demonstrate an acceptance of other groups.[53]

The five-step model for **majority identity** development follows a similar first stage, *unexamined identity*, where identity is of little concern. *Acceptance*, the second stage, is characterized by acquiescence to existing social inequities, even though such acceptance may be at a subconscious level. At the next stage, *resistance*, members of the dominant culture become more aware of existing social inequities, begin to question their own culture, and increase association with minority culture members. Achievement of the fourth and fifth stages, *redefinition* and *reintegration*, brings an increased understanding of one's dominant culture identity and an appreciation of minority cultures.[54]

In the first stage of Martin and Nakayama's **biracial identity** development model, biracial individuals may rotate through three phases where they (1) become conscious of differences in general and the potential for discord, (2) gain an awareness of their personal differences from other children, and (3) begin to sense they are not part of the norm. The second stage entails a struggle to be accepted and the development of feelings that they should choose one race or another. In the third and final stage, biracial individuals accept their duality, becoming more self-confident.[55] This development model is demonstrated in the historical experience of Japanese biracial children, called *hafu* (half) in Japanese. The occupation of Japan by Allied forces after WWII saw the birth of increasing numbers of biracial children, who generally encountered derision and overt discrimination. However, as their numbers increased, especially in the wake of globalization, they have become common figures in the contemporary social order. Recently, they established a formal, worldwide organizational structure and launched an ongoing project that organizes events and public lectures to create "a dialogue about being in between cultures."[56]

Identities can also be classified as *ascribed* or *avowed*, based on how they are achieved.[57] This distinction refers to whether your identities were obtained involuntarily or voluntarily. Racial, ethnic, and sexual identities are assigned at birth and are considered *ascribed*, or involuntary. In hierarchical cultures where social status is often inherited, such as is Mexico's, a person's family name can be a strong source of ascribed identity. By contrast, your identity as a university student is *avowed* because you voluntarily elected to attend the school. Even though being a university student is a voluntary identity, your culture has established expectations that delineate appropriate and inappropriate social behavior for college students. When enacting your student identity, you will normally try to conform to those socially appropriate expectations, sometimes consciously and at other times subconsciously.

ESTABLISHING AND ENACTING CULTURAL IDENTITY

By now you should have a clear understanding of what constitutes identity, an awareness of some of your many identities, and insight into how identities are acquired. This background will help you understand how cultural identities are established and expressed.

As you go about your daily routine, stepping into and out of various contexts, different identities are established, re-established, and displayed. By interacting with others you continually create and re-create your cultural identity through communication.[58] As Molden notes, "It is through communication that we are able to express and (hence make known) our similarities and dissimilarities to others."[59] Communication employed to create and enact identity can take a variety of forms, including "conversation, commemorations of history, music, dance, ritual, ceremonial, and social drama of all sorts."[60] The stories told by family members tie us to the past and provide a "sense of identity and connection to the world."[61] These stories are also infused with cultural beliefs and values, which become part of one's identity.

Culture's influence in establishing identity is demonstrated by contrasting student interaction styles in U.S. and Japanese schools. In the United States individualism is stressed, and even young children are taught to be independent and develop their personal identity. Schools in the United States encourage competition in the classroom and on the playing field. Students quickly learn to voice their ideas and feel free to challenge the opinions of others as a means of asserting their own identity.

Being different is a common and valued trait. This is in contrast to the collective societies found in South America, West Africa, and Northeast Asia, where children learn the importance of family dependence and interdependence, and identity is "defined by relationships and group memberships."[62] This produces activities that promote identity tied to the group. In Japanese preschool and elementary classrooms students are frequently divided into small groups (*han*), where they are encouraged to solve problems collectively rather than individually.[63] Through this procedure young Japanese students are taught the importance of identifying with a group.

Identities are also established and displayed in cultural rites of passage, which are used to help adolescents gain an increased awareness of who they are as they enter adulthood.[64] In some underdeveloped societies the rite can involve a painful physical experience, such as male or female circumcision, but in developed nations, the ceremony is usually less harsh and is often a festive occasion. The bar mitzvah, for instance, is used to introduce Jewish boys into adulthood, when they become more responsible for religious duties. In Mexican culture girls look forward to celebrating their fifteenth birthday with a *Quinceañera*. This festivity is a means of acknowledging that a young woman has reached sexual maturity and is now an adult, ready to assume additional family and social responsibilities. In addition, the celebration is intended to reaffirm religious faith, good morals, and traditional family values.[65] In the dominant U.S. culture rites of passage into adulthood are generally not as distinct, but are often associated with the individual attaining a greater degree of independence.[66] Graduation from high school or college, for example, brings increased expectations of self-sufficiency and a new identity.

Once established, identities are enacted in many ways, beginning in childhood and progressing through adolescence into the adult years. For instance, individuals in almost every culture have ways of displaying their religious or spiritual identity. Many Jews wear yarmulkes or other distinctive clothes, and among Christians it is common to see a cross worn as an item of personal jewelry. Throughout the world, Muslim women are seen wearing the traditional headscarf (*hijab*) as a means of conveying their religious identity. Some men and women wear a red dot (*pottu*) on their forehead as a sign of their devotion to the Hindu religion. Adherents of Shikism commonly wear a turban as part of their devotion. Each of these symbols identifies the wearer as belonging to a specific religious group and thus is a sign of both inclusion and exclusion.

Identity can also be signaled by involvement in commemorative events. The Fourth of July in the United States, Bastille Day in France, and Independence Day in Mexico are celebrations of national identity. The annual Saint Patrick's Day parade in New York City is an opportunity for people of Irish heritage to take pride in their ethnic identity. Oktoberfest celebrations allow people to rekindle their German identity, and the Lunar New Year is a time for the Chinese and many other Asian cultures to observe traditions that reaffirm their identities.

While many customs of identity enactment are tradition-bound, evolving circumstances can bring about new ways. This type of change was discovered by David and Ayouby's study of Arab minorities in the Detroit, Michigan, area. They found that a division existed between how early immigrants and later arrivals understood Arab identity. Immigrants who arrived in the United States years earlier were satisfied "with meeting and enacting their ethnicity in a ritualistic fashion by eating Arabic food, perhaps listening to Arabic music, and even speaking Arabic to their limited ability."[67] The more recent Arab immigrant arrivals, however, had a "more politicized

Strong feelings of identity can be signaled and reinforced by involvement in commemorative events.

Edwin McDaniel

identity,"[68] resulting from their experiences in the conflicts and political turmoil of the Middle East. They felt that being an Arab involved taking a more assertive role in events in their native land, such as sending money back or becoming politically active.[69]

There are certainly many more ways of establishing and evincing your identity than we have discussed here. For instance, we did not address the obvious cultural identity markers of language, accents, or family names. But this overview should convince you of the complexity of your identities and how they are shaped by culture.

IDENTITY IN INTERCULTURAL INTERACTIONS

We have pointed out that identity is established through communicative interaction with others. According to Hecht and his colleagues, identity is also "maintained and modified through social interaction. Identity then begins to influence interaction through shaping expectations and motivating behavior."[70] As was previously discussed, you are constantly moving through various identities as you interact with other people, and with each identity you employ a set of communicative behaviors appropriate for that identity and context. Culture has shaped your understanding and expectations of correct communication practices for various social settings—for example, a classroom, hospital, or sales meeting. However, what is appropriate in one culture may be inappropriate in another. We have already pointed out how students and teachers in Japan and the United States have quite different culturally established standards for classroom communicative behavior. However, what if a Japanese student were placed in a U.S. classroom, or vice versa?

In an intercultural meeting the varying expectations for identity display and communication style carry considerable potential for creating anxiety, misunderstandings, and even conflict. This is why Imahori and Cupach consider "cultural identity as a focal element in intercultural communication."[71] Continuing with our student/teacher example, try to imagine how students from a culture that does not value communicative assertiveness would feel in a typical U.S. classroom. Being unaccustomed to having the instructor query students, they would probably be reluctant to raise their hands and would likely consider U.S. students who challenged the teacher to be rude or even arrogant. To avoid potential problems during intercultural interaction, you need to develop what Collier calls intercultural competence, which is achieved when an avowed identity matches the ascribed identity.

> For example, if you avow the identity for an assertive, outspoken U.S. American and your conversational partner avows himself or herself to be a respectful, nonassertive Vietnamese, then each must ascribe the corresponding identity to the conversational partner. You must jointly negotiate what kind of relationship will be mutually satisfying. Some degree of adjustment and accommodation is usually necessary.[72]

Collier is saying that in order to communicate effectively in an intercultural situation, an individual's avowed cultural identity and communication style should match the identity and style ascribed to him or her by the other party. But since the communication styles are likely to be different, the participants will have to search for a middle ground, and this search will require flexibility and adaptation. As a simple illustration, the Japanese traditionally greet and say goodbye to each other by bowing. However, in Japanese-U.S. business meetings, the Japanese have learned to bow only slightly while shaking hands. In doing this, they are adjusting their normal greeting practice to accommodate U.S. visitors. Longtime U.S. business representatives to Japan have learned to emulate this behavior. Thus, a mutually satisfying social protocol has evolved. In achieving this, the participants have demonstrated the principal components of intercultural communication competence: motivation, knowledge, and skills.

IDENTITY IN A GLOBALIZED SOCIETY

There is no denying that the contemporary world social order is increasingly characterized by multiculturalism. In Chapter 10, we will talk about how business is now routinely conducted in a transnational environment, cross-cultural health care is a growing field, and multicultural education is a salient challenge. Contrary to the belief of some, globalization is not producing a homogeneous global society. We agree with Giddens, who claims that rather than homogeneity, a result of globalization is increased cultural diversity and "a revival of local cultural identities in different parts of the world."[73] This trend was recently displayed in San Diego, California, where local Vietnamese have called for an area of the city to be recognized as "Little Saigon." The district is populated by many former South Vietnam refugees and hosts a variety of Vietnamese businesses. Backers of the drive feel that the designation would "promote cultural identity" and help younger generations better define their cultural heritage.[74] In European countries, there is growing concern about how traditional national identities might be impacted by the increasingly vocal immigrant communities and the rising numbers of new arrivals. So great is this concern that France has launched a "government-sponsored debate over national identity."[75]

From another perspective, multiple cultural identities are becoming more commonplace. The globalized economy, immigration, ease of foreign travel, communication technologies, and intercultural marriage are bringing about an increased mixing of cultures, and this mixing is producing people who possess multiple cultural identities.

Chuang notes that "cultural identity becomes blurry in the midst of cultural integration, bicultural interactions, interracial marriages, and the mutual adaptation processes."[76] Martin, Nakayama, and Flores further support this idea by reporting that "increasing numbers of people are living 'in between' cultural identities. That is, they identify with more than

one ethnicity, race, or religion."[77] An example of this is a series of ads in *The Economist* magazine sponsored by a large Brazilian bank. The ads feature photos of prominent Latin American sports and cultural arts personalities with the caption "I am a Global Latin American." This message implies that in addition to their national identity, the celebrities are also adopting a larger, more inclusive, regional identity.

In the United States, immigration, intercultural marriage, and multiracial births are creating a social environment where the younger generations consider cultural diversity a normal part of social life.[78] Kotkin and Tseng contend that among U.S. Americans there is "not only a growing willingness—and ability—to cross cultures, but also the evolution of a nation in which personal identity is shaped more by cultural preferences than by skin color or ethnic heritage."[79] Hitt points out "more and more Americans have come to feel comfortable changing out of the identities they were born into and donning new ethnicities in which they feel more at home."[80]

The global marketplace is giving rise to what Onwumechili and his colleagues have termed "intercultural transients." These are "travelers who regularly alternate residence between their homeland and a host foreign country,"[82] and must manage frequent cultural changes and identity renegotiations.[83] Over the past decade, a growing number of nations have made dual citizenship available, which has added to the number of intercultural transients. Carlos Ghosn serves as a model example of an intercultural transient. Born in Brazil of Lebanese immigrant parents, Ghosn attended schools in Lebanon and France, and speaks multiple languages. A citizen of Lebanon, he is the Chairman, President, and CEO of Nissan (a Japanese company) and CEO and President of Renault (a French firm), positions he holds concurrently.[84] To fulfill his responsibilities, Ghosn has to divide his time between Japan, France, the United States, and the many other countries where his organizations own and manage subsidiary operations. In his daily activities, Mr. Ghosn must adjust to the intricacies of each culture. Although this is a somewhat extreme example, it is clear that the ranks of intercultural transients are expanding as organizations compete internationally for employees.

Issues of identity can be expected to remain complex—and perhaps become more so—as multiculturalism increasingly characterizes contemporary society. It is clear, however, that the old understanding of a fixed cultural identity or ethnicity is outdated, and identity is rapidly becoming more of an "articulated negotiation between what you call yourself and what other people are willing to call you."[85] But regardless of how they are achieved, the form they take, or how they are acquired, your identities will remain a product of culture.

THE DARK SIDE OF IDENTITY

By now you should have a clear idea of what identity is and how it can influence intercultural communication interactions. It should be equally clear that, fundamentally, identity is about similarities and differences.[86] In other words, you identify with something as a result of preference, understanding, familiarity, or socialization. You may prefer the hip-hop style of dress instead of cowboy boots and jeans. You may understand American football better than cricket, and you may be more familiar with hamburgers and French fries than with a Vegemite sandwich. You will likely have greater tolerance toward the people and things you prefer, understand, and find familiar. But by definition, intercultural communication involves people from dissimilar cultures, and this makes difference a normative condition. Thus your reaction to, and ability to manage, those differences is key to successful intercultural interactions. A preference for things you understand and are familiar with can adversely influence your perception of, and attitude toward, new and different people and things. This can lead to stereotyping, prejudice, racism, and ethnocentrism.

STEREOTYPING

When confronted with a lack of familiarity or similarity, we often resort to stereotypes. Because we meet so many strangers and are often faced with unusual circumstances, stereotyping is a common occurrence. Thus, stereotyping can be a natural way of dealing with the unknown, but problems frequently arise from a failure to recognize negative stereotypes.

STEREOTYPES DEFINED

Stereotyping is a complex form of categorization that mentally organizes your experiences with, and guides your behavior toward, a particular group of people. It becomes a means of organizing your perceptions into simplified categories that can be used to represent an entire collection of things or people. Psychologists Abbate, Boca, and Bocchiaro offer a more formal definition: "A stereotype is a cognitive structure containing the perceiver's knowledge, beliefs, and expectancies about some human social groups."[87] The reason for the pervasive nature of stereotypes is that human beings have a psychological need to categorize and classify. The world is too big, too complex, and too dynamic to comprehend in all its detail. Hence, you tend to classify and pigeonhole. The main problem is not in the pigeonholing or categorizing, but rather "the difficulty lies with the overgeneralization and the often negative evaluations (attitudes and prejudices) that are directed toward members of the categories."[88]

Stereotypes can be positive or negative. Those that refer to a large group of people as lazy, coarse, vicious, or moronic are obviously negative. There are, of course, positive stereotypes, such as the assumption that all Asian students are hardworking, well mannered, and intelligent. However, because stereotypes (as the word is currently defined) narrow our perceptions, they usually jeopardize intercultural communication and take on a negative tone. This is because stereotypes tend to overgeneralize the characteristics of a group of people. For example, we know that not all Asian students are hardworking and intelligent and that there is no large group of people in which everyone is lazy.

LEARNING STEREOTYPES

Stereotypes are everywhere and they seem to endure. Why? Perhaps one way to understand the power and lasting impact of stereotypes is to examine how they are acquired. Remember, you are not born with stereotypes; they are learned, and like culture, they are learned in a variety of ways. The most obvious, and perhaps most important, agent of stereotypes is the socialization process, which begins with our parents. While many parents try to avoid teaching their children to think in stereotypes, we tend to agree with Schneider when he notes that often parents directly or indirectly actually promote them.[89] Children who hear their parents say, "All those illegal immigrants are taking our jobs" are learning stereotypes. Once children enter school, peers become an important carrier of stereotypes. Of course, the socialization process continues as children become members of various religious and social groups. These groups, while teaching the virtues of a particular point of view, might also intentionally or unintentionally impart stereotypes about an opposite view. For example, by learning one particular view of religion and at the same time hearing of the "evils of religious terrorists," children might be acquiring stereotypes about Muslims.

Many stereotypes are generated by the mass media and widely disseminated through a variety of formats such as advertisements, movies, and TV sitcoms, soap operas, and reality shows. Television has been guilty of providing distorted images of many ethnic groups, the elderly, and gay people. Media has also played a role in perpetuating certain stereotyped perceptions of women and men. Wood offers an excellent summary of television's portrayal of men and women when she writes, "Media most often represents boys and men as active, adventurous, powerful, sexually aggressive, and largely uninvolved in human relationships, and represents girls and women as young, thin, beautiful, passive, dependent, and often incompetent."[90] When the media highlights incidents of crime committed by illegal immigrants, an image is created that all immigrants are engaged in criminal activities. In other words, a series of isolated behaviors by a few members of a group unfairly engenders a generalized perception that is applied to all members of the group. Stereotypes can also evolve out of fear of people from groups that differ from one's own. People who dress differently, speak another language, practice an unfamiliar religion, and celebrate holidays different from the mainstream population can easily become targets of suspicion and derision.

STEREOTYPES AND INTERCULTURAL COMMUNICATION

In most instances, stereotypes are the result of limited, lazy, and misguided perceptions and the resulting problems created by these misperceptions are both numerous and serious. Adler reminds us of the harmful effect stereotypes can have on intercultural communication:

> Stereotypes become counterproductive when we place people in the wrong groups, when we incorrectly describe the group norm, when we evaluate the group rather than simply describing it, when we confuse the stereotype with the description of a particular individual, and when we fail to modify the stereotype based on our actual observations and experience.[91]

Let us look at four additional reasons why stereotypes hamper intercultural communication. *First*, stereotypes are a kind of filter; they only allow in information that is consistent with information already held by the individual. In this way, what might be the truth can be filtered out. For example, women were stereotyped for many years as a rather one-dimensional group confined to the role of homemaker. That stereotype often kept women from advancing in the workplace. *Second*, it is not the act of classifying that creates intercultural problems. Rather, it is the assumption that culture-specific information applies to every member of a particular cultural group.[92] Stereotypes conjecture that all members of a group have exactly the same traits. *Third*, stereotypes also keep you from being a successful communicator because they are oversimplified, exaggerated, and overgeneralized. Stereotypes distort because they are based on half-truths and often-untrue premises and assumptions. Guirdham reaffirms this important point when he notes that stereotypes alter intergroup communication because they lead people to base their preparation, transmission, and reception of messages on false assumptions.[93] *Fourth*, stereotypes are resistant to change. Because they are usually developed early in life and are repeated and reinforced by the in-group, stereotypes tend to intensify with the passage of time. Contact between in-groups and out-groups may only buttress the stereotype. As Meshel and McGlynn point out, "Once formed, stereotypes are resistant to change, and direct contact often strengthens the pre-existing associations between the target group and the stereotypical properties."[94]

AVOIDING STEREOTYPES

Because both culture and stereotypes are learned early in life, the first stage of avoiding stereotypes should begin in childhood. Research indicates that children who have positive face-to-face contact with other groups hold fewer negative stereotypes than children who do not have the opportunity for such contact.[95] Some studies suggest that positive contact among children can diminish many of the effects of stereotyping.[96] Through this interaction, fictitious and negative stereotypes can be proven false.

To assess the stereotypes you currently hold, ask yourself some of the following questions:

- Who is the target of my stereotype?
- What is the content of my stereotype?
- What is the source of my stereotype?
- Why do I believe the stereotype is accurate?
- How much actual contact do I have with the target of the stereotype?

Another method for controlling stereotypes is advanced by Ting-Toomey and Chung, who ask you "to learn to distinguish between inflexible stereotyping and flexible stereotyping."[97] As the words indicate, inflexible stereotyping is rigid, intransigent, and occurs almost automatically. Because these stereotypes are so deeply entrenched, you refuse to accept perceptions that run counter to the categorization. When you try to engage in flexible stereotyping, you begin by being aware of your natural tendency to engage in categorization. The two most important aspects of being flexible are "being open to new information and evidence" and "being aware of your own zone of discomfort."[98]

PREJUDICE

In the broadest sense, prejudices are deeply held negative feelings associated with a particular group. These sentiments often include anger, fear, aversion, and anxiety. Macionis offers a detailed definition of prejudice:

> Prejudice amounts to a rigid and irrational generalization about a category of people. Prejudice is irrational to the extent that people hold inflexible attitudes supported by little or no direct evidence. Prejudice may target people of a particular social class, sex, sexual orientation, age, political affiliation, race, or ethnicity.[99]

In a communication setting, according to Ruscher, the negative feelings and attitudes held by those who hold a prejudicial perspective are often exhibited through the use of group labels, hostile humor, or speech that alleges the superiority of one group over another.[100] As you can see, hostility toward others is an integral part of prejudice.

As with stereotypes, beliefs linked to prejudices have certain characteristics. First, they are directed at a social group and its members. Often those groups are marked by race, ethnicity, gender, age, and the like. Second, prejudices involve an evaluative dimension. According to Brislin, prejudices deal with "feelings about what is good and bad, right and wrong, moral and immoral, and so forth."[101] These either/or feelings often cause discussions of prejudiced attitudes to turn into heated debates. Third, they possess centrality, which refers "to the extent to which a belief is important to an individual's attitude about others."[102] The less intense the belief, the more success you will have in changing prejudice.

FUNCTIONS OF PREJUDICE

Prejudices, like stereotypes, are learned and serve a variety of functions for the people who hold them. For example, prejudices provide some people with feelings of superiority and power. Let us spend a moment looking at four of the most common functions prejudices fulfill.[103]

(1) The *ego-defensive function* allows individuals to hold a prejudice while denying to themselves that they possess negative beliefs about a group. An example is the statement, "I didn't get the promotion because they needed to fill their affirmative action quota." This type of remark allows the speaker to articulate a prejudicial statement while avoiding self-examination to determine why he/she was not promoted.

(2) The *utilitarian function* permits people to believe that their prejudicial beliefs produce a positive outcome. This is often found in situations where economic gain is involved. For instance, someone hiring illegal immigrants might think, "Those immigrants have so little education and training that they are lucky to have the jobs we offer them." This sort of statement reflects a utilitarian prejudice because the holder can use the belief as a justification for offering minimal pay to the workers in question.

(3) The *value-expressive function* occurs when people maintain their prejudice in the belief that their attitudes represent the highest and most moral values of the culture. This usually revolves around values related to religion, government, and politics. Someone who believes their religion is the only true faith and denigrates other beliefs is being prejudicial against people who celebrate different religious convictions.

(4) The *knowledge function* enables people to categorize, organize, and construct their perceptions of other people in a manner they see as rational—even if that perception is woefully inaccurate. This makes dealing with the world much simpler as people can be viewed as a homogeneous group rather than individually. This results in an abundance of labels. People are seen not as individuals with a variety of characteristics, but rather as "Jews," "Mexicans," "gays," or "feminists." The labels deny the existence of the person's unique characteristics.

EXPRESSIONS OF PREJUDICE

Prejudice is expressed in a variety of ways—at times subtle and indirect, but on other occasions overt and direct. Over 50 years ago Gordon Allport's research revealed five escalating levels of prejudice.[104] That scale remains relevant today and many contemporary scholars continue to cite Allport's classic work, which we discuss below.

First, prejudice can be expressed through what Allport refers to as *antilocution*, which involves talking about a member of the target group in negative and stereotypical terms. Ethnic jokes are a form of antilocution, as are remarks such as "All Italians belong to the Mafia." Another example is the statement, "Don't give those homeless people any money. They will only waste it on dope or alcohol," which attributes negative behavior to an entire group of people.

Second, people act out prejudice through *avoidance*. This occurs when people avoid and/or withdraw from contact with the disliked group. Unfortunately, this can be a somewhat common occurrence in U.S. schools, when a group of students decides to exclude another group of students from certain activities or attempt to ostracize them socially. On a larger scale, this is seen at the national level when Israeli and Palestinian government officials refuse to engage in peace talks.

Third, when *discrimination* is the expression of prejudice, the prejudiced person will attempt to exclude all members of the group in question from access to certain types of employment, residential housing, political rights, educational and recreational opportunities, churches, hospitals, or other social institutions. Often in cases of discrimination, we observe ethnocentrism, stereotyping, and prejudice coming together in a form of fanaticism that completely obstructs any form of successful intercultural communication. When discrimination replaces communication, you see overt and covert expressions of anger and hate that restrict one group's opportunity or access to opportunities that rightly belong to everyone. An apartment manager's refusal to rent to minority members is discrimination. When businesses promote less qualified men instead of competent women, you have discrimination.

The fourth level of prejudice involves *physical attacks*, which often escalate in hostility and intensity if left unchecked. From the burning of churches, to the writing of anti-Semitic slogans on Jewish synagogues, to attacks on gays, physical acts occur when minorities are the targets of this level of prejudicial activity. Historical examples include the violence committed against Blacks during the segregation era, pogroms against Jews in Russia, and more recently attacks on Muslims and mosques in the United States following the 9/11 incident.

The fifth, and most alarming, form of prejudice is *extermination*. This expression of prejudice leads to acts of physical violence with the objective of removing or eliminating all or major segments of the target group community. History is replete with examples of lynchings, massacres, and programs of genocide. In cases such as Hitler's "master plan," the "killing fields" of Cambodia, the Serbian "ethnic cleansing," tribal warfare in Rwanda, and the religious and tribal conflicts in Iraq and Afghanistan, you see attempts to destroy an entire ethnic group. Nor should we forget the U.S. government's efforts to remove the American Indians from their native lands in the 1800s.

CAUSES OF PREJUDICE

There are no simple explanations for the causes of prejudice, which in most instances are multiple. Experts have isolated a few of the basic motivations of prejudice, and we will look at three of these in order to better understand how prejudice can be a major deterrent to successful intercultural interaction.

(1) *Societal sources*: A great deal of prejudice is built into the major organizations and institutions of a society. According to Oskamp, these organizations produce norms, rules, regulations, and laws that give rise to societal prejudice and help "maintain the power of the dominant groups over subordinate ones."[105] The era of apartheid rule in South Africa is a classic example of how the social structure can be used to establish, enforce, and sustain prejudice.

(2) *Maintaining social identity*: At the beginning of this chapter we pointed out the important role that identity plays in connecting people to their culture. This link is very personal and emotional because it creates the bond that binds people and culture together. Anything that threatens that connection, such as out-group members, can become a target of prejudice. For example, the growing U.S. Hispanic population is viewed by some members of the dominant culture as a threat to present-day social values and their established way of life.

(3) *Scapegoating*: Scapegoating occurs when a particular group of people, usually a minority, is singled out to bear the blame for certain events or circumstances, such as economic or social hardships, that adversely affect the dominant group. Scapegoating generates arguments and justifications based on fear and imagined threats posed by an out-group. According to Stephan and Stephan, these assumed, unsubstantiated threats can be political, economic, or social concerns believed to threaten "the physical or material wellbeing of the in-group or its members."[106] Throughout history, black people, Jews, immigrants, gays, and other minority groups have been used as scapegoats in order for the dominant group to avoid responsibility.

AVOIDING PREJUDICE

Avoiding prejudice is not an easy assignment because like most aspects of cultural perception, racial and cultural prejudices are learned early and are reinforced through repeated exposure. Nevertheless, research has revealed that two techniques are often successful in dispelling prejudicial views: personal contact and education.[107] Research on the value of personal contact as a method of reducing prejudice has a history dating from the early 1950s. The rationale for personal contact, at least in its expression, is a simple one: the greater the frequency of positive contacts between in-group and out-group individuals, the lower the level of perceived prejudice. According to Oskamp, the contact needs to meet certain conditions to be successful, the most important being "equal status between groups" and cooperation "toward common goals."[108]

There are two types of educational programs that psychologists have used to help reduce prejudice. The first type centers on what are called *multicultural education curricula*, which Stephan and Stephan describe as "usually [consisting] of materials on the history and cultural practices of a wide array of racial and ethnic groups."[109] These materials are often presented from the point of view of the minority groups rather than from the perception of the dominant culture. The second type program, *cultural diversity training*, is used mainly in business and organizational settings and consists of programs designed "to teach managers and employees to value group differences, increase understanding between groups, and help individuals recognize that their own behavior is affected by their background."[110] Regardless of the program selected, the explicit goals remain the same—to reduce prejudice through intergroup contact and dialogue.

RACISM

It is sad but true that racism has been present throughout history. In the past 100 years, African Americans have been forced to ride in the back of buses, Jews were required to wear a yellow Star of David, Japanese Americans were confined to concentration camps during the Second World War, and South Africa was divided along racial lines. We are well into the twenty-first century and it is evident that Martin Luther King, Jr.'s dream that children "will be judged not by the color of their skin but by the content of their character" remains just that, a dream. As Vora and Vora point out, "Both blatant and very subtle forms of racism permeate organizational and personal levels of our society, from governmental, business, and educational institutions to our everyday interactions."[111] Racist acts in these institutions, and in society in general, target many groups of people and for a host of reasons. Gold notes that "Forms of racism are experienced by groups such as Asian Americans, Latinos, Arabs, and American Indians, whose racialization is associated with factors such as religion, foreignness, clothing, culture, citizenship, gender and language."[112] Expressions of racism have even been directed toward the holder of the United States' highest office. Netter points out that President Obama has been subjected to "racial taunts and innuendos that have slyly, or sometimes blatantly, been circulated on the Internet, in e-mails and cartoons."[113] Manifestations of racism continue today in the form of offensive graffiti, property damage, intimidation, and even physical violence. People also practice more subtle forms of racism, such as uttering racial slurs or telling ethnic jokes. Nor is racism a problem confined to the United States. Many studies point out that racism is on the rise throughout the world,[114] and this is particularly evident in the growing resentment against immigrants in Western Europe. Although racism exists for many reasons, experts seem to agree that at its core racism is driven by "culture, economics, psychology and history."[115]

It is difficult to make a complete assessment of the consequences of racism because the effects are both conscious and subconscious. What we do know is that racism is damaging to those who are the recipients of this destructive behavior as well as to the racists themselves. It devalues the target person by denying his or her identity, and it destroys the culture by creating divisions and eroding social cohesion. This occurs when a selected group of people are excluded from access to social, economic, and educational institutions.

> **REMEMBER THIS**
>
> *Racism occurs when people believe their race is inherently superior to another race. Racist individuals will often engage in discrimination against people of another group.*

RACISM DEFINED

Racism, in many ways, is an extension of stereotyping and prejudice, as demonstrated in Leone's classic definition:

> Racism is the belief in the inherent superiority of a particular race. It denies the basic equality of humankind and correlates ability with physical composition. Thus, it assumes that success or failure in any societal endeavor will depend upon genetic endowment rather than environment and access to opportunity.[116]

It is important to notice the word "superiority" in this explanation, because this idea of superiority allows one group of people to mistreat another group on the basis of race, color, national origin, ancestry, religion, or sexual preference. The folly of racist thinking is that it is not only unethical and cruel, but it is also founded on false premises. There is no biologically based ability that differentiates groups of people. It is common knowledge, for those who are willing to accept it, that "the big differences among human groups are the result of culture, not biological inheritance or race. All human beings belong to the same species and the biological features essential to human life are common to us all."[117] Yet in spite of this truth and wisdom, racism remains a major hindrance to successful intercultural communication.

EXPRESSIONS OF RACISM

Racism can be expressed in a variety of forms, some of which are almost impossible to detect while others are blatant and transparent. In general, these forms can be categorized as either personal or institutional. "Personal racism consists of racist acts, beliefs, attitudes, and behaviors on the part of the individual persons."[118] Referring to institutional racism, Bloom is very specific when he writes, "Institutional racism refers to racial inferiorizing or antipathy perpetrated by specific social institutions such as schools, corporations, hospitals, or the criminal justice system as a totality."[119] While "institutional racism may be intentional or unintentional,"[120] its consequences have a detrimental effect on targeted groups specifically and on the greater society as well.

AVOIDING RACISM

Although views about race are often deeply entrenched, there are four steps you can take to help reduce racism. First, *try to be honest* with yourself when deciding if you hold any racist views. It is a simple point to state, but a difficult one to accomplish. Yet, confronting personal racist views is an important first step. Second, *object to racist jokes and insults* whenever you hear them. This daring and sometimes courageous act will send a message to other people that you denounce racism in whatever form it may take. Third, as straightforward as it sounds, *respect freedom*. The Constitution of the United States specifies, "nor shall any state deprive any person of life, liberty, or property, without due process of law; nor deny to any person within its jurisdiction the equal protection of the laws." From this declaration, it follows that to preserve liberty all individuals must be seen as being free from political and social limitations. Fourth, examine the *historical roots of racism*. The rationale for such an examination is clearly documented by Solomos and Back when they note that before the full impact of racism can be grasped and challenged, one must be able to understand and explain "both the roots of contemporary racist ideas and movements and the sources of their current appeal."[121]

We conclude by reminding you that racism, stereotyping, and prejudice are pervasive because they are often learned early in life and like much of culture, become part of our way of seeing the world. The noted author Maya Angelou uses an eloquent metaphor to make this same point. "The plague of racism is insidious, entering into our minds as smoothly and quietly and invisibly as floating airborne microbes enter into our bodies to find lifelong purchase in our bloodstreams."[122]

ETHNOCENTRISM

People from one culture might view people who eat whale meat as being barbaric and inhumane. But the people who eat whale meat might consider people in other cultures as uncaring and self-centered because they commonly assign the elderly to nursing homes. Both ways of thinking demonstrate an ethnocentric attitude. At the core of ethnocentrism are judgments about what is right, moral, and rational. These judgments pervade every aspect of a culture's existence. Examples range from the insignificant ("Tattoos should not be visible") to the significant ("Christianity is the only true religion"). There is a very natural tendency to use one's own culture as a starting point when evaluating the behavior of other people and cultures. Nanda and Warms provide a contemporary explanation of ethnocentrism:

> Ethnocentrism is the notion that one's own culture is superior to any other. It is the idea that other cultures should be measured by the degree to which they live up to our cultural standards. We are ethnocentric when we view other cultures through the narrow lens of our own culture or social position.[123]

It is this "narrow lens" that links ethnocentrism to the concepts of stereotyping, prejudice, and racism. Even a simple statement like "They drive on the wrong side of the road in that country" conveys a degree of ethnocentrism.

CHARACTERISTICS OF ETHNOCENTRISM

Levels of Ethnocentrism

Ethnocentrism can be viewed as having three levels: *positive*, *negative*, and *extremely negative*. The first, *positive*, is the belief that one's own culture is preferred over all others. This is natural because individuals draw much of their personal identity and many beliefs from their native culture. At the *negative* level, ethnocentrism begins to take on an evaluative dimension. This is demonstrated in the belief that one's own culture is the center of everything, and all other cultures should be measured and rated by its standards. This evolves when an individual, or group, believes that their personal beliefs and values are unquestionably correct. Finally, in the *extremely negative* form, it is not enough to consider one's culture as the most valid and useful. The person or group believes their values and customs should be adopted by other cultures.

Ethnocentrism Is Universal

Anthropologist generally agree that, "Most people are ethnocentric, and a certain degree of ethnocentrism probably is essential if people are to be content with their lives and if their culture is to persist."[124] Like culture, ethnocentrism is usually learned at the unconscious level.

For example, schools that teach mainly the history, geography, literature, language, and government of their own country and exclude those of others are encouraging ethnocentrism. A history book that contains only the accomplishments of white males is subliminally teaching ethnocentrism. Politicians who advocate the idea of "American Exceptionalism" are promoting ethnocentrism. U.S. Americans exposed to limited perspectives can develop the belief that the United States is the world's

Ethnocentrism is learned early in life and is continuously being reinforced by specific activities.

Robert Fonseca

best country, and they begin to judge other nations by U.S. standards. This phenomenon is also characteristic of other cultures. When children in Iran are exposed to only the Koran, they are learning to judge all religious truths by a singular standard. And when Chinese students, as they have done for thousands of years, write the name of their country using ideograms meaning "Central Kingdom," they are learning to view their nation as the center of the world. Even the stories and folktales that each culture tells its young people contribute to ethnocentrism. For example, a culture's creation story almost inevitably gives primacy to itself.

Ethnocentrism Contributes to Cultural Identity

Another reason ethnocentrism is so pervasive is that it provides members of a culture with feelings of identity and belonging. As Rusen points out, being a part of a particular group, nation, or civilization provides an individual a sense of self-esteem and pride in the "achievements of their own people."[125] The manner in which this idea translates into ethnocentrism is clearly brought out by Haviland and his colleagues:

> To function effectively, we may expect a society to embrace at least a degree of ethnic pride and a loyalty to its unique cultural traditions, from which its people derive psychological support and a firm social bond to their group. In societies where one's self-identification derives from the group, ethnocentrism is essential to a sense of personal worth.[126]

Ethnocentrism is strongest in moral and religious contexts, where emotionalism may overshadow rationality and cause the type of hostility the world witnessed on September 11, 2001. Explaining the link between ethnocentrism and devotion to one's culture, Brislin observes, "If people view their own group as central to their lives and as possessing proper behavioral standards, they are likely to aid their group members when troubles arise. In times of war the rallying of ethnocentric feelings makes a country's military forces more dedicated to the defeat of the (inferior) enemy."[127]

There can be serious consequences if you engage in negative ethnocentrism at the same time you are trying to practice successful intercultural communication. One of the major interpersonal consequences of ethnocentrism is anxiety. The argument is simple and is clearly enunciated by Gamble and Gamble: "The more ethnocentric you are, the more anxious you are about interacting with other cultures; when we are fearful, we are less likely to expect a positive outcome from such interactions, and less willing to trust someone from another culture."[128]

AVOIDING ETHNOCENTRISM

Avoiding ethnocentric perceptions and behavior is not an easy task. We can, however, offer two suggestions that might help you to reduce the negative consequences of ethnocentrism. *First*, try to avoid dogmatism. You can begin by asking yourself to think about the following questions:

- Jews cover their heads when they pray, but Protestants do not. Is one practice more correct than the other?
- Catholics have one God, Buddhists have no god, and Hindus have many gods. Is one belief more correct than the others?

- In parts of the Middle East, women cover their faces with veils, whereas women in the United States do not. Is one behavior more correct than the other?
- In China, Korea, and Japan, people eat with chopsticks, while in the United States and Europe they use metal or plastic utensils. In some parts of the world people eat with their hands. Is one method more correct than the other?

These sorts of rhetorical questions are limitless. We urge you to remember that it is not the questions that are important but rather the dogmatic answers that they often generate. The danger of ethnocentrism is that it is strongest in political, moral, and religious settings. In these contexts it is easy to let culturally restricted views overshadow rationality. Avoiding this problem requires that you be alert to intolerance and narrowness in any form. St. Thomas Aquinas said much the same thing hundreds of years ago: "Beware of the man of one book."

Second, learn to be open to new views. This is clearly evident in Triandis' proposal that "When we make a comparative judgment that our culture is in some ways better than another, we need to learn to follow this judgment with two questions: Is that really true? What is the objective evidence?"[129] One of the main missions of this book is to expose you to a variety of cultures so that you might be able to carry out Triandis' advice by knowing the "truth" about other cultures and how they view the "truth." This lack of knowledge is a major cause of ethnocentrism.

CHAPTER 8

Verbal Messages: Language

Change your language and change your thoughts.

KARL ALBRECHT

The limits of my language mean the limits of my world.

LUDWIG WITTGENSTEIN

Language is the roadmap of a culture. It tells you where its people came from and where they are going.

RITA MAE BROWN

The role and importance of language in daily life is self-evident. Language enables humans to symbolize. That ability allows the exchange of information, including abstract ideas, which is what sets us apart from all other animals. Language lets you convey to others your beliefs, values, attitudes, worldviews, emotions, aspects of identity, and myriad other personal features. Even your name is a function of language. Without language there would be no need for Facebook, Twitter, LinkedIn, or any of the other social networking media; YouTube would have only silent videos, and iTunes would be limited to instrumental music. There would be no Internet!

Language and culture are the indispensable components of intercultural communication. Together, they form a synergy, each working to sustain and perpetuate the other while creating a greater phenomenon—language allows the dissemination and adoption of culture, while culture gives rise to and shapes language. Combined, they enable societal organization and collective activities. With the exception of co-culture members, in almost every intercultural interaction one of the participants will be speaking a language other than their native language. And even with co-cultures, you are likely to encounter unfamiliar, specialized English usage, such as argot and slang, which are a function of culture.

The objective of this chapter is to provide you with an appreciation and understanding of verbal language and its role in intercultural communication. We will begin by examining some of the functions of language. Next, some examples will illustrate how different cultures actually use language and how language reflects the values of those cultures. Several features of the interpretation and translation process, a critical link in intercultural communication, are then examined. We next explore some aspects of language in communication technology. The chapter concludes with a look at language considerations that can increase intercultural communication competence.

FUNCTIONS OF LANGUAGE

Contemporary society, both domestic and international, is increasingly characterized by interactions between people from different cultures speaking different languages. For example, a 2009 U.S. Census report disclosed that over 19 percent of the U.S. population, five years of age or older, speak a language other than English at home.[1] This statistic offers a compelling reason to understand how culture and language

Language allows people to express and exchange ideas and thoughts with others.

David Frazier/PhotoEdit

complement each other. In this section we begin that journey by looking at how language functions in social interaction, provides a means of social cohesion, and facilitates expressions of identity.

SOCIAL INTERACTION

Everyone makes daily use of language. Stop for a minute and consider some of your daily activities that require language. These activities include talking with friends before class, listening to a lecture, using your cell phone, surfing the Internet, reading an assignment, writing a report, coordinating with co-workers, or chilling with your iPad. All of these activities, and many more, form a part of your daily schedule. Without language, however, none of these events would be possible. Language allows you to speak, read, write, listen to others, and even talk to yourself—or to think.

Language also serves important communicative functions other than directly expressing and exchanging ideas and thoughts with others. For example, language allows you to verbally convey your internal emotions and relieve stress by simply uttering a phrase (darn it) or a swear word (damn). You use language to express pain (ouch), elation (great!), disappointment (oh no!), and amazement or surprise (OMG!).[2] Often, these or similar expressions are used subconsciously, even when no one is around. Language is also employed to invoke assistance from the supernatural. A Jewish rabbi, a Buddhist priest, a Mongolian shaman, the Pope, a Muslim, or a small child reciting a prayer are all using language to appeal to a greater power.

SOCIAL COHESION

A common language allows individuals to form social groups and engage in cooperative efforts. A shared vocabulary enables a group to record and preserve past events, albeit often with a selective interpretation. Because the past is an important means for teaching children their culture's normative behaviors, these recordings provide the people with a communal history that becomes a unifying force for future generations. As you may recall from Chapter 2, language allows a group of people to maintain a record of the cultural values and expectations that bind them together. The rules a cultural group establishes for using language provide a form of social-bonding and predictability.[3] The maintenance of social relations also relies on language for more than communicating messages. For example, the type of language used to express intimacy, respect, affiliation, formality, distance, and other emotions can help you sustain a relationship or disengage from one.[4] Unfortunately, the unity created by a shared language can also become a divisive force when people identify too strongly with their native tongue, become ethnocentric, and feel threatened by someone speaking a different language.

EXPRESSIONS OF IDENTITY

Language plays an important role in the formation and expression of your identity, particularly national identity. Recall the ongoing controversy over making English the official language of the United States, which is often seen as a reaction to the rising tide of illegal immigrants. While they represent only 22 percent of the Canadian population, French speakers have made French "the official language of Québec."[5] Noted for taking extraordinary measures to ensure the purity of its national language, France established the Académie Française in 1635 to "codify and regulate the French tongue."[6] In the Baltic nation of Estonia, a part of the former Soviet Union, approximately 30 percent of the population uses Russian as their first language. In an effort to bolster national identity, the government created the National Language Inspectorate, which is charged with ensuring that state employees possess and utilize a proficiency in Estonian.[7] Language related conflict between French and Flemish speakers in Belgium actually led to dissolution of the government in 2010.[8] Language can also be used to construct a new national identity, as was done with Hebrew in Israel in 1948, when there was an urgent need to unify extremely diverse groups from many different nations who spoke a variety of languages.[9]

Language plays a part in establishing and expressing ethnic identity. Black English Vernacular (BEV), or Ebonics, helps create and reinforce a sense of mutual identity among African Americans. Dialects or accents can also be a part of one's identity. Think for a minute about the stereotypical southern drawl, the variety of accents encountered in the metropolitan areas of Boston and New York City, or the surfer's lingo heard in southern California. Each of these different linguistic conventions contributes to the user's regional identity.

Language usage can categorize people into groups according to factors such as age and gender. The terminology used can easily mark one as young or old. Recall how you sometimes thought the words used by your parents or grandparents sounded old fashioned. Additionally, language is part of your gender identity. Women and men use language differently, both in word choice and behaviors. Among U.S. English speakers, women tend to ask more questions, listen more, and use a supportive speech style. Men, on the other hand, are more prone to interrupting, asserting their opinions, and are poor listeners.[10] In Japan, women employ more honorific terms and the two genders often use a different word to say the same thing. Language has also been used to categorize people into varying social and economic levels. "Historically, the way that people speak carries an unimaginable weight in how they are perceived in the society. They are viewed to be civilized or uncivilized, sophisticated or unsophisticated and 'high class' or 'low class' by the language that they speak."[11]

LANGUAGE AND MEANING

WHAT IS LANGUAGE?

At the most basic level, language is a set of shared symbols or signs that a cooperative group of people has mutually agreed to use to help them create meaning. The relationship between the selected sign and the agreed meaning is quite often arbitary.[12] This concept is easily illustrated by looking at some of the varied symbols used by different cultures to identify a familiar household pet. In Finland they have settled on *kissa*, but in Germany *katze* has been chosen, and Swahili speakers use *paka*. The Japanese decided on *neko* (猫), Tagalog speakers in the Philippines prefer *pusa*, and in Spanish-speaking countries *gato* has been selected. In the English language *cat* is the term used. As you can see, none of the words has any relation to the actual characteristics of a cat. They are simply arbitrary symbols that each language group uses to call to mind the common domestic pet, or sometimes a larger wild animal such as a

> ## REMEMBER THIS
>
> *A language is a set of symbols that a cultural group has agreed to use to create meaning. The symbols and their meanings are often arbitrary.*

tiger, lion, or leopard. These differences in symbols also extend to how people of a cultural group hear natural sounds.[13] For instance, in the United States pigs are heard to make an "oink, oink" sound, but the Japanese hear the sound as "bu–bu."

When you applaud an outstanding performance in the United States, the sound is "clap-clap," but in Japan it's "pachi-pachi." It is also common to find significant differences within a major language group. While English can vary within national boundaries, more prominent differences, such as pronunciation, spelling, and terminology, can be found when comparing English-speaking countries such as Australia, England, and the United States. For example, in England, the trunk of a car is a "boot" and the hood is the "bonnet." Australians pronounce the "ay" sound as "ai." Imagine the confusion and consternation when an Australian asks his U.S. friend how she will celebrate "Mother's Dai."

Pronunciation differences, or accents, between the English-speaking countries are a product of early immigration and the natural evolution of the language. Rubenstein provides a clear explanation of this process: "Again, geographic concepts help explain the reason for the differences. From the time of their arrival in North America, colonists began to pronounce words differently from the British. Such divergence is normal, for interaction between the two groups was largely confined to exchange of letters and other printed matter rather than direct speech."[14] However, variations in spelling between American English and that used in England are the result of a calculated effort to create a new national identity and loosen the colonies' ties to England. When Noah Webster sat down to write his early American dictionary, the underlying objective was to "create a uniquely American dialect of English."[15]

Of course, English is not the only language to have significant deviations across international borders. The differences in spelling between the Portuguese used in Portugal and that used in Brazil and the former Portuguese colonies in Africa is so great that in 2008 Portugal adopted a standardization measure requiring "hundreds of words to be spelled the Brazilian way."[16] Even within the Spanish language there are major linguistic differences in what is used in Spain, South America, Central America, Mexico, and other Spanish-speaking nations.[17]

LANGUAGE VARIATIONS

In addition to the differences discussed above, cultures are also characterized by a number of internal linguistic variations. These differences are usually culturally influenced and frequently offer hints as to the nation or region where a person lives or grew up, their age, level of education, and socioeconomic status.[18] It is particularly important to have both an awareness of these distinctions and an appreciation of their role in intercultural communication. With this knowledge you will be able to avoid erroneous, misinformed judgments derived from a person's accent, dialect, or other language trait.

Accent

As we mentioned earlier, accents are simply variations in pronunciation that occur when people are speaking the same language. These are often a result of geographical or historical differences, such as those among English speakers in Australia, Canada, England, South Africa, and the United States. In the United States you often hear regional accents characterized as "Southern," "New England," or "New York."

Dialect

In addition to pronunciation variations that characterize accents, during communicative exchanges you may have already encountered regional differences in language usage. In intercultural communication an additional challenge to competency is presented by these regional distinctions or dialects, which are distinguished by differences in vocabulary, grammar, and even punctuation.[19] The Japanese, often considered a homogeneous culture, have a number of dialects, and some, like Kagoshima-*ben* and Okinawa-*ben* in the extreme south, are very difficult for other Japanese to understand. Chinese is usually considered to have eight distinct, major dialects (Cantonese, Mandarin, Hakka, etc.), which are bound by a common writing system but are mutually unintelligible when spoken. Indeed, some scholars consider the dialects as separate languages.[20] The most common dialect categories of German are High, Middle, and Low, but there are numerous sub-dialects of these classifications that are often unintelligible to someone speaking Standard German. There are different dialects of the Spanish language spoken in Spain, such as Andalusian in the south, Castilian in the center, and Galician in the northwest. Significant dialectical differences exist between the Spanish spoken in Europe and that used in North and South America, and most regions have their own unique variations.

English spoken in the United States is characterized by a number of dialects. Black English Vernacular (BEV), which we referred to earlier, represents a very distinct dialect in the United States, as does Hawaiian "pidgin." Among U.S. white, native English speakers, a 2004 survey identified six regional dialects prevalent for middle-class, college-educated participants between 18 and 25 years of age: (1) New England, (2) Mid-Atlantic, (3) North, (4) Midland, (5) South, and (6) West.[21] Take a moment and place yourself in the position of an international visitor, using English as a second language, confronted with a group of Americans speaking several of these dialects.

Argot

Argot is a private vocabulary unique to a co-culture, group, organization, or profession. In the United States many individuals employ a specialized vocabulary that identifies them as a member of a particular co-culture or group, such as prisoners or those engaged in criminal activities, gays, street gangs, and professional or sporting groups. Members of these groups may employ a specialized vocabulary to obscure the intended meaning or to create a sense of identity. "By changing the meaning of existing words or inventing new ones, members of the 'in-group' can communicate with fellow members while effectively excluding outsiders who may be within hearing range."[22]

While technically an argot, professional terminology is often referred to as jargon.[23] Workers in vocational fields such as medicine, engineering, or computer science make extensive use of professional jargon. Each branch of the U.S. military uses jargon specific to their mission and particular type of activity. The contract you signed for your cell phone is an excellent example of argot used in the legal system.

Slang

Slang designates those non-standard terms, usually used in instances of informality, which serve as a "means of marking social or linguistic identity."[24] Slang can be regionally based, associated with a co-culture, or used by groups engaged in a specific endeavor. Contemporary speech used by Japanese students provides an example of regional slang. In the Tokyo area McDonald's (*Maku Donarudo*) is referred to as *Maku*, but further to the west, in Osaka, it becomes *Makudo*. And in both locations Starbucks is *Sutaba*. The word "dude" can help you understand how slang evolves. Originally, "dude" was a term used by rural inhabitants to belittle someone from the city. Later, it became popular among the early Southern California surfing community and then spread to the general population, where it is now commonly used to address or refer to another person.

CONVERSATIONAL TABOOS

All cultures have taboos related to the use of language. These can be cultural restrictions against discussing a topic in a particular setting, or prohibitions against using certain words. Crystal tells us that a culture's verbal taboos generally relate "to sex, the supernatural, excretion, and death, but quite often they extend to other aspects of domestic and social life."[25] Because they believe that death can be brought on by talking about it, the Navajo refrain from discussing the topic. Additionally, names of the dead are never spoken again.[26]

From personal experience you know that at first meetings, whether for business or pleasure, people usually engage in "small talk" as a way of getting to know each another. However, the choice of topics discussed during these meetings must follow established cultural norms. In intercultural interactions this requires that you learn which topics are acceptable and which are taboo. In the United States early conversations often center on the weather or some aspect of the physical setting, such as the scenery or furnishings in a room. As the interaction becomes more comfortable, topics relating to sports, food, or travel may be discussed.[27] If both parties continue the conversation, which is a positive sign, they begin gathering information about each other through personal questions related to likes and dislikes and family matters. For American businesspersons personal questions are not actually considered taboo in the business context. Hence, you might hear the most well-intentioned American ask questions such as "What do you do?" "How long have you been with your company?" "Do you have a family?" But those personal topics are considered taboo in many cultures.

In the United States we are taught that it is impolite to ask a person's age, sexual orientation, or religion, and to refrain from arguing about politics. However, in many European nations vigorous debates about political activities are quite acceptable. In Saudi Arabia asking about a person's family can cause considerable offense.[28] It is common to begin a meeting or a presentation in the United States with a joke, but this can prove disastrous in an international setting. This is because humor does not travel well, if at all, across cultures. What is funny in one culture can be offensive in another.

> ### REMEMBER THIS
>
> *Language and culture cannot be separated. Language is vital to understanding our unique cultural perspectives. Language is a tool that is used to explore and experience our cultures and the perspectives that are embedded in our cultures.*
>
> Buffy Sainte-Marie (American singer and song writer)

LANGUAGE AND CULTURE
THE SYNERGY OF LANGUAGE AND CULTURE

As mentioned at the beginning of this chapter, language and culture form a synergistic relationship. Language provides the means for a group of people to create a collective societal structure encompassing political, economic, social support, and educational institutions. Culture fashions the template for those institutions, and as you would expect, the organizations are structured around, and replicate, the values of that culture. What you might find surprising, however, is that a culture's values are also embodied in the content and use of language.

A well-known and widely debated theoretical concept, the Sapir-Whorf hypothesis, holds that language is a dominant influence in shaping one's worldview and perception of reality. In general, most scholars today agree that the hypothesis originally overstated the effect of language, which is now considered to have a more selective influence on how one views reality.[29] Critics do agree, however, that a culture's linguistic vocabulary emphasizes what is considered important. Salzmann contends "those aspects of culture that are important for the members of a society are correspondingly highlighted in the vocabulary."[30] This culture-language synergy is easily illustrated by comparing a food staple from the United States with one from Japan. As Table 8.1 reveals, each nation has a large vocabulary for the product that is important, but few words for the less used product. In the United States "rice" refers to the grain regardless of context—whether it is cooked, found in the store, or still in the field. Similarly, when discussing "beef" the Japanese use only the traditional word *gyūniku* or the adopted English of *bifu* or *bifuteki*.

> ### REMEMBER THIS
>
> *Developed in the early twentieth century, the Sapir-Whorf hypothesis holds that language defines your perceptions of the world.*

TABLE 8.1	English and Japanese Words Reflecting Culturally Important Items
U.S. CUTS OF BEEF	**JAPANESE RICE**
• chuck	• *ine* – rice growing in the field
• rib	• *momi* – rice with the husk still on
• short loin	• *genmai* – unpolished (brown) rice
• sirloin	• *kome* – uncooked white rice (e.g., at the store)
• round	• *shinmai* – rice harvested this year
• brisket	• *komai* – rice harvested last year
• fore shank	• *gohan* – steamed glutinous rice
• short plank	• *okayu* – rice gruel

Source: © Cengage Learning 2013

USING LANGUAGE

The concept that language influences perception is echoed by the words of the late Austrian philosopher Ludwig Wittgenstein, "If we spoke a different language, we would perceive a somewhat different world." To gain a better understanding of how language serves this adaptive function, we now look at several cultures and the different ways they employ language.

Spanish

An exploration of how the Spanish language is used in Mexico can provide insight into Mexican society and further demonstrate the codependency of language and culture. First, communicative interaction, especially conversation, is an important part of Mexican life, and Mexicans readily engage in casual talk. Condon reports that during interactions, even in a business setting, puns, double-entendres, and colloquialisms are frequently interjected,[31] which gives conversations a feeling of liveliness and warmth. This is in contrast to the logic based U.S. style that Mexicans often see as cold and remote.

The male orientation that characterizes Mexican society is clearly evident in the Spanish language use of gendered nouns and pronouns. For instance, men in an all-male group are referred to as *ellos*, and women in an all-female group are *ellas*, the *o* ending denoting masculine and the *a* ending being feminine. However, *ellos* is used for a group of several men and one woman, as well as a gathering of women and one male. Small girls in a group are called *niñas*, but if a boy joins the girls, *niños* is used.

The Spanish use of separate verb conjugations for formal and informal speech also helps Mexicans express the formality that is important in their culture. To understand this distinction, we can look at the pronoun *you*. In formal speech, *usted* is used, but when talking to family, friends, or in informal situations, *tú* is more appropriate. The use of titles, such as *Profesor*, *Doctor*, or *Licenciado*, is widespread in Mexico and illustrates the value placed on status and hierarchy.[32]

Finally, the Mexican preference for indirectness and face-saving tactics is evident in their use of language. Interpersonal relationships are very important among Mexicans, and they try to avoid situations that carry the potential for confrontation or loss of face. High-context communication and etiquette are employed to help ensure harmonious interactions.[33] Among U.S. Americans this indirect politeness can sometimes be misconstrued as dishonesty or aloofness, when it is actually a sign of respect and an opportunity for the other person to save face.

Northeast Asian Cultures

The languages of China, Korea, and Japan are quite different, but there are commonalities in how those respective languages are used. All three nations are considered high-context cultures and commonly employ language in an indirect manner to promote harmony and face-saving measures. Politeness can take precedence over truth, which is consistent with the cultural emphasis on maintaining social stability. Members of these three cultures also expect their communication partners to be able to recognize the intended meaning more from the context than the actual words used. The languages of the Northeast Asian cultures also reflect the importance placed on formality and hierarchy and vary sharply from the more direct, informal, low-context speech common among Americans. This contrast is, in part, a result of varying perceptions of the reason for communication. In Northeast Asia communication is used to reduce one's selfishness and egocentrism. This is diametrically opposite to the Western perspective that views communication as a way to increase one's esteem and guard personal interests.[34] To provide more insight, we will examine some specific examples of the similarities between how Chinese, Korean, and Japanese are used.

Chinese. Wenzhong and Grove suggest that the three most fundamental values of Chinese culture are (1) collectivism or a group orientation, (2) intragroup harmony, and (3) societal hierarchy.[35] The latter two values are easily discernible in the Chinese's use of language. For instance, the focus on social status and position among the Chinese is of such importance that it also shapes how individuals communicatively interact. Accordingly, a deferential manner is commonly used when addressing an authority figure.[36] The widespread use of titles is another way of showing respect and formality in the Chinese culture. Among family members, given names are usually replaced with a title, such as "younger" or "older" brother, which reflects that individual's position within the family.[37]

The Chinese exhibit the importance of in-group social stability, or harmony, through a number of different communication protocols. Rather than employing precise language, as is done in the United States, the Chinese will be vague and indirect, which leaves the listener to discern the meaning.[38] Conflict situations among ingroups will be avoided when possible and intermediaries are used to resolve disputes. Any criticism will be issued in an indirect manner.[39] The concern for others' face can be pervasive, and to demonstrate humility, the Chinese will frequently engage in self-deprecation, and attentively listen to others, especially seniors or elders.[40]

Korean. The cultural values of collectivism, status, and harmony are also prevalent in the way Koreans use language. For instance, the family represents the strongest ingroup among Koreans and a common way of introducing one's parent is to say "this is our mother/father" rather than using the pronoun "my." This demonstrates the Korean collective orientation by signaling that one's family is a comprehensive unit, encompassing parents and siblings, extending beyond self-considerations.[41] Status is another important cultural value and one's position as a senior or a junior will dictate the appropriate communication style. As a result, Koreans will use small talk in an effort to ascertain each other's hierarchical position.[42] Because Korea is also a high-context culture, communicative interactions are often characterized by indirectness, with the meaning imbedded in the context of how something is expressed rather than what is actually said. For example, instead of asking a subordinate to work on a project over the weekend, a Korean manager may say, "The success of this project is important to the company, and we cannot miss the deadline."

Japanese. As with China and Korea, Japan is a high-context, hierarchical culture with a distinct group orientation emphasizing social harmony, and these cultural characteristics are manifest in the Japanese language, which is highly contextual and often ambiguous. There are many words that have identical pronunciations and written form, but quite different meanings. For instance, *sumimasen* can mean "excuse me," "sorry," or "thank you," or can be used simply to attract someone's attention. The listener is left to determine the meaning from the context. *Osoi* is another word that has dual meanings ("slow" or "late"), but is written and pronounced identically. Japanese verbs come at the end of sentences, which impedes a full understanding until the sentence has been completed and allows the speaker to gage listeners' reaction before deciding on which verb form to use.

Social position, or status, is an important consideration among the Japanese and is very evident in their use of language. One's social position will determine the type of language and choice of words to use during every interaction. Women will use more honorific words than men. Juniors will employ polite speech when addressing their seniors, who may reply with informal speech. Terms of address are also determined by one's hierarchical positioning. Given names are rarely used between Japanese, who prefer to use last names followed by a suffix term that is determined by the type or level of the relationship. Professor Mari Suzuki's students, for example, would call her Suzuki *sensei* (teacher), and she would refer to the students by their last name and the *–san* (Mr. or Ms.) suffix. There are many other hierarchically determined suffix terms used with an individual's name. In addition to the Japanese concern for social position, this practice also indicates that Japan is a formal culture.

Arabic

Linguistic identity as an Arab transcends ethnic origins, national borders and, with certain exceptions (e.g., Coptic, Jewish), religious affiliation.[43] Among Arabs "anyone whose mother tongue is Arabic" is considered an Arab. Thus, language is what defines and unites the greater Arab community. The importance placed on language is, in part, a function of their history. Recall from Chapter 4 that the early Arabs developed cultural expressions, such as poetry and storytelling, which were suited to their nomadic life. Nydell provides an insightful summation of the prominence of language among Arabs: "The Arabic language is their [Arabs] greatest cultural treasure and achievement, an art form that unfortunately cannot be accessed or appreciated by outsiders…. In the Arab world, how you say something is as important as what you have to say."[44] Thus, Arabs see their language as possessing an emotional content. Arabs approach the language as a "social conduit in which emotional resonance is stressed," which is in contrast with the western view that language is a means of transferring information.[45]

In Chapter 6 we indicated that Arab societies are characterized by the cultural values of collectivism, hierarchy, and a present orientation, which are mirrored in how Arabic is used. As with almost every collective society, social harmony among in-group members is valued among Arabs, who rely on indirect, ambiguous statements to lessen the potential for loss of face during interactions.[46] While employing indirectness to ensure smooth relations, Arabs will engage in repetition and exaggeration to appeal to the audience's emotions. The noisy, animated speech form often associated with the Arab communication style is normally limited to interactions with social peers. When engaging elders or superiors "polite deference is required,"[47] which demonstrates the value placed on hierarchy. Arabs also tend to focus more on the present and consider future events with some degree of incertitude. This attitude is evident in the frequent use of *inshallah* (if God wills) when discussing future events. Additionally, when connected to some action, the phrase can be used to indicate "yes," but at an unspecified future time, "no" in order to avoid personal responsibility, or an indirect "never."[48]

English

The cultural values characterizing Americans are quite evident in their use of English. Think for a moment on how frequently you use "I" in conversation and writing. When constructing your resume personal accomplishments and rewards take precedence over group efforts. During communicative interactions you will probably be more concerned with protecting your own face than that of others. This leads to a very direct, forthright style of communication that promotes the individuality so valued in the United States. The cultural value of equality also influences how Americans use English. With certain exceptions—such as judges, doctors, figures in higher education, and political office holders—titles are rarely used, and Americans prefer to move quickly to a first name basis when meeting new people.

However, as we briefly noted earlier in this chapter, the English language in other national cultures can vary in usage, vocabulary, and even spelling. For instance, the British place more emphasis on social status, or class, which can be reflected through one's accent. Additionally, they tend to be more formal and first names are normally not used until a relationship has been established. "The Queen's English" also has a large vocabulary of terms that vary from those employed in the United States—soldiers leaving the U.S. military are "discharged," but in England and Australia they are "demobbed." In the United States being "pissed" implies irritation or anger, but in England, Australia, and New Zealand it means being intoxicated. A "bum" in the United States refers to a vagrant or shiftless person, but in England it is that part of the body you sit on.

INTERPRETING AND TRANSLATING

The impact of globalization on the world community and the ever increasing level of intercultural communication activity is a theme running through every chapter of this text. The work of interpreters and translators is instrumental to the success of increased communication activities across cultural boundaries. Their importance in our globalized, multicultural society is exemplified by the requirements of the European Union. Today, the EU must manage meetings and correspondence in its 23 official languages,[49] as well as several others, such as Arabic, Chinese, and Russian. This requires approximately 135,000 interpreter days per year.[50] Nations with large immigration populations are faced with interpretation and translation requirements that often exceed those of the European Union. For example, the written exam for a

As interactions with people from other cultures speaking different languages continue to increase, the ability to work through an interpreter or translator becomes essential to ensuring your message is conveyed correctly and that you understand the other party's meaning.

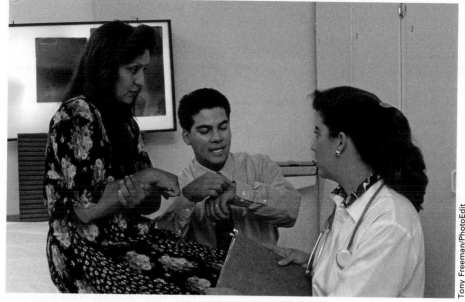

Tony Freeman/PhotoEdit

California state driver license is available in 31 languages in addition to English.[51] The Los Angeles County court system maintains a pool of interpreters representing over 100 languages.[52] In addition to these examples, and on a larger scale, government, business, and social institutions must structure their messages, products, and advertisements to appeal to culturally diverse communities.

The term "translating" is often used in a broad sense to refer to changing messages, written or signed, from one language to another. However, in professional settings, "translation" is taken to mean working with written messages. "Interpretation," on the other hand, implies changing oral or signed messages from one language into another. Awareness of this difference is especially important when dealing with organizations that must continually manage information in two or more languages. The European Commission, for instance, has both a Directorate General for Interpretation and a Directorate General for Translation.

INTERPRETATION

In today's multicultural society the presence of interpreters is commonplace. In the United States interpretation services are frequently used in health care centers, courtrooms, business conferences, and even classrooms. Television news clips of international meetings often show participants with headsets or earphones. Almost any un-posed photo of a U.S. president conversing with a foreign government leader will show one or two individuals hovering near the participants interpreting the conversation. The presence of either an interpreter or participants wearing earphones usually suggests the type of translation being done—consecutive or simultaneous. *Consecutive* translation is most often used in high-level private activities, business meetings, and small, informal gatherings. In this method the speaker will talk for a short time and then stop to allow the interpreter to convey the message to the other party. *Simultaneous* translation uses audio equipment, with the translator located in a soundproof booth away from the participants. This is a much more demanding method because the speaker does not pause, which requires the translator to listen and speak simultaneously. In each method, a high degree of fluency in the target languages is obviously necessary.

TRANSLATION

As we mentioned above, a translator's task is to convert written text from one language into another. Types of texts can vary widely, including official government documents, international contracts, scientific papers, and even novels and poetry. Translators have the advantage of being able to consult references if needed and are not subject to the same time constraints that interpreters must work under. However, they are usually required to be knowledgeable in, and possess a comprehensive vocabulary of, a specific subject area. These vocabularies can be highly technical, such as for a scientific document, or consist of contemporary jargon or slang like that used in novels or even *manga* (Japanese comics) publications. Research in machine translation is a growing field and significant advances are being made. However, language variations in grammar, sentence structure, and cultural differences encompassing humor, irony, sarcasm, and the like, make this a daunting task. Although machines have lessened the burden of some elementary, routine translations, linguistic experts think it will be some time before human translators are replaced by machines.[53] Part of the difficulty lies in a machine's inability to detect the subtle aspects of language, such as emotions and sarcasm, which can be conveyed by the way words are *used* rather than the actual words. Moreover, machines cannot read nonverbal communication.

CULTURAL CONSIDERATIONS IN INTERPRETATION AND TRANSLATION

The process of translation and interpretation is much more complicated than merely taking a word from one language and replacing it with one from another language. There are numerous cultural considerations that come into play. Often, there is no single word equivalency or the word may have a different meaning in another language. Football, for instance, means something quite different in Europe and South America than in the United States or Canada. In the United States, the suggestion to "discuss" something connotes a desire to talk over a topic in a mutually agreeable, friendly manner, but in Spanish, *"discusión"* implies a more intense, discordant attitude.

An applied example can illustrate how cultural factors can compound the interpretation process. In previous chapters we pointed out that some cultures (e.g., China, Japan, and Korea) rely on an indirect communication style and others (e.g., United States) use a straightforward, direct style. In cross-cultural negotiations with a U.S. group, representatives from one of the Northeast Asian countries might respond to a request with "maybe," "I will try my best," or "we will have to consider this" to signal a negative reply. In this case, a literal translation devoid of any cultural nuances can be potentially misleading. Members of the U.S. team are conditioned to hearing a more direct reply, such as a simple "no" or even "that is out of the question." Thus, they could easily misconstrue a literal interpretation to be a positive reply.

Translation tasks can also require an extensive awareness of cultural factors. As an illustration, if translating a Japanese novel into English, the translator would need to be aware of contemporary colloquialisms and slang. For example, if the novel mentions a large truck (*oki torakku*), it could become "eighteen-wheeler" or "semi" in American English, but in the United Kingdom, "articulated lorry" would be a more appropriate term. Similarly, if the Japanese novel mentioned an "American dog" (*Amerikan doggu*), the Australian version would use "Dagwood Dog" and the U.S. adaptation would be "corn dog."

The Spanish word *ahora* offers another example. Among Spanish speakers the common meaning is that something will be done within a few minutes to several hours. However, the word is usually translated into English as "now," which implies immediately or right away. To add greater urgency, the Spanish speaker would use *ahorita* or *ahoritita*. Even *within* the Spanish language there are major linguistic differences between what is used in Spain, South America, Central America, Mexico, and other Spanish speaking nations. These variations are so great that it is impossible to translate "a given text in a way that would fully satisfy all of these people."[54]

WORKING WITH INTERPRETERS AND TRANSLATORS

As interactions with people from other cultures speaking different languages continue to increase, the ability to work through an interpreter or translator becomes essential to ensuring your message is conveyed correctly and that you properly understand the other party's meaning. Use of an interpreter or translator involves establishing a three-way rapport between you, the interpreter or translator, and the audience. Thus, it is important to select an interpreter or translator that best suits your particular situation. The following are some of the more obvious considerations.

- **Language knowledge**: The individual selected needs to be completely bilingual. Moreover, this knowledge should encompass contemporary usage which includes metaphors, slang, and idioms.
- **Dialect knowledge:** In addition to language, the individual should also have a facility in any dialect that may come into play. While this may seem minor, during the 2010 Gulf of Mexico oil spill, to work with the Vietnamese speaking residents of the Gulf area, BP hired interpreters who spoke a North Vietnamese dialect and used what was considered "Communist terminology." This caused the Gulf Coast Vietnamese, originally from South Vietnam, to view the interpreters with suspicion.[55]
- **Specialized terminology:** The specialized terminology used in different fields can be very confusing to an outsider. Therefore, it is essential that an interpreter or translator be well versed in the terms, jargon, and acronyms of the topic being addressed. For instance, an interpreter unfamiliar with medical terminology would be an impediment to effective intercultural communication in a health care setting.

- **Cultural knowledge:** There is a growing recognition that interpreters and translators must be culturally competent, and this requires knowledge of own culture as well as that of the target language culture.

COMMUNICATION TECHNOLOGY AND LANGUAGE

The digital age has greatly enhanced the ability of people around to world to easily and quickly "connect" with others through a variety of media. Although the Internet enables people from different cultures to interact with individuals and groups across vast distances, they must find and use a common language. Because the Internet is such a dynamic communication forum, new innovations are continually being introduced. Thus, it is not our intention to provide you a comprehensive examination of the nexus between technology and culture, an endeavor far beyond the scope of this book. Rather, we wish to offer you a perspective on the variety of languages used to access the Internet.

English continues to be the most common language among Internet users, which has raised concern of it becoming the world's dominant language.[56] There are two rather obvious reasons for English being the principal language among Internet users: (1) the system was conceived and implemented in the United States and was, therefore, designed for English speakers, and (2) English "is the lingua franca of scientific and academic publishing."[57]

However, Internet usage statistics over the past decade suggest that other languages are gaining a greater presence. Looking at Table 8.2, for example, we see that China has the largest number of all Internet users, but they represent less than one-third of the country's population. In contrast, the United States is the second largest user with over three quarters of the population going online. Thus, China has a much greater

The digital age has greatly enhanced the ability of people around the world easily and quickly to "connect" with others through a variety of media.

Simone D. McCourtie/World Bank Group

TABLE 8.2	Internet Usage by Country[58]		
COUNTRY	**PERCENT OF COUNTRY POPULATION THAT ARE USERS**	**PERCENT OF WORLD USERS**	**2000–2010 INCREASE**
China	31.6 %	21.4 %	1,766.7 %
United States	77.3 %	12.2 %	151.6 %
Japan	78.2 %	5.0 %	110.6 %
India	6.9 %	4.1 %	1,520.0 %
Brazil	37.8 %	3.9 %	1,418.9 %

Source: © Cengage Learning 2013

potential for increasing its number of Internet users, as do the other developing nations of India and Brazil.

Just as previous Western media, such as television, music, and videos, increased the world's exposure to English, so has the Internet. But Danet and Herring suggest that "the possibility of a single language prevailing over all others seems remote."[59] What seems possible, however, is "an oligarchy of the world's largest languages—Chinese, Spanish, English, Arabic, Malay, Hindi, Russian—each of them dominating in its geographical region, where it also enjoys economic and cultural influences."[60]

Language can also play a role in the selection of which social media outlet a culture favors. A mid-2010 report indicated that while 62 percent of U.S. Internet users were on Facebook, only 3 percent of the Japanese were. However, more than 16 percent of Japanese Internet users "tweeted," compared to 9.8 percent in the United States. One reason for this variation is that the Japanese language (as well as Chinese) enables users to say considerably more in the 140 character limit than can be said in English.[61] For example, the word "Japan" requires five characters in English, but only two (日本) in Japanese.

LANGUAGE AND INTERCULTURAL COMPETENCE

As we stated at the outset of this chapter, almost every intercultural communication interaction involves one or more individuals relying on a second language. Thus, it is impossible to discuss even a small number of the many scenarios where language is used to create understanding. Later in the book we devote an entire chapter to intercultural communication interactions in business, health care, and education contexts, and discuss a broad spectrum of factors that influence understanding. But here we want to acquaint you with some general measures relating to language use that can enhance your intercultural communication competence.

IMPROVING INTERPERSONAL INTERACTIONS

During interactions with someone speaking a second language, there is a very high potential for miscommunication, unless the person is fluent and culturally knowledgeable. When using your own language while conversing with a non-native speaker, the following considerations should help you reduce the potential for misunderstandings.

Being Mindful

In any intercultural communication interaction it is especially important that you be *mindful*. This is defined as creating new categories, being receptive to new information, and realizing that other people may not share your perspective.[62] Creating new categories means moving beyond the broad, general classifications you may have been using for many years. As an example, instead of categorizing someone as an Asian, you should try to form a more specific classification that considers gender, age, national and regional identity, occupation, and such (e.g., "a young Chinese male college student from Beijing"). Being receptive to new information may mean something as simple as learning that some people consider horse meat a delicacy or do not wear shoes inside their homes. Yet learning about different perspectives can also be as complicated as trying to understand why another culture sees nothing wrong in bribing government officials or aborting a fetus because it is not a male.

Being mindful can also entail being aware that using a second language is more physically and cognitively demanding than speaking one's native language. During a conversation, someone speaking a second language must be more alert to what the other person is saying and how it is being said. They must simultaneously think about how to respond. Depending on the degree of fluency, this may require the second language speaker to mentally convert the received message into his or her native language, prepare a response in the native language, and then cognitively translate that response into the second language. If their second language vocabulary is limited, the cognitive demands are even greater. This difficulty is increased if the second language speaker is unfamiliar with the native speaker's accent. As you can see, the second language speaker is confronted with a much greater mental task than the native speaker. This cognitive process can produce both mental and physical fatigue. Thus, the native speaker must be alert for signs that the second language speaker is tiring.[63]

Speech Rate

One problem encountered by second language speakers is that native speakers often seem to talk quite fast. For example, if you are interacting with someone who is using English as a second language, you cannot automatically assume that he or she is completely fluent. Therefore, until the other person's level of language competence is determined, you should speak a bit more slowly and distinctly than you normally do. By closely monitoring feedback from the second language speaker, you can adjust your speech rate accordingly. It is also important to look in the direction of the other person, as this can aid in understanding a second language.

Vocabulary

Determining the second language speaker's vocabulary level is also important. Until you are sure that the other person has the requisite second language ability, avoid professional vocabulary, technical words, and acronyms. In a health care setting, instead of using "inflammation," it might be more effective to say, "The area will get red and a little sore." Metaphors, slang, and colloquialisms can also impede understanding and should not be used. In the United States, for instance, the phrase "we are on a parallel course" is used to indicate that you agree with the other party's proposal. However, in Japan, it means that the proposal will never be accepted because parallel lines never meet. In addition, please recall our earlier warning that humor does not travel well across cultures.

Attend to Nonverbal Behaviors

When interacting with a second language user, you need to be alert to the individual's nonverbal responses. This can provide cues about your speech rate, type of vocabulary, and whether the individual understands what you are saying. Moreover, in an intercultural situation you need to be aware of cultural differences in nonverbal cues, which will be discussed more in depth in Chapter 9. For instance, if your Japanese counterpart is giggling at something you said, which you know is not humorous, it might be a signal that your message is not fully understood. At the same time you should expect a second language speaker to exhibit unfamiliar nonverbal behaviors. Standing farther apart than you are used to, being less demonstrative, refraining from smiling, or avoiding direct eye contact may be normal nonverbal behaviors in their culture.

Checking

By "checking," we mean that you should employ measures to help ensure your intercultural partner understands your messages. If you feel the second language speaker is having difficulty comprehending something said, simply say, "Let me say that another way," and rephrase your statement. Also, while checking for understanding, try to do so from a subordinate position. That is, instead of asking, "Do you understand?" which places the burden on the other person, ask, "Am I being clear?" In this manner you take responsibility for the conversation and lessen the potential for embarrassing the other person. This can be of considerable importance when interacting with someone from a culture where face is highly valued. Another means of checking is to write out a few words of the message you are trying to convey. Some people's second language reading skills may be greater than their listening ability.

As you have read throughout this book, globalization has made the world much smaller. As more and more people from different cultures come together, knowing another language becomes increasingly beneficial. The following section will note some of the benefits of learning a second language.

SECOND LANGUAGE BENEFITS

It should be clear at this stage of the chapter that learning another language can be extremely demanding, requiring considerable time and effort, but the advantages are so numerous as to make the effort worthwhile. Obviously, knowledge of a second language will help you communicate with other people. Additionally, it also tells the native speakers that you are interested in them and their culture. Using another language can also help you better express yourself or explain certain concepts or items. Lal, a native Hindi speaker, explained that English, his second language, had no "words for certain kinds of [Hindi] relationships and the cultural assumptions and understandings which go with them."[64] Wong, who speaks Chinese (Mandarin and

Edwin McDaniel

Knowledge of a second language will help you function more effectively as you move from culture to culture.

Cantonese) and English echoes this: "Relying only on English, I often cannot find words to convey important meanings found in Chinese."[65] Thus, learning a second language can provide greater insight into the emotions and values of another culture, which will increase your intercultural understanding and competence, and also provide a greater awareness of cultural influences in general.

> ### REMEMBER THIS
>
> *There are over 6,900 first languages spoken in the world. People in the United States speak 364 languages—176 indigenous languages and 188 immigrant languages.[66]*

A Belgian businessman explained that one of the first questions asked during employment interviews is, "Do you speak languages?"[67] This priority is a product of Belgium's small geographical size, which creates a need for international commerce, and as a member of the European Union. In many ways the language ability the people of Belgium need to effectively interact within the greater sphere of the European Union is a microcosm of globalization. As world society becomes more interconnected and more integrated, there is a corresponding need to speak more than one language. While bilingualism is official in only a small number of nations—such as Switzerland, Belgium, India, and Canada—it is practiced in almost every country.[68] The criticality of language to successful interactions in a globalized world is seen in the European Commission's goal of a "Europe where everyone can speak at least **two other languages** in addition to their own mother tongue."[69] A similar objective was voiced on the other side of the world by the Japanese Minister of Education, Culture, Sports, Science and Technology (MEXT), "Since we are living in a globalized society, I am keenly aware of the necessity of children acquiring the ability to communicate in foreign languages."[70]

Nonverbal Communication: The Messages of Action, Space, Time, and Silence

Silence is sometimes the answer.

ESTONIAN PROVERB

To know what people think, pay regard to what they do, rather than what they say.

RENÉ DESCARTES

Finally! After more than four years of life as a university student, graduation day is only weeks away. No more late night cram sessions, boring mass lecture classes, endless meals of instant ramen, and a dead end part-time job. Life begins today! Your first interview at the company went well, and today's follow-up is the final hurdle before being offered your dream job. Knowing the importance of making a good first impression, and recalling what you learned about nonverbal messages in a communication class, you pay particular attention to every detail of your appearance. After showering and a quick glance in the mirror, you begin to wonder about your short beard. After a moment of reflection, including a fleeting thought about selling your soul to corporate America, off goes the beard, followed by a dash of after-shave for that clean scent. Next comes the freshly ironed shirt (white, of course), new tie (stylish but not flashy), and the shined business shoes. As you pick up the thin leather briefcase (purchased just for the occasion) and head for the door, your roommate offers a "thumbs up" for good luck.

At precisely 9:20 AM, right after popping a small breath mint into your mouth, you enter the building, approach the receptionist, and inform her you are there for a 9:30 appointment. Ten minutes later you are ushered into a large, carpeted corner office. A carved wooden nameplate on the elegant oak desk lets you know this is the office of the Executive VP for Human Resources. The smartly dressed woman seated behind the desk smiles, rises, and walks around to meet you. Returning the smile, you step forward and firmly grasp her outstretched hand to signal your self-confidence. With a nod of her head, she invites you to sit in a comfortable overstuffed chair, while she takes a seat in another chair across the coffee table from you. The interview is about to begin.

This hypothetical (and perhaps exaggerated) episode was intended to demonstrate a few of the many and subtle ways nonverbal communication affects your life. In our little drama it was assumed, and rightly so, that the interviewer would have positive responses to your nonverbal "messages" of punctuality, grooming, apparel, expression, handshake, odor, and the like. But would these same behaviors be as successful if you were applying for a position in another country? The answer is **no**. Before we explain our negative response, however, we ask you to reflect on a few more nonverbal examples.

Early in the Iraq conflict, as American troops drove through the streets of Baghdad, they believed they were being greeted by throngs of people who were happy to see them. They observed hundreds of children lining the streets giving them the "thumbs-up" sign. However, as Woodward points out, the Americans "did not realize that in Iraq the thumbs-up sign traditionally was the equivalent of the American middle-finger salute."[1] That same middle finger used in Dubai would get you deported. Misinterpreting the nonverbal actions of people of different cultures is commonplace. In Mexico it is not unusual to see both men and women greet each other by hugging in public. Arab men often greet by kissing on both cheeks. In Japan men and women greet by exchanging bows. Recall that you greeted the interviewer with a simple handshake. In Thailand, to signal another person to come near, one wags their fingers back and forth with the palm down. The interviewer sent you a beckoning message with her palm facing up. In Vietnam that same motion is reserved for someone attempting to summon a dog. In Italy, and in various Arab countries, it is not uncommon for people to be thirty minutes tardy for an appointment. And there you were making sure you were on time for your interview!

All of the examples offered in the last few paragraphs were presented for two reasons. First, we hoped to arouse your interest in the subject of nonverbal communication. Second, we wanted to demonstrate that although much of nonverbal communication is universal, many nonverbal actions are shaped by culture. What might be a clear "message" in one culture could well produce confusion in another. This potential for misinterpretation is at the core of this chapter.

To appreciate fully the significance of nonverbal communication to human interaction, reflect for a moment on the countless times, besides employment interviews, that you send and receive nonverbal messages. Barnlund highlights some of those occasions:

> Many, and sometimes most, of the critical meanings generated in human encounters are elicited by touch, glance, vocal nuance, gestures, or facial expression with or without the aid of words. From the moment of recognition until the moment of separation, people observe each other with all their senses, hearing pause and intonation, attending to dress and carriage, observing glance and facial tension, as well as noting word choice and syntax. Every harmony or disharmony of signals guides the interpretation of passing mood or enduring attribute. Out of the evaluation of kinetic, vocal, and verbal cues, decisions are made to argue or agree, to laugh or blush, to relax or resist, or to continue or cut off conversation.[2]

REMEMBER THIS

The nonverbal messages you send, and the responses they produce, are rooted in culture.

THE FUNCTIONS OF NONVERBAL COMMUNICATION

Not only is nonverbal communication omnipresent and an essential ingredient in human interaction, it also occurs for specific reasons. Examining a few of those reasons will illustrate why any study of intercultural interaction must include information about nonverbal communication.

EXPRESSING INTERNAL STATES

Nonverbal communication is important because people use this message system to express ideas, attitudes, feelings, and emotions. As Guerrero and Floyd point out, "Nonverbal communication is the predominant means of conveying meaning from person to person."[3]

Consciously and unconsciously, intentionally and unintentionally, people make important judgments concerning your internal state by the nonverbal messages you generate. If you see someone with a clenched fist and an inhospitable expression, you do not need words to tell you that the person is not happy. If you hear someone's voice quaver and witness their hands tremble, you may infer that the person is fearful or anxious, despite what might be said. If someone smiles as you approach them, you feel far more at ease than if they were scowling.

Be it fear, joy, anger, or sadness, your posture, face, and eyes can convey your feelings without you ever uttering a word. For this reason most people rely heavily on what they perceive through their eyes. In fact, research indicates that you will usually believe nonverbal messages instead of verbal messages when the two contradict.[4]

Be it fear, joy, anger, or sadness, your posture, face, and eyes can convey your feelings without you ever uttering a word.

Kathleen K. Parker

You can even appraise the quality of your relationships according to the interpretations assigned to nonverbal messages. From the amount of touching that takes place, to the tone of voice being used, to the distance between you and your partner, you can gather clues to the closeness of your relationship. The first time you move from holding hands with your partner to touching his or her face, you are sending a message, and that message takes on added significance if your touch is returned. In short, "people use nonverbal cues to define the social and emotional nature of their relationships and interactions."[5]

CREATING IDENTITY

Nonverbal communication is important in human interaction because it is partially responsible for establishing identity. The nonverbal inferences people use to construct their identities are drawn from a variety of messages. From personal experience you know how judgments are often made about another person based on such things as skin color, use of makeup, facial expression, manner of dress, accent, jewelry, and even the type of handshake offered. This use of nonverbal symbols to express a person's identity is universal, as expressed in the following quote about tattoos.

In New Guinea, a swirl of tattoos on a Tofi woman's face indicates her family lineage. The dark scrawls on a Cambodian monk's chest reflect his religious beliefs. A Los Angeles gang

In nearly every culture, and in many co-cultures, tattoos express an indelible identity.

Edwin McDaniel

member's sprawling tattoos describe his street affiliation, and may even reveal if he's committed murder. Whether the bearer is a Maori chief in New Zealand or a Japanese mafia lord, tattoos express an indelible identity.[6]

REGULATING INTERACTION

Nonverbal actions offer clues regarding how people navigate conversation. In a classroom you might raise your hand to signal that you want to talk. In other situations you could lean forward, point a finger, pause, or change the direction of your gaze as a way of altering the conversation. These and other actions communicate to your partner "when to begin a conversation, whose turn it is to speak, how to get a chance to speak, how to signal others to talk more, and how to end a conversation."[7]

REPEATING THE MESSAGE

A common function of nonverbal communication is that it can be used for repetition. If someone is offering what you consider to be a substandard plan, you can move your head from side to side at the same time you utter the word "no." While pointing in a certain direction you can say to the other person, "The computer lab's over there." In both of these examples the gestures and the words you use have similar meanings and reinforce one another.

SUBSTITUTING FOR WORDS

Nonverbal messages can be used as substitutes for words. For example, there are many occasions when someone who is carrying bad news will end up signaling their sorrow without uttering a sound. Or think of all the occasions when you approach a very special friend with a large smile and open arms. A teacher will often place an index finger to the lips as an alternative to saying, "Please be quiet." In each of these examples an action is replacing a verbal utterance and that action becomes the language. To help you understand the language of nonverbal communication, and its role in intercultural communication, we will (1) define nonverbal communication, (2) offer some guidelines for studying nonverbal communication, (3) link nonverbal communication to culture, (4) discuss the major classifications of nonverbal messages, and (5) offer some advice on how to better employ nonverbal communication within the intercultural context.

DEFINING NONVERBAL COMMUNICATION

Because the central concern of this chapter is to examine how and why people communicate nonverbally, we begin with a definition of nonverbal communication. A single definition, like our definitions of "culture" and "communication" in Chapter 2, is hard to pin down. For example, a common and very general definition of nonverbal communication is: "Nonverbal behavior refers to actions as distinct from speech."[8] Because this definition is so broad as to include nearly every aspect of non-linguistic communication, we offer a slightly different view of nonverbal communication that is consistent with current thinking in the field and also reflects the cultural orientation of this book. We propose that *nonverbal communication involves all those nonverbal stimuli in a communication setting that are generated by both the source and his or her use of the environment, and that have potential message value for the source and/or receiver.*

It is not by chance that our definition is somewhat lengthy. We wanted to offer a definition that would not only establish the boundaries of nonverbal communication, but would also reflect how the process actually functions. Part of that functioning involves (1) intentional and unintentional messages, and (2) the reciprocal relationship between verbal and nonverbal messages.

INTENTIONAL AND UNINTENTIONAL MESSAGES

Our definition permits us to include *intentional* as well as *unintentional* behavior. One of the features that separate humans from most other animals is that humans can usually plan certain actions before they execute them. Observing a friend approaching, you offer a broad smile as part of your greeting. This is an intentional act. Yet nonverbal messages are most often produced without a conscious awareness that they may have meaning for other people. These are unintentional messages. For example, frowning because the sun is in your eyes may make someone mistakenly believe you are angry; looking upset after receiving a phone call could make a person approaching you think that you're unhappy to see him or her; and touching someone's hand for an extended time could cause that person to think you are flirting when that was not your intent. These are all examples of how your actions, unintentionally, can send messages to others. The sociologist Goffman describes this fusing of intentional and unintentional behavior:

> The expressiveness of the individual (and therefore his capacity to give impressions) appears to involve two radically different kinds of sign activity: the expression that he gives and the impression that he gives off. The first involves verbal symbols or their substitutes, which he uses admittedly and solely to convey the information that he and the other are known to attach to these symbols. This is communication in the traditional and narrow sense. The second involves a wide range of action that others can treat as symptomatic of the actor (communicator), the expectation being that the action was performed for reasons other than the information conveyed in this way.[9]

VERBAL AND NONVERBAL MESSAGES

We have already indicated that nonverbal communication is a multidimensional activity where nonverbal messages can serve as substitutes for verbal messages. We now add that verbal and nonverbal messages often work in unison. Knapp and Hall emphasize this idea when they write, "We need to understand that separating verbal and nonverbal behavior into two separate and distinct categories is virtually impossible."[10] The interfacing of the verbal with the nonverbal is reflected in a number of ways. For example, you often use nonverbal messages to repeat a point you are trying to make verbally. You could place your index finger over your lips at the same time you were whispering "please don't yell" to someone who was shouting. You can also observe the reciprocal relationship between words and actions if you tell someone you are pleased with his or her performance while patting them on the shoulder.

STUDYING NONVREBAL COMMUNICATION

Because the study of nonverbal communication has become part of "popular culture," this complex and multifaceted subject is often trivialized. Fox News Network, for example, frequently employees an "expert" in nonverbal communication to inform viewers of what politicians are "really saying." This marginalizing often means that nonverbal communication is presented in a misleading and frivolous manner. Therefore, we need to pause before pursuing the topic any further and mention some potential problems and misconceptions associated with this area of study.

NONVERBAL COMMUNICATION CAN BE AMBIGUOUS

Part of the ambiguity associated with nonverbal messages is contextual, which can be seen if someone brushes against you in an elevator: Was it merely an accident, or was it an opportunistic sexual act? As Osborn and Motley tell us, "Meanings and interpretations of nonverbal behaviors often are on very shaky ground."[11] You saw that "shaky ground" when people, both in and out of the media, interpreted a fist bump exchanged by President Barack Obama and his wife Michelle as a "terrorist greeting" instead of a simple sign of camaraderie between husband and wife. Our intention is to remind you that "different situations or environments produce different nonverbal messages."[12]

MULTIPLE FACTORS INFLUENCE NONVERBAL COMMUNICATION

Nonverbal communication, like much of your behavior, is produced by a host of variables, and culture is but one of them. Nonverbal interactions are influenced by factors such as "cultural background, socioeconomic background, education, gender, age, personal preferences and idiosyncrasies."[13] Simply stated, not everyone in a particular culture engages in the same nonverbal actions, so interpretations of nonverbal behaviors must be carefully evaluated before generalizations can be made.

THE STUDY OF NONVERBAL COMMUNICATION INCLUDES CULTURAL UNIVERSALS

Although the bulk of this chapter will focus on nonverbal differences across cultures, we need to point out that there are many similarities in how cultures employ this communication system. Intercultural parallels have been at the core of a lingering academic debate that goes back to the work of Charles Darwin. While much of the debate deals with facial expressions, the arguments touch all dimensions of nonverbal communication. Here lies the question: Is there a universal language of facial expressions? One position holds that anatomically similar expressions may occur in everyone, but the meanings people attach to them differ from culture to culture.[14]

The majority opinion among scholars is that there are universal facial expressions for which people have similar meanings. Ekman, the driving force behind this position, advances the following point of view: "The subtle creases of a grimace tell the same story around the world, to pre-literate New Guinea tribesmen, to Japanese and American college students alike. As noted, this was also Darwin's thesis but now here's hard evidence that culture does not control the face."[15] Ekman and others present the theory that there is "a basic set of at least six facial expressions that are innate, universal, and carry the same basic meaning throughout the world."[16] The six pan-cultural and universal emotions conveyed by facial expressions are happiness, sadness, fear, anger, disgust, and surprise.

Despite the biologically based nature of facial expressions, there seem to be clear cultural expectations and norms that often dictate when, where, how, and to whom facial expressions are displayed.[17] This means that different cultures construct their own rules for what are appropriate facial expressions, as well as what aspects of that behavior should be attended to.[18]

NONVERBAL COMMUNICATION AND CULTURE

We have just finished discussing how culture is but one of the dynamics that influence the manner in which people send and receive nonverbal messages. However, while granting the assorted causes behind human behavior, we nevertheless advocate that nonverbal communication mirrors the learned behaviors imbedded in a culture. Speaking of this link, Wood writes, "Most nonverbal communication isn't instinctual, but is learned in the process of socialization."[19] Rosenblatt confirms this same idea by noting, "What emotions are felt, how they are expressed, and how they are understood are matters of culture."[20] What is key in Rosenblatt's sentence is that your culture has taught you what nonverbal actions to display (crying or laughing), the meaning of those actions (sadness or happiness), and the contextual backdrop of those actions (funeral or wedding). Our thesis should be clear: Nonverbal communication "plays a crucial and necessary part in communicative interactions between people from different cultures."[21]

As a student of intercultural communication, learning about the connection between culture and nonverbal behavior will help to improve the manner in which you engage in intercultural interactions. Hall underscores the need to learn about nonverbal behaviors in the following:

> I remain convinced that much of our difficulty with people in other countries stems from the fact that so little is known about cross-cultural communication…. Formal training in the language, history, government, and customs is only a first step. Of equal importance is an introduction to the nonverbal language of the country. Most Americans are only dimly aware of this silent language, even though they use it every day.[22]

By understanding cultural differences in nonverbal behavior you will also be able to gather clues about underlying attitudes and values being expressed by your communication partner. How far people stand from each other during normal conversation can offer clues to their views on privacy. Bowing tells you that a culture values formality, rank, and status. It is not by chance that Hindus greet each other by placing their palms together in front of themselves while tilting their heads slightly downward. This salutation reflects their belief that the deity exists in everyone.

CLASSIFICATIONS OF NONVERBAL COMMUNICATION
MESSAGES OF THE BODY

As we begin our discussion of the classifications of nonverbal communication you will notice that our analysis of each category starts with the behaviors found in the dominant culture of the United States. We also remind you of the integrated nature of these categories. "Messages generated by each category do not exist in isolation but rather exist in the company of messages from other categories, verbal messages, contexts, and people functioning as message receivers."[23] Most classifications divide nonverbal messages into two comprehensive categories: those that are primarily produced by the body (appearance, movement, facial expressions, eye contact, touch, and paralanguage), and those that the individual combines with the setting (space, time, and silence).

APPEARANCE

From hair sprays to hairpieces, from fat-reducing diets to 24-hour fitness centers, from false eyelashes to blue contact lenses, and from cosmetic surgery to tanning salons, people show their concern for how they appear to others. Many people in the United States now use body piercing and tattooing to alter their appearance. A study in 2010 conducted by the Pew Research Center found that 38 percent of Americans between the ages of 18 and 29 have at least one tattoo.[24] Keating clearly underscores the sway your outer shell has on others when she writes, "The power of communication to draw others near or to drive them away derives as much from how we appear as from the language we deploy."[25] What Keating is suggesting is, of course, what you observe daily in your personal life. Whom you approach and whom you avoid, particularly in regard to first impressions, might well determine future interaction, or indeed, if there will be any interaction. "Initial attraction from one person to another is frequently the precursor to actual interaction, whereas a lack of attraction may preclude people from taking any steps toward relational development."[26]

Judgment of Beauty

Concern with personal appearance is not unique to the United States. As Peoples and Bailey point out, "People around the world are highly creative in altering their physical appearance."[27] And we add that they have been doing so for a long time. As far back as the Upper Paleolithic period (about forty thousand years ago) your ancestors were using bones for necklaces and other bodily ornaments. From that period to the present, historical and archaeological evidence has shown that people are fixated on their bodies. They have painted them, fastened objects to them, dressed them, undressed them, and even deformed and mutilated them in the name of beauty. According to Keesing, "The use of the body for decoration appears to be a cultural universal."[28]

An important component of appearance is the perception of attractiveness and judgments regarding beauty, both of which are influenced by culture.

Steve Harrington

An important component of appearance is the perception of beauty. Studies show that in the United States, being overweight reduces one's income, lowers one's chances of getting married, and helps decrease the amount of education one receives.[29] People use a person's attractiveness to make inferences (often faulty) about that individual's "intelligence, gender, age, approachability, financial well-being, class, tastes, values, and cultural background."[30] In intercultural communication, appearance is important because "One's body image and the satisfaction with it result from comparisons with an implicit cultural ideal and standard."[31] In the United States, people tend to value the appearance of men with muscular bodies and women who are tall and slender.[32] This view of attractiveness is not the rule in all cultures. For example, in large parts of Africa plumpness is considered a sign of beauty, health, and wealth, and slimness is evidence of unhappiness, disease, or mistreatment at the hands of one's husband.[33] Among the Chinese, you can see yet another cultural standard for female attractiveness. As Wenzhong and Grove note, "Many women keep their hairstyles simple (often one or two braids) and make little attempt to draw attention to themselves through self-decoration such as colorful scarves, jewelry, or makeup."[34] In major Chinese cities today, however, judgments of beauty are being influenced by an influx of Western images.

The judgment of beauty across cultures is a perception that is ripe for ethnocentrism. What happens is that "people intolerant of different cultural practices often fail to realize that had they been raised in one of those other cultures, they would be practicing those allegedly disgusting or irrational customs."[35] As we have just noted, one of those "customs" is what defines attractiveness. The link between ethnocentrism and beauty arises from "what is seen as beautiful in one culture may look hideous to people from another culture."[36]

> The many exotic rituals we often see in PBS documentaries or in the pages of *National Geographic*, such as neck stretching, lip enlargements, earlobe plugs, teeth filing, and so on, represent the beautifying practices common in many parts of the world. Of course, liposuction, hair implants, facelifts, laser surgery, and the like, while not the least bit extraordinary to many Westerners, may seem abhorrent to people from other parts of the world.[37]

Because cultures are always in a state of flux, it will be interesting to observe if perceptions of attractiveness begin to change as cultures have greater contact with one another. Even today doctors are reporting an increase in plastic surgeries in places like China, Korea, and Brazil.

Skin Color

Perhaps we should have begun our discussion of appearance with skin color, since it is the first characteristic people notice when they approach a stranger, and the one that has the greatest impact on perception and interaction. In fact "skin color is the first racial marker children recognize and can be considered the most salient of phenotypic attributes."[38] Often that marker is perceived negatively. In an effort to replicate the classic "Doll Test" from the 1940s, where both black and white children preferred white dolls over black, Spencer recently designed a similar study and found that color still mattered in 2010. According to her research, "white children, as a whole, responded with a high rate of what researchers called white bias, identifying the color of their own skin with positive attributes and darker skin with negative attributes."[39] This conclusion, and others like it, is noteworthy in intercultural communication since skin color is a clear symbol of differences. Knapp and Hall note, "In many respects, permanent skin colors have been the most potent body stimulus for determining inter-personal responses in our culture."[40] Skin color "may also be the basis of the allocation of economic and psychological privileges to individuals relative to the degree those privileges are awarded to valued members of the dominant culture."[41]

The United States is not the only location where members of a culture are judged by their skin tone and seek various means to alter that tone. South Asian and Chinese women often avoid sunlight so that their skin remains light. They, along with women from Brazil, Jamaica, and India, are even using an assortment of creams and lotions as a means of achieving a paler tone to their skin.

Attire

You know from your own experiences that clothing goes well beyond protection from the elements. As Adler and Rodman state, "Clothing can be used to convey economic status, education, social status, moral standards, athletic ability and/or interests, belief system (political, philosophical, religious), and levels of sophistication."[42] In the United States, you can also observe how clothing can be a sign of group identification. Whether it is a military uniform, the

sweatshirt that carries a logo of a favorite football team, the specific tilt of a baseball cap, or the attire of the hip-hop co-culture, clothing attempts to tell other people something about your identity. Among gang members in East Los Angeles, even the color of a bandana is a proclamation of group affiliation—blue for Crips and red for Bloods.[43] The notion of trying to make a statement with attire is so strong that recently, young boys at a high school in California were sent home from school because they were wearing T-shirts that looked like the American flag. According to school officials, they were wearing the American flag T-shirts on the same day that Cinco de Mayo was being celebrated by the Mexican students at the high school. School administrators believed that the conspicuous American flag apparel could provoke fights.

Nowhere is the incendiary nature of clothing more apparent than in the various types of scarves, veils, and robes associated with Muslim women. The first is called the *hijab*, which basically covers only the head, while the second scarf, known as the *al-amira*, is a two-piece veil that also includes a scarf. There is also the *niqab*, a more extensive veil that only leaves an area open around the eyes. However, the most controversy has been generated by the *burqa*, which consists of a robe and veils over the entire face of the woman. Even the eyes are covered with the exception of a mesh screen that allows the woman to see what is in front of her. These coverings, particularly the ones over the entire face, have been a point of contention in some non-Muslim countries. In many European nations there have been government attempts to ban the veils from being worn in public places.[44] For example, countries such as Britain, The Netherlands, Italy, Denmark, Belgium, Austria, and Switzerland are all deliberating proposals that, in one form or another, would prohibit the wearing of some veils in

The message that can be communicated by clothing is apparent in the various types of scarves, veils, and robes associated with Muslim women.

Susan Van Etten / PhotoEdit

schools and other public places. France has already taken the first step in this debate with the bold action of banning Muslim headscarves and other so-called religious symbols from classrooms.[45] Attempts at outlawing the veils have even come to North America where "Lawmakers in Quebec are pushing a bill that would deny public services—including health care and education—to Muslim women who wear the *niqab*."[46]

The arguments for and against an imposed dress code are complex, particularly since Muslim women wear scarves, veils, and the *burqa* as nonverbal symbols of womanhood, identity, and more importantly, as a manifestation of their religious beliefs. Throughout the Koran, women are told to be modest and wear clothing that does not draw attention to themselves. Al-Kaysi develops this point in more detail when he speaks of the links between modesty and dress among Muslim women: "The main garment must be a 'flowing' one, that is, a woman must avoid tight or clinging clothes which exaggerate her figure, or any part of it, such as breasts, legs or arms."[47] Young girls and women are also urged in the Koran to dress in garments that do not resemble the clothes of nonbelievers. For these and other reasons, many Muslims and non-Muslims believe the banning of certain religious attire by any government violates the rights of a religion to offer "instruction" to its adherents. Those who support the ban advance arguments about freedom, female equality, secular traditions within a country, and even fears of terrorism.[48] There is, of course, no simple solution to this dilemma. Some Arab countries have attempted to mediate the controversy by outlawing some of the religious clothing while permitting the wearing of a few specific garments. Syria and Turkey (secular countries with Muslim majority populations) have forbidden students and teachers from wearing the *niqab* in school, but have attempted to avoid extending these rulings off campus.

The issue of dress for Muslim women has even found its way to the United States in a location that in many ways is an icon of the United States—Disneyland. A young woman received an internship to work at Disneyland without having to be interviewed for the position. When she appeared for her first day of employment she was wearing a *hijab*. She was told to remove the *hijab*. She refused and was relegated to a room at Disneyland where she did not have any contact with park visitors. The woman is now pursuing legal action against Disneyland. This example, and all the others in this section, demonstrates just how powerful an impact nonverbal communication can have on human behavior.

Muslim men, like the women, have attire that differs from that found in the West. And like the attire of women, there is often a link between religion and dress. The traditional attire for men in Arabic nations would "include a long loose robe called a *dishdasha* or *thobe* and a headpiece, a white cloth *kaffiya* banded by a black *egal* to secure it."[49] The subtlety of color in garments "tells others" about their status and affiliation. An all-white *kaffiya* means the person wearing the headpiece has not yet made the pilgrimage to Mecca.

The link between cultural values and clothing can be seen in nearly every culture. For example, as a symbolic gesture of their faith, the Amish dress in clothing that demonstrates humility and a severance from the dominant culture. Both males and females dress in clothing that is simple, unadorned, and predominantly dark in color. You can also observe the relationship of values and beliefs to dress in German culture, a culture where status and authority are significant. Hall and Hall write:

> Correct behavior is symbolized by appropriate and very conservative dress. The male business uniform is a freshly pressed dark suit and tie with a plain shirt and dark shoes and socks. It is important to emulate this conservative approach to both manners and dress.

Personal appearance, like the exterior appearance of their homes, is very important to Germans.[50]

Japan is another place that merges attire and a culture's value system, as seen in, "The general proclivity for conservative dress styles and colors emphasizes the nation's collectivism and, concomitantly, lessens the potential

for social disharmony arising from nonconformist attire."[51] Like so many cultural values, this Japanese desire for dark and unobtrusive attire has its roots deep in Japanese culture.[52]

In much of the world people still dress in very traditional garments. Clothing styles, according to Peoples and Bailey, "have historically served as the most overt single indicator of ethnic identity."[53] Whether it be the women of Guatemala wearing their colorful tunics (*huípiles*), or African men in white *dashikis*, traditional garments are still common in many cultures. Whether they are Sikhs in white turbans, women in Iran wearing their *hijabs*, the Japanese in kimonos, Hasidic Jews in black yarmulkes, or the dark attire of the Amish in the United States, you need to learn to be tolerant of others' external differences and not let them impede communication.

BODY MOVEMENT

We remind you that the major thesis of this chapter is that communication involves much more than words. Imai underscores this point when he writes: "The world is a giddy montage of vivid gestures—traffic police, street vendors, expressway drivers, teachers, children on playgrounds, athletes with their exuberant hugging, clenched fists and 'high fives.' People all over the world use their hands, heads, and bodies to communicate expressively."[54]

The study of how movement communicates is called *kinesics*. Kinesic cues are those visible body shifts and movements that can send both intentional and unintentional messages. For example, your attitude toward the other person can be shown by leaning forward to "communicate" that you are comfortable with him or her. You might show your emotional state by tapping on a table because you are nervous. Something as simple as walking can also send messages. Americans, particularly males, tend to walk in a manner that is distinct from most other cultures. Stevenson highlights this distinguishing gait thusly: "We walk big—swinging arms, letting our legs amble wide—in a manner that's fitting for folks from a country with plenty of empty space. Citizens of densely populated Europe exhibit a far more compact posture, with elbows and knees tucked tight and arm swings restrained."[55]

In attempting to understand the influence of body movement, a few points need to be clarified. First, in most instances the messages the body generates operate in combination with other messages. People usually smile and say "hello" to a friend at the same time. In Mexico, when asking someone to wait for "just a minute, please" (*un momento, por favor*), the speaker also makes a fist and then extends the thumb and index finger so that they form a sideways "U," as though measuring a short span of time. Second, while body language is universal, the meanings it evokes are attached to culture. Third, it is often difficult to control kinesic behavior. That is to say, in most instances you have at least a fraction of a second to think about what you are going to say, but a great deal of body action is spontaneous. Finally, there are thousands of distinct physical signs. Hence, any attempt at cataloging them would be both frustrating and fruitless. Our basic purpose is to point out that while all people use movements to communicate, culture teaches them how to use and interpret the movements. In the upcoming sections we look at a few cultural differences in a person's (1) posture and (2) movements (gestures) that convey ideas and feelings.

Posture

Posture can indicate whether or not people are paying attention, the degree of status in the encounter, if people like or dislike each other, feelings of submissiveness, and even sexual intentions.[56] One study revealed "that body posture may be as important as the face in communicating emotions such as fear."[57] Think for a moment of all the meanings associated with slouching, being stiff, slumping over, crouching, kneeling, pulling back one's shoulders, twitching one's legs, putting one's hands in pockets, bowing, and the like.

On an intercultural level, posture can offer insight into a culture's value system. President Obama discovered this firsthand when he visited Japan and engaged in a polite bow in front of Japan's Emperor Akihito. The arguments surrounding this seemingly innocuous nonverbal action created a firestorm of media attention. *Newsweek* magazine summarized the positions on both sides of the argument in the following two sentences: "The President was pilloried last week for his deep bow to Japan's Emperor Akihito during a visit to Tokyo. Was he groveling before a foreign leader—or just being polite?"[58] The problem is, "In the West, bowing is associated with the indignity of feudal bondage."[59] Hence, for many, Obama was engaging in an act of subservience. For the Japanese, the bow (*ojigi*) is not a sign of capitulation, but rather it mirrors their value of status and respect.[60] Actually, the Japanese have a wide range of uses for the bow. It can be a nonverbal way of expressing "thank you," a greeting, an apology, a congratulatory gesture, and much more.

To outsiders the act of bowing appears simple. The actual Japanese ritual is rather complicated. For example, the person who occupies the lower station begins the bow, and his or her bow must be deeper than the other person's. The superior, on the other hand, determines when the bowing is to end. When the participants are of equal rank, they begin the bow in the same manner and end at the same time. In fact, there are so many nuances to the act of bowing in Japan that young children begin to learn about this nonverbal behavior at a very early age. Many large companies even hold classes in correct bowing protocol for their employees.

Thai people use a bow that is similar to the one employed by the Japanese. This movement (called the *wai*) is made by pressing both palms together in front of one's body, with the fingertips reaching to about neck level. While the basic value behind the bow is to demonstrate respect, it is also used to "say" "thank you." Many Buddhists will also keep the hands in the *wai* position while listening to a Dharma talk (Buddhist teaching).

Another nonverbal greeting pattern linked to religion is used in the Indian culture, where the *namaste* (Indian bow) is carried out by making a slight bow and bringing both hands together in front of the heart. This practice of greeting someone reflects the Hindu belief that God is in everything—including other people. Hence, all human beings, along with all the gods of Hinduism, are to be honored and respected.

Hindus will even bow before eating as a way of bestowing thanks for yet another one of God's gifts.

As eccentric as it sounds, the way people sit is often a reflection of important cultural characteristics. In the United States, being casual and friendly is valued, and people often demonstrate this through their manner of sitting. The casual sitting position for males "includes a slump and leaning back and a type of sprawl that occupies a lot of space."[61] American males often, consciously or unconsciously, sit with their feet up on their desk as a sign of being relaxed. In many countries, such as Germany, Sweden, and Taiwan, where lifestyles tend to be more formal, slouching is considered a sign of rudeness and poor manners. In fact, "German children are still taught to sit and stand up straight, which is a sign of good character. Slouching is seen as a sign of a poor upbringing."[62] Even the manner in which you position your legs while sitting has cultural overtones. Remland offers further instances of the crossing of legs when he notes, "An innocent act of ankle-to-knee leg crossing, typical of most American males, could be mistaken for an insult (a showing of the sole of the foot gesture) in Saudi Arabia, Egypt, Singapore, or Thailand."[63] People in Thailand also believe there is something special about the bottoms of the feet. For them, the feet are the lowest part of the body, and they should never be pointed in the direction of another person.[64]

In the United States, co-cultural differences exist in how people move, stand, and sit during interaction. Women often hold their arms closer to their bodies than men do. They usually keep their legs close together. Their posture is more restricted and less relaxed than the posture of males. Most of the research in the area of gender communication concludes that these differences are related to issues such as status, power, and affiliation.[65] Posture and stance also play important roles in the African-American co-culture. This is evident in the walk assumed by many young African-American males. "The general form of the walk is slow and casual with the head elevated and tipped to one side, one arm swinging and the other held limply."[66] The walk is often used to "show the dominant culture that you are strong and proud, despite your status in American society."[67]

Gestures

Consider all of the messages that can be sent by waving, placing hands on hips, folding the arms, scratching the head, biting fingernails, pointing, making a fist, shaking a finger, etc. Gestures are a nonverbal "vocabulary" that people use, both intentionally and unintentionally, to share their internal states. Reflect for a moment about "signing" as a major form of communication utilized by the deaf co-culture in the United States. Here you can observe a rich and extensive vocabulary composed almost exclusively of gestures. Another example of the power of gestures can be found in the hand signals

CONSIDER THIS

You met someone who has recently arrived in the United States and they ask your help in deciding what certain gestures mean. What would you tell them the following gestures mean in United States culture?

- *Fingers crossed*
- *Thumbs up*
- *Thumbs down*
- *Making a round ring (O) with the thumb and index finger*
- *Pointing at a person*

After you explain the above gestures, they ask you if those gestures can have more than one meaning. What would you answer?

used by various urban gangs. The slightest variation in performing a certain gesture can be the catalyst for a violent confrontation. Inability to "read" the meaning of a gesture, particularly in an intercultural communication setting, has the potential for confusion and awkwardness. You can witness some of the uncertainty of intercultural gestures in the following few examples.

- The "thumbs-up" gesture in the United States has positive connotations because it indicates that "everything is okay" or "you are doing very well." However, "in Australia and West Africa it is seen as a rude gesture."[68]
- In the United States, pointing at someone usually does not carry negative connotations. In fact, directions are often given by pointing in one direction or another with the index finger. Germans point with the little finger, while in Japan pointing is done with the entire hand with the palm held upward. In China, pointing can be taken as a sign of rudeness. In much of the Arab world, pointing is thought to be an offensive gesture. And in much of Asia, pointing the index finger at a person is considered rude.
- In the United States "making a circle with one's thumb and index finger while extending the others is emblematic of the word 'okay'; in Japan (and Korea) it traditionally signifies 'money'[69] (*okane*); and among Arabs this gesture is usually accompanied by a baring of teeth, signifying extreme hostility."[70] To a Tunisian, the gesture means, "I'll kill you." And in some Latino cultures the circle with the thumb and index finger is "an obscene gesture."[71]

We could present many more examples, since there are thousands of gestures prevalent in every culture. Therefore, instead of presenting a random catalog of gestures from all over the world, we will present enough examples to demonstrate how gestures and culture are linked. In so doing we examine (1) *idiosyncratic gestures*, (2) *beckoning*, (3) *agreement*, and variations related to the (4) *frequency and intensity* of the gestures.

Idiosyncratic Gestures. As we have already indicated, there are limitless *idiosyncratic gestures* found in each culture. These are the distinctive gestures whose meanings are the feature and property of a particular culture. Nonverbal ways of communicating admiration can be one of the most idiosyncratic categories of all gestures. For example, "the Frenchman kisses his fingertips, the Italian twists an imaginary moustache, and the Brazilian curls one hand in front of another as if he is looking through an imaginary telescope."[72] The Japanese have a gesture whose actual movement is not unique to that culture, yet the meaning is exclusive to that culture. The gesture is made by pointing both index fingers above the head, at the top of the ears, as if they were the horns of an ogre. The gesture means the man's wife is angry.[73] In China, if you place your right hand over your heart, it means you are making a sincere promise. In Iraq, the same gesture can mean "thank you." For the French, pulling the skin down below the right eye can mean "I don't believe you." In Argentina, one twists an imaginary mustache to signify that everything is "okay."

Meanings for gestures with sexual connotations may also be exclusive to a specific culture. In the United States someone might use the middle finger to send an insulting, obscene gesture. This sexual insult gesture is not universal. For the Japanese, the thumb protruding out between the index finger and the middle finger is a sexual sign with a variety of interpretations. This same gesture is the letter "T" in American sign language.[74]

Beckoning Gestures. The sign used for *beckoning* is also attached to culture. In the United States when a person wants to signal a friend to come, he or she usually makes the gesture with one hand, palm up, fingers more or less together, and moving toward the body. In much of Latin America this gesture takes on romantic connotations. Koreans signal someone to come by cupping "the hand with the palm down and drawing the fingers toward the palm."[75] This same beckoning sign is used by the Vietnamese. When they see this gesture, many Americans think the other person is waving good-bye. In Germany and much of Scandinavia, tossing the head back constitutes a beckoning motion. For many Arabs, holding the right hand out, palm upward, and opening and closing the hand is nonverbally asking someone to "come here."[76] And to beckon someone in Spain, you stretch your arm out, palm downward, and make a scratching motion toward your body with your fingers.

Agreement Gestures. Movements and gestures denoting agreement represent another example of culturally based gestures. In the United States, moving your head up and down is perceived as a sign of agreement. This same movement can have different meanings in different cultures. "Among Native American, Middle Eastern, and Pacific Island groups, it often means, 'I hear you speaking.' It does not signal that the listener understands the message nor does it suggest that he or she agrees."[77] Greeks express "yes" with a nod similar to the one used in the United States, but when communicating "no," they jerk their head back and raise their faces. Lifting one or both hands up to the shoulders strongly emphasizes the "no." In India, gestures for "yes" and "no" also differ from those used in the United States. Indians demonstrate they agree with you by tossing the head from side to side. To show disagreement they nod up and down.[78] These gestures are virtually reversed in the United States. In Japan people have "learned" to strike the palm of one hand with a clenched fist to show agreement,[79] but this is an obscene gesture in Indonesia.[80]

Frequency and Intensity of Gestures. There are also cultural differences that regulate the frequency and intensity of gestures. It is generally accepted that Italians, most Latinos, Africans, and people from the Middle East are more demonstrative and employ gestures with greater frequency and intensity than do cultures such as the Japanese, Chinese, Finns, and Scandinavians.[81] Italians, for example, "speak" with their hands as well as their voices. Berry and his colleagues reaffirm this idea when they mention the "excited impression" Italians make "because of their lively movement patterns."[82] "Brazilians say that if you tie their hands they cannot speak. They use hand gestures and broad arm gestures as they talk."[83] The use of gestures to promote meaning is also common among Arab men. Here you can see large gestures and "the waving of arms used to accompany almost every spoken word."[84] Members of many Asian cultures perceive such outward activity quite differently, often equating vigorous action with a lack of manners and restraint.[85] Germans are also made uncomfortable by bold hand gestures. These types of gestures, by their standards, are too ostentatious and flamboyant.[86] Ruch offers the following advice to American executives who work with German corporations: "Hands should be used with calculated dignity. They should never serve as lively instruments to emphasize points in conversation. The entire game plan is to appear calm under pressure."[87] The Germans are not alone in their aversion to large and ostentatious

used with far more discretion, generally only with those persons one knows and really likes."[106]

Even within a culture, there are groups and co-cultures that use facial expressions differently from the dominant culture. For example, when compared to men, women use more facial expressions, are more expressive, smile more, are more apt to return smiles, and are more attracted to others who smile.[107]

Eye Contact and Gaze

The eyes, and their power and sway, have always been a topic of interest and fascination. You can witness the potential communication component of eye contact when professional poker players seek to hide behind their dark glasses or a hooded sweat shirt during a tournament. The impact of eye contact on communication is also seen in the countless literary and musical allusions to eyes made over hundreds of years. Emerson wrote, "The eyes indicate the antiquity of the soul." Shakespeare also knew the communicative potency of the eyes when he wrote, "Thou tell'st me there is murder in mine eye." Bob Dylan underscored the same potency in his lyrics: "Your eyes said more to me that night than your lips would ever say." Even the concept of "the evil eye" has been present in nearly every culture for centuries. The notion of an "evil eye" means being able to send another person a thought (transmitted through the eyes) that can cause damage in a host of ways. By some estimates there are approximately 70 cultures covering nearly every part of the world that believe in the influence of the evil eye.[108] Belief in the power of the evil eye (*mal de ojo*) is seen in Mexico and Puerto Rico, where "Mothers may isolate their children for fear of having one become a victim of *mal de ojo*."[109]

Eye contact and gaze are essential to the study of human communication for a number of reasons. First, eyes express emotions, monitor feedback, indicate degrees of attentiveness and interest, regulate the flow of the conversation, influence changes in attitude, define power and status relationships, and help modify impression management.[110]

Second, eyes are significant to the communication process because of the number of messages they can send. We have all heard some of the following words used to describe a person's eyes: *direct, sensual, sardonic, cruel, expressive, intelligent, penetrating, sad, cheerful, worldly, hard, trusting,* and *suspicious.* Finally, and perhaps most importantly for our purposes, much of eye contact is directly related to culture. On both a conscious and unconscious level you have "learned" the significance of eye contact and the "rules" for employing (or not employing) eye contact. As Tubbs and Moss point out, "The many rules implicit in our culture about looking at others are a tacit admission that eye contact is perhaps the single most important facial cue we use in communicating."[111] These rules become quite evident when people are in an elevator with strangers. Also, reflect on the discomfort felt when someone stares at you for a long period of time.

Before offering some comparisons that demonstrate culture's influence, we shall briefly discuss how eye contact is used by the dominant culture in the United States. As Triandis notes, looking another person directly in the eye is very common in the United States.[112] Not only is it the rule, but for most members of the dominant culture, eye contact is highly valued.[113] "For Americans, a direct gaze signals a positive connection from one person to another and communicates caring and common courtesy. If we turn away when speaking to others, we communicate that the words we are saying are difficult or we are thinking about other things."[114] The implication is that if you fail to use direct eye contact you risk being perceived as showing a lack of interest, trying to hide something, or even being deceitful.

But what is normal in the United States can be unacceptable in other cultures. In Japan prolonged eye contact may be considered discourteous and disrespectful. It is not uncommon for the Japanese to look down or away or even close their eyes while engaging in conversation. You can probably appreciate the problems that might arise if Americans are not aware of the Japanese use of eye contact. Americans who are culturally unaware often interpret Japanese eye contact, or lack of it, "as signs of disagreement, disinterest, or rejection."[115]

Dresser notes that "People from many Asian, Latino, and Caribbean cultures also avoid eye contact as a sign of respect."[116] This same orientation toward eye contact is found in many parts of Africa, where "Making eye contact when communicating with a person who is older or of higher status is considered a sign of disrespect or even aggression ... where respect is shown by lowering the eyes."[117] There is even a Zulu saying: "The eye is an organ of aggression." India and Egypt provide two additional examples of eye contact mirroring a cultural value. "In India, the amount of eye contact that is appropriate depends on one's social position (people of different socioeconomic classes avoid eye contact with each other)."[118] In Egypt, where the issue is not social status but gender, "Women and men who are strangers may avoid eye contact out of modesty and respect for religious rules."[119] We should point out, at least as it applies to gender and globalization, the use of eye contact involving women is "changing as more women throughout the world enter the job market and rise to higher levels."[120]

The avoidance of direct eye contact is not the case among Arabs who use very direct eye contact between same-sex communicators. This contact is not only direct, but extends over a long period of time. For "outsiders" this directness often appears as a form of staring. Yet for Arab males this visual intensity is employed so that they can infer the "truthfulness" of the other person's words.[121] Notice how the words "same-sex" were used in our portrayal of Arab eye contact. The reason is that where gender segregation is the norm (such as in Saudi Arabia) direct eye contact between men and women is often avoided.[122]

Germans also engage in very direct eye contact. And because of this, problems can arise. Nees notes: "Germans will look you directly in the eye while talking, which some Americans find vaguely annoying or disconcerting. From the German point of view, this is a sign of honesty and true interest in the conversation. For Americans it can seem too intense and direct."[123]

In North America the prolonged stare is frequently part of the nonverbal code used in the gay male co-culture. When directed toward a member of the same sex, an extended stare, like certain other nonverbal messages, is often perceived as a signal of interest and sexual suggestion.[124] A few other differences in the use of eye contact in the United States are worth noting. Eye contact, or a lack of it, can create misunderstandings between African Americans and members of the dominant culture. The reason is simple: African Americans often do not find it necessary to engage in direct eye contact at all times during a conversation.[125] This same uncomfortable feeling toward direct and prolonged eye contact can be found among Mexican Americans who "consider sustained eye contact when speaking directly to someone as rude. Direct eye contact with superiors may be interpreted as insolence. Avoiding direct eye contact with superiors is a sign of respect."[126]

Among members of the dominant culture in the United States there are also gender variations in how people use their eyes to communicate. Research on the subject of gender differences in the use of eye contact indicates that in most instances, "women are much more visually oriented than are men."[127] This characteristic manifests itself by the fact that "Women look more at other people, attempt to make more eye contact, and are also looked at more than men."[128] As you might expect, eye contact is a very important consideration when communicating with members of the deaf community who are employing American Sign Language. Among members of the deaf co-culture who are "signing," there is a belief that eye contact is an especially important part of their communication process.[129] Turning your back to people who are "signing" is essentially the same as ignoring them. So delicate is the use of eye contact that you seldom realize the modifications you make when communicating. For example, the next time you are speaking with a disabled person, perhaps someone in a wheelchair, notice how little eye contact you have in comparison with someone who is not disabled. This practice is all too common and, unfortunately, may be interpreted as a lack of interest and concern.

Touch

Touch as a form of communication can be as effortless as holding your mate's hand, or as powerful and frightening as being touched in a sexual manner by a stranger. The meanings you assign to being touched, and your reasons for touching others, offer insights into the communication encounter. This is vividly illustrated by the character Holden Caulfield in the American classic *The Catcher in the Rye*:

> I held hands with her all the time. This doesn't sound like much, but she was terrific to hold hands with. Most girls, if you hold hands with them, their goddam hand *dies* on you, or else they think they have to keep *moving* their hand all the time, as if they were afraid they'd bore you or something.[130]

Touch, often considered the most fundamental of all your senses, is a primitive and indispensable form of communication.

> Tactile sensitivity may be the first sensory process to become functional, and it is the most developed sense at birth. In fetal life, the child begins to respond to vibrations of the mother's pulsating heartbeat, which impinge on the child's entire body and are magnified by the amniotic fluid. In one sense, our first input about what life itself will be like comes from the sense of touch.[131]

Soon after birth infants utilize all their senses as a means of defining the reality that confronts them. During this period they are highly involved in tactile experiences with other people. They are being held, nuzzled, cuddled, getting cleaned, patted, kissed, and in many cases being breast-fed. As you move from infancy into childhood, you learn the rules of touching. You are taught whom to touch and where they may be touched. By the time you reach adolescence, your culture has taught you the "rules" of touch behavior. You have learned about shaking hands by employing various types of handshakes—firm, gentle, etc. You even have become skilled at knowing whom to hug and the intensity and location of contact associated with the person you are hugging (parent, friend, lover). Culture has also "taught you" what occasions (greeting, expression of affection, etc.) call for a hug.

In the dominant U.S. culture, there are six basic types of touching:

1. *Accidental touching* is when someone inadvertently bumps into you.

2. *Professional touching* is carried out by individuals such as doctors, nurses, hairdressers, or even a swimming coach moving the arms of a pupil.

3. *Social politeness* touching is usually associated with greeting and showing appreciation. These contacts can range from a handshake to a respectful pat on the back.

4. *Friendship touches* demonstrate concern and caring between family members and close friends. In this type of touching you might see actions from an extended embrace to an arm placed on a shoulder.

5. *Love-intimacy touches* are those touches that usually occur in romantic relationships (caressing, hugging, embracing, kissing, and the like).

6. *Sexual touch*, the most intimate type, is used for sexual arousal.[132]

As is the case with all the topics in this book, each culture has subtle directives aimed at its members concerning how to use this means of communication. "Every culture has a well-defined set of meanings connected with touching. That is, each culture defines who can touch whom, on what parts of the body, and under what circumstances."[133] So prescriptive are these "cultural definitions" regarding touch that in the United Arab Emirates a British couple was sentenced to one-month in prison for kissing in public. You may recall the upheaval created in Great Britain when First Lady Michelle Obama was introduced to Queen Elizabeth and touched the queen as part of her greeting. Shaking hands and even hugging dignitaries is common in the United States; it is taboo in Great Britain.

Perhaps one of the best locations to observe cultural variations in touch behavior is an international airport. Drawing from a study involving these variations, Andersen offers the following observations:

> A family leaving for Tonga formed a circle, wove their arms around each other's back, and prayed and chanted together. A tearful man returning to Bosnia repeatedly tried to leave his sobbing wife; each time he turned back to her, they would grip each other by the finger-tips and exchange a passionate, tearful kiss and a powerful embrace. Two Korean couples departed without any touch, despite the prolonged separation that lay ahead of them.[134]

Let us add to Andersen's list and examine a few other cultural examples. We begin with Arabs, a group of people who employ a great deal of touching behavior as part of their communication style.[135] In fact, it is not uncommon to see men in such places as Saudi Arabia holding hands while walking. Men will often kiss each other on the cheek in many Arab countries. This type of contact as a greeting has led Feghali to note that "Touching in Arab societies 'replaces' the bowing and handshaking rituals of other societies."[136] Because of religious and social traditions, Arab Muslims eat and do other things with the right hand, but do not greet (touch) with the left hand because this is a social insult. The left hand is used to engage in basic biological functions. Muslim women seldom touch or are touched by individuals outside of their family.

In South America and Mexico touch is routine. Brazilians, for example, engage in "embraces and back-thumping between men,"[137] and "kiss each other on alternating cheeks."[138] In Mexico a physical embrace, called an *abrazo*, is commonplace among both males and females. "Hugs, pats on backs, and other physical contact are an important part of communication in Mexico."[139] The use of touch as a form of communication is also found in Costa Rica where women greet each other with a kiss on one cheek and a hand on the shoulder.[140] A high frequency of touching is also prevalent among the people of Eastern Europe, Spain, Greece, Italy, Portugal, and Israel.[141]

Touching is not a common form of communication in Asia.[142] Chinese men and women seldom "show physical affection in public."[143] In Japanese business practices, "Touching fellow workers and associates is not common.... Patting someone on the back or putting a friendly arm around them is not done."[144] Even the simple act of kissing has cultural overtones. Although one of the uses of mouth-to-mouth kissing is sexual in Western cultures, it is not widespread in many parts of Asia. In fact, the Japanese have for centuries rhapsodized about the appeal of the nape of the neck as an erotic zone. Having no word for kiss in their language, the Japanese borrowed the English word and *kisu* is now used. In some cultures, touch can have a religious meaning. For instance, "Many southeast Asians believe that touching their heads places them in jeopardy because that is where their spirits reside."[145]

Gender differences also occur in the use of touch as a form of communication. Women, for example, tend to welcome touch more than do men when it is from the same sex, and they initiate touch behavior more than men.[146] During the last decade gender differences as they apply to touch, particularly in the workplace, have become the source of many sexual harassment cases. A male colleague who strokes a female co-worker on the arm, or even pats her on the back, might be perceived as engaging in sexual or condescending behavior. Hence, you need to remember that touching is contextual and often carries multiple meanings. While being greeted with a hug at a party with friends might seem appropriate, that same contact can be highly inappropriate in the workplace, especially between supervisors and subordinates.

Co-cultures within the United States often employ touch in ways that are unique to their members. A limited number of studies reveal that African Americans engage in more interpersonal touch than do whites.[147] One study has shown that "black females touch each other almost twice as often as white females."[148]

Because some cultural "rules" are subject to change, a new approach to using touch as a greeting has emerged among many young people. Growing weary of the handshake, the high-five, and fist bump, some are greeting each other with hugs. Kershaw writes, "Girls embracing girls, girls embracing boys, boys embracing each other—the hug has become the favorite social greeting when teenagers meet or part these days."[149]

Paralanguage

When the German poet Klopstock wrote, "The tones of human voices are mightier than strings or brass to move the soul," he knew that the sounds people produce contain subliminal messages that influence how people feel. Most of you probably have viewed a foreign film with subtitles. During those intervals when the subtitles were not on the screen, you heard the actors speaking an unfamiliar language but could understand some of what was happening just from the sound of the voices. Perhaps you inferred that the performers were expressing anger, sorrow, or joy, or recognized who the hero was and who was cast in the role of the villain. The rise and fall of voices also may have told you when one

REMEMBER THIS

Paralanguage is concerned with the communicative characteristics of the voice and with how people use their voices. Paralanguage includes such things as giggles, laughter, accents, groans, sighs, pitch, tempo, volume, and resonance.

person was asking a question and when another was making a statement or issuing a command. Whatever the case, certain vocal cues provided you with information with which to make judgments about the characters' personalities. You could only speculate on the exact meaning of the words being spoken, but voice inflections still revealed a great deal about what was happening. Research reveals that *how* a person's voice sounds can influence perceptions related to the individual's emotional state, social class, credibility, comprehension, and personality.[150] What we have been talking about is called *paralanguage*. It denotes the features that accompany speech and contribute to the meanings people assign to the overall transaction. Most classifications divide paralanguage into three categories: (1) *vocal qualities*, (2) *vocal characterizers*, and (3) *vocal segregates*.

Vocal Qualities (Volume, Rate, Pitch, Tempo, Resonance, Pronunciation, Tone)

As we just indicated, a great many inferences about content and character can be made from the paralinguistic sounds people produce. For example, paralanguage cues assist you in drawing conclusions about an individual's emotional state, socioeconomic status, height, ethnicity, weight, age, intelligence, race, regional background, and educational level.[151] Let us pause for a moment and look at some paralanguage behaviors that have message value in particular cultures.

While vocal qualities have numerous components, cultural differences are most apparent in the use of volume. Arabs speak with a great deal of volume because for them it connotes strength and sincerity. A softer voice suggests weakness and even deceitfulness.[152] Germans conduct their business with a "commanding tone that projects authority and self-confidence."[153] On the other end of the continuum, there are cultures that have a very different view toward loud voices. For example, "People from the Philippines speak softly, as they believe that this is an indication of good breeding and education."[154] A visitor from Thailand once asked one of the authors if the loud voices she was hearing in America meant Americans were upset or mad at a specific person or event. Her question made a great deal of cultural sense. In Thailand people speak in soft voices and believe it a sign of anger when a person elevates their volume. In Japan, raising one's voice often implies a lack of self-control. For the Japanese, a gentle and soft voice reflects good manners and helps maintain social harmony—two important values in Japanese culture.

Co-cultures also use vocal qualifiers in subtle and unique ways. For example, many African Americans use more inflection and employ a greater vocal range than most white Americans.[155] Differences in paralanguage also mark the communication patterns of males and females. Wood offers the following summary: "Men's voices tend to have louder volume, lower pitch, and less inflection, features that conform to cultural views of men as assertive and emotionally controlled. Women's voices typically have higher pitch, softer volume, and more inflection, features consistent with cultural views of women as emotional and deferential."[156]

Vocal Characteristics (Laughing, Crying, Moaning, Whining, Yawning)

Vocal characteristics are vocalizations that convey a learned meaning for members of a specific culture. In both France and Argentina it is considered rude to yawn in public. And in much of Europe whistling during a public performance is a message of disapproval and ridicule. For many Muslims the simple act of sneezing is interpreted as "a blessing from God."[157] In fact, after a sneeze a Muslim would say *Al-hamduillah* (praise and thanks to God). Laughing also sends different messages, depending on the culture. Lynch and Hanson do an excellent job of noting this difference when they write:

> Laughing and giggling are interpreted as expressions of enjoyment among most Americans—signals that people are relaxed and having a good time.... Among other cultural groups, such as Southeast Asians, the same behavior may be a sign of extreme embarrassment, discomfort, or what Americans might call "nervous laughter" taken to the extreme.[158]

Vocal Segregates ("uh-huh," "shh," "uh," "oooh," "um," "mmmh," "hmmm")

Vocal segregates are sounds that are audible but are not actual words. These sounds are used as substitutes for words. A case in point is the "shh" sound produced by Americans when they are asking someone to be silent. In many cultures certain sounds also take on special meanings. For instance, the Maasai in Africa use a number of sounds that have significance. The most common one is the "eh" sound, which the Maasai draw out and which can mean "yes," "I understand," or "continue."[159] In Kenya, the "iya" sound tells the other person that everything is okay. In Jamaica, the "kissing" or "sucking" sound expresses anger, exasperation, or frustration. The Japanese make use of vocal segregates in their conversations. To demonstrate reluctance or concern, a Japanese worker might "suck in his breath, look doubtful and say 'Saa....'"[160] Japanese will also make small utterances to demonstrate their attentiveness, such as *hai* (yes, certainly, all right, very well), *so* which has the same sound as the English "so" (I hear that, or an indication of agreement), or *eto* (well... or let me see...).[161] Many members of the African-American co-culture are familiar with the "whoop" used by many Preachers, a sound to arouse members of the church. This sound has been employed in African-American churches since slavery.

Having previously examined how body movement communicates, we now move to a review of how space, time, and silence communicate. Although these variables are external to the communicator, they are used and manipulated in ways that send messages. For example, imagine your reaction to someone who stands too close to you, arrives late for an important appointment, or remains silent after you reveal some personal information. In each of these instances you would find yourself reading meaning into your communication partner's use of (1) *space and distance*, (2) *time*, and (3) *silence*.

SPACE AND DISTANCE

The variation in distance between you and the people with whom you interact is as much a part of the communication experience as the words being exchanged.

The study of this message system, called *proxemics*, is concerned with such things as (1) *personal space*, (2) *seating*, and (3) *furniture arrangement*.

PERSONAL SPACE

The significance of personal space is highlighted by Hall and Hall:

> Each person has around him an invisible bubble of space which expands and contracts depending on his relationship to those around him, his emotional state, his cultural background, and the activity he is performing. Few people are allowed to penetrate this bit of mobile territory, and then only for short periods of time.[162]

Your personal space is that area you occupy and call your own. As the owner of this area, you usually decide who may enter and who may not. When your space is invaded, you react in a variety of ways. You may retreat, stand your ground, or sometimes even react violently. Use of personal space is learned on both the conscious and unconscious levels. Hall classified how personal space was used in the United States by proposing the following four categories that demonstrate how space can communicate.[163]

1. *Intimate distance* (actual contact to 18 inches) is normally reserved for very personal relationships. You can reach out and touch the person at this distance. Because of the closeness of the participants, voices are usually in the form of a whisper.

2. In *personal distance* (18 inches to 4 feet) there is little chance of physical contact, and you can speak in a normal voice. This is distance reserved for family and close friends.

3. *Social distance* (4 to 12 feet) is the distance at which most members of the dominant culture conduct business and take part in social gatherings.

4. *Public distance* is usually used in public presentations and can vary from relatively close to very far.

As with most forms of communication, space is associated with cultural values. A good example of the link between the use of space and culture can be seen in the values of individualism and collectivism. Cultures that stress individualism and privacy (England, United States, Sweden, Germany, and Australia) generally demand more space than do collective cultures. According to Triandis, Arabs, Latin Americans, and U.S. Hispanics fall into this collective category,[164] where people are more interdependent and "the members work, play, live and sleep in close proximity to one another."[165] With regard to Arabs, Ruch writes, "Typical Arab conversations are at close range. Closeness cannot be avoided."[166] This closeness is even reflected when people stand in line. When waiting, "Egyptians do not stand in neat lines ... everyone pushes their way toward the front."[167]

As we have noted elsewhere, a person's use of space is directly linked to their value system and culture. In some Asian cultures students do not sit close to their teachers or stand near their superiors; the extended distance demonstrates deference and esteem. In Germany personal space is sacred.[168] For Germans "this distancing is a protective barrier and psychological symbol that operates in a manner similar to that of the home."[169] You find the opposite view toward space in Brazil where "physical

The way people use space, including how they arrange themselves in a group, is often rooted in their culture.

Curt Carnemark/World Bank Group

contact, closeness, and human warmth," are important, hence, conversation takes place with less room between participants.[170]

SEATING

Like so many features of nonverbal communication, seating arrangements send both inconspicuous and obvious messages. The sending of a very subtle message could be witnessed at an important diplomatic meeting between the Turkish ambassador and his counterpart from Israel. The Turkish representative was extremely distressed that he was asked to sit on a sofa that was lower than the one occupied by the Israeli officials. His anger was so intense that he refused to allow the media to take a picture of the meeting since he felt it humiliated him and his country. This real-life example vividly demonstrates that seating arrangements can be a powerful form of nonverbal communication. Notice that when you are a member of a group in the United States, people tend to talk with those opposite them rather than those seated beside them. This same pattern controls how the group might designate their leader. In most instances, the person sitting at the head of the table is the leader.

When we turn to China we witness a very different orientation toward seating arrangements. Because of their Confucian background, China is a culture that respects proper etiquette and ritual. Therefore, seating arrangements are frequently dictated by cultural and historical norms, particularly at formal events such as banquets, and diplomatic and business meetings. At banquets, which are very common in China, seating arrangements place the honored person (often decided by seniority and age) facing east or facing the entrance to the hall. The higher a person's status, the closer they sit to the person of honor.[171] At business meetings the Chinese experience alienation and uneasiness when they face someone directly or sit opposite them at a desk or table.[172] If you view a news story about American diplomats meeting with government officials from China, you might observe that the meeting is taking place with people sitting side by side—frequently on couches. In Korea seating arrangements reflect status and role distinctions. In a car, office, or home, the seat on the right is considered to be the place of honor.

For the Japanese, much like the Chinese, seating at any formal event is determined based on hierarchy. When conducting business or diplomatic negotiations, the Japanese will arrange themselves with the most senior person sitting in the middle and those next highest in rank sitting to the left and right of this senior position. Low-ranking members will sit away from the table, behind the other representatives.[173]

FURNITURE ARRANGEMENT

The way people arrange furniture (chairs, tables, desks, etc.) also communicates. The importance of seating arrangement as a form of communication is seen in the Chinese traditional philosophy of *feng shui* that dates back over 3,000 years. This approach to the arrangement of furniture and space is part of the Chinese philosophy that stresses the need for people and nature to live in harmony. The heart of this perspective is that people must live with, rather than against, their environment. Further, it is believed that striking the balance between self and one's physical environment brings good health, happiness, and wealth. You can observe the signs of this philosophy in Chinese homes and the way some Chinese arrange themselves at a table. For example, when at a business meeting, Chinese executives will often seek out a seat that they believe is in sync with the environment. In recent years many Westerners have found this perception of space so intriguing there are now both books and classes on the art of *feng shui*.

Just as *feng shui* reflects some of the history and values of China, furniture arrangement can also reflect some of the values found in the United States, where furniture is often arranged to achieve privacy and interpersonal isolation. It is a way of circumventing interaction. People who value conversation, such as the French, Italians, and Mexicans, are often surprised when they visit the United States and see that the furniture in the living room is pointed toward the television set so people can focus on the television program rather than the other people in the room. They believe such an arrangement is rude and stifles conversation.

In Japan offices are usually open, shared with many colleagues, and the furnishings are, like the workers, placed in close proximity. The contrast between office arrangements in the United States and Japan can, of course, create problems. As Nishiyama notes, "Because of its lack of privacy, Westerners, especially individualistic Americans, might find the Japanese office arrangement very uncomfortable and annoying."[174]

The arrangement of furniture in offices can also give you a clue to the character of a people. "French space is a reflection of French culture and French institutions. Everything is centralized, and spatially the entire country is laid out around centers."[175] Hence, offices are organized around the manager, who is at the center. In Germany, where privacy is stressed, office seating is dispersed throughout the office.[176] By comparison, in Japan, where group effort and hierarchy are important, office seating is arranged according to seniority, with desks abutting each other.

CONSIDER THIS

The next time you are at an airport, supermarket, or shopping mall where people from different cultural backgrounds might be interacting, try to observe the interactions by referencing the items listed below:

a. *What are the average distances between the people you observed? Were there differences related to culture?*
b. *What differences did you observe in touching behavior? How did people greet each other? Did people hug, kiss, shake hands, etc.?*
c. *What differences did you observe in facial expressions? Were people animated, reserved, etc.?*
d. *Did you notice any differences in gestures? Did some people use more or fewer gestures?*

Some co-cultures have their own special use of space. In prisons, where space is limited and controlled, space and territory are crucial forms of communication. New inmates quickly learn the culture of prison by finding the correct ways to use space. They soon learn how and when to enter another cell, what part of the exercise yard they can visit, how a reduction of a person's space is a form of punishment, and that they must form lines for nearly all activities.

Women and men also use space differently. For example, women normally "establish closer proximity to others" than do men.[177] In summarizing gender differences in the use of space, Leathers has concluded:

Men use space as a means of asserting their dominance over women, as in the following: (a) they claim more personal space than women; (b) they more actively defend violations of their territories—which are usually much larger than the territories of women; (c) under conditions of high density, they become more aggressive in their attempts to regain a desired measure of privacy; and (d) men more frequently walk in front of their female partner than vice versa.[178]

There is also research concerning the co-cultures of African Americans and Hispanic Americans and their use of space. "Most studies reveal that interactions involving black and white communication occur at greater distances than those involving persons of the same race,"[179] and Hispanic Americans communicate at a closer distance than most other groups.[180]

Spatial distance is also a variable when interacting with members of the deaf culture. For example, when using American Sign Language (ASL), it is necessary for the person signing to sit far enough away from the other person so that they can be seen. It would not be uncommon for two signers to sit across from one another at a distance that hearing people might perceive as impersonal.[181]

TIME

When the Dutch mathematician Christian Huygens built the first pendulum clock over three centuries ago, he probably had little idea that his invention would have such an impact on people's lives. We all strap timepieces to our wrists, hang them on our walls, see them on our computer screens and cell phones, and give them the power to control everything from moods to relationships. Rapport and Overing underscore the importance of time to human behavior when they write, "To cut up life into moments of being, in sum, is for the individual to possess a means by which that life can be filled, shaped and reshaped in significant ways."[182] Some reflection will reveal how time communicates. If you arrive 30 minutes late for an important appointment and offer no apology, you send a certain message about yourself. Telling someone how guilty you feel about your belated arrival also sends a message. Studies point out that one of the markers of a successful and intimate relationship is the amount of time people spend together and how patient they are with each other.[183]

Of course, there is much more to time than what it says about your relationships. "Our temporal perspective influences a wide range of psychological processes, from motivation, emotion and spontaneity to risk-taking, creativity and problem-solving."[184] The connection of time to culture is profound, and like most aspects of culture, is part of the enculturation process early in life.

> Culture begins to educate each of us at an early age as to the value of and the means by which we distinguish time. Each culture has its own particular time norms, which are unconsciously followed until violated. When such violations occur, however, they are perceived as intentional messages associated with that particular culture. In this regard, each culture teaches its people what is appropriate or inappropriate with regard to time.[185]

Experience tells you that in the United States most members of the dominant culture adhere to Benjamin Franklin's pronouncement that "Time is money." Think of what is being said about the use of time in the common expressions: "Don't put off until tomorrow what you can do today," "He who hesitates is lost," and "Just give me the bottom line." For Americans, "time is fixed and measurable, and where we feel seconds ticking away, we attach much significance to schedules. We measure our efficiency according to our ability to meet deadlines and cross off items on our checklist by the end of the day. Getting things done on schedule has a value in itself."[186] For Gannon, "Time is also limited in America because there are so many things to do in one's lifetime. The society develops technologically at horrendous speed, and it's difficult to keep up. One has to be continuously on the move. This is America: there is little time for contemplating or meditating."[187]

As is the case with all aspects of nonverbal communication, culture plays a substantial role in how you perceive and manipulate time in order to communicate different messages. "The existence and proliferation of objective, independent time-measuring devices is itself a cultural by-product, and the uniform seconds, minutes, and hours that clocks appear to 'measure' also are culturally constructed."[188] When cultures employ time in dissimilar ways, misunderstandings and even antagonisms can occur. To better recognize some contradictory ways of using time we will examine two cultural perspectives: (1) *informal time* and (2) *monochronic and polychronic classifications*.

Informal Time

Informal time is usually composed of two interrelated components—punctuality and pace.

Punctuality. Rules that apply to punctuality are taught implicitly and explicitly. On a conscious level, young children are taught the importance of being prompt. They are told that a lack of punctuality means "that you don't care about the person/event that was scheduled; that you are lazy, disorganized, careless, disrespectful, carefree, and so forth."[189] In addition to these conscious messages there are numerous messages sent and learned on an unconscious level. You would probably have some difficultly remembering where you learned some of the following informal rules: The boss can arrive late for a meeting without anyone raising an eyebrow. A late secretary might receive a reprimand in the form of a stern glance. A rock star or a physician can keep people waiting for a long time, but the warm-up band and the food caterer had better be at the event on time. In short, you know these "rules" about time, but cannot point to the moment you learned them because they usually function below the level of consciousness.

Cultures vary in their punctuality standards:

> How late is "late"? This varies greatly. In Britain and America, one may be 5 minutes late for a business appointment, but not 15 and certainly not 30 minutes late, which is perfectly normal in Arab countries. On the other hand, in Britain it is correct to be 5 to 15 minutes late for an invitation to dinner. An Italian might arrive 2 hours late, an Ethiopian after, and Japanese not at all—he had accepted only to prevent his host from losing face.[190]

Status relationships can influence punctuality in Japan. As Nishiyama points out, "The time usage in Japan is usually determined by the status relationships between the people involved."[191] In other words, someone in Japan would wait much longer for a person of higher status to arrive than if the person were of lower status. For the Japanese, a person's use of time is yet another way of showing respect.

A few additional examples will help illustrate how reactions to punctuality are rooted in culture. In Spain, Italy, and in many Arab countries, it is typical for people to be 30 minutes, or more, late for a meeting or dinner appointment. "Punctuality is not considered a virtue in Saudi Arabia. Your client may be late for an appointment or not show up at all."[192] In Africa, people often "show up late for appointments, meetings, and social engagements."[193] There is even a Nigerian expression that says, "A watch did not invent man." These views of tardiness would be perceived as rudeness in Germany where, "Promptness is taken for granted … in fact, it's almost an obsession."[194]

Pace.   You can also determine a culture's attitude toward time by examining the pace at which members of that culture perform specific acts. Because of the pace of life in the United States, to "outsiders" Americans always appear to be in a hurry. As Kim observes, "Life is in constant motion. People consider time to be wasted or lost unless they are doing something."[195] From fast-food restaurants to gas stations where you can do your marketing while you are putting gas in your car, to microwave cooking, to computers that use the fastest available processors, Americans live life at a very hectic pace. Even the expression "rush hour" describes how commuters in major cities are hurrying and dashing to get from point "A" to point "B." Children in the United States grow up hearing others tell them not "to waste so much time" and to "hurry up and finish their homework." Think how those expressions differ from the Latin proverb, "Haste manages all things badly," or the Mexican saying, "You don't have to get there first, you just have to know how to get there."[196]

Because people in other cultures use time differently, they live life at a pace different from that found in the United States. For instance, "the French do not share the American sense of urgency to accomplish tasks."[197] Japanese culture treats time in ways that often appear at cross-purposes with American goals. Brislin illustrates how the Japanese pace is reflected in the negotiation process:

> When negotiating with the Japanese, Americans like to get right down to business. They were socialized to believe that "time is money." They can accept about fifteen minutes of "small talk" about the weather, their trip, and baseball, but more than that becomes unreasonable. The Japanese, on the other hand, want to get to know their business

counterparts. They feel that the best way to do this is to have long conversations with Americans about a wide variety of topics.[198]

Indonesians are another group that perceives time as a limitless pool, and there is "a phrase in Indonesia describing this concept that translates as 'rubber time,' so that time stretches or shrinks and is therefore very flexible."[199] The Chinese also value a slow pace. For them, the completion of the mission is what matters, regardless of the amount of time it takes. The Chinese proverb, "With time and patience the mulberry leaf becomes a silk gown," captures the notion of time being unhurried. In Africa, where a slow pace is the rule, "People who rush are suspected of trying to cheat."[200]

The idea that nonverbal behavior is directly linked to a culture's religious and value orientation is manifest among Arabs. Earlier we pointed out that Muslims believe that their destiny is predetermined. The connection between this religious view and the pace of life is pointed out by Abu-Gharbieh: "Throughout the Arab world, there is nonchalance about time and deadlines: the pace of life is more leisurely than in the West. Social events and appointments tend not to have a fixed beginning or end."[201]

MONOCHRONIC (M-TIME) AND POLYCHRONIC (P-TIME)

Hall established a classic taxonomy for examining the link between culture and time. He proposed that cultures organize time in one of two ways—either *monochronic* (M-time) or *polychronic* (P-time),[202] which represents two approaches to perceiving and utilizing time. Although M-time and P-time are presented as two distinct categories, it is much more realistic to perceive the two classifications as points along a continuum. There are many cultures that do not fall precisely into one of the two categories, but instead contain degrees of both M-time and P-time.

M-time

As the word *monochronic* implies, this concept views time as linear, sequential, and segmented. More specifically, "A monochronic view of time believes time is a scarce resource which must be rationed and controlled through the use of schedules and appointments, and through aiming to do only one thing at any one time."[203] Cultures with this orientation perceive time as being *tangible*. When speaking of the M-time orientation Hall states, "People talk about time as though it were money, as something that can be 'spent,' 'saved,' 'wasted,' and 'lost.'"[204] To act out this view of time would mean to value punctuality, good organization, and the judicious use of time. The English naturalist Charles Darwin glorified this approach when he wrote, "A man who dares to waste one hour of time has not discovered the value of life."

Cultures that can be classified as M-time include Germany, Austria, Sweden, Norway, England, Finland, Canada, Switzerland, and the dominant U.S. culture.[205] As Hall explains, "People of the Western world, particularly Americans, tend to think of time as something fixed in nature, something around us and from which we cannot escape; an ever-present part of the environment, just like the air we breathe."[206] In the business setting, M-time culture people schedule appointments in advance, try not to be late to meetings, try to be succinct in making presentations, and have "a strong preference for following initial plans."[207]

P-time

People from cultures on *polychronic* time live their lives quite differently than do those who move to the monochronic clock. The pace for P-time cultures (Arab, African, Indian, Latin American, South Asian, and Southeast Asian) is more leisurely than the one found in M-time cultures. In P-time cultures human relationships, not tasks, are important. "A polychronic view of time sees the maintenance of harmonious relationships as the important agenda, so that use of time needs to be flexible in order that we do right by the various people to whom we have obligations."[208] These cultures are normally collective and deal with life in a holistic manner. For P-time cultures, time is less tangible and people are usually not in a hurry to finish an assignment or chore. In addition, P-time participants can interact with more than one person or do more than one thing at a time. Because P-time has this notion of multiple activities and flexibility, Dresser believes it "explains why there is more interrupting in conversations carried on by people from Arabic, Asian, and Latin American cultures."[209] African cultures also place great stock in the activity that is occurring at the moment, and emphasize people more than schedules. The person they are interacting with is far more important than someone or something that is someplace else. In short, "Time for Africans is defined by events rather than the clock or calendar."[210]

As we conclude this section on how time communicates, it is important to remember that specific settings and occasions can influence how a person "acts out" M-time or P-time. In one context, you might be extremely prompt (M-time); in another situation, you might decide that what you are doing at that moment is essential and postpone meeting your next appointment (P-time). Two cultural examples will further underscore the contextual nature of the use of time. While Arab culture manifests all the characteristics of P-time cultures, "Modernization has influenced approach to time in the Arab regions, particularly in regional business centers and other urban environments."[211] Hall offers another instance of how the setting can determine which orientation a person utilizes: "The Japanese time system combines both M-time and P-time. In their dealings with foreigners and their use of technology, they are monochronic; in every other way, especially in interpersonal relations, they are polychronic."[212]

Table 9-1 summarizes the basic aspects of monochronic and polychronic time. The table takes many of the ideas we have mentioned and translates them into specific behaviors.

CONSIDER THIS

David Thorn was sent to Mexico by his employer, a computer chip company, to try to negotiate a large contract that would allow his company to start producing chips in Mexico. The contract would mean a savings of millions of dollars for the company. His Mexican contact person, Santiago Guzman, invited David to a dinner party that he and his wife were hosting. Santiago told David the party would start "around eight on Friday night." David arrived a few minutes before eight so he could make a good impression. When he arrived, Santiago and his wife were still dressing and had not even begun to prepare to receive guests.

What do you think went wrong?

SILENCE

"The spoken word sometimes loses what silence has won." This Spanish proverb is a fitting introduction to our discussion of silence. Observe the poignant use of silence when the classical composer strategically places intervals of orchestration so that the ensuing silence marks a contrast in expression. Silence can be a powerful message. There is a story of how the American philosopher Ralph Waldo Emerson "talked" in silence for hours to the

TABLE 9.1	A Comparison of Monochronic and Polychronic Cultures

MONOCHRONIC TIME PEOPLE	POLYCHRONIC TIME PEOPLE
• Do one thing at a time	• Do many things at once
• Concentrate on the job	• Easily distracted and subject to interruption
• Take time commitments (deadlines, schedules) seriously	• Consider time commitments an objective to be achieved, if possible
• Are low context and need information	• Are high context and already have information
• Are committed to the job	• Are committed to people and human relationships
• Adhere to plans	• Change plans often and easily
• Are concerned about not disturbing others; follow rules of privacy	• Are more concerned with people close to them (family, friends, close business associates) than with privacy
• Show great respect for private property; seldom borrow or lend	• Borrow and lend things often and easily
• Emphasize promptness	• Base promptness on the relationship
• Are accustomed to short-term relationships	• Have tendency to build lifetime relationships

Source: Adapted from E.T. Hall and M.R. Hall, *Understanding Cultural Differences: Germans, French, and Americans* (Yarmouth, ME: Intercultural Press, 1990), 15.

famous English writer Thomas Carlyle. It seems that Emerson, on a visit to Europe, arranged to meet with Carlyle, who was his idol. Emerson maintains they sat together for hours in perfect silence until it was time for him to go, then parted company cordially, congratulating each other on the fruitful time they had had together.

Periods of silence affect interpersonal communication by providing an interval in an ongoing interaction during which the participants have time to think, check or suppress an emotion, encode a lengthy response, or inaugurate another line of thought. Silence also provides feedback, informing both sender and receiver about the clarity of an idea or its significance in the overall interpersonal exchange. In most Western cultures talk is highly valued, and it is often difficult to determine the meaning behind someone's silence, because it can be interpreted as an indication of agreement, anger, lack of interest, injured feelings, or contempt. For young children in the United States silence often takes on negative connotations when used as a punishment. Reflect for a moment about the secondary message being sent when a misbehaving child is given a "time-out"—a period when they are expected not to talk or have any sort of human interaction. For many Americans "silence can be a very frightening experience. There are often occasions when it is embarrassing, humiliating or makes us appear to be fools when we remain silent."[213] This is one reason Americans will usually try to fill up the silence with "small talk."

The intercultural implications of silence as a means of interpreting ongoing verbal interactions are as diverse as those of other nonverbal cues:

> Cross-cultural differences are common over when to talk and when to remain silent, or what a particular instance of silence means. In response to the question, "Will you marry

me?" silence in English would be interpreted as uncertainty.... In Igbo, it would be considered a denial if the woman were to continue to stand there and an acceptance if she ran away. [214]

Knowing how various cultures use silence is essential information for anyone who interacts with a different culture. As Braithwaite points out: "One of the basic building blocks of competence, both linguistic and cultural, is knowing when not to speak in a particular community. Therefore, to understand where and when to be silent, and the meaning attached to silence, is to gain a keen insight into the fundamental structure of communication in that world."[215]

As already noted, silence is not a meaningful part of the life of most members of the dominant U.S. culture. Talking at coffee houses, talking on cell phones (even when driving an automobile), watching television, or listening to music on an iPod keeps Americans from silence. Reflect for a moment on the popularity of radio and television programs called "talk shows." Members of the dominant culture not only enjoy talking and avoiding silence, but also "feel responsible for starting a conversation or keeping it going, even with strangers."[216] Because Americans have this orientation toward silence, they "often experience problems when they go international and place themselves in face-to-face contacts with more silent people of the world."[217]

Americans are not the only group of people who prefer noise and talking over silence. In the commercial world, "a silent reaction to a business proposal would seem negative to American, German, French, Southern European and Arab executives."[218] It seems that there is a link between cultures that emphasize social interaction (Jewish, Italian, French, Arab, and others) and their perception of and use of silence. In fact, talking in these cultures is highly valued. In Greek culture there is also a belief that being in the company of other people and engaging in conversation are signs of a good life. The concepts of solitude and silence are overshadowed in Greek history and literature, which contain numerous allusions to rhetoric and dialogues. The culture that produced Aristotle, Plato, and Socrates is not one that will find silent meditation appealing. This is in sharp contrast to cultures where a hushed and still environment is the rule. We now will look at a few cultural variations in the use of silence, so that you might better understand how a lack of words can influence the outcome of a communication event.

In the Eastern tradition the view of silence is much different from the Western view. As you learned when we examined Buddhism in Chapter 5, many people feel comfortable with the absence of noise or talk and actually believe that words can contaminate an experience. They maintain that inner peace and wisdom come only through silence. This idea is brought out by the Buddhist scholar A.J.V. Chandrakanthan:

> In the stories and discourses attributed to Buddha, one can clearly see a close link between Truth and Silence. Wherever Truth is mentioned in references to Buddha it is always said in relation to silence. In fact, popular Buddhist religious tradition attests that whenever someone asked Buddha to explain truth, he invariably answered in Silence.[219]

Barnlund links this Buddhist view of silence to communication, "One of its tenets is that words are deceptive and silent intuition is a truer way to confront the world; mind-to-mind communication through words is less reliable than heart-to-heart communication through an intuitive grasp of things."[220] Silence is also used by many

Asian people as a means of avoiding conflict. "A typical practice among many Asian peoples is to refuse to speak any further in conversation if they cannot personally accept the speaker's attitude, opinion, or way of thinking about particular issues or subjects."[221]

Silence is both important and complex among the Japanese. In many instances, people are expected to know what another person is thinking and feeling without anything being said. Some scholars even refer to this mode of communication as "implying rather than saying."[222] The Japanese emphasis on silence serves a variety of purposes. First, among family members, silence is actually seen as a way of "talking." The following example offers an explanation of how silence takes the place of words for the Japanese: "When people say 'There's no communication between parents and children,' this is an American way of thinking. In Japan we didn't need spoken communication between parents and children. A glance at the face, a glance back, and we understand enough."[223]

Second, silence in Japan is linked to credibility. Someone who is silent is often perceived as having higher credibility than someone who talks a great deal. "Reticent individuals are trusted as honest, sincere, and straightforward. Thus silence is an active state, while speech is an excuse for delaying activity."[224] Finally, the Japanese also use silence to avoid both conflict and embarrassment.[225] The Japanese view of silence is reflected in the following proverbs: "It is the duck that squawks that gets shot," and "A flower does not speak." Compare these perceptions of silence with the American saying, "the squeaky wheel gets the grease," or with the words of Ralph Waldo Emerson, "Speech is power: Speech is to persuade, to convert, to compel." You can easily imagine how these two uses of silence might create communication problems when Americans and Japanese come together. For example, during business negotiations between Japanese and Americans, each will give a different interpretation to the same silent period. The Japanese use the silence to "consider the Americans' offer; the Americans interpret the silence as rejection and respond by making concessions."[226]

Silence plays a central role in the Indian culture. Hindus believe that "self-realization, salvation, truth, wisdom, peace, and bliss are all achieved in a state of meditation and introspection when the individual is communicating with himself or herself in silence."[227] Many Scandinavians also have a view of silence that differs from the dominant U.S. culture. In Finland, Sweden, Denmark, and Norway, silence conveys interest and consideration. In fact, your silence tells the other person that you want them to continue talking.[228]

Some U.S. co-cultures also use silence differently than does the dominant U.S. culture. As Hoeveler points out, "Silence is a major value in Native American culture, for silence is the token of acceptance, the symbol of peace and serenity, and the outward expression of harmony between the human and natural worlds."[229] American Indians also believe that silence, not speaking, is a sign of an extraordinary person. Remaining silent shows respect to persons of authority, age, and wisdom. To respond too quickly when asked a question is considered immature, as it indicates that the person did not have the insight to use a period of silence to think about their response.

IMPROVING NONVERBAL COMMUNICATION SKILLS

In the Preface, and during many of the discussions that followed, we accentuated the idea that *communication is an activity*. This was a way of saying that communication is

CONSIDER THIS

What is meant by: "Communication is an activity"?

a behavior that you engage in and that others respond to. We conclude the chapter by offering a brief section on how you can exercise some control over that behavior to produce positive results.

MONITOR YOUR NONVERBAL ACTIONS

As simplistic as it sounds, what *you* bring to the communication event greatly influences the success or failure of that event. Although "know thyself" is an overused expression, it is, nevertheless, worth repeating. The novelist James Baldwin made the idea of self-knowledge clear when he wrote, "The questions which one asks oneself, begin, at last, to illuminate the world, and become one's key to the experiences of others." Hence, our initial advice is to *monitor your actions so that you better understand the experiences of others*. By knowing how you "present" yourself you can gain insight into how people are reacting to the types of messages you are sending. As Dunn and Goodnight point out, "Keep in mind that others may interpret your nonverbal messages differently from the way you had intended."[230] We urge you to consider some of the following questions that will help you understand the responses displayed by your intercultural communication partner.

• Is my behavior making people feel comfortable or uncomfortable?
• Am I adjusting my nonverbal messages to the feedback I am receiving from my communication "partner"?
• How are people reacting to my use of space, touch, paralanguage, time, and the like?
• If my messages are being misinterpreted is it because my unintentional messages, rather than my intentional messages, are impacting my communication "partner"?

MONITOR FEEDBACK

Using feedback is directly related to the preceding suggestion regarding the notion of self-monitoring. Both suggestions ask you to be aware of the interactive nature of communication; that is to say, the recipients of your messages are not passive observers. They receive your verbal and nonverbal symbols and respond in a variety of ways. As explained in Chapter 2, these responses are known as *feedback*. Hence, our next suggestion is that you *encourage feedback as a way of improving the accuracy of your perceptions of the communication encounter*. Utilizing both verbal and nonverbal feedback devices allows you to make qualitative judgments about the communication encounter. Feedback also affords you the opportunity to immediately correct and adjust your next message.

Because feedback is critical, you need to create an atmosphere that encourages it. Communication skills that promote feedback include smiling, head nodding, leaning forward, and even laughing. Although the four actions just mentioned are found in Western cultures, they often produce positive reactions in other cultures as well. Each of these nonverbal activities contributes to a relaxed atmosphere that fosters an accurate "reading" of your receiver's nonverbal response to your messages.

BE SENSITIVE TO THE CONTEXT

As you have already learned, *communication is rule-governed*. Some self-reflection tells you that your behavior is different as you move from place to place. Think of all the "rules" that are in operation in school rooms, courtrooms, churches, business meetings, parties, restaurants, sporting events, funerals, and the like. Each of these settings requires behaviors that you have learned as part of the acculturation process. When trying to improve nonverbal communication skills you need to understand how each situation might influence meaning given a specific action. During a job interview a person's actions might reflect a degree of nervousness brought about by the formal setting (fidgeting, talking fast, etc.), while at home that same person might be relaxed and speak at a slower pace.

Culturally you can also observe vast differences in how people respond nonverbally when thrust into an unfamiliar environment. In North American classrooms students move around and interact with the teacher and other students. In Japan and China nonverbal behavior is much more subdued and restrained as students follow the classroom "rules" in these cultures. There, silence and constrained gestures are the rule. When trying to improve your ability to read nonverbal behaviors, ask yourself if the observed actions are appropriate for the setting.

BE AWARE OF NONVERBAL AMBIGUITY

At the beginning of this chapter we noted that nonverbal messages can be intentional (waving goodbye to a friend) or unintentional (frowning because you are looking into the sun and your friend believes you are upset). It would be as if you were nonverbally "saying" two different things at once. That confusion can also be seen if you tell someone, "I am so happy to see you again," while at the same time you are pulling away as they try to embrace you. *This multiple meaning dimension of nonverbal communication puts an increased burden on you whether you are the sender or the receiver.*

KNOW YOUR CULTURE

Recommending that you need to know your own culture should be obvious at this stage of the book. Your culture "told you" how to use all of the nonverbal action discussed in this chapter. Therefore, a certain degree of introspection about your own culture is an important step in improving nonverbal behavior.

> Each of us is a product of our culture, including gender, ethnicity, family, age, religion, profession, and other life experiences. Our cultural inventory provides us with valuable insights for understanding our beliefs and attitudes, our values and assumptions. It is critical that we reflect on the various aspects of our own cultural identity and examine their positive impacts on our personal and professional development.[231]

In many ways this observation is a fitting conclusion to both this chapter and the discussion of how to enhance your use of nonverbal communication. Therefore, we close this chapter by harking back to the idea that cultural affiliation influences both how you send messages and how other people react to those messages.

CHAPTER 10

Communication Contexts and Cultural Influences

Live together like brothers and do business like strangers.

ARAB PROVERB

Human history is increasingly a race between intercultural education and disaster.
If education is not intercultural, it is probably not education, but rather the
inculcation of nationalist or religious fundamentalism.

DAVID COULBY

If you are not in tune with the universe, there is sickness in the heart and mind.

NAVAJO SAYING

CULTURE AND CONTEXT

In Chapter 2 we introduced the idea that communication is contextual when we noted that communication does not occur in a social void. All human interaction is influenced to some degree by the cultural, social, and physical settings in which it occurs. These settings are called *communication contexts*. Social interaction is neither arbitrary nor disorderly, but is patterned by *interaction rituals* that specify normative ways of speaking and behaving in specific social situations such as business meetings, parties, or sports events.[1]

When communication rules are shared the rules configure and orchestrate their social interaction in accord with these norms and communication proceeds smoothly. If, however, communication rules are not shared, or if speakers actively resist these norms, then communication may break down. In the case of intercultural interaction, communication rules often diverge, and accordingly there is a greater risk of misunderstandings.[2]

Culture helps determine the appropriate communicative behavior within a variety of social and physical contexts by prescribing certain rules. When communicating with members of your own culture, you and your cohorts rely on deeply internalized cultural rules that delineate the normative behaviors for specific communication situations. These rules facilitate your ability to communicate effectively with each other. And since they are integrated into your personality, you do not have to think consciously about which rules to use.

When engaging in intercultural communication, however, things can be different because you and your communication partners may not be operating under the same sets of rules. Indeed, communication rules display a great deal of cultural diversity. You must be fully aware of the differences, otherwise, you may encounter a variety of surprises—some of which could be embarrassing, detrimental, or both! This chapter is about some of the contexts where people frequently find themselves engaged in intercultural communication: the *business setting*, the *health care setting*, and the *education setting*.

So that you may understand just how important the social context is in intercultural communication, we will look at three basic assumptions about human communication that apply directly to the setting: (1) communication is rule governed, (2) context prescribes appropriate communication rules, and (3) communication rules are culturally diverse.

UNDERLYING ASSUMPTIONS ABOUT CONTEXT

COMMUNICATION IS RULE GOVERNED

Both consciously and unconsciously, people expect that their interactions will follow appropriate and culturally determined rules—rules that inform both parties about what is appropriate communicative behavior for specific situations. Communication rules act as guidelines for both your actions and the actions of others. These rules, as Wood notes, "are shared understandings of what communication means and what kinds of communication are appropriate in particular situations."[3]

Communication rules govern both verbal and nonverbal behaviors and specify not only what should be said, but also how it should be said. Nonverbal rules, as we saw in Chapter 9, apply to touch, facial expressions, eye contact, and paralanguage. Verbal rules govern such things as topic selection, turn taking, voice volume, and the formality of language.

There are also rules that people follow in their personal relationships. Morreale, Spitzberg, and Barge point out that there is a long set of rules that govern friendships (emotionally trusting the other person versus keeping secrets) and conflict (raising your voice versus not showing any emotion).[4] What is interesting about these cultural rules is that they, like most of culture, are learned, integrated into the self, and followed.

CONTEXT HELPS SPECIFY COMMUNICATION RULES

Our second assumption about communication is that the context specifies the appropriateness of the rules to be employed. As Shimanoff states, communication rules are "a followable prescription that indicates what behavior is obligated, preferred, or prohibited in a certain context."[5] Your personal experiences should validate Shimanoff's observations. Consider for a moment how such diverse contexts as a classroom, bank, church, hospital, courtroom, wedding, funeral, or sporting event determine which communication rules you follow. In a job interview you might use formal or respectful words such as "sir" or "ma'am" when responding to your potential employer. Yet at a football or basketball game your language would be far less formal, incorporating slang phrases and quite possibly good-natured derogatory remarks about the opposing team. For that job interview you might wear a dark suit with white or blue shirt and conservative tie for men, or a dark suit with a white or pastel blouse for women. For a sports event jeans or cut-offs and a T-shirt could be appropriate. Your nonverbal behavior would also be different. At the interview you would probably shake hands with your prospective employer, but at the football game with friends you might embrace them when you see them, slap them on the back, or hit a "high-five."

COMMUNICATION RULES ARE CULTURALLY DIVERSE

Our third assumption is that communication rules are, to a large extent, determined by your culture. Although cultures have many similar social contexts (business meetings, classrooms, hospitals, and the like), their members frequently adhere to different sets of rules when interacting within those environments. Consequently, concepts of dress, time, language, manners, and nonverbal behavior differ significantly among cultures. A few examples will help to illustrate our point about these different behaviors.

When doing business in America, for instance, it is not uncommon for men and women to welcome each other to a meeting by shaking hands. In the Middle East,

The specific context of any communication event can influence everything from seating arrangements to attire.

Edwin McDaniel

however, some Muslim businessmen may choose to avoid shaking hands with a woman. This should not be perceived as rude or insulting, but may reflect the man's religious proscriptions.[6] In a college classroom setting you may notice that an Asian student seems shy and reserved and reluctant to engage in conversation. This may be due to his or her cultural rules about the hierarchy that governs interaction between students and professors. Slight contextual differences may be found when you compare business dining in Turkey and the United States. In Turkey, for example, your Turkish colleagues will be adamant about paying for everything associated with entertaining you. Turkish hospitality is legendary, and they will not even permit you to pay for any part of the meal.[7]

There is a reason we have selected the business, education, and health care settings for further analysis. These three "locations" represent contexts in which you are likely to encounter people of cultures different from your own. To be successful in those settings, it is essential to be aware of your own culture's rules and how they might differ from the rules of the person with whom you are interacting. Before examining some of these differences, however, we will discuss some variables that tend to remain consistent across cultures.

ASSESSING THE CONTEXT

There are three important communication variables found in every communication setting. These are general rules that apply across all cultures and all social settings. In every social context you will find culture-based communication rules that apply to: (1) the appropriate degrees of formality and informality, (2) the influence of assertiveness and interpersonal harmony, and (3) the influence of power distance relationships. Each variable plays an important role in how people respond to their interpersonal and organizational environments.

FORMALITY AND INFORMALITY

Cultures can have views regarding events and people that range from extremely informal to very formal. The manifestations of informality and formality take many forms.

Informality

Grounded in a strong belief in individualism and equality, the United States has long been considered an informal culture. "In North America people tend to treat others with informality and directness. They avoid the use of formal codes of conduct, titles, honorifics, and ritualistic manners in their interactions with others."[8] This informality and openness displayed by U.S. Americans can be a source of confusion and misunderstanding for people from more formal cultures. Crouch, making the same point about North American business executives doing business in Mexico, notes, "Our disregard for formality sometimes makes international business more difficult."[9]

Formality

In contrast to the level of informality found in the United States, there are many cultures that place a high value on formality. In Egypt, Turkey, and Japan, for instance, the student-teacher relationship is very formal. This may be seen in the

Egyptian proverb "Whoever teaches me a letter I should become a slave to him forever." In these countries when the teacher enters the room, students will assume a subordinate attitude and in some cases may even stand and bow. Students encountering their teachers on the street will show deference to them. Contrast this with the relaxed, informal student-teacher relationships found in the United States.

Formality is also evident in how cultures use forms of address. Not knowing these differences can cause embarrassing problems. Germans, for example, address others and conduct themselves in a very formal manner, which many U.S. Americans would consider stiff and extreme. Hall and Hall note, "American informality and the habit of calling others by their first names make Germans acutely uncomfortable, particularly when young people or people lower in the hierarchy address their elders or their superiors by their first names."[10] Germany is not the only place where forms of address are directly linked to perception and values. The Mexican culture is another that values formality:

> Mexicans also make heavy use of honorific titles to show respect. New acquaintances met at a party are addressed as *señor, señora,* and *señorita.* In business, people address managers with titles like director, doctor, *ingeniero* (engineer), or *licenciado* (someone who has a higher education degree).[11]

In addition to Mexico, there are other places where cultures value formality over informality. China is a good example because the Chinese tend to be very formal and non-revealing about their personal lives. You can easily imagine the outcome of trying to negotiate a cross-cultural business venture if, at the initial meeting, the U.S. Americans were speaking in an informal manner, using their counterparts' first names, and offering personal information about themselves, while their Chinese counterparts were doing the opposite.

ASSERTIVENESS AND INTERPERSONAL HARMONY

The second important dimension of culture that affects the communication context is the manner in which people present themselves to others. While there are many aspects of communication styles, assertiveness and interpersonal harmony directly influence the intercultural setting—be it in a business meeting, classroom, or health care context.

Assertiveness

The United States is widely known for its assertive communication style. Think about the style of communication displayed on "talk radio" or the MSNBC or Fox News television political shows where participants frequently end up shouting at each other in an effort to make a point. In the sports arena, "trash talk" is commonplace between members of opposing teams, be they high school, collegiate, or professional. While the communication styles in these two examples are exaggerations of the norm, they illustrate the positive value placed on communicative assertiveness in the United States.

While a forceful and assertive communication style might be part of the American experience, in many cultures, and in a variety of settings, forceful behavior makes people feel uncomfortable. For example, in the health care environment, according to Purnell and Paulanka, Filipino and Chinese nurses working in the United States often feel uncomfortable with the "outspoken" and "aggressive" behavior of their U.S. American health care co-workers.[12]

Interpersonal Harmony

Although cultures such as those of the United States, Germany, and Israel see assertiveness as an asset, other cultures consider it threatening and detrimental to genial interpersonal relations. Among Northeast and Southeast Asian cultures mutual agreement, loyalty, and reciprocal obligations underlie the importance placed on harmonious relations. The Filipino culture, as we noted with our example regarding nurses, values interpersonal harmony. For Filipinos, "The ultimate ideal is one of harmony—between individuals, among the members of a family, among the group divisions of society, and of all life in relationship with God."[13]

Maintaining harmonious relations and avoiding what appears to be aggressive behavior is also a primary consideration among Chinese in-groups. Confucius held that the basic unit of society is the family and that harmony must be preserved in relationships.[14] So strong is that concern for the feelings of others that Chinese avoid the word "no," which they find harsh. Since deviance is considered threatening and disruptive, most Chinese willingly accept and follow normative expectations during social and professional interactions.

Mexicans also value smooth interpersonal relationships and encourage polite behavior. In the business setting this view toward harmonious relations "demands a low-key, respectful, and sometimes, a seemingly obsequious posture."[15] Avoiding confrontations can make the concept of "truth" situational in Mexico, and in order to sustain positive relations or make the other person feel better, Mexicans may slightly alter facts or withhold possibly important negative information.

The education setting is also a context where differences in assertiveness and harmony are acted out. Fish describes a multicultural classroom in which Israeli and Vietnamese students demonstrated very different behavioral patterns as they apply to aggressive and complacent behaviors. According to Fish, the Vietnamese children, fearful that whatever they say will appear to be rude, will not speak during class.[16] On the other hand, Fish reports that her Israeli students not only take an active role in class, but also often criticize the teacher. You can imagine how these two different sets of rules regarding classroom behaviors could influence the learning environment.

POWER DISTANCE RELATIONSHIPS

The third communication variable that influences nearly all communication settings relates to a culture's perception of and response to hierarchy. As we pointed out in Chapter 6 when we examined Hofstede's notion of power distance, we saw that every culture and organization has specific culturally based protocols that guide interaction between people of differing social positions. Using a broad classification scale, a culture can be placed along a continuum bounded by *egalitarian*, which has a low level of concern for social distance, and *hierarchical*, which places significant emphasis on status and rank.

Egalitarian

Egalitarianism facilitates and encourages openness among communication participants, stresses informal interaction between subordinates and seniors, and minimizes the expectation of deference and formality. A person's status is usually acquired through individual effort such as success in business or achievement of an advanced degree—avenues that are open to everyone. This creates an environment of social mobility by encouraging the belief that everyone has the opportunity to improve his or her social status. The United States, Australia, Israel, and New Zealand are considered highly egalitarian cultures. Many U.S. Americans are not very concerned with differences in social status and power.

Hierarchical

Cultures with a hierarchical view of social status are essentially the opposite of egalitarian cultures. In these societies status is normally acquired by birth, appointment, or age. In countries like Brazil, China, and India, real power is held by a few individuals who may have achieved their position by means of family connections, level of education, marriage, or simply age. Merit and ability are often secondary considerations. Interactions between subordinates and seniors are conducted in a formal manner, and titles are always used.

Having looked at the potential impact of the overarching variables of informality, formality, assertiveness, interpersonal harmony, and status relationships, we are ready to apply these and others to various intercultural settings. We now move from the general to the specific as we turn to the international business context. We will now examine the interaction between culture and communication by looking at (1) international business settings, (2) domestic business settings, (3) business cultures, and (4) negotiation and conflict resolution.

INTERCULTURAL COMMUNICATION IN THE BUSINESS CONTEXT

THE INTERNATIONAL BUSINESS SETTING

We agree with Max Weber who wrote, "If we learn anything from the history of economic development, it is that culture makes all the difference."[17] For example, trade and exploitation were principal motives for the establishment of European colonies in Africa, the Americas, Southeast Asia, and the Pacific Islands. As Friedman points out, "In this era, countries and governments (often inspired by religion or imperialism or a combination of both) led the way in breaking down walls and knitting the world together, driving integration."[18] The shift from an agrarian to an industrial society, brought about by the Industrial Revolution in the latter half of the nineteenth century, expanded and accelerated cross-cultural trade.

Following the end of the Cold War, dramatic improvements in transportation systems, telecommunications technologies, and increasingly advanced product distribution significantly reduced, or even eliminated time- and distance-related barriers.

The importance of national borders has diminished in an era characterized by international joint ventures, mergers, licensing agreements, foreign capital investment, and offshore production. These events have led to increased economic interdependencies among nations. This global interdependence was clearly demonstrated on March 11, 2011, when the world experienced a ripple effect from the devastating earthquake in Japan that disrupted the supply of Japanese produced parts needed by manufacturers worldwide. In addition, the sovereign debt of a number of European Union countries such as Greece, Ireland, and Portugal is having a negative impact on the world economy. These events support the accuracy of our notion from Chapter 1 that what happens in one part of the world can have effects all over the world. What is transpiring today, mainly because of globalization, is that interdependence, rather than dominance, is the watchword for doing business. In this new era, "While globalization has opened new markets to rich-world companies, it has also given birth to a pack of fast-moving, sharp-toothed new multinationals that is emerging from the poor world."[19]

All of the intercultural changes that we have been discussing create an environment where "doing business" requires people from different cultures to work together. For example, the German company Siemens has 277,000 employees abroad, the Mexican company Cemex has 32,790 employees abroad, the U.S. company Walmart has 700,000 employees abroad, and the Korean company Samsung has 95,000 employees abroad.[20] McDonald's operates outlets in over 100 nations.[21] The world's largest coffee chain, Starbucks, operates more than 5,000 stores overseas,[22] including over 500 in mainland China.[23] "U.S. multinational companies increased employment overseas by 2.4 million in the 2000s, even as they cut their U.S. workforces by 2.9 million. Overall, big-name firms employed 21.1 million people in the United States in 2009 and 10.3 million abroad."[24] In 2010 a Chinese state-owned offshore oil and gas company acquired a one-third interest in a 600,000-acre lease in a South Texas oil and gas field.[25]

In addition, small business franchises for such companies as Dunkin Donuts, Pizza Hut, Ace Hardware, Napa Auto Parts, Century 21, and Kay's Fine Jewelry are located in many parts of the world. What should be obvious at this point is that both developed and developing nations are now tied directly to an international system of economic interdependence, and most countries have at least one asset within their borders that is needed by another country.

The economic integration we have been discussing has created a need for knowledge and understanding of how to conduct business in a manner that accommodates different cultural rules. In the contemporary business

CONSIDER THIS

Annie had been working for a number of years in the office of a large manufacturing company. She was happy with her position and the people she worked with—particularly her immediate supervisor. However, just before Christmas, Annie was told the company was merging with another company, and that many of the employees from the new firm would be coming to Annie's building around January 2. She was also told that she would be working for a "new boss," but that her position was secure. Annie was pleased, since jobs in her town were hard to locate.

On the first day that the two workforces were combined, Annie noticed something that upset her. It seemed that some members of the male staff had made changes to the community coffee and snack room. Not only did they put wine and beer in the icebox, but they also hung a few pin-up pictures of women in swimsuits from the Sports Illustrated magazine's swimsuit edition. Annie asked the other female staff members what they thought about the alterations in the workroom. Most of them were also troubled by the pictures, but did not want to lose their jobs, so they remained silent. However, the pictures bothered Annie, so she decided to talk to her new supervisor. He told her to relax and not to worry about it. He said he liked the new atmosphere. Annie quit her job.

What do you believe Annie should have done?

environment knowledge of cultural differences, cross-cultural teamwork, and multicultural collaboration are essential for an organization's success. It is obvious that globalization results in individuals from one culture working with, and also for, individuals from another culture.

THE DOMESTIC BUSINESS SETTING

Not only has the impact of intercultural contact altered the way international business is conducted, but events within the borders of the United States have made the need to understand different cultures a twenty-first century imperative. Perhaps the clearest statement of how the demographics of the United States are changing can be found in the data from the *American Community Survey* conducted by the U.S. Census Bureau. The 2008 survey revealed that 19.8 percent, or nearly one in five, of the people living in the United States spoke a language other than English at home.[26] Minority co-cultures are now the fastest-growing segment of the United States demography. In the future it is estimated that more than 80 percent of the growth in the United States will come from immigration. It is apparent that through birthrates and immigration the United States has become a nation characterized by extensive cultural diversity.

As the population of minority co-cultures has increased, it has impacted the United States in both the marketplace and workforce. Businesses have adapted their operations to meet the needs of these new residents. Walmart has opened Hispanic-focused supermarkets called Supermercado de Walmart in Phoenix and Houston and as an analog to its Sam's Club membership stores, Sam's Más Club in Houston. In all large cities nearly every market has entire sections set aside for the ethnic shoppers who frequent their stores.

According to the U.S. Census Bureau, in the year 2050 whites will no longer make up the majority of Americans.[27] The Hispanic population grew four times faster than the total population between 2000 and 2010.[28] Under the Census Bureau's predictions, by 2050 Blacks will make up 12.2 percent, Hispanics will rise to 28 percent, and Asians are expected to increase to 6 percent of the population.[29]

In addition to the larger number of co-cultural workers in today's labor force, the number of minority entrepreneurs is also expanding. In 2007 the United States Department of Commerce found that minority-owned businesses grew by 45.6 percent overall between 2002 and 2007 with most of the growth taking place in the states of Alabama, Florida, Georgia, Nevada, and North Carolina.[30] Hispanic businesses alone grew at a rate of 43.7 percent in the five-year period between 2002 and 2007 so that there are now more than 2.3 million businesses in the United States owned by Hispanics.[31]

CONSIDER THIS

Most advertisers are well aware of the fact that there are specific cultural audiences for their products. Therefore, they often advertise in magazines tailored to those audiences. Go to a magazine stand or a library and look at some popular magazines aimed at a co-culture audience. Compare the advertisements and images in those magazines with those found in some "mainstream" publications.

All of these data and figures translate into the fact that internationally and within the United States' domestic workforce, most business transactions involve culturally diverse populations. What this means is that successful management of this diverse labor force demands increased awareness and acceptance of various cultural values and greater intercultural communication competence. Many American corporations, recognizing the importance of cultural diversity among workers, have instituted training programs designed to increase employee awareness of cultural differences and raise intercultural competence. Managers in this culturally varied environment will also have to be constantly alert to the hazards of discrimination, ethnocentrism, and sexual harassment. The multicultural business setting demands workers and employers who can adapt to this contemporary workplace. The remainder of this section seeks to help you with that adaptation process.

COMMUNICATION IN THE MULTICULTURAL BUSINESS CONTEXT

In discussing how contextual rules help determine communicative behavior we indicated that when business negotiators come from cultures with different rules, communication problems may arise. This was clearly demonstrated in a case study involving chains of pizza restaurants in China and a packaging company in Canada. The pizza companies relied on local Chinese suppliers for their pizza boxes but were dissatisfied with their quality and irregular delivery schedule as well as the cost. The Canadian packaging company, wishing to extend its activities into the area of convenience foods, found a Chinese producer that could manufacture pizza boxes to their specifications with assurances that they could deliver the boxes within set deadlines at a very reasonable cost. Intensive negotiations by email and telephone led both the Chinese and the Canadians to schedule face-to-face meetings. Arrangements were made for the Chinese to visit the Canadians first, with the Canadians returning the visit two weeks later.

The Canadian company went all out with their reception for the Chinese visitors. Although the Chinese were greeted by the Canadian company's president and management team with lavish words of praise in front of a hundred guests, they remained reticent and very formal. Later, during a dinner, the Chinese did not seem to

Globalization has created a climate where business executives from all over the world are meeting face-to-face to establish joint ventures and negotiate contracts.

Eric Miller/World Bank Group

appreciate the meal and said very little despite attempts by the Canadians to keep the conversation going. The evening ended in silence on both sides when the Chinese delegation made their excuses and quietly returned to their rooms. The Canadians were surprised and disappointed. What had gone wrong?[32]

The explanation lies in the different cultural rules that govern initial business meetings. Although the Chinese were very polite and hospitable, they were on what they thought of as a normal business visit. Thus, they only expected an ordinary welcome. The welcome they received seemed extraordinary, caused them to feel ill at ease, and prompted the early departure to their rooms.[33]

This case study illustrates that developing effective business communication skills for a globalized economy is not a simple matter. The diversity among business cultures can frequently lead to confusion, misunderstandings, and failures in cross-cultural commercial endeavors. In the business sector culture determines such dynamics as (1) protocol, (2) management, (3) leadership, (4) decision-making processes, and (5) negotiation and conflict management. We now turn our attention toward business protocol and introduce you to some of the cultural variations for making initial contacts and culturally appropriate forms of greeting behavior.

BUSINESS PROTOCOLS

Protocol involves forms of ceremony, etiquette, dress, and appropriate codes of conduct, and it is important to understand and follow the prevailing customs when conducting business in another culture. Although informality may be the norm in the United States, this view is not shared in all cultures.

Making Initial Contacts

In international business the way you make *initial contacts* is very important. The methods used to establish these contacts can range from sending an e-mail, to placing an unsolicited telephone call, to writing a formal letter requesting a meeting, to using a "go-between" or emissary to obtain your appointment. Which procedure you should use is related directly to the culture of the person you wish to contact. Failure to follow expected protocol may be perceived as a breach of etiquette and result in your failure to gain access to an organization. A few examples will illustrate this point.

We begin with China. An unsolicited call or a letter of introduction will usually not work with the Chinese. The most effective means of establishing a business connection is by using your country's Department of Trade or Commerce to arrange appointments with local Chinese businesses.[34] India has much the same attitude about initial contacts because Indian culture is based on established relationships. First exchanges are best made under the auspices of common business associates. In Latin American cultures, such as Brazil's, the best approach is to employ a local *pessoa bem conectada* (well-connected person) to arrange introductions and contacts for you. Again, eliciting support from your country's Department of Trade or Commerce will assist in making these contacts.

Greeting Behavior

Meeting, speaking, and being understood are necessary if you are to build global business relationships. It is necessary, therefore, that you learn the basic history and culture of the country you are visiting and a few phrases in their language. Although English may be the international language of business, learning key phrases, such as "Do you speak English?" "Yes," "No," "Good day," "Good night," "Excuse me," "Where is the restroom?" "Thank you," and "Help" can be helpful.[35]

First impressions are powerful and serve to create the expectation of positive relationships. Your chances of making a good first impression increase enormously if you have prepared yourself and know what to expect during initial meetings.[36] When greeting someone for the first time, be sure you know the proper form of address. Determine whether you use a first name, last name, or title. Generally, for a first meeting it is a good idea to use the formal "Mr. Wong" or "Mrs. Macias" until you are invited to use their first names. If someone has a title, it is proper and will be appreciated if you include the title as you are introduced, so you would address the person as "Dr. Wong" or "*Profesora* Macias."[37]

Regardless of the culture in which you may find yourself interacting with others, here is a list of basic protocols you should observe:

- Remember your hosts' names and how they are properly pronounced.
- Use appropriate ranks and titles.
- Be aware of the local uses of time and punctuality.
- Create an appropriate impression by wearing suitable attire.
- Practice behavior that demonstrates your concern for others by employing tact and discretion.
- Enjoy social events while observing local customs relative to food and drink.[38]

We have introduced you to some of the general approaches to greeting behavior with examples from several cultures. We will now look at appropriate greeting behaviors for the specific cultures we will be considering for the remainder of this section.

Brazil. Brazilians are generally warm and friendly. Extended handshakes are common during first meetings, progressing to embraces once a friendship has developed. Women frequently kiss each other on alternate cheeks. It is common to shake hands with everyone present both upon arrival and departure.[39] Forms of address should include titles such as "Doctor," or "Professor," or the term *Senhor* or *Senhora* may be used before the surname when a title is unknown or absent. Brazilians may even introduce themselves using their titles and their first names such as "I'm Dr. Agusto."[40]

China. The Chinese business community is much more formal than that of the United States. Chinese usually greet the most senior person first and use titles that clearly reflect their cultural emphasis on hierarchy.[41] The order of Chinese personal names is reversed from that in the West. The Chinese place their family name (surname) first and their given name last. For example, in the name *Wang Jintao*, Wang is the family name and Jintao is the given name; thus, in English, the proper form of address would be Mr. Wang. The Chinese have widely adopted the Western handshake for initial and subsequent greetings. This, however, does not extend to the common Western practice of placing a hand on the back or an arm around the shoulder. As Morrison and Conaway indicate, a slight bow and a brief shake of the hand is most appropriate.[42]

Negotiating with Brazilians

Brazilian interaction styles differ from those in the United States. Frequently, two or more people may be talking at the same time during a conversation with few or no pauses. For Americans, normal conversational pauses provide opportunities for turn-taking. When speaking with Brazilians, you may have to be more assertive in order to enter the conversation.[89] English is the recognized language among members of the international business community in Brazil, and more often than not, people in managerial positions at Brazilian multinational companies speak some degree of English.[90]

Although there is a sense of fatalism among Brazilians, the general attitude while doing business and negotiating is more along the lines of "take your time." Negotiations cannot be rushed; business is done with friends, and friendships take a long time to build. Because personal relationships form the basis of trust in business deals, nepotism and preferential treatment to friends is common in both companies and government. The following are some characteristics of negotiating styles in Brazil.

- *Particular over universal.* When making decisions, Brazilians like to look at the details involved in each particular situation, instead of applying universal rules or patterns of behavior to all situations.
- *Relationship over task.* Brazilians feel that a good relationship must be in place before anything can be accomplished, and it is never a good idea to damage a relationship that is intact, even if it means not completing a task.
- *Polychronic over monochronic.* Brazilians tend to view the concept of time in a polychronic way, often discussing the details of a proposal in a random order instead of sequentially.
- *Group over individual.* Although this depends on the circumstances, Brazilians feel that the group and relationships within the group are more important than individual aspirations. This has implications concerning methods of motivation. Sometimes an individual manager would prefer to share a bonus with his subordinates or coworkers instead of keeping it all for him- or herself.
- *Flexible over inflexible.* Due to constant changes in Brazilian laws, as well as the uncertainty brought by fluctuations in exchange rates, interest rates, and inflation rates, Brazilians have become very adept at "going with the flow." They consider people who always follow standard procedures to be unimaginative and lacking intelligence.[91]

Negotiating with the Chinese

In several earlier chapters we have mentioned the role that history plays in the Chinese worldview. That history also influences the Chinese approach to negotiations. According to McGregor, two factors play a role in establishing a context for international negotiations with the Chinese: the memory of over 200 years of domination and isolation by Western powers, and the Chinese sense of cultural ethnocentrism derived from their historical legacy. Thus, when entering into negotiations, the Western negotiator may well encounter Chinese dual feelings of entitlement and cultural superiority. Moreover, the Chinese are quite proficient at discerning foreigner attitudes and respect plays an important role in the negotiation process. The Chinese have a preference for following a specific protocol when conducting negotiations. Opening discussions will usually be very formal. The host side will first describe themselves—who they are, what they do—with many statistics. Then they will expect the guests to do the same. None of this has any real bearing on the issue being negotiated, but this form is important. For Chinese, the preference for form and correct manner preserves harmony and provides the context within which the negotiations will take place.[92]

In China, the status of team members is significant. The most important member of the negotiating team is the one who is most senior in age. Seniority, along with membership in the Communist party, is a key to the Chinese workplace hierarchy.[93] The inclusion of high-ranking company officers or individuals from influential families is often an indication that the company is serious about negotiations. Also, the number of people assigned to the team will also signal the level of importance attached to the negotiations—the more participants, the greater the importance. In addition, Chinese negotiators prefer to take a long-term view toward business ventures. They first work on building relationships, establishing levels of trust, and determining the desirability of entering into an extended association with the other organization.

A Chinese negotiator's verbal communication style, particularly as it applies to the direct and indirect use of language, can also be a source of difficulties in international business. Because the Chinese place considerable value on maintaining positive relations with their negotiation counterparts, they rely on an indirect communication style. Sensitive issues with the potential to create conflict or cause discord are handled with care and normally are addressed in an indirect manner. Chinese are reluctant to give a direct negative reply, relying instead on what Lee calls the "soft no." A reply, such as "we think the proposal is worth additional study," is a means of saving everyone's face and maintaining harmony among the negotiators. This indirectness can be the source of consternation to Western negotiators, who are used to "getting to the point" and "not beating around the bush," what Lee refers to as a "hard no."[94]

The Western concern for time and adhering to schedules promotes a desire to move the negotiations along rapidly, but this is not a popular approach among the Chinese. China is a group-oriented society, which implies that negotiations must cover the interests of many different parties. In meetings, the Chinese will examine a counterpart's attitude and speech and apply it to the problem solving. Technical competence is critical and some negotiators have requested more seasoned technical people join their negotiating team midway through negotiations.[95] Negotiators from the United States strive to bring about a written contract that takes into account as many detailed eventualities as possible. The Chinese, by way of contrast, are more likely to insist on a much less detailed contract, one that tends to emphasize the more generalized relationship between the two parties.[96] For the Chinese, a contract is not a rigid agreement to which the parties are expected to adhere precisely to the various provisions. They see the negotiations as designed to establish the parameters of the relationship, and the contract should serve only as an outline or guide.

The use of mutual empathy where one negotiating team attempts to put itself into the cultural perspective of the other, at the same time the other team is trying to do the same, is an ideal approach to communication; but as you will see, it does not always work. Motorola University prepared a carefully crafted presentation to be made in China titled "Relationships do not retire." The idea was to convince the Chinese that Motorola was coming to China to stay and help the economy create wealth. Relationships with Chinese suppliers, subcontractors, and employees would constitute a permanent commitment. The Chinese audience listened politely to this presentation, but was quiet when invited to ask questions. Finally, one manager put up his hand and said: "Can you tell us about pay for performance?" What happened here was that both sides attempted to put themselves into each other's cultural perspective and ended up passing each other invisibly like ships in the night.[97]

Negotiating with Indians

Business in India is personal, and it is necessary to establish personal relationships with those with whom you will be negotiating. The American "time is money" penchant for efficiency and speedy movement through a negotiation to a final agreement does not work in India. As far as Indian negotiating style is concerned, negotiations must follow formal procedures although the atmosphere may be friendly and relaxed.[98]

Although highly collectivist in their local group, Indians develop a sense of individuality when dealing on their own with outsiders. They are adroit at the negotiations of buying and selling. An example of this may be seen by examining an Indian strategy of selling, which they apply with great skill. Their negotiation plan proceeds in a series of steps that may take place over a period of days or weeks. Some of the steps that Indian business representatives from a family owned business may employ in their negotiating strategy are summarized below.

- I don't want to sell at all.
- This business is at the top of all the businesses my family controls.
- We don't need the money.
- I really don't intend to sell this business, but if I did, I would sell it to you.
- Perhaps I would like to sell to you, but I will never be able to convince my family to agree.
- I have to tell you that we have received a very serious higher bid from another company.
- I am willing to give the deal to you because I promised I would sell to you.

Ultimately, after days or weeks of negotiation following some of the ploys given above, an agreement may be reached, and the sale finalized.[99] You must realize, however, that as with most everything in India, decisions are arrived at slowly. For Western negotiators, this unhurried process may be extremely frustrating, but there is no point in trying to impose deadlines.

Although we applied the family culture metaphor to our discussion of Brazilian business culture, it is also applicable to India. Indian business organizations are also high-context and even higher in the power distance dimension. These cultural dynamics affect the manner in which Indians enter into and conduct negotiations. Relationships tend to be diffuse. The father or elder brother is influential in all negotiations even when others present are better qualified in the area under discussion.[100] And, as in other high-context cultures, the preservation of individuals' feelings is important. For Indians, feelings may be far more persuasive than facts. Indians, therefore, follow in the same tendency as many Asian cultures and find the use of "no" to be harsh. Evasive refusals are common and considered to be more polite. Indians conduct business at a leisurely pace and anyone engaging in negotiations in India must be prepared to spend a great deal of time arriving at a final agreement. Although there may be many participants representing the Indian side in a negotiation, you must realize that the ultimate decisions are made at the top. This is a reflection of the "family-culture" of Indian business organizations.[101]

Below are a set of guidelines you should find useful when preparing to engage in negotiations with Indians.

- Acquire knowledge about the general attitudes of the individual negotiators. Diversity of attitudes among Indians can be extreme, and it will be to your advantage to know the position of those with whom you will be negotiating.
- Although Indians may engage in a seemingly relaxed negotiation atmosphere, they are prone to adhere to rules that govern professional conduct and negotiating procedures, as well as hospitality. Also, do not let their behavior deceive you into thinking the Indians are not focused on reaching a concluding agreement.
- Be sure and discuss the underlying issues apt to be brought up by both sides with your fellow negotiators. It is best to be in agreement on issues than to have differing ideas expressed by members of your team.
- Although Indians may believe that feelings are more persuasive than facts, they nevertheless prefer arguments that are supported by facts. Do not assume that a "win/win" negotiating approach will be found appealing. If the Indians take a "win/lose" approach, emphasize your concessions and their gains.
- As in other high-context cultures, some Indians will view definitive contract terms as being too rigid. You must, however, negotiate specific contract terms even if some negotiators object to their rigidity.
- It is a good idea to build momentum toward a final agreement by negotiating agreement on smaller issues as the negotiation process advances.
- Identify the leader of the Indian negotiating team and build a strong rapport with that person, but do not ask personal questions until you are friends.
- Remember, decisions are from the top, and you want to be on the best of terms with that leader. On the other hand, do not ignore mid-level negotiators because they may have the capacity to form a consensus and/or influence decisions made at the top.[102]

Developing Intercultural Negotiation Skills

We conclude this section on the negotiation process across cultures with a bit of advice:

1. *Be prepared.* The overriding message embedded in our first suggestion asks you to learn all you can about the host culture before negotiations begin. This means learning about the behaviors that we have discussed in this chapter as they relate to formality, status, nonverbal actions, the use of language, and the like.

2. *Develop sensitivity to the use of time.* This admonition asks you to learn to adapt to a slower pace than you might be used to if you are from the U.S. dominant culture. It also advises being patient when dealing with cultures that use a different tempo than the one found in your culture.

3. *Listen carefully.* Part of concentrating on the proceedings is learning to remain comfortable with silence and realize that a lack of words is also a form of communication.

4. *Learn to tolerate ambiguity.* Many intercultural encounters are characterized by confusion and a search for meaning,

REMEMBER THIS

Cultures have very different "personalities" when engaging in intercultural negotiations. There are differences with regard to:

- *Being direct or indirect when speaking*
- *Respecting age or respecting youth*
- *Being formal or informal*
- *Working at a slow pace or a rapid pace*
- *Encouraging group harmony or individual assertiveness*
- *Working collectively or as individuals*

which can translate into a high degree of ambiguity—the quality of having more than one meaning. Therefore, we urge you to be tolerant of the unknown as you seek to make sense of what is new and often hard to characterize.

5. *Try to locate areas of agreement.* Since both sides in a negotiation want to gain something, it should be a simple matter to isolate areas of agreement. If both parties can be made to see these areas, everyone benefits.

THE EDUCATION CONTEXT
CULTURALLY DIVERSE EDUCATIONAL SYSTEMS

An ancient Chinese proverb tells us that "by nature all men are alike, but by education widely different." This difference is mainly due to the influence of culture on the world's educational systems. In earlier chapters, we emphasized that cultures impress upon each generation their worldviews, values, and perceptual filters. Yet, as writer Paul Goodman observed, "There is only one curriculum, no matter what the method of education: what is basic and universal in human experience and practice, the under-lying structure of culture." What is taught in a culture, therefore, is crucial to the maintenance and perpetuation of that culture and usually is a major responsibility of the formal educational systems within a culture. Cultures with formal educational systems tend to teach many of the same things: literacy, mathematics, science, history, religion, and so forth. Yet, significant differences may be found in both what and how cultures teach.

The teaching of history is common in all cultures, but each culture emphasizes its own past. This natural tendency to emphasize one's past is succinctly expressed by the scholar and diplomat Abba Eban, who noted, "A nation writes its history in the image of its ideal." In the United States, that ideal involves events such as the signing of the Declaration of Independence, the American Revolution, the settling of the American West, the Industrial Revolution, and the many victories achieved on the battlefield. In Mexico, however, the focus might be on the cultural heritage of the pre-Columbian Indians and the Mexican Revolution. The teaching of language is also common in all cultures, but, as with history, cultures first teach their own language. When schoolchildren are taught a culture's history and language, their society is passing on its culture and reinforcing its beliefs and values—as well as its prejudices.

Every culture, whether consciously or unconsciously, tends to glorify its historical, scientific, economic, and artistic accomplishments, frequently minimizing the achievements of other cultures. In this way, schools in all cultures impart ethnocentrism. For instance, the next time you look at a world map, notice that the United States is probably located in the center—unless, of course, you are looking at a map designed by an African, Chinese, or Russian cartographer. Many students in the United States, if asked to identify the great books of the world, would produce a list of texts authored mainly by dead, Western, white, male authors. This subtle ethnocentrism, which reinforces a culture's values, beliefs, and prejudices, is not a uniquely American phenomenon. Studying only the Koran in Pakistani schools, or only the Torah in Israeli classrooms, while disregarding other religious texts, is also a quiet form of ethnocentrism. Since what is taught in educational systems varies between cultures, you should not be surprised to find there are also differences in how students and teachers participate in the learning process. Being familiar with what a culture teaches can give you insight into that culture. Knowing how teaching occurs within a culture is just as important, because it (1) provides knowledge about the nature of the culture, (2) helps you understand interpersonal relationships among students and between students and teachers, and (3) illustrates the importance a culture places on education.

MULTICULTURAL EDUCATION

The cultural and linguistic diversity of the nation's student body has increased to the point where immigrants and students from a wide range of cultures and co-cultures make up some 45 percent of the public school enrollment, and more than one in five is a Latino student.[103] Over half of the children now born in the United States are nonwhite.[104] Census data from 2009 indicated that 21 percent of the children from 5–17 years old did not speak English in their home and 5 percent had difficulty with English.[105] From these statistics you can see that education in America has become a multicultural activity involving various ethnicities, worldviews, and life and learning styles.[106] In order to provide adequate educational opportunities for this culturally diverse student population, the educational establishment must accommodate to this multicultural population. Change is difficult; sometimes welcomed, but frequently not. But, as Segal indicates, "even in today's society, some classrooms seem to be focusing on the differences and difficulties involved in multicultural education rather than embracing these differences as enriching, desirable, inevitable, natural, and positive forces."[107] Change, however, compels re-examination—looking at something as if for the first time. These refreshed perceptions, as Lu suggests, can prompt recognition of new opportunities. Alternatively, these reflections may give rise to feelings of apprehension about the future. Neither fitful nor intermittent, these feelings are continuous and encompass societies, institutions, and the people who compose them. These are, however, the images that spark reform.[108]

Although much of the material found here will be primarily of use to future teachers, we believe that many of you will profit from this knowledge regardless of your future employment. In the business world, for instance, you might become a corporate trainer working with culturally diverse clients. If, on the other hand, you become a health care professional, you might find yourself "teaching" culturally diverse clients about appropriate prenatal care. In each instance you can profit from knowledge about cultural diversity in education.

In the United States, multicultural education is perceived as teaching and learning based upon democratic values and beliefs that affirm cultural pluralism in an interdependent society.

In a pluralistic democracy such as the United States, multicultural education holds that the primary goal of public education is to foster the intellectual, social, and personal development of all students to their highest potential. In contemporary U.S. society, however, these goals present challenges that have resulted in tension and disagreement among persons of good will. Tosolt indicates that a "fundamental

REMEMBER THIS

1. Enrollment in U.S. schools is at an all-time high.
2. The U.S. student body is becoming increasingly culturally and linguistically diverse.
3. Students from culturally and linguistically diverse cultures make up 43 percent of the U.S. public school enrollment.
4. Over 20 percent of U.S. public school students speak a language other than English at home.

belief of multicultural education is that schooling in the United States is founded on European American cultural characteristics and that students who do not share these cultural characteristics have difficulties navigating that system."[109] Glasgow, McNary, and Hicks add, "Teachers must not only acknowledge the more obvious diversity issues such as color and physical disability, but also be aware of the cultural diversity of students and families."[110]

In this section we will explore how U.S. schools are responding to the challenge of cultural diversity. First, we examine the challenges of multicultural education, and second, we look at diversity in cultural learning preferences.

CHALLENGES OF MULTICULTURAL EDUCATION

The need for effective multicultural education is an issue that must be faced by the educational establishment. Regardless of a student's native culture or co-cultural membership, the goal of multicultural education must be to prepare students to become functioning, productive members of society. The wide array of immigrant students' home and school experiences pose a major challenge for teachers in the American educational system. The character of this challenge is illustrated by Gollnick and Chinn, who state:

> Educators today are faced with an overwhelming challenge to prepare students from diverse cultural backgrounds to live in a rapidly changing society and a world in which some groups have greater societal benefits than others because of race, ethnicity, gender, class, language, religion, ability, or age. Schools of the future will become increasingly culturally diverse.
>
> It is not only ethnic and racial diversity that is challenging schools. During the past 35 years, new waves of immigrants have come from parts of the world unfamiliar to many Americans. With them have come their religions, which seem even stranger to Americans than these new people.[111]

In addition, "differences in majority and minority cultures play themselves out in visible ways in classrooms across the country"[112] thus increasing the challenge. Also, the process by which teachers can build cultural bridges between students' diverse home experiences and their educational experiences is complicated by the differences in the demographic profiles of both the K–12 teaching profession and student populations.[113] To meet this challenge educational systems will have to constantly adapt to the ever-changing cultural dynamics found in U.S. classrooms.

The spirit of multiculturalism demands that educators face these problems head-on and recognize and affirm everyone's commonality. Thus, a multicultural student body is important to the experiences of members of both the dominant culture and of co-cultures. Such an approach to education requires an educational strategy in which students' cultural backgrounds are used to develop effective classroom instruction and school environments. It supports and extends the concepts of culture, diversity, equality, social justice, and democracy in the formal school setting.[114]

CONSIDER THIS

What are the major challenges facing education in the United States? How does the influx of culturally and linguistically diverse students impact U.S. public schools?

Robert Fonseca

Children from a host of cultures are now bringing different backgrounds in curriculum and learning styles to classrooms in the United States.

In the next section we will turn our attention to the connection between culture and learning so that you can both understand that relationship and use that knowledge to help you better construct effective messages for the multicultural classroom context.

CULTURE AND LEARNING

Aristotle once wrote, "To learn is a natural pleasure, not confined to philosophers, but common to all men." While learning itself may be instinctive in humankind, people differ in *how* they learn. Each person has his or her own preferred ways of gathering and processing information. Barmeyer calls these personal cognitive choices, which are acquired in the course of a long socialization process, *learning preferences*.[115] Each culture has likewise adopted approaches to learning that best fit its collective needs. Hofstede describes this process as one in which "our cognitive development is determined by the demands of the environment in which we grew up: a person will be good at doing things that are important to him or her and that she or he has occasion to do often. Cognitive abilities are rooted in the patterns of a society."[116] The strength of the link between culture and learning is emphasized by Nieto when she says "learning is influenced by the particular individual personalities of students and the values of the cultures in which they have been raised."[117]

While there are a variety of culturally influenced learning preferences, "there is no agreement on the number or range of learning styles that actually exist."[118] It is important to note that no learning approach is "better" or "worse" than another.[119] In fact, diverse learning preferences may serve as an advantage to education. As Gay points out, learning preferences should be looked upon as tools to improve the educational achievement of diverse students by creating more cultural congruity in the teaching/learning process.[120] Additionally, research indicates that "when students are permitted to learn difficult academic information or skills through their identified learning style preferences, they tend to achieve statistically higher test and aptitude scores than when instruction is dissonant with their preferences."[121]

Students entering the multicultural classroom come from diverse backgrounds and bring with them different ideas about education. This gives rise to two topics relevant to multicultural education: (1) cultural ways of knowing and (2) cultural learning preferences. Both of these issues affect how students learn and participate in the educational process.

Cultural Ways of Knowing

Ways of knowing refers to the mental processes people employ to think about and become aware of their universe. Although the field of philosophy includes *epistemology*, the systematic study of thought, we have chosen a different approach to this topic. We will introduce you to the thinking processes of two traditional cultures to demonstrate how diverse the acts of seeking and acquiring knowledge can be.

Although today many cultures rely on science and scientific methods to gain new knowledge, indigenous cultures frequently depend on traditional knowledge, which is gained through direct experience. Knowledge from experience accumulates over time "as a result of new experiences that modify or add to the storehouse of wisdom."[122] Traditional knowledge is, according to Chisenga, characterized as being based on experience, tested over centuries of use, adapted to local culture and environments, dynamic, and subject to change.[123]

Many traditional native Hawaiians believe that thinking comes from the intestines, the "gut" that links the heart and the mind. In Hawaiian culture, feelings and emotions are inseparable from knowing, wisdom, and intelligence. In addition, according to Spring, for the Hawaiian, learning must include an aesthetic or practical dimension. Knowledge must link the spirit and the physical self and help foster interpersonal relationships.[124] This Hawaiian view is distinctly different from the Western rational view in which the cognitive domain of intellectual activity comes from the head/brain and is separate from the affective domain of emotion.

Holistic ways of knowing are a characteristic of the Kwara'ae people of the Solomon Islands. In their system, there is no detachment of the knower from the known. Knowledge is gained through sensory experiences, which are characterized as five kinds of "seeing": (1) physical seeing with the eyes; (2) seeing with the mind, which consists of insight or foresight; (3) seeing the unseen or spirits; (4) seeing beyond temporal boundaries, such as seeing something that indicates a future event; and (5) seeing through a medium or traditional healer to reveal the nature of an illness or the outcome of an event seen in a dream.[125]

REMEMBER THIS

There is a strong link between culture and learning and knowing that is reflected in how people prefer to learn and to know.

Our purpose has not been to provide you with an exhaustive examination of how people come to know, but to give you a brief glimpse of the diverse processes employed in some cultures to gain knowledge. We will now turn our attention to the influence of culture on cognitive styles.

Cultural Learning Preferences

A *learning preference* may be considered as the manner in which individuals prefer to receive and process information. It is an internal manner of processing information that envelops an individual's cultural elements.[126] Cognitive styles reflect a learner's preferred sensing modalities (auditory, visual, and kinesthetic), their preference for cooperative versus competitive approaches to learning, and their perceived value of education and schooling.[127] There are significant differences among learners within ethnic groups, and these differences are not due just to culture but to social class, the language spoken at home, the number of years or generations in the United States, and simple individual differences.[128]

Education researchers have investigated cognitive styles and teaching methods to determine how children from diverse backgrounds best learn. Below we will examine an approach to cognitive styles that uses four bipolar scales to identify continua that reflect four diverse cognitive styles.

Field Independence versus Field Dependence. Field independent learners perceive objects as separate and individualized, that is, separate from the field. Field dependent learners tend to perceive information through a global perspective taking in the totality rather than individual aspects. Field independent students prefer to work independently, are generally task oriented, and prefer to receive rewards that are based on individual competition. Field dependent students prefer to work with others, seek guidance from their teachers, and favor rewards based on group outcomes.[129]

Low-context, highly industrialized, individualistic societies such as the United States are predominantly field independent. High-context, traditional, collectivistic societies like Mexico and Japan tend toward field sensitivity. According to Leung, African American, Asian American, Latino, American Indian, and Hmong students generally prefer a field-sensitive, holistic learning style.[130] Kush indicates, however, that while children raised in traditional Mexican settings are inclined to develop a field dependent learning style, children raised in Mexican-American families that have assimilated some aspects of the Anglo culture tend to embrace a more field independent style.[131]

Cooperation versus Competition. This cognitive style describes students who prefer to work together in a cooperative environment or to work independently in competition with one another. Students from collective cultures expect and accept group work; in fact, they often work harder in a group than they do individually. Students in individualistic cultures usually expect to be graded on individual work. Cultures do, however, differ in the degree to which they stress cooperation or competition. Latino cultures, says Grossman, teach their children to cooperate and work collectively in groups. U.S. Americans, on the other hand, teach their young to work individually and to compete with one another.[132] In addition to Latinos, African Americans, Asian Americans, Pacific Rim Americans, Filipino Americans, and Hawaiians tend to raise their children cooperatively. Among Hawaiian families, for example, multiple caretakers, particularly older siblings, bring up children. According to Hollins, King, and Haymen, this behavior extends into the classroom and is evidenced by "high rates of peer interaction, frequently offering help to peers or requesting assistance from them."[133] In another example, Cleary and Peacock indicate that Native Americans usually do better in cooperative rather than competitive learning environments.[134]

Trial and Error versus "Watch, Then Do."
Some students with a fondness for risk-taking enjoy engaging themselves in a task, and learning to do it through trial and error. Others seek to minimize risk, preferring demonstrations and observing before attempting a task. Many mainstream American students prefer to solve problems and reach conclusions through trial and error. This approach, however, is not common in all cultures. As Grossman notes, in many cultures, "individuals are expected to continue to watch how something is done as many times and for as long as necessary until they feel they can do it."[135] Many American Indian students, say Cleary and Peacock, prefer to watch others until they feel competent to engage in an educational activity.[136]

Tolerance versus Intolerance for Ambiguity. This dimension reflects how well people contend with ambiguity in learning situations. Students from some cultures are open-minded about contradictions, differences, and uncertainty. Students from other cultures prefer a structured, predictable environment with little change. Although U.S. culture generally shows a high tolerance for ambiguity, the classroom tends to be an exception. The U.S. school day is frequently quite structured, with students moving from subject to subject, and often from room to room, based on the clock. Tolerance or intolerance for ambiguity also affects what is taught in the classroom. For example, U.S. culture emphasizes right/wrong, correct/incorrect, and yes/no answers, and values logic, rationalism, and cause-and-effect relationships. In contrast, many non-Western cultures are less tied to logic and rationalism. American Indian cultures, for instance, give little regard to seeking truth in absolute terms.

LINGUISTIC ISSUES IN MULTICULTURAL EDUCATION

As you discovered in Chapter 8, language is an important and significant cultural dynamic. It is an integral part of life and an integral part of every social system and reflects the richness and diversity of its culture.[137] "Historically, the way people speak carries an unimaginable weight in how they are perceived in the society. They are viewed to be civilized or uncivilized, sophisticated or unsophisticated, and 'high class' or 'low class' by the language that they speak."[138] "Words are a part of language, and language is a part of culture. They can be used to uplift or demean people."[139] Because culture and language are so closely tied to how people communicate and relate with one another and thus affect the classroom and learning process, we will look at three aspects of language that affect the educational context. These are (1) the extent of cultural and linguistic diversity in American schools, (2) the relationship between culturally and linguistically diverse students and the maintenance of their cultural identity, and (3) the educational problems associated with culturally and linguistically diverse students.

LINGUISTIC DIVERSITY

As we pointed out earlier, culturally and linguistically diverse students make up as much as 45 percent of the public school enrollment and that number is expected to grow. Multicultural learners are appearing with regularity in rural areas as well as urban areas like New York City, where students come from approximately 100 native language backgrounds.[140] Consequently, the educational system must recognize and accommodate to the needs of these culturally and linguistically diverse learners and provide not only academic instruction but English language learning (ELL) as well.

Because there is no common language in American classrooms, "teachers encounter communication dilemmas when teaching language and verbal skills."[141] The dialects and languages spoken by students influence teachers' perceptions of students' academic ability, their learning opportunities, evaluations of their contributions to class, and the way they are grouped for instruction. Language also can be the basis for categorization and the formation of in-groups and out-groups, especially within an institutional context where the languages spoken have unequal status. Languages are often symbols of group boundaries and, therefore, can be the sources of intergroup conflicts and tensions.[142] The educational system's response to this problem has not always been appropriate.[143] Although we believe, as does Delpit, that "all people have the right to their own language,"[144] discrimination against students who use non-standard language is quite common in various policies and school practices, even those that call for linguistic tolerance.[145]

If English language learners from varied cultural backgrounds and languages are to succeed educationally, it is imperative that educators understand and respect students for whom English is a second language. This requires demonstrating patience and valuing students' contribution to the class. To this end, educators need to model respectful yet challenging communication and questioning skills that show respect for the diverse modes of language and student learning[146] because, as Delpit suggests, "we cannot constantly correct children and expect them to continue to want to talk like us."[147] In addition, teachers must recognize that their students' ethnic identity is tied directly to their native language.

LANGUAGE AND IDENTITY

As we noted in Chapter 8, language performs the vital function of helping individuals construct and maintain their ethnic identities. As Dicker notes, "It is not surprising that our native language is often referred to as our 'mother tongue,' a term which recalls our earliest memories and influences."[148] A person's native language has deep significance because it is the seed of identity that blossoms as children grow.[149] Language helps individuals construct an identity that ties them to their in-group and at the same time sets them apart from other possible reference groups.[150] When non- or limited-English-speaking students enter the U.S. school system, they are encouraged to assimilate into the English-speaking culture. This is because academic proficiency in English-language skills affects students' abilities to adapt socially at school and is also highly predictive of academic success. The ability to perform on multiple-choice tests, extract meaning from written text, and argue a point, both orally and in writing, are essential to high levels of academic attainment.[151] But schools teach more than academics. "As socializing agents of students, schools have the opportunity to profoundly influence identity construction through their pedagogical and curricular stance."[152] Teachers can facilitate this process by showing respect for their students' native languages and thus ease students' adaptation to an English-speaking culture.

CULTURALLY AND LINGUISTICALLY DIVERSE STUDENTS

It should now be apparent that culturally and linguistically diverse (CLD) students may have a hard time in school. Their difficulty involves both cognitive and linguistic issues. McKeon has identified four sources of difficulty for CLD students. First, they must be concerned with both the cognitive aspects of learning the subject matter and the linguistic problems of simultaneously learning English. These students "must decipher the many structures and functions of the language before any content will make sense."[153] They must not only grasp the subject content but also make the new language express what they have learned. CLDs, therefore, must perform at a much higher cognitive and linguistic level than their English-speaking peers, who need only to deal with the cognitive aspects of learning. A second problem faced by CLDs is academic insufficiency. Developing higher cognitive and linguistic levels is often difficult because of academic delays. Many students who enter U.S. schools are academically deficient in their native language. As a result, it is very difficult for them to function at prescribed grade levels, let alone at higher cognitive and linguistic levels.[154] A third problem for CLDs is that they enroll in U.S. schools at various points in their academic careers— kindergarten, second grade, eleventh grade, and so on. The problem this creates, according to McKeon, is that "the higher the grade level, the more limited English proficiency is likely to weigh on students because at higher levels of schooling, the cognitive and linguistic loads are heavier."[155] Finally, the fourth complication for these students is that they arrive from countries that may emphasize different curricular sequences, content objectives, and instructional pedagogies.

A deductive instructional approach is generally used in the United States, but many Asian cultures frequently use an inductive approach. United States schools emphasize written education, whereas African and Middle Eastern schools emphasize oral education. Additionally, education in the United States is student-centered, which is characterized by an informal student-teacher relationship. In many cultures, however, education is teacher-centered, with the student-teacher relationship being very formal.

CONSIDER THIS

Think about your own experiences with cultural and linguistic diversity, and then answer the following questions.

1. *When was your first school interaction with someone from another culture, from another country?*
2. *What were your feelings following the interaction?*
3. *Did this interaction lead you to develop friendships with fellow students who were from different cultures?*
4. *Are students today benefiting from contact with culturally linguistically diverse students?*

CULTURALLY RESPONSIVE CLASSROOM COMMUNICATION

One important conclusion should have emerged by now: "Communication in the learning environment is influenced by cultural, psychological, and contextual factors and it involves the application of interpersonal and intrapersonal values."[156] Every classroom is a cultural community that is a product of the subject material, textbook authors, students, and the teachers. Successful educational outcomes depend upon teaching that is responsive to cultural diversity and require an approach where both teachers and students are responsible for understanding the perspectives of others and for understanding their own perspectives and how they acquired them. In addition to cultural knowledge, culturally responsive teachers must possess communicator qualities that aid in their presentation of the curriculum. Three such qualities, which we will discuss below, are self-efficacy, immediacy, and empathy.

COMMUNICATOR CHARACTERISTICS

Self-Efficacy

Self-efficacy is an individual's belief in her or his ability to organize and execute the courses of action required to successfully accomplish a specific teaching task in a particular context.[157] It is a person's belief that he or she can influence how well students learn and correlates positively with student outcomes. Teachers who have a high sense of efficacy are more satisfied with teaching, experience less stress, and exhibit greater enthusiasm for teaching.[158] Self-efficacy stems from lifelong experiences resulting in beliefs and perceptions affecting how people see themselves individually and collectively.[159]

Immediacy

Teachers may use *immediacy*, which incorporates approach and avoidance behaviors to optimize their teacher–student communication and enhance their credibility. Immediate teachers are viewed as approachable, friendly, open, responsive to student needs, as well as perceived as warm and relaxed. Non-immediate teachers are frequently perceived as cold, distant, and unfriendly.[160]

Immediacy involves the presentation of verbal and nonverbal behaviors that enhance physical and psychological closeness. Immediacy displays include such behaviors as praising, using humor, addressing others by name, making use of personal examples, using the words *our* and *we*, smiling, maintaining eye contact, and displaying changes in vocal and facial expression.[161]

Research has revealed a positive relationship between immediacy and cognitive learning, as well as between immediacy and credibility, across numerous cultures. Even in high-power distance cultures such as Kenya, say Johnson and Miller, students seem to benefit from seeing their teachers as approachable.[162] Additionally, Jazayeri reports that immediacy has been related to students' perceptions of teacher effectiveness in Mexico, Norway, China, Japan, and Australia, as well as in the United States.[163]

Empathy

The practice of empathy by both teachers and students is an indispensable quality found in the multicultural classroom environment. *Empathy* is the ability of one to assume the role of another and, by imagining the world as the other sees it, predict accurately the motives, attitudes, feelings, and needs of the other. Empathy in a classroom involves two steps. First, empathic teachers are able to imagine how it must be for immigrant students to adapt to a classroom where surroundings, language, and behavior are often unfamiliar. Second, empathy involves communicating in ways that are rewarding to the student who is the object of empathic prediction.[164]

Accurate prediction requires accepting people for who they are and thus understanding what can realistically be expected of them. Because you accept other people for who they are does not mean that you must agree with what they say or do. Although you may accept students' feelings, ideas, and behavior as legitimate, that does not mean you necessarily have to agree with them. Students do, however, react positively to empathic understanding—to the realization that they are not being evaluated or judged, and they are understood from their own point of view rather than from someone else's.[165] The empathic teacher, therefore, will let students use their own cultural resources and voices to develop new skills and to critically explore subject matter.[166]

The ability to communicate empathically requires learning specific behaviors and practices; it does not happen automatically. Cooper and Simonds offer four guidelines that you should follow in order to become an empathic communicator:

- *Communicate a supportive climate.* Community classrooms are supposed to create a supportive climate. To nourish this climate, you must create messages that indicate you understand your students' feelings and needs, rather than expressing judgments of student behavior.[167]
- *Attend to a student's nonverbal behavior as well as his or her verbal communication.* Effective interpretation of messages requires that you respond to the cognitive content of the message as well as to the meta-communication expressed nonverbally.[168] For instance, many Puerto Ricans use a nonverbal wrinkling of the nose to signify "what?" In one classroom, when the teacher asked if they had understood the lesson, some students would invariably wrinkle their noses. Not understanding this gesture, the teacher simply went on with the lesson, assuming that the nose wrinkling had no meaning.[169]
- *Accurately reflect and clarify feelings.* There is a tendency to respond more to the content of what others say—the ideas, thoughts, opinions, and attitudes expressed—than to the feelings that they are expressing. Feelings are more difficult to respond to because in the mainstream U.S. culture most people have less experience responding to feelings than to ideas.
- *Be genuine and congruent.* You are not likely to foster a good relationship with students if you communicate in false or misleading ways. A truly constructive relationship is one in which the participants respond to each other in an honest and genuine fashion. Your communication is congruent when the things that you do and say accurately reflect your real thoughts and feelings.[170] An important factor in classroom empathic behavior is demonstrating that teachers care about their students. Student perceptions of teacher behaviors perceived as caring include:
  - Listening to my side of the story
  - Encouraging me to keep trying
  - Writing helpful comments on my papers
  - Intervening when other kids are picking on me
  - Making sure I understand directions

- Insisting that I do my very best work most of the time
- Smiling at me
- Seeking my opinion[171]

In addition to the communication characteristics we have just discussed, effective multicultural classroom communication requires the employment of appropriate communication strategies.

COMMUNICATION STRATEGIES

Communicating effectively in a culturally diverse educational setting is not easy. Effective communication depends, in part, on the use of appropriate communication strategies. A first consideration in developing effective strategies is to consider the culture for which messages are being constructed. For example, in a traditional U.S. classroom situation, if a teacher has a disciplinary problem with a student, he or she might warn the student that further inappropriate behavior will result in a trip to the vice principal's office. In a remote Alaskan village, however, the teacher might use a very different message, such as "I'll be steaming with your mother tonight." In this cultural situation homes in the village have no running water and bathing takes place in communal gender-specific steam rooms as a group activity. For the student, this message could translate as "I'll be seeing your mother tonight, so shape up or I'll talk to her about your behavior." In a more general sense, effective communication strategies should be based upon a number of relevant factors and assumptions. We will list a few of the most important assumptions below.

- Provide ample opportunities to discuss global topics of interest and relevance with students. Always encourage perspective taking during such conversations.
- Avoid conversations that perpetuate "us" and "them" discussions. Foster a collective sense of being in the classroom.
- Allow discussion about unique cultural beliefs and practices and how they differ from those who misuse them to sustain terrorist activity.
- Be sensitive to cultural customs that might differ from the mainstream, particularly in regard to dress and personal rituals (such as daily prayer and fasting for Ramadan). Actively seek information about these unique customs, and promote accurate understanding with all students in your class.
- Remind students that school is a safe place of learning for students of *all* cultural backgrounds. If they do not feel safe, it is your obligation as an educator to directly address their feelings of insecurity and/or discomfort.
- Use culturally relevant proverbs as a teaching tool. Select similar proverbs from the diverse cultures in the classroom community to make a lesson point as well as to reveal the similarities among cultures.[172]

Another strategy is to create a harmonious communicative process by establishing the rules of discourse or communication. The social interaction styles of some urban ethnic groups or cultures can be misidentified as disrespectful. For example, some Asian cultures use ritualized laughter to maintain harmony and avoid conflicts with authority. Certain African-American groups use a social interaction style referred to as "call response." Here, students may frequently speak while the teacher is speaking as a response to their feelings about a teacher's comments. This is not rude behavior but is a cultural strategy to enter into the conversation through personal assertiveness rather than waiting for an "authority" to give permission.[173]

Self-questioning is another appropriate strategy. Teachers should ask themselves questions such as will this example or assignment make a student feel uncomfortable with regard to his or her race, religion, ethnicity, sexual orientation, or cultural background. What about the student who doesn't celebrate Christian or Jewish holidays? Rather than asking students to write a story about their favorite Christmas memory, a teacher could ask students to write about a favorite family tradition.[174]

A final suggested strategy focuses on teachers making good connections with their students both personally and intellectually. To this end, you might ask students to share information about their interests, their learning styles, and how you can successfully interact with them. Since so many students are computer literate, questions such as "Can anyone give an example of something they saw on Facebook or YouTube that is relevant to this topic?" are another way to honor their knowledge and make connections.[175]

We hope that at this point you understand and appreciate the impact cultural diversity has on the U.S. classroom. And we hope you will acknowledge that an education system that fails to understand cultural diversity will lose the richness of values, worldviews, lifestyles, and perspectives of the diverse U.S. co-cultures.

THE HEALTH CARE CONTEXT

When the American physician entered the examination room to greet Seyyed, his Iranian patient, he found him huddled on the floor, mumbling in a seemingly incoherent manner. His first thought was that the patient was in distress and may have fainted, fallen off the examination table, and perhaps even struck his head. But when he tried to assist him, the patient became agitated and resisted his help.[176]

During the evening hours, a Chinese-born surgeon phoned the night nurse to check on a patient scheduled for surgery the next morning. The nurse advised the physician that she had noticed a new hesitancy in the patient's attitude. "To tell you the truth, doctor, I think Mrs. Colby is getting cold feet."[177] The physician, hearing the term "cold feet," suspected a possible lower limb circulation problem and ordered a number of unnecessary vascular tests.

As he was being wheeled into an operating room, the American patient asked his Korean-born surgeon if he was going to "kick the bucket." The Korean physician, wanting to reassure the patient that his upcoming surgery would be successful, responded affably, "Oh, yes, you are definitely going to kick the bucket."[178]

These three examples reveal how confusion and unintended consequences may occur during intercultural health care communication. The first circumstance demonstrates how language differences and ignorance of other cultures can lead to a misunderstanding and adversely affect communication. Seyyed spoke little English, and the doctor did not comprehend the cultural circumstance. If the doctor had known that Seyyed was a Muslim and had understood Islamic religious requirements, he would have realized that his patient was most likely praying and would have given him some privacy.[179] In the second and third situations, failure to recognize culture-specific idiomatic expressions led to misunderstandings, first by the doctor who ordered unnecessary tests, and second on the part of the patient who was not reasonably assured that he would survive his surgery.

The goal of medicine is to provide appropriate health care for all patients. This requires that health care providers have "the ability to understand and work effectively with patients whose beliefs, values, and histories differ from one's own."[180] Competent health care delivery requires effective communication among all of the individuals who are involved: patients, physicians, health care professionals, language interpreters, and family members.[181] Galanti adds:

> In a multiethnic society, this goal can be accomplished only if the health care providers understand such things as why Asian patients rarely ask for pain medication whereas patients from Mediterranean countries seem to need it for the slightest discomfort; why Middle Easterners will not allow a male physician to examine their women; and that coin rubbing is an ancient form of Asian medical treatment, not a form of child abuse.[182]

Supporting Galanti's view, Andersen and Taylor hold the following position:

> One of the challenges for the health care system in a society with increasing diversity is responding to the different cultural orientations of various groups in society. Immigrants, for example, who may have limited English language skills and may have come from cultures with very different health care practices, may be especially confused by the practices within the U.S. health care system.[183]

Kundhal and Kundhal echo this concern when they write, "the cultural and ethnic backgrounds of patients can shape their views of illness and well-being in both the physical and spiritual realm and affect their perceptions of health care as well as the outcome of their treatment."[184]

People from different cultures frequently hold quite dissimilar beliefs about illness, health care, and death which can be very different from Western views.[185] "In the face of such diversity, and recognizing that clinical encounters abound with cultural signs and meanings, immigrant patients and their physicians need skills in intercultural communication in order to receive and provide satisfactory health care."[186]

In this section we will discuss some of these needed skills by examining (1) diverse beliefs about health and the treatment of illness, (2) the requisites for effective intercultural health care communication, (3) the communication problems caused by language diversity, and (4) strategies for effective health care communication.

> **REMEMBER THIS**
>
> *Cultural diversity in worldviews may hinder effective communication between patients and health care providers.*

DIVERSE HEALTH CARE BELIEF SYSTEMS

Although beliefs about health and the causes, treatment, and prevention of illness are found in all cultures, these beliefs often vary from one culture to another and lead to different and sometimes idiosyncratic concepts of illness. As Aghadiuno notes,

> Culture and the meaning we give to illness and health are closely bound. Illness is synonymous with sickness, disease, affliction, disability; while health equates with haleness, robustness, vigour, well-being and strength.[187]

Culture and ethnicity, therefore, present unique sets of beliefs and perceptions about health and illness which in turn influence how illness is recognized, to what it is attributed, how it is interpreted, and how and when health services are sought.[188]

Cultural notions about health and illness differ not only around the world but also among co-cultures in the United States. Spector notes that in Chinese medicine, which is practiced by millions of the Chinese who live in the United States, a prevailing belief posits that "health is a state of spiritual and physical harmony with nature."[189] Many Chinese "may use meditation, exercise, massage, and prayer. Drugs, herbs, food, good air, and artistic expression may also be used. Good-luck charms are cherished and traditional and nontraditional medicines are used."[190] In addition, many Africans and African Americans frequently perceive pain as a sign of illness or disease and often employ folk medicine to cure their illnesses.[191] It is imperative, therefore, that health care professionals deepen their "understanding of the health beliefs and practices of individuals in cultural communities to meet their diverse, and often unmet, health care needs and expectations."[192]

Andrews puts forth a comprehensive paradigm in which health belief systems are divided into three major categories: *supernatural/mágico/religious*, *holistic*, and *scientific/biomedical*, each with its own set of related premises and beliefs.[193] We will use Andrews' paradigm to organize our discussion of the various cultural beliefs about the causes, treatment, and prevention of illness.

SUPERNATURAL/MÁGICO/RELIGIOUS TRADITION

Underlying Premises

Religious and spiritual factors are significant in health care because they influence beliefs about the nature of illness.[194] The supernatural/mágico/religious health care belief system is based on the assumption that people live in a world inhabited by supernatural forces.[195] Andrews describes this system as one where "the fate of the world and those in it, including humans, depends on the actions of God, or the gods, or other supernatural forces for good or evil."[196] Followers of this tradition believe quite strongly that sorcery, magic, and evil spirits can negatively affect them in their daily lives.

Causes of Illness

In this belief system both religion and spirituality "can play a key role in the way disease is perceived and addressed in different cultures. In fact, religion and spirituality include traditions and values that may affect people's understanding of the causes of illness, compliance to treatment and physician recommendations, or feeling of optimism or fatalism about disease outcomes to name just a few examples."[197] Illness is often attributed to spiritual factors such as "sorcery, breaching a taboo, intrusion of a disease object, intrusion of a disease-causing spirit, and loss of the soul."[198] In some cultures people may believe that illness results from the possession of the body by evil spirits or possibly from the casting of evil spells.[199] In other cultural groups people may believe that illness is a sign of weakness, a punishment for evildoing, or retribution for shameful behavior such as disrespect toward one's elders. The ill person is, therefore, receiving a deserved punishment rendered by a supernatural agent.[200]

REMEMBER THIS

People who subscribe to a supernatural/mágico/religious worldview believe that one's state of health may be affected by sorcery, magic, or evil spirits.

Treatment of Illness

For those who subscribe to the super-natural/mágico/religious tradition, cultural health care practices arising from religious beliefs and practices can have a profound impact on health. Aghadinuo has made the observation that "For some the term spirituality is analogous to religion and for others it embraces everyone with or without a religious affiliation. Spirituality is described as a vast realm of human potential dealing with ultimate purposes, with high entities, with God, with life, with comparison and with purpose."[201]

Spiritual needs, therefore, may become quite intense when a sudden illness takes away activity, interests, and the very meaning of existence.[202] Mexican Americans, for instance, may embrace the thought *ayúdate que Dios te ayudara* (help yourself so that God will help you) by placing the responsibility for care and caring with the entire family and God. As such, the family is essential to promote the caring that leads to health.[203] Muslims, on the other hand, may believe that God created human beings and gave them their bodies as gifts to be cared for. On the Day of Judgment, God will ask what

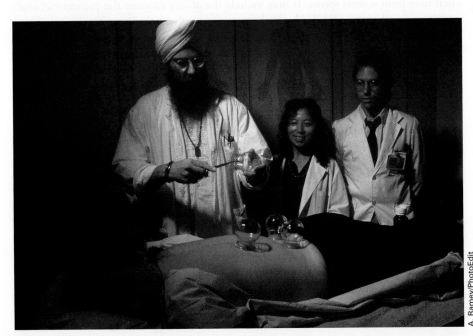

Cultures differ in their understanding of the causes, treatments, and prevention of illness.

A. Ramey/PhotoEdit

CONSIDER THIS

You are a teacher in an American middle school. One day you notice that one of your Vietnamese students has bruise-like marks on her arms, legs, neck, and face. You are a culturally competent teacher working in a multicultural environment and have learned about the practices of cupping, spooning, and coining as folk treatments for illness. Yet, the laws of your state mandate that you report any suspicion of child abuse to Child Protective Services, which has the authority to remove children from their homes if they suspect abuse.

What action would you take?

they did with their bodies and their health. Human beings express gratitude to God for their good health through worship and by not harming their bodies.[204]

The supernatural/mágico/religious tradition seeks to treat illness by achieving a positive association between the patient and the relevant spirits, deities, and so forth.[205] Treatment may be administered by traditional priests or carried out by healer-practitioners recognized by their communities as shamans. The word "shaman" is derived from an ancient Siberian language and means "spirit healer." It denotes a person who works with supernatural entities. Shamanism is found today in many parts of the world among people who live by mystical participation or a sense of spiritual connection that they believe exists between everyone and everything in the universe. Shamanism is neither a religion nor a science, but an activity that takes place in a world that is ordinary yet spiritual. It can be viewed as a healing or helping technology—the technology of the sacred—instead of a set of beliefs or customs.[206]

Generally, priests or shamans seem to invoke energies that are greater than the ordinary physical power found in everyday life. The healing capability of a shaman may be invoked by a hands-on power to heal that removes harmful spirit maladies from the body and restores the body's energy; the visionary ability to see into the body of a sick person; and the capability to retrieve the lost soul or spirit of the sick. Shamanism may also provide a spiritual connection with animals, and the ability to elicit help from animal spirits. It may include the ability to sense the presence of one's ancestors or other friendly dead who have come to give help.[207]

Korean folk medicine follows the practice of *hanyak*, which has its roots in ancient Chinese medicine. According to Clark, *hanyak* involves diagnosing imbalances in the body that are believed to cause illness and then prescribing appropriate natural remedies that restore the body's ability to maintain its balance.[208] A *hanyak* practitioner who has arrived at a diagnosis will prescribe from a wide and varied *hanyak* pharmacopoeia. These are drugs taken from roots, flowers, leaves, and vines and are the sources of many of the drugs used today in Western medicine. Quinine, for example, is an ancient Eastern drug that has been adopted in the West to treat malaria.[209]

Many Cubans, Puerto Ricans, and Brazilians follow a belief in *Santería* (a type of religion). When someone of this belief becomes sick, a *santero* or folk healer is contacted who consults an *Orisha* (saint-like deity) to assist in finding a cure. Similarly, it is not uncommon for Haitians to consult voodoo priests and priestesses for treatments that can involve candles, baths, charms, and spirit visits.[210]

In the United States many African Americans will draw upon their ancestral

REMEMBER THIS

The supernatural tradition comes from a belief system in which the world is perceived as an arena filled with magic, sorcery, and evil spirits. Illness is attributed to evil spiritual forces. Treatment is carried out by healers who invoke special powers to cast out the evil forces.

roots and utilize folk practitioners selected from among spiritual leaders, grandparents, elders of the community, or voodoo doctors or priests.[211] Although some of these treatments may seem unusual or even bizarre from a Western perspective, health care practitioners in other cultures have successfully employed these methods for centuries.

HOLISTIC TRADITION

Underlying Premises

Followers of the holistic tradition believe the earth is a system consisting of such components as air, land, water, plants, and animals. Holistic health is based on the principle that a whole is made up of interdependent, interacting parts. In the same way, an individual is a whole made up of interdependent parts, which are known as physical, mental, emotional, and spiritual. Yet, each individual is unique and holism underlines this uniqueness. "Holism sees people as parts of a family, culture and community and regards people as entities with physical, psychological, socio-cultural and spiritual aspects."[212] If life is to be sustained, these parts cannot be separated, because what is happening to one part of a system is also felt by all of the other parts. When one part of an individual is not working at its best, all of the other parts of that person are affected. Furthermore, this whole person, including all of his or her parts, is in constant interaction with everything in the surrounding environment. For instance, if an individual is anxious about an examination or an employment interview, his or her nervousness may result in a physical reaction such as a headache or a stomachache. When someone suppresses anger over a long period, he or she often develops a serious illness such as migraine headaches, emphysema, or arthritis.[213]

Holistic health is about more than just not being sick; it is actually an approach to life.[214] Rather than focusing on a specific illness or specific parts of the body, holism refers to "health practices, approaches, knowledge and beliefs incorporating plant, animal and mineral-based medicines, spiritual therapies, manual techniques, applied singularly or in a combination to treat, diagnose, and prevent illness or maintain well-being."[215] It is concerned with the connection of mind, body, and spirit and how persons interact with their environment. The goal is to achieve maximum well-being, where everything is functioning in the very best way possible. With holistic health, people accept responsibility for their own level of well-being, and everyday choices are used to take charge of one's own health.[216]

Causes of Illness

Holistic or naturalistic approaches to the cause of illness assume there are natural laws that govern everything and every person in the universe. For people to be healthy they must remain in harmony with nature's laws and willingly adjust and adapt to changes in their environment.[217] In reviewing beliefs about holistic causes among Asian cultures, Giger and Davidhizar suggest that many people of Asian origin (Chinese, Filipinos, Koreans, Japanese, and Southeast Asians) do not believe they have control over nature. They possess a fatalistic perspective in which people must adjust to the physical world rather than controlling or changing the environment.[218] According to Murillo-Rhode, Holistic Mexican and Puerto Rican medical beliefs are derived from the Greek humoral theory that specifies four humors of the body: "blood—hot and wet; yellow bile—hot and dry; phlegm—cold and wet; and black bile—cold and dry."[219] An imbalance of one of the four body humors is seen as a cause of illness.[220] According to Spector, people of African, Haitian, or Jamaican origin also frequently view illness as a result of disharmony with nature.[221]

Although there are many American Indian tribes with somewhat different worldviews, there is enough similarity among them to allow us to make some valid generalizations. First, we can generalize that American Indians consider the earth "to be a living organism—the body of a higher individual, with a will and a desire to be well. For them, ill health is something that must be."[222] American Indian belief systems maintain that a person should respect his or her body, just as the earth should be treated with respect. Spector reports that American Indians tend to believe in a reciprocal relationship whereby if the earth is harmed, humankind itself is harmed, and "conversely, when humans harm themselves they harm the earth. The earth gives food, shelter, and medicine to humankind, and for this reason, all things of the earth belong to human beings and nature."[223]

As you can see, the holistic worldview results in multiple approaches to understanding the causes of illness. And, as we will discuss next, it yields a variety of ways to treat illness.

Treatment of Illness

Holistic treatments for illness may be viewed from two perspectives. The first is the centuries old traditional holistic folk-healing approach. The second perspective is frequently referred to as Complementary Alternative Medicine (CAM) and is practiced in contemporary developed cultures.

The traditional holistic approach to treating illness is to achieve or maintain balance among the natural elements and forces acting within and upon the human body. Traditional Chinese medicine, for example, attempts to restore balance between the natural *yin* and *yang* forces. Matocha explains this process:

> The Chinese believe that health and a happy life can be maintained if the two forces of the yang and the yin are balanced. The hollow organs (bladder, intestines, stomach, and gallbladder), head, face, back, and lateral parts of the body are the yang. The solid viscera (heart, lung, liver, spleen, kidney, and pericardium), abdomen, chest, and the inner parts of the body are the yin. The yin is cold and the yang is hot. Health care providers need to be aware that the functions of life and the interplay of these functions, rather than the structures, are important to Chinese.[224]

Frequently, Mexicans and Mexican Americans consult folk healers such as *curanderos/as* to treat illness. Folk healers are recognized by the state government of New Mexico as a significant collaborative influence on the State's Midwifery Consultant Program. The midwives work with the *curanderas-parteras* (folk healers/midwives) to improve basic childbirth practices. In 1979 New Mexico established regulations requiring all practicing *curanderas-parteras* to obtain a formal education and pass a licensing exam.[225]

Mexican folk medicine looks beyond symptoms of illness and seeks to locate imbalances in an individual's relationship with the environment, negative emotional states, and harmful social, spiritual, and physical factors. When one becomes ill, folk healers use foods and herbs to restore the desired balance. A "hot" disease is treated with cold or cool foods. A "cold" disease is treated by hot foods. *Hot* and *cold* do not refer to the temperature of the foods, but to their intrinsic nature. Hot foods include chocolate, garlic, cinnamon, mint, and cheese. Cold foods include avocados, bananas, fruit juice, lima beans, and sugarcane.[226]

> ## REMEMBER THIS
>
> *The holistic tradition is based on a balanced system of relationships among the body, mind, and spirit. Illness occurs when there is an imbalance among any of these aspects of the system. Cures are effected by restoring balance to the system.*

Many physicians who have been trained in the scientific/biomedical tradition have come to recognize that the scientific/biomedical model "does not take into account current knowledge that most diseases and their prognoses are heavily influenced by social and cultural habits, as well as the individual's psychological status. Health conditions such as obesity, diabetes, and depression are clearly influenced by external factors, which can include lifestyle issues, emotional stress, and cultural beliefs and preferences."[227] These physicians are now following holistic principles utilizing complementary alternative medicine (CAM) in conjunction with standard scientific/biomedical practices. As Geist-Martin, Sharf, and Jeha relate, "Holistic health practitioners use therapeutic modalities on the physical body in order to restore the 'whole' person—all aspects including both the body and the soul."[228] Complementary alternative medicine practices may employ such forms of treatment as herb and dietary supplement therapy, mind-body medicine which may include biofeedback, hypnosis, meditation, music therapy, tai chi, and yoga. Other forms of alternative medicine include acupuncture, *reiki*, massage, spinal manipulation, homeopathy, and traditional Chinese medicine practices.

SCIENTIFIC/BIOMEDICAL TRADITION

Underlying Premises

The scientific/biomedical model has existed for many centuries and is based on the assumption that poor health is a physical phenomenon that can be explained, identified, and treated with physical means.[229] This health care system focuses on the objective diagnosis and scientific explanation of disease. It uses an evidence-based approach that relies on procedures such as laboratory tests to verify the presence and diagnosis of disease. The scientific/biomedical model, therefore, does not take into account the person's psychological conditions, individual and social beliefs, attitudes and norms, or other factors that can affect health and illness. Andrews states that this paradigm supports the belief that "life is controlled by a series of physical and biochemical processes that can be studied and manipulated by humans. Human health is understood in terms of physical and chemical processes."[230] The scientific/biological perspective is the dominant health-related belief system in the United States and the Western world and the medical establishment promotes an almost exclusive belief in and reliance on it.[231] Most Western physicians and other health care professionals are trained in this tradition.

> ## REMEMBER THIS
>
> *The Western scientific/biomedical worldview toward health holds that illness is caused by a breakdown in a patient's physical and chemical processes.*

Causes of Illness

The scientific/biological tradition emphasizes biological concerns and is primarily interested in discovering abnormalities in the body's physical structure or its chemical functioning. Disease is held to be present when a person's condition is seen to deviate from clearly established norms based on biomedical science. Causes are thought to be the result of an invasion of bacteria or viruses, deterioration of skeletal structures or organs, abnormal cell growth, arteriolar deposits, and the like. Luckmann believes that adherents to this approach view the model as "more 'real' and significant in contrast to psychological and sociological explanations of illness."[232]

Treatment of Illness

Scientific/biomedical treatment protocols seek to destroy or remove the illness-causing agent, repair the affected body part, or control the affected body system. These approaches are the dominant form of treatment in the United States as well as most developed nations. Treatments to return the body to its normal state include surgery, medications, or other therapeutic interventions that destroy or remove the cause of illness. Following this approach, for example, surgery, chemotherapy, or radiation therapy may be employed to battle cancer. Antibiotics may be prescribed to destroy illness-causing bacteria and antiviral medications may be administered to treat viral infections. In some cases, nutritional supplements such as vitamins and minerals may be prescribed to help return the body to its normal state.

Having discussed diverse belief systems about the causes and treatment of illness, we now turn to helping you become an effective communicator in a multicultural health care environment. There are three important aspects of communication you need to understand in order to develop your health communication skills: (1) the impact of language diversity on health care communication, (2) the requisites you need to help you acquire health care communicator skills, and (3) the development of effective health care communication strategies.

LANGUAGE DIVERSITY AND HEALTH CARE COMMUNICATION

LANGUAGE DIVERSITY

The general relationships between language and culture were considered in Chapter 8. However, the role of language diversity in the health care setting needs to be explored here because "language barriers impair discussions of symptoms and recommended therapies resulting in misdiagnoses or poor treatment decisions. Communication barriers also impede adherence to treatment regimes."[233] Ferguson and Candib explain that "race, ethnicity, and language all affect the quality of the doctor patient relationship."[234] Likewise, Purnell contends that

> a lack of knowledge of clients' language abilities and cultural beliefs and values can result in serious threats to life and quality of care for all individuals. Organizations and individuals who understand their clients' cultural values, beliefs, and practices are in a better position to be co-participants with their clients in providing culturally acceptable care.[235]

Lacking a similar linguistic background, physicians may fail to understand information given by the immigrant patient. Consequently, treatment advice may not be properly understood by the patient, making it difficult for the physician to arrive at the right diagnosis.

It is clear that language differences can complicate medical interactions. How does a young Latina woman who speaks no English explain to a medical team in a hospital emergency ward that the liquid drops she put into her baby's mouth (which were intended for the baby's ears) have made her child worse? Think for a moment about the potential for confusion if a Western doctor speaks of a woman's "period" to someone whose culture does not use this metaphor. Similarly, a patient's literal translation of the phrase "have your tubes tied" may lead to a misunderstanding that the tubes can just as easily be "untied." Medical situations resulting from such miscommunication can be detrimental to the patient.

EMPLOYING INTERPRETERS

Need for Interpreters

Although the topic of interpreters and translators was discussed earlier in Chapter 8, we revisit the subject here as it applies to the health care context. There are at least three reasons for using a medical interpreter: (1) legal reasons, (2) quality-of-care reasons, and (3) financial reasons.[236] An interpreter is necessary if the physician and the patient are not fluent in the same language. Additionally, patients may be reluctant to reveal that they do not understand what the health care provider is saying. Even minor misunderstandings between patients and health care professionals can lead to critical errors in diagnosis and treatment.[237]

Selecting and Using Interpreters

Although family members may be the most convenient interpreters, Cole believes that using non-professional interpreters or family members is dangerous. "They may modify the questions we physicians ask out of their concern for privacy, or they may change the answer our patients provide for a variety of well-meaning reasons."[238] For example, Haffner reports that a Mexican woman whose son usually interpreted for her suffered a great deal before the doctor discovered her actual problem—a fistula in her rectum. She was so embarrassed about her condition that she was reluctant to reveal her symptoms through her son. Only when a professional interpreter was called did she reveal her true symptoms.[239] Also, the use of a family member or friend as an interpreter may breach confidentiality laws, cause confusion because a family member or friend does not understand medical terminology, or make it difficult to assess sensitive issues such as sexuality and domestic violence. Therefore, as Purnell recommends, a trained medical interpreter should be used because "providers who know ethnoculturally specific knowledge are less likely to demonstrate negative attitudes, behaviors, ethnocentrism, stereotyping, and racism."[240]

Below are some helpful guidelines when using interpreters.

- Use interpreters who can decode the words and provide the meaning behind the message.
- Use dialect-specific interpreters whenever possible.

- Use interpreters trained in the health care field.
- Give the interpreter time alone with the client.
- Provide time for translation and interpretation.
- Use same-gender interpreters whenever possible.
- During the assessment, direct your questions to the patient, not to the interpreter.
- Ask one question at a time and allow interpretation and a response before asking another question.
- Remember that clients can usually understand more than they can express; thus, they need time to think in their own language. They are alert to the health care provider's body language, and they may forget some or all of their English in times of stress.
- Review responses with the patient and interpreter at the end of a session.[241]

We have shown how health care can be compromised when provider and client speak different languages. We have also given you some insights into the problems associated with using an interpreter. Next, we will turn to developing effective health care communication. In so doing, we will examine the skills and knowledge you need to be an effective multicultural health care communicator and then discuss specific strategies you can use to enhance communication with culturally diverse clients.

EFFECTIVE INTERCULTURAL HEALTH CARE COMMUNICATION

In health care delivery the influence of culture is present at every step of the process. Spector adds to this theme: "In many situations, this is not difficult; in other situations, it seems impossible.... [T]he needs most difficult to meet are those of people whose belief systems are most different from the 'mainstream' health-care provider culture."[242] Thus, in order to attain a goal of optimal health care for everyone in the culturally diverse United States, health care providers and institutions must be effective intercultural communicators.

REQUISITES FOR EFFECTIVE MULTICULTURAL HEALTH CARE COMMUNICATION

Providing competent health care to a culturally diverse population demands that clinicians "become aware of their own biases, values and ethno-cultural background as well as the implicit assumptions of the subculture of Western medicine."[243] In addition, "knowledge of the patient's culture of origin is regarded as helpful, but physicians are warned of the risk of stereotyping and oversimplification."[244]

Know Your Own Culture

Before health care providers can widen their knowledge about other cultures, they must be aware of their own beliefs and recognize how culture affects their ability to look at, understand, and appreciate other belief systems. Perceptions, beliefs, and understandings of what constitutes health and health care are developed through social acculturation and shaped by cultural experiences.[245] In the United States, health care providers—physicians, nurses, social workers, dietitians, laboratory and

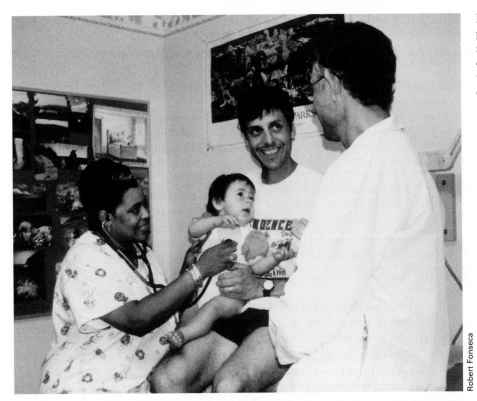

Health care professionals need special communication skills when dealing with diverse cultures.

Robert Fonseca

departmental professionals—are socialized into the culture of their profession and, for the most part, are educated in the Western scientific/biomedical worldview. This professional socialization teaches practitioners to hold and accept a set of beliefs, practices, habits, likes, dislikes, norms, and rituals consistent with the scientific/biomedical orientation.[246] Thus, health care providers should self-examine their personal orientations to become acutely aware of their beliefs, biases, and reactions to alternate health care beliefs.

Learn About Diverse Health Care Beliefs

The more you can learn about the health care beliefs and practices found in various cultures, the better your care and treatment plans can take into account a client's worldview and expectations. Experience in multicultural environments can enhance the ability to communicate with patients from other cultures.[247] The belief perspectives of both provider and patient are influenced by the social and cultural factors that define each person, different worldviews can undermine the trust and cooperation necessary for a successful healing and therapeutic relationship.[248] When working in a multicultural environment, you should first understand the beliefs of the patient and his or her family, especially toward treatment goals. Second you must develop a treatment plan that is acceptable to the patient, the family, and the health care team.

Concern about families is important because in many cultures health care decisions are not made by the individual patient but by the family as a team. Galanti reported that "when asked to name their most common problem in dealing with non-Anglo

REMEMBER THIS

Anderson, Scrimshaw, and Fullilove suggest four things that should be considered in intercultural health care interactions:

1. *Does the patient value individuality and personal choice, or does the patient focus more on family and collective choices?*
2. *Does the patient value open communication or does the patient tend to draw cues from the context of the situation?*
3. *Does the patient believe people can and should influence their health?*
4. *Does the patient believe in a Western biomedical view of illness, or does the patient hold an alternative or blended view of illness?*[249]

Although the above questions are not exhaustive, they do illustrate a way to obtain the kind of knowledge you will need to provide effective health care.

ethnic groups, most nurses respond, 'their families.'"[250] This is understandable because of cultural differences in a number of issues related to families, including decision making and the role of family members when someone is ill. In many cultures, including Romany (Gypsy), Asian, Middle Eastern, and Hispanic, males are traditionally the authority figures. Unless they are well acculturated, it is often best to consider them as the spokespersons for the family. They are often the ones who will make the decisions. This recommendation may be difficult for those with pro-feminist leanings, but it is likely to be the most productive approach. Age is also a sign of authority in Romany and Asian cultures, so initial conversations should be addressed to the eldest male.[251] Because Americans commonly possess a strong sense of independence, they may be used to making their own decisions about their own health care. Therefore, it is a useful to ask patients if there is anyone they would like to consult with before making a health care decision.

For the Western-oriented health care provider, biomedical information is usually of primary concern, sometimes to the exclusion of everything else; but it is essential to remember that a patient's, and his or her family's, perception and understanding of the origin and meaning of well-being, illness, and recovery can be major factors in the health care process. It is important to remember this potentially different perception, because, according to Rundle, Carvalho, and Robinson, a provider may not appreciate a family's reliance on a shaman or spiritual healer.[252]

We have described some of the cultural factors than can impede effective health care communication. Now, we want to call your attention to communication strategies that can be used to engage in effective interaction with culturally diverse patients.

DEVELOPING EFFECTIVE HEALTH CARE COMMUNICATION STRATEGIES

Health care communication strategies offer advice and suggestions about gaining insight into a patient's background and health care beliefs. Strategies are also valuable in helping overcome barriers to effective communication between caregivers and patients. In our examination of communication strategies, we will look at (1) avoiding stereotypes and generalizations, (2) conducting interviews, and (3) discussing end-of-life situations.

Avoid Stereotypes

One danger inherent in working with people from diverse cultures is relying on stereotypes, which results in ascribing a characteristic to a person or group of people that may not be true. For instance, if you were to meet a Mexican woman and assume that she has a large family, that would be a stereotype. And if your interaction with people is based on stereotypes, you can make errors in judgments and assumptions that interfere with effective communication. For example, you are stereotyping if you assume that all Muslim families have a strong patrilineal tradition where women are subordinate to men and young people are subordinate to older people. In many situations this may be true. But if you apply that assumption in all cases and believe that the husband will talk for his wife and make decisions about her health care, you could be wrong. And if you are wrong, that assumption could easily interfere with the ability to establish rapport and trust with clients.

Conducting Interviews

Interviews are the primary technique used by physicians and other caregivers to elicit information. As we have indicated, communicating with patients from different cultures is often complicated by language differences. Health care professionals face a far greater challenge when they must communicate with patients who have limited or no English language proficiency. During a cross-cultural interview, the health care provider should ask the patient a series of questions that will elicit the information necessary to determine effective treatment. Juckett has proposed a list of cross-cultural interview questions, which we quote below:

1. What do you call the illness?

2. What do you think has caused the illness?

3. Why do you think the illness started when it did?

4. What problems do you think the illness causes? How does it work?

5. How severe is the illness? Will it have a long or short course?

6. What kind of treatment do you think is necessary? What are the most important results you hope to receive from this treatment?

7. What are the main problems the illness has caused you?

8. What do you fear most about the illness?[253]

We would add to this list a ninth question: What treatments, if any, are you receiving, and are you using folk remedies?

As you can see from the above discussion, conducting cross-cultural health care interviews is not an easy task. Until you overcome language barriers, your customary assessment and teaching skills will be seriously hampered, and the patient's care may be compromised.

Communication about Death and Dying

In Chapter 3 when we discussed religion, we noted that cultures have evolved many different ways to deal with the feelings of loss and grief associated with the termination of life. They range from actively participating in discussions to completely ignoring the issue. In the health care professions, however, death cannot be ignored. Effective and timely communication can help patients and their families gather relevant health information about significant threats to health and assist them in developing plans for responding appropriately to those threats. Wright, Sparks, and O'Hair rightly note that "an increasing problem for providers is how to communicate health information that is bad news to patients."[254] We now turn our attention to communication about unpleasant prognoses and terminal illness.

U.S. Americans emphasize patient autonomy and a patient's "right to know." These beliefs have resulted in right to privacy laws that prohibit sharing medical information without the patient's written consent. Galanti notes, however, that "one of the first cultural issues that arise with regard to the end of life is whether or not to reveal a terminal diagnosis to the patient."[255] In the U.S. American culture, where individualism and autonomy are values, the patient is told if she or he has a terminal condition because it is a basic right of patients to know. However, the situation becomes complicated when the patient is from a culture that values the family over the individual.[256]

Cultural diversity in beliefs about death and dying can intensify the communication process for health care workers and their clients. In many non-Western societies the reference group for an individual is his or her kin, relationships that may extend far beyond the ties of the nuclear family that form the norm for so many in the United States and Europe. In these societies, families are often drawn into the decision-making processes that influence individual lives about issues that in the West would be considered an individual's "private matter."

When patients and health care workers have diverse cultural backgrounds, patients frequently want to follow their cultural belief systems, which can hinder effective communication. Bowman and Singer believe that "these differences in perspective, when unacknowledged, can lead to a complete breakdown in communication."[257] The custom in many cultures, including Mexican, Filipino, Chinese, and Iranian, is for the patient's family to be the first to know about an unpleasant prognosis. After receiving this news, it becomes the family's responsibility to decide whether and how much to tell the patient. A care giver must be aware of such cultural differences and discuss with the patient in advance just who should be given information regarding the patient's condition, thus avoiding unnecessary stress for the patient and his or her family.[258]

Discussions with patients and their families about death and dying must take into account not only the initial revelation of the diagnosis and prognosis, but the treatment and care of the patient who is terminally ill. In broaching the topic of terminal illness, some families may approach the discussion of death in an open and disclosing manner, but others may avoid the topic, or use sarcasm and dark humor to reduce its emotional intensity.[259] Members of some cultures may perceive telling a patient that he or she is dying as being insensitive because they believe such news will create a sense of hopelessness and hasten the dying process.

Many Mexican Americans believe that the stress of knowing your condition would only cause an illness to get worse. The very devout may believe that only God knows when someone will die. Among the Hmong, to tell someone they are dying is thought to curse them. "How could you know they will die unless you plan to kill them yourself?"[260] In some cultures talking of death is actually taboo. Navajos, for instance, hold a cultural taboo that you should not think negatively about something or it will happen. It is difficult, therefore, to discuss death and dying with members of the Navajo culture because such a discussion is believed to bring it about. This characteristic is also found among some Zuni and Koreans who believe that speaking of a person's death can bring sadness or hasten their demise.[261]

Cultural groups have different beliefs about using treatment or artificial nutrition with a feeding tube. "African Americans typically want assertive treatment"[262] and may want even more aggressive care during an end-of-life situation, such as requesting life-sustaining therapy such as cardiopulmonary resuscitation, intensive care unit admissions, artificial ventilation, and tube feeding. They are less likely to sign advance directives or "Do Not Resuscitate" (DNR) orders or to accept hospice care.[263]

Many African Americans prefer to have a spiritual leader participate in end-of-life discussions, and many believe that it is the duty of the health care worker to help organize and participate in the meeting.[264] In regard to the relative importance of preserving life at all costs versus preserving quality of life or a "life worth living," African Americans often believe in the possibility of a "miracle," and that a patient must be kept alive indefinitely so that the miracle can occur.[265]

As we conclude, we again remind you that the primary motivation behind this chapter is to provide an understanding of the influence that cultural contexts have on communication styles and individual belief systems. Simply stated, this understanding will assist you when engaged in the professions associated with business, education, and health care.

Chapter Review

CHAPTER 1

SUMMARY

- Globalization, domestic diversity, and immigration make acquiring intercultural communication skills imperative.

- Communication technology is making interaction between people from different cultures increasingly common.

- Intercultural communication involves communicative interaction between people from varying cultures.

- The dominant culture controls the societal institutions—government, education, and social.

- Co-cultures may share some dominant culture characteristics but also exhibit different communication behaviors.

- A society can encompass more than one culture.

- Venturing into a new culture can cause anxiety and emotional dissonance.

- Culture shock is a mental state that comes from the transition that occurs when you go from a familiar environment to an unfamiliar one and find that your established patterns of behavior are ineffective.

- According to the U-Curve model, culture shock has four phases: exhilaration, disenchantment, adjustment, and effective functioning.

- International immigration creates culturally and ethnically diverse societies whose members must learn to interact with each other.

- Cultural adaptation strategies include learning about the language of the host culture, guarding against ethnocentrism, and working to maintain contact with your own culture.

- Ethics focuses on appropriate behavior in interpersonal interactions, both within your own culture and when you are in another culture.

- There are two major perspectives on ethics: fundamentalism and relativism.

- Because intercultural messages elicit responses, ethical communicators are mindful of their actions, show respect to others, seek commonalities, recognize cultural differences, and accept responsibility for their actions.

- Some of the problems with studying intercultural communication involve individual uniqueness, generalizing, and a lack of objectivity.

ACTIVITIES

1. Working with others, think of some of the ways that the changing U.S. demography will likely affect your lives.

2. Explain the link between culture and communication.

3. Working with others, discuss the various ways the dominant culture influences and controls the values, attitudes, and behaviors of co-cultures.

4. In a class or online group, discuss the components of an intercultural ethic. How would you recommend that such an ethic be internalized so that it is always present during intercultural communication?

5. Go to YouTube and type in "Examples of culture shock." After viewing some of the videos, try to isolate some of the most common causes of culture shock.

CONCEPTS AND QUESTIONS

1. What are some of the communication challenges that will have to be managed over the next 50 years?

2. How do you think the United States becoming a "minority majority" nation will influence dominant culture values?

3. If you were planning a trip to another country, what preparations would you make to minimize the effects of culture shock?

4. Why do you believe so many immigrants have a difficult time adapting to a new culture? What suggestions do you have for making that process less troublesome?

5. What are the relative merits of a fundamentalist and a relativist approach to developing an intercultural ethic?

6. As a member of a host culture, what responsibilities do you believe you have to make immigrants feel comfortable in their new cultural environment?

CHAPTER 2

SUMMARY

- Communication helps create identities, assists in gathering information about other people, helps fulfill interpersonal needs, and allows you to influence other people.

- Communication is a dynamic process in which people attempt to share their internal states with other people through the use of symbols.

- The components of communication include source, encoding, messages, channel, receiver, decoding, feedback, and noise.

- Communication is dynamic, symbolic, contextual, learned, and has a consequence.

- Culture and communication are so intertwined that it is easy to think that culture is communication and communication is culture.

- Culture is a set of human-made objective and subjective elements that in the past have increased the probability of survival and resulted in satisfaction for the participants in an ecological niche, and thus became shared among those who could communicate with each other because they had a common language and lived in the same time and place.[106]

- Culture informs its members regarding life; therefore, it reduces confusion and helps them predict what to expect from life.

- The elements that compose culture are religion, history, values, social organizations, and language.

- Culture is learned, transmitted from generation to generation, based on symbols, and is a dynamic and integrated system.

ACTIVITIES

1. Early in this chapter we discussed the notion that "Communication has a consequence." List at least two occasions when you have experienced a consequence due to a communication.

2. Attend a meeting (church service, lecture, social event, etc.) of a culture or co-culture different from you own. Try to notice the various ways cultural characteristics of that culture are being reflected in the interaction.

3. Make a list of the changes in your culture that you have observed in your lifetime. Discuss with a group of your classmates how those changes have affected intercultural communication.

4. Go to YouTube and search for "culture and folk tales." View some folktales from a variety of cultures. Note the "lessons" being taught in each folktale.

CONCEPTS AND QUESTIONS

1. What is meant by the statement: "In studying other cultures, we do so very often from the perspective of our own culture"[107]?

2. Explain how and why communication and culture are linked.

3. Why is it said that much of culture is invisible?

4. Explain what is meant by the phrase: "Communication is contextual." Can you think of examples of how context has influenced your behavior?

5. How does intercultural communication differ from everyday forms of communication?

CHAPTER 3

SUMMARY

- The deep structures of a culture, which include such elements as family (clans), state (community), and religion (worldview), are important because they carry a culture's most significant beliefs. Their messages endure, are deeply felt, and help supply much of a culture's identity.

- Families can take a variety of forms. The two most common are nuclear and extended.

- Traditional definitions of "family" are undergoing major changes in the United States.

- The influence of globalization (mass media and shifting migration patterns) in recent years has had a major impact on traditional family structures throughout the world.

- Families perform a series of key functions in all cultures. These functions include teaching members of the culture about reproduction, economics, socialization, values and religion, identity, and communication.

- The family also teaches gender roles, views on individualism and collectivism, perceptions of aging, and social skills.

ACTIVITIES

1. Interview someone from a culture different from your own using questions about child-rearing practices. You might inquire about methods of discipline, toys, games, topics discussed at the dinner table, and so forth. During the discussion share with them some "do's" and "don'ts" you were taught in your family.

2. Working with others, have each person discuss the "stories" that helped form his or her family and cultural identity.

3. Go to YouTube and search for "Jewish family Passover." View some of the family videos as they apply to how family rituals are taught to the children who are sharing the religious service associated with the Passover dinner.

4. Working with others, discuss the following question: Are child-rearing practices throughout the world more alike than they are different?

- Although all religions have some unique features, they share many similarities. These include, among other things, speculation about the meaning of life, sacred writings, rituals, and ethics.

- The six most prominent religious traditions are Christianity, Judaism, Islam, Hinduism, Buddhism, and Confucianism. These traditions present their members with advice on how to live life, and they offer explanations about death.

ACTIVITIES

1. Working with others, answer the following: "Why has religion been relevant to humankind for more than ten thousand years?"

2. Go to YouTube and search for videos that show a religious service inside a Catholic Church, an Islamic Mosque, and a Buddhist Temple. Make note of the rituals, messages, art, music, and space that you deem offer insight into each religious tradition. Also, what do these services have in common and how do they differ?

3. Working with others, discuss the following question: "How does my view of death compare with the beliefs found in the six great religious traditions?" As part of your discussion, include observations on how a person's perception of death might influence his or her behavior.

4. In a group, identify and discuss the common principles and practices you see among all of the major religions.

CONCEPTS AND QUESTIONS

1. Explain how its religious views are linked to a culture's lifestyle.

2. Explain the statement: "Religion is only one kind of worldview."

3. What common set of ethics can you identify from the six religious traditions discussed in this chapter?

4. Answer the question: "Is globalization good or bad for religion?"

5. What role might religion play in an intercultural communication encounter?

CHAPTER 6

SUMMARY

- Perception may be defined as the process whereby people convert external events and experiences into meaningful internal understanding.

- Perception is the primary mechanism by which you develop your worldview.

- Perception is selective, learned, culturally determined, consistent, and inaccurate.

- Values are enduring attitudes about the preference for one belief over another.

- Cultural pattern taxonomies are used to illustrate the dominant beliefs and values of a culture.

- When applying cultural patterns, you should keep in mind, we are more than our culture; cultural patterns are integrated, dynamic, and can be contradictory.

- According to Kohls, the dominant American cultural patterns include personal control over the environment, change, time and its control, equality, individualism/privacy, self-help, competition, future orientation, action/work orientation, informality, directness/openness/honesty, practicality/efficiency, and materialism/acquisitiveness.

- A prominent taxonomy of diverse culture patterns that explains both perceptual and communication differences is Hofstede's Values Dimension, which includes (1) individualism/collectivism, (2) uncertainty avoidance, (3) power distance, (4) masculinity/femininity, (5) long-term/short-term orientation, and (6) indulgence/restraint.

- Minkov has recently revealed the monumentalism/flexhumility value dimension.

- The Kluckhohn and Strodtbeck Value Orientation taxonomy includes (1) human nature, (2) the perception of nature, (3) time, (4) activity, and (5) relationships.

- In Hall's Context Orientation, high-context and low-context describe the degree to which individuals rely on internalized information.

- The GLOBE study examined personal and institutionalized values in 61 societies using cultural dimensions from Hofstede and Kluckhohn and Strodtbeck.

- For some dimensions, the GLOBE study found differences between personal and institutionalized values.

- The GLOBE study constructed 10 societal groupings and used statistical procedures to examine similarities and differences between those groups.

- For Ting-Toomey, face and facework take different forms and are valued differently across cultures.

- Face is a function of group affiliation in collectivistic cultures and is self-derived in individualistic cultures.

- In conflict situations, collectivistic cultures focus on other-face and mutual face, while individualistic cultures focus on self-face.

ACTIVITIES

1. Working with others, list the American cultural values mentioned in this chapter. Try to think of other values that are not included in the text. Then find examples from American advertising campaigns that illustrate those values. For example, the advertising slogan, "Just do it," from an athletic-shoe manufacturer, reflects the American values of perseverance and accomplishment.

2. Working with others and using Hofstede's value dimensions, make a list of behaviors found in American culture that reflect individualism, uncertainty avoidance, and femininity.

3. Working with others, make a list of typical American behaviors that relate to evil, good and evil, and good. How widespread are these behaviors within the culture?

4. Examine your behavior and determine how well you fit into the various degrees of time orientation.

5. Think about a recent conflict situation in which you participated (e.g., an argument with your significant other, your parents, or a stranger). What communication strategies did you use to give, maintain, or take face?

CONCEPTS AND QUESTIONS

1. How does a study of cultural values help you understand other cultures?

2. What differences in behavior are exhibited by people who come from cultures that have different activity orientations?

3. Examine the concept of high- and low-context cultures. What problems can you anticipate when you are communicating with someone who holds a different context orientation?

4. How can cultural differences in social perception affect the intercultural communication process?

5. What cultural values help explain why face is more important in Asian societies than in the United States?

CHAPTER 7

SUMMARY

- Identity is a highly abstract, dynamic, multifaceted concept that defines who you are.

- Identities can be categorized as human, social, and personal. Another classification scheme uses personal, relational, and communal.

- Every individual has multiple identities—racial, ethnic, gender, national, regional, organizational, personal, and perhaps cyber/fantasy—that act in concert. The importance of any single identity is a result of the context.

- Identity is acquired through interaction with other members of one's cultural group. The family exerts a primary influence on early identity formation.

- Identities are established through group membership and are enacted in a variety of ways, including rites of passage, personal appearance, and participation in commemorative events. Concepts of identity within the same group can change over time.

- Competent intercultural communication is achieved when the participants find commonality in ascribed and avowed identities.

- As society becomes increasingly multicultural, new concepts of cultural identity are evolving.

- Stereotyping occurs when people categorize experiences about another group of people and allow those categorizations to guide behavior. Stereotypes are applied to the behavioral norm of an entire group of people, not individual persons.

- A prejudice is a strong feeling or attitude toward a particular social group or thing.

- Racist individuals believe that their race/ethnicity is superior to another race/ethnicity of people.

- Ethnocentrism occurs when people believe their culture is superior to other cultures.

ACTIVITIES

1. Construct a list of as many of your identities as you can. Using the list, draw a pie chart with each identity receiving space proportional to that identity's importance to you. Compare your chart with other classmates' charts. Do members of the dominant and minority cultures differ in the amount of space allotted to their racial/ethnic identity? If so why?

2. Select an ethnicity other than your own and try to answer the five questions relating to avoiding stereotypes on page 224.

3. Working with some members of your class, try to compile a list of what you believe to be examples of American ethnocentrism.

4. What is the relationship among stereotypes, prejudice, racism, and ethnocentrism?

5. To learn more about your personal biases and preferences, take one of the Implicate Association Tests (IAT), sponsored by Harvard University. The tests can be taken anonymously online with results provided immediately. Go to "Project Implicit" at https://implicit.harvard.edu/implicit/demo/

CONCEPTS AND QUESTIONS

1. Why is an awareness of identity important in your personal life? What are some of the situations in which this awareness would be beneficial?

2. How would you define identity? How would you explain your identities to another person?

3. What are some of your different identities and how did you acquire them? What are some differences between your identities and those same identities in another culture?

4. How did you establish some of your identities? How do you enact those identities?

5. Discuss the following statement: "Prejudice can never be eliminated because it is so deeply rooted in human nature."

CHAPTER 8

SUMMARY

- Language allows people to exchange information and abstract ideas, and it is an integral part of identity. Based on the language they use, people are often categorized into groups such as age, gender, and socio-income level.

- The use of a common language enables people to organize and perform collective activities.

- Language is a set of shared symbols used to create meaning. The relationship between the symbol and the meaning is often arbitrary. There are usually variations within language groups, such as accents, dialects, argot, and slang.

- Corporate brands (i.e., names, logos, and slogans) are often understood across cultures irrespective of language.

- Every culture has conversational taboos—restrictions against some topics in certain contexts.

- Culture and language form a symbiotic relationship; without one, the other could not exist.

- Cultural values, or dimensions, can be reflected in the language used by a culture.

- Interpreters work with spoken or signed language and translators work with written messages. Consecutive interpretation is when you stop every minute or so to allow the translator to relay your message in the other language. Simultaneous interpretation is done while the speakers are talking in their native language. A good interpreter/translator should have knowledge of the target language, dialect, special terminology, and culture.

- English is the most common language used on the Internet at this time. The increasing number of Chinese users could alter this in the future. Some scholars have predicted a future oligarchy of major world languages—Chinese, Spanish, English, Arabic, and Russian.

- In any intercultural communication interaction it is probable that someone will be using a second language. Using a second language can be both physically and cognitively demanding.

- When speaking to someone who is using a second language, you should be mindful; monitor your speech rate, vocabulary, and nonverbal feedback; and check to ensure that the other person understands your message.

- One way of enhancing your intercultural communication competency is to study another language.

ACTIVITIES

1. Take four different English proper nouns (other than someone's name) and use online translation dictionaries to translate each noun into five different European languages. Do some of the translated nouns have a resemblance to the English nouns? If so, what are some possible reasons?

2. Talk with two or three people over sixty years of age and ask them for some examples of the slang they used in their younger days (e.g., "groovy man"). Try to compare it with slang that is

popular now. You can also do this by watching a movie made before 1960.

3. Working with an ESL speaker, compile a list of animals that are common to both of you, then compare the sounds that each of you hear those animals make.

4. Meet with one or two ESL speakers to identify the kinship terms they use in their native language (e.g., mother, brother, aunt, etc.). Do they have

kinship terms that vary with age differences? Do their kinship terms differ between own kin and other's kin? What cultural values do you think their terms reflect?

5. A Google search for "Where is the Speaker From?" should take you to the PBS website regional dialect quiz. Take the quiz. Explore the "Do You Speak American" site for additional information on U.S dialects. (The quiz is at http://www.pbs.org/speak/seatosea/americanvarieties/map/map.html)

CONCEPTS AND QUESTIONS

1. What images come to mind when you hear someone speaking English with an accent? Do different accents create different images? Try to decide why you form those images? Talk with others to see if they have the same experience.

2. Some countries have an official language (or languages), but others do not. What are the advantages and disadvantages of a country having an official language? Should the United States have an official language? Why?

3. How many "brands" can you think of that have international recognition? What type of meaning

(e.g., style, reliability, etc.) do you usually associate with those brands? Do other people assign the same meaning to them?

4. Construction of a simple sentence in English is Subject-Verb-Object (S-V-O). In Japanese and Korean it is S-O-V. What kind of problems might this present for simultaneous translation?

5. Some scholars think the world is moving toward an "oligarchy" of major economic power languages. Do you think this would be a good or bad occurrence? Why? What will happen to minority languages, and what will be the result?

CHAPTER 9

SUMMARY

- Nonverbal communication is important to the study of intercultural communication because people use nonverbal communication to express internal states, create identity, regulate interaction, repeat messages, and substitute actions for words.

- Nonverbal communication is culture-bound.

- Nonverbal communication involves all nonverbal stimuli in a communication setting that (1) are generated by both the source and his or her use of the environment and (2) have potential message value for the source and/or the receiver.

- Nonverbal messages may be intentional or unintentional.

- Nonverbal messages can work alone or in tandem with verbal messages.

- When studying nonverbal communication it should be remembered that nonverbal behaviors can be ambiguous, contain multiple meanings, and include cultural universals.

- Nonverbal behaviors and culture are similar in that both are learned, both are passed from generation to generation, and both involve shared understandings.

- The body is a major source of nonverbal messages. These messages are communicated by means of general appearance, skin color, attire, body movements (kinesics), posture, gestures, facial expressions, eye contact, touch, and paralanguage.

- Cultures differ in their perception and use of personal space, seating, and furniture arrangement.

- A culture's sense of time can be understood by learning how members of that culture view informal time and whether or not their orientation toward time is monochronic or polychronic.

- The use of silence varies from culture to culture.

- You can improve your nonverbal communication skill by monitoring your nonverbal actions, being sensitive to the context, employing feedback, being aware of nonverbal ambiguity, and knowing your culture.

ACTIVITIES

1. Go to YouTube and view video of services of three different religions: Catholic, Buddhist, and Jewish. Observe the nonverbal elements, noting particularly the differences in how members of each group use paralanguage, space, and touch.

2. Attend an event—social, religious, etc.—populated by people from a culture different from your own. Make note of any differences between your culture and the culture you are visiting as they apply to greeting behavior, eye contact, voice volume levels, seating arrangements, dress, and the like.

3. Locate pictures from magazines and newspapers that you believe are showing the following emotions through facial expressions: (a) anger, (b) joy,

(c) sadness, (d) fear, and (e) revulsion. Show these pictures to people from various cultures and see what interpretations they give to the facial expressions.

4. Go to YouTube and type in "Culture and body language." View some of the videos for examples of how cultures differ in their use of body language.

5. Watch a foreign film and look for examples of proxemics, touch, and facial expressions. Compare these to those of the dominant culture of the United States.

6. Explain the phrase: "Our nonverbal actions usually reflect our culture."

CONCEPTS AND QUESTIONS

1. Why is it useful to understand the nonverbal language of a culture?

2. What are some potential obstacles to accurately reading the nonverbal messages of other people?

3. What is meant by the following: "Most nonverbal communication is learned on the subconscious level."

4. Give your culture's interpretation of the following nonverbal actions:

- Two people are speaking loudly, waving their arms, and using many gestures.
- A customer in a restaurant waves his hand over his head and snaps his fingers loudly.
- An elderly woman dresses entirely in black.
- A young man dresses entirely in black.
- An adult pats a child's head.
- Two men kiss in public.

5. How can studying the intercultural aspects of nonverbal behavior assist you in discovering your own ethnocentrism? Give personal examples.

6. How late can you be for the following: (a) a class, (b) work, (c) a job interview, (d) a dinner party, or (e) a date with a friend? Ask this same question of members of two or three cultures other than your own.

7. What is meant by "Nonverbal communication is rule-governed"?

CHAPTER 10

SUMMARY

- The communication context is the socio-cultural environment in which communication takes place.

- Culturally diverse communication rules prescribe the appropriate behaviors for a variety of social contexts.

- Rules concerning informality, formality, assertiveness, interpersonal harmony, and social status can be found in every communication setting.

- Intercultural communication occurs in both international and domestic business settings.

- Business cultures influence management styles, leadership, and decision making.

- Negotiation styles differ across cultures, and differences are revealed in how cultures view the selection of negotiators and the actual negotiation process.

- Conflict in negotiations can frequently be reduced by identifying the cause, keeping an open mind, slowing down, and focusing on ideas rather than people.

- Schools are the primary means for pass a culture's history and traditions from generation to generation.

- Schools teach both formal and informal knowledge as well as the values of a culture.

- U.S. schools have become culturally and linguistically diverse.

- Learning preferences are particular ways in which individuals receive or process information.

- Culturally and linguistically diverse students face numerous obstacles in the classroom.

- Self-efficacy, immediacy, and empathy are especially important communicator qualities for educators working in a multicultural classroom.

- The development of appropriate communication strategies is requisite for creating effective classroom messages.

- Culture and language diversity are a source of problems in health care communication.

- Health belief systems can be divided into three categories—supernatural/mágico-religious, holistic, and scientific/biomedical—each with their own set of underlying premises.

- Cultural diversity leads to differences in beliefs about the causes and treatment of illness.

- Health care practices must accommodate a culturally diverse population.

- Health care practitioners should use an interpreter if they are not fluent in the language of their clients.

- Family members and friends are usually not good interpreters because of their connection to the patient and should only be used when there is no other alternative.

- Cultural diversity affects individual beliefs about death and dying, which can lead to conflicts between providers and families about when, if, and how to communicate bad news to patients.

ACTIVITIES

1. Working with others, determine some of the cultural problems that can arise in both a multinational and a domestic workforce. What are the problematic differences and similarities between the two workforces?

2. Working with others, develop a protocol for entering into negotiations with a team of Brazilian, Chinese, or Indian negotiators. What considerations must you give to their business culture in developing your plan?

3. Looking back upon your school experiences, devise a plan to integrate the various cultures in a multicultural classroom into a classroom community.

4. Working with others, devise a plan that would reconcile the different learning preferences of students in a sixth-grade classroom with the following student balance: six Latinos, eight European Americans, five African Americans, four Japanese, and one Iranian.

5. Identify the differences that exist between your various beliefs about the causes and treatment of illness and those found in another culture.

6. Examine your worldview and determine how important spirituality is to your health care.

7. Interview people from other cultures and ask them if they have encountered communication problems when seeking health care.

8. Ask members of other cultures how they view death and dying. Determine the role family plays in their approach to end-of-life decisions.

CONCEPTS AND QUESTIONS

1. What are some of the typical behaviors of U.S. negotiators that might create problems in a negotiation session with business representatives from another culture? What recommendations would you make for dealing with these problem areas?

2. Because many managers must now deal with a variety of cultures, they must learn to adapt to a variety of cultural differences in the workplace and at the bargaining table. Which cultural values and behaviors are the most important for the intercultural manager to learn about?

3. In a graduate seminar, a college professor has a new graduate student from China with excellent reading fluency in English but limited oral proficiency. What should be the professor's expectations of the Chinese student's participation in seminar discussions?

4. What training is necessary for health care providers to become effective intercultural communicators?

5. What policies should be in effect at a health care facility to determine when interpreters should be used?

6. Why might it be important to incorporate more than one medical belief system into the treatment plans of patients in a multicultural health care setting?

7. What are some cultural differences in beliefs about death and dying? How do these different belief systems affect the manner in which caregivers relate to their clients?

Notes

Chapter 1

1. "Action: The World Is Watching," *San Diego Union Tribune* (August 6, 2010), E-1.

2. *UNWTO Tourism Highlights: 2011 Edition*, (World Tourism Organization (UNWTO): United Nations, n.d.), 1, 6. http://mkt.unwto.org/sites/all/files/docpdf/unwtohighlights11enlr_0.pdf (accessed September 13, 2011).

3. "The house that Saud built," *The Economist* (July 23, 2011), 39.

4. "Will they still come?" *The Economist* (August 7, 2010), 55–56.

5. Ibid., 57.

6. A. Labi, "Collaborative International Degrees Are on the Rise," *The Chronicle of Higher Education* (September 11, 2011), http://chronicle.com/article/Joint-International-Degrees/128924/ (accessed September 13, 2011).

7. J. Gillis and C.W. Dugger, "U.N. Forecasts 10.1 Billion People by Century's End," *New York Times* (May 3, 2011), http://www.nytimes.com/2011/05/04/world/04population.html (accessed September 13, 2011).

8. "Crisis prevention," *The Economist* (February 26, 2011), 12.

9. "The others," *The Economist* (December 19, 2009), 107.

10. H. Yen, "Nation's population now 35 percent minorities," *San Diego Union-Tribune* (June 11, 2010), A6.

11. K.R. Humes, N.A. Jones, and R.R. Ramirez, *Overview of Race and Hispanic Origin: 2010* (U.S. Department of Commerce Economics and Statistics Administration, U.S. Census Bureau, March 2011), 3–5; S.R. Ennis, M. Ríos-Vargas, and N.G. Albert, *The Hispanic Population: 2010* (U.S. Department of Commerce Economics and Statistics Administration, U.S. Census Bureau, May 2011), 2–11.

12. W.H. Frey, *America's Diverse Future: Initial Glimpses at the U.S. Child Population from the 2010 Census* (Washington, D.C.: Metropolitan Policy Program at Brookings, 2011), 6–8.

13. R. Brownstein, "The Gray And The Brown: The Generational Mismatch," *National Journal* (January 30, 2011), http://www.nationaljournal.com/magazine/the-gray-and-the-brown-the-generational-mismatch-20100724?print=true (accessed September 16, 2011).

14. L.M. Howden and J.A. Meyer, *Age and Sex Composition: 2010* (U.S. Department of Commerce Economics and Statistics Administration, U.S. Census Bureau, May 2011).

15. D. Cave, "A Generation Gap Over Immigration," *New York Times* (May 17, 2010), http://www.nytimes.com/2010/05/18/us/18divide.html (accessed September 16, 2011).

16. Brownstein, 2011.

17. Ibid.

18. J.Q. Adams and J.R. Welsch, "Multiculturalism: The Manifest Destiny of the U.S.A.: An Interview With Ronald Takaki," *Multicultural Perspectives*, 11:4 (October–December, 2009), 227.

19. "Nation's Foreign-Born Population Nears 37 Million," *Newsroom: US Census Bureau* (October 19, 2010), http://www.census.gov/newsroom/releases/archives/foreignborn_population/cb10-159.html (accessed September 17, 2010).

20. S. Tavernise and R. Gebeloff, "Immigrants Make Paths to Suburbia, Not Cities," *New York Times* (December 15, 2010), A13; "One nation, divisible," *The Economist* (November 20, 2010), 33.

21. E. Schumacher-Matos, "To 'out-innovate,' we must let more immigrants in," *Washington Post*, (January 28, 2011), http://www.washingtonpost.com/wp-dyn/content/article/2011/01/27/AR2011012704371.html (accessed September 17, 2011).

22. C. Page, "How to do multiculturalism right," *Houston Chronicle* (February 20, 2011), http://www.chron.com/disp/story.mpl/editorial/outlook/7438689.html (accessed September 7, 2011).

23. T.L. Friedman, "A Theory of Everything (Sort Of)," *New York Times* (August 13, 2011), http://www.nytimes.com/2011/08/14/opinion/sunday/Friedman-a-theory-of-everyting-sort-of.html?partner=rssnyt&emc=rss (accessed August 22, 2011).

24. "Statistics," *facebook* (2011), http://www.facebook.com/press/info.php?statistics (accessed October 31, 2011).

25. M. Magnier, "In India, anti-corruption activist declares victory," *Los Angeles Times* (August 28, 2011), A3.

26. "A new sort of togetherness," *The Economist* (May 22, 2010), 64.

27. J. Wildens, "Beyond Belief," *San Diego Union-Tribune* (January 23, 2011), F-4.

28. N.D. Kristof, "The Daily Me," *New York Times* (March 19, 2009), http://www.nytimes.com/2009/03/19/opinion/19kristof.html (accessed September 19, 2011).

29. "Schumpter: The wiki way," *The Economist* (September 25, 2010), 82; "Love at first byte," *The Economist* (January 1, 2011), 51–53; R. Bansal, "India's Remix Generation," *Current History*, 106: 699 (April 2007), 171.

30. C. Seymour-Smith, *Dictionary of Anthropology* (Boston, MA: G.K. Hall, 1986), 262; P. Whitten, "Society," in *Encyclopedia of Anthropology*, D.E. Hunter and P. Whitten (eds.) (New York: Harper & Row, 1976), 361; A.G. Johnson, *The Blackwell Dictionary of Sociology*, 2nd ed. (Malden, MA: Blackwell, 2000), 297–98.

31. R.W. Nolan, *Communicating and Adapting Across Cultures* (Westport, CT: Bergin and Garvey, 1999), 19.

32. G. Ferraro and S. Andreatta, *Cultural Anthropology: An Applied Perspective*, 8th ed. (Belmont, CA: Wadsworth Cengage Learning, 2010), 192.

33. H. Triandis, *Culture and Social Behavior* (New York: McGraw-Hill, 1994), 265.

34. S. Lysgaard, "Adjustment in a Foreign Society: Norwegian Fulbright Grantees Visiting the United States," *International Social Science Bulletin*, 7 (1955), 45–51; K. Oberg, "Culture Shock: An Adjustment in New Cultural Environments," *Practical Anthropology*, 7 (1960), 177–182; J.T. Gullahorn and J.E. Gullahorn, "An Extension of the U-Curve Hypothesis," *Journal of Social Issues*, 19:3 (1963), 33–47.

35. D. Nash, "The Course of Sojourner Adaptation: A New Test of the U-Curve Hypothesis," *International Journal of Intercultural Relations*, 50:3 (1991), 283–286; C. Ward, Y. Okura, A. Kennedy, and T. Kojima, "The U-Curve on Trial: A Longitudinal Study of Psychological and Sociocultural Adjustment During Cross-Cultural Transition," *International Journal of Intercultural Relations*, 11:2 (1998), 168–180; F.L. Hamela, K. Chikamori, Y. Ono, and J. Williams, "First contact: Initial responses to cultural disequilibrium in a short term teaching exchange program," *International Journal of Intercultural Relations*, 34 (2010), 600–614; K.F. Gaw, "Reverse culture shock in students returning from overseas," *International Journal of Intercultural Relations*, 24 (2000), 83–104; N.M. Sussman, "Testing the cultural identity model of the cultural transition cycle: sojourners return home." *International Journal of Intercultural Relations*, 26 (2002), 391–408.

36. N.J. Adler, *International Dimensions of Organizational Behavior*, 5th ed. (Mason, OH: Thompson South-Western, 2008), 278; Y.Y. Kim, *Becoming Intercultural* (Thousand Oaks, CA: Sage, 2001), 54–61.

37. A. Kosic and K. Phalet, "Ethnic Categorization of Immigrants: The Role of Prejudice, Perceived Acculturation Strategies and Group Size," *International Journal of Intercultural Relations*, 30 (2006), 770.

38. A. Mak, M. Westwood, and F. Ishiyama, "Optimising Conditions for Learning Sociocultural Competencies for Success," *International Journal of Intercultural Relations*, 23 (1999), 80.

39. J.W. Berry, "Acculturation: Living Successfully in Two Cultures," *International Journal of Intercultural Relations*, 29 (2005), 698–699.

40. C. Ward, S. Bochner, and A. Furnham, *The Psychology of Culture Shock*, 2nd ed. (New York: Routledge, 2001), 271.

41. A. Harper, "Cultural Adaptation and Intercultural Communication: Some Barriers and Bridges," paper presented to the Annual Convention of the Western Speech Communication Association, Monterey, CA, Feb 1997, 13.

42. C. Gouttefarde, "Host National Culture Shock: What Management Can Do," *European Business Review*, 92 (4) (1992), 1.

43. "The future of mobility," *The Economist* (May 28, 2011), 87.

44. R.K. Johannesen, *Ethics in Human Communication*, 4th ed. (Prospect Heights, IL: Waveland Press, 1996), 1.

45. M.G. Harper, "Ethical Multiculturalism: An Evolutionary Concept Analysis," *Advances in Nursing Science*, 29 (2), 2006, 110–124, 112.

46. M.C. Brannigan, *Ethics Across Cultures: An Introductory Text with Readings* (Boston: McGraw Hill, 2005), 13.

47. Harper, 2006, 12.

48. G. Harman and J.J. Thomson, *Moral Relativism and Moral Objectivity* (Cambridge, MA: Blackwell, 1996), 3.

49. W.A. Haviland, H.E.L. Prins, D. Walrath, and B. McBride, *Anthropology: The Human Challenge*, 13th ed. (Belmont, CA: Wadsworth Cengage Learning, 2011), 337.

50. C.J. Robertson and W.F. Crittenden, "Mapping Moral Philosophies: Strategic Implications for Multinational Firms," *Strategic Management Journal*, 24 (4), (April 2003), 386.

51. S. Boorstein, *It's Easier Than You Think: The Buddhist Way to Happiness* (New York: HarperCollins, 1997), 60.

52. N. Burbules, *Dialogue in Teaching* (New York: Teacher's College Press, 1993), 81–82.

53. Johannesen, 1996, 257.

54. M.K. DeGenova, *Families in Cultural Context: Strength and Challenges in Diversity* (Mountain View, CA: Mayfield Publishing Company, 1997), 6.

55. J. Beverluis, *A Source Book for the Earth's Community of Religions* (New York: Global Education Associates, 1995), 138.

56. S. Huntington, *The Conflict of Civilizations and the Remaking of World Order* (New York: Simon and Schuster, 1996), 320.

57. D.C. Barnlund, *Communication Styles of Japanese and Americans* (Belmont, CA: Wadsworth, 1989), 92–93.

58. R. Evanoff, "A Communicative Approach to Intercultural Dialogue on Ethics," in *Intercultural Communication: A Reader*, 13th ed., L.A. Samovar, R.E. Porter, and E.R. McDaniel, eds. (Boston, MA: Wadsworth Cengage Learning, 2011), 477.

59. S. Pinker, *The Blank Slate: The Modern Denial of Human Nature* (New York: Viking, 2002), 34.

60. J. Hooker, *Working Across Cultures* (Stanford, CA: Stanford University Press, 2003), 60.

61. R.L. Coles, *Race and Family: A Structural Approach* (Thousand Oaks, CA: Sage Publications, 2006), xi.

62. *English Dictionary* (allwords.com), http://www.allwords.com/word-objectivity.html (accessed September 14, 2011).

63. Ferraro and Andreatta, 2010, 15.

64. H.L. Tischler, *Introduction to Sociology*, 10th ed. (Belmont, CA: Wadsworth Cengage Learning, 2011), 53.

Chapter 2

1. C.F. Keating, "World Without Words: Messages from Face and Body," in *Psychology and Culture*, W.J. Lonner and R.S. Malpass, eds. (Boston: Allyn and Bacon, 1994), 175.

2. J.T. Wood, *Communication Mosaics*, 6th ed. (Boston, MA: Wadsworth Cengage Learning, 2011), 181.

3. See R.E. Porter and L.A. Samovar, "Cultural Influences on Emotional Expression: Implications for Intercultural Communication," in *Handbook of Communication and Emotion: Research, Theory, Applications, and Contexts*, P.A. Andersen and L.K. Guerrero, eds. (New York: Academic Press, 1998), 451–472.

4. R.B. Adler and R.F. Proctor II, *Looking Out, Looking In*, 13th ed. (Boston, MA: Wadsworth Cengage Learning, 2011), 8.

5. F.E.X. Dance and C.E. Larson, *Speech Communication: Concepts and Behavior* (New York: Holt, Rinehart, and Winston, 1972).

6. D.M. Dunn and L.J. Goodnight, *Communication: Embracing Difference*, 3rd ed. (Boston, MA: Allyn & Bacon, 2011), 11.

7. S. Trenholm and A. Jensen, *Interpersonal Communication*, 6th ed. (New York: Oxford University Press, 2008), 5.

8. S.W. Littlejohn, *Theories of Human Communication*, 3rd ed. (Belmont, CA: Wadsworth, 1989), 152.

9. S. Shimanoff, *Communication Rules: Theory and Research* (Beverly Hills, CA: Sage Publications, 1980), 57.

10. E.T. Hall and M.R. Hall, *Understanding Cultural Differences: Germans, French, and Americans* (Yarmouth, ME: Intercultural Press, 1990), 18.

11. R.M. Berko, L.B. Rosenfeld, and L.A. Samovar, *Connecting: A Culture-Sensitive Approach to Interpersonal Communication*, 2nd ed. (New York: Harcourt Brace, 1997), 10.

12. J.T. Wood, *Interpersonal Communication: Everyday Encounters*, 5th ed. (Belmont, CA: Thomson Wadsworth, 2007), 30.

13. E.T. Hall, *Beyond Culture* (Garden City, NY: Anchor Doubleday, 1977), 14.

14. J. Peoples and G. Bailey, *Humanity: An Introduction to Cultural Anthropology*, 8th ed. (Belmont, CA: Wadsworth Cengage Learning, 2009), 23.

15. G.A. Rodriguez, *Bringing up Latino Children in a Bicultural World* (New York: Fireside, 1999), 20.

16. E.T. Hall, *The Silent Language* (New York: Doubleday, 1959), 169.

17. Wood, 2011, 157.

18. G. Hofstede, *Culture's Consequences: Comparing Values, Behaviors, Institutions, and Organizations Across Nations*, 2nd ed. (Thousand Oaks, CA: Sage Publications, 2001), 10.

19. R.W. Nolan, *Communicating and Adapting Across Cultures: Living and Working in the Global Village* (Westport, CT: Bergin and Garvey, 1999), 3.

20. W.A. Haviland, H.E.L. Prins, D. Walrath, and B. McBride, *Cultural Anthropology: The Human Challenge*, 13th ed. (Belmont, CA: Wadsworth Cengage Learning, 2011), 325.

21. C. Chiu and Y. Hong, *Social Psychology of Culture* (New York: Psychology Press, 2006), 17.

22. L.E. Harrison and S.P. Huntington, eds. *Culture Matters: How Values Shape Human Progress* (New York: Basic Books, 2000), xv.

23. W.J. Lonner and R.S. Malpass, "When Psychology and Culture Meet: Introduction to Cross-Cultural Psychology," in *Psychology and Culture*, W.J. Lonner and R.S. Malpass, eds. (Boston: Allyn and Bacon, 1994), 7.

24. H. Triandis, *Culture and Social Behavior* (New York: McGraw-Hill, 1994), 23.

25. T. Sowell, "Cultural Diversity: A World View," in *Intercultural Communication: A Reader*, 12th ed., L.A. Samovar and R.E. Porter, eds. (Belmont, CA: Wadsworth, 2009), 430.

26. G. Ferraro, *Cultural Anthropology: An Applied Perspective*, 7th ed. (Belmont, CA: Thomson Wadsworth, 2008), 344–347.

27. G. Bailey and J. Peoples, *Essentials of Cultural Anthropology*, 2nd ed.

(Belmont, CA: Wadsworth Cengage Learning, 2011), 26.

28. J.J. Macionis, *Society: The Basics*, 4th ed. (Upper Saddle River, NJ: Prentice Hall, 1998), 34.

29. R.H. Lavenda and E.A. Schultz, *Core Concepts in Cultural Anthropology*, 4th ed. (New York: McGraw Hill, 2010), 90.

30. C.M. Parkes, P. Laungani, and B. Young, eds. *Death and Bereavement Across Cultures* (New York: Routledge, 1997), 15.

31. Haviland, Prins, Walrath, and McBride, 2011, 331.

32. Nolan, 1999, 3.

33. Haviland, Prins, Walrath, and McBride, 2011, 369.

34. G. Bailey and J. Peoples, 2011, 36.

35. Haviland, Prins, Walrath, and McBride, 2011, 324.

36. S.P. Huntington, "The West Unique, Not Universal," *Foreign Affairs*, Nov/ Dec 1996, 28.

37. R. Brislin, *Understanding Culture's Influence on Behavior*, 2nd ed. (Fort Worth, TX: Harcourt College Publishers, 2000), 10.

38. H.L. Shapiro, *Aspects of Culture* (New Brunswick, NJ: Rutgers University Press, 1956), 54.

39. Haviland, Prins, Walrath, and McBride, 2011, 31,

40. H.W. Gardiner and C. Kosmitzki, *Lives Across Cultures: Cross-Cultural Human Development*, 4th ed. (Boston: Allyn and Bacon, 2008), 66–67.

41. E.T. Hall, *The Hidden Dimension* (New York, NY: Doubleday, 1966).

42. J.T. Wood, *Communication in Our Lives*, 5th ed. (Belmont, CA: Wadsworth Cengage Learning, 2009), 169.

43. E. Schuster, "Proverbs: A Path to Understanding Different Cultures," *Journal of Extension*, 36:1 (1998), http://www.joe.org/joe/1998february/tt2.php (accessed June 6, 2011).

44. J.M. Sellers, *Folk Wisdom of Mexico* (San Francisco: Chronicle Books, 1994), 7.

45. E.G. Seidensticker, in *Even Monkeys Fall from Trees, and Other Japanese*

Proverbs, D. Galef, ed. (Rutland, VT: Charles E. Tuttle, 1987), 8.

46. W. Mieder, *Encyclopedia of World Proverbs: A Treasury of Wit and Wisdom Through the Ages* (New Jersey: Prentice Hall, 1986), xi.

47. Ibid., x.

48. C. Roy, "Mexican *Dichos*: Lessons through Language," in *Intercultural Communication: A Reader*, 13th ed., L.A. Samovar and R.E. Porter, eds. (Belmont, CA: Wadsworth Cengage Learning, 2009), 288.

49. For a further listing of international proverbs, see S. Arnott, *Peculiar Proverbs: Weird Words of Wisdom from Around the World* (New York: St. Martin's Press, 2008; L.P. Canlas, *International Proverbs* (Philadelphia: Infinity Publishing, 2000); G. De Lay, P. Darbo and K. Potter, *International Dictionary of Proverbs* (New York: Hippocrene Books, Inc., 1998); J. Speake, *The Oxford Dictionary of Proverbs* (New York: Oxford University Press, 2003); G. Titelman, *Popular Proverbs and Sayings* (New York: Gramercy Books, 1997).

50. J. Yolen, ed. *Favorite Folktales From Around the World* (New York: Pantheon Books, 1986), 8.

51. R. Bini, ed. *A World Treasury of Myths, Legends, and Folktales* (New York: Harry N. Abrams, Inc., 2000), 6.

52. G. Ferraro and S. Andreatta, *Cultural Anthropology: An Applied Perspective* (Belmont, CA: Wadsworth Cengage Learning, 2010), 390.

53. "World Folktales," ESL Station (ESL Department, San Jose City College, n.d.), http://www.eslstation.net/the REALWF/Introduction.htm (accessed June 6, 2011).

54. G.A. Rodriguez, *Bringing up Latino Children in a Bicultural World* (New York: Fireside, 1999), 269.

55. Ibid., 270.

56. P'u Sung-ling, "The Taoist Priest of Lao-Shan [Folktale]," in *Children and Youth in History*, Item #204, http://chnm.gmu.edu/cyh/primary-sources/204 (accessed June 6, 2011).

57. C. Tomlinson, "Myth of Invincibility Draws Children to Battles in Zaire," *San Diego Union-Tribune*, (Dec 17, 1996), A21.

58. Ferraro, 2008, 382.

59. R. Erdoes and A. Ortiz, eds. *American Indian Myths and Legends* (New York: Pantheon, 1984), xv.

60. J. Campbell, *The Power of Myth* (New York: Doubleday, 1988), 6.

61. "Give Us Back Our Treasures," *This Week* (April 30, 2010), 8.

62. G.F. Will, "Understanding America through Art," *The San Diego Union-Tribune* (December 25, 2008), B6.

63. C. Strickland, *Art History* (New York: Sterling Publishing Co., 2006), 1.

64. S. Nanda, *Cultural Anthropology*, 5th ed. (Belmont, CA: Wadsworth, 1994), 403.

65. Ferraro and Andreatta, 2010, 381.

66. Ibid.

67. E.H. Gombrich, *The Story of Art* (New York: Phaidon, 1955), 102.

68. A. Hunter and J. Sexton, *Contemporary China* (New York: St. Martin's Press, 1999), 158.

69. J. Campbell, *Myths to Live By* (New York: Penguin, 1972), 106.

70. Ibid.

71. Haviland, Prins, Walrath, and McBride, 2011, 619.

72. Ibid.

73. M. Sedgwick, *Islam and Muslims* (Boston: Intercultural Press, 2006), 132.

74. Haviland, Prins, Walrath, and McBride, 2011, 606.

75. Wood, 2010, 296.

76. F. Williams, *The New Communications*, 2nd ed. (Belmont, CA: Wadsworth, 1989), 269.

77. "New Study Finds Children Age Zero to Six Spend As Much Time With TV, Computers and Video Games As Playing Outside," *Kaiser Family Foundation* (October 28, 2003), http://www.kff.org/entmedia/entmedia102803nr.cfm (accessed June 6, 2011).

78. F.P. Delgado, "The Nature of Power Across Communicative and Cultural Borders" (paper presented at the Annual Convention of the Speech Communication Association, Miami Beach, FL, Nov 1993), 12.

79. See G. Gerbner, L. Gross, M. Morgan, and N. Signorielli, "Living With Television: The Dynamics of the Cultivation Process," in *Perspectives on Media Effects*, J. Bryant and D. Zillman, eds. (Hillsdale, N. J.: Lawrence Erlbaum, 1986), 17–40; G. Gerbner, "Advancing on the Path of Righteousness (Maybe)," in *Cultivation Analysis: New Directions in Media Effects Research*, N. Signorielli and M. Morgan, eds. (Newbury Park, CA: Sage, 1990); J.D. Robinson, "Media Portrayals and Representations," in *21st Century Communication: A Reference Handbook*, W.F. Eadie, ed. (Thousand Oaks, CA: Sage, 2009), 497–505.

80. Ibid.

81. S. Tubbs and S. Moss, *Human Communication*, 11th ed. (New York: McGraw-Hill Higher Education, 2008), 535.

82. J.C. Hersey and A. Jordan, *Reducing Children's TV Time to Reduce the Risk of Childhood Overweight: The Children's Media Use Study* (Atlanta: Centers for Disease Control and Prevention; Nutrition and Physical Activity Communication Team (NuPAC), March 2007), 8, http://www.cdc.gov/obesity/downloads/TV_Time_Highlights.pdf (accessed June 6, 2011).

83. Peoples and Bailey, 2009, 236.

84. Macionis, 1998, 69.

85. J.T. Wood, *Gendered Lives: Communication, Gender, and Culture* (Boston, MA: Wadsworth Cengage Learning, 2011), 145.

86. See M.J. Gannon and R. Pillai, *Understanding Global Cultures: Metaphorical Journeys Through 29 Nations, Clusters of Nations, Continents, and Diversity*, 4th ed. (Thousand Oaks, CA: Sage Publications, 2010).

87. Ibid., xiii.

88. R. Brislin, *Understanding Culture's Influence on Behavior* (Fort Worth, TX: Harcourt Brace Jovanovich, 1993), 6.

89. J.M. Charon, *The Meaning of Sociology*, 6th ed. (Upper Saddle River, NJ: Prentice Hall, 1999), 4.

90. Ibid., 94.

91. Ferraro, 2008, 29.

92. Bailey and Peoples, 2011, 27.

93. Macionis, 1998, 33.

94. H.L. Weinberg, *Levels of Knowing and Existence* (New York: Harper and Row, 1959), 157.

95. D.G. Bates and F. Plog, *Cultural Anthropology*, 3rd ed. (New York: McGraw-Hill, 1990), 20.

96. M.V. Angrosino, *The Culture of the Sacred: Exploring the Anthropology of Religion* (Prospect Heights, IL: Waveland Press, Inc., 2004), 202.

97. Haviland, Prins, Walrath, and McBride, 2011, 335.

98. Lavenda and Schultz, 2010, 32.

99. L. Beamer and I. Varner, *Intercultural Communication in the Global Workplace*, 5th ed. (New York: McGraw-Hill Irwin, 2011), 25.

100. Haviland, Prins, Walrath, and McBride, 2011, 409.

101. D.C. Barnlund, *Communicative Styles of Japanese and Americans: Images and Realities* (Belmont, CA: Wadsworth, 1989), 192.

102. E.T. Hall, *Beyond Culture* (New York: Doubleday, 1976), 13–14.

103. Ferraro and Andreatta, 2010, 41.

104. R. Benedict, *Patterns of Culture*, 2nd ed. (New York: Mentor, 1948), 2.

105. R. Benedict, *Patterns of Culture* (Boston: Houghton Mifflin, 1934), 21–22.

106. Triandis, 1994, 23.

107. A. Giddens, *Runaway World*, 2nd ed. (New York: Routledge, 2003), 10.

Chapter 3

1. W.A. Haviland, H.E.L. Prins, D. Walrath, and B. McBride, *Cultural Anthropology: The Human Challenge*, 13th ed. (Belmont, CA: Wadsworth Cengage Learning, 2011), 331.

2. D.G. Bates and F. Plog, *Cultural Anthropology*, 3rd ed. (New York, McGraw-Hill, 1990), 285.

3. S. Roberts, "Ethnic Clashes in China: Uighurs vs. Han Chinese." *The Washington Post* (July 8, 2009), http://www.washingtonpost.com/wp-dyn/content/discussion/2009/07/07/DI2009070701491.html (accessed May 28, 2011).

4. "The Perpetual War," *The Week*, October 22, 2010, 15.

5. S.P. Huntington, "The Clash of Civilizations," *Foreign Affairs*, 72 (1993), 22.

6. Ibid., 25.

7. F.P. Delgado, "The Nature of Power Across Communicative and Cultural Borders" (paper delivered at the Annual Convention of the Speech Communication Association, Miami Beach, FL, Nov 1993), 11.

8. "Kenyan anti-cartoon protester shot," *World: CNN.com* (Feb 9, 2006), http://edition.cnn.com/2006/WORLD/asiapcf/02/10/cartoon.protests/index.html (accessed July 2, 2008); A. Akram, "Muslim Americans split on cartoons," *The Christian Science Monitor* (Feb 9, 2006), http://www.csmonitor.com/2006/0209/p02s01-ussc.html (accessed May 29, 2011).

9. J.M. Charon, *The Meaning of Sociology*, 6th ed. (Upper Saddle River, NJ: Prentice Hall, 1999), 27.

10. S.P. Huntington, *The Clash of Civilizations and the Remaking of World Order* (New York: Simon and Schuster, 1996), 128.

11. S. Kakar, *The Colors of Violence: Cultural Identities, Religion, and Conflict* (Chicago: University of Chicago Press, 1996), 189.

12. Huntington, 1996, 21.

13. M. Guirdham, *Communicating Across Cultures* (West Lafayette, IN: Ichor Business Books, 1999), 63.

14. E.L. Lynch and M.J. Hanson, *Developing Cross-Cultural Competence: A Guide for Working with Young Children and Their Families* (Baltimore: Paul H. Brookes, 1992), 358.

15. M.L. Andersen and H.F. Taylor, *Sociology: The Essentials*, 6th ed. (Belmont, CA: Wadsworth Cengage Learning, 2011), 314.

16. D.E. Brown, *Human Universal* (New York: McGraw-Hill, 1991).

17. E.Y. Kim, *The Yin and Yang of American Culture* (Yarmouth, ME: Intercultural Press, 2001), 159.

18. Ibid.

19. B.G. Farrell, *Family: The Making of an Idea, an Institution, and a Controversy in American Culture* (Boulder, CO: Westview Press, 1999), 5.

20. F.I. Nye and F.M. Berardo, *The Family: Its Structures and Interaction* (New York: Macmillan, 1973), 3.

21. R. Rhodes, *1001 Unforgettable Quotes about God, Faith, & the Bible* (Eugene, OR: Harvest House, 2011), 92.

22. D.E. Smith and G. Mosby, "Jamaican Child-Rearing Practices: The Role of Corporal Punishment," *Adolescence*, 28 (2003), 369.

23. M.K. DeGenova and F.P. Rice, "Why Examine Family Background?" in *Making Connections: Readings in Relational Communication*, 4th ed., K.M. Galvin and J.P. Cooper, eds. (Los Angeles: Roxbury Press, 2006), 104.

24. A. Swerdlow, R. Bridenthal, J. Kelly, and P. Vine, *Families in Flux* (New York: Feminist Press, 1989), 64.

25. B. Strong, C. DeVault, and T.F. Cohen, *The Marriage and Family Experience*, 11th ed. (Belmont, CA: Wadsworth Cengage Learning, 2011), 11.

26. M.A. Lamanna and A. Riedman, *Marriage and Families: Making Choices in a Diverse Society*, 10th ed. (Belmont, CA: Thomson Wadsworth, 2009), 9.

27. Ibid.

28. J. Yerby, N. Buerkel-Rothfuss, and A.P. Bochner, *Understanding Family Communication*, 2nd ed. (Scottsdale, AZ: Gorsuch Scarisbrick Publishers, 1995), 13.

29. G. Ferraro and S. Andreatta, *Cultural Anthropology: An Applied Perspective*, 8th ed. (Belmont, CA: Wadsworth Cengage Learning, 2010), 226.

30. Ibid., 227.

31. H.C. Triandis, *Culture and Social Behavior* (New York: McGraw-Hill, 1994), 159.

32. Haviland, Prins, Walrath, and McBride, 2011, 493.

33. H.L. Tischler, *Introduction to Sociology*, 10th ed. (Belmont, CA: Wadsworth Cengage Learning, 2011), 269.

34. Triandis, 1994, 159.

35. R.M. Berko, L.B. Rosenfeld, and L.A. Samovar, *Connecting: A Culture-Sensitive Approach to Interpersonal Communication Competency* (Fort Worth, TX: Harcourt Brace Jovanovich, 1997), 331.

36. Tischler, 2011, 267.

37. B. Strong, C. DeVault, and T.F. Cohen, 2011, 74.

38. U.S. Census Bureau, "*U.S. Census Bureau Reports Men and Women Wait Longer to Marry*" (November 10, 2010), http://www.census.gov/newsroom/releases/archives/families_households/cb 10-174.html (accessed December 16, 2010).

39. Andersen and Taylor, 2011, 319–323.

40. M.A. Lamanna and A. Riedman, *Marriage and Families: Making Choices in a Diverse Society*, 10th ed. (Belmont, CA: Thomson Wadsworth, 2009), 62.

41. "After 40 Years, Interracial Marriage Flourishing," www.msnbc.com (April 15, 2007), http://www.msnbc.msn.com/id/18090277/ (accessed May 29, 2011).

42. Pew Social Trends Staff, *The Decline of Marriage and the Rise of New Families* (Pew Social and Demographic Trends: November 18, 2010), http://pewsocialtrends.org/2010/11/18/the-decline-of-marriage-and-rise-of-new-families/2/#ii-overview (accessed May 29, 2011).

43. Ibid.

44. G. Bailey and J. Peoples, *Essentials of Cultural Anthropology*, 2nd. ed. (Belmont, CA: Wadsworth Cengage Learning, 2011), 11.

45. S. McGregor, "Globalization, Family Well-Being, and a Culture of Peace," *Journal of Family and Consumer Sciences*, 95 (2003), 60.

46. B.S. Trask, *Globalization and Families: Accelerated Systemic Social Change*, (New York: Springer, 2010), v.

47. R.H. Lavenda and E.A. Schultz, *Core Concepts in Cultural Anthropology*, 4th ed. (New York: McGraw-Hill Higher Education, 2010), 189.

48. Ibid.

49. Bailey and Peoples, 2011, 254–255.

50. S.D. Smith, "Global Families," in *Families in Global and Multicultural Perspective*, 2nd ed., B.B. Ingoldsby and S.D. Smith, eds. (Thousand Oaks, CA: Sage Publications, 2006), 21.

51. "UNFPA State of World Population 2006'" *United Nations Population Fund* (2006), http://www.unfpa.org/swp/2006/english/chapter_1/index.html (accessed May 18, 2011).

52. Ibid.

53. Smith, 2006, 18.

54. M. Hefti, "Globalization and Migration" (paper presented at the European Solidarity Conference on the Philippines, *Responding to Globalization*, Zurich, Switzerland, Sep 1997), http://www.philsol.nl/solcon/Anny-Misa.htm (accessed June 30, 2008).

55. Haviland, Prins, Walrath, McBride, 2011, 498.

56. Basler, "Hong Kong Journal: Underpaid, Overworked and From the Philippines," the *New York Times*, (August 28, 1990), http://www.nytimes.com/1990/08/28/world/hong-kong-journal-underpaid-overworked-and-from-the-philippines.html (accessed May 29, 2011).

57. Hefti, 1997.

58. Bailey and Peoples, 2011, 254.

59. J. Bunim, "Forgotten Families," *Mother Jones* (April 21, 2006), http://www.motherjones.com/interview/2006/04/heymann.html (accessed May 29, 2011).

60. A. Giddens, *Runaway World: How Globalization Is Reshaping Our Lives* (New York: Routledge, 2003), 4.

61. Strong, DeVault, and Cohen, 2011, 13.

62. Tischler, 2011, 269.

63. Lamanna and Riedmann, 2011, 30.

64. Strong, DeVault, and Cohen, 2011, 14.

65. K.J. Christiano, "Religion and the Family in Modern American Culture," in *Family, Religion and Social Change in Diverse Societies*, S.K. Houseknecht and J.G. Pankhurst, eds. (New York: Oxford University Press, 2000), 43.

66. J.W. Berry, Y.H. Poortinga, M.H. Segall, and P.R. Dasen, *Cross-Cultural Psychology: Research and Application* (New York: Cambridge University Press, 1992), 22.

67. M.I. Al-Kaysi, *Morals and Manners in Islam: A Guide to Islamic Ābāb* (United Kingdom: The Islamic Foundation, 1986), 36.

68. A. Burguiere, C. Klapisch-Zuber, M. Segalen, and F. Zonabend, *A History of the Family* (Cambridge, MA: Harvard University Press, 1996), 9.

69. K.K. Lee, "Family and Religion in Traditional and Contemporary Korea," in *Religion and the Family in East Asia*, G.A. De Vos and T. Sofue, eds. (Berkeley, CA: University of California Press, 1986), 185.

70. K.A. Ocampo, M. Bernal, and G.P. Knight, "Gender, Race, and Ethnicity: The Sequencing of Social Constancies," in *Ethnic Identity: The Formation and Transmission among Hispanic and Other Minorities*, M.E. Bernal and G.P. Knight, eds. (New York: State University of New York Press, 1993), 106.

71. *Cultural Perspective on Families* (Center for Cross-Cultural Research Western Washington University, n.d.) http://www.ac.wwu.edu/~culture/unit13.htm (accessed July 4, 2008).

72. P.B. Smith, M.H. Bond, and Çiğdem Kağitçibaşi, *Understanding Social Psychology across Cultures: Living and Working in a Changing World* (Thousand Oaks, CA: Sage Publications, 2006), 82.

73. S. Trenholm and A. Jensen, *Interpersonal Communication*, 6th ed. (New York: Oxford University Press, 2008), 259.

74. T.K. Gamble and M.W. Gamble, *Contacts: Interpersonal Communication in Theory, Practice, and Context*,

(New York: Houghton Mifflin, 2005), 422.

75. J.G. Pankhurst and S.K. Houseknecht, "Introduction," in *Family, Religion and Social Change*, S.K. Housekecht and J.G. Pankhurst, eds. (New York: Oxford University Press, 2000), 28.

76. B.L. Rodriguez and L.B. Olswang, "Mexican-American and Anglo-American Mothers' Beliefs and Values About Child Rearing, Education, and Language," *American Journal of Speech-Language Pathology*, 12 (2003), 369.

77. J.T. Wood, *Gendered Lives: Communication, Gender, and Culture*, 9th ed. (Belmont, CA: Wadsworth Cengage Learning, 2011), 161.

78. R.H. Robbins, *Cultural Anthropology: A Problem-Based Approach*, 4th ed. (Belmont, CA: Thomson Wadsworth, 2006), 203.

79. Tischler, 2011, 253.

80. Ocampo, Bernal, and Knight, 1993, 14.

81. R.L. Coles, *Race and Family: A Structural Approach* (Thousand Oaks, CA: Sage Publications, 2006), 90.

82. K.W. Galvin and P.J. Cooper, *Making Connections: Reading in Relational Communication*, 4th ed. (Los Angeles: Roxbury Publishing, 2006), 90. Also see Wood, 2011, 165.

83. C. Wade and C. Tavris, "The Long War: Gender and Culture," in *Psychology and Culture*, W.J. Lonner and R.S. Malpass, eds. (Boston: Allyn and Bacon, 1994), 126.

84. L. Reese, "Gender Difference in History Women in China and Japan" (Women in World History Curriculum: Essays, 2003), http://www.womeninworldhistory.com/essay-04.html (accessed May 29, 2011).

85. Ibid.

86. M. Kim, "Transformation of Family Ideology in Upper-Middle-Class Families in Urban South Korea," *International Journal of Cultural and Social Anthropology*, 32 (1993), 70.

87. Ibid., 70.

88. L.E. Davis and E.K. Proctor, *Race, Gender and Class: Guidelines with Individuals, Families, and Groups* (Englewood Cliffs, NJ: Prentice Hall, 1989), 67.

89. W.R. Jankowiak, *Sex, Death, and Hierarchy in a Chinese City: An Anthropological Account* (New York: Columbia University Press, 1993), 166.

90. V. Hildebrand, L.A. Phenice, M.M. Gray, and R.P. Hines, *Knowing and Serving Diverse Families*, 3nd ed. (Upper Saddle River, NJ: Merrill Prentice Hall, 2008), 134.

91. T.V. Tran, "The Vietnamese-American Family," in *Ethnic Families in America: Patterns and Variations*, 4th ed., C.H. Mindel, R.W. Habenstein, and R. Wright, eds. (Upper Saddle River, NJ: Prentice Hall, 1998), 261.

92. L. Schneider and A. Silverman, *Global Sociology: Introducing Five Contemporary Societies*, 5th ed. (Boston, MA: McGraw Hill Higher Education, 2010), 39.

93. E.T. Hall and M.R. Hall, *Hidden Differences: Doing Business with the Japanese* (New York: Anchor Books, 1990), 47.

94. J. Hendry, *Understanding Japanese Society* (New York: Routledge, 1987), 5.

95. Hildebrand, Phenice, Gray, and Hines, 2008, 94.

96. E.S. Kras, *Management in Two Cultures* (Yarmouth, ME: Intercultural Press, 1995), 64.

97. R.M. Becerra, "The Mexican-American Family," in *Ethnic Families in America: Patterns and Variations*, 4th ed., C.H. Mindel, R.W. Habenstein, and R. Wright, eds. (Upper Saddle River, NJ: Prentice Hall, 1998), 159.

98. Ibid.

99. Ibid.

100. M. Ferguson, *Feminism and Postmodernism* (Durham, NC: Duke University Press, 1994).

101. Strong, DeVault, and Cohen, 2011, 125.

102. G.A. Rodriguez, *Bringing up Latino Children in a Bicultural World* (New York: Fireside, 1999), 299.

103. M.J. Gannon and R. Pillai, *Understanding Global Culture*, 4th ed. (Thousand Oaks, CA: Sage Publications, Inc., 2010), 517.

104. R.H. Dana, *Multicultural Assessment Perspective for Professionals* (Boston: Allyn and Bacon, 1993), 70.

105. Schneider and Silverman, 2010, 91.

106. Lamanna and Riedmann, 2009, 64.

107. C.E. Henderson, *Culture and Customs of India* (Westport, CT: Greenwood Press, 2002), 128.

108. Tischler, 2011, 249

109. Henderson, 2002, 130.

110. Gannon, 2010, 478.

111. U.A. Segal, "The Asian Indian-American Family," in *Ethnic Families in America: Patterns and Variations*, 4th ed., C.H. Mindel, R.W. Habenstein, and R. Wright, eds. (Upper Saddle River, NJ: Prentice Hall, 1998), 335.

112. Henderson, 2002, 131.

113. Ferraro and Andreatta, 2010, 215.

114. S. Wolpert, *India*, 3rd ed. (Berkeley, CA: University of California Press, 2005), 137.

115. "India's Female Workforce Grows," *Rediff India Abroad: Business* (December 5, 2006), http://rediff.com///money/2006/dec/05women.htm (accessed May 10 2011).

116. Hildebrand, Phenice, Gray, and Hines, 2008, 153.

117. M. Sedgwick, *Islam and Muslims: A Guide to Diverse Experience in a Modern World* (Boston: Intercultural Press, 2006), 90.

118. Schneider and Silverman, 2010, 201.

119. D.L. Daniel and A.A. Mahdi, *Culture and Customs of Iran* (Westport, CT: Greenwood Press, 2006), 158.

120. Al-Kaysi, 1986, 41.

121. R. Patai, *The Arab Mind* (New York: Scribner's, 1973), 31–79.

122. M.S. Sait, "Have Palestinian Children Forfeited Their Rights?" *Journal of Comparative Family Studies*, 2 (2004), 214.

123. Schneider and Silverman, 2010, 203.

124. S. Irfan and M. Cowburn, "Disciplining, Chastisement and Physical Abuse: Perceptions and Attitudes of the British Pakistani Community," *Journal of Muslim Affairs*, 24 (2004), 96.

125. Lamanna and Riedmann, 2009, 97.

126. B.S. Trask, "Families in the Islamic Middle East," in *Families in Global and Multicultural Perspective*, 2nd ed., B.B. Ingoldsby and S.D. Smith, eds. (Thousand Oaks, CA: Sage Publications, 2006), 243.

127. Tischler, 2011, 256.

128. Schneider and Silverman, 2010, 209.

129. "Saudi King Cracks Down on Photos of Women," *FoxNews.com* (May 16, 2006), http://www.foxnews.com/story/0,2933,193743,00.html (accessed May 20, 2011).

130. S. Nanda and R.L. Warms, *Cultural Anthropology*, 6th ed. (Belmont, CA: Wadsworth Publishing Company, 1998), 221.

131. Lynch and Hanson, 1992, 161–162.

132. Triandis, 1994, 172.

133. W.V. Schmidt, R.N. Conaway, S.E. Easton, and W.J. Wardrope, *Communicating Globally: Intercultural Communication and Intercultural Business* (Los Angeles: Sage Publications, 2007), 25.

134. R. West and L.H. Turner, *Understanding Interpersonal Communication: Making Choices in Changing Times*, 2nd ed. (Boston, MA: Wadsworth Cengage Learning, 2009), 93–94.

135. D.C. Thomas and K. Inkson, *Cultural Intelligence: People Skills for Global Business* (San Francisco: Berrett-Koehfer, 2004), 31.

136. L. Veysey, "Growing Up in America," in *American Issues: Understanding Who We Are*, W.T. Alderson, ed. (Nashville, TN: American Association for State and Local History, 1976), 118.

137. K. McDade, "How We Parent: Race and Ethnic Differences," in *American Families: Issues in Race and Ethnicity*, C.K. Jacobson, ed. (New York: Garland Publishing, 1995), 283.

138. Ferraro and Andreatta, 2010, 133.

139. H.C. Triandis, *Individualism and Collectivism* (San Francisco: Westview Press, 1995), 63.

140. N. Nomura, Y. Noguchi, S. Saito, and I. Tezuka, "Family Characteristics and Dynamics in Japan and the United States: A Preliminary Report from the Family Environment Scale," *International Journal of Intercultural Relations*, 19 (1995), 63.

141. Schneider and Silverman, 2010, 264.

142. Smith, Bond, et al., 2006, 261.

143. Wolpert, 2005, 133–134.

144. Schneider and Silverman, 2010, 89.

145. B.B. Ingoldsby, "Families in Latin American," in *Families in Global and Multicultural Perspective*, 2nd ed., B.B. Ingoldsby and S.D. Smith, eds. (Thousand Oaks, CA: Sage Publications, 2006), 275.

146. Rodriguez, 1999, 327.

147. Y. Sanchez, "Families of Mexican Origin," in *Families in Cultural Context: Strengths and Challenges of Diversity*, M.K. DeGenova, ed. (Mountain View, CA: Mayfield Publishing Company, 1997), 66.

148. M.B. Zinn and A.Y.H. Pok, "Traditional and Transition in Mexican-Origin Families," in *Minority Families in the United States: A Multicultural Perspective*, 3rd ed., R.L. Taylor, ed. (Upper Saddle River, NJ: Prentice Hall, 2002), 84.

149. T. Novinger, *Communicating with Brazilians: When Yes Means No* (Austin, TX: University of Texas Press, 2003), 82.

150. Z.E. Suárez "Cuban-American Families," in *Ethnic Families in America*, 4th ed., C. H. Mindel, R.W. Habenstein, and R. Wright, eds. (Upper Saddle River, NJ: Prentice Hall, 1998), 186.

151. H. Carrasquillo, "Puerto Rican Families in America," in *Families in Cultural Context: Strengths and Challenges in Diversity*, M.K. DeGenova, ed. (Mountain View, CA: Mayfield Publishing Company, 1997), 159.

152. S.W. Wilson and L.W. Ngige, "Families of Sub-Saharan Africa," in *Families in Global and Multicultural Perspective*, 2nd ed., B.B. Ingoldsby and S.D. Smith, eds. (Thousand Oaks, CA: Sage Publications, 2006), 250.

153. Ibid., 247.

154. K. Peltzer, "Personality and Person Perception in Africa," in *Intercultural Communication: A Reader*, 11th ed., L.A. Samovar, R.E. Porter, and E.R. McDaniel, eds. (Belmont, CA: Wadsworth, 2006), 135.

155. Y. Richmond and P. Gestrin, *Into Africa: Intercultural Insights* (Yarmouth, ME: Intercultural Press, 1998), 3.

156. J. Esherick, *Women in the Arab World* (Philadelphia: Mason Crest Publishers, 2006), 68.

157. S.K. Farsoun, *Culture and Customs of the Palestinians* (Westport, CT: Greenwood Press, 2004), 33.

158. Schneider and Silverman, 2010, 214.

159. Gannon, 2010, 63.

160. Hildebrand, Phenice, Gray, and Hines, 2008, 151.

161. Ferraro and Andreatta, 2010, 151.

162. D. Cheal, *Sociology in Family Life* (New York: Palgrave, 2002, 25.

163. R. Shorto, "Made-in-Japan Parenting," *Health*, 23 (1991), 54.

164. Ibid.

165. C.I. Murray and N. Kimura, "Families in Japan," in *Families in Global and Multicultural Perspective*, 2nd ed., B.B. Ingoldsby and S.D. Smith, eds. (Thousand Oaks, CA: Sage Publications, 2006), 303.

166. T. Bestor and H. Hardacre, "The Japanese Family," Contemporary Japan: Culture and Society (Asian Topics on Asia for Educators: Columbia University, 2004), http://afe.easia.columbia.edu/at_japan_soc/ (accessed May 29, 2011).

167. G. Redding and G.Y.Y. Wong, "The Psychology of Chinese Organizational Behavior," in *The Psychology of the Chinese People*, M.H. Bond, ed. (NY: Oxford University Press, 1987), 274.

168. J.J. Ponzetti, ed., *International Encyclopedia of Marriage and Family*, 2nd

ed. (New York: The Gale Group, 2003), 1207.

169. G.C. Chu and Y. Ju, *The Great Wall in Ruins: Communication and Culture Change in China* (Albany, NY: State University of New York Press, 1993), 9–10.

170. Hildebrand, Phenice, Gray, and Hines, 2008, 170.

171. R. John, "Native American Families," in *Ethnic Families in America: Patterns and Variations*, 4th ed., C.H. Mindel, R.W. Habenstein, and R. Wright, eds. (Upper Saddle River, NJ: Prentice Hall, 1998), 383.

172. T. Cheshire, "American Indian Families: Strength and Answers from Our Past," in *Families in Global and Multicultural Perspective*, 2nd ed. (Thousand Oaks, CA: Sage Publications, 2006), 318.

173. D.W. Sue and D. Sue, *Counseling the Culturally Different*, 2nd ed. (New York: John Wiley and Sons, 1990), 177.

174. Haviland, Prins, Walrath, and McBride, 2011, 527.

175. R. Frisk, "Roles of Elderly," http://mnsu.edu/emuseum/culture/aging/roles.html (accessed January 29, 2011).

176. Haviland, Prins, Walrath, and McBride, 2011, 527.

177. Andersen and Taylor, 2011, 91.

178. Ferraro and Andreatta, 2010, 126.

179. J. Tyndale, "Respect for the Elderly," *The Wall Street Journal Classroom Edition* (May 2005), http://www.wsjclassroomedition.com/archive/05/related_05may_teacher_elderly.htm (accessed January 24, 2011).

180. H.W. Gardiner and C. Kosmitzki, *Lives Across Cultures: Cross-Cultural Human Development*, 2nd ed. (Boston: Allyn and Bacon, 2002), 100.

181. Sue and Sue, 1990, 232.

182. M. Sánchez-Ayéndez, "The Puerto Rican Family," in *Ethnic Families in America: Patterns and Variations*, 4th ed., C.H. Mindel, R.W. Habenstein, and R. Wright, eds. (Upper Saddle River, NJ: Prentice Hall, 1998), 199.

183. Hildebrand, Phenice, Gray, and Hines, 2008, 97.

184. Ibid., 155.

185. A. Mir, *The American Encounter with Islam* (Broomall, PA: Mason Crest Publishers, 2004), 85.

186. J. Tyndale, "Respect for the Elderly," *The Wall Street Journal Classroom Edition* (May 2005), http://wsjclassroom.com/archive/05may/related_05may_teacher_elderly.htm (accessed February 2, 2011).

187. D.E. Long, *Culture and Customs of Saudi Arabia* (Westport, CT: Greenwood Press, 2005), 38.

188. A.M. Lutfiyya, "Islam in Village Culture," in *Readings in Middle Eastern Societies and Cultures*, A.M. Lutfiyya and C.W. Churchill, eds. (Paris: Mouton, 1970), 55.

189. Tischler, 2011, 94.

190. T. Plate, "The Age of Insecurity: The Elderly in Asia versus America," *The Japan Times: Online* (June 6, 2004), http://search.japantimes.co.jp/cgi-bin/eo20040606tp.html (accessed May 30, 2011).

191. P. Min, "The Korean-American Family," in *Ethnic Families in America: Patterns and Variations*, 4th ed., C.H. Mindel, R.W. Habenstein, and R. Wright, eds. (Upper Saddle River, NJ: Prentice Hall, 1998), 232.

192. D.N. Clark, *Culture and Customs of Korea* (Westport, CT: Greenwood Press, 2000), 36.

193. H. Wenzhong and C.L. Grove, *Encountering the Chinese: A Guide for Americans*, rev. ed. (Yarmouth, ME: Intercultural Press, 1999), 7.

194. M.G. Wong, "The Chinese-American Family, " in *Ethnic Families in America: Patterns and Variations*, 4th ed., C.H. Mindel, R.W. Habenstein, and R. Wright, eds. (Upper Saddle River, NJ: Prentice Hall, 1998), 303.

195. J. Carlson, Y. Kurato, E. Rui, K-M Ng, and J. Yang "A Multicultural Discussion About Personality Development," *The Family Journal: Counseling and Therapy for Couples and Families*, 12 (2004), 113.

196. M. Izuhara, "Changing Families and Policy Responses to an Aging Japanese Society," in *The Changing Japanese Family*, M. Rebick and

A. Takenaka, eds. (New York: Routledge, 2006), 162–163.

197. Schneider and Silverman, 2010, 59.

198. "Native American Elderly," http://cas.umkc.edu/casww/natameers.htm, (accessed February 3, 2011).

199. M. Yellowbird and C.M. Sniff, "American Indian Families," in *Minority Families in the United States*, 3rd ed., R.L. Taylor, ed. (Upper Saddle River, NJ: Prentice Hall, 2002), 240.

200. Hildebrand, Phenice, Gray, and Hines, 2008, 171.

201. H. P McAdoo, "African American Families," in *Ethnic Families in America: Patterns and Variations*, 4th ed., C.H. Mindel, R.W. Habenstein, and R. Wright, eds. (Upper Saddle River, NJ: Prentice Hall, 1998), 362.

202. J. Campinha-Bacaote, "African-Americans," in *Transcultural Health Care: A Culturally Competent Approach*, L.D. Purnell and B.J. Paulanka, eds. (Philadelphia: F.A. Davis, 1998), 57.

203. D.S. Ruiz, "The Changing Roles of African American Grandmothers Raising Children: An Exploratory Study in the Piedmont Region of North Carolina," in *The Western Journal of Black Studies* (March 22, 2008), http://highbeam.com/doc/1G1-1897501.html (accessed February 6, 2011).

204. Andersen and Taylor, 2011, 78.

205. M.H. DeFleur, P. Kearney, T. Plax, and M.L. DeFleur, Fundamentals of Human Communication (New York: McGraw-Hill, 2005) 157.

206. O.L. Taylor, *Cross-Cultural Communication: As Essential Dimension of Effective Education*, rev. (Chevy Chase, MD: The Mid-Atlantic Equity Center, 1990), 11, http://www.maec.org/pdf/taylor.pdf (accessed May 30, 2011).

207. K.M. Galvin and B.J. Brommel, *Family Communication: Cohesion and Change*, 3rd ed. (New York: HarperCollins, 1991, 22.

208. F.M. Moghaddam, D.M. Taylor, and S.C. Wright, *Social Psychology in Cross-Cultural Perspective* (New York: W.H. Freeman, 1993), 125.

209. Wood, 2011, 294.

210. Hildebrand, Phenice, Gray, and Hines, 2008, 141.

211. R. Cooper and N. Cooper, *Thailand: A Guide to Customs and Etiquette* (Portland, OR: Graphic Arts Center, 1982), 83.

212. Moghaddam, Taylor, and Wright, 1993, 124.

213. Coles, 2006, 182.

214. L. Sparks and M. Villagran, *Patient and Provider Interaction* (Malden, MA: Polity Press), 75.

215. Trenholm and Jensen, 2008, 262.

216. Freakonomics, "How Culture Influences Decision-Making," *New York Times* (August 11, 2010) http://freakonomics.blogs.nytimes.com/2010/08/11/how-culture-influences-decision-making/ (accessed February 6, 2011).

Chapter 4

1. P.N. Stearns, "Why Study History?," *American Historical Association* (1998), http://www.historians.org/pubs/free/WhyStudyHistory.htm (accessed May 20, 2011).

2. W. Huber, "The Judeo-Christian Tradition," in *The Cultural Values of Europe*, H. Joasand K. Weigandt, eds. (Translated by Alex Skinner) (Liverpool: Liverpool University Press, 2009), 43.

3. T. Bender, *A Nation Among Nations: American's Place in World History* (New York: Hill and Wang, 2006), 3–4.

4. B. Lewis, *The Shaping of the Modern Middle East* (New York: Oxford Press, 1994), 11.

5. B. Lewis, *The Middle East: A Brief History of the Last 2,000 Years* (New York: Scribner, 1995), 67.

6. Stearns, 1998.

7. B. Kerblay, *Modern Soviet Society* (New York: Pantheon, 1983), 271.

8. J.H. McElroy, *American Beliefs: What Keeps a Big Country and Diverse People United* (Chicago: Ivan R. Dee, 1999), 51.

9. Ibid., 220.

10. C.S. Fischer. *Made in America* (Chicago: University of Chicago, 2010), 12.

11. A. Chua, *Day of Empire* (New York: Doubleday, 2007), 239.

12. Data contained in the "Country Statistics" tables in this chapter were obtained from the CIA *World Factbook*, https://www.cia.gov/library/publications/the-world-factbook/ and State Department *Background Notes*, http://www.state.gov/r/pa/ei/bgn/ (accessed November 30, 2011).

13. C. Van Doren, *A History of Knowledge* (New York: Ballantine Books, 1991), 224.

14. G. Althen, *American Ways*, 2nd ed. (Yarmouth, ME: Intercultural Press, 2003), 120.

15. J.H. McElroy, *Finding Freedom: America's Distinctive Cultural Formation* (Carbondale, IL: Southern Illinois University Press, 1987), 65.

16. S.D. Cohen, *An Ocean Apart* (Westport, CT: Praeger, 1998), 141.

17. E.C. Stewart and M. J. Bennett, *American Cultural Patterns*, rev. ed. (Yarmouth, ME: Intercultural Press, 1991), 136.

18. Fischer, 2010, 10.

19. McElroy, 1987, 143.

20. "The U.S. Military Presence Abroad," *International Debates*, 8:6 (Sep 2010), 1.

21. Bender, 2006, 188.

22. Ibid, 187–188.

23. R. Griswold del Castillo, *The Treaty of Guadalupe Hidalgo: A Legacy of Conflict* (Norman, OK: University of Oklahoma Press, 1990), 4.

24. Steward and Bennett, 1991, 119–123.

25. G.E. Curtis, ed. *Russia: A Country Study* (Washington: GPO for the Library of Congress, 1996), http://countrystudies.us/russia/ (accessed May 19, 2011).

26. J. Kohan, "A Mind of Their Own," (*Time*, Dec 7, 1992), 66.

27. A.C. Kuchins, "Why Russia is so Russian," *Current History*, 108:720 (2009): 318–324.

28. R.V. Daniels, *Russia: The Roots of Confrontation* (Cambridge, MA: Harvard University Press, 1985), 55.

29. A. Esler, *The Human Venture*, 3rd ed. (Upper Saddle River, NJ: Prentice Hall, 1996), 668.

30. Kuchins, 2009, 320.

31. "Background Note: Russia," *Country Background Notes* (Washington: U.S. Department of State, 14 June 2010), http://www.state.gov/r/pa/ei/bgn/3183.htm (accessed May 19, 2011).

32. "The Uses and Abuses of History," *The Economist* (May 7, 2005), 43.

33. M. Bergelson, "Russian Cultural Values and Workplace Communication Patterns," in *Intercultural Communication: A Reader*, 13th ed., L.A. Samovar, R.E. Porter, and E.R. McDaniel, eds. (Boston, MA: Wadsworth Cengage, 2012), 191.

34. "Background Note: Russia," 2010.

35. P. Kolsto, "Nation-Building in Russia: A Value Oriented Strategy," in *Nation Building and Common Values in Russia*, P. Kolsto and H. Blakkisrud, eds. (Lanham, MD: Rowman & Littlefield, 2004), 2.

36. Kuchins, 2009, 323.

37. D. Treisman, *The Return: Russia's Journey from Gorbachev to Medvedev* (New York: Free Press, 2011), 344.

38. "Frost at the Core," *The Economist*," (December 11, 2010), 30.

39. N. Eberstadt, "The Enigma of Russian Mortality," *Current History*, 109:729 (2010): 288–294.

40. M. Schwirtz, "Russian Trial to Bare a Face of Nationalism," *New York Times* (February 19, 2011), http://www.nytimes.com/2011/02/20/world/europe/20russia.html?_r=1&hpw=&pagewanted=all (accessed May 19, 2011); M. Elder, "Putin reinforces Russian nationalism," *Global Post* (December 23, 2010), http://www.globalpost.com/dispatch/russia/101222/vladimir-putin-russian-nationalism (accessed May 19, 2011).

41. Treisman, 2011, 388.

42. J. Mathews and L. Mathews, *One Billion: A China Chronicle* (New York: Random House, 1983), 11.

43. I. Morris, *Why the West Rules—For Now* (New York: Farrar, Straus and Giroux, 2010), 123.

44. "Background Note: China," *Country Background Notes* (U.S. Department of State, August, 5, 2010), http://www.state.gov/r/pa/ei/bgn/18902.htm#history (accessed May 20, 2011).

45. C.O. Hucker, *China's Imperial Past* (Stanford, CA: Stanford University Press, 1975), 2.

46. Morris, 2010, 285.

47. "Background Note: China," 2010.

48. J.C. Ramo, "Hu's Visit: Finding a Way Forward on U.S.-China Relations," (*Time*, Apr 8, 2010), http://www.time.com/time/world/article/0,8599,1978640-1,00.html (accessed May 20, 2011); O. Schell, "China's Agony of Defeat," *Newsweek* (August 4, 2008), 39.

49. F. Dikötter, *Mao's Great Famine* (New York: Walker Publishing, 2010), x.

50. "China," *CIA World Factbook* (Washington, D.C.: Central Intelligence Agency, 2011), https://www.cia.gov/library/publications/the-world-factbook/geos/ch.html (accessed May 20, 2011).

51. D. Shambaugh, "New China Requires a New US Strategy," *Current History* 109:728 (September 2010), 219–226.

52. "Clashing with the Foreign Devils," *The Economist* (February 19, 2011), 92.

53. J. Chapman, "David Cameron Rejects Chinese Requests to Remove 'Offensive' Poppies During Visit," *Mail.Online* (November 11, 2010), http://www.dailymail.co.uk/news/article-1328311/David-Cameron-rejects-China-request-remove-offensive-poppies.html# (accessed May 20, 2011).

54. S. L. Shirk. *China: Fragile Superpower* (New York: Oxford University Press, 2002), 20–32.

55. W. Feng and M. Hvistendahl, "China's Population Destiny: The Looming Crisis," *Current History*, 728:244 (September 2010), 250.

56. J. Fallows, "Dirty Coal, Clean Coal," *The Atlantic* (December 2010), http://www.theatlantic.com/magazine/archive/2010/12/dirty-coal-clean-future/8307/ (accessed May 20, 2011).

57. J.W. Dower, *Embracing Defeat: Japan in the Wake of World War II*, (New York: W.W. Norton, 1999), 29.

58. E.O. Reischauer and M.B. Jansen, *The Japanese Today: Change and Continuity*, (Cambridge, MA: Harvard University Press, 1995), 32.

59. H. Tabuchi, "Japan Keeps a High Wall for Foreign Labor," *The New York Times* (January 2, 2011), http://www.nytimes.com/2011/01/03/world/asia/03japan.html?_r=1&ref=hirokotabuchi (accessed May 20, 2011).

60. M.B. Jansen, *The Making of Modern Japan* (Cambridge, MA: Belknap Press, 2000), 97; A. Gordon, *A Modern History of Japan* (New York: Oxford University, 2003), 16.

61. B.L. De Mente, *Behind the Japanese Bow* (Chicago: Passport Books), 1–2, 12.

62. J. Kingston, *Contemporary Japan: History, Politics, and Social Change Since the 1980s* (Chichester, UK: John Wiley & Sons, 2011), 17.

63. T.S. Lebra, *Japanese Patterns of Behavior*, (Honolulu, HI: University of Hawaii Press, 1976), Various.

64. "Japan," *CIA World Factbook* (Central Intelligence Agency, May 17, 2011), https://www.cia.gov/library/publications/the-world-factbook/geos/ja.html (accessed May 20, 2011).

65. Jansen, 2000, 111.

66. Reischauer and Jansen, 1995, 15–16.

67. Jansen, 2000, 111.

68. K. Elwood, "Cultural Conundrum: Keeping in line with the Joneses, *Daily Yomiuri Online* (Dec 28, 2010), http://www.yomiuri.co.jp/dy/features/language/T101221001750.htm (accessed May 20, 2011).

69. J. Hendry, *Understanding Japanese Society*, 3rd ed. (New York: RoutledgeCruzon, 2003), 18.

70. D. McCargo, *Contemporary Japan* (London: Palgrave, 2000), 169.

71. "Chapter 2. Population: Declining Birth Rate and Aging Population," *Statistical Handbook of Japan 2010* (Tokyo: Ministry of Internal Affairs and Communications: Statistics Bureau, Director-General for Policy Planning (Statistical Standards) & Statistical Research and Training Institute, 2010), http://www.stat.go.jp/english/data/handbook/c02cont.htm#cha2_2, (accessed May 20, 2011); Kingston, 2011, 41.

72. Kingston, 2011, 19–20.

73. M. Foster, "For Japan, 2010 was a year to forget," *Newsday.com* (December 27, 2010), http://www.newsday.com/business/for-japan-2010-was-a-year-to-forget-1.2570984 (accessed May 20, 2011).

74. Y. Sugimoto, *An Introduction to Japanese Society*, 3rd ed. (New York: Cambridge University), 190.

75. S. Wolpert, *India*, 3rd ed. (Berkeley, CA: University of California Press, 2005), 2.

76. H. Timmons, "Outsourcing to India Draws Western Lawyers," *New York Times* (August 4, 2010), http://www.nytimes.com/2010/08/05/business/global/05legal.html (accessed May 20, 2011).

77. M. Kripalani, "Indian Americans Come Out," *Los Angeles Times* (January 21, 2007), http://www.latimes.com/news/printedition/asection/la-oe-kripalani20jan20,0,1385820.story (accessed May 20, 2011).

78. T. Parti, "The Rise of the Indian-American Candidate, as Nikki Haley and Others Run, *The Christian Science Monitor* (June 11, 2010), http://www.csmonitor.com/USA/Politics/2010/0611/The-rise-of-the-Indian-American-candidate-as-Nikki-Haley-and-others-run (accessed May 20, 2011).

79. Data for this description was taken from the following sources: "Background Note: India," *Country Background Notes* (U.S. Department of State, July 14, 2010), http://www.state.gov/r/pa/ei/bgn/3454.htm#people (accessed May 20, 2011); N. Grihault, *Culture Smart! India* (London: Kuperard, 2007); C. E. Henderson, *Culture and Customs of India* (Westport, CT: Greenwood Press, 2002); "India," *CIA World Factbook* (Central Intelligence

Agency, May 17, 2011), https://www.cia.gov/library/publications/the-world-factbook/geos/in.html (accessed May 20, 2011).

80. Grihault, 2007, 24; Henderson, 2002, 13; D.R. SarDesai, *India: The Definitive History* (Boulder, CO: Westview, 2008), 18; Wolpert, 2005, 25–27.

81. Henderson, 2002, 13–15; Wolpert, 2005, 29–38.

82. Wolpert, 2005, 40–41.

83. Henderson, 2002, 15.

84. Wolpert, 2005, 42.

85. D. Brown, *A New Introduction to Islam*, (Malden, MA: Blackwell, 2004), 192; Henderson, 2002, 26.

86. Henderson, 2002, 17.

87. Grihault, 2007, 29.

88. Wolpert, 2005, 51.

89. Ibid.

90. Grihault, 2007, 28; Henderson, 2002, 21; Wolpert, 69.

91. "Country Comparison: GDP," *CIA World Factbook* (Central Intelligence Agency, 2011), https://www.cia.gov/library/publications/the-world-factbook/rankorder/2001rank.html?countryName=India&countryCode=in&regionCode=sas&rank=5#in (accessed May 20, 2011).

92. SarDesai, 2008, 10.

93. R. Bansal, "India's Remix Generation," *Current History*, 106: 699 (2007), 168.

94. Ibid., 171.

95. "India," in *The World Factbook* (Central Intelligence Agency, February 14, 2011), https://www.cia.gov/library/publications/the-world-factbook/geos/in.html (accessed May 20, 2011).

96. Ibid.; R. Mukherji, "A Tiger Despite the Chains: The State of Reform in India," *Current History*, 109:726 (2010), 149.

97. "A Village in a Million," *The Economist* (December 18, 2010), 63.

98. S. Ganguly, "India Held Back," *Current History*, 107:712 (November 2008), 370.

99. Ibid, 373.

100. "Background Note: Mexico," *Country Background Notes* (U.S. Department of State, December 14, 2011), http://www.state.gov/r/pa/ei/bgn/35749.htm (accessed May 20, 2011).

101. N.G. Albert, *The Hispanic Population: 2010* (U.S. Department of Commerce Economics and Statistics Administration, U.S. Census Bureau, May 2011), 2–11; "Power in Numbers," *The Economist* (January 9, 2010), 31.

102. L. Schneider and A. Silverman, *Global Sociology: Introducing Five Contemporary Societies*, 5th ed. (Boston: McGraw-Hill, 2010), 72.

103. L.V. Foster, *A Brief History of Mexico*, (New York: Facts on File, 1997), 2; J.D. Cockcroft, *Mexico's Hope: An Encounter with Politics and History* (New York: Monthly Review Press, 1998), 13; Schneider and Silverman, 2010, 60.

104. Norman, *Guide to Mexico* (Garden City, NY: Doubleday, 1972), 53.

105. Schneider and Silverman, 2010, 72–73.

106. Cockcroft, 1998, 19.

107. Foster, 1997, 65–66.

108. Ibid., 96.

109. F. Merrell, *The Mexicans: A Sense of Culture* (Boulder, CO: Westview Press, 2003), 53–56.

110. Schneider and Silverman, 2010, 74.

111. Foster, 1997, 111.

112. C.J. Johns, *The Origins of Violence in Mexican Society* (Westport, CT: Praeger, 1995), 202.

113. M.V. Meed, *The Mexican War 1846-1848* (Oxford, GB: Osprey Publishing, 2002), 7.

114. "The Treaty of Guadalupe Hidalgo," *Hispanic Reading Room* (Library of Congress, February 14, 2011), http://www.loc.gov/rr/hispanic/ghtreaty/ (accessed May 20, 2011).

115. Griswold del Castillo, 1990, xii.

116. J. Samora and P.V. Simon, *A History of Mexican-American People* (London: University of Notre Dame Press, 1977), 98.

117. A. Esler, *The Human Venture*, 3rd ed. (Upper Saddle River, NJ: Prentice Hall, 1996), 613.

118. Schneider and Silverman, 2010, 75.

119. L. Alvarez and J.M. Broder, "More and More, Women Risk All to Enter U.S.," *The New York Times* (January 10, 2006), http://www.nytimes.com/2006/01/10/national/10women.html, (accessed May 20, 2011).

120. "Background Note: Mexico," 2011.

121. H. Siddique, "Mexico Drug Wars Have Killed 35,000 People in Four Years," *The Guardian* (January 13, 2011), http://www.guardian.co.uk/world/2011/jan/13/mexico-drug-deaths-figures-calderon (accessed May 20, 2011).

122. F.E. Gonzalez, "Mexico's Drug Wars Get Brutal," *Current History*, 108:715 (2009), 74–75; Schneider and Silverman, 2010, 775–76.

123. *The Future of the Global Muslim Population: Projections for 2010-2030*, (Pew Research Center: Forum on Religion & Public Life January 2011), 13, 155.

124. Ibid, pp. 15, 20.

125. I.R. Manners & B. M. Parmenter, "The Middle East: A Geographic Preface," in *Understanding the Contemporary Middle East*, 2nd ed., D.J. Gernerand, J. Schwedler, eds. (Boulder, CO: Lynne Riemmer Publishers, 2004), 5–32; A. Goldschmidt, Jr. "The Historical Context," in *Understanding the Contemporary Middle East* (2nd ed.), D.J. Gerner and J. Schwedler, eds. (Boulder, CO: Lynne Riemmer Publishers, 2004), 33–78.

126. A. L. W. Admec, *Historical Dictionary of Islam* (Lanham, MD: Scarecrow Press, 2001), 132.

127. Goldschmidt, Jr., 2004, 39.

128. Ibid.

129. F.M. Donner, "Muhammad and the Caliphate," in *The Oxford History of Islam*, J.L. Esposito, ed. (New York: Oxford University Press, 1999), 11.

130. P. Lunde, *Islam* (New York: DK Publishing, 2002), 8.

131. Donner, 1999, 11.

132. Ibid., 13.

133. Lunde, 2002, 52, 61.

134. *Mapping the Global Muslim Population: A Report on the Size and Distribution of the World's Muslim Population* (Pew Research Center:

Forum on Religion & Public Life, October, 2009), p. 8–9.

135. Ibid., 10.

136. J.L. Esposito, *What Everyone Needs to Know About Islam* (New York: Oxford University Press, 2002), 47.

137. Lunde, 2002, 54–56.

138. J.I. Smith, "Islam and Christendom," in *The Oxford History of Islam*, J.L. Esposito, ed. (New York: Oxford University Press, 1999), 312, 337.

139. E. Rogers and E.M. Steinfatt, *Intercultural Communication* (Prospect Heights, IL: Waveland Press, 1999), 9.

140. Smith, 1999, 339.

141. B. Lewis, *The Crisis of Islam* (New York: Random House, 2004) 59.

142. S.V.R. Nasr, "European Colonialism and the Emergence of Modern Muslim States," in *The Oxford History of Islam*, J.L. Esposito, ed. (New York: Oxford University Press, 1999), 552.

143. Lewis, 2004, xix.

144. D. Brown, *A New Introduction to Islam* (Malden, MA: Blackwell, 2004), 18–19.

145. Lewis, 1994, 27.

146. Esposito, 2002, 169; E.E. Curtis, ed., *The Columbia Sourcebook of Muslims in the United States* (New York: Columbia University Press, 2008).

147. B. Lewis, "The Revolt of Islam," *The New Yorker* (November, 19, 2001), 52.

148. "Waking from Its Sleep: A Special Report on the Arab World," *The Economist*, (July 25, 2009), 1–16.

149. Esposito, 2002, 44.

150. A.M. Shahrur, "A Call for Reformation," in "Voices within Islam: Four Perspectives on Tolerance and Diversity," B. Baktiari and A.R. Norton, *Current History*, 104:658 (2005), 39–43.

151. "Waking," 2009, 11.

152. Ibid., 14.

Chapter 5

1. G. Bailey and J. Peoples, *Essentials of Cultural Anthropology*, 2nd ed. (Belmont, CA: Wadsworth Cengage Learning, 2011), 31.

2. R.H. Lavenda and E.A. Schultz, *Core Concepts in Cultural Anthropology*, 4th ed. (New York: McGraw-Hill Higher Education, 2010), 68.

3. S. Ishii, P. Cooke, and D. Klopf, "Our Locus in the Universe: Worldview and Intercultural Misunderstandings/Conflicts," *Dokkyo International Review*, 12 (1999), 301–317.

4. E.A. Hoebel, *Man in the Primitive World* (New York: McGraw-Hill, 1958), 159.

5. R.O. Olayiwola, "The Impact of Islam on the Conduct of Nigerian Foreign Relations," *Islamic Quarterly*, 33 (1989), 19–26.

6. B. Toelken, *Dynamics of Folklore*, rev. and expanded (Logan, UT: Utah State University Press, 1996), 245.

7. W.A. Haviland, H.E.L. Prins, E. Walrath, and B. McBride, *Cultural Anthropology: The Human Challenge*, 12th ed. (Belmont, CA: Wadsworth, 2008), 298.

8. R.H. Dana, *Multicultural Assessment Perspective for Professional Psychology* (Boston: Allyn and Bacon, 1993), 9.

9. D.L. Pennington, "Intercultural Communication," in *Intercultural Communication: A Reader*, 4th ed., L.A. Samovar and R.E. Porter, eds. (Belmont, CA: Wadsworth, 1985), 32.

10. T. Biaquis, *A History of the Family*, vol. 4, A. Burguiere, gen. ed. (Cambridge, MA: Harvard University Press, 1996), 618.

11. Genesis 1:26, *The Holy Bible: The New King James Version* (NY: American Bible Society, 1990).

12. M.P. Fisher and R. Luyster, *Living Religions* (Englewood Cliffs, NJ: Prentice Hall, 1991), 153–156.

13. P.U. Spencer, "A Native American Worldview," *Noetic Sciences Review*, (Summer 1990), http://ratical.com/many_worlds/NAworldview.html (accessed June 28, 2011).

14. R. Bartels, "National Culture-Business Relations: United States and Japan Contrasted," *Management International Review*, 2 (1982), 5.

15. R.E. Nisbett, *The Geography of Thought* (New York: The Free Press, 2003), 100.

16. P. Gold, *Navajo and Tibetan Sacred Wisdom: The Circle of the Spirit* (Rochester, VT: Inner Traditions, 1994), 60.

17. S. Ishii, D. Klopf, and P. Cooke, "Our Locus in the Universe: Worldview and Intercultural Communication," in *Intercultural Communication: A Reader*, 11th ed., L.A. Samovar, R.E. Porter, and E.R. McDaniel, eds. (Belmont, CA: Wadsworth, 2006), 32–38.

18. K.A. Roberts, *Religion in Sociological Perspective*, 4th ed. (Belmont, CA: Wadsworth Cengage Learning, 2004), 11.

19. M.D. Coogan, "Introduction," in *The Illustrated Guide to World Religion*, M.D. Coogan, ed. (New York: Oxford University Press, 1998), 6.

20. M. Futrell, "Worldview Sampler: What is a worldview?" (Teaching About Religion, August 18, 2006), http://www.worldvieweducation.org/worldview.html (accessed July 3, 2011).

21. I.S. Markham, *A World Religions Reader*, 2nd ed. (Malden, MA: Blackwell, 2000), 43.

22. H.L. Tischler, *Introduction to Sociology*, 10th ed. (Belmont, CA: Wadsworth Cengage Learning, 2011), 308.

23. The Pew Forum on Religion and Public Life, *U.S. Religious Landscape Survey* (June 23, 2008), http://religions.pewforum.org/reports (accessed July 3, 2011).

24. "Losing Our Religion," *The Week*, November 6, 2009, 13.

25. "Major Religions of the World Ranked by Adherents" (August 9, 2007), http://www.adherents.com/Religions_By_Adherents.html (accessed July 3, 2011).

26. "What is Secular Humanism?" *Council for Secular Humanism* (n.d.), http://www.secularhumanism.org/index.php?section=main&page=what_is (accessed July 3, 2011).

27. D.C. Halverson, "Secularism," in *The Compact Guide to World Religions*, D.C. Halverson, ed.

(Minneapolis, MN: Bethany House Publishers, 1996), 185.

28. C. Hitchens, *God Is Not Great* (New York: Hachette Book Group USA, 2007), 10.

29. "Humanism: A Positive Approach to Life," *BBC: Religions* (October 22, 2009), http://bbc.co.uk/religion/religions/atheism/types/humanism.shtml (accessed July 3, 2011).

30. S. Jacoby, *Freethinkers: A History of American Secularism* (New York: Metropolitan Books, 2004), 10.

31. Ibid., 11.

32. R.B. Bragg, "Humanist Manifesto I," *The New Humanist* (1933; American Humanist Association, 1977), http://www.americanhumanist.org/Who_We_Are/About_Humanism/Humanist_Manifesto_I (accessed July 3, 2011).

33. Halverson, 1996, 186.

34. I.S. Markham and C. Lohr, "Secular Humanism," in *A World Religions Reader*, 3rd ed. (Oxford, UK: Wiley-Blackwell, 2009), 298.

35. W.A. Haviland, H.E.L. Prins, D. Walrath, and B. McBride, *Cultural Anthropology: The Human Challenge*, 13th ed. (Belmont, CA: Wadsworth Cengage Learning, 2011), 578.

36. R.A. Carvalho and M. Robinson, eds., *Cultural Competence in Health Care: A Practical Guide* (San Francisco: Jossey-Bass, 1999), 102.

37. L. Schmidt, *Restless Souls: The Making of American Spirituality* (New York: HarperCollins, 2005), 12.

38. C. Kimball, *When Religion Becomes Evil* (New York: HarperCollins Publishers, 2002), 196.

39. T.L. Friedman, *The Lexus and the Olive Tree* (New York: Farrar, Straus and Giroux, 1999).

40. M. P. Osborne, *One World, Many Religions: The Ways of Worship* (New York: Alfred A. Knopf, 1996), vii.

41. A. Malefijt, *Religion and Culture: An Introduction to Anthropology of Religion* (Prospect Heights, IL: Waveland Press, 1968), 145.

42. S. Nanda and R.L Warms, *Cultural Anthropology*, 6th ed. (Belmont, CA: Wadsworth, 1998), 276.

43. H. Smith, *The World's Religions* (New York: HarperCollins, 1991), 9.

44. G. Ferraro, *Cultural Anthropology: An Applied Perspective*, 6th ed. (Belmont, CA: Thomson Wadsworth, 2006), 356–360.

45. Tischler, 2011, 302.

46. Haviland, Prins, Walrath, and McBride, 2011, 576.

47. Roberts, 2004, 373.

48. G.W. Braswell, Jr., *Understanding World Religions* (Nashville, TN: Broadman & Holman Publishers, 1994), 3.

49. G. Ferraro and S. Andreatta, *Cultural Anthropology: An Applied Perspective* (Belmont, CA: Wadsworth Cengage Learning, 2010), 364.

50. Roberts, 2004, 397.

51. M. Wilson, ed., *World Religion* (Farmington Hills, MI: Thomas Gale, 2006), 15.

52. F. Ghitis, "Anti-Semitism Increasing Worldwide," *San Diego Union-Tribune*, February 3, 2009, B-5.

53. S. Al-Marayati and S. Ghori, "Islamophobia: Bigotry Toward Muslims Is Growing in the United States," *San Diego Union-Tribune*, December 15, 2006, B-7.

54. W.E. Paden, *Religious Worlds: The Comparative Study of Religion* (Boston: Beacon, 1994), 170.

55. M. Wilson, 2006, 21.

56. "Major Religions of the World Ranked by Number of Adherents," (August 9, 2007), http://www.adherents.com/Religions_By_Adherents.html (accessed July 3, 2011).

57. N. Smart, *The World's Religions*, 2nd ed. (New York: Cambridge University Press, 1998), 319–321; 541–546.

58. D.L. Carmody and J.T. Carmody, *In the Path of the Masters: Understanding the Spirituality of Buddha, Confucius, Jesus, and Muhammad* (New York: Paragon House, 1994), Preface.

59. Smith, 1991, 3.

60. Ferraro and Andreatta, 2010, 365.

61. J.J. Macionis, *Society: The Basics*, 4th ed. (Upper Saddle River, NJ: Prentice Hall, 1998), 319.

62. R.E. Van Voorst, *Anthology of World Scriptures*, 7th ed. (Boston, MA: Wadsworth Cengage Learning, 2011) xvii.

63. W. Matthews, *World Religions*, 6th ed. (Belmont, CA: Wadsworth Cengage Learning, 2010), 3.

64. Van Voorst, 2011, 5.

65. D. Crystal, *The Cambridge Encyclopedia of Language*, 2nd ed. (New York: Cambridge University Press, 2003), 224.

66. N. Smart, *Worldview: Crosscultural Explorations of Human Beliefs*, 3rd ed. (Upper Saddle River, NJ: Prentice Hall, 2000), 9–10.

67. Matthews, 2010, 3.

68. Haviland, Prins, Walrath, and McBride, 2010, 588.

69. M.V. Angrosino, *The Culture of the Sacred: Exploring the Anthropology of Religion* (Prospect Heights, IL: Waveland Press, 2004), 97.

70. Paden, 1994, 96.

71. T.A. Robinson and H. Rodrigues, *World Religions: A Guide to Essentials* (Peabody, MA: Hendrickson Publishers, 2006), 14.

72. Smart, 1998, 18.

73. J.L. Esposito, D. J. Fasching, and T. Lewis, *World Religions Today*, 3rd ed. (New York: Oxford University Press, 2009), 11.

74. Smart, 2000, 9.

75. Matthews, 2010, 91.

76. Smart, 2009, 9.

77. Matthews, 2010, 194.

78. H. Smith, *The Illustrated World's Religions: A Guide to Our Wisdom Traditions* (New York: HarperCollins, 1994), 210.

79. Ibid.

80. Coogan, 1998, 10.

81. J. Hendry, *Understanding Japanese Society*, 3rd ed. (New York: Routledge Curzon, 2003), 122.

82. W.C. Smith, *Modern Culture from a Comparative Perspective* (Albany, NY: State University of New York Press, 1997), 32.

83. "Major Religions of the World Ranked by Number of Adherents,"

(August 9, 2007), http://www.adher-ents.com/Religions_By_Adherents. html (accessed March 16, 2011).

84. Ferraro and Andreatta, 2010, 365.

85. *Newsweek* 16, 2001, 49.

86. Braswell, 1994, 95.

87. B. Wilson, *Christianity* (Upper Saddle River, NJ: Prentice Hall, 1999), 16.

88. S. Prothero, *God Is Not One* (New York: HarperCollins, 2010) 67.

89. R.D. Hale, "Christianity," in *The Illustrated Guide to World Religions*, M.D. Coogan, ed. (New York: Oxford University Press, 1998), 54.

90. Esposito, Fasching, and Lewis, 2009, 149.

91. M.J. Weaver and D. Brakke, *Introduction to Christianity*, 4th ed. (Belmont, CA: Wadsworth Cengage Learning, 2009), 8.

92. Markham and Lohr, 2009, 194.

93. A. Romagosa, "Christianity and Community," (n.d.), http:// aromagosa.easycgi.com/christianhu manism/preamble/Christianity.htm (accessed July 3, 2011).

94. Ibid.

95. Carmody and Carmody, 1994, 116.

96. Ibid.

97. McGuire, 2001, 302.

98. Ibid.

99. K.L. Woodard, "2000 Years of Jesus," *Newsweek*, April 5. 1999, http:// www.newsweek.com/id/87939 (accessed July 13, 2011).

100. H.T. Blanche and C.M. Parkes, "Christianity," in *Death and Bereavement Across Cultures*, C.M. Parkes, P. Laungani, and B. Young, eds. (New York: Routledge, 1997), 145.

101. Woodward, 1999.

102. Ibid.

103. B. Storm, *More Than Talk: Communication Studies and the Christian Faith* (Dubuque, IA: Kendall/Hunt, 1996).

104. Smart, 2000, 113.

105. Wilson, 1999, 26.

106. Smith, 1994, 210.

107. Weaver and Brakke, 2009, 161.

108. Ibid., 162.

109. M.L. Andersen and H.F. Taylor, *Sociology: The Essentials*, 6th ed. (Belmont, CA: Wadsworth Cengage Learning, 2011), 335.

110. T.C. Muck, *Those Other Religions in Your Neighborhood: Loving Your Neighbor When You Don't Know How* (Grand Rapids, MI: Zondervan, 1992), 165.

111. Blanche and Parkes, 1997, 145.

112. Carmody and Carmody, 1994, 104.

113. R. France, "Jesus," in *Eerdmans' Handbook to the World's Religions*, (Grand Rapids, MI: Eerdmans, 1982), 339.

114. Ibid.

115. K.P. Kramer, *The Sacred Art of Dying: How World Religions Understand Death* (Mahwah, NJ: Paulist Press, 1988), 1.

116. Matthews, 2011, 320.

117. Kramer, 188, 142.

118. I Peter 1:3–4 (CEV).

119. B. Wilson, 1999, 105.

120. C.J. Johnson and M.G. McGee, eds., *How Different Religions View Death and Afterlife*, 2nd ed. (Philadelphia, PA: The Charles Press, 1998), 266.

121. M. Connolly, "After Death— Heaven", *Spirituality for Today*, 1:9, April 1996, http://www.spirituality. org/is/009/page06.asp (accessed July 13, 2008).

122. Matthews, 2011, 320.

123. C. Panati, *Sacred Origins of Profound Things* (New York: Penguin Books, 1996), 461.

124. Ibid.

125. "Christian Funerals: Christian Death and Burial, *BBC Religions* (June 23, 2009), http://www.bbc.co.uk/ religion/religions/christianity/ ritesrituals/funerals.shtml (accessed June 26, 2011).

126. "Major Religions of the World Ranked by Number of Adherents," (August 9, 2007), http://www.adher ents.com/Religions_By_Adherents. html (accessed July 3, 2011).

127. Prothero, 2010, 245.

128. Smith, 1991, 271.

129. Matthews, 2011, 240.

130. Ibid., 341.

131. S.M. Matlins and A.J. Magida, *How To Be A Perfect Stranger*, 4th ed. (Woodstock, VT: SkyLight Paths, 2006), 132.

132. D. Prager and J. Telushkin, *The Nine Questions People Ask About Judaism* (New York: Simon and Schuster, 1981), 112.

133. D.J. Boorstin, *The Creators* (New York: Random House, 1992), 43.

134. R.L. Torstrick, *Culture and Customs of Israel* (Westport, CT: Greenwood Press, 2004), 28.

135. C.S. Ehrlich, "Judaism," in *The Illustrated Guide to World Religion*, M.D. Coogan, ed. (New York: Oxford University Press, 1998), 16.

136. R. Robinson, "Judaism and the Jewish People," in *The Compact Guide to World Religion*, D.C. Halverson, ed. (Minneapolis, MN: Bethany House, 1996), 125.

137. Torstrick, 2006, 31.

138. Matthews, 2011, 268.

139. Prothero, 2010, 267.

140. Robinson, 1996, 124.

141. Tischler, 2011, 268.

142. Osborne, 1996, 7.

143. Prothero, 2010, 267.

144. Ibid., 269.

145. Fisher and Luyster, 1991, 175.

146. C. Van Doren, *A History of Knowledge* (New York: Ballantine Books, 1991), 16.

147. B.A. Robinson, "Two Millennia of Jewish Persecution: Anti-Judaism: 70 to 1200 CE," Ontario Consultants on Religious Tolerance, (February 7, 2010), http://www. religioustolerance.org/jud_pers1.htm (accessed June 26, 2011).

148. B.A. Robinson, "Two Millennia of Jewish Persecution: Anti-Judaism: 1201 to 1800 CE," Ontario Consultants on Religious Tolerance, (May 2, 2009), http://www.religioustoler ance.org/jud_pers3.htm (accessed June 26, 2011).

149. Prothero, 2010, 272.

150. Prager and Telushkin, 1981, 29.

151. Esposito, Fasching, and Lewis, 2009, 131.

152. Markham and Lohr, 2009, 131.

153. U.S. Department of State, *Contemporary Global Anti-Semitism: A Report Provided to the United States Congress* (March 2008), http://www.state.gov/documents/organization/102301.pdf (accessed November 7, 2011).

154. Van Doren, 1991, 16.

155. Braswell, 1994, 81.

156. E. Peters, *Judaism, Christianity and Islam: The Classical Texts and Their Interpretation* (Princeton, NJ: Princeton University Press, 1990).

157. L. Rosten, *Religions of America* (New York: Simon and Schuster, 1975), 143.

158. Ibid.

159. Tischler, 2011, 314.

160. Markham and Lohr, 2009, 174.

161. Prager and Telushkin, 1981, 46.

162. Smith, 1994, 189.

163. Prothero, 2010, 253.

164. "What is Judaism: The Jewish People Are A Family," *Judaism 101* (n.d.), http://www.jewfaq.org/judaism.htm (accessed July 3, 2011).

165. Matlins and Maglins, 2006, 139.

166. M. Langley, *Eyewitness Religion* (New York: D K Publishing, Inc., 2005), 46.

167. Rosten, 1975, 575.

168. A.L. Ponn, "Judaism," in *How Different Religions View Death and Afterlife*, 2nd ed., C.J. Johnson and M.G. McGee, eds. (Philadelphia, PA: The Charles Press, 1998), 147.

169. "Afterlife," *The Jewish Virtual Library* (American-Israeli Cooperative Enterprise, 2006), http://www.jewishvirtuallibrary.org/jsource/Judaism/afterlife.html (accessed June 26, 2011).

170. Kramer, 1988, 123.

171. Matthews, 2010, 274.

172. Markham, 2000, 243.

173. Prothero, 2010, 25.

174. Esposito, Fasching, and Lewis, 2009, 216.

175. Ferraro and Andreatta, 2010, 340–341.

176. Ibid., 314.

177. D. Belt, "The World of Islam," *National Geographic*, January 2002, 76.

178. The Pew Forum on Religion and Public Life, *Mapping the Global Muslim Population* (October 7, 2009), http://pewforum.org/Mapping-the-global-Muslim-Population.aspx (accessed June 26, 2011).

179. V. Hildebrand, et al., *Knowing and Serving Diverse Families*, 3rd ed. (Upper Saddle Back, NJ: Merrill Prentice Hall, 2008), 149.

180. M. Sedgwick, *Islam and Muslims: A Guide to Diverse Experience in a Modern World* (Boston: Intercultural Press, 2006), 4.

181. K.L. Woodward, "In the Beginning, There Were the Holy Books," *Newsweek*, Feb 11, 2001, 52.

182. T. Reagan, *Non-Western Educational Traditions: Alternative Approaches to Educational Thought and Practice*, 2nd ed. (Mahwah, NJ: Lawrence Erlbaum, 2000), 183.

183. M.S. Gordon, "Islam," in *The Illustrated Guide to World Religion*, M.D. Coogan, ed. (New York: Oxford University Press, 1998), 92.

184. "Muslim-Majority Countries," The Future of the Global Muslim Population: Projections for 2010-2030, Pew Research Center: Forum on Religion & Public Life (January 27, 2011), http://pewforum.org/future-of-the-global-muslim-population-muslim-majority.aspx (accessed July 7, 2011).

185. E.E. Calverley, "World-Center Islam," in *World-Center: Today and Tomorrow*, R.N. Anshen, ed. (New York: Harper and Brothers, 1956), 65.

186. Koran, 112: 1–4.

187. Braswell, 1994. 119.

188. A. Schimmel, *Islam: An Introduction* (Albany, NY: State University of New York Press, 1992), 82.

189. Panati, 1996, 372.

190. Langley, 2005, 56.

191. Van Voorst, 2011, 297.

192. Prothero, 2010, 42.

193. J.J. Elias, *Islam* (Upper Saddle River, NJ: Prentice-Hall, 1999), 21.

194. D.L. Daniel and A.A. Nahdi, *Culture and Customs of Iran* (Westport, CT: Greenwood Press, 2006), 38.

195. C.E. Farah, *Islam*, 7th ed. (Hauppauge, NY: Barron's Educational Series, Inc., 2003), 120.

196. Ibid.

197. Koran, 3:145.

198. Ibid., 87:2–3.

199. L. Schneider and A. Silverman, *Global Sociology: Introducing Five Contemporary Societies*, 5th ed. (New York: McGraw-Hill, 2010), 194.

200. Fisher and Luyster, 1991, 289.

201. E.M. Caner and E.F. Caner, *Unveiling Islam* (Grand Rapids, MI: Kregel Publications, 2002), 122.

202. M.K. Nydell, *Understanding Arabs: A Guide for Modern Times*, 4th ed. (Boston: Intercultural Press, 2006), 85.

203. Prothero, 2010, 33.

204. Matthews, 2010, 336.

205. Schneider and Silverman, 2010, 197.

206. Esposito, Fasching, and Lewis, 2009, 241.

207. S.K. Farsoun, *Culture and Customs of the Palestinians* (Westport, CT: Greenwood, 2004), 77.

208. Prothero, 2010, 34.

209. J.J. Elias, *Islam* (Upper Saddle River, NJ: Prentice-Hall, 1999), 71.

210. Caner and Caner, 2002, 130.

211. Prothero, 2010, 34.

212. B. Handwerk, "What Does 'Jihad' Really Mean to Muslims?" *National Geographic News*, October 24, 2003, http://news.nationalgeographic.com/news/pf/48665454.html (accessed June 26, 2011).

213. C. Bennett, *Studying Islam* (New York: Continuum International Publishing Group, 2010), 62.

214. Schneider and Silverman, 2010, 198.

215. Elias, 1999, 73.

216. Ibid.

217. K. Armstrong, *A History of God: The 4000-Year Quest of Judaism, Christianity, and Islam* (New York: Knopf, 1994), 344.

218. K.E. Richter, E.M. Rapple, J.C. Modschiedler, and R. Peterson, *Understanding Religion in a Global Society* (Belmont, CA: Wadsworth, 2005), 366.

219. Nydell, 2006, 81.

220. Elias, 1999, 61.

221. A. Esler, *The Human Venture*, 2nd ed. (Englewood Cliffs, NJ: Prentice Hall, 1992), 257–258.

222. Prothero, 2010, 49.

223. "Sharia," *BBC Religions* (March 09, 2009), http://www.bbc.co.uk/religion/religions/islam/beliefs/sharia_1.shtml (accessed July 3, 2011).

224. A. Claverie, "Group Tries to Separate Islam from Sharia Law," *North County Times*, September 21, 2010.

225. Prothero, 2010, 55.

226. L. Taraki, "The Role of Women," in *Understanding The Contemporary Middle East*, 2nd ed., D.J. Gerner and J. Schwedler, eds. (Boulder, CO: Lynne Rienner Publishers, 2004), 335.

227. Sedgwick, 2006, 90–91.

228. J. Esherick, *Women in the Modern Arab World* (Philadelphia: Mason Crest Publishers, 2005), 53.

229. Ibid.

230. Esposito, Fasching, and Lewis, 2009, 247.

231. Elias, 1999, 107.

232. J. Hughes, "Muslim Women Find an Ally for More Rights: The Koran," *The Christian Science Monitor - CSMonitor.com*, May 13, 2010, htt://www.csmonitor.com/Commentary/John-Hughes/2010/0513/ Muslim-women-find-an-ally-for-more-rights-the-Koran (accessed July 3, 2011).

233. "Cairo," *The Week*, March 18, 2011, 10.

234. Farah, 2006, 415.

235. Nydell, 2006, 45.

236. Ibid.

237. A. Mir, *The American Encounter with Islam* (Broomall, PA: Mason Crest Publishers, 2004), 88.

238. Robinson and Rodrigues, 2006, 131.

239. Elias, 1999, 64.

240. Smith, 1986, 318.

241. "World Hindu Population," Malaysia Hindu Dharma Mamandram (n.d.), http://www.mamandram.org/tools/world-hindu-population.html (accessed June 26, 2011)

242. V. Narayanan, "Hinduism," in *The Illustrated Guide to World Religion*, M.D. Coogan, ed. (New York: Oxford University Press, 1998), 126.

243. Boorstin, 1992, 5.

244. Smart, 1998, 44.

245. Esposito, Fasching, and Lewis, 2009, 301.

246. C. Shattuck, *Hinduism* (Upper Saddle River, NJ: Prentice Hall, 1999), 17.

247. Matthews, 2010, 67.

248. Narayanan, 1998, 130.

249. R.E. Van Voorst 2011, 22.

250. D.M. Knipe, "Veda," in *The Perennial Dictionary of World Religions*, K. Crim, ed. (New York: HarperCollins, 1989), 785.

251. S. Prabhavanda and F. Manchester, *The Upanishads: The Breath of the Eternal* (Hollywood, CA: Vedanta Press, 1978), xvii.

252. B. Usha, *A Ramakrishna-Vedanta Handbook* (Hollywood, CA: Vedanta Press, 1971), 79–80.

253. "Bhagavad Gita," *The Columbia Encyclopedia*, 6th ed. (2008), http://www.encyclopedia.com/topic/Bhagavad-Gita.axpx#3 (accessed June 26, 2011).

254. Robinson and Rodrigues, 2006, 165.

255. Shattuck, 1999, 39.

256. Markham and Lohr, 2009, 64.

257. V. Narayanan, *Understanding Hinduism* (London: Duncan Baird Publishers, 2006), 23.

258. Boorstin, 1992, 4–5.

259. D. Jurney, ed., *Gems of Guidance: Selections from the Scriptures of the World* (Kidlington, UK: George Ronald, Publisher, 1992), 48.

260. R. Kumer and A.K. Sethi, *Doing Business in India* (New York: Palgrave Macmillan, 2005), 57.

261. Johnson and McGee, 1998, 112.

262. Smart, 1998, 87.

263. N. Jain and E.D. Kussman, "Dominant Cultural Patterns of Hindus in India," in *Intercultural Communication: A Reader*, 9th ed., L.A. Samovar and R.E. Porter, eds. (Belmont, CA: Wadsworth, 2000), 83.

264. S. Prabhavanda, *The Spiritual Heritage of India*, 2nd ed. (Hollywood, CA: Vedanta Press, 1969), 335.

265. M.B. McGuire, *Religion: The Social Context*, 5th ed. (Belmont, CA: Wadsworth, 2002), 166.

266. Braswell, 1994, 31.

267. V. Jayaram, "The Hindu Way of Life, According to Hindu Dharma for Self Realization," *Hindu Website.com* (n.d.), http://www.hinduwebsite.com/hinduwaycorrect.asp (accessed July 3, 2011).

268. Richter, Rapple, Modschiedler, and Peterson, 2005, 89.

269. T.K. Venkateswaran, "Hinduism: A Portrait," in *A Source Book for Earth's Community of Religions*, J. D. Beversluis, ed. (Grand Rapids, MI: CoNexus Press, 1995), 40.

270. C.E. Henderson, *Culture and Customs of India* (Westport, CT: Greenwood Press, 2002), 32.

271. M.K. DeGenova, *Families in Cultural Context: Strengths and Challenges in Diversity* (Mountain View, CA: Mayfield Publishing Company, 1997), 174.

272. Prothero, 2010, 161.

273. Johnson and McGee, 1998, 115.

274. A. Dhand, "The Dharma of Ethics, the Ethics of Dharma: Quizzing the Ideals of Hinduism," *Journal of Religious Ethics*, 30 (2002), 347–372.

275. Prothero, 2010, 146.

276. Matthews, 2010, 75.

277. Kumar and Sethi, 2005, 58.

278. See Braswell, 1994, 37; Esposito, Fasching, and Lewis, 2009; Matthews, 2011, 79; Van Voorst, 2011, 37.

279. Matthews, 2011, 78.

280. Narayanan, 2004, 90.

281. Matlins and Magida, 2006, 107.

282. Johnson and McGee, 1998, 124–127.

283. A. Powell, *Living Buddhism* (Berkeley, CA: University of California Press, 1989), 10.

284. N. Thera, *An Outline of Buddhism* (Singapore: Palelai Buddhist Temple Press, n.d.), 19.

285. K. Armstrong, *Buddha* (New York: Penguin Books, 2001), xxi.

286. Esposito, Fasching, and Lewis, 2009, 398.

287. H. Smith and Novak, *Buddhism: A Concise Introduction* (New York: HarperCollins, 2003), 4.

288. P. Garfinkel, "Buddha Rising," *National Geographic*, December 2005, 96.

289. D.N. Clark, *Culture and Customs of Korea* (Westport, CT: Greenwood Press, 2000), 31.

290. R.H. Robinson, W.L. Johnson, and T. Bhikku, *Buddhist Religions: A Historical Introduction*, 5th ed. (Belmont, CA: Wadsworth, 2005), 7.

291. Prothero, 2010, 181.

292. M. Wood, *India* (New York: Basic Books, 2007) 65.

293. Smith and Novak, 2003, 3–4.

294. Ibid., 4.

295. K. Armstrong, *The Great Transformation: The Beginnings of Our Religious Traditions* (New York: Alfred A. Knopf, 2006), xiii.

296. B. Bodhi, *The Buddha and His Dhamma* (Sri Lanka: Buddhist Publication Society, 1999), 15.

297. B. Bodhi, *Nourishing the Roots and Other Essays on Buddhist Ethics* (Sri Lanka: Buddhist Publication Society, 1978), 7.

298. Powell, 1989, 23.

299. Smith, 1991, 99.

300. W. Metz, "The Enlightened One: Buddhism," in *Eerdmans' Handbook of the World's Religions*, (Grand Rapids, MI: Eerdmans, 1982), 231–232.

301. Bodhi, 1999, 25.

302. Esposito, Fasching and Lewis, 2009, 404.

303. "The Four Noble Truths," *BBC: Religion* (November 17, 2009), http://www.bbc.co.uk/religion/ buddhism/beliefs/fournobletruths_1. shtml#h3 (accessed June 26, 2011).

304. Prothero, 2010, 183.

305. For a more detailed description of the Eightfold Path see Bodhi, 1999, 32; B.H. Gunaratana, *Eight Mindful Steps to Happiness* (Boston: Wisdom Publications, 2001); Esposito, Fasching, and Lewis, 2009, 404–405; Halverson, 1996, 58–59; Matthews, 2010, 111; A. Newberg, *Why We Believe What We Believe* (New York, NY: Free Press, 2006), 172; Powell, 1989, 24–25; and Van Voorst, 2011, 82–83.

306. R. Brabant-Smith, "Two Kinds of Language," *The Middle Way: Journal of the Buddhist Society*, 68 (1993), 123.

307. T. Thien-An, *Zen Philosophy, Zen Practice* (Emeryville, CA: Dharma, 1975), 17.

308. A.J.V. Chandrakanthan, "The Silence of Buddha and His Contemplation of the Truth," *Spirituality Today*, 40:2 (1988), http://www.spiritualitytoday.org/ spir2day/884025chandrak.html (accessed June 27, 2011).

309. Smith and Novak, 2003, 56.

310. Ibid, 112.

311. "Fundamentals of Buddhism: Karma," *Buddanet.com* (Buddha Dharma Education Association Inc. (n.d.), http://www.buddhanet.net/ fundbud9.htm (accessed July 3, 2011).

312. K.N. Jayatilleke, *The Message of the Buddha* (Sri Lanka: Buddhist Publication Society, 2000), 141.

313. Novak, 1994, 67.

314. R. Bogoda, *A Simple Guide to Life* (Sri Lanka: Buddhist Publication Society, 1994), 43.

315. Markham and Lohr, 2009, 94.

316. J. Carse, "Death," in *The Perennial Dictionary of World Religions*, K. Crim, ed. (New York: HarperCollins, 1989), 210.

317. A. Ottama, *The Message in the Teachings of Kamma, Rebirth, Samsara* (Sri Lanka: Buddhist Publication Society, 1998), 43.

318. S.O. Long, *Final Days: Japanese Culture and Choice at the End of Life* (Honolulu, HI: University of Hawaii Press, 2005) 69.

319. Johnson and McGee, 1998, 55.

320. C. Lamb, "Buddhist Rites of Passage," *Inquiring Mind*, 27 (Spring 2011), 8–9.

321. R.L. Taylor, *Confucianism* (Philadelphia, PA: Chelsea House Publications, 2004), 3.

322. Prothero, 2010, 104.

323. L.E. Harrison, "Promoting Progressive Cultural Change," in *Culture Matters: How Values Shape Human Progress*, L.E. Harrison and S.P. Huntington, eds. (New York: Basic Books, 2000), 296.

324. Van Voorst, 2011, 139.

325. Prothero, 2010, 105.

326. R.L. Taylor, "Confucianism," in *The Perennial Dictionary of World Religions*, K. Crim, ed. (New York: HarperCollins, 1989), 188–189.

327. Scarborough, 1998, 27.

328. Taylor, 1989, 192.

329. Oldstone-Moore, "Chinese Traditions," in *The Illustrated Guide to World Religion*, M.D. Coogan, ed. (New York: Oxford University Press, 1998), 205.

330. I.P. McGreal, *Great Thinkers of the Eastern World* (New York: HarperCollins, 1995), 3.

331. Matthews, 2010, 183.

332. T.I.S. Leung, "Confucianism," in *The Compact Guide to World Religions*, D.C. Halverson, ed. (Minneapolis, MN: Bethany Publishers, 1996), 75.

333. Van Voorst, 2011, 148.

334. S. Dragga, "Ethical Intercultural Technical Communication: Looking Through the Lens of Confucian Ethics," in *Intercultural Communication: A Reader*, 11th ed., L.A. Samovar, R.E. Porter, and E.R. McDaniel, eds. (Belmont, CA: Wadsworth, 2006), 421.

335. J.O. Yum, "Confucianism and Interpersonal Relationships and Communication Patterns in East Asia," in *Intercultural Communication: A Reader*, 9th ed., L.A. Samovar

and R.E. Porter, eds. (Belmont, CA: Wadsworth, 2000), 64.

336. Van Voorst, 2011, 149.

337. Esposito, Fasching, and Lewis, 2009, 486.

338. Langley, 2005, 30.

339. Smith, 1994, 110.

340. Matthews, 2010, 185.

341. Ibid., 184.

342. Smith, 1994, 111.

343. M.J. Gannon and R. Pillai, *Understanding Global Cultures*, 4th ed. (Thousand Oaks, CA: Sage Publications, 2010), 438.

344. Smith, 1994, 111.

345. M. Soeng, *Trust Your Mind* (Boston: Wisdom Publications, 2004), 42.

346. C. Chiu and Y. Hong, *Social Psychology of Culture* (New York: Psychology Press, 2006), 178.

347. G. Chen and J. Chung, "The Impact of Confucianism on Organizational Communication," *Communication Quarterly*, 42 (1994), 97.

348. Novak, 1994, 120.

349. G. Gao and S. Ting-Toomey, *Communicating Effectively with the Chinese* (Thousand Oaks, CA: Sage Publications, 1998), 75.

350. Yum, 2000, 70.

351. Prothero, 2010, 106.

352. Kramer, 1988, 200.

353. Prothero, 2010, 106.

354. T.L. Friedman, "A War We Can't Win with Guns Only," *San Diego Union-Tribune*, Nov 28, 2001, B-8.

355. Esposito, Fasching, and Lewis, 2009, 593.

356. Prothero, 2010, 334–335.

357. Friedman, 2001, B-8.

Chapter 6

1. R. L. Merz, *A Declaration of American Business Values* (Cherry Hill, NJ: Values of America, 2006), 19.

2. S. Hawking and L. Mlodinow, *The Grand Design* (New York: Bantam Books, 2010), 46.

3. B.L. De Mente, *Japan Unmasked* (Tokyo: Tuttle, 2005), 131.

4. W. B. Gudykunst, *Bridging Differences: Effective Intergroup Communication*, 4th ed. (Thousand Oaks, CA: Sage Publications, 2004), 105.

5. P.R. Harris and R.T. Moran, *Managing Cultural Differences: Leadership Strategies for a New World of Business* (Houston, TX: Gulf, 1996), 274.

6. N.J. Adler with A. Gunderson, *International Dimensions of Organizational Behavior*, 5th ed. (Mason, OH: Thomson South-Western, 2008), 73.

7. H. Nordby, "Values, Cultural Identity and Communication: A Perspective from Philosophy of Language," *Journal of Intercultural Communication*, 17 (June 2008), http://www.immi.se/intercultural/ (accessed May 20. 2011).

8. "The Debate Over Universal Values," *The Economist* (October 2, 2010), 43.

9. Charlemagne, "Help them to help themselves," *The Economist* (Jun 26, 2010), 56.

10. M. L. Andersen and H. F. Taylor, *Sociology: The Essentials*, 6th ed. (Belmont, CA: Wadsworth Cengage Learning, 2011), 37.

11. G. Bailey and J. Peoples, *Essentials of Cultural Anthropology*, 2nd ed. (Belmont, CA: Wadsworth Cengage Learning, 2011), 26.

12. R. D'Andrade, *A Study of Personal and Cultural Values* (New York: Palgrave Macmillan, 2008), 4.

13. J. M. Charon and L. G. Vigilant, *The Meaning of Sociology*, 8th ed. (Upper Saddle River, NJ: Pearson Prentice Hall, 2009), 87.

14. E. Y. Kim, *The Yin and Yang of American Culture: A Paradox* (Yarmouth, ME: Intercultural Press, 2001), xv.

15. "Robert Kohls," *Washington Post* (September 2, 2006), http://www.washingtonpost.com/wp-dyn/content/article/2006/09/01/AR2006090101637.html (accessed May 20, 2011).

16. Table adapted from L. Robert Kohls, *The Values Americans Live By* (1986), http://www.claremontmckenna.edu/pages/faculty/alee/extra/American_values.html (accessed May 20, 2011).

17. G. Althen, *American Ways*, 2nd ed. (Yarmouth, ME: Intercultural Press, 2003), 57.

18. A. R. Lanier, *Living in the USA*, 6th ed., rev. by J.C. Davis (Boston, MA: Intercultural Press, 2005), 82–83.

19. M. J. Gannon and R. Pilai, *Understanding Global Cultures*, 4th ed. (Thousand Oaks, CA: Sage, 2011), 263.

20. *Declaration of Independence*, http://www.archives.gov/exhibits/charters/declaration_transcript.html (accessed May 20, 2011).

21. *Constitution of the United States*, Section 9, http://www.archives.gov/exhibits/charters/constitution_transcript.html (accessed May 20, 2011).

22. M. J. Hanson, "Families with Anglo-European Roots," in *Developing Cross-Cultural Competence: A Guide for Working with Children and Their Families*, 2nd ed., E. W. Lynch and M. J. Hanson, eds. (Baltimore: Paul H. Brookes, 1998), 104–105.

23. M. K. Datesman, J. Crandall, and E.N. Kearny, *American Ways: An Introduction to American Culture*, 3rd ed. (White Plains, NY: Pearson, 2005), 29.

24. E. C. Stewart and M. J. Bennett, *American Cultural Patterns: A Cross-Cultural Perspective* (Yarmouth, ME: Intercultural Press, 1991), 133.

25. Datesman, Crandall, and Kearny, 2005, 29.

26. C.S. Fischer, *Made in America* (Chicago: University of Chicago, 2010), 12.

27. Gannon and Pillai, 2010, 255.

28. Adler and Gunderson, 2008, 33.

29. Lanier, 2005, 17–18.

30. Stewart and Bennett, 1991, 119.

31. Althen, 2003, 27.

32. "You choose," *The Economist* (December 18, 2010), 123.

33. T. Bender, *A Nation Among Nations: America's Place in World History* (New York: Hill and Wang, 2006), 187.

34. G. Hofstede, *Culture's Consequences: International Differences in Work-Related Values*, 2nd ed. (Beverly

Hills, CA: Sage Publications, 2001). See also G. Hofstede, G.J. Hofstede, and M. Minkov, *Cultures and Organizations: Software of the Mind*, 3rd ed. (New York: McGraw-Hill, 2010).

35. P. B. Smith, M.H. Bond, and Ç. Kağitçibaşi, *Understanding Social Psychology Across Cultures* (Thousand Oaks, CA: Sage, 2006), 34.

36. J. O. Yum, "The Impact of Confucianism on Interpersonal Relationships and Communication Patterns," in *Intercultural Communication: A Reader*, 8th ed., L.A. Samovar and R.E. Porter, eds. (Belmont, CA: Wadsworth, 1997), 78.

37. P. A. Andersen, M.L. Hecht, G.D. Hoobler, and M. Smallwood, "Nonverbal Communication Across Cultures," in *Cross-Cultural and Intercultural Communication*, W.B. Gudykunst, ed. (Thousand Oaks, CA: Sage Publications, 2003), 77.

38. H. C. Triandis, *Individualism and Collectivism* (Boulder, CO: Westview8Press, 1995). See also H.C. Triandis, "Cross-Cultural Studies of Individualism and Collectivism," in *Cross-Cultural Perspectives*, J.J. Berman, ed. (Lincoln, NE: University of Nebraska Press, 1990), 41–133.

39. D. Brooks, "Harmony and the Dream" *New York Times* (August 11, 2008), http://www.nytimes.com/2008/08/12/opinion/12brooks.html (accessed May 21, 2011).

40. Hofstede, Hofstede, and Minko, 2010, 90.

41. C. Triandis, "Cross-Cultural Studies of Individualism and Collectivism," in *Cross-Cultural Perspectives*, J.J. Berman, ed. (Lincoln, NE: University of Nebraska Press, 1990), 52.

42. D. Etounga-Manguelle, "Does Africa Need a Cultural Adjustment Program?" in *Culture Matters: How Values Shape Human Progress*, L. Harrison and S.P. Huntington, eds. (New York: Basic Books, 2000), 71.

43. M. L. Hecht, M.J. Collier, and S.A. Ribeau, *African American Communication: Ethnic Identity and Interpretation* (Newbury Park, CA: Sage Publications, 1993), 97.

44. T.Y.J. Shim, M.S. Kim, and J.N. Martin, *Changing Korea: Understanding Culture and Communication* (New York: Peter Lang, 2008), 27.

45. K. Belson and N. Onishi, "In Deference to Crisis, a New Obsession Sweeps Japan: Self-Restraint," *New York Times* (March 27, 2011), http://www.nytimes.com/2011/03/28/world/asia/28tokyo.html?ref=world (accessed May 21, 2011).

46. Hofstede, Hofstede, and Minko, 2010, 191.

47. K. Makihara, "Too Tall for Japan," *New York Times* (July 7, 2010), http://www.nytimes.com/2010/07/08/opinion/08iht-edkumiko.html (accessed May 21, 2011).

48. Hofstede, Hofstede, and Minko, 2010, 205.

49. Ibid., 55.

50. Ibid., 61.

51. W. B. Gudykunst, *Asian American Ethnicity and Communication* (Thousand Oaks, CA: Sage Publications, 2001), 41.

52. R. Brislin, *Understanding Culture's Consequence on Behavior*, 2nd ed. (Fort Worth, TX: Harcourt College Publishers, 2000), 288.

53. C. Calloway-Thomas, P.J. Cooper, and C. Blake, *Intercultural Communication: Roots and Routes* (Boston: Allyn and Bacon, 1999), 196.

54. Hofstede, Hofstede, and Minko, 2010, 74.

55. Adler and Gunderson, 2008, 57–58.

56. Hofstede, Hofstede, and Minko, 2010, 140.

57. Adler and Gunderson, 2008, 57.

58. *Women in Elective Office, 2011: Fact Sheet*, Center for American Women and Politics (CAWP), Eagleton Institute of Politics, Rutgers University (March 2011), http://www.cawp.rutgers.edu/fast_facts/levels_of_office/documents/elective.pdf (accessed May 21, 2011).

59. Hofstede, Hofstede, and Minko, 2010, 140.

60. "Norway," in *Global Database of Quotas for Women* (November 17, 2009), http://www.quotaproject.org/uid/countryview.cfm?country=165 (accessed May 21, 2011).

61. R. Hausmann, L.D. Tyson, and S. Zahidi, *The Global Gender Gap Report 2010* (Geneva, Switzerland: World Economic Forum, 2010), http://www3.weforum.org/docs/WEF_GenderGap_Report_2010.pdf (accessed May 21, 2011).

62. Gudykunst, 2001, 47.

63. Chinese Culture Connection, "Chinese Values and the Search for Culture-Free Dimensions of Culture," *Journal of Cross-Cultural Psychology*, 18 (1987), 143–164; See also G. Hofstede and M.H. Bond, "Confucius and Economic Growth: New Trends in Culture's Consequence," *Organizational Dynamics*, 16 (1988), 4–21.

64. Hofstede 2001, 351, 354.

65. Ibid., 351, 355.

66. For information on the World Values Survey, see: http://www.worldvaluessurvey.org/

67. M. Minkov and G. Hofstede, "Hofstede's Fifth Dimension: New Evidence from the World Values Survey," *Journal of Cross-Cultural Psychology* (December 15, 2010), 2. DOI: 10.1177/0022022110388567

68. Ibid, 9.

69. Hofstede, Hofstede, and Minko, 2010, 239, 254.

70. Minkov and Hofstede, "Hofstede's Fifth Dimension," 9.

71. Hofstede, Hofstede, and Minko, 2010, 251.

72. Ibid., 2010, 281.

73. M. Minkov, "Monumentalism versus Flexumility," SIETAR Europa Congress (2007), www.sietar-europa.org/congress2007/files/congress2007_paper_Michael_Minkov.doc (accessed May 21, 2011); Hofstede, Hofstede, and Minko, 2010, 252.

74. F. R. Kluckhohn and F. L. Strodtbeck, *Variations in Value Orientations* (New York: Row and Peterson), 1960.

75. P-J. Fu, "Human Nature and Human Education: On Human Nature as Tending Toward Goodness," in *Chinese Foundations for Moral*

Education and Character Development, T.V. Doan, V. Shen, and G. McLean, eds. (Washington, D.C.: The Council for Research in Values and Philosophy, 1991), 20.

76.   N. C. Jain and E. D. Kussman, "Dominant Cultural Patterns of Hindus in India," in *Intercultural Communication: A Reader*, 9th ed., L.A. Samovar and R.E. Porter, eds. (Belmont, CA: Wadsworth, 2000), 89.

77.   G. C. Chu and Y. Ju, *The Great Wall in Ruins* (Albany, NY: State University of New York Press, 1993), 222–223.

78.   E. T. Hall and M. R. Hall, *Understanding Cultural Differences* (Yarmouth, ME: Intercultural Press, 1990), 87.

79.   J. Luckmann, *Transcultural Communication in Nursing* (Albany, NY: Delmar Publishers, 1999), 31.

80.   N. J. Adler and M. Jelinek, "Is 'Organization Culture' Culture Bound?" in *Culture, Communication and Conflict: Readings in Intercultural Relations*, 2nd ed., G.R. Weaver, ed. (Boston: Pearson, 2000), 130.

81.   Kim, 2001, 115.

82.   E. T. Hall, *Beyond Culture* (Garden City, NY: Doubleday, 1976), 91.

83.   Ibid., 85.

84.   Hall and Hall, 1990, 6.

85.   Hall, 1976, 91.

86.   Hall and Hall, 1990, 6.

87.   D. A. Foster, *Bargaining Across Borders* (New York: McGraw-Hill, 1992), 280.

88.   Gudykunst, 2001, 32.

89.   H-C. Chang, "Communication in the *Analects* of Confucius," in *The Global Intercultural Communication Reader*, M.K. Asante, Y. Miike, and J. Yin, Eds. (New York: Routledge, 2008), 97.

90.   Hall and Hall, 1990, 7.

91.   Althen, 2003, 42.

92.   R. J. House, "Illustrative Examples of GLOBE Findings," in *Culture, Leadership, and Organizations: The GLOBE Study of 62 Societies*, R.J. House, P.J. Hanges, M. Javidan,

P.W. Dorfman, and V. Gupta, eds. (Thousand Oaks, CA: Sage, 2004), 3–8. Problems with data from the Czech Republic resulted in that country being dropped from the study, reducing the number of societies to 61.

93.   For the other two dimensions, there was a positive correlation for Gender Egalitarianism, but the In-Group Collectivism correlation was insignificant. M. Javidan, R. House, P.W. Dorfman, P.J. Hanges and M. Sulleyde Luque, "Conceptualizing and Measuring Cultures and their consequences: A Comparative Review of GLOBE's and Hofstede's Approaches," *Journal of International Business Studies*, 37 (2006), 900–901.

94.   D'Andrade, 2008, 121–126.

95.   R. J. House and M. Javidan, "Overview of GLOBE," in *Culture, Leadership, and Organizations: The GLOBE Study of 62 Societies*, R.J. House, P.J. Hanges, M. Javidan, P.W. Dorfman, and V. Gupta, eds. (Thousand Oaks, CA: Sage, 2004), 11–13; R. House, M. Javidan, P. Hanges, and P. Dorfman. "Understanding Cultures and Implicit Leadership Theories across the Globe: An Introduction to Project Globe." *Journal of World Business*, 37 (2002), 3–10.

96.   For over ten years, this conflict between individual desires (personal values) and the expected organizational practices (institutionalized values) has been a constant theme in informal conversations between Japanese workers and the third author.

97.   V. Gupta and P.H. Hanges, "Regional and Climate Clustering of Societal Cultures," in *Culture, Leadership, and Organizations: The GLOBE Study of 62 Societies*, R.J. House, P.J. Hanges, M. Javidan, P.W. Dorfman, and V. Gupta, eds. (Thousand Oaks, CA: Sage, 2004), 178–189.

98.   G. Bakasci, T. Sándor, K. András, I. Viktor, "Eastern European Cluster: Tradition and Transition," *Journal of World Business*, 37 (2002), 75.

99.   N. M. Ashkansky, E. Trevor-Roberts, L. Earnshaw, "The Anglo Cluster: Legacy of the British Empire," *Journal of World Business*, 37 (2002), 28, 35; V. Gupta, G. Surie, M. Javidan, and J. Chhokar, "Southern Asia Cluster: Where the Old Meets the New?, *Journal of World Business*, 37 (2002), 14.

100.   V. Gupta, P.J. Hanges, and P. Dorfman, "Cultural Clusters: Methodology and Findings," *Journal of World Business*, 37 (2002), 14.

101.   E. Szabo, F.C. Brodbeck, D.N.D. Hartog, G. Reber, J. Weibler, and R. Wunder, "The Germanic Europe Cluster: Where Employees have a Voice," *Journal of World Business*, 37 (2002), 64; Gupta and Hanges, 2004, 199.

102.   G. Bakasci, T. Sándor, K. András, I. Viktor, "Eastern European Cluster: Tradition and Transition," *Journal of World Business*, 37(2002), 75.

103.   J. C. Jesuino, "Latin Europe Cluster: From South to North," *Journal of World Business*, 37 (2002), 84–85.

104.   Gupta and Hanges, 2004, 188, 200.

105.   H. Kabasakal, M. Bodur, "Arabic Cluster: A Bridge Between East and West," *Journal of World Business*, 37 (2002), 40–54.

106.   Gupta, Hanges, and Dorfman, 2002, 14.

107.   Gupta and Hanges, 2004, 200.

108.   Gupta, Surie, Javidan, and Chhokar, 2002, 20–23.

109.   K. Domenici and S.W. Littlejohn, *Facework: Bridging Theory and Practice* (Thousand Oaks, CA: Sage Publications, 2006), 10.

110.   Ting-Toomey, "The Matrix of Face: An Updated Face-Negotiation Theory," in *Theorizing About Intercultural Communication*, W. B. Gudykunst, ed. (Thousand Oaks, CA: Sage Publications, 2005), 73.

111.   Domenici and Littlejohn, 2006, 11.

112.   R.M. March, *Reading the Japanese Mind* (Tokyo: Kodansha, 1996), 28.

113.   G. Gao and S. Ting-Toomey, *Communicating Effectively with the Chinese* (Thousand Oaks, CA: Sage Publications, 1998), 54.

114. P.B. Smith, M.H. Bond, and Ç. Kağitçibaşi, 2006, 159.

115. M.-S. Kim, *Non-Western Perspectives on Human Communication* (Thousand Oaks, CA: Sage Publications, 2002), 65.

116. S. Ting-Toomey and A. Kurogi, "Facework Competence in Intercultural Conflict: An Updated Face-Negotiation Theory," *International Journal of Intercultural Relations*, 22 (1998), 202.

117. Ibid.

Chapter 7

1. J.S. Pinney, "A Three-Stage Model of Ethnic Identity Development in Adolescence," in *Ethnic Identity: Formation and Transmission Among Hispanics and Other Minorities*, M.E. Bernal and G.P. Knight, eds. (Albany, NY: State University of New York Press, 1993), 62.

2. K.R. Humes, N.A. Jones, and R.R. Ramirez, *Overview of Race and Hispanic Origin: 2010* (Washington, D.C.: U.S. Census Bureau), http://www.census.gov/prod/cen2010/briefs/c2010br-02.pdf (accessed August 26, 2011), 4, 9–10.

3. A. Brittingham and P. de la Cruz, *Ancestry: 2000*, (Washington, D.C.: Census 2000 Brief, U.S. Census Bureau), 9. www.census.gov/prod/2004pubs/c2kbr-35.pdf (accessed August 26, 2011).

4. Ibid., 3.

5. M.L. Hecht, R.L. Jackson, II, and S.A. Ribeau, *African American Communication: Exploring Identity and Culture*, 2nd ed. (Mahwah, NJ: Lawrence Erlbaum, 2003), 62.

6. G. Marranci, *The Anthropology of Islam* (New York: Berg, 2008), 89.

7. H.W. Gardiner and C. Kosmitzki, *Lives Across Cultures: Cross-Cultural Human Development*, 4th ed. (Boston: Pearson Education, 2008), 154.

8. S. Ting-Toomey, "Identity Negotiation Theory: Crossing Cultural Boundaries," in *Theorizing About Intercultural Communication*, W.B. Gudykunst, ed. (Thousand Oaks, CA: Sage Publications, 2005), 212.

9. J.N. Martin and T.K. Nakayama, *Intercultural Communication in Contexts* 5th ed. (New York: McGraw-Hill, 2010), 162.

10. M. Fong, "Identity and the Speech Community," in *Communicating Ethnic and Cultural Identity*, M. Fong and R. Chuang, eds. (Lanham, MD: Rowman and Littlefield, 2004), 6.

11. Ibid.

12. M.W. Lustig and J. Koester, *Intercultural Competence: Interpersonal Communication Across Cultures*, 6th ed. (Boston: Allyn and Bacon, 2010), 142.

13. S. Ting-Toomey and L.C. Chung, *Understanding Intercultural Communication* (Los Angeles: Roxbury, 2005), 93.

14. I.E. Klyukanov, *Principles of Intercultural Communication* (Boston: Pearson Education, 2005), 12.

15. J.C. Turner, *Rediscovering the Social Group: A Self-Categorization Theory* (Oxford: Basil Blackwell, 1987), 45.

16. B.J. Hall, *Among Cultures*, 2nd ed. (Belmont, CA: Thomson-Wadsworth, 2005), 108–109.

17. Ibid., 109.

18. W.B. Gudykunst, *Bridging Differences: Effective Intergroup Communication*, 4th ed. (Thousand Oaks, CA: Sage Publications, 2004), 77.

19. T.T. Imahori and W.R. Cupach, "Identity Management Theory: Face Work in Intercultural Relations," in W.B. Gudykunst, ed., *Theorizing About Intercultural Communication* (Thousand Oaks, CA: Sage Publications, 2005), 196.

20. W.A. Haviland, H.E.L. Prins, D. Walrath, and B. McBride, *Cultural Anthropology: The Human Challenge*, 13th ed. (Belmont, CA: Wadsworth Cengage Learning, 2010), 24.

21. Fong, 2004, 14.

22. P.B. Smith, M.H. Bond, and C. Kagitcibasi, *Understanding Social Psychology Across Cultures* (Thousand Oaks, CA: Sage, 2006), 224.

23. "Explore the Form" *United States Census 2010*, http://2010.census.gov/

2010census/about/interactive-form.php (accessed August 27, 2010).

24. C.P. Kottak and K.A. Kozaitis, *On Being Different*, 2nd ed. (New York: McGraw-Hill, 2003), 92.

25. M.J. Collier, "Researching Cultural Identity: Reconciling Interpretive and Postcolonial Perspectives," in *Communication and Identity Across Cultures*, D.V. Tanno and A. Gonzalez, eds. (Thousand Oaks, CA: Sage Publications, 1998), 38.

26. V. Chen, "(De)hyphenated Identity: The Double Voice of The Woman Warrior" in *Our Voices*, 4th ed., A. González, M. Houston, and V. Chen, eds. (Los Angeles: Roxbury, 2004), 20.

27. Martin and Nakayama, 2010, 191.

28. Ting-Toomey, 2005, 213.

29. P. Cohen, "Professor is a Label That Leans to the Left," *New York Times* (January 18, 2010), http://www.nytimes.com/2010/01/18/arts/18liberal.html (accessed August 28, 2011).

30. Haviland, et al., 2010, 149–50.

31. H. Beech, "Where the 'Ladyboys' Are," *Time World* (July 07, 2008), http://www.time.com/time/world/article/0,8599,1820633,00.html (accessed August 28, 2011).

32. "A question of sex," *The Economist* (October 17, 2010), 2009.

33. T.R. Reid, *The United States of Europe* (New York: Penguin Press, 2004), 200.

34. "Critics Slam French Immigration Ministry," *Japan Times* (June 24, 2007), 7.

35. "The difficulty of trying to stop it happening ever again," *The Economist* (April 11, 2009), 45.

36. K. Maurer, "Afghan commandos' esprit de corps transcends tribe." *Seattle Times* (September 12, 2009), http://seattletimes.nwsource.com/html/nationworld/2009854105_apasafghancommandos.html (accessed August 28, 2011).

37. G.W. Allport, *The Nature of Prejudice* (Reading, MA: Addison-Wesley, 1954), 116.

38. H. Hirayama, *Breakthrough Japanese* (Tokyo: Kodansha, 2004), 15–16.

39. H. Markus and S. Kitayama, "Culture and the Self: Implications for Cognition, Emotion, and Motivation," *Psychological Review*, 98 (1991), 224.

40. J. Suler, "Identity Management in Cyberspace," *Journal of Applied Psychoanalytic Studies*, 4 (2002), 455.

41. Ibid., 457.

42. "Eat, Pray, Tweet," *The Economist* (January 8, 2011), 64.

43. "No Mao suits here," *The Economist* (August 6, 2011), 58.

44. C. Reid and H. MacDonald, "Comics, Digital Delivery and a Few Movies Rule Comic-Con 2011," *Publisher's Weekly* (July 29, 2011), http://www.publishersweekly.com/pw/by-topic/industry-news/trade-shows-events/article/48173-comics-digital-delivery-and-a-few-movies-rule-comic-con-2011.html (accessed October 9, 2011).

45. Ting-Toomey, 2005, 211.

46. Ibid., 212.

47. Phinney, 1993, 61–79.

48. Ibid., 66.

49. J.N. Martin, R.L. Krizek, T.K. Nakayama, and L. Bradford, "Exploring Whiteness: A Study of Self Labels for White Americans, *Communication Quarterly*, 44 (1996), 125.

50. Phinney, 1993, 69.

51. D.V. Tanno, "Names, Narratives, and the Evolution of Ethnic Identity," in *Our Voices*, 4th ed., A. González, M. Houston, and V. Chen, eds. (Los Angeles: Roxbury, 2004), 39.

52. Phinney, 1993, 76.

53. Martin and Nakayama, 2011, 172–80.

54. Ibid.

55. Ibid.

56. "Background," *'Hafu'/Half Japanese* (2010), http://www.hafujapanese.org/index.html (accessed August 28, 2011).

57. Hall, 2005, 117.

58. G.A. Yep, "My Three Cultures: Navigating the Multicultural Identity Landscape," in *Readings in Intercultural Communication*, J.N. Martin, T.K. Nakayama, and L.A. Flores, eds. (Boston: McGraw-Hill, 2002), 63.

59. D. Molden, "Seven Miles from Independence: The War, Internee Identity and the Manzanar Free Press," dissertation, University of Minnesota, 1998, 21–22.

60. A.D. Buckley and M.C. Kenney, *Negotiating Identity: Rhetoric, Metaphor, and Social Drama in Northern Ireland* (Washington, D.C.: Smithsonian Institution Press, 1995).

61. J.A. Drzewiecka and N. Draznin, "A Polish Jewish American Story: Collective Memories and Intergroup Relations," in L.A. Samovar, R.E. Porter, and E.R. McDaniel, eds., *Intercultural Communication: A Reader*, 11th ed. (Belmont, CA: Thomson-Wadsworth, 2005), 73.

62. H.C. Triandis, *Individualism and Collectivism* (Boulder, CO: Westview Press, 1995), 71; see also Martin and Nakayama, 2008, 91.

63. M.Y. Ishikida, *Japanese Education in the 21st Century* (New York: iUniverse, 2005), 59.

64. H.W. Gardiner and C. Kosmitzki, *Lives Across Cultures*, 4th ed. (Boston: Allyn and Bacon, 2008), 71.

65. D.H. Palfrey (1997) *La Quinceañera*. www.mexconnect.com, http://www.mexconnect.com/articles/3192-la-quincea%C3%B1era-a-celebration-of-budding-womanhood (accessed August 28, 2011).

66. Gardiner and Kosmitzki, 2008, 73.

67. G. David and K.K. Ayouby, "Being Arab and Becoming Americanized: Forms of Mediated Assimilation in Metropolitan Detroit," in *Muslim Minorities in the West*, Y.Y. Haddad and J.I. Smith, eds. (Walnut Creek, CA: Altamira Press, 2002), 131.

68. Ibid.

69. Ibid.

70. Hecht, Jackson, and Ribeau, 2003, 61.

71. T.T. Imahori and W.R. Cupach, "Identity Management Theory: Face Work in Intercultural Relations," in W.B. Gudykunst, ed., *Theorizing About Intercultural Communication* (Thousand Oaks, CA: Sage Publications, 2005), 197.

72. M.J. Collier, "Cultural Identity and Intercultural Communication," in *Intercultural Communication: A Reader*, 11th ed., L.A. Samovar, R.E. Porter, and E.R. McDaniel, eds. (Belmont, CA: Thomson-Wadsworth, 2006), 59.

73. A. Giddens, *Runaway World: How Globalization is Reshaping our Lives* (New York: Rutledge), 13.

74. F. Vuong and T. Nguyen, "Time for San Diego to Establish a Little Saigon," *San Diego Union-Tribune* (July 11, 2010), B-7.

75. S. Erlanger, "French Mosque's Symbolism Varies With Beholder," *New York Times* (December 27, 2009), http://www.nytimes.com/2009/12/28/world/europe/28marseille.html?pagewanted=all (accessed August 30, 2011).

76. R. Chuang, "Theoretical Perspective: Fluidity and Complexity of Cultural and Ethnic Identity," in *Communicating Ethnic and Cultural Identity*, M. Fong and R. Chuang, eds. (Lanham, MD: Rowman and Littlefield, 2004), 65.

77. J.N. Martin, T.K. Nakayama, and L.A. Flores, "Identity and Intercultural Communication" in *Readings in Intercultural Communication*, J.N. Martin, T.K. Nakayama, and L A. Flores, eds. (Boston: McGraw-Hill, 2002), 33.

78. J. Hit, "The Newest Indians," *New York Times Magazine* (August 21, 2005), 38.

79. J. Kotkin and T. Tseng, "Happy to Mix It All Up," *Washington Post*, (June 8, 2003), B-1.

80. Ibid.

81. U.S. Department of State, *Table XVI (A)*, *Classes of Nonimmigrants Issued Visas, Fiscal Years 1992-2010* (n.d.), http://travel.state.gov/pdf/MultiYearTableXVI.pdf (accessed August 30, 2011).

82. C. Onwumechili, P.O. Nwosu, R.L. Jackson II, and J. James-Hughes, "In the Deep Valley with Mountains to Climb: Exploring Identity and

Multiple Reacculturation," *International Journal of Intercultural Relations*, 27 (2003), 42.

83. Ibid., 40, 50.

84. "Executive Profile: Carlos Ghosn," *Bloomberg Business Week* (August 29, 2011), http://investing.businessweek.com/businessweek/research/stocks/people/person.asp?personId=752502&ticker=NSANY:US (accessed August 30, 2011); "Carlos Ghosn," *Encyclopedia of World Biography* (n.d.), http://www.notablebiographies.com/supp/Supplement-Fl-Ka/Ghosn-Carlos.html (accessed August 30, 2011).

85. Hitt, 2005, 40.

86. R. Jenkins, "Social Identity," in *The Meaning of Sociology: A Reader*, 9th ed., J.M. Charon and L.G. Vigilant, eds. (Upper Saddle River, NJ: Pearson, 2009), 31.

87. C.S. Abbate, S. Boca, and P. Bocchiaro, "Stereotyping in Persuasive Communication: Influence Exerted by Disapproved Source," *Journal of Applied Social Psychology*, 34 (2004), 1192.

88. J.W. Berry, Y.H. Segall, and P.R. Dasen, *Cross-Cultural Psychology: Research and Application* (New York: Cambridge University Press, 1992), 299.

89. D.J. Schneider, *The Psychology of Stereotypes* (New York: Guilford Press, 2004), 341.

90. J.T. Wood, *Gendered Lives: Communication, Gender and Culture*, 6th ed. (Belmont, CA: Wadsworth/Thomson Learning, 2005), 234.

91. N.J. Adler, *International Dimensions of Organizational Behavior*, 5th ed. (Eagan, MN: Thomson/South Western, 2008), 79.

92. E.W. Lynch and M.J. Hanson, *Developing Cross-Cultural Competence: A Guide for Working with Young Children and Their Families* (Baltimore, MD: Paul H. Brookes, 1992), 44.

93. M. Guirdham, *Communicating Across Cultures* (West Lafayette, IN: Purdue University Press, 1999), 163.

94. D.S. Meshel and R.P. McGlynn, "Intergenerational Contact, Attitudes, and Stereotypes of Adolescents and Older People," *Educational Gerontology*, 30 (2004), 461.

95. Meshel and McGlynn, 2004, 462.

96. W. Stephan, *Reducing Prejudice and Stereotyping in Schools* (New York: Teachers College Press, 1999), 17–19.

97. S. Ting-Toomey and L.C. Chung, *Understanding Intercultural Communication* (Los Angeles: Roxbury Publishing Company, 2005), 238–55.

98. Ibid., 239.

99. J.J. Macionis, *Society: The Basics*, 4th ed. (Upper Saddle River: NJ: Prentice Hall, 1998), 217.

100. J.B. Rusher, *Prejudice Communication: A Social Psychological Perspective* (New York: Guilford Press, 2001), 6.

101. R. Brislin, *Understanding Culture's Influence on Behavior*, 2nd ed. (New York: Harcourt College Publishers, 2000), 209.

102. H.D. Fishbein, *Peer Prejudice and Discrimination: The Origins of Prejudice* (Mahwah, NJ: Lawrence Erlbaum, 2002), 61.

103. For a more detailed account of the functions of prejudice, see Brislin, 2000, 208–213; D. Katz, "The Functional Approach to the Study of Attitudes," *Public Opinion Quarterly*, 24 (1960), 164–204; Hall, 2005, 218–220.

104. A.G. Allport, *The Nature of Prejudice* (Cambridge, MA: Addison-Wesley, 1954).

105. S. Oskamp, "Multiple Paths to Reducing Prejudice and Discrimination," in *Reducing Prejudice and Discrimination*, S. Oskamp, ed. (Mahwah, NJ: Lawrence Erlbaum, 2000), 3.

106. W.G. Stephan and C.W. Stephan, "An Integrated Threat Theory of Prejudice," in *Reducing Prejudice and Discrimination*, S. Oskamp, ed. (Mahwah, NJ: Lawrence Erlbaum, 2000), 25.

107. Oskamp, 2000, 7; Stephan and Stephan, 2000, 40–41.

108. Oskamp, 2000, 9.

109. Stephan and Stephan, 2000, 40.

110. Ibid.

111. E. Vora and J.A. Vora, "Undoing Racism in America: Help from a Black Church," *Journal of Black Studies*, 32 (2002), 389.

112. S.J. Gold, "From Jim Crow to Racial Hegemony: Evaluating Explanations of Racial Hierarchy," *Ethnic and Racial Studies*, 27 (2004), 957.

113. S. Netter, "Racism in Obama's America One Year Later," *ABC World News* (January 27, 2010), http://abcnews.go.com/WN/Obama/racism-obamas-america-year/story?id=9638178 (accessed August 31, 2011).

114. L.D. Bobo and C. Fox, "Race, Racism, and Discrimination: Bridging Problems, Methods, and Theory in Social Psychology Research," *Social Psychology Quarterly*, 66 (2003), 324.

115. Gold, 2004, 953.

116. B. Leone, *Racism: Opposing Viewpoints* (Minneapolis, MN: Greenhaven Press, 1978), 1.

117. S. Nanda and R.L. Warms, *Cultural Anthropology*, 10th ed. (Belmont: CA: Wadsworth, 2011), 14.

118. L. Blum, *I'm Not a Racist, But....* (Ithaca, NY: Cornell University Press, 2002), 9.

119. Ibid.

120. Gudykunst and Kim, 2003, 143.

121. J. Solomos and L. Back, *Racism and Society* (New York: St. Martin's Press, 1996), 216.

122. M. Angelou, *Critical Multicultural Pavilion: Social Justice Quips & Quotes* (2010), http://www.edchange.org/multicultural/language/quotes_alpha.html (accessed September 2, 2011).

123. Nanda and Warms, 2011, 10.

124. G. Bailey and J. People, *Essentials of Cultural Anthropology* (Belmont, CA: Wadsworth Cengage, 2011), 13.

125. J. Rusen, "How to Overcome Ethnocentrism: Approaches to a Culture of Recognition by History in the Twenty-First Century," *History and Theory*, Theme Issues, 43 (Dec 2004), 121.

126. W.A. Haviland, H.E.L. Prins, D. Walrath, and B. McBride, *Cultural Anthropology: The Human*

Challenge 12th ed. (Belmont, CA: Thomson Higher Education, 2008), 376.

127. Brislin, 2000, 45.

128. T.K. Gamble and M.W. Gamble, *Contacts: Interpersonal Communication in Theory, Practice, and Context* (Boston: Houghton Mifflin, 2005), 281.

129. Triandis, 1994, 39.

Chapter 8

1. "S1601. Language Spoken at Home," *American Community Survey* (US Census Bureau, 2009), http://factfinder.census.gov/servlet/STTable?_bm=y&-geo_id=01000US&-qr_name=ACS_2009_5YR_G00_S1601&-ds_name=ACS_2009_5YR_G00_ (accessed May 16, 2011).

2. D. Crystal, *The Cambridge Encyclopedia of Language*, 2nd ed. (New York, NY: Cambridge University Press, 2003), 10.

3. M.G. Aldridge, "What is the Basis of American Culture," *Intercultural Communication*, 5 (2002), http://www.immi.se/intercultural/nr5/aldridge.htm (accessed May 16, 2011).

4. Crystal, 2003, 42.

5. "Background Note: Canada," *U.S. Department of State: Bureau of Western Hemisphere Affairs* (September 2010), http://www.state.gov/r/pa/ei/bgn/2089.htm (accessed May 16, 2011); "The "The Charter of the French Language," *Éditeur officiel du Québec* (April 2011), http://www2.publicationsduquebec.gouv.qc.ca/dynamicSearch/telecharge.php?type=2&file=/C_11/C11_A.html (accessed May 16, 2011).

6. "Sarkozy Can't Speak Proper," *The Economist* (January 15, 2011), 55.

7. C.J. Levy, "Estonia raises Its Pencils to Erase Russian," *New York Times* (June 7, 2010), http://www.nytimes.com/2010/06/08/world/europe/08estonia.html (accessed May 16, 2011).

8. S. Daley, "The Language Divide, Writ Small, in Belgian Town," *New York Times* (July 15, 2010), http://www.nytimes.com/2010/07/16/world/europe/16belgium.html (accessed May 16, 2011).

9. Crystal, 2003, 34.

10. Ibid, 21.

11. F.E. Obiakor, D. J. Smith, and M. Sapp, "Understanding the Power of Words in Multicultural Education," *Multicultural Perspectives*, 9:2 (2007), 36.

12. E. Finegan, *Language: Its Structure and Use*, 5th ed. (Boston: Thomson Wadsworth, 2007), 8.

13. Ibid.

14. J.M. Rubenstein, *An Introduction to Human Geography*, 9th ed. (Upper Saddle River, NJ: Pearson Prentice Hall, 2008), 151.

15. Ibid.; Crystal, 2003, 109.

16. "Portugal adopts Brazilian spelling," *Japan Times* (May 18, 2008), 2.

17. M. Sofer, *The Translator's Handbook*, 6th rev. ed. (Rockville, MD: Schreiber Publishing, 2006), 48.

18. B.F. Shearer, "Context: The Land, the People, the Past, the Present," in *Culture and Customs of the United States*, vol. 1, B.F. Shearer, ed. (Westport, CT: Greenwood Press, 2008), 31.

19. Finegan, 2008, 348; Crystal, 2003, 24.

20. Crystal, 2003, 314.

21. C.G Clopper and D.B. Pisoni, "The Nationwide Speech Project," (paper delivered at the 147th meeting of the Acoustical Society of America, New York, NY, May 27, 2004), http://www.acoustics.org/press/147th/clopper.htm (accessed May 16, 2011).

22. W.A. Haviland, H.E.L. Prins, D. Walrath, and B. McBride, *Anthropology: The Human Challenge*, 13th ed. (Belmont, CA: Wadsworth Cengage, 2011), 376.

23. Finegan, 2008, 322.

24. Crystal, 2003, 53.

25. Ibid., 8.

26. D.B. Daitz, "With Poem Broaching the Topic of Death," *New York Times* (January 24, 2011), http://www.nytimes.com/2011/01/25/health/25navajo.html (accessed May 16, 2011).

27. L. H. Chaney and J. S. Martin, *Intercultural Business Communication*, 4th ed. (Upper Saddle River, NJ: Pearson Prentice Hall, 2007), 102.

28. Ibid., 103.

29. G. Bailey and J. Peoples, *Essentials of Cultural Anthropology*, (Belmont, CA: Wadsworth Cengage, 2011), 50–51; M. L. Andersen and H. F. Taylor, *Sociology: The Essentials*, 6th ed. (Boston, MA: Wadsworth Cengage, 2011), 33; G. Ferraro, *Cultural Anthropology: An Applied Perspective*, 7th ed. (Belmont, CA: Thompson Wadsworth, 2008), 129.

30. Z. Salzmann, *Language, Culture, and Society: An Introduction to Linguistic Anthropology*, 4th ed. (Boulder, CO: Westview Press, 2007), 58.

31. J.C. Condon, *Good Neighbors: Communicating with the Mexicans* (Yarmouth, ME: Intercultural Press, 1985), 50; F. Merrel, *The Mexicans: A Sense of Culture* (Boulder, CO: Westview, 2003), 10.

32. Salzmann, 2007, 59; E.S. Kras, *Management in Two Cultures*, rev. ed. (Yarmouth, ME: Intercultural Press, 1995), 32, 36.

33. Merrel, 2003, 15; Condon, 1985, 62; Kras, 1995, 32.

34. Y. Miike, "An Asiacentric Reflection on Eurocentric Bias in Communication Theory," *Communication Monographs*, 74:2 (June 2007), 274.

35. H. Wenzhong and C. Grove, *Encountering the Chinese*, 3rd ed. (Boston, MA: Intercultural Press, 2010), xxv–xxvii.

36. G. Gao and S. Ting-Toomey, *Communicating Effectively with the Chinese* (Thousand Oaks, CA: SAGE, 1998), 17.

37. Wenzhong and Grove, 2010, 4.

38. C. Lee, *Cowboys and Dragons*, (Chicago, IL: Dearborn Trade Publishing, 2003), 81,

39. Gao and Ting-Toomey, 1998, 60–81.

40. Wenzhong and Grove, 2010, 39–42.

41. T.Y. Shim, M-S. Kim, and J.N. Martin, *Changing Korea: Understanding Culture and Communication* (New York: Peter Lang, 2008), 57.

42. Ibid., 65.

43. R. Patai, *The Arab Mind*, rev. ed. (New York: Hatherleigh Press, 2002), 45–46; "A God-given way to communicate," *The Economist* (Apr 24, 2010), 47.

44. M.K. Nydell, *Understanding Arabs*, 4th ed. (Boston, MA: Intercultural Press, 2006). 95, 97.

45. R.S. Zaharna, "Understanding Cultural Preferences of Arab Communication Patterns," *Public Relations Review*, 21:3 (1995), 245–246.

46. Ibid., 249.

47. Nydell, (2006), 99.

48. E. Feghali, "Arab Cultural Communication Patterns," *International Journal of Intercultural Relations*, 21:3 (1997), 361.

49. "Languages of Europe: Official EU Languages," *European Commission: Multilingualism* (Dec 13, 2010), http://ec.europa.eu/education/languages/languages-of-europe/doc135_en.htm (accessed May 16, 2011).

50. "What We Do: DG Interpretation in Key Figures," *Directorate General for Interpretation, European Commission* (June 14, 2010), http://ec.europa.eu/education/languages/languages-of-europe/index_en.htm (accessed May 16, 2011).

51. "Driver License and Identification (ID) Card Information," *California Department of Motor Vehicles* (2011), http://www.dmv.ca.gov/dl/dl_info.htm#languages (accessed May 16, 2011).

52. V. Kim. "American Justice in a Foreign Language, *Los Angeles Times* (February 21, 2009), http://articles.latimes.com/2009/feb/21/local/me-interpret21 (accessed May 16, 2011).

53. Crystal, 2003, 353.

54. Sofer, 2006, 48.

55. J. Ravitz, "Vietnamese fishermen in Gulf fight to not get lost in translation," *CNN.com* (Jun 25, 2010), http://articles.cnn.com/2010-06-24/us/vietnamese.fishermen.gulf.coast_1_vietnamese-speaking-fishermen-gulf-coast?_s=PM:US (accessed May 16, 2011).

56. B. Danet and S.C. Herring, "Introduction," in *The Multilingual Internet: Language, Culture, and Communication Online*, B. Danet and S.C. Herring, eds. (New York: Oxford University Press, 2007), 3.

57. Ibid, 5.

58. Adapted from: "Top 20 Countries with Highest Number of Internet Users," *Internet World Stats* (March 26, 2011), http://www.internetworldstats.com/top20.htm (accessed May 16, 2011).

59. Danet and Herring, 2007, 22.

60. Ibid.

61. Y. Kageyama "Twitter a hit in Japan as millions 'mumble online'," *msnbc.com* (Jun 18, 2010). http://www.msnbc.msn.com/id/37778965/ns/technology_and_science-tech_and_gadgets/t/twitter-hit-japan-millions-mumble-online/ (accessed May 15, 2002).

62. W.G. Gudykunst, *Bridging Differences*, 4th ed. (Thousand Oaks, CA: SAGE, 2004), 32.

63. D. Morales, "Battling language's law of diminishing returns," *Japan Times* (Oct 20, 2011), 13.

64. B.B. Lai, "Three Worlds: Inheritance and Experience," in *Translating Lives: Living with Two Languages and Cultures*, M. Besemeres and A. Wierzbicka, eds. (Queensland, Australia: University of Queensland, 2007), 27.

65. J. Wong, "East Meets West, or Does It Really?" in *Translating Lives: Living with Two Languages and Cultures*, M. Besemeres and A. Wierzbicka, eds. (Queensland, Australia: University of Queensland, 2007), 22.

66. P.M. Lewis (ed.), *Ethnologue: Languages of the World*, 16th ed. (Dallas, Tex.: SIL International. Online version, 2009), http://www.ethnologue.com/ (accessed May 16, 2011).

67. Personal conversation with Bert Adams, Metris Company, Nagoya, Japan, July 2008.

68. Crystal, 2003, 362.

69. "EU Languages and Language Policy," *European Commission: Multilingualism* (November 24, 2010), http://ec.europa.eu/education/languages/languages-of-europe/index_en.htm (accessed May 16, 2011).

70. T. Fukada, "Takaki Stresses Value of Foreign Languages," *Japan Times* (Oct 13, 2011), 3.

Chapter 9

1. B. Woodward, *State of Denial* (New York: Simon & Schuster, 2006), 290.

2. D.C. Barnlund, *Interpersonal Communication: Survey and Studies* (Boston: Houghton Mifflin, 1968), 536–537.

3. L.K. Guerrero and K. Floyd, *Nonverbal Communication in Close Relationships* (Mahwah, NJ: Laurence Erlbaum Associates, Publisher, 2006), 2.

4. J.K. Burgoon, D.B. Buller, and W.G. Woodall, *Nonverbal Communication: The Unspoken Dialogue* (New York: Harper and Row, 1989), 9–10.

5. S.P. Morreale, B.H. Spitzberg, and J.K. Barge, *Human Communication: Motivation, Knowledge, and Skills*, 2nd ed. (Belmont, CA: Thomson Wadsworth, 2007), 113.

6. A. Tucker, "The Body of Work," *Smithsonian* (October 2010), 56. For a further examination of nonverbal communication and identity see J.T. Wood, *Communication Mosaics* (Boston, MA: Wadsworth Cengage Learning, 2011), 103.

7. L.K. Guerrero, J.A. DeVito, and M.L. Hecht, *The Nonverbal Communication Reader: Classic and Contemporary Readings*, 2nd ed. (Prospect, IL: Waveland Press, 1999), 9.

8. A. Mehrabian, *Nonverbal Communication* (New Brunswick, CT: Aldine Transaction, 1972), 1.

9. E. Goffman, *The Presentation of Self in Everyday Life* (New York: Doubleday, 1957), 2.

10. L. Knapp and J.A. Hall, *Nonverbal Communication in Human Interaction*, 7th ed. (Boston, MA: Wadsworth Cengage, 2010), 5.

11. S. Osborn and M.T. Motley, *Improving Communication* (Boston: Houghton Mifflin, 1999), 50.

12. M. Hickson, D.W. Stacks, and N. Moore, *Nonverbal Communication: Studies and Applications* (Los Angeles, CA: Roxbury Publishing Company, 2004), 26.

13. L. Beamer and I. Varner, *Intercultural Communication in the Global Workplace* (New York: McGraw-Hill, 2001), 160.

14. F. Davis, *Inside Intuition* (New York: Signet, 1975), 47. See also Ray L. Birdwhistell, *Kinesics and Context* (Philadelphia: University of Pennsylvania Press, 1970).

15. P. Ekman, "Face Muscles Talk Every Language," *Psychology Today* (September, 1975), 35–39. See also P. Ekman, W. Friesen, and P. Ellsworth, *Emotion in the Human Face: Guidelines for Research and an Integration of the Findings* (New York: Pergamon Press, 1972). See also P. Ekman, W. Friesen, and P. Ellsworth, *Emotion in the Human Face: Guidelines for Research and an Integration of the Findings* (New York: Pergamon Press, 1972).

16. P.A. Andersen, "The Basis of Cultural Differences in Nonverbal Communication," in *Intercultural Communication: A Reader*, 13th ed., L.A. Samovar, R.E. Porter, and E.R. McDaniel, eds. (Boston, MA: Wadsworth Cengage Learning, 2011), 294.

17. R.E. Porter and L.A. Samovar, "Cultural Influences on Emotional Expression: Implications for Intercultural Communication," in *Handbook of Communication and Emotion: Research, Theory Applications, and Contexts*, P.A. Andersen and L.K. Guerrero, eds. (San Diego, CA: Academic Press, 1998), 454.

18. D. Matsumoto, *Unmasking Japan: Myths and Realities About the Emotions of the Japanese* (Stanford, CA: Stanford University Press, 1996), 54.

19. Wood, 2011, 99.

20. P.C. Rosenblatt, "Grief in Small-Scale Societies," in *Death and Bereavement Across Cultures*, C.M. Parks, P. Laungani, and B. Young, eds. (New York: Routledge, 1997), 36.

21. B. Vandenabeele, "The Need for Essences: On Non-verbal Communication in First Inter-Cultural Encounters," *South African Journal of Philosophy*, 21 (2002), 1.

22. E.T. Hall, *The Silent Language* (New York: Fawcett, 1959), xii–xiii.

23. P. Richmond, J.C. McCracken, and S.K. Payne, *Nonverbal Communication in Interpersonal Communication*, 2nd ed. (New Jersey: Prentice Hall, 1991), 13.

24. D. Klingensmith, "Do You Tattoo," *North County Times*, October 17, 2010, G-1.

25. C.F. Keating, "World without Words: Messages from Face and Body," in *Psychology and Culture*, W.J. Lonner and R.S. Malpass, eds. (Boston: Allyn and Bacon, 1994), 175.

26. Guerrero and Floyd, 2006, 60.

27. J. Peoples and G. Bailey, *Humanity: An Introduction to Anthropology*, 7th ed. (Belmont, CA: Thomson Wadsworth), 2006, 309.

28. F. Keesing, *Cultural Anthropology: The Science of Custom* (New York: Holt, Rinehart, and Winston, 1965), 203.

29. "Obesity: A Heavy Burden Socially," *San Diego Union-Tribune* (September 30, 1993), A-14.

30. B.D. Ruben, *Communication and Human Behavior*, 3rd ed. (Englewood Cliffs, NJ: Prentice Hall, 1992), 213.

31. H.W. Gardiner and C. Kosmitzki, *Lives Across Cultures: Cross-Cultural Human Development*, 2nd ed. (Boston: Allyn and Bacon, 2002), 145.

32. Gardiner and Kosmitzki, 2002, 146. Also see Wood, 2011, 102.

33. Y. Richmond and P. Gestrin, *Into Africa: Intercultural Insights* (Yarmouth, ME: Intercultural Press, 1998), 45.

34. H. Wenzhong and C.L. Grove, *Encountering the Chinese* (Yarmouth, ME: Intercultural Press, 1991), 135.

35. G. Ferraro, *Cultural Anthropology: An Applied Perspective*, 6th ed. (Belmont, CA: Thomson Wadsworth, 2006), 35.

36. M.S. Remland, *Nonverbal Communication in Everyday Life* (New York: Houghton Mifflin, 2000), 113.

37. Ibid., 113–114.

38. L.A. Vazquez, E. Garcia-Vazquez, S.A. Bauman, and A.S. Sierra, "Skin Color, Acculturation, and Community Interest among Mexican American Students: A Research Note," *Hispanic Journal of Behavioral Sciences*, 19 (1997), 337.

39. "Study: White and black children biased toward lighter skin," CNN U.S. (May 13, 2010), http://articles.cnn.com/2010-05-13/us/doll.study_1_black-children-pilot-study-white-doll?_s=PM:US (accessed May 30, 2011).

40. Knapp and Hall, 2010, 195.

41. G.E. Codina and F.F. Montalvo, "Chicano Phenotype and Depression," *Hispanic Journal of Behavioral Sciences*, 16 (1994), 296–306.

42. R.B. Adler and G. Rodman, *Understanding Human Communication*, 8th ed. (New York: Oxford University Press, 2003), 171.

43. H.H. Calero, *The Power of Nonverbal Communication* (Aberdeen, WA: Silver Lake Publishers, 2005), 169.

44. "Women and Veils: Running for Cover," *The Economist* (May 15, 2010), http://www.startribune.com/world/94258084.html?page=2&c=y (accessed May 23, 2010).

45. J. Bowen, "'Why the French Don't Like Headscarves,'" *New York Times* (April 1, 2007), http://www.nytimes.com/2007/04/01/books/chapters/0401-1st-bowe.html?pagewanted=all (accessed May 31, 2011).

46. "Helping to Free Muslim Women," *The Week* (April 16, 2010), 15.

47. M.I. Al-Kaysi, *Morals and Manners in Islam: A Guide to Islamic d b* (London: The Islamic Press, 1986), 84.

48. "The Islamic veil across Europe," BBC News (June 15, 2010), http://newsvote.bbc.co.uk/mpapps/pagetools/print/news.bbc.co.uk/2/hi/europe/5414098.stm (accessed May 31, 2011).

49. W.V. Ruch, *International Handbook of Corporate Communication* (Jefferson, NC: McFarland, 1989), 242.

50. E.T. Hall and M.R. Hall, *Understanding Cultural Differences: Germans, French and Americans* (Yarmouth, ME: Intercultural Press, 1990), 53.

51. E. McDaniel, "Nonverbal Communication: A Reflection of Cultural

Themes," in *Intercultural Communication: A Reader*, 11th ed., L.A. Samovar, R.E. Porter, and E.R. McDaniel, eds. (Boston: Wadsworth, Cengage Learning, 2006), 260.

52. A. Horvat, *Japanese Beyond Words* (Berkeley, CA: Stone Bridge Press, 2000), 23.

53. Peoples and Bailey, 2006, 357.

54. T.J. Whande, "Look! My body is talking to you," Sunday Standard. Online Edition (July 22, 2007), http://www.sundaystandard.info/print_article.php?NewsID=1796 (accessed May 31, 2011).

55. S. Stevenson, "How to be Invisible," *Newsweek*, (April 19, 2010), 12.

56. Ferraro, 2006, 79.

57. S. Loygren, "Fear Is Spread by Body Language, Study Says," *National Geographic News* (Nov 16, 2004), http://news.nationalgeographic.com/news/2004/11/1116_041116_fear_-posture.html (accessed May 31, 2011).

58. "Row Over the Bow," *Newsweek*, (November 30, 2009), 15.

59. Horvat, 2000, 25.

60. S. Ishii, "Characteristics of Japanese Nonverbal Communication Behavior," *Communication*, 2 (1973), 163–180.

61. T. Novinger, *Intercultural Communication: A Practical Guide* (Austin, TX: University of Texas Press, 2001), 64.

62. G. Ness, *Germany: Unraveling an Enigma* (Yarmouth, ME: Intercultural Press, 2000), 93.

63. Remland, 2000, 229.

64. R. Cooper and N. Cooper, *Culture Shock: Thailand* (Portland, OR: Graphic Arts Center, 1994), 22–23.

65. For a more detailed account of posture and other nonverbal differences between males and females, see P. Anderson, *Nonverbal Communication: Forms and Functions*, 2nd ed. (Long Grove, IL: Waveland Press, Inc., 2008), 124; L.P. Arliss, *Gender and Communication* (Englewood Cliffs, NJ: Prentice Hall, 1991), 87; J.A. Doyle and M. A. Paludi, *Sex and Gender: The Human Experience*, 2nd ed. (Dubuque, IA: Wm. C. Brown, 1991), 235; M. Hickson, D.W. Stacks, and N. Moore, *Nonverbal Communication: Studies and Applications*, 5th ed. (New York: NY: Oxford University Press, 2010), 28; J.C. Pearson, R.L. West, and L.H. Turner, *Gender and Communication*, 3rd ed. (Dubuque, IA: Wm. C. Brown, 1995), 126; L.P. Steward, P.J. Cooper, and S.A. Friedley, *Communication Between the Sexes: Sex Differences and Sex Role Stereotypes* (Scottsdale, AZ: Gorsuch Scarisbrick, 1986), 75; J.T. Wood, *Gendered Lives: Communication, Gender and Culture*, 6th ed. (Belmont, CA: Wadsworth, 2005), 138.

66. M.L. Hecht, M.J. Collier, and S.A. Ribeau, *African American Communication: Ethnic Identity and Cultural Interpretation* (Newbury Park, CA: Sage Publications, 1993), 102.

67. D. Glanton, "Obama's Ways Cool to Some, New to Others," *Chicago Tribune* (January 25, 2009).

68. L.H. Channey and J.S. Martin, *Intercultural Business Communication*, 4th ed. (Upper Saddle River, NJ: Prentice Hall, 2007), 127.

69. D. Archer, "Unspoken Diversity: Cultural Differences in Gestures," *Qualitative Sociology*, 20 (1997), 81.

70. R.G. Harper, A.N. Wiens, and J.D. Matarazzo, *Nonverbal Communication: The State of the Art* (New York: Wiley, 1978), 164.

71. E.W. Lynch and M.J. Hanson, *Developing Cross-Cultural Competence*, 2nd ed. (Baltimore, MD: Paul H. Brookes, 1998), 74.

72. Ferraro, 2006, 147.

73. Hamiru-aqui, *70 Japanese Gestures: No Language Communication*, (Minato, Tokyo: IBC Publishing, 2004), 49.

74. Ibid., 99.

75. *Handbook for Teaching Korean-American Students* (Sacramento, CA: California Department of Education, 1992), 95.

76. M.K. Nydell, *Understanding Arabs*, 4th ed. (Boston: Intercultural Press, 2006), 37.

77. Lynch and Hanson, 1998, 74.

78. T. Morrison, W.A. Conaway, and J.J. Douress, *Doing Business Around the World* (Paramus, NJ: Prentice Hall, 2001), 172.

79. Hamiru-aqui, 2004, 41.

80. T. Morrison and W.A. Conaway, *Kiss, Bow, or Shake Hands*, 2nd ed. (Avon, MA: Adams Media, 2006), 245.

81. R.D. Lewis, *When Cultures Collide: Managing Successfully Across Cultures* (London: Nicholas Brealey, 1999), 135.

82. J.W. Berry, Y.H. Poortinga, M.H. Segall, and P.R. Dasen, *Cross-Cultural Psychology: Research and Applications* (New York: Cambridge University Press, 1992), 87–88.

83. T. Novinger, *Communicating with Brazilians* (Austin, TX: University of Texas Press, 2003), 173.

84. Beamer and Varner, 2001, 166.

85. M. Kim, "A Comparative Analysis of Nonverbal Expression as Portrayed by Korean and American Print-Media Advertising," *Howard Journal of Communications*, 3 (1992), 321.

86. R. West and L.H. Turner, *Understanding Interpersonal Communication: Making Choices in Changing Times* (Belmont, CA: Thomson Wadsworth, 2006), 201.

87. Ruch, 1989, 191.

88. Morrison and Conaway, 2006, 78.

89. Andersen, 2008, 123.

90. Hecht, Collier, and Ribeau, 1993, 112.

91. Calero, 2005, 66.

92. Ferraro, 2006, 102.

93. Mehrabian, 2007, 144.

94. M. Patterson, "Evolution and Nonverbal Behavior: Functions and Mediating Processes, *Journal of Nonverbal Behavior*, 3 (2003), 205.

95. Keating, 1994, 181.

96. D.G. Leathers, *Successful Nonverbal Communication: Principles and Applications*, 2nd ed. (New York: Macmillan, 1992), 32.

97. M. Maynard, "An Apology From Toyota's Leader" *New York Times* (February 24, 2010), http:www.nytimes.com/2010/02/25/business/global/25toyota.html?pagewanted=print (accessed May 30, 2011).

98. D.W. Sue and D. Sue, *Counseling the Culturally Different*, 2nd ed. (New York: Wiley, 1990), 54.

99. Kim, 1992, 321.

100. R.E. Porter and L.A. Samovar, "Cultural Influences on Emotional Expression: Implications for Intercultural Communication," in *Handbook of Communication and Emotion Research, Applications, and Context*, P.A. Andersen and L.K. Guerrero, eds. (San Diego, CA: Academic Press, 1998), 454.

101. Matsumoto, 1996, 54.

102. R.E. Kruat and R.E. Johnson, "Social and Emotional Messages of Smiling," in *The Nonverbal Communication: Classic and Contemporary Reading*, 2nd ed., L.K. Guerrero, J.A. De Vito, and H.L. Hecht, eds. (Prospect Heights, IL: Waveland Press, 1999), 75.

103. K. Nishiyama, *Doing Business in Japan: Successful Strategies for Intercultural Communication* (Honolulu, HI: University of Hawaii Press, 2000), 22.

104. Matsumoto, 1996, 54.

105. N. Dresser, *Multicultural Manners*, rev. ed. (New York: Wiley, 2005), 21.

106. G. Nees, *Germany: Unraveling an Enigma* (Yarmouth, ME: Intercultural Press, Inc., 2000), 93.

107. Moore, Hickson, and Stacks, 2010. See also Pearson, West, and Turner, 1995, 123; Andersen, 2008, 123.

108. "The Evil Eye: A Stare of Envy," *Psychology Today* (December, 1977), 154.

109. M.E. Zuniga, "Families with Latino Roots," in *Developing Cross-Cultural Competence*, 2nd ed., E.W. Lynch and M.J. Hanson, eds. (Baltimore, MD: Paul H. Brookes, 1998), 231.

110. D. Leathers, *Successful Nonverbal Communication: Principles and Applications* (New York: Macmillan, 1986), 42.

111. S. Tubbs and S. Moss, *Human Communication: Principles and Context*, 11th ed. (Boston, MA: McGraw-Hill, 2008), 120.

112. H. Triandis, *Culture and Social Behavior* (New York: McGraw-Hill, 1994), 198.

113. E.W. Lynch, "From Culture Shock to Cultural Learning," in *Developing Cross-Cultural Competence: A Guide for Working with Young Children and Their Families*, E.W. Lynch and M.J. Hanson, eds. (Baltimore, MD: Paul H. Brookes, 1992), 19–33.

114. K.S. Young and H.P. Travis, *Communicating Nonverbally* (Long Grove, IL: Waveland Press, Inc., 2008), 31.

115. Richmond, McCracken, and Payne, 1991, 301.

116. Dresser, 2005, 22.

117. Richmond and Gestrin, 1998, 88.

118. J. Luckmann, *Transcultural Communication in Nursing* (Albany, NY: Delmar, 1999), 57.

119. F. Meleis and M. Meleis, "Egyptian-Americans," in *Transcultural Health Care: A Culturally Competent Approach*, L.D. Purnell and B.J. Paulanka, eds. (Philadelphia: F.A. Davis, 1998), 221.

120. E.A. Tuleja, *Intercultural Communication for Business* (Mason, OH: Thomson South-Western, 2005), 47.

121. E. Feghali, "Arab Cultural Communication Patterns," *International Journal of Intercultural Relations*, 21 (1997), 346.

122. D. C. Herberg, *Frameworks for Cultural and Racial Diversity* (Toronto: Canadian Scholars' Press, 1993), 48.

123. Nees, 2000, 93.

124. For a discussion of homosexual nonverbal communication, see W.F. Eadie, "In Plain Sight: Gay and Lesbian Communication and Culture," in *Intercultural Communication: A Reader*, 13th ed., L.A. Samovar, R.E. Porter, and E.R. McDaniel eds. (Boston, MA: Wadsworth Cengage, 2011), 254–267.

125. Sue and Sue, 1990, 55.

126. L.D. Purnell, "Mexican-Americans," in *Transcultural Health Care: A Culturally Competent Approach*, L.D. Purnell and B.J. Paulanka, eds. (Philadelphia: F.A. Davis, 1998), 400.

127. Andersen, 2008, 124.

128. Ibid.

129. "Eye contact," *Handspeak.com* (n.d.). http://www.handspeak.com/byte/e/index.php?byte=eyecontact (accessed June 2, 2011).

130. J.D. Salinger, *The Catcher in the Rye* (New York: Grosset and Dunlap, 1945), 103.

131. Knapp and Hall, 2010, 263.

132. R.M. Bereko, L.B. Rosenfeld, and L.A. Samovar, *Connecting: A Culture-Sensitive Approach to Interpersonal Communication Competency*, 1st Canadian ed. (Canada: Harcourt-Brace Canada, 1998). See also Knapp and Hall, 2010, 270.

133. G. Ferraro, 2006, 147.

134. P.A. Andersen, 1999, 78.

135. W.B. Gudykunst and Y.Y. Kim, *Communication with Strangers*, 4th ed. (New York: McGraw-Hill, 2003), 256.

136. Feghali, 2006, 364.

137. Morrison, Conaway, and Douress, 2001, 38.

138. Ibid.

139. J. Condon, *Good Neighbors: Communicating with the Mexicans* (Yarmouth, ME: Intercultural Press, 1985), 60.

140. C. Helmuth, *Culture and Customs of Costa Rica* (Westport, CT: Greenwood Press, 2000).

141. Moore, Hickson, and Stacks, 2010, 69.

142. E. McDaniel and P.A. Andersen, "International Patterns of Interpersonal Tactile Communication," *Journal of Nonverbal Communication Behavior*, 22 (Spring 1998) 70.

143. L.K. Matocha, "Chinese-Americans," in *Transcultural Health Care: A Culturally Competent Approach*, L.D. Purnell and B.J. Paulanka, eds. (Philadelphia: F.A. Davis, 1998), 184.

144. D. Rowland, *Japanese Business Etiquette* (New York: Warner, 1985), 53.

145. Dresser, 2005, 15.

146. Knapp and Hall, 2010, 432.

147. Guerrero and Floyd, 101–102.

148. Leathers, 1986, 138–139.

149. S. Kershaw, "Hellos Give Way to Hugs for Current Crop of Teens," *San Diego Union-Tribune*, (May 28, 2009), A-1.

150. Knapp and Hall, 2010, 378–381.

151. V.P. Richmond, J.C. McCracken, and S.K. Payne, *Nonverbal Communication in Interpersonal Relations*, 2nd ed. (Englewood Cliffs, NJ: Prentice Hall, 1991), 94–109.

152. Feghali, 1997, 368.

153. Ruch, 1989, 191.

154. Chaney and Martin, 2004, 111.

155. Hecht, Collier, and Ribeau, 1993, 113.

156. Wood, 2011, 108. See also P. Andersen, 2008, 125–126.

157. Al-Kaysi, 1996, 55.

158. Lynch and Hanson, 1998, 26.

159. L. Skow and L. Samovar, "Cultural Patterns of the Maasai," in *Intercultural Communication: A Reader*, 9th ed., L.A. Samovar and R.E. Porter, eds. (Belmont, CA: Wadsworth, 2000), 97.

160. E.T. Hall and M.R. Hall, *Hidden Differences: Doing Business With the Japanese* (New York: Anchor Books, 1990), 113.

161. E.R. McDaniel, "Japanese Nonverbal Communication: A Review and Critique of Literature," paper presented at the Annual Convention of the Speech Communication Association, Miami Beach, FL, November 1993, 18.

162. Hall and Hall, 1990, 12–13.

163. E.T. Hall, *The Silent Language* (New York: Fawcett, 1959). See also Remland, 2000, 148–149.

164. Triandis, 1994, 201.

165. Andersen, 2008, 92–93.

166. Ruch, 1989, 239.

167. Morrison, Conaway, and Douress, 2001, 136.

168. Hall and Hall, 1990, 38.

169. M.J. Gannon and R. Pillai, *Understanding Global Culture*, 4th ed. (Thousand Oaks, CA: Sage, 2010), 187.

170. Gannon and Pillai, 2010, 102.

171. "Seating Arrangement," China Highlights (n.d.), http://www.chinahighlights.com/travelguide/chinese-food/seating-arrangement.htm (accessed June 2, 2011).

172. Matocha, 1998, 167.

173. McDaniel, 2006, 270.

174. Nishiyama, 2000, 26.

175. Hall and Hall, 1990, 91.

176. Beamer and Varner, 2001, 175.

177. M.S. Remland, T.S. Jones, and H. Brinkman, "Interpersonal Distance, Body Orientation, and Touch: Effects of Culture, Gender and Age," *Journal of Social Psychology*, 135 (1995), 282.

178. Leathers, 1986, 236. See also Andersen, 2008, 120; Young and Travis, 2008, 58; Wood, 2011, 105.

179. Knapp and Hall, 2010, 151. See also Mehrabian, 2007, 7.

180. Ibid.

181. L.A. Siple, "Cultural Patterns of Deaf People," *International Journal of Inter-cultural Relations*, 18 (1994), 345–367.

182. N. Rapport and J. Overing, *Social and Cultural Anthropology: The Key Concepts* (New York: Routledge, 2000), 261.

183. K.L. Egland, M.A. Stelzner, P.A. Andersen, and B.H. Spitzberg, "Perceived Understanding, Nonverbal Communication and Relational Satisfaction," in *Intrapersonal Communication Process*, J. L. Aitken and L. Shedletsky, eds. (Annandale, VA: Speech Communication Association, 1997), 386–395. See also Guerrero and Floyd, 2006, 112.

184. A. Gonzalez and P.G. Zimbardo, "Time in Perspective," in *The Nonverbal Communication Reader: Classic and Contemporary Reading*, 2nd ed., L.K. Guerrero, J.A. De Vito, and H.L. Hecht, eds. (Prospect Heights, IL: Waveland Press, 1999), 227.

185. Moore, Hickson, and Stacks, 2010, 291.

186. N. Crouch, *Mexicans and Americans: Cracking the Cultural Code* (Yarmouth, ME: Nicholas Brealey Publishers, 2004), 34.

187. Gannon and Pillai, 2010, 267.

188. D.I. Ballard and D.R. Seibold, "Time Orientation and Temporal Variation Across Work Groups: Implications for Group and Organizational Communication," *Western Journal of Communication*, 64 (2000), 219.

189. Moore, Hickson, and Stacks, 2010, 293.

190. M. Argyle, "Inter-cultural Communication," in *Cultures in Contact: Studies in Cross-Cultural Interaction*, S. Bochner, ed. (New York: Pergamon Press, 1982), 68.

191. Nishiyama, 2000, 28.

192. Morrison and Conaway, 2006, 432.

193. Richmond and Gestrin, 1998, 108.

194. Hall and Hall, 1990, 35.

195. E.Y. Kim, *The Yin and Yang of American Culture: A Paradox* (Yarmouth, ME: Intercultural Press, 2001), 115.

196. Crouch, 2005, 39.

197. G. Asselin and R. Maston, *Au Contraire! Figuring Out the French* (Yarmouth, ME: Intercultural Press, 2001), 233.

198. R. Brislin, *Understanding Culture's Influence on Behavior* (Fort Worth, TX: Harcourt Brace Jovanovich, 1993), 211.

199. P.R. Harris and R.T. Moran, *Managing Cultural Differences*, 4th ed. (Houston, TX: Gulf, 1996), 266.

200. Ruch, 1989, 278.

201. P. Abu Gharbieh, "Arab-American," in *Transcultural Health Care: A Culturally Competent Approach*, L.D. Purnell and B.J. Paulanka, eds. (Philadelphia: F.A. Harris, 1998), 140.

202. E.T. Hall, *The Dance of Life: Other Dimensions of Time* (New York: Anchor Press/Doubleday, 1983), 42.

203. P.B. Smith and M.H. Bond, *Social Psychology Across Cultures: Analysis and Perspective* (Boston: Allyn and Bacon, 1994), 149.

204. Hall and Hall, 1990, 16.

205. Andersen, 2008, 80.

206. E.T. Hall, *The Silent Language* (New York: Fawcett, 1959), 19.

207. F. Trompenaars and C. Hampden-Turner, *Riding the Waves of Culture: Understanding Diversity in Global*

Business, 2nd ed. (New York: McGraw-Hill, 1998), 143.

208. Smith and Bond, 1999, 147.

209. Dresser, 2005, 26.

210. Richmond and Gestrin, 1998, 109.

211. Feghali, 1997, 376.

212. Hall and Hall, 1990, 18.

213. Calero, 2005, 61.

214. D. Crystal, *The Cambridge Encyclopedia of Language*, 2nd ed. (New York: Cambridge University Press, 1997), 174.

215. C. Braithwaite, "Cultural Uses and Interpretations of Time," in *The Nonverbal Communication Reader: Classic and Contemporary Reading*, 2nd ed., L.K. Guerrero, J.A. De Vito, and H.L. Hecht, eds. (Prospect Heights, IL: Waveland Press, 1999), 164.

216. Beamer and Varner, 2001, 184.

217. T.J. Bruneau, "How Americans Use Silence and Silences to Communicate," *China Media Research*, 4 (2008), 83.

218. Lewis, 1999, 13.

219. A.J.V. Chandrakanthan, "The Silence of Buddha and his Contemplation of the Truth," *Spirituality Today*, 40:2 (Summer 1988), 145, http://www.spiritualitytoday.org/spir2day/884025chandrak.html (accessed May 30, 2011).

220. D.C. Barnlund, *Communicative Styles of Japanese and Americans: Images and Realities* (Belmont, CA: Wadsworth, 1989), 142.

221. S. Chan, "Families with Asian Roots," in *Developing Cross-Cultural Competence*, 2nd, ed., E.W. Lynch and M.J. Hanson, eds. (Baltimore, MD: Paul H. Brookes, 1998), 321–322.

222. R.L. De Mente, *Japan Unmasked: The Character and Culture of the Japanese* (Tokyo: Tuttle Publishing, 2005), 179.

223. A. Kerr, *Dogs and Demons: Tales from the Dark Side of Japan* (New York: Hill and Wang, 2001), 105.

224. A. Jaworski, "The Power of Silence in Communication," in *The Nonverbal Communication Reader: Classic*

and Contemporary Reading, 2nd ed., L.K. Guerrero, J.A. De Vito, and H.L. Hecht, eds. (Prospect Heights, IL: Waveland Press, 1999), 161.

225. Ibid.

226. N. Adler, *International Dimensions of Organizational Behavior*, 3rd. ed. (Cincinnati, OH: South-Western) 1997, 217.

227. N. Jain and A. Matukumalli, "The Functions of Silence in India: Implications for Intercultural Communication Research," paper presented at the Second International East Meets West Conference in Cross-Cultural Communication, Comparative Philosophy, and Comparative Religion, Long Beach, CA (1993), 7.

228. Smith and Bond, 1999, 141.

229. D.L. Hoeveler, "Text and Context: Teaching Native American Literature," *The English Journal*, 77:5 (September, 1988), 20.

230. D.M. Dunn and L.J. Goodnight, *Communication: Embracing Difference*, 3rd ed. (Boston, MA: Allyn & Bacon, 2011), 97.

231. Kim, 2001, 207.

Chapter 10

1. J. Charlebois, "The Social Construction of Demeanor through Deference Rituals," in L.A. Samovar, R.E. Porter, and E.R. McDaniel, eds., *Intercultural Communication: A Reader*, 13th ed. (Boston: Wadsworth Cengage Learning, 2012), 458.

2. Ibid.

3. J.T. Wood, *Interpersonal Communication: Everyday Encounters*, 6th ed. (Boston: Wadsworth Cengage Learning, 2010), 101.

4. S.P. Morreale, B.H. Spitzberg, and J.K. Barge, *Human Communication: Motivation, Knowledge, and Skills*, 2nd ed. (Belmont, CA: Thomson Wadsworth, 2007), 168–169.

5. S.B. Shimanoff, *Communication Rules: Theory and Practice* (Beverly Hills, CA: Sage Publications, 1980), 57.

6. M.K. Nydell, *Understanding Arabs: A Guide for Westerners*, 4th ed. (Boston: Intercultural Press, 2006), 63.

7. T. Morrison and W.A. Conway, *Kiss, Bow, or Shake Hands: Europe: How to do Business in 25 European Countries* (Avon, MA: Adams Media, an F+W Publications Company, 2007a), 294.

8. A. Javidi and M. Javidi, "Cross-Cultural Analysis of Interpersonal Bonding: A Look at East and West," in *Intercultural Communication: A Reader*, 8th ed., L.A. Samovar and R.E. Porter, eds. (Belmont, CA: Wadsworth, 1997), 89.

9. N. Crouch, *Mexicans and Americans: Cracking the Cultural Code* (Yarmouth, ME: Nicholas Breadley Publishing, 2004), 134.

10. E.T. Hall and M.R. Hall, *Understanding Cultural Differences: Germans, French, and Americans* (Yarmouth, ME: Intercultural Press, 1990), 48.

11. L. Schneider and A. Silverman, *Global Sociology: Introducing Five Contemporary Societies* (New York: McGraw-Hill, 1997), 70.

12. L.D. Purnell and B.J. Paulanka, *Transcultural Health Care: A Culturally Competent Approach* (Philadelphia, PA: F.A. Davis Company, 1998), 47, 172.

13. T. Gochenour, *Considering Filipinos* (Yarmouth, ME: Intercultural Press, 1990), 23.

14. T. Morrison and W.A. Conaway, *Kiss, Bow, or Shake Hands: Asia* (Avon, MA: Adams Media an F+W Publications Company, 2007b), 5–6.

15. E.A. Kras, *Management in Two Cultures: Bridging the Gap Between U.S. and Mexican Managers* (Yarmouth, ME: Nicholas Brealey Publishing, 1995), 33.

16. L. Fish, "Building Blocks: The First Steps of Creating a Multicultural Classroom," http://www.edchange.org/multicultural/papers/buildingblocks.html (accessed August 20, 2011).

17. As quoted in D.S. Landes, *The Wealth and Poverty of Nations* (New York: W.W. Norton, 1998), 516.

18. T.L. Friedman, *The World Is Flat* (New York: Farrar, Straus and Giroux, 2005), 9.

19. "Globalization's Offspring: How the Multinationals Are Remaking the Old," *The Economist*, (April 7, 2007), 11.

20. "Developing Your Global Know-How," *Harvard Business Review*, (March 2011), 72–75.

21. *McDonalds Corporation Annual Report 2010*, 8. http://www.aboutmcdonalds.com/etc/medialib/aboutMcDonalds/investor_relations3.Par.56096.File.dat/2010%20Annual%20Report%20(print).pdf (accessed 19 August 2011).

22. *Starbucks Coffee International* (2011), http://www.starbucks.com/business/international-stores (accessed August 19, 2011).

23. *Starbucks Corporation Annual Report 2010* (2011), http://phx.corporate-ir.net/External.File?item=UGFyZW50SUQ9NzkzODl8Q2hpbGRRRD0tMXxUeXBlPTM=&t=1 (accessed August 19, 2011).

24. "Talking Points," *The Week* (April 29, 2011), 42.

25. "China Invests in Texas Oil Field," *New York Times* (2010, October 10), http://www.nytimes.com/2010/10/11/business/11oil.html (accessed August 19, 2011).

26. U.S. Census Bureau, "Language Spoken at Home," 2008, *American Community Survey*, www.census.gov/compendialstatab/2011/tables/11s0053.pdf (accessed July 15, 2011).

27. N. Santa Cruz, "White Americans' majority to continue until 2050, report says," *Los Angeles Times* (December 17, 2009), http://articles.latimes.com/2009/dec/17/nation/la-na-white-minority17-2009dec17 (accessed August 20, 2011).

28. E. Aguilera, "Hispanics nationwide: a snapshot," *San Diego Union Tribune* On-Line, (June 7, 2011), http://www.signonsandiego.com/news/2011/jun/07/hispanics-nationwide-a-snapshot/ (accessed August 20, 2011).

29. Santa Cruz, Ibid.

30. "Census Bureau Reports Minority Business Ownership Increasing at More Than Twice the National Rate," (2010, July 13), http://www.census.gov/newsroom/releases/archives/economic_census/cb10-107.html (accessed August 19, 2011); "Minority-Owned Firms," U.S. Census Bureau (2010, July 13), http://www2.census.gov/econ/sbo/07/prelim/minority_state_map.pdf (accessed August 19, 2011).

31. "Census Bureau Reports Hispanic-Owned Businesses Increase at More Than Double the National Rate," *Survey of Business Owners: U.S. Census Bureau* (2010, September, 21), http://www.census.gov/newsroom/releases/archives/business_ownership/cb10-145.html (accessed August 19, 2011).

32. M-J. Browaeys and R. Price, *Understanding Cross-Cultural Management* (Edinburgh Gate, Harlow, England: Pearson Education Limited 2008), 35.

33. Ibid.

34. Morrison and Conaway, 2007b, 9.

35. J.S. Martin and L.H. Chaney, *Global Business Etiquette* (Westport, CT: Prager Publishers 2008), 23.

36. M.M. Bosrock, *Asian Business Customs and Manners: A Country-by-Country Guide* (New York: Meadowbrook Press, 2007), 18.

37. Martin and Chaney, 2008, 24–25.

38. R.T. Moran, P.R. Harris, and S.V. Moran, *Managing Cultural Differences: Leadership Skills and Strategies for Working in a Global World*, 8th ed. (Burlington, MA: Elsevier, 2011), 226.

39. T. Morrison and W.A. Conaway, *Kiss, Bow, or Shake Hands: Latin America* (Avon, MA: Adams Media an F+W Publications Company, 2007c), 48.

40. Ibid.

41. Morrison and Conaway, 2007b, 12–13

42. Ibid., 12.

43. Ibid., 31.

44. Morris, Harris, and Moran, 2011, 347.

45. R.D. Lewis, *When Cultures Collide: Managing Successfully Across Cultures* (London: Nicholas Brealey Publishing, 1998), 296.

46. R. Kumar and A.K. Sethi, *Doing Business in India: A Guide for Western Managers* (New York: Palgrave, 2005), 110.

47. Morrison and Conaway, 2007b, 31.

48. M. Guirdham, *Communication Across Cultures at Work*, 2nd ed. (West Lafayette, IN: Purdue University Press, 2005), 304–305.

49. N.J. Adler, *International Dimensions of Organizational Behavior*, 5th ed. (Cincinnati, OH: South-Western College Publishing, 2008), 30.

50. Moran, Harris, and Moran, 2011, 302.

51. "Background Note: Brazil," *Country Background Notes* (Washington: U.S. Department of State, March 8, 2011), http://www.state.gov/r/pa/ei/bgn/35640.htm (accessed August 19, 2011).

52. Harris, Moran, and Harris, 2011, 304.

53. Browaeys and Price 2008, 51.

54. Harris, Moran, and Harris, 2001, 309.

55. Ibid., 304.

56. G. Ferraro, *The Cultural Dimension of International Business*, 6th ed. (Boston: Prentice-Hall, 2010), 267.

57. Browaeys and Price, 2008, 51.

58. F. Trompenaars and C. Hampden-Turner, *Riding the Waves of Culture: Understanding Diversity in Global Business*, 2nd ed. (New York: McGraw-Hill, 1998), 163.

59. Ibid., 164.

60. Browaeys and Price, 2008, 60.

61. T.H. Becker, *Doing Business in the New Latin America* (Westport, CT: Praeger, 2004), 164.

62. Ibid., 124–125

63. S.L. Shirk. *China: Fragile Superpower* (New York: Oxford University Press, 2002), 4.

64. J. McGregor. *One Billion Customers.* (New York, NY: Free Press, 2005), 273.

65. I. Varner and L. Beamer, *Intercultural Communication in the Global Workplace,* 5th ed. (New York: McGraw-Hill Irwin, 2011), 440–441.

66. Varner and Beamer, 2011, 127.

67. Ibid., 306.

68. Lewis, 1998, 276.

69. Moran, Harris, and Moran, 2011, 332.

70. Varner and Beamer, 2011, 306.

71. "Background Note: India," *Country Background Notes* (Washington: U.S. Department of State, July 14, 2010), http://www.state.gov/r/pa/ei/bgn/3454.htm (accessed August 20, 2011).

72. Moran, Harris, and Moran, 2011, 343.

73. Ibid.

74. Ibid., 341.

75. Ibid., 344–35.

76. "Developing Your Global Know-How," *Harvard Business Review,* (March 2011), 72–75.

77. Browaeys and Price, 2008, 66.

78. L. Beamer and I. Varner, *Intercultural Communication in the Global Workplace,* 2nd ed. (New York: McGraw-Hill Irwin, 2001), 84.

79. Browaeys and Price, 2008, 65–66.

80. Lewis 1988, 81, 297.

81. Ibid., 296–297.

82. Varner and Beamer, 2011, 164.

83. P. Cappelli, H. Singh, J.V. Singh, and M. Useem, "Leadership Lessons from India: How the Best Indian Companies Drive Performance by Investing in People," *Harvard Business Review* (March 2010), 90–93.

84. M.M. Magnier, "Indian activist is likely to leave prison soon," *Los Angeles Times* (August 19, 2011), A8.

85. S.W. Littlejohn and K. Domenici, *Communication, Conflict, and the Management of Difference* (Long Grove, IL: Waveland, 2007), 26.

86. Ibid., 117.

87. Varner and Beamer, 2011, 331.

88. Ferraro, 136.

89. Ibid., 69.

90. Ibid., 310–311.

91. Ibid., 335.

92. J. McGregor, *One Billion Customers* (New York: Free Press, 2005), 50–51; Varner and Beamer, 2011, 335.

93. Ibid.

94. C. Lee, *Cowboys and Dragons* (Chicago, IL: Dearborn Trade Publishing, 2003), 171–172.

95. Moran, Harris, and Moran, 2011, 334–335.

96. Ferraro, 136.

97. Trompenaars and Hampden-Turner, 1998, 204.

98. L.E. Metcalf, A. Bird, M. Shankarmahesh, Z. Aycan, J. Larimo, and D.D. Valdelamar, "Cultural tendencies in negotiation: A comparison of Finland, India, Mexico, Turkey, and the United States," *Journal of World Business,* 41 (2006), 390.

99. Lewis, 1998, 297–298.

100. Moran, Harris, and Moran, 2011, 164.

101. Ibid.

102. Ibid.

103. Institute for Educational Sciences. *The Condition of Education 2011: Overview* (Washington, D.C.: National Center for Education Statistics: U.S. Department of Education, 2011), http://nces.ed.gov/programs/coe/overview.asp (accessed August 20, 2011).

104. "Majority of U.S. Babies Are Non-White for First Time, Census Finds" *Huffington Post* (June 23, 2011), http://www.huffingtonpost.com/2011/06/23/census-whites-now-make-up-minority-of-babies_n_883082.html (accessed August 20, 2011).

105. Institute for Educational Services, 2011.

106. N.A. Glasgow, S.J. McNary, and C.D. Hicks, *What Successful Teachers Do in Diverse Classrooms: Research-Based Classroom Strategies for New and Veteran Teachers* (Thousand Oaks, CA: Corwin Press, 2006), 2.

107. W.E. Segall, *School Reform in a Global Society* (Lanham, MD: Rowman & Littlefield Publishers, 2006), 1.

108. Ibid.

109. B. Tosolt, "Gender and Race Differences in Middle School Students' Perceptions of Caring Teachers," *Multicultural Perspectives,* 12:3 (July-September, 2010), 145.

110. Glasgow, McNary, and Hicks, 2006, 2.

111. D.M. Gollnick and P.C. Chinn, *Multicultural Education in a Pluralistic Society,* 7th ed. (Upper Saddle River, NJ: Merrill Prentice Hall, 2006), 4.

112. Tosolt, 2010, 145.

113. S. Dillon, "Top Test Scores from Shanghai Stun Educators," *New York Times,* December 7, 2010, http://www.nytimes.com/2010/12/07/education/07education.html (accessed August 21, 2011).

114. Gollnick and Chinn, 2006, 5.

115. C.L. Barmeyer, "Learning Styles and Their Impact on Cross-Cultural Training: An International Comparison in France, Germany and Quebec," *International Journal of Intercultural Relations,* 26:6 (November, 2004), 577–594.

116. G. Hofstede, "Cultural Differences in Teaching and Learning," *International Journal of Intercultural Relations,* 10 (1986), 305.

117. S. Nieto, *The Light in Their Eyes: Creating Multicultural Learning Communities* (New York: Teachers College Press, 1999), 8.

118. Ibid., 64.

119. C. Calloway-Thomas, P.J. Cooper, and C. Blake, *Intercultural Communication: Roots and Routes* (Boston: Allyn and Bacon, 1999), 199.

120. G. Gay, *Culturally Responsive Teaching: Theory, Research, and Practice,* 2nd ed. (New York: Teachers College Press, 2010), 124.

121. Calloway-Thomas et al., 1999, 199.

122. J. Spring, *The Intersection of Cultures: Multicultural Education in the United States and the Global Economy,* 4th ed. (New York: Lawrence Erlbaum, 2008), 106.

123. J. Chisenga, "Indigenous Knowledge: Africa's Opportunity to Contribute to Global Information Content," *South African Journal of Library & Information Sciences*, 68:1 (2002) 3.

124. Spring, 2008, 77–78.

125. D.W. Gegeo and K.A. Watson-Gegeo "'How We Know': Kwara'ae Rural Villagers Doing Indigenous Epistemology," *The Contemporary Pacific*, 13:1, (Spring 2001), 63.

126. S. Nieto, *Affirming Diversity: The Sociopolitical Context of Multicultural Education*, 4th ed. (Boston: Pearson-Allyn and Bacon, 2004), 149.

127. P.A. Cordeiro, T.G. Reagan, and L.P. Martinez, *Multiculturalism and TQE* (Thousand Oaks, CA: Sage Publications, 1994), 3.

128. Nieto, 2004, 149–150.

129. J.C. Kush, "Field-Dependence, Cognitive Ability, and Academic Achievement in Anglo-American and Mexican-American Students, *Journal of Cross-Cultural Psychology*, 27:5 (September, 1996), 563.

130. B.P. Leung, "Culture as a Study of Differential Minority Student Achievement," *Journal of Educational Issues of Language Majority Students*, 13 (1994).

131. Kush, 1996, 563.

132. H. Grossman, *Educating Hispanic Students: Cultural Implications for Instruction, Classroom Management, Counseling, and Assessment* (Springfield, IL: Charles C. Thomas, 1984).

133. E.R. Hollins, J.E. King, and W.C. Haymen, *Teaching Diverse Population: Formulating a Knowledge Base* (New York: State University of New York Press, 1994), 19.

134. Cleary and Peacock, 1998. L.M. Cleary and T.D. Peacock, *Collected Wisdom: American Indian Education* (Boston: Allyn and Bacon, 1998).

135. H. Grossman, *Teaching in a Diverse Society* (Boston: Allyn and Bacon, 1995), 270.

136. Cleary and Peacock, 1998.

137. E.E. Obiakor, D.J. Smith, and M. Sapp, "Understanding the Power of Words in Multicultural Education," *Multicultural Perspectives*, 9 (June, 2007), 36.

138. S. York, "Culturally Speaking: English Language Learners," *Library Media Connection* (April/May 2008), 26.

139. Ibid.

140. Ibid.

141. L. Delpit, "No Kinda Sense" in L. Delpit and J.K. Dowdy, eds., *The Skin That We Speak: Thoughts on Language and Culture in the Classroom* (New York: The New Press, 2008), 33.

142. J. Abrams and J. Ferguson, "Teaching Students from Many Nations," *Educational Leadership* (December/January, 2005), 87.

143. J. Le Roux, "Effective Educators Are Culturally Competent Communicators," *Intercultural Education*, 13:1 (2001), 274–275.

144. Delpit, 2008.

145. S.J. Dicker, *Languages in America: A Pluralist View* (Philadelphia: Multilingual Matters, 1996), 2.

146. Ibid., 4.

147. Delpit, 2008.

148. Dicker, 1996, 2.

149. J.A. Banks, "Multicultural Education: Characteristics and Goals" in J.A. Banks and C.A. McGee Banks, eds., *Multicultural Education: Issues and Perspectives*, 5th ed. (Hoboken, NJ: Wiley, 2004), 41.

150. S.A. Reyes and T.L. Vallone, "Toward an Expanded Understanding of Two-Way Bilingual Immersion Education: Constructing Identity through a Critical, Additive Bilingual/Bicultural Pedagogy," *Multicultural Perspectives*, 9:3 (July 2007), 9–10.

151. D. McKeon, "When Meeting Common Standards is uncommonly Difficult," *Educational Leadership*, 51 (1994), 45–49.

152. Ibid.

153. McKeon, 1994, 45–49.

154. Glasgow, McNary, and Hicks, 2006, 7.

155. McKeon, 1994, 46.

156. K.N. Robins, R.B. Lindsey, D.B. Lindsey, and R.D. Terrell, *Culturally Proficient Instruction: A Guide for People Who Teach* (Thousand Oaks, CA: Corwin Press, 2002), 4.

157. K.O. Siwatu, "Predicting Preservice Teachers' Self-Efficacy to Resolve a Cultural Conflict Involving an African American Student," *Multicultural Perspectives*, 12:2 (January-March, 2010), 10–17.

158. P.J. Cooper and C.J. Simonds, *Communication for the Classroom Teacher*, 8th ed. (Boston: Pearson Education, 2007), 29.

159. N.P. Gallavan, "Seven Perceptions Influencing Novice Teachers' Efficacy and Cultural Competence," *Praxis*, 2:1 (Fall, 2007), 7.

160. Cooper and Simonds, 2007, 3.

161. Ibid.

162. S.D. Johnson and A.N. Miller, "A Cross-Cultural Study of Immediacy, Credibility, and Learning in the U.S. and Kenya," *Communication Education*, 52:3 (July 2002), 289.

163. A.S. Jazayeri, "Immediacy and Its relationship to Teacher Effectiveness: A Cross-Cultural Examination of Six Cultures," paper presented at the annual meeting of the National Communication Association, Chicago 1999.

164. P.J. Cooper and C.J. Simonds, *Communication for the Classroom Teacher*, 7th ed. (Boston: Allyn and Bacon, 2003), 67.

165. Ibid.

166. Gollnick and Chinn, 2006, 7.

167. Cooper and Simonds, 2003, 67.

168. Ibid.

169. S. Nieto, *Affirming Diversity: The Sociopolitical Context of Multicultural Education*, 4th ed. (Boston: Pearson Education, 2004), 153.

170. I.G. Malcolm, "Invisible Culture in the Classroom: Minority Pupils and the Principle of Adaptation," in *English Across Cultures, Cultures Across English: A Reader in Cross-Cultural Communication*, O. Garcia and R. Otheguy, eds. (New York: Mouton de Gruyter, 1989), 134.

171. Tosolt, 2010, 148.

172. S.V. Taggar, "Headscarves in the headlines! What does this mean for

educators?" *Multicultural Perspectives*, 8:3 (2006) 9.

173. Glasgow, McNary, and D. Hicks, 2006, 25.

174. Ibid., 2–3.

175. A.M. Blankstein, "Terms of Engagement: Where Failure is Not an Option," in A.M. Blankstein, R.W. Cole, and P.D. Houston, eds., *Engaging Every Learner* (Thousand Oaks, CA: Corwin Press, 2007), 8.

176. D.L. Pennachio, *Cultural Competence: Caring for Your Muslim Patients* (May 2005), http://medicaleconomics.modernmedicine.com/memag/content/printContentPopup.jsp?id=158977 (accessed August 6, 2011).

177. G-A. Galanti, *Caring for Patients from Different Cultures*, 3rd ed. (Philadelphia: University of Pennsylvania Press, 2004), 20.

178. Ibid., 3.

179. Pennachio, 2005, 4.

180. J. Capell, E. Dean, and G. Veenstra, "The Relationship Between Cultural Competence and Ethnocentrism of Health Care Professionals," *Journal of Transcultural Nursing*, 19:2 (April 2008), 121.

181. L. Calderón and R.A. Beltrán, "Pitfalls in Health Communication: Health Care Policy, Institution, Structure, and Process," *Medscape General Medicine*, 6:1 (2004), 1, http://www.ncbi.nlm.nih.gov/pmc/articles/PMC1140704/ (accessed August 21, 2011).

182. G-A. Galanti, *Caring for Patients from Different Cultures*, 4th ed. (Philadelphia: University of Pennsylvania Press, 2008), 1.

183. M.L. Andersen and H.F. Taylor, *Sociology: Understanding a Diverse Society*, 4th ed. (Belmont, CA: Thompson-Wadsworth, 2007), 367.

184. K.K. Kundahl and P.S. Kundhal, "Cultural Diversity: An Evolving Challenge to Physician-Patient Communication," *Journal of the American Medical Association*, 298:1 (January 1, 2003), 94.

185. K.B. Wright, L. Sparks, and H.D. O'Hair, *Health Communication in the 21st Century* (Malden, MA: Blackwell Publishing, 2008), 9–10.

186. E. Rosenberg, C. Richard, M-T. Lussier, and S.N. Abdoll, "Intercultural communication competence in family medicine: Lessons from the field," *Patient Education and Counseling* 61 (2006), 236–245.

187. M. Aghadiuno, *Soul Matters: The Spiritual Dimension within Healthcare* (Oxford, UK: Radcliffe Publishing, 2010), 8.

188. L.M. Anderson, S.C. Scrimshaw and M.T. Fullilove, "Culturally Competent Healthcare Systems: A Systematic Review," *American Journal of Preventive Medicine*, 24:Suppl.1 (April 2003), 68–79.

189. R.E. Spector, *Cultural Diversity in Health and Illness*, 6th ed. (Upper Saddle River, NJ: Pearson/Prentice Hall, 2004), 212.

190. L.D. Purnell, *Guide to Culturally Competent Health Care*, 2d ed. (Philadelphia: F.A. David Company, 2009), 98.

191. J. Camphinha-Bacote, "African Americans," in *Transcultural Health Care: A Culturally Competent Approach*, J.D. Purnell and B.J. Paulanka, eds. (Philadelphia: F.A. Davis, 1988), 68.

192. C.V. Angelelli and P. Geist-Martin, "Enhancing Culturally Competent Health Communication: Constructing Understanding Between Providers and Culturally Diverse Patients" in E.B. Ray, ed., *Health Communication in Practice: A Case Study Approach* (Mahwa, NJ: Lawrence Erlbaum Associates, 2005), 282.

193. M.M. Andrews, "The Influence of Cultural and Health Belief Systems on Health Care Practices," in *Transcultural Concepts in Nursing Care*, 4th ed., M.M. Andrews and J.S. Boyle, eds. (Philadelphia: Lippincott Williams & Wilkins, 2003), 75.

194. R. Schiavo, *Health Communication: From Theory to Practice* (San Francisco: Jossey-Bass, 2007), 75.

195. Andrews, 2003, 75.

196. Ibid.

197. Schiavo, 2007, 76.

198. Andrews, 2003, 75.

199. J. Luckmann, *Transcultural Communication in Health Care* (Albany, NY: Delmar/Thomson Learning, 2000), 44.

200. A. Fadiman, *The Spirit Catches You and You Fall Down* (New York: Farrar, Straus and Giroux, 1997).

201. Aghadiuno, 2010, 36.

202. Spector, 2004, 256.

203. D.B. Stasiak, "Culture Care Theory with Mexican-Americans in an Urban Context," in M.M. Leininger, ed., *Culture Care Diversity and Universality: A Theory of Nursing* (Boston: Jones and Bartlett Publishers, 2001), 183.

204. A.R.O. Yosef, "Health Beliefs, Practice and Priorities for Health Care of Arab Muslims in the United States," *Journal of Transcultural Nursing*, 19:3 (July 2008), 284.

205. M. Aghadiuno, *Soul Matters: The Spiritual Dimension within Healthcare* (Oxford, UK: Radcliffe Publishing, 2010), 36.

206. E. Turner, "Shamanism and Spirit," *Expedition*, 46:1 (2004), 13.

207. Ibid.

208. D.N. Clark, *Culture and Customs of Korea* (Westport, CT: Greenwood Press, 2000), 111–112.

209. Ibid., 112.

210. D. Grossman, "Cuban Americans," in *Transcultural Health Care: A Culturally Competent Approach*, L.D. Purnell and B.J. Paulanka, eds. (Philadelphia: F.A. Davis, 1998), 208; G.A. Galanti, *Caring for Patients from Different Cultures: Case Studies from American Hospitals* (Philadelphia: University of Pennsylvania Press, 1991), 101.

211. J. Camphinha-Bacote, "African Americans," in *Transcultural Health Care: A Culturally Competent Approach*, J.D. Purnell and B.J. Paulanka, eds. (Philadelphia: F.A. Davis, 1988), 68.

212. Aghadiuno, 2010, 14.

213. S. Walter, "Holistic Health" in *The Illustrated Encyclopedia of Body-Mind Disciplines*, N. Allison, ed. (New York: The Rosen Publishing Group,

1999), 7–9, http://www.eso-garden.com/specials/the_illustrated_encyclopedia_of_body_mind_disciplines.pdf (accessed August 21, 2011).

214. Ibid., 2.

215. P. Geist-Martin, B. Sharf, and N. Jeha, "Communicating healing holistically" in H.M. Zoller and M.J. Dutta, eds., *Emerging Perspectives in Health Communication: Meaning, Culture, and Power* (New York: Routledge/Taylor & Francis Group, 2008), 87.

216. Walter, 1999, 1.

217. J. Luckmann, *Transcultural Communication in Nursing*, (Albany, NY: Delmar Publishers, 1999), 49.

218. Giger and Davidhizar, 1995, 404.

219. I. Murillo-Rhode, "Hispanic American Patient Care," in *Transcultural Health Care*, G. Henderson and M. Primeaux, eds. (Menlo Park, CA: Addison-Wesley, 1981), 59–77.

220. N. Dresser, *Multicultural Manners: New Rules of Etiquette for a Changing Society* (New York: Wiley, 1996), 246.

221. R. Spector, "Cultural Concepts of Women's Health and Health-Promoting Behavior," *Journal of Obstetric, Gynecologic and Neonatal Nursing* 24:3 (March/April 1995), 243.

222. Spector, 2004, 189.

223. Ibid.

224. L.K. Motocha, "Chinese Americans," in *Transcultural Health Care: A Culturally Competent Approach*, L.D. Purnell and B.J. Paulanka, eds. (Philadelphia: F.A. Davis, 1998), 181.

225. R. Amerson, "Reflections on a conversation with a Curandera," *Journal of Transcultural Nursing*, 19:4 (2008), 384.

226. Murillo-Rhode, 1981.

227. Schiavo, 2007, 55.

228. Geist-Martin, Sharf, and Jeha, 2008, 96.

229. Schiavo, 2007, 55.

230. Andrews, 2003, 76.

231. Luckmann, 2000, 75.

232. Ibid., 117.

233. R. Lavizzo-Mourey, "Improving quality of US health care hinges on improving language services," *Journal of General Internal Medicine*, 22: Supplement 2 (2007), 279.

234. W.J. Ferguson and L. Candib, "Culture, Language, and the Doctor-Patient Relationship," *Family Medicine*, 34:5 (2002), 359.

235. L.D. Purnell, "Transcultural Diversity and Health Care" in L.D. Purnell and B.J. Paulanka, eds., *Transcultural Health Care: A Culturally Competent Approach*, 3rd ed. (Philadelphia: F.A. Davis, 2008), 1–2.

236. Luckman, 2000, 156.

237. Ibid., 158.

238. P.M. Cole, "Cultural Competence Now Mainstream Medicine. Responding to Increasing Diversity and Changing Demographics," *Postgraduate Medicine*, 116:6 (2004), 51–53.

239. L. Haffner, "Translation is Not Enough: Interpreting in a Medical Setting," *Western Journal of Medicine*, 157 (1992), 256.

240. Purnell, 2008, 2.

241. L.D. Purnell, "The Purnell Model for Cultural Competence" in L.D. Purnell and B.J. Paulanka, eds. *Transcultural Health Care: A Culturally Competent Approach*, 3rd ed. (Philadelphia: F.A. Davis, 2008), 26-27.

242. Spector, 2004, 4.

243. E. Rosenberg, L.J. Kirmayer, S. Xenocostas, M.D. Dao, and C. Loignon, "GP's strategies in intercultural clinical encounters," *Family Practice*, 24 (2007), 146.

244. Ibid.

245. Wright, Sparks, and O'Hair, 2008, 27.

246. Spector, 2000, 91.

247. D.W. Gibson and M. Zhong, "Intercultural Communication Competence in the Healthcare Context," *International Journal of Intercultural Relations*, 29:5 (2005), 632–634.

248. J.R. Betancourt, A.R. Green, and J.E. Carrillo, "The Challenges of Cross-cultural Healthcare—Diversity, Ethics, and the Medical Encounter," *Bioethics Forum*, 16:3 (2000), 27.

249. L.M. Anderson, S.C. Scrimshaw, and M.T. Fulilove, "Culturally Competent Healthcare Systems: A Systematic Review," *American Journal of Preventive Medicine*, 24, (Suppl. 1), April 2003, 68-79.

250. Galanti, 2008, 94–95.

251. Ibid.

252. A. Rundle, M. Carvalho, and M. Robinson, eds., *Cultural Competence in Health Care: A Practical Guide* (San Francisco, CA: Jossey-Bass, 1999), xxi.

253. G. Juckett, "Cross Cultural Medicine," *American Family Physician*, 72:11 (2005), 2269.

254. Wright, Sparks, and O'Hair, 2008, 60–61.

255. Galanti, 2008, 167.

256. Ibid.

257. Bowman and Singer, 2001, 11.

258. G-A Galanti, "An introduction to cultural differences," *Culture and Medicine*, 172 (May 2000), 335–336.

259. S. Planalp and M.R. Trost, "Communication Issues at the End of Life: Reports from Hospice Volunteers," *Health Communication*, 23 (2008), 222–233.

260. Galanti, 2008, 167–168.

261. M.L. Andersen and H.F. Taylor, *Sociology: Understanding a Diverse Society*, 4th ed. (Belmont, CA: Thompson-Wadsworth, 2007), 367.

262. W.H. Shrank, J. S. Kutner, T. Richardson, R.A. Mularski, S. Fisher, and M. Kagawa-Singer, "Focus group findings about the influence of culture on communication preferences in end-of-life care," *Journal of General Internal Medicine*, 22: Supplement 2 (2000), 703.

263. Ibid., 706.

264. Ibid., 705.

265. Ibid., 707.

Index